The Politics of
Federal
Judicial Administration

The Politics of

Federal
Judicial Administration

Peter Graham Fish

Princeton University Press, Princeton, New Jersey

LCC 76-39785
ISBN 0-691-09226-5 (hardcover edition)
ISBN 0-691-10013-6 (limited paperback edition)

This book has been composed in
Linotype Caledonia

Printed in the United States of America
by Princeton University Press.
Princeton, New Jersey

To My Mother and Father

Contents

Illustrations
[following page 240]

1. Members of the Second Conference of Senior Judges of the United States Circuit Courts of Appeals calling on President Calvin Coolidge at the White House, September 23, 1923. (French Collection, Library of Congress)

2. Chief Justice Charles Evans Hughes and members of the Conference of Senior Circuit Judges following a meeting with President Franklin D. Roosevelt at the White House, September 27, 1934. (Underwood & Underwood)

3. Judges Lobbying Congress. Chief Justice Hughes flanked by Associate Justices Willis Van Devanter and Louis D. Brandeis testifying before the Senate Judiciary Committee, March 26, 1935. (Underwood & Underwood)

4. President Franklin Roosevelt signing into law the bill establishing an Administrative Office of the United States Courts and the circuit judicial councils, August 7, 1939. (Wide World Photos)

5. Interchange among judges of the appellate courts at the Judicial Conference of the Third Circuit, 1945. (Courtesy of John Biggs, Jr.)

6. Unveiling of the dedicatory plaque in the courtyard of the Federal Judicial Center, November 1, 1968. (Courtesy of General Services Administration)

7. A session of the Judicial Council of the District of Columbia Circuit in the 1960s. (Courtesy of Nathan Paulson and the Smithsonian Institution)

8. The Judicial Conference Committee on Court Administration meeting on June 8, 1969, in the Federal Building

Preface

THE LITERATURE on judicial administration is extensive and growing every year. The bulk of it, however, is technical and reform-oriented. Only in a peripheral fashion has it attempted to place the subject of administration in the broad context of the judicial process. This study surveys a dimension of that process which has received little scholarly attention since Frankfurter and Landis wrote their seminal work on *The Business of the Supreme Court* in 1928. I begin essentially where they ended. Thereafter, I delineate the development and politics of major national and regional institutions of federal judicial administration through the Chief Justiceship of Earl Warren.

In short, I seek to illuminate an important function of the court system of the United States. As Senior Circuit Judge John J. Parker wrote long ago to the Chief Justice of the Ohio Supreme Court Carl V. Weygandt: "It seems to me that the importance of the administrative side of the courts, if not as great as the subject of the substantive law, is such that it holds at least the position of very close second."

Although administrative policy-making may lack the luster associated with judicial decision-making, both constitute vital elements of the judicial process. Lawyers and scholars have traditionally been concerned with the adjudicative role of judges and with the substantive law emanating from the courts, particularly the Supreme Court of the United States. Because American courts enjoy the power to resolve disputes in an authoritative fashion, their judicial decisions have a decided ring of finality about them. Thus it is hardly unexpected that scholarship has emphasized the legal product of judicial lawmakers.

Administrative decisions, on the other hand, typically relate to the manner in which the courts organize their litigation process. Such decisions are not final. Yet they may well have a decisive influence on the quality as well as quantity of justice dispensed by the Third Branch. And, conversely, court decisions may require adjustments in administrative policies. Then, too, the line between administration and adjudication is sometimes blurred. After all, some federal judges wear two hats; they are judicial as well as administrative policy-makers. This book considers federal judges in the latter capacity.

Judges as administrators become deeply involved in politics. Yet they play politics in a system largely screened from public gaze. Partisan politics, characteristic of fights over issues of judicial selection and Supreme Court jurisdiction, rarely emerge. Interest groups so visible in great hallmark cases recede into the background. And even judges who loom large as jurisprudential "greats" are scarce. So, too, the Supreme Court fades from the scene.

The parameters of this study encompass primarily administration of the congressional-created inferior courts of the United States. The focus is on the lower courts: district courts, courts of appeals, and the special courts. Yet the perspective is that from Washington. The book does not purport to be a comprehensive survey of the administration of over one hundred individual courts, nor of even a single court. Nor does it attempt to exhaust the subject of judicial rule-making which merits separate study. This book is rather a study of the structure and politics of national judicial administration. Within this framework enduring issues are raised: Shall local federal judges be wholly independent or must they conform to uniform standards of law and administration? Shall administration be separate and diffused or united and centralized? Shall politics be superior or subordinate to so-called standards of "efficiency"? Shall the interests of trial judges prevail over or be subordinate to the regional and national interests of appellate judges? How shall money, manpower, jurisdictional, and structural changes be distributed among the courts? To what extent, if any, should judges modify their behavior or institutions to meet external criticism? All of the above are issues decidedly political in nature, and resolution of conflicts involving them may depend less on rationalism and efficiency than on the exigencies of intra- and extra-judicial politics.

Many individuals have made contributions to the research, organization, and writing of this study. Foremost among the contributors was the late Professor Carl Brent Swisher of The Johns Hopkins University. As a scholar, teacher, and adviser, his wisdom, experience, and patient understanding provided guidance and encouragement of inestimable value. To Professors Francis E. Rourke and J. Woodford Howard of Johns Hopkins I owe a deep debt of gratitude for their cogent criticisms and helpful advice. Professor Alpheus T. Mason of Princeton University deserves special mention. While his research assistant in the summers of 1960 and 1961, I surveyed the William Howard Taft Papers, which stimulated me to undertake further study of federal judicial administration.

During the course of my research many people gave me courteous and useful assistance. Among those whose help was of immeasurable aid were: Patricia H. Collins and William Beach of the Department of Justice; Dorothy H. Gersack of the Records Appraisal Division of the General Services Administration; John B. Hansley of the Federal Records Center in Alexandria, Virginia; Hardee F. Allen and Buford Rowland of the National Archives; David C. Mearns of the Manuscripts Division of the Library of Congress; Anne Freudenberg and Elizabeth Ryall of the Alderman Library at the University of Virginia; Nancy C. Prewitt of the Western Historical Manuscripts Collection at the University of Missouri; Elias Clark, son of the late Judge Charles E. Clark and Master of Silliman College, Yale University, who permitted me to examine his father's papers; Martin Schmitt of the University of Oregon Library, who loaned material from the Samuel Driver Collection to The Brookings Institution Library; Joseph F. Spaniol, Jr. of the Administrative Office of the United States

Courts; Hubert H. Finzel and M. Albert Figinski of the Senate Subcommittee on Improvements in Judicial Machinery; Henry P. Chandler, former director of the Administrative Office of the United States Courts; and the Honorable John Biggs, Jr., Senior Circuit Judge. William P. Brandon, James Pou, and Wayne L. Wilson, students at Duke University, rendered valuable assistance in the final preparation of the manuscript. Mrs. Doris Ralston provided me with essential secretarial assistance and expediting services.

I appreciate permission granted by the following journals to use materials printed in their pages: the *Journal of Politics, University of Chicago Law Review, Journal of the National Conference of Referees in Bankruptcy* (now the *American Bankruptcy Law Journal*), and the *Western Political Quarterly*, which is quoted by permission of the University of Utah, copyright holder. I am also indebted to the many individuals who took the time and effort to grant me specific permission to quote from their own correspondence or from that of a deceased relative.

I am grateful for the financial assistance received from The Johns Hopkins University and its Public Affairs Committee for a Ford Foundation Grant for Research in Public Affairs which facilitated extended research in the files of the Department of Justice, the Administrative Office of the United States Courts, and in the papers of several judges of the United States courts. The Brookings Institution made a substantial contribution to this study by providing me with the privileges of a Guest Scholar during 1964-65. The Duke University Research Council contributed vital financial support in the later stages of the project.

Finally, my wife, Barbara Maly Fish, gave not only encouragement but also material assistance in the typing and editing of this manuscript.

P.G.F.

Durham, North Carolina
January 1973

xiv

The Politics of
Federal
Judicial Administration

Sources Frequently Cited
in the Notes

Administrative Office Correspondence = Correspondence of the Administrative Office of the United States Courts, Record Group 116, Federal Records Center, Alexandria, Virginia

Chandler, "Some Major Advances" = Henry P. Chandler, "Some Major Advances in the Federal Judicial System, 1922-1947," *Federal Rules Decisions*, 31 (1963), 307-517

Department of Justice Files = Judicial Districts Administration Files, Record Group 60, National Archives, Washington, D.C.

Judicial Conference Report = (For the period covered by this book, the reports from 1924 to 1944 were included in the *Annual Report of the Attorney General*; from 1945 to 1969 they were issued with the *Annual Report of the Director of the Administrative Office of the United States Courts*. See Appendix A for a complete listing.)

Legislative Files = Legislative Files, National Archives, Washington, D.C.

CHAPTER 1

Administrative Heritage and Reform, 1789–1922

The Framework

FROM its inception, the hallmarks of the federal judiciary's administrative system have been independence, decentralization, and individualism. The courts in their judicial decision-making were rendered independent of the executive and legislative branches of government by Article III of the Constitution. That Article's guarantee of tenure during good behavior and undiminished salary while a judge held office reinforced judicial independence and promoted the administrative autonomy of each magistrate.

Congress, however, retained great power over the judicial branch, for it might, in its discretion, "ordain and establish" courts inferior to the Supreme Court. As it turned out, legislative exercise of this power assured the creation of a decentralized system of inferior federal courts reflecting the demands of local constituencies. Local influences would be felt not only in the realm of structure, but also in selection, for the Constitution defined judges of the inferior courts as "superior" officers subject to Senate approval.[1]

[1] Article II, Section 2 of the Constitution provides that the President "shall nominate, and by and with the Advice and Consent of the Senate, shall appoint . . . Judges of the Supreme Court, and all other Officers of the United States, whose appointments are not herein otherwise provided for, and which shall be established by Law. . . ." Congress may, on the other hand, vest the appointment of "inferior" officers "in the President alone, in the Courts of Law, or in the Heads of Departments." Inferior officers "are usually officers intended to be subordinate to those in whom their appointment is vested; but the requirement is by no means absolute." Edward S. Corwin, Norman J. Small, Lester S. Jayson, eds., *The Constitution of the United States of America: Analysis and Interpretation* (Washington, 1964), p. 504.

Such judges were likely to be local residents, approved by the Senate, adjudicating in their own home area, and subject to the continuing influence of their environment.[2]

The autonomy of courts and judges for which the Constitution laid a foundation was further promoted by the Judiciary Act of 1789.[3] The Act itself represented a compromise between anti-nationalists and nationalists in the First Congress. As the Federalists had hoped, it created a court system separate from that of the several states. The measure included, however, important provisions which emphasized decentralizing of state and local administrative and political influences. Established was a judicial structure hierarchically organized in three tiers. At the peak was the court of final review—the Supreme Court of the United States. It alone among federal courts traced its existence to a specific provision of Article III. The first Judiciary Act created two additional tiers of inferior courts. One was composed of circuit courts exercising important original as well as some appellate jurisdiction. The other tier contained district courts which were courts of first instance.

The 1789 Act also divided the country into three circuits: Southern, Middle, and Eastern. The boundaries of each one coincided with the boundaries of the several states which made up each circuit and thus opened the courts to state and sectional influences and practices. Reflecting the territorial expansion of the United States, the number of circuits grew to six in 1802[4] and to nine in 1866,[5] where it remained until 1893, when Congress created the District of Columbia Circuit.[6] Then, in 1929, the Tenth Circuit was organized,[7] bringing the number of circuits to its present eleven circuits.[8]

---

[2] Richard J. Richardson and Kenneth N. Vines, *The Politics of Federal Courts: Lower Courts in the United States* (Boston, 1970), p. 21.
[3] 1 *Stat.* 73.   [4] 2 *Stat.* 157.   [5] 14 *Stat.* 209.
[6] 27 *Stat.* 434; see also 42 *Stat.* 162, 58 *Stat.* 925.
[7] 45 *Stat.* 1346.
[8] 62 *Stat.* 870; see Erwin C. Surrency, "A History of Federal

4

For each circuit, there existed a circuit court consisting of two members of the Supreme Court, known as circuit justices, and one of the district judges residing within the circuit.[9] Primary responsibility for the light and often mundane workloads of these courts devolved on the local district judges[10] rather than on the justices from the Supreme Court.[11] As business before the highest tribunal increased during the nineteenth century, the presence of circuit justices became virtually impossible. In 1869 Congress provided each circuit with "a circuit judge, who shall reside in his circuit."[12] He enjoyed the same judicial powers exercised by the circuit-riding Supreme Court justices as well as administrative power to appoint the clerk of his court.

The landmark 1891 Court of Appeals Act[13] retained the old circuit courts, circuit duty for the justices of the Supreme Court, and the existing circuit structure. The meas-

Courts," *Missouri Law Review*, 28 (Spring 1963), 224-26; *United States Government Organization Manual: 1969-70* (Washington, 1969), p. 46.

[9] There "shall be held annually in each district of said circuit, two courts, which shall be called Circuit Courts, and shall consist of any two justices of the Supreme Court, and the district judge of such districts, any two of whom shall constitute a quorum" (1 *Stat.* 74, 75). The Act of April 29, 1802 amended the above provision; it stated that each circuit court should consist of one justice of the Supreme Court who, except in the Second Circuit, resided in the circuit, ". . . and the district judge of the district where such court shall be holden" (2 *Stat.* 157, 158).

[10] See John P. Frank, *Justice Daniel Dissenting: A Biography of Peter V. Daniel, 1784-1860* (Cambridge, 1964), pp. 281-84; Richardson and Vines, pp. 21-25; Charles Warren, *The Supreme Court in United States History* (Boston, 1926), i, 62.

[11] Chief Justice Salmon P. Chase urged a court assistant to aid District Judge George W. Brooks of North Carolina in properly arranging the circuit court business prior to his arrival. See Salmon P. Chase to D. A. Goodlow, May 30, 1867, Salmon P. Chase Papers (Library of Congress, Washington, D.C., cited hereafter as Chase Papers, Washington).

[12] 16 *Stat.* 44.   [13] 26 *Stat.* 826.

ure, however, added circuit judges, laid the groundwork for terminating Supreme Court circuit duties, abolished the appellate jurisdiction of the circuit courts, and established tribunals with clearly-defined intermediate appellate jurisdiction. The old circuit courts, shorn of their appellate jurisdiction, lingered on for another two decades,[14] while the new circuit courts of appeals expanded in size and jurisdiction during the twentieth century.[15]

In addition to the circuit courts, the first Judiciary Act divided the country, then composed of eleven states, into thirteen districts with a court for each district. The boundary of no single district extended beyond that of the state in which it was located. Although Massachusetts and Virginia both received two districts under the 1789 Act, both were contained within each state.[16] Thus the lowest tier of the federal judicial system consisted of thirteen districts, one or more to a state. With a few exceptions, these districts were in turn self-contained within circuits composed of several states.[17] Those states organized into two or more districts always lay wholly within a single circuit: they were never divided among different circuits.[18] The early nineteenth-century system of single districts comprising an entire state and single district judges gradually became transformed into one in which nearly half the states have two or more districts and all district courts except Wyoming, New Hampshire, and Maine have multi-judge tribunals. Thus, from a handful of single-judge district courts in 1789 the number of federal trial courts had soared to

[14] 36 *Stat.* 1087.
[15] See Surrency, "A History of Federal Courts," p. 234.
[16] See 1 *Stat.* 73.
[17] See Surrency, p. 216, n. 8. Referring to the district courts in Maine and Kentucky which exercised circuit as well as district court jurisdiction (1 *Stat.* 79), Surrency states (pp. 216-17) that never during the existence of the old circuit courts were all the districts included within a circuit.
[18] *Ibid.*, p. 225.

eighty-nine in 1969, composed of 327 district judges in regular active service.[19]

From the Act of 1789 and subsequent measures pertaining to the structure of the federal judiciary emerged three important characteristics: independence, decentralization, and individualism. These characteristics were particularly apparent in judicial administration. Here courts in all three tiers enjoyed virtual autonomy. Judges in administrative matters were not only independent of Congress and of the President but of each other as well. Congress, in the words of Felix Frankfurter and James Landis, had "created a hierarchical system of courts, not of judges."[20] No significant supervisory power over judges was lodged in any court. And participation by members of the Supreme Court in the legal work of the lower courts little mitigated the centrifugal thrust built into the judicial institution.

The Circuit Justices

The "circuit riding" required by the Act of 1789 proved highly unpopular with the justices, who were obligated to hold circuit courts in far-flung and almost inaccessible places.[21] Once at their destinations, articulation of national

[19] Eighty-eight district courts in fifty states and one in the District of Columbia. See *United States Government Organization Manual: 1969-70*, p. 46. There were 331 district judgeships in 1969 but only 327 permanent district judges. See *Reports of the Proceedings of the Judicial Conference of the United States—Annual Report of the Director of the Administrative Office of the United States Courts: 1969* (Washington, 1970), p. 93.

[20] Felix Frankfurter and James M. Landis, *The Business of the Supreme Court* (New York, 1928), p. 218.

[21] All members of the Supreme Court under Chief Justice John Jay complained of their circuit duties which required that they hold "twenty-seven Circuit Courts a year, in the different States, from New Hampshire to Georgia, besides two sessions of the Supreme Court . . . , in the two most severe seasons of the year," and that they "pass the greater part of their days on the road, and at inns, and at a distance

law and assimilation of state and local values,[22] not administrative duties, consumed the time and energy of the judges from Washington. Nevertheless, while on circuit they participated in the adoption of "sundry rules and regulations" for proceedings in the circuit courts,[23] and in the appointment of subordinate circuit court officers.[24] Some degree of communication with the district judges in remote areas was maintained during the terms of the Supreme Court. The Chief Justice, in particular, received information on the state of judicial business in the far-flung districts,[25] commented on the quality of jury charges given by district judges,[26] and interpreted recent Supreme Court decisions for the benefit of uncertain lower court magistrates.[27]

The Chief and his colleagues on the High Court even enjoyed a real capacity for influencing the substance and, to

---

from their families. . . ." Quoted in Warren, *The Supreme Court*, I, 88-89. For a vivid description of mid-nineteenth-century circuit duty, see Frank, *Justice Daniel Dissenting*, ch. XVII.

[22] See Warren, I, 58-62.   [23] *Ibid.*, I, 59, n. 1.

[24] The Act of February 20, 1812 provided "that it shall be lawful for the circuit court of the United States . . . to appoint . . . so many discreet persons, in different parts of the district, as such court shall deem necessary, to take acknowledgements of bail and affidavits . . ." (2 *Stat.* 679-81). The Act of April 29, 1802 provided that "the clerk of each district court shall be also clerk of the circuit court in such district, except as is herein after excepted" (2 *Stat.* 158). But presumably at least one Circuit Justice had a voice in selecting a clerk because the same Act provided "that the circuit court and district courts for the district of North Carolina shall appoint clerks for the said courts respectively . . ." (2 *Stat.* 163).

[25] John Erskine to Salmon P. Chase, October 10, 1868; John C. Underwood to Salmon P. Chase, May 21, 1866; Richard Busteed to Salmon P. Chase, November 24, 1866; Chase Papers, Washington.

[26] Busteed to Chase, November 24, 1866, *ibid.*

[27] Chase to Robert A. Hill, March 1, 1867, *ibid.*; see Peter Graham Fish, "Chief Justice Salmon Portland Chase: His Concept of the Office and Powers of the Chief Justice," pp. 221-22 (unpub. thesis, Department of Politics, Princeton University, 1960; cited hereafter as "Salmon Portland Chase").

some extent, the administration of district court business within their circuits. "It is only as a Circuit Judge that the Chief Justice or any other Justice of the Supreme Court has, individually, any considerable power," Chief Justice Salmon P. Chase observed in 1868.[28] But the exercise of this power was most pronounced and effective on issues of law arising in the two-judge circuit courts.[29] In administrative matters, it often took the form of advice on convening of the circuit court,[30] how to settle conflicts over the jurisdiction of federal military courts in the post-Civil War South,[31] and the equalization of work among district judges within the circuit.[32]

On occasion, however, the Circuit Justice's tone could become quite admonitory as did that of Justice Samuel Miller, who criticized the work of one district court clerk in a Supreme Court opinion.[33] Chief Justice Chase also played an active role in lower court administration. The former Radical Republican Ohio governor ordered a United States marshal in North Carolina to make no distinctions because of race or color in selecting grand and petit jurors.[34] Even judges were not exempt from supervision, as Circuit Judge Hugh L. Bond learned when Chase notified him to "take up and decide" a case because "under the circumstances, [it] . . . as well as the others should, perhaps, be promptly decided."[35] And to another judge, suspected of "leaking" his opinion in advance of decision day, Chase noted that news-

[28] Salmon P. Chase to J. D. Van Buren, March 25, 1868, Chase Papers (Historical Society of Pennsylvania, Philadelphia, Pa.; cited hereafter as Chase Papers, Philadelphia).
[29] See Fish, "Salmon Portland Chase," pp. 227-30.
[30] Salmon P. Chase to George W. Brooks, March 20, 1866, Chase Papers, Philadelphia.
[31] Ibid.
[32] Charles Fairman, Mr. Justice Miller and the Supreme Court: 1862-1890 (Cambridge, 1939), p. 414.
[33] Russell v. Ely, 67 U.S. 575, 580-81 (1862).
[34] The American Annual Cyclopaedia (New York, 1872), vii, 548.
[35] Chase to Hugh L. Bond, September 28, 1870, Chase Papers, Washington.

paper correspondents seemed to "know as much (and probably more) of your opinions and future decisions as you yourself! I take it for granted that you keep your own counsel."[36]

Judicial patronage as well as administrative and ethical problems led the Chief Justice to intervene in district court administration. Section 3 of the Bankruptcy Act of March 2, 1867 empowered him to nominate and recommend candidates for Registers of Bankruptcy to the district judges who actually appointed them.[37] Chase believed that "the District Judge should have the whole of this business of appointment in his own hands, for he must know much better than the Chief Justice how to select so as to meet all circumstances."[38] But when Judge Bland Ballard of the District of Kentucky denied an appointment to two of the Chief's old political acquaintances, Chase tactfully suggested that the judge could reconsider his action with "perfect propriety."[39] Less circumspect was the Chief's response to objections from bench and bar to his candidate for United States Commissioner in Baltimore.[40] Informed that the individual was "totally unfit for the place,"[41] he nevertheless demanded the appointment of a loyal Republican in order that there "be equality in numbers if not in value and position."[42]

Chief Justice Salmon P. Chase intervened in lower court administration for reasons closely related to his political attitudes and to the peculiar administrative problems and judicial business of the Fourth Circuit during his circuit jus-

[36] Chase to John C. Underwood, May 13, 1867, John C. Underwood Papers (Library of Congress, Washington, D.C.).
[37] 14 *Stat.* 518. See Fish, "Salmon Portland Chase," pp. 67-68.
[38] Chase to C. L. Benedict, May 15, 1867, Chase Papers, Washington.
[39] Chase to Bland Ballard, June 22, 1867, *ibid.*
[40] 2 *Stat.* 679.
[41] Hugh L. Bond to Salmon P. Chase, March 9, 1867, Chase Papers, Washington.
[42] Chase to William F. Giles, March 16, 1867, *ibid.*; see Fish, "Salmon Portland Chase," pp. 231-33.

ticeship. Neither he nor his predecessor or immediate successors sought or exercised, formally or informally, continuous supervision over the geographically dispersed courts of the United States. Nor was Congress much concerned with creating an administratively integrated federal court system.

Reform, Expansion, and Judicial Autonomy

Relief of the Supreme Court justices from congested dockets and arduous circuit duties and the bringing of federal justice to newly-settled regions of the country constituted the foremost problems in judicial administration during the nineteenth century. In 1790, members of the Supreme Court, aided by those interests favorable to expanded federal jurisdiction, began to labor for creation of an intermediate court of appeals.[43] But efforts to establish a separate intermediate tribunal largely failed until the last decade of the nineteenth century.[44] Then, the court of appeals bill, formally endorsed by the justices of the Supreme Court and supported by the bar[45] became law.[46]

The 1891 Court of Appeals Act laid the foundation for the judicial and administrative ascendency of the appellate courts during the twentieth century. As Leon Green observed, "the early appellate court, made up as it was of a group of trial judges, neither had nor sought a dominant position in the judicial system. From the moment that the appellate courts became a separate organization from trial courts, a silent and probably unconscious struggle for supremacy began. . . ."[47] Green found that by 1930 this appellate judicial supremacy had resulted "not only in complete

[43] See Warren, *The Supreme Court*, i, 85.
[44] See 2 *Stat.* 89; 2 *Stat.* 132; Richardson and Vines, p. 28.
[45] Willard L. King, *Melville Weston Fuller: Chief Justice of the United States, 1888-1910* (Chicago, 1967), pp. 150-51.
[46] 26 *Stat.* 826.
[47] Leon Green, *Judge and Jury* (Kansas City, Mo., 1930), p. 380.

11

subordination of trial judges but also of juries."[48] On the administrative side, however, the impact of the 1891 Act became evident more slowly.

Policies relating to district court administration during the nineteenth century involved a quantitative expansion of the system as Congress gradually brought to the people crucial components of federal justice—judges and courthouses. The criteria for locating these components were hit-and-miss.[49] Complained one congressman in 1872: "The first proposition is to establish a new place of holding court; the next is to create a new district with a district judge, marshal, and attorney; the next step is to build a courthouse-post office; and if this system has to go on . . . we shall have in the United States as many places of holding courts as there are counties, and instead of having sixty or seventy district judges you will have six or seven hundred."[50]

Once established, each court administratively constituted an independent and autonomous unit. With complete discretion over patronage, the single district judge, who in most cases constituted the full court, appointed everyone from court clerk to bankruptcy receiver. The lines of authority and responsibility in matters of judicial conduct thus radiated no farther than his own court unless "high crimes and misdemeanors" were involved. This autonomy continued into the twentieth century, when President Franklin Roosevelt's Attorney General, Homer Cummings, complained of the absence of a "general administrative officer in the district or outside of it who is responsible for the arrangement of the judicial business, the handling of the docket, or any other matters that would tend to expedite or facilitate the disposition of litigation."[51]

[48] *Ibid.*
[49] See James B. Weaver, *Congressional Record*, 46th Cong., 2d Sess., 1880, vol. 10, part 4, 3444. See also David A. DeArmond, *Congressional Record*, 58th Cong., 2d Sess., 1904, vol. 38, part 5, 5004ff.
[50] Lyman Trumbull, *Congressional Globe*, 42d Cong., 2d Sess., 1872, vol. 45, part 4, 3574.
[51] U.S., Congress, Senate, Committee on the Judiciary, *Hearings, on*

The decentralizing features of the Act of 1789 were everywhere in evidence. Throughout the country appeared a multitude of single-judge district courts which, until the Court of Appeals Act of 1891,[52] disposed of a major share of all litigation in the federal courts.[53] Isolated and sometimes underworked district judges[54] thus stood at the crossroads of the federal judicial system. In an era of limited federal jurisdiction, mastery of the law lay well within their grasp.[55] They became lions on their relatively remote thrones. However they might find or make the law, delay or accelerate the flow of cases, reward or punish friends and foes with patronage and favorable bench rulings, concerned none but themselves. Only appellate court reversals on points of law and impeachment for crimes and misdemeanors limited their conduct.

Psychic security flowing from isolation, real power without checks, and mastery of the then relatively small corpus of federal law provided a source of independence. It also fostered a type of personality not always appreciated by bar, litigants, or even by some sensitive judges. "I have found," wrote one distinguished appellate judge, "fellow judges, especially those who have been on the bench for a

---

S. 3212, *Administrative Office of the United States Courts*, 75th Cong., 3d Sess., 1938, p. 3.

[52] 26 *Stat.* 826.

[53] See James W. Hurst, *The Growth of American Law: The Law Makers* (Boston, 1950), pp. 111ff.

[54] According to John P. Frank, biographer of District Judge and later Supreme Court Justice Peter V. Daniel: "The office of Federal district judge for the eastern district of Virginia was a post of more honor than labor, and little financial reward. Daniel himself estimated that the office left him with almost ninety percent of his time free. . . . The total number of all of the cases handled in the district court at the Richmond sessions during Daniel's five years of service was under fifty. . . . Daniel's circuit court work, though not heavy, was more substantial" (*Justice Daniel Dissenting*, pp. 143-44, 146).

[55] Nationwide, the bulk of mid-nineteenth-century district court business consisted of admiralty and criminal cases. Surrency, "A History of Federal Courts," pp. 215-16.

long time, to be of the rugged individualistic type." This condition was regrettable, but unavoidable, because "their living and their position is conducive to the development of trends which the same individual probably would not manifest if he were in competitive business."[56]

A Mobile Judiciary

No aspect of the federal judiciary more clearly symbolized its historic administrative system than the immobility of the inferior court judges. For many years the organization of the federal courts was based not only on frozen district boundaries but on frozen judges within those confines as well. Not until 1850 was it possible for a district judge to sit in a district other than his own. Even then the assignment was confined to districts within his own circuit or to those in a contiguous circuit for the sole purpose of assisting a sick or disabled judge.[57]

But this principle of immobility was subject to continuous erosion. In 1907 Congress permitted the Chief Justice to assign a judge from any foreign circuit to aid a circuit encumbered with a disabled judge. As a prerequisite, a certificate of disability issued by the circuit judge of the receiving circuit was required; this he issued only after determining the actual disability of his judge and the impracticability of designating a judge from another district within his own circuit.[58]

General intercircuit assignments received a major impetus six years later. That year Congress responded to the entreaties of the senior circuit judges of the Second Circuit who, with the help of two attorneys general, had been campaigning for "a law permitting the overworked circuit to have . . . the assistance of district judges in other circuits

[56] Evan A. Evans to D. Lawrence Groner, January 3, 1939, Duncan Lawrence Groner Papers, Box 11 (Alderman Library, University of Virginia, Charlottesville, Virginia; cited hereafter as Groner Papers).
[57] 9 Stat. 442. [58] 34 Stat. 1417.

14

who are not fully occupied."[59] Applicable only to the Second Circuit, the Act of October 13, 1913 enabled the Chief Justice of the United States to dispatch a district judge from any one of the nine circuits to the Second Circuit on certification by the senior circuit judge in New York of a need for it. In addition it required the consent of the designated district judge to the assignment. He went to a far district only of his own volition; no judge, not even the Chief Justice, could compel him to go.[60] Whether or not the Act relieved the chronically congested courts in New York "for all time" as Senior Circuit Judge E. H. Lacombe had predicted,[61] it did provide an entering wedge for more extensive reforms.

After 1913 efforts were made to expand the assignment power then restricted to the Second Circuit. The able senior circuit judge of the Sixth Circuit, Arthur C. Denison, sought a broad construction of the 1913 measure as well as of Section 13 of the Judicial Code permitting intercircuit assignments to relieve disabled judges. Chief Justice Edward Douglas White, however, interposed fatal objections. Refusing to approve the transfer of a Texas judge to sit in Detroit's congested federal district court, he ruled that the limited intent of Congress as revealed in the Act of 1913 barred any expansive interpretation of another section of the Code.[62] Thus, only a judge's physical or mental deficiencies, not delays arising from a heavy volume of business, re-

[59] H. Snowden Marshal to James C. McReynolds, September 9, 1913, Correspondence of the Administrative Office of the United States Courts, Record Group 116, 52-A-18, Box 3 (Federal Records Center, Alexandria, Virginia; cited hereafter as Administrative Office Correspondence).

[60] 38 *Stat.* 203.

[61] E. H. Lacombe to George W. Wickersham, December 24, 1909, Administrative Office Correspondence, 52-A-18, Box 3.

[62] Arthur C. Denison to Andrew J. Volstead, July 8, 1921, Legislative Files, House, H.R. 7110, 67th Cong. (National Archives, Washington, D.C.; cited hereafter as Legislative Files). See also Arthur C. Denison to A. Mitchell Palmer, December 31, 1919, Administrative Office Correspondence, 52-A-18, Box 3.

mained the sole criteria for valid use of the assignment power.[63]

Attempts by the Department of Justice and Judge Denison to amend the Judicial Code received a cool reception from Chief Justice Edward D. White. Although his objections were technical, he apparently entertained real qualms about the implications of an integrated federal judiciary. One feature of the Act of 1913 particularly disturbed him. That provision prevented a senior circuit judge from refusing to release his district judges for service in a foreign circuit unless the business of the designated justice's district was in arrears. The condition of the other districts in the circuits was irrelevant to the operation of the Act, an important factor to those circuits "from which judges were taken for the purpose of being assigned to duty elsewhere."[64]

Although the Chief Justice had "often wished that some comprehensive plan might be devised to cure the gross inequality which now prevails between the districts," he felt that maintenance of the *status quo* offered the safest course because "of the difficulty which that consideration would involve, and the possible harm which might come to the whole system by attempting to deal with it."[65] In the face of this attitude, efforts to meet his objections[66] came to naught,[67] and the Department of Justice abandoned its pro-

[63] U.S., Congress, Senate, Committee on the Judiciary, *Increase of Judges of United States District Courts: Letter from Hon. Arthur C. Denison, United States Circuit Judge, to Hon. Knute Nelson, Chairman of the Committee on the Judiciary, Relative to H.R. 9103, Together with General Comments and Suggestions on Said Bill and an Analysis and Explanatory Note of a Proposed Substitute Therefor*, December 30, 1921, Committee Print, 67th Cong., 2d Sess., 1921, p. 2.

[64] Edward D. White to Arthur C. Denison, February 9, 1920, Administrative Office Correspondence, 52-A-18, Box 3.

[65] *Ibid.*

[66] Arthur C. Denison to Edward D. White, February 28, 1920, *ibid.*; A. C. King to Charles E. Stewart, April 28, 1920, *ibid.*

[67] Edward D. White to A. Mitchell Palmer, May 12, 1920, *ibid.*

16

posal.[68] Judge Denison, however, refused to surrender. Working through Congressman Andrew Volstead, his drafts reached the Sixty-sixth and Sixty-seventh Congresses,[69] but until Chief Justice White's departure from the scene these proposals remained in limbo. In the meantime, powerful social and political forces began an assault on a judicial system which in its procedures and administrative organization had changed little since its founding a century before.

Protest and Response

The chief justiceship of Edward Douglas White (1910-1921) coincided with important changes in the American political and judicial climate, changes which had far-reaching implications for procedural and administrative reform of the federal judicial system. In large measure, these reforms would be a response to vitriolic criticisms leveled at the federal courts by the Populist-Progressive coalition. There existed two judicial systems "for two classes of people," argued Senator George W. Norris, "one for the poor and the other for the well-to-do."[70] The overriding issue to critics like Norris lay not with the federal judiciary's administrative deficiencies, but with its substantive decisions. "The public complains less that decisions are a long time in coming than it does that they are wrong when they come," commented another coalition spokesman.[71]

Such decisions as *Lochner v. New York*,[72] *Lowe v. Lawlor*,[73] and *Coppage v. Kansas*[74] were "wrong" because they effectively stymied state and federal social welfare legislation in the name of private property rights. The blame lay with the magistrates on the federal trial and appellate

[68] William L. Frierson to Arthur C. Denison, January 14, 1921, *ibid.*
[69] S. 4977, 66th Cong.; S. 2046 and H.R. 7110, 67th Cong.
[70] *New York Times*, April 23, 1922, sec. VI, p. 5.
[71] Gilbert E. Roe, *Our Judicial Oligarchy* (New York, 1912), p. 189.
[72] 198 U.S. 45 (1905).   [73] 208 U.S. 274 (1908).
[74] 236 U.S. 1 (1915).

17

benches. These men, argued Senator Norris, were "not responsive to the pulsations of humanity [because] the security of a life position and a life salary makes them forget too often the toiling masses who are struggling for an existence."[75] Thus the Populist-Progressives during the early decades of the century sought to infuse federal judicial institutions with elements of popular democracy, to alter the substance of judicial decisions,[76] to change the selection of federal judges,[77] and to circumscribe their power[78] and the jurisdiction of their courts.[79]

Influential members of the bench and bar challenged the attacks and programs of "that radical section of the community which would overthrow existing social, economic, and political institutions."[80] Warned William Howard Taft, in his 1914 Presidential Address to the American Bar Association: "The agitation with reference to the courts, the general attacks upon them, the grotesque remedies proposed of recall of judges and recall of judicial decisions, and the resort of demagogues to the unpopularity of courts as a means of promoting their own political fortunes, all impose on us, members of the Bar and upon judges of the courts and legislatures, the duty to remove . . . grounds for just criticism of our judicial system."[81]

[75] *New York Times*, April 23, 1922, sec. VI, p. 5.
[76] Theodore Roosevelt, "Judges and Progress," *Outlook*, vol. 100, January 6, 1912, pp. 40-48. See also *New York Times*, May 16, 1923, p. 21.
[77] *Ibid.*, September 30, 1924, p. 3.
[78] H.R. 9354, 65th Cong. See also: "Notes: Judicial Administration in the Federal Courts," *Harvard Law Review*, 31 (May 1928), 1012; *Congressional Record*, 67th Cong., 2d Sess., 1922, vol. 62, part 5, 5108.
[79] *Ibid.* See also S. 3151, 70th Cong.; Robert C. Brown, "The Jurisdiction of the Federal Courts Based on Diversity of Citizenship," *University of Pennsylvania Law Review*, 78 (December 1929), 179-94.
[80] "Report of the Committee on the Establishment of a Permanent Organization for the Improvement of the Law Proposing the Establishment of an American Law Institute," *American Law Institute, Proceedings*, 1 (1923), 1.
[81] "Address of President American Bar Association," *Report of the*

To Taft and his fellow members of the legal community, the substance of judicial decisions was emphatically not "grounds for just criticism." Progressive protests notwithstanding, Taft unhesitatingly discounted charges of economic bias in judicial decisions and attitudes. "The complaints that the courts are made for the rich and not for the poor," he asserted, were unrelated to the attitude of the courts toward substantive legal issues for the simple reason that "the judges of this country are . . . free from prejudice."[82] Thus reform must follow a path different from that advocated by the Populist-Progressives. As Roscoe Pound put it, "Public opinion must affect the administration of justice through the rules by which justice is administered rather than through the direct administration."[83]

Cumbersome procedures and defective judicial administration thus became the focus of attention for reformers as disparate jurisprudentially as Taft and Pound. In the words of the latter, these two weak pillars in the temple of justice constituted the "most efficient causes of dissatisfaction with the present administration of justice in America."[84] Their most obvious symptom was delayed justice. Delays in the administration of justice, said Taft, were "likely to grow in importance, as the inequality between the poor and rich in our civilization is studied."[85]

They were likely to grow quantitatively because the Roosevelt-Wilson era witnessed a mass of federal regulations ranging from the Federal Employers Liability Act[86] to the Volstead Act.[87] Consequently, much new litigation

---

37th Annual Meeting of the American Bar Association, 39 (1914), 384-85.

[82] William Howard Taft, "The Delays of the Law," *Yale Law Journal*, 18 (November 1908), 35.

[83] Roscoe Pound, "The Causes of Popular Dissatisfaction with the Administration of Justice," *Journal of the American Judicature Society*, 20 (February 1937), 180.

[84] *Ibid.*, p. 183.

[85] Taft, "The Delays of the Law," p. 30.

[86] 35 *Stat.* 65.　　　　　　　　　　[87] 41 *Stat.* 305.

came to the doors of federal courthouses. This condition, accompanied by congested dockets and delays, arose, commented Taft, because "every reformer thinks if he can only get his case into Federal Court he'll make a killing."[88]

To meet this challenge, conservative reformers proposed not an infusion of more democracy into the judicial process, but a regeneration of the existing judicial institution. In a climate of reform then pervading the country, they took the same goals as those sought by bureaus of municipal research and President Taft's pioneering Commission on Economy and Efficiency, which had called for "the integration of all administrative agencies of the Government . . . into a unified organization for the most effective and economical dispatch of public business."[89]

Across the land slogans echoed, calling for economy, efficiency, effectiveness, simplicity, integration, and coordination.[90] And the federal courts were a likely subject for the application of these principles, for an efficient federal court system offered a model to be emulated by state and local judicial reformers.[91]

The reform movement itself followed two major paths, one leading toward modernization of federal procedure and the other toward reform of the judiciary's administrative organization. The separation of powers doctrine could conceivably have provided the federal courts with a ra-

[88] William Howard Taft, "Address to the Bar Association of Chicago," December 27, 1921, p. 2, William Howard Taft Papers, Addresses and Articles (Library of Congress, Washington, D.C.; cited hereafter as Taft Papers).

[89] U.S., Congress, House, *President's Special Message to Congress Accompanied by a Report on the Outline of the United States Government Prepared by His Committee on Economy and Efficiency*, 62d Cong., 2d Sess., 1912, House Exec. Doc. 458, p. 4.

[90] William Howard Taft, "Proceedings of the Judicial Section," *Report of the 39th Annual Meeting of the American Bar Association*, 41 (1916), 742ff.

[91] See "Message of the President," *Congressional Record*, 62d Cong., 3d Sess., 1912, vol. 49, part 1, 210.

tionale for developing inherent plenary power over their own procedures and administration.[92] But instead, judges and their allies looked then, and would continue to look, to Congress for enabling legislation.[93] The fountainhead of congressional power was Article III which authorized Congress to establish the inferior courts. This power, implemented by the "necessary and proper" clause, constituted authority for extensive legislative control over the lower federal courts.[94]

The leaders of the well-documented campaign for procedural reform[95] consequently looked to Congress for means of alleviating delays and confusion in the administration of justice arising from the Conformity Act of 1872.[96]

[92] "Memorandum—Constitutionality of a Statutory Alternative to Impeachment," in U.S., Congress, Senate, Subcommittee on Improvements in Judicial Machinery of the Committee on the Judiciary, *Hearings, on S. 1506, S. 1507, S. 1508, S. 1509, S. 1510, S. 1511, S. 1512, S. 1513, S. 1514, S. 1515, and S. 1516, Judicial Reform Act,* 91st Cong., 1st and 2d Sess., 1969 and 1970, p. 224.

[93] Joseph D. Tydings, "The Courts and Congress," *Public Administration Review,* 31 (March/April 1971), 115.

[94] Art. I, sec. 8, cl. 18 reads: "To make all laws which shall be necessary and proper for carrying into execution . . . all other powers vested by this Constitution in the Government of the United States, or in any department or officer thereof." See also *Wayman v. Southard,* 10 Wheat., 1, 21-22 (1825); William H. Rehnquist, U.S., Congress, Senate, Subcommittee on Separation of Powers of the Committee on the Judiciary, *Hearings, on the Independence of Federal Judges,* 91st Cong., 2d Sess., 1970, p. 341.

[95] The literature is voluminous. See, generally, William W. Barron and Alexander Holtzoff (rev. Charles A. Wright), *Federal Practice and Procedure with Forms,* Rules Edition (St. Paul, 1960), I, 8-24; Henry P. Chandler, "Some Major Advances in the Federal Judicial System, 1922-1947," *Federal Rules Decisions,* 31 (1963), 477-516; Charles E. Clark, "Two Decades of the Federal Rules," *Columbia Law Review,* 58 (April 1958), 435-51; Charles E. Clark, "Code Pleading and Practice Today," in Alison Reppy, ed., *David Dudley Field: Centenary Essays* (New York, 1941), pp. 55-72; William D. Mitchell, "The Federal Rules of Civil Procedure," in *ibid.,* pp. 73-82; Edson R. Sunderland, "Modern Procedural Services," in *ibid.,* pp. 83-97.

[96] 17 *Stat.* 197, Sec. 5.

21

Requiring the adherence by federal courts to state procedures in all civil cases at common law, that act spawned a great diversity of procedures in the federal tribunals. These variations reflected, of course, the different state procedures on which, by the act, the federal procedure was patterned. Thus, common law pleadings, rooted in the old forms of action, characterized federal procedure in some United States district courts, while modern code pleading typified that in adjacent districts.

Under the leadership of Roscoe Pound, William Howard Taft, and Thomas W. Shelton, its congressional lobbyist, the American Bar Association launched, in 1912, what became a long-term battle for a uniform system of law pleadings.[97] Ten years later, the proposed reform was expanded to include not merely modernization of procedures at law, but also the merger of law and equity procedures in one form of civil action.[98]

In spite of strenuous efforts on the part of Taft, Shelton, and key congressmen, the procedural reform movement remained stalled throughout the 1920s. Repeatedly, bills introduced in Congress were beaten down by Senator Thomas J. Walsh of Montana, whom Taft considered "one of the most narrow-minded men" he knew.[99] To Walsh, procedural reform meant inconvenience for small-town lawyers required to learn both federal and state court procedures,[100] and, above all, it meant that the Supreme Court would formulate any such rules. Such delegation of the rule-making power would, he believed, set a precedent for

[97] "Report of the Committee on Judicial Administration and Remedial Procedures," *Report of the 35th Annual Meeting of the American Bar Association*, 37 (1912), 434-36.

[98] "Report of the Committee on Uniform Judicial Procedures," *Report of the 45th Annual Meeting of the American Bar Association*, 47 (1922), 80-82, 370-87.

[99] William Howard Taft to Horace Dutton Taft, December 7, 1924, Taft Papers.

[100] Thomas J. Walsh, *Reform of Federal Procedure*, Senate Doc. 105, 69th Cong., 1st Sess., 1926, pp. 2-3.

22

legislative delegation of power to determine "what inferior courts should be constituted, what jurisdiction they shall have, how causes shall be removed from the State to the Federal courts, what salaries the judges shall have."[101]

Although Senator Walsh's resistance so discouraged the Bar Association that in 1933 it terminated all organized efforts to secure procedural reforms,[102] those who were campaigning for reform of the judiciary's administrative organization had, in the meantime, met with success at local, state, and national levels. The Chicago Municipal Court was organized in 1906 and thereafter became a model for judicial reformers across the country. Its Chief Justice had extensive administrative powers; he was empowered to classify the business of the court, to assign judges to various classes of cases, to confer with his colleagues in administrative matters, and to assemble and publish a statistical record of judicial business.[103]

Meanwhile reform of judicial administration in the states had begun, led, characteristically, by Wisconsin. Its Board of Circuit Judges, established in 1913, was the precursor of many state judicial councils created to facilitate fair distribution of work among the courts, and to provide greater efficiency in the mundane administrative tasks of court housekeeping.[104] These councils were, in effect, central executive agencies designed to meet the demand "for some central clearing house of information and ideas which will focus attention upon the existing system and encourage suggestions for its improvement. . . ."[105]

---

[101] *Ibid.*, p. 13.

[102] "Report of the Committee on Uniform Judicial Procedure," *Report of the 56th Annual Meeting of the American Bar Association*, 58 (1933), 108-10.

[103] Herbert Harley, "Administering Justice in Cities," *Annals of the American Academy of Political and Social Science*, 136 (March 1928), 89-90.

[104] William F. Willoughby, *Principles of Judicial Administration* (Washington, 1929), pp. 264ff.

[105] Quoted in *ibid.*, p. 266.

23

The role of such state organs in promoting communications among dispersed courts, formulating administrative policies, and transmitting them to the legislature were among the reform proposals advocated by and activities chronicled in the pages of the *Journal of the American Judicature Society*. Founded early in the century by Herbert Harley, the *Journal* articulated the views and accomplishments of the conservative reformers. Integrated judicial administration, it repeated again and again, was the answer to congested dockets. "Closer co-ordination of judges," it urged in 1919, was "the remedy indicated for the avoidance of individual eccentricities."[106]

Taft and Judges-at-Large

Confirmation of William Howard Taft as Chief Justice brought to the Supreme Court a leading conservative reformer. As senior judge of the court of appeals in the Sixth Circuit, he had demonstrated an abiding interest in centralized administration of that court. There, he assumed personal responsibility for those cases which had been pending before the court for long periods of time.[107] Later, impressed by the operation of the then recently established Chicago Municipal Court, Taft would urge on members of the bench and bar that court's "plan of executive management of the judicial force and [its] making the head of the court responsible for the disposition of all the judicial business."[108]

His campaign for administrative integration of the judiciary achieved an evanescent fulfillment during his presi-

[106] "Our Comprehensive Programme," *Journal of the American Judicature Society*, 2 (April 1919), 167.

[107] William H. Taft to Harry M. Daugherty, July 3, 1921, Department of Justice Files, Judicial Districts Administration Files, Record Group 60, No. 144446, Sec. 2 (National Archives, Washington, D.C.; cited hereafter as Department of Justice Files).

[108] William H. Taft, "Attacks on the Courts and Legal Procedure," *Kentucky Law Journal*, 5 (November 1916), 17.

dency. In 1910 Congress established the United States Commerce Court, composed of judges-at-large assignable by the Chief Justice. To Taft's Attorney General, George W. Wickersham, its organization represented "the first step" toward an administratively integrated federal judicial system.[109]

But it proved a brief first step because the ill-fated court came under devastating attack from the Progressives in Congress. Throughout the struggle over its survival, Attorney General Wickersham endeavored to save the members of the court, who were "a body of five circuit judges at large, who may be sent to places where there is a congestion of business or a shortage of judges."[110] Although Congress abolished the court, it spared the judicial offices from a like fate. Hence, the mobile magistrates who had held these offices remained on the federal bench as circuit judges-at-large.[111]

After his departure from the White House in March 1913, Taft became a leading proponent of an integrated federal judiciary with mobile judges. From many platforms he pressed his campaign for "a system by which the whole judicial force of circuit and district judges could be distributed to dispose of the entire mass of business promptly."[112]

Appointed Chief Justice, he did more than talk; he acted. Convinced that his nomination had been accelerated because of Attorney General Daugherty's desire for assistance

[109] George W. Wickersham to Alexander W. Smith, December 9, 1910, Department of Justice Files, No. 144446, Sec. 1. See Act of June 18, 1910. 36 *Stat.* 539.

[110] George W. Wickersham to Francis E. Warren, June 4, 1912, quoted in *Congressional Record*, 62d Cong., 2d Sess., 1912, vol. 48, part 8, 7972.

[111] Act of October 22, 1913. 38 *Stat.* 219. For legislative history see Frankfurter and Landis, *The Business of the Supreme Court*, pp. 168-73. Also see U.S., Congress, Senate, Committee on the Judiciary, *Legislative History of the United States Circuit Courts of Appeals and the Judges who Served During the Period 1801 through March, 1958*, Committee Print, 85th Cong., 2d Sess., 1958, pp. 21-26.

[112] "Address of President," *Report of the 37th Annual Meeting of the American Bar Association*, 39 (1914), 384.

in initiating judicial reforms,[113] he wrote Daugherty within hours after his confirmation as Chief Justice. In a long letter, Taft set forth his grand design for federal judicial reform. He did it, he told Daughterty, in order "that you may see what was running in my mind so you could take them up and wipe them off the slate or modify them as may seem wise."[114]

Uppermost in his mind was the securing of district judges-at-large. In language almost identical to that which he had used seven years before in his Presidential Address to the American Bar Association,[115] he called for the application of the judicial force "at points where . . . arrears have a tendency to accumulate by some one made responsible by law and given authority to direct its use where needed."[116] A five-man committee of district judges and United States attorneys appointed by the Attorney General[117] promptly echoed Taft by reporting in favor of judges-at-large who "may be mobilized through designation by the Chief Justice at the suggestion of the Attorney General and senior circuit judges at points most needed and so marshalled as to render the most efficient service."[118]

That the committee's recommendation followed the

[113] William Howard Taft to Helen H. Taft, July 2, 1921, Taft Papers.

[114] Taft to Harry M. Daugherty, June 3, 1921, Department of Justice Files, No. 144446, Sec. 2.

[115] "Address of President," *Report*, 39 (1914), 384.

[116] Taft to Daugherty, July 3, 1921, Department of Justice Files, No. 144446, Sec. 2.

[117] The members were Judge John E. Sater of the Sixth Circuit (chairman); Judge John C. Pollack, Eighth Circuit; Judge William I. Grubb, Fifth Circuit; William H. Hayward, U.S. attorney for the Southern District of New York; and Charles F. Clyne, U.S. attorney for the Northern District of Illinois (secretary).

[118] U.S., Congress, Senate, Committee on the Judiciary, *Additional Judges for the Federal Courts: Report of the Committee Selected by the Attorney General to Suggest Emergency Legislation to Relieve the Federal Courts of Their Congested Condition*, Committee Print, 67th Cong., 1st Sess., 1921, p. 2.

course urged by the Chief Justice was hardly accidental. Not only had Taft expounded his ideas to the Attorney General in writing[119] and in person,[120] but he also met with the Attorney General's committee.[121] Following a long session, he wrote that the members had "agreed substantially on my plan."[122]

So strongly did the Chief Justice feel about the need for freely assignable judges that he pressed the Attorney General to double the proposed number from nine to eighteen.[123] The plan was then presented to Congress as a palliative for an expensive and congested judicial process. It was cheap, the Attorney General assured Congress, because transient judges did not require clerks and marshals as did permanent judges.[124] It was efficient, said Taft, who confidently predicted that "if we have those 18 judges thus to be disposed of through the country, we can make a great hole in the docket. . . ."[125]

The plan, however, represented a significant deviation from existing practices, and some judges, lawyers, and a number of congressmen remained unconvinced of its efficacy. The senior circuit judge of the Seventh Circuit, Francis E. Baker, thought "the bill for peripatetic judges . . . all wrong,"[126] because it would jeopardize district court cal-

[119] Taft to Daugherty, July 3, 1921, No. 144446, Sec. 2.
[120] Taft to Helen H. Taft, July 12, 1921, Taft Papers.
[121] Harry M. Daugherty, U.S., Congress, Senate, Committee on the Judiciary, *Hearings, on S. 2432, S. 2433, S. 2523, Additional Judges, United States District Courts,* 67th Cong., 1st Sess., 1921, p. 20 (cited hereafter as *Hearings on S. 2432*).
[122] Taft to Helen H. Taft, July 15, 1921, Taft Papers.
[123] See George W. Strong, "Memorandum for Attorney General," August 15, 1921, Department of Justice Files, No. 144446, Sec. 2; Taft to Harry M. Daugherty, August 8, 1921, Taft Papers; Daugherty to Taft, August 11, 1921, *ibid.*
[124] Harry M. Daugherty to Andrew J. Volstead, August 19, 1921, Legislative Files, House, H.R. 8875, 67th Cong.
[125] Senate Committee on the Judiciary, *Hearings on S. 2432*, p. 12.
[126] Francis E. Baker to James E. Watson, December 15, 1921, Department of Justice Files, No. 144446, Sec. 3.

endar systems. Members of the bar, argued one lawyer, "will hesitate to bring their matters before the judge-at-large [because] the itinerant character of the judge-at-large would make him inaccessible to the attorneys."[127] Their objections went deeper, however. An outside judge whose judicial philosophy was unknown and whose decisions might reflect norms prevalent elsewhere was automatically suspect. As Taft had perceived, they were suspect precisely because of their freedom from "those ameliorating local influences so dear to a man who is 'up against it.' "[128] As Senator Lee S. Overman of North Carolina asked rhetorically in assailing the assignment of a North Carolina judge to Wisconsin: "What does he know about the law in Wisconsin? What does he know about your people? What does he know about . . . conditions existing there?"[129]

Congressional opposition was strong, and Taft's own speech-making did little to alleviate it. Traveling about the country in quest of bar support for judges-at-large, he constantly alluded to them as a "flying squadron of judges"[130] and as a "Light Horse Cavalry"[131] available for "massing . . . in the particular districts that most need additional judicial force."[132] His assurances that such judges were only "a temporary provision to meet the emergency" and would be assigned to fixed districts on termination of the existing congestion crisis proved unavailing.[133] In the House Judiciary Committee the opportunity died for equipping the federal judiciary with judges whose service would "be really of a

[127] Thomas W. White to Harry M. Daugherty, October 26, 1921, *ibid.*, Sec. 2.
[128] Taft to Daugherty, July 3, 1921, *ibid.*
[129] *Congressional Record*, 67th Cong., 2d Sess., 1922, vol. 62, part 5, 5097-98.
[130] See William H. Taft, "Possible and Needed Reforms in the Administration of Justice in the Federal Courts," *Report of the 45th Annual Meeting of the American Bar Association*, 47 (1922), 250-51.
[131] Handwritten margin comment in William H. Taft, "Address to the Bar Association of Chicago," Taft Papers, p. 4.
[132] *Ibid.*   [133] *Ibid.*

national character."[134] With it went Taft's hope for a dramatic reform of judicial administration. His dissatisfaction would eventually be assuaged by the authorization of twenty-four additional judgeships, the largest single increase since 1789.[135]

Defeat of the mobile judge proposal still left open the possibility of universalizing the inter-circuit assignment provision then applicable only to the Second Circuit. This course had been noted by the Attorney General's committee which saw "no good reason why the district judges in any circuit who are not sufficiently employed in their own districts and circuits should not be available in any of the congested districts in any circuit, or why they should be assignable in the second circuit only."[136]

However, the Act of 1913 contained defects which had reduced its effectiveness. One was a requirement that the district judge selected by the Chief Justice to sit in New York "shall have consented in writing to such designation and appointment."[137] This voluntary procedure, as distinguished from a compulsory system advocated by Attorney General James C. McReynolds,[138] reflected a congressional belief that "district judges take office . . . with the understanding of a sort of contractual relation with the public in the discharge of their duty, to the effect that they would perform their services in their circuits. . . ."[139]

Less than a decade later, both Chief Justice Taft and Attorney General Daugherty successfully assailed this position in winning a House committee recommendation "that

[134] John E. Sater, Senate Committee on the Judiciary, *Hearings on S. 2432*, p. 27.

[135] 42 *Stat.* 839.

[136] Senate Committee on the Judiciary, *Report of the Committee Selected by the Attorney General*, 1921, p. 4.

[137] 38 *Stat.* 203.

[138] James C. McReynolds to H. Snowden Marshal, May 16, 1913, Administrative Office Correspondence, 52-A-18, Box 3.

[139] Henry D. Clayton, *Congressional Record*, 63d Cong., 1st Sess., 1913, Vol. 50, Part 6, 5209.

the matter of assignment to another district ought not to rest on the assent of the judge proposed to be transferred, ... but ... it should be the duty of such judge to accept the assignment."[140] Later, the enacted measure would incorporate this suggestion.[141]

Another feature of the Second Circuit Act had been the relative absence of control by the senior circuit judge over the departure of his district judges.[142] To soothe their antagonism toward "any plan for increasing . . . foreign drafts,"[143] Circuit Judge Arthur C. Denison urged broader discretion for the senior circuit judge in certifying the departures of his designated district judges.[144] A bill drafted by him incorporated this idea.[145] It provided for certification by the senior circuit judge of the receiving circuit as to the necessity for outside assistance and for the consent to the district judge's assignment by the senior circuit judge of the sending circuit. With these arrangements complete, the Chief Justice might then officially designate and assign the district judge.[146]

The Judicial Conference of Senior Circuit Judges

Intimately linked to this modified assignment power was a conference of judges. For William Howard Taft the creation of a single or multi-judge agency for exercising such power had long seemed a vital step toward administrative

[140] U.S., Congress, House, Committee on the Judiciary, *Additional District Judges for Certain Districts, etc.*, Report to Accompany H.R. 8875, H. Rept. 482, 67th Cong., 1st Sess., 1921, p. 4.

[141] 42 *Stat.* 839, sec. 3.

[142] 38 *Stat.* 203.

[143] Arthur C. Denison to Andrew J. Volstead, July 8, 1921, Legislative Files, House, H.R. 7110, 67th Cong.

[144] See Arthur C. Denison to William L. Frierson, February 3, 1921, Administrative Office Correspondence, 52-A-18, Box 3.

[145] S. 2523, 67th Cong.

[146] 42 *Stat.* 839, Sec. 3. See also Knute Nelson to William Howard Taft, October 1, 1921, Taft Papers.

integration of the inferior federal courts. His first thoughts on its design were expressed in 1914. Then, he had proposed that the power be conferred "upon the head of the Federal judicial system, either the Chief Justice, or a council of judges appointed by him, or by the Supreme Court to consider each year the pending Federal judicial business of the country and to distribute the Federal judicial force of the country through the various districts and intermediate appellate courts. . . ."[147] As Chief Justice, however, he revised and clarified his original views. In July 1921, he urged that decisive administrative power be exercised by "the Chief Justice and the Senior Circuit Judges of the nine circuits upon conference with the Attorney General."[148] Judicial assignments in the lower courts would then be made on the initiative of the Attorney General. This conference, Taft thought, might meet annually "at a convenient season . . . at Washington to consider the prospect for the year and to make all possible provision for it."[149]

The following month a measure in draft form received the Chief's approval,[150] but not before he had urged two amendments. He suggested that district judges should do more than merely communicate to their senior circuit judges the number of cases on the court dockets; they should express their "best judgment as to the amount of arrears, if any. . . ."[151] In addition, he recommended that the Attorney General not simply attend the conference, but that he "take part therein as a member."[152] This recommendation accorded with his wish, expressed earlier, to work

[147] Taft, "Attacks on the Courts and Legal Procedure," pp. 14-15.
[148] Taft to Daugherty, July 3, 1921, Department of Justice Files, No. 144446, Sec. 2.
[149] *Ibid.*
[150] Taft to Daugherty, August 8, 1921, *ibid.*
[151] *Ibid.* See also H.R. 8875, sec. 2, para. 3, 67th Cong. 42 *Stat.* 838, sec. 2, para 2.
[152] George E. Strong, "Memorandum for Attorney General," August 15, 1921, Department of Justice Files, No. 144446, Sec. 2. See also H.R. 8875, 67th Cong., sec. 2, para. 4.

closely with the Attorney General in assigning judges.[153]

Like the proposal for judges-at-large, the modified conference-assignment provision drew strong criticism from Congress. Basic attachment to a loosely-structured judicial institution,[154] reluctance to delegate some of its supervisory powers over the inferior courts thereby endowing ex-President Taft with much enhanced administrative prerogatives,[155] and apprehension, heightened by the prominent lobbying role of the Anti-Saloon League,[156] over the use of that power, combined to threaten defeat of the vital conference-assignment provision.[157]

So pervasive were these cross-currents of opposition that at one point in the legislative process this section had been stricken from the bill, reconsidered, and replaced.[158] Later, a single-vote margin allowed its emergence from the fifteen-member Senate Judiciary Committee which then included a strong representation of the Populist-Progressive coalition.[159]

The Conference's Purpose

As modified to meet the demands of the Progressives as well as those of Chief Justice Taft, the bill in final form provided for a conference, composed of the Chief Justice and

[153] Taft to Daugherty, July 3, 1921, Department of Justice Files, No. 144446, Sec. 2.

[154] John K. Shields, *Congressional Record*, 67th Cong., 2d Sess., 1922, vol. 62, part 5, 4862.

[155] *Ibid.*, 4853; George W. Norris, *ibid.*, 5113-14.

[156] Unsigned Memorandum, "Reasons for Section 2 of amended H.R. 9103 Providing for an Annual Conference of the Chief Justice and Senior Circuit Judges," George W. Norris Papers (Library of Congress, Washington, D.C.), Tray 6, Box 8. See also Wayne B. Wheeler to George W. Norris, February 24, 1922, *ibid.*

[157] H.R. 9103, sec. 2, 67th Cong.

[158] *Congressional Record*, 67th Cong., 2d Sess., 1922, vol. 62, part 5, 4849.

[159] George E. Strong, "Memorandum for Attorney General, Re:

the senior circuit judges, but not of the Attorney General. As counsel for the most important litigant in the federal courts, his membership was attacked as "a monstrous proposition" by one senator.[160] Under such pressure, the Senate Judiciary Committee eliminated the Attorney General's membership, but not his participation.[161] The fundamental purpose of the conference, "to prepare plans for assignment and transfer of judges to or from" congested districts or circuits, remained intact.[162]

On its face, and, as soon became apparent in practice, the measure hardly transformed the Chief Justice into a commander-in-chief of an obedient group of subordinate judges. Instead, the Chief Justice actually enjoyed less formal assignment authority in relation to all the circuits than had Chief Justice White in respect to the Second. This paradox arose from the interposition of a senior circuit judge between the Chief Justice and the district judge available for assignment. Although the district judge could not, in theory, refuse an assignment, his superior within the circuit could do it for him. Chief Justice Taft recognized this limitation when he told the American Bar Association that "Gentlemen have suggested that I would send dry judges to wet territory and wet judges to dry territory, oblivious of the fact that the Chief Justice has not the means of assigning them to any particular work in any particular district to which he may assign them. . . ."[163]

On the other hand, the expanded assignment power clearly enhanced the status of the Chief Justice as leader of

Judgeship Bill," February 24, 1922, Department of Justice Files, No. 144446, Sec. 3. The vote stood 8 to 7.

[160] John K. Shields, *Congressional Record*, 67th Cong., 2d Sess., 1922, vol. 62, part 5, 4857.

[161] *Congressional Record*, 67th Cong., 2d Sess., 1922, vol. 62, part 5, 4857. See also *ibid.*, part 11, 11765.

[162] 42 *Stat.* 838, sec. 2, para. 3.

[163] Taft, "Possible and Needed Reforms in the Administration of Justice in the Federal Courts," *American Bar Association Journal*, 8 (October 1922), 601-02.

the federal judiciary. It endowed him with a power useful in rewarding friends and, possibly, for punishing enemies. Taft so indicated in a letter to Clarence Hale, a retired district judge originally appointed by President Theodore Roosevelt. "If the bill goes through . . . giving the Chief Justice more power in respect to the assignment of Judges to other circuits," he suggested, "it may be that you and I can agree occasionally on your hearing cases in one of the Southern Districts in the winter time when the beauties of living in Maine are a matter of retrospect or prospect."[164]

The mobility of the judicial manpower, the motives, real and suspected, of the Chief Justice in urging it, and the fears of Congress in approving it, had dominated the legislative history of the measure which ultimately became the Act of September 14, 1922.[165] Other purposes of the Act, especially those involving the contemplated functions of the conference of senior circuit judges, remained obscure. Nevertheless, the congressional debates and statutory language indicate that the framers perceived this new institution as an important step toward administrative integration, albeit one intimately related to effective use of the intercircuit assignment power. "Instead of having occasional and disjointed and disconnected communications between the Chief Justice and the various circuit judges," asserted Senator Albert B. Cummins of Iowa, "we have provided for a meeting at which the requirements of all the districts can be considered and compared."[166] This purpose was manifested in the statutory requirement that the "conference shall make a comprehensive survey of the condition of business in the courts of the United States."[167]

The newly-created conference thus provided the federal

[164] William H. Taft to Clarence Hale, November 14, 1921, Taft Papers.
[165] 42 *Stat.* 837.
[166] *Congressional Record*, 67th Cong., 2d Sess., 1922, vol. 62, part 4, 4854.
[167] 42 *Stat.* 838, sec. 2, para. 3.

judiciary with a catalyst for its tenuous lines of communication stretching thousands of miles across nine circuits. From each of these circuits, the senior circuit judge came to Washington. He would bring, said Chief Justice Taft, "what he ought to know, namely, the condition of his circuit acquired from the reports . . . filed with him by the district judges."[168] The report of the Attorney General was designed to make available additional information and analyses obtained through the special facilities of the Justice Department.[169]

Except for the assignment of judges, the use of this information was left vague. Conceivably, it might form the basis for recommendations to Congress. Traditionally, recommendations for legislation relating to the federal judiciary had emanated from and been pressed on Congress by the Attorney General,[170] by the American Bar Association,[171] and by individual judges acting on their own initiative.[172] No judicial legislative program nor agency for formulating and proposing one had ever existed.

The Conference of Senior Circuit Judges was not specifically authorized to fill the void. In fact, little attention had been devoted to this subject during the congressional debates although one opponent of the measure had perceived, perhaps as an afterthought, its potential develop-

[168] Senate Committee on the Judiciary, *Hearings on S. 2432*, p. 12. See also 42 *Stat.* 838, sec. 2, para. 21.

[169] 42 *Stat.* 839, sec. 2, para. 4.

[170] See George W. Wickersham to J. C. Pritchard, May 10, 1910, Administrative Office Correspondence, 52-A-18, Box 144; U.S., *Annual Report of the Attorney General of the United States for 1909* (Washington, 1909), p. 26.

[171] U.S., Congress, Senate, *Courts of the United States* (Edward Wetmore to George F. Hoar, February 27, 1899), Senate Doc. 142, 55th Cong., 3d Sess., 1899, pp. 1, 4; also, *Congressional Record*, 61st Cong., 3d Sess., vol. 46, part 2, 1542.

[172] William H. Sawtelle to Henry D. Clayton, November 21, 1916, George Sutherland Papers (Library of Congress, Washington, D.C.), Box 3. See also Thomas B. Felder to William T. Newman, May 25, 1918, *ibid.*

ment. He had predicted that "eventually . . . our Federal judiciary in conference assembled will become the propaganda organization for legislation for the benefit of the Federal judiciary." Especially would it "give official color to the judiciary's recommendations to Congress to create more judgeships."[173]

His prediction proved accurate, for Chief Justice Taft had long conceived of the conference or a like body playing just such a role. The Supreme Court, he suggested in 1914, might constitute a suitable forum. Free of those personal and political influences which the legal community associated with Congress, the high Court could objectively determine "how many judges are needed and where, and the judicial force could be increased to meet the real exigency."[174] Seven years later, Taft had changed his mind about the role of the Court, but envisioned the conference as performing the same task. It might "make recommendations to the Attorney General as to the need of additional Judicial force and where and of what rank." In this way Congress could "have the benefit of judgment formed on nothing but the need of service."[175] Whatever the congressional intent, that of the Chief Justice was unmistakably clear.

The power of the conference to act directly upon individual judges also remained ill-defined. Other than the transmission of information on docket conditions, the district judges appeared affected only by a provision enabling the conference to "submit such suggestions to the various courts as may seem in the interest of uniformity and expedition of business."[176] However, the vesting of this power in a central agency constituted an important departure

173 Clarence F. Lea, *Congressional Record*, 67th Cong., 2d Sess., 1921, vol. 62, part 1, 203.

174 "Address of President," *Report*, 39 (1914), 384.

175 Taft to Daugherty, July 3, 1921, Department of Justice Files, No. 144446, Sec. 2.

176 42 *Stat.* 838-39, sec. 2, para. 3.

from the autonomy historically enjoyed by the federal trial courts.

It had thus become a target of criticism during the congressional debates. Senator Thomas E. Watson of Georgia had warned that "the language of the bill is so vague that the convention [Judicial Conference] may virtually give orders to every district judge in the Union."[177] The senior circuit judges would, he continued, compel a district judge "to obey them, else they will make him feel sorry that he did not; they will punish him in some way."[178] Protested another senator, the power was "an entering wedge for . . . an assault upon the independence of the judiciary, which may grow and grow and sap and undermine that independence."[179]

In part, these fears had been stimulated by the rhetoric used by Chief Justice Taft in his testimony to the Senate Judiciary Committee. There, he publicly articulated thoughts previously expressed only to Attorney General Daugherty.[180] "This bill," he explained, "introduces a reasonable system of watching and supervising conditions by the judges of the courts of appeals."[181] The "mild annual observation" so contemplated afforded at least a slight counterweight to the judge whose "power not infrequently leads to a kind of indifference, . . . [and] he thinks that the people are made for the court instead of the court for the people."[182]

In the Chief Justice's mind the scope of the conference's scrutiny apparently extended no further than to an exami-

[177] *Congressional Record*, 67th Cong., 2d Sess., 1922, vol. 62, part 5, 5280.
[178] *Ibid.*
[179] John K. Shields, *ibid.*, 4863; also *ibid.*, part 11, 11669.
[180] Taft to Daugherty, July 3, 1921, Department of Justice Files, No. 144446, Sec. 2.
[181] Senate Committee on the Judiciary, *Hearings on S. 2432*, p. 11.
[182] *Ibid.*, p. 12.

nation of a judge's capacity to dispose of his case load.[183] This fixation on efficient utilization of the existing institution reflected his perception of the kind of crisis then challenging the federal judicial system. Others saw in the conference an instrument for promoting broad reform in judicial administration. Congressman Joseph Walsh of Massachusetts, House floor manager for the conference-assignment bill, contended that this power, as well as the mere communication of ideas at the meeting, would pave the way for greater uniformity throughout the nation in the manner of holding court, in procedure, and in sentencing.[184]

Even ethical misconduct was considered by at least one congressman as within the competence of the conference. A controversy involving a district judge's acceptance of employment as baseball arbitrator at a salary of $42,500 inspired an attempt to amend the pending measure. The proposal that $7,500-a-year district judges be barred from extra-judicial employment found little support, but it did lead one proponent of the bill to assert that the conference might facilitate the elimination of this and similar ethical problems.[185]

Sponsors of the conference-assignment provision disclaimed any intent to permit coercion of the judges. The report of the House committee denied "that such conference should result in any mandatory interference with the district courts." Nor would it "pursue any inquisitorial course."[186] Anxious to assure Congress of the innocuous consequences of any supervision of the inferior courts undertaken by the conference, Taft emphasized the new agency's

[183] William H. Taft, "Informal Address," *Report of the 44th Annual Meeting of the American Bar Association*, 46 (1921), 564.

[184] U.S., *Congressional Record*, 67th Cong., 2d Sess., 1921, vol. 62, part 1, 152, 202. See also Warren F. Martin to Francis J. Trimble, January 17, 1923, Department of Justice Files, No. 144446, Sec. 4.

[185] Joseph Walsh, *Congressional Record*, 67th Cong., 2d Sess., 1921, vol. 62, part 1, 151.

[186] House Committee on the Judiciary, *Additional District Judges for Certain Districts, etc.*, 1921, p. 3.

inability to criticize a judge. It might only inquire about the state of his work.[187] Yet the Chief Justice placed great confidence in publicity of docket conditions as a means of promoting efficient administration of justice. With it, he believed that peer-group influence would induce a fellow judge "to cooperate much more readily in an organized effort to get rid of business and do justice."[188]

Hardly a central office with managerial power, the conference established by the Act of 1922[189] constituted only a first step toward a more integrated administrative system. It was seen by those at the time as a medium for strengthening an already existing sense of professional identity and transforming it into an institutional one. To this end each senior circuit judge implicitly became a key link in a nationwide communications network. Through him information on judicial conditions and practices flowed into the Washington meeting. There, through a process of group interaction, ideas and policies were considered, and, in turn, disseminated to dispersed district judges and to Congress. The Act, in essence, created an institutional framework with administrative leadership and informal responsibility lodged in the Chief Justice and the presiding officers of the intermediate appellate courts.

[187] Senate Committee on the Judiciary, *Hearings on S. 2432,* p. 12.
[188] Taft, "Informal Address," 564.
[189] 42 *Stat.* 838, sec. 2.

CHAPTER 2

The Judicial Conference:
Formative Years under Taft and Hughes

Organization and Composition

THE first meeting of the Judicial Conference, held in December 1922, established the pattern of organization to which subsequent Conferences would conform. To this session came the senior circuit judges of each of the nine circuits as required by statute.[1] Six years later, creation of the Tenth Circuit out of the sprawling Eighth[2] brought an additional senior circuit judge to the Conference.[3] Then, in 1937, circuit representation was increased to eleven with the admission of the Chief Justice of the Court of Appeals for the District of Columbia. Although this tribunal was a "court of the United States" and the Conference considered the business of all such courts,[4] its presiding officer had been designated not as a "senior circuit judge" but as "Chief Justice." This "wholly inadvertent"[5] language effectively excluded him from membership in the Conference until 1937 when Congress amended the statute[6] on the recommendation of the Judicial Conference.[7]

The senior circuit judges or their designated substitutes

---

[1] 42 *Stat.* 838.   [2] 45 *Stat.* 1346.

[3] "Recommendations of Conference of Senior Circuit Judges," in U.S., *Annual Report of the Attorney General of the United States, 1929* (Washington, 1929), p. 2. (Cited hereafter as *Judicial Conference Report*. For a complete title-source listing, see Appendix A.)

[4] 42 *Stat.* 838.

[5] U.S., Congress, Committee on the Judiciary, *Representation of the United States Court of Appeals for the District of Columbia on Annual Conference of Senior Circuit Judges*, 1937, S. Rept. No. 736, to accompany H.R. 2703, 75th Cong., 1st Sess., 1937.

[6] 50 *Stat.* 473.

[7] *Judicial Conference Report, 1936*, p. 8.

who participated in the Conference under Chief Justice Taft ranged in age from youthful Martin Manton of the Second Circuit, who was 47 in his first year at the Conference, to 82-year-old Walter H. Sanborn of the Eighth Circuit. Collectively, the median age of the senior circuit judges varied from 64 in 1928 to 70 in 1925.[8]

The age discrepancies increased somewhat during the longer Hughes period. In 1939, John Biggs, Jr. of the Third Circuit, then 44 years old, began a quarter century of service on the Conference, while at the other end Judge William B. Gilbert of the Ninth terminated his career in 1930 at age 83. Although the outer limits of the age spectrum exhibited marked similarity to that of the Taft Conference, the median age of the senior circuit judges revealed an infusion of youth; it ranged from 68 years in 1930 to 59 years in 1934. However, after Hughes' first year, 1930, the median age never rose above 66 years.

Whatever their ages, these senior circuit judges were hardly new to the federal judiciary. Some brought as many as thirty years of experience on the appellate bench to the Taft Conference, while one judge brought thirty-eight years to those under Hughes. The average judge, however, came with substantial, but much less, experience. Typically in the Taft Conference, he had served on the federal bench for 11.3 years, while in those of Taft's successor, he had served for 10.5 years. As might be expected, however, the number of Conference members who had served for five or more years on the Conference increased by a third.

One characteristic which changed little was the Republicanism of the senior circuit judges in the two decades from 1922 to 1941. Appointed by a string of Republican presidents, prior to and after Woodrow Wilson's administration, a majority of them identified with the G.O.P. Thus, 52.4 per-

[8] Comparative data for *all* judges of the federal courts of appeals is found in John R. Schmidhauser, "Age and Judicial Behavior: American Higher Appellate Judges," in Wilma Donahue and Clark Tibbits, eds., *Politics of Age* (Ann Arbor, 1962), pp. 108-13.

cent in the Taft Conference and 53.8 percent in the Hughes Conference were aligned with that party.[9] In addition to the judges, a succession of attorneys general, accompanied by their assistants[10] and the solicitors general,[11] appeared at the Taft and Hughes conferences. Occasionally other interested parties joined them. Members of the Board of United States Tax Appeals attended the 1926 Conference[12] to join in discussion of uniform appellate court rules for review of Tax Board decisions.[13] The following year saw members of the Committee on Jurisprudence and Law Reform of the American Bar Association present suggestions to the Conference, probably on the proposed realignment of the circuits.[14]

The Chief's Long Shadow

The Chief Justice, as chairman *ex officio*, presided over the assemblage of nine to eleven ranking appellate court judges, the Attorney General, and, on rare occasions, invited guests. The statute merely empowered him to preside; he was not explicitly made a member of the Conference.[15] But Chief Justice Taft immediately established his membership by casting votes on several motions coming before the early Conferences.[16]

[9] Taft Conference (N = 21): 11 Republicans, 10 Democrats, data on one judge unavailable. Hughes Conference (N = 26): 14 Republicans, 11 Democrats, 1 independent.

[10] *Judicial Conference Report, 1925,* p. 6.

[11] *Ibid.,* 1928, p. 3.　　　　　　[12] *Ibid., 1926,* pp. 9-10.

[13] See William Howard Taft to Edmund Waddill, Jr., April 5, 1926, John J. Parker Papers, Box 53 (Southern Historical Manuscripts Collection, University of North Carolina, Chapel Hill, North Carolina; cited hereafter as Parker Papers).

[14] *Judicial Conference Report, 1927,* p. 4. See "Report of the Committee on Jurisprudence and Law Reform," in *Annual Report of the American Bar Association,* 51 (1926), 431.

[15] 42 *Stat.* 838.

[16] See Henry P. Chandler, "Some Major Advances in the Federal

Taft, as chairman, was the staff as well as the presiding officer of the Judicial Conference. From the first, he assumed the task of issuing the call of the Conference and preparing the agenda.[17] But the Chief's efforts sometimes went unheeded. Arriving late on the last day of the 1925 Conference, Judge Joseph Buffington of the Third Circuit announced that he "did not get into my mind the time of this session. I haven't done a blame thing. You got me out of bed at three o'clock this morning and I am on the job now."[18]

As the date of the first Conference session approached in 1922, Taft reminded the senior circuit judges that the law required district judges to submit to the senior circuit judges data on judicial business in their districts. "I suggest to you that you at once request the [district] judges to prepare a statement as to the condition of business with them on the first of October [1922]," he wrote the senior judges who might but dimly perceive their obligations to the newly-created Conference. The statement, Taft directed, should include "the prospect of the disposition of business during the ensuing Court year, together with recommendations as to the extra judicial force needed."[19] Meanwhile, he had pressed "the Attorney General to make a similar call upon the Clerks of the District Courts and generally to prepare a statement to be presented to the judicial council when it meets."[20]

Committees of the Conference emerged at the first session.[21] But as with the development of the congressional

---

Judicial System, 1922-1947," in *Federal Rules Decisions*, 31 (1963), 331, n. 3. See also *Judicial Conference Report, 1929*, p. 6.

[17] Chandler, pp. 331-33.

[18] "Report of the Fourth Conference of Senior Circuit Judges Called Pursuant to the Act of Congress, September 14, 1922," June 1925, p. 110, carbon copy, Parker Papers, Box 53.

[19] William H. Taft to Joseph Buffington, October 5, 1922, Taft Papers.

[20] *Ibid.*

[21] "The Federal Judicial Council," *Texas Law Review*, 2 (June, 1924), 459.

committee system, the early committees were largely *ad hoc* or select. The Chief Justice played a leading part in the creation of these precursors of an extensive committee network. It was a role which he would retain, as indicated by a resolution of the 1927 Conference, which delegated to him the power to establish "if at any time it seems necessary . . . ," a committee from the conference to recommend legislation on the fees charged by clerks.[22] Typically, the Conference charged committees with investigating a particular subject, collecting the relevant facts or opinions of judges, and presenting at a subsequent Conference session a written report accompanied by specific proposals.[23] These essentially "clearing-house"[24] duties were then performed by committees of small numbers of senior circuit judges, with no resources beyond those ordinarily available to such judges. Thus, the few Conference members who composed the first committees were "authorized to associate with them, as members thereof, circuit and district judges of convenient residence to act with them."[25]

From the first, the power to appoint committee members was a prerogative of the Chief Justice as chairman.[26] Specific authorization by the 1937 Conference permitting Chief Justice Hughes to enlarge a committee at his discretion only confirmed the existing practice.[27] Criteria for committee appointments varied. Often appointments went to the senior circuit judge who took the initiative in proposing creation, reconstitution, or expansion of committees or their duties.[28]

[22] *Judicial Conference Report, 1927*, p. 4.
[23] "The Federal Judicial Council," p. 459.
[24] *Judicial Conference Report, 1938*, pp. 22-23.
[25] "The Federal Judicial Council," p. 462.
[26] "Report of the Fourth Conference," p. 36.
[27] "Report of the Third Conference of Senior Circuit Judges Called by the Chief Justice Pursuant to the Act of September 14, 1922," October 1924, carbon copy, Parker Papers, Box 53.
[28] *Judicial Conference Report, 1931*, pp. 9-11. See also Francis E. Baker to Kimbrough Stone, July 6, 1923, Kimbrough Stone Papers, Box 11 (Western Historical Manuscripts Collection, University of

Taft deemed representation important when, in 1925, he suggested and obtained enlargement of a committee on law books for district court libraries "so as to include one more man to represent the other seven Circuits."[29] Similarly, in constituting a committee to investigate alleged malfunctioning of the bankruptcy system, the Chief selected "Judge Buffington, Judge Rogers, Judge Baker and Judge Bingham within whose circuits are the large cities of Philadelphia, New York, Chicago, and Boston, in which abuses are charged to exist."[30] Not until 1938, however, did the Conference formally expand committee membership to include district as well as appellate judges. That year, it established the Committee on District Court Rules, composed wholly of trial judges.[31]

Judicial specialists with needed expertise or political connections were recruited for some committees. The Chief Justice recognized Judge Martin Manton as a "politician down to the ground,"[32] and as one with wide experience in congressional lobbying when he selected the Second Circuit Judge for a committee to secure legislative authorization for law clerks.[33] Amending the Judicial Code required a different kind of expertise. For that task, Taft chose Senior Circuit Judge Arthur C. Denison, a judge with long experience in legislative drafting and widely respected by the judiciary committees of Congress.[34]

Chief Justice Taft reportedly conducted the sessions of

Missouri, Columbia, Missouri; cited hereafter as Kimbrough Stone Papers).

[29] Francis E. Baker to Kimbrough Stone, *ibid.*
[30] William H. Taft, "Memorandum for the Press," October 28, 1923, Speeches and Articles, Taft Papers.
[31] *Judicial Conference Report, 1938*, pp. 22-23.
[32] Alpheus T. Mason, *William Howard Taft: Chief Justice* (New York, 1965), p. 170.
[33] Martin T. Manton to John G. Sargent, October 4, 1927, Administrative Office Correspondence, 52-A-18, Box 141.
[34] See Martin T. Manton to George W. Norris, April 9, 1930, Norris Papers, Tray 42, Box 3.

the Judicial Conference with "rare charm and effectiveness."[35] He took a relatively small part in discussions on
such a technically complex subject as revision of the bankruptcy statutes, a realm in which he deferred to his Bankruptcy Committee.[36] But on issues requiring congressional
legislation, he played a prominent role. The 1924 Conference abruptly tabled a motion to recommend a court reporter system after Taft suggested that other agencies
should press for the measure.[37] At the same Conference, a
senior circuit judge dropped his effort to secure endorsement of a federal probation system when Taft indicated a
potentially negative congressional reaction to it. The popular trend, he suggested, "was towards more severity."[38]

The former President's creditability in legislative matters
sprang from his political experience and apparent expertise.
When the senior circuit judge of the Fifth Circuit queried
whether a term of the appeals court at Fort Worth might
be eliminated, the Chief had an answer which could only
enhance his own authority: "You write to Representative
[Hatton] Sumners and tell him you made this statement
here and that I said I would take it up with him, because he
is . . . the most powerful man on the Democratic side of the
[House Judiciary] Committee."[39]

Taft, however, did not emerge the victor on all issues. He
occasionally acted precipitously and thereby opened himself not so much to defeat on a formal vote, but rather to
criticism and inaction on the part of the other judges. The
1925 Conference refused to follow his recommendation that
it ascribe congestion in federal courts to the failure of some
states to enact "little Volstead" statutes. "To state it that way

[35] J. Warren Davis to William Howard Taft, November 2, 1927,
Taft Papers.
[36] See "Report of the Third Conference," p. 24.
[37] Ibid., p. 38. The vote was 8 to 1, Sanborn voting nay.
[38] Ibid., p. 39. Taft misjudged the legislative climate; five months
later the Act of March 4, 1925 created a federal probation system
(43 Stat. 1259).
[39] "Report of the Fourth Conference," pp. 99-100.

and publish it," protested one aged member, "would result in a very blatant attack from all parts of the country upon the Conference and the Courts."[40] Nor did the Conference approve Taft's proposal that it publicly favor replacement of the United States Attorney in the Northern District of West Virginia. That prosecutor had allegedly inspired impeachment charges against the district judge who was subsequently vindicated.[41] The ensuing hostility between the two officials had paralyzed judicial business in the district. After presenting his argument, Taft asked his fellow judges: "What do you say, gentlemen, are you willing to vote on that? We are called upon to help out. That is what this Conference is for."[42] But other members had a different sense of the proprieties and the subject was dropped.[43]

Some issues by their very nature generated conflict. Members of the 1924 Conference differed widely over the trial judges' responsibility for affirmatively expediting cases on his docket.[44] Strong opposition greeted a proposed Conference recommendation that "Continuances by agreement of counsel to another term shall not be allowed."[45] Over objections that the rule was "too harsh," the judges adopted it in an unusually close six to four vote.[46]

However much Chief Justice Taft sought unity and teamwork, conferences under his direction did not act as "rubber stamps." Dissent was endemic on some issues; and Taft lacked an appreciation of opposition, loyal or otherwise. He complained of Conference members who refused to work.[47]

---

[40] Walter H. Sanborn, *ibid.*, pp. 38-39.

[41] *Ibid.*, pp. 103-106. The judge was William E. Baker. See Joseph Borkin, *The Corrupt Judge: An Inquiry into Bribery and Other High Crimes and Misdemeanors in the Federal Courts* (New York, 1962), pp. 222-23.

[42] *Ibid.*, p. 105.   [43] *Ibid.*, pp. 105-06.

[44] "Report of the Third Conference," p. 23.

[45] *Ibid.*

[46] *Ibid.*, Bingham, Denison, Alschuler, and Sanborn voting nay.

[47] Taft to Helen H. Taft, September 27, 1923, Taft Papers.

47

Among them were "many who talk,"[48] and others who persistently advanced their ideas in a "desultory uninformed manner."[49] Then there existed a small coterie of purely "reactionary members who are impatient with all suggestions of reform."[50]

The nature of intra-Conference proceedings changed under Chief Justice Hughes, whose personality differed markedly from that of his predecessor. With a mind "trained to work with the precision of a fine watch,"[51] Hughes ran the Conferences in much the same way he conducted conferences of his own court.[52] The chairman's role, as he perceived it, lay in "dispatching business and reducing random talk."[53] It meant taking "the initiative . . . in most if not all" resolutions adopted by the Conference[54] as well as unhesitatingly expressing his "views on nearly every controversial question."[55] Finally, his role entailed stating the question and calling for the votes "beginning at one end of the table and going the rounds."[56]

The net result of Hughes' forceful leadership was reduced dissent in the conferences. It was a result fostered by the application of strong persuasion on those judges who evinced wayward tendencies,[57] and the simple charging of

[48] Ibid.
[49] Taft to Arthur C. Denison, March 19, 1925, ibid.
[50] Taft to Helen H. Taft, September 28, 1923, ibid.
[51] Orie L. Phillips to Henry M. Bates, in Henry M. Bates to Harlan Fiske Stone, December 17, 1945, Harlan Fiske Stone Papers (Library of Congress, Washington, D.C.), Box 3.
[52] See Alpheus T. Mason, Harlan Fiske Stone: Pillar of the Law (New York, 1956), p. 789.
[53] D. Lawrence Groner to Harlan Fiske Stone, September 8, 1941, Groner Papers, Box 12.
[54] Henry P. Chandler to Merlo Pusey, December 14, 1949, Administrative Office Correspondence, 59-A-532, Box 4.
[55] Groner to Harlan F. Stone, September 8, 1941, Groner Papers, Box 12.
[56] Ibid.
[57] Kimbrough Stone to John J. Cochran, December 21, 1931, Kimbrough Stone Papers, Box 11.

Conference committees to produce reports and proposals acceptable to him.[58] Such leadership had its effect, as explained by Senior Circuit Judge Kimbrough Stone, who left one of the last Conferences chaired by Hughes with an "uncomfortable feeling" that his colleagues had "acted upon quite a few matters of considerable importance without mature consideration and rather in a snap judgment sort of way."[59] Resolutions had been adopted, he contended, with "no thought or investigation before they were brought up for discussion."[60] As will be seen, this strategy would have far-reaching consequences for the Conference as an institution.

As Conference chairman, the Chief Justice necessarily became its public relations director. Recognizing that Taft "was the man to secure adequate publicity," at his suggestion the members of the 1924 Conference authorized him "to publish at his discretion" any portions of the minutes which "he thought should be made public."[61] So authorized, the Chief gave "to the press resolutions addressed to our Court, resolutions addressed to Congress, and resolutions addressed to the District Judges."[62] These reports, as could be expected, largely reflected the personalities of Taft and Hughes. Those by Taft were highly personal, rhetorical, and quite informal; those of his successor largely omitted Taft's "rollcall" of dilatory and efficient judges, substituting instead a highly organized and impersonal format.[63]

[58] Interview with Orie L. Phillips, February 22, 1965, Washington, D.C.
[59] Kimbrough Stone to Charles Evans Hughes, May 17, 1941, Kimbrough Stone Papers, Box 10.
[60] Kimbrough Stone to D. Lawrence Groner, August 2, 1941, Groner Papers, Box 8.
[61] "Report of the Third Conference," pp. 36-37.
[62] William Howard Taft to Horace Dutton Taft, December 7, 1924, Taft Papers. Also see Taft to the Chairman of the House of Representatives Judiciary Committee, February 13, 1924, Legislative File, H.R. 3318, 68th Cong.
[63] See Judicial Conference Report, 1929, p. 5; ibid., 1932, pp. 8-10.

49

In addition to the reports and press releases, Taft and Hughes promoted Conference-endorsed programs through appearances at meetings of bar associations[64] and the American Law Institute. The latter became the unofficial platform for the Chief Justice's annual address on the state of the federal judiciary. Taft, "one of the godfathers of the Institute,"[65] presided at the Institute's earlier sessions[66] and began the tradition of an address by the Chief Justice in 1927.[67] Hughes continued it. He used the forum provided by the Institute to urge that Congress promptly meet the needs of the federal courts for personnel and for procedural reforms.[68]

The very nature of the Conference with its geographically separated membership and infrequent meetings meant that during the yearlong interim between formal sessions, Taft and later Hughes not only spoke for the Conference, but acted for it as well. Sometimes they did so in pursuit of a specific Conference resolution,[69] or after polling the senior circuit judges and obtaining their approval for a contemplated course of action.[70] Occasionally, the Chief Justice, as Conference chairman, took the initiative without prior clearance from the senior judges. This procedure was noted by Attorney General John G. Sargent in 1927, when he told Senator George W. Norris that in spite of the omission of "the Northern District of New York . . . among the districts for which the Conference of Senior Circuit Judges has rec-

[64] William Howard Taft, "Possible and Needed Reforms in Administration of Justice in Federal Courts," *American Bar Association Journal*, 8 (October 1922), 601-07; *New York Times*, September 30, 1931, p. 26.

[65] "Mr. Wickersham," *The American Law Institute, Proceedings*, 5 (1927), 133. See also *ibid.*, 2 (1923-24), 93-94.

[66] William Howard Taft, remarks, *ibid.*

[67] *The American Law Institute, Proceedings*, 5 (1927), 133.

[68] "Address of the Chief Justice," *ibid.*, 12 (1934-35), 54-55.

[69] *Judicial Conference Report, 1925*, p. 8.

[70] Taft to Edmund Waddill, Jr., April 5, 1926, Parker Papers, Box 53.

ommended additional district judges, Chief Justice Taft . . . has, since the last meeting of the Conference, specially examined the situation in the Northern District of New York and concluded that an additional district judge is needed there."[71] And Taft's policy-making strategy was right out of Byzantium. When a Congressman from Florida requested his endorsement of an additional judgeship for the Southern District of that state, the following exchange ensued:

Taft:	How far is it from Jacksonville to Key West?
Cong.:	Five hundred and twenty-two miles.
Taft:	How far is it from Jacksonville to Pensacola?
Cong.:	Four hundred miles.
Taft:	How long is your coast-line?
Cong.:	About 1,400 miles.
Taft:	That is enough; I am convinced.[72]

The Chief Justice commanded the Conference. For Taft, it was command with a purpose, for the two- to five-day sessions afforded him a means of giving "unity to the Federal judicial force."[73] The social as well as the business aspects of the meetings were intended to inculcate a national perspective among the ranking federal judges. To this end, the Chief Justice arranged for Conference members to visit the White House and meet the President,[74] and "gave them a luncheon at the Metropolitan Club."[75] Judges from Port-

[71] John G. Sargent to George W. Norris, February 11, 1927, Department of Justice Files, 33-N-11; see also Charles Evans Hughes to Franklin Delano Roosevelt, February 22, 1935, Department of Justice Files, 109-X-11.

[72] U.S., Congress, House, Committee on the Judiciary, *Hearings, on H.R. 7730, Additional Judge for the Southern District of Florida*, 70th Cong., 1st Sess., 1928, p. 2. See also pp. 3-4.

[73] Taft to Felix Frankfurter, February 23, 1926, Taft Papers.

[74] *New York Times*, October 2, 1924, p. 13; September 28, 1926, p. 3.

[75] Taft to Robert A. Taft, October 2, 1927, Taft Papers.

land, Oregon to Concord, New Hampshire, and from Grand Rapids, Michigan to Huntsville, Alabama,[76] mingled with the associate justices of the Supreme Court, the solicitor general, and the Attorney General and his assistants.[77] They had informal exchanges with those who reviewed their cases on appeal, and buttonholed the Attorney General on the administrative needs of their courts.[78] Among themselves, they lined up support behind aspirants for the presidency of the American Bar Association. At the conclusion of the 1931 Conference, Senior Circuit Judge Kimbrough Stone informed an ultimately successful candidate for the association presidency that he had spoken with "Judges Buffington, Manton, Bryan, and Parker and each of them told me their men were all right for you."[79]

This social side of the conferences proved a great success. Even Associate Justice James McReynolds who attended the 1923 affair "expecting to be bored . . . was much pleased to find that he greatly enjoyed it."[80] Commented Taft: "That from a grouch like him was a great concession."[81] More importantly, from the Chief's point of view, the social activities strengthened the entire Conference, for they encouraged the members when they left for their circuits to feel "that the privilege of attending a Conference as a Senior Circuit Judge was worth while."[82] Nevertheless, the real significance of the Conference lay in its substantive work.

[76] *New York Times*, October 2, 1924, p. 13.

[77] See Taft to Helen H. Taft, September 27, 1923, Taft Papers. See also Chandler, "Some Major Advances," p. 333.

[78] Kimbrough Stone to William B. Mitchell, October 21, 1932, Administrative Office Correspondence, 52-A-18, Box 148; also Kimbrough Stone to Charles E. Stewart, October 24, 1930, *ibid.*

[79] Kimbrough Stone to Guy A. Thompson, October 7, 1931, Kimbrough Stone Papers, Box 15. Guy A. Thompson of St. Louis, Missouri was ABA President, 1931-32.

[80] Taft to Helen H. Taft, September 29, 1923, Taft Papers.

[81] *Ibid.*

[82] Taft to Robert A. Taft, October 2, 1927, Taft Papers.

52

The Attorney General's Report

The formal sessions of each Conference followed a stereotyped pattern. After appointment of the Conference secretary, usually the Chief Justice's own law clerk or personal secretary, and adoption of the minutes of the preceding meeting, the Attorney General of the United States reported on the business of the federal courts,[83] including a statistical overview of the state of the dockets. These were obtained from the court clerks and compiled by the Division of Accounts in the Justice Department. The statistics, together with the Attorney General's own interpretation of them, characteristically emphasized the department's abiding interest in the flow of government litigation, particularly criminal cases.[84] The usefulness of the statistics, however, left something to be desired. Taft thought them "unintelligible,"[85] while Hughes regarded the "statistics given us by the Attorney General, great as was the labor of their production, as of very little value."[86]

The Attorney General's report typically included something more than cold statistics. It also set forth complaints about judicial behavior received from United States attorneys in the field as well as recommendations for changes in judicial practice advantageous to the work of the Justice Department. Demanding that federal judges impose more severe sentences in criminal, especially Prohibition, cases, then Attorney General Harlan F. Stone deprecated "a tendency on the part of some judges to go light on those who

[83] Report of the Committee on Procedure of the Conference, "Report of the Third Conference of Senior Circuit Judges," pp. 20-21.

[84] See Henry P. Chandler, "An Administrative Office for State Courts," *Journal of the American Judicature Society*, 26 (June 1942), 9. See also "Memorandum for Mr. Will Shafroth, Re: Statistical Tables for Annual Reports," July 30, 1940, Administrative Office Correspondence, 60-A-328, Box 7.

[85] *Judicial Conference Report, 1926*, p. 7.

[86] 1930 Judicial Conference transcript, p. 257, in Chandler, "Some Major Advances," p. 355.

plead 'guilty.'"[87] Other attorneys general called for more motion days, fewer delays, more uniformity in sentencing,[88] and "more care in the appointment of United States commissioners,"[89] as well as requests for Conference endorsement of portions of the department's legislative program.[90]

The assembled senior circuit judges rarely received the Attorney General's complaints in silence. They availed themselves of the forum provided by the Conference to communicate their positions and, if possible, to secure his cooperation in resolving their problems. To Stone's complaint about criminal sentences, a Conference member responded that trial judges were compelled to hand out lenient sentences because "federal agents refused to go after 'big bootleggers' and brought in trivial cases."[91] Were district courts congested? If so, the judges requested that the Attorney General withdraw protracted mail fraud cases and institute them elsewhere.[92]

The great majority of complaints and requests, however, related to the department's role as the administrative agency of the federal courts charged with an endless array of sensitive housekeeping duties. Senior circuit judges complained of the need for adequate law libraries,[93] for additional judgeships,[94] and for court facilities and personnel.[95] Aside from requests for inclusion of larger judicial appropriations in the department's budget,[96] they called on that agency's resources for staff services. In 1930 the Conference urged the Attorney General to study consolidation of judi-

[87] "Report on the Third Conference," p. 3.
[88] *Judicial Conference Report, 1936*, p. 7.
[89] "The Federal Judicial Council," *Texas Law Review*, 2 (1924), 460.
[90] *Judicial Conference Report, 1931*, pp. 9-11.
[91] "Report of the Third Conference," p. 3.
[92] *Ibid.*, p. 4; "Report of the Fourth Conference," pp. 11-12.
[93] "Report on the Third Conference," p. 5.
[94] Chandler, "Some Major Advances," pp. 335-36, 341.
[95] "The Federal Judicial Council," p. 458.
[96] *Judicial Conference Report, 1927*, p. 6; *ibid., 1936*, pp. 7-8.

cial districts.[97] The following year, the senior circuit judges suggested that he examine delay and expense in the administration of justice caused by the requirement of both a preliminary examination and a grand jury presentment when the accused intended to plead guity.[98] Informally as well as by formal resolution, the judges pressed the Attorney General to improve his staff work not only for the Conference[99] but also for the individual courts for which his office then bore administrative responsibility.[100]

Reports of the Senior Circuit Judges

As required by the Act of 1922, the senior circuit judges reported on judicial business in their circuits. Proceeding in numerical order, they presented statistics on cases filed, pending, and terminated in the several district courts within their respective circuits.[101] They noted, usually on the initiative of the trial judge, personnel requirements,[102] as well as procedural[103] and administrative problems in the lower courts.[104]

Statistical data on civil and criminal business was obtained from district judges who, in turn, had secured it from the same source used by the Department of Justice,

[97] Ibid., 1930, p. 7.

[98] Ibid., 1931, p. 11. The senior circuit judges favored Justice Department sponsorship of a bill permitting waiver of grand jury proceedings in such cases.

[99] Ibid., p. 9.

[100] See Chandler, "Some Major Advances," pp. 365-66.

[101] "Report on the Third Conference of Senior Circuit Judges," p. 20.

[102] William C. Coleman to John J. Parker in which the former, a judge of the District Court for Maryland, expressed gratification that Parker would "further my plea for law clerks for District Judges as far as you appropriately can, at the next Conference of Senior Circuit Judges in September." June 13, 1938, Parker Papers, Box 27.

[103] "The Federal Judicial Council," pp. 461-62.

[104] 1934 Judicial Conference transcript, p. 73, in Chandler, "Some Major Advances," p. 347.

namely the court clerk. Thus, the accuracy was no better than that of the Attorney General's report. "I get no help at all from these general figures that are given here," declared Chief Justice Hughes after examining statistics presented by the judges. "I know nothing about the work of the districts from telling me that there are so many United States civil cases, and so many private civil cases begun and ended. I would not know whether the work was being done or not."[105]

However, the senior judges' statistical statement was usually accompanied by a "full and informal statement . . . as to the real and actual conditions. . . ."[106] The Conference forum permitted an explanation of the statistics, rather than their mere presentation. It was this information function which proved the value of the Conference. Said Hughes, "It is the interpretation of the man who does know, and who comes here, that will help."[107]

Thus, for the first time the performance of the individual judges, or the lack thereof, as well as special difficulties plaguing particular courts came before the ranking federal appellate judges.[108] Prodded by the Chief Justice, the senior circuit judges discussed the quantity and quality of judicial output in the trial courts.[109] "Does Judge [George A.] Carpenter do his end of the work?" queried Taft, who, as President, had appointed Carpenter to the federal bench.[110] When the senior circuit judge indicated a negative answer, the Chief Justice complained that Carpenter had reportedly adjourned a trial "while he went on a shooting trip down in New Orleans."[111]

More serious were allegations of misdeeds. A judge in the

[105] 1931 Judicial Conference transcript, p. 257, in Chandler, pp. 355-56.

[106] *Judicial Conference Report, 1926*, p. 6.

[107] 1931 Judicial Conference transcript, p. 257, in Chandler, p. 356.

[108] *Judicial Conference Report, 1928*, pp. 3-5; *ibid.*, *1929*, pp. 3-5. See also Chandler, p. 335.

[109] *Judicial Conference Report, 1928*, pp. 41-43.

[110] *Ibid.*, p. 71.   [111] *Ibid.*, pp. 71-72.

Western District of Tennessee had been implicated in a Memphis bank failure, a charge which Senior Circuit Judge Arthur C. Denison denounced as "quite unfounded."[112] But then there was District Judge George W. English of the Eastern District of Illinois. He had already been examined by a committee of the House of Representatives, and his senior circuit judge informed the Conference of unofficial reports that English would be impeached.[113]

Conference discussions concerned not only dilatory, corrupt, ill, and aged judges,[114] but also the luminaries of the federal trial bench. "We have a young man forty-one years old who does excellent work," declared Senior Circuit Judge Walter Sanborn. "His name is Phillips and he is from New Mexico."[115] Judge Martin J. Wade of the Southern District of Iowa received similar accolades. Both Sanborn and Taft lauded him as ". . . a fine man, . . . an American clear through . . . a great patriot . . ." and one who accomplished ". . . a great deal during the War."[116] After America's entry into World War I, the Iowa judge had gained wide fame for his narrow construction of the First Amendment and vigorous application of the harsh provisions of the 1917 Espionage Act, including its 20-year maximum sentence.[117]

The Judicial Conference did not restrict its scrutiny to the work, attitudes, and character of federal magistrates, because neither the cause nor the solution of all administrative problems lay with the judges. "The United States Attorney here is not efficient," reported a Conference mem-

[112] *Ibid.*, p. 67. The judge was John W. Ross.
[113] *Ibid.*, p. 69. See Borkin, *The Corrupt Judge*, pp. 203-04. Judge English resigned his office November 4, 1926.
[114] "Report of the Third Conference," pp. 7-9.
[115] "Report of the Fourth Conference," p. 133. Orie L. Phillips became Judge of the United States District Court for New Mexico in 1923. President Hoover appointed him to the Court of Appeals for the newly-created Tenth Circuit in 1929, and from 1940 to 1955 Phillips served as chief judge of that court.
[116] "Report of the Fourth Conference," p. 77.
[117] See Zechariah Chafee, Jr., *Freedom of Speech* (New York, 1920), pp. 62-64, 83.

57

ber, "the particular trouble being that he had a nephew in the office who was constantly in the way."[118] Congestion plagued some federal courts because of discretionary decisions made by prosecutors and lawyers. One judge was widely known for imposing long sentences on criminal defendants, while another was allegedly a lenient judge. Consequently, stated the senior circuit judge, "the Federal officers bring their cases before Judge [Edwin Y.] Webb, and Judge Webb's criminal docket does not present as good an appearance as does Judge [Henry G.] Connor's."[119] Elsewhere, personal-injury lawyers crowded the federal courts with their cases, "because the State court was behind in its work and was subject to two appeals, and was often reversed, whereas the decision of the Federal Court was subject to only one appeal, and was not often reversed."[120]

Intercircuit Assignments

A perennial subject before the Taft and Hughes Conferences was the insufficiency of judges in urban courts with congested dockets. The intercircuit assignment of judges constituted one means of meeting the need for additional judges. Under Taft, "the massing of [the judicial] force at points where the congestion requires more than the regular number of judges" became an important goal of the Conference.[121]

The senior circuit judges in their reports pleaded for assignment to their circuits of available judges from other circuits.[122] The Chief Justice, the Attorney General, and the Committee on the Need and Possibility of Transferring

[118] "Report of the Third Conference," p. 10.
[119] *Ibid.*, Judge Webb sat in the Western District of North Carolina and Judge Connor in the Eastern District of the state.
[120] *Ibid.*, p. 13.
[121] William Howard Taft to Felix Frankfurter, February 23, 1926, Taft Papers. See also Taft to Joseph Buffington, October 5, 1922, *ibid.*
[122] Chandler, "Some Major Advances," p. 337.

Judges established at the first Conference responded. They contributed information and suggestions derived from their own considerable investigating efforts.[123] Thus at the 1927 Conference "the names of district judges who could be transferred from one circuit to another at different times during the year were furnished by the judges of circuits from which such judges could be taken without interference with the business of their own districts."[124]

Available judges, however, were hard to find.[125] Once found, their transfer became the subject of intense bargaining between the affected Conference members.[126] Many senior circuit judges had no more enthusiasm for losing their district judges to the congested courts in the East[127] than did the assignable judges for going. One South Carolina trial judge was "fond of admiralty work" and the Southern District of New York needed someone to try such cases. But New York's winter climate lacked appeal for him.[128] Other candidates resisted transfer to the same city on grounds that the dockets there contained a "large number of liquor violation cases"[129] which rendered the courts in "New York . . . just another garbage barrel."[130]

Even when the Conference discovered a district judge available for intercircuit duty, attention was given to his judicial attitudes. But relatively few candidates received the scrutiny accorded Judge George M. Bourquin of the

[123] "The Federal Judicial Council," p. 459; Taft to Walter H. Sanborn, September 1, 1925, Administrative Office Correspondence, 52-A-18, Box 3; Taft to Harlan Fiske Stone, July 12, 1924, Taft Papers.

[124] *Judicial Conference Report, 1927*, p. 4.

[125] Chandler, p. 337.

[126] "Report on the Third Conference," p. 15.

[127] 1931 Judicial Conference transcript, pp. 214-20, in Chandler, p. 337.

[128] "Report of the Third Conference," p. 10.

[129] Kimbrough Stone to Walter H. Saunders, May 26, 1932, Kimbrough Stone Papers, Box 9.

[130] Arthur C. Denison to William J. Donovan, August 27, 1925, Administrative Office Correspondence, 52-A-18, Box 3.

District of Montana. Chief Justice Taft considered him "a man of great character and of a great deal of originality of expression and of intellectual force."[131] A substantial portion of these resources, however, had been devoted to denunciations of the Volstead Act accompanied by minimum sentences against its violators.[132] Complaints about Bourquin's performance had reached the Chief Justice from "the ladies of the Women's Christian Temperance Union."[133] Senior Judge Henry W. Rogers of the Second Circuit advanced doubts about his transfer to New York. The following discussion among Taft, Rogers, and Bourquin's Senior Circuit Judge, William B. Gilbert then ensued:

Gilbert: He is a splendid equity lawyer.

Rogers: We have equity cases for him. I don't suppose he has had many patent cases?

Gilbert: No.

Taft: He is a good trial lawyer. . . . Put him on some of your jury cases.

Rogers: All right. We will take him. We won't give him Volstead cases.[134]

In spite of the efforts of senior circuit judges, transferred judges were sometimes given a chilly reception. Such judges met with criticism from local lawyers who complained that their "time of arrival . . . is uncertain, the length of their stay is likewise uncertain, and frequently they are unfamiliar with local peculiarities."[135] Congressmen joined in the chorus of disapproval, assailing the decisions of visiting judges as partial, unequal, and unfair,[136]

[131] "Report of the Fourth Conference," p. 19.
[132] *Ibid.*, p. 10.   [133] *Ibid.*   [134] *Ibid.*, p. 87.
[135] "Report of the Special Committee of the Association of the Bar of the City of New York, May 11, 1926," *Congressional Record*, 69th Cong., 1st Sess., 1926, vol. 67, part 10, 10943.
[136] Emanuel Celler, *Congressional Record*, 70th Cong., 2d Sess., 1929, vol. 70, part 2, 1744.

and the power itself as conducive to "judicial 'joy riding'" at government expense.[137]

Responding partly to these complaints and partly to clear evidence of the inherent shortcomings in the assignment process, the 1931 Conference "deemed undesirable, . . . except where absolutely necessary," service by judges outside their own circuits.[138] "Each circuit, as far as possible, should deal with its own needs."[139] The Conference had proved inadequate to the task of making the intercircuit assignment power work on a large scale, as even Chief Justice Taft admitted.[140]

Legislative Clearance

A function less emphasized by Taft in pressing for the creation of the Judicial Conference developed rapidly after 1922. That was the Conference's role as an instrument of legislative clearance. Some proposals transmitted to Congress originated with the Conference and its committees,[141] others with federal trial and appellate judges and the Attorney General. Wherever their origin, Taft as chairman sought to funnel them through the Conference to discourage random and solo efforts, particularly by individual judges, to secure legislation.[142]

The Act of 1922 had not explicitly empowered the Conference to recommend legislation, but from the first the senior circuit judges exercised this power. Undoubtedly they were influenced by Chief Justice Taft, who perceived the Conference as enabling "the judiciary to express itself

[137] Fiorello LaGuardia, *Congressional Record*, 72d Cong., 1st Sess., 1932, vol. 75, part 9, 10345.
[138] *Judicial Conference Report, 1931*, p. 6.
[139] *Ibid.*
[140] 1927 Judicial Conference transcript, p. 22, in Chandler, "Some Major Advances," p. 338.
[141] "The Federal Judicial Council," pp. 460-63.
[142] William Howard Taft to Henry Wade Rogers, November 21, 1923, Taft Papers.

in respect of certain subjects in such a way as to be helpful to Congress."[143] Nowhere was this power spelled out, but, as Taft told the House Judiciary Committee in 1924, the Conference "assumed to make recommendations for the betterment of the general system of the Federal judiciary where the subject-matter has come immediately under the examination of the members of the council."[144]

The Chief apparently regarded such lobbying as an inherent power of the judiciary and one warranted by the "separation of powers" doctrine. And, given the nature of the legislative process, lobbying was unavoidable. In 1924, the same year in which Taft indicated that the Conference had "assumed" the legislative role, he squelched a senior circuit judge's opposition to it by observing that "Congress was waiting upon the Conference for such recommendations."[145] Nevertheless, the Judicial Conference enjoyed discretion in exercising its prerogative to speak on legislative matters. If the subject appeared particularly complex and the time likely to be consumed by its consideration great, then Taft and other senior circuit judges felt under no obligation to act even in the face of an informal request from a congressional committee.[146]

The power of the Conference to recommend changes in rules of procedure remained uncertain. The 1923 Conference issued a general resolution urging Congress to enact "legislation looking to a simplified procedure and the unification of forms of action,"[147] but doubts about the Conference's authority in the realm of rule-making persisted.[148] Anxious that the Conference be developed, Chief Justice

[143] Taft to Robert A. Taft, October 2, 1927, Taft Papers.

[144] U.S., Congress, House, Committee on the Judiciary, *Additional Judges for the Eighth Circuit*, H. Rept. 102 to accompany H.R. 661, 68th Cong., 1st Sess., 1924, p. 2.

[145] "Report of the Third Conference," p. 37.

[146] "Report of the Fourth Conference," pp. 124-25. The subject matter related to changes in the Bankruptcy Rules.

[147] "The Federal Judicial Council," p. 461.

[148] *Judicial Conference Report, 1926*, pp. 9-10.

62

Hughes sided with the doubters.[149] He feared that unilateral assumption of the rule-making power, without specific legislative authorization, could spark a congressional backlash and rejection of Conference proposals.[150]

Thus Hughes sought a formal delegation of the rule-making power to the Conference, a step which Felix Frankfurter, then a professor at Harvard Law School, urged on George Norris, chairman of the Senate Judiciary Committee.[151] By resolution the 1930 Conference called on Congress to empower the Judicial Conference to recommend "such changes in the statutory law affecting the jurisdiction, practice, evidence, and procedure of and in the different district courts and circuit courts of appeals as may to the Conference seem desirable."[152]

The need for such authority was never more pressing. For many years the American Bar Association, under Thomas Shelton's leadership, had campaigned to vest rule-making power in the Supreme Court.[153] Shelton passed from the scene in 1930, and the movement languished under the influence of unsympathetic association members.[154] Then Hughes took up the torch. For four years, he unsuccessfully sought to lodge the rule-making power in the Judicial Conference.[155] Early in 1934, however, his efforts were complemented by those of Attorney General Homer

[149] "Address of the Honorable Charles Evans Hughes," *American Law Institute, Proceedings*, 9 (1930-31), 46, 49.

[150] 1932 Judicial Conference transcript, pp. 227-29, in Chandler, "Some Major Advances," p. 354.

[151] Felix Frankfurter to George W. Norris, March 11, 1932, Norris Papers, Tray 42, Box 7.

[152] *Judicial Conference Report, 1930*, p. 8.

[153] "Report of the Committee on Judicial Administration and Remedial Procedure," *Annual Report of the American Bar Association*, 37 (1912), 434-36.

[154] Chandler, pp. 382-83.

[155] See "Address of the Honorable Charles Evans Hughes," p. 9; *Judicial Conference Report, 1930*, p. 8; *ibid.*, 1931, p. 12; *ibid.*, 1932, p. 12; *ibid.*, 1933, p. 5.

Cummings.[156] Little more than three months after Cummings began to champion the all but moribund cause of procedural reform, Congress authorized the Supreme Court to frame the rules.[157] No formal role was provided for the Judicial Conference.

Instead, the Supreme Court, led by Chief Justice Hughes, announced its intention in June 1935 to formulate "a unified system of general rules for cases in equity and actions at law." It appointed a 14-man Advisory Committee on the Rules of Civil Procedure to assist in drafting the rules.[158] During the summer of 1936, a preliminary draft prepared by Dean Charles E. Clark of the Yale Law School, the committee's reporter, was circulated among members of the bench and bar, debated, revised and then recirculated the following spring.[159] Finally, in December 1937, the Supreme Court adopted the rules recommended by its Advisory Committee[160] and, almost a year later, after clearing high congressional hurdles, they became effective.[161] The 1938 rules superseded all the forms of declaration used at common law and obliterated the distinction between pleadings in law and equity. For all causes, they provided a single form of civil action. Moreover, the new rules mitigated the sometimes harsh impact on litigants of the adversary process; discovery procedures were broadened and pretrial proceedings encouraged.[162]

[156] Homer Cummings, "Immediate Problems for the Bar," *American Bar Association Journal*, 20 (April 1934), 213. See also, Chandler, p. 483.

[157] 48 *Stat.* 1064.

[158] *Appointment of Committee to Draft Unified System of Equity and Law Rules: Order*, 295 U.S. 774 (1934).

[159] See Chandler, "Some Major Advances," pp. 489-95.

[160] *Orders re Rules of Procedure*, 302 U.S. 783 (1937).

[161] *Congressional Record*, 76th Cong., 1st Sess., 1939, vol. 84, part 8, 8473-79.

[162] See Chandler, pp. 499-502; U.S., Congress, House, Committee on the Judiciary, *Rules of Civil Procedure for the District Court of the United States*, House Rept. 2743, 75th Cong., 3d Sess., 1938, p. 4.

64

Although long excluded from the rule-making function, both the Taft and Hughes Conferences had made recommendations on a wide variety of legislative proposals. In the Taft period, these had been directed to Congress,[163] but under his more punctilious successor, some were directed to the Attorney General for subsequent presentation to Congress.[164] With one exception, the Conference's recommendations called on Congress to act affirmatively on a pending or proposed measure. The sole exception involved a reappearance of the "Caraway Bill" to bar federal judges from commenting on evidence in their jury charges; Chief Justice Taft and the American Bar Association had waged unrelenting warfare against this bill during the 1920s.[165] The 1937 Conference followed suit and called on the Attorney General "to oppose its enactment."[166]

Recommendations for money and additional judges emanated from the earliest Conferences.[167] The first one called on Congress to appropriate funds for additional court personnel to accommodate the expected rush of idle judges assigned to congested districts.[168] Finding "no law library worthy of the name" in several circuits and that an inadequate library "hampers and delays the administration of justice," the 1924 Conference issued a blanket appeal to "the President of the United States, the Attorney General, the Director of the Budget, and the Congress of the United States" to rectify the condition.[169] Subsequent conferences made similar requests for new library and salary appropriations.[170]

Although expectations were high that the intercircuit as-

163 *Judicial Conference Report, 1928*, p. 5.
164 *Ibid., 1931*, p. 11.
165 See Walter F. Murphy, *Elements of Judicial Strategy* (Chicago, 1964), pp. 163-65.
166 *Judicial Conference Report, 1937*, p. 18.
167 "The Federal Judicial Council," p. 458.
168 *Ibid.*
169 *Judicial Conference Report, 1924*, facing p. iii.
170 *Ibid., 1926*, p. 9; see also *ibid., 1931*, p. 11.

signment system would alleviate congested courts and reduce the need for additional permanent judgeships, the
shortcomings of the system were recognized by the mid-
twenties. Even Chief Justice Taft, its leading exponent, admitted that ambulatory magistrates were not "anything like
as helpful as permanent judges would be."[171] And so as
early as 1923 the senior circuit judges began to use the Conference to bombard Congress with requests for additional
judgeships.[172] Their recommendations reflected exigencies
revealed by statistics, as well as by legislative politics. The
judges of the Southern District of New York might feel
their chances of securing additional judges would improve
if legislation were introduced for two rather than three new
judgeships. Not so, argued the Chief Justice. "If they ask for
three, we can probably get one Democrat, and if you get
one Democrat, you will get the bill through."[173] But the going was often rough, especially in the then solid Democratic
South. As Taft noted, "Democratic Congressmen take little
interest in promoting legislation to give judicial places for
a Republican President to fill."[174] And ardent states-righters
in Congress had little use for the federal judiciary anyway.
"As long as Tom Watson was in the Senate," recalled Senior
Circuit Judge Richard W. Walker of the Fifth Circuit, "he
did not believe in United States judges at all, and there was
no interest [in additional judgeships or new districts] in the
Congressional delegation."[175]

Political considerations continued to influence some Judicial Conference policies during Charles Evans Hughes' tenure. To meet what it described as "special conditions," the
1937 session urged creation of an additional judgeship for
Kansas.[176] The "special conditions," however, turned out to

[171] 1927 Judicial Conference transcript, p. 22, in Chandler, p. 338.
[172] "The Federal Judicial Council," p. 463. See also *Judicial Conference Report, 1929*, pp. 4-5; *ibid., 1937*, pp. 15-17.
[173] "Report of the Fourth Conference," p. 44.
[174] *Ibid.*, p. 56.
[175] *Ibid.*
[176] *Judicial Conference Report, 1937*, p. 16.

be unrelated to the volume of judicial business, which had actually declined in the preceding five years.[177] Rather, they related to the manner in which the substance of that business had been processed. Old guard Republicans and lawyers representing Kansas business interests chafed under the lone incumbent's progressive jurisprudence. And they complained of his failure to favor them with lucrative "receivership cases so as to give the boys the gravy."[178] Thus the Conference-endorsed "move to add a second Federal judge in Kansas" was challenged by one local newspaper as "a bit of low-down partisan politics."[179] It merely sought "to relieve lawyers who hate [the incumbent judge] from having to practice in his court."[180]

Legislative recommendations were not restricted to the appropriations and personnel requirements of the courts. Various Conferences urged Congress to enact or amend existing statutes on a wide range of subjects, including those relating to more effective law enforcement. When publicity-seeking prohibition agents crowded court dockets with "trivial, futile, and unimportant cases" which did nothing to "really deter the principal offenders," the 1924 Conference suggested transfer of the prohibition unit from the Treasury Department to the Department of Justice.[181] The judges believed that the latter department could reach larger conspiracies then beyond the capacities of the Treasury Department and bring to trial only the relatively few "big

[177] See "Re: Condition of Docket in Federal District Court in Kansas," U.S., Congress, House, Subcommittee No. 1 and 3 of the Committee on the Judiciary, *Hearings, Additional United States Judges,* Part I, 75th Cong., 3d Sess., 1938, p. 85.

[178] W. P. Lambertson, U.S., Congress, Senate, Subcommittee of the Committee on the Judiciary, *Hearings, on S. 3233, Additional Judges for Federal Courts,* Part III, 75th Cong., 3d Sess., 1938, p. 185. See also *ibid.,* pp. 39-40.

[179] "[*Coffeyville Daily Journal,* February 11, 1938], 'Second Judge Unneeded,' " in *ibid.,* Part II, p. 57.

[180] *Ibid.*

[181] *Judicial Conference Report, 1924,* facing p. iii.

cases."[182] With the twin values of judicial efficiency and effective law enforcement at stake, Chief Justice Taft unhesitatingly stated "that he thought it was within the proprieties of the Conference to make recommendations in this regard."[183] Calls on Congress to reorganize agencies within the executive branch became less common after Taft's death, but even his cautious successor found it politic to join the Attorney General in advancing legislative recommendations of interest primarily to the Department of Justice.[184]

The senior circuit judges did maintain discreet silence on some issues for reasons of propriety, but not very often, given Taft's broad view of the Conference's role. The 1924 Conference considered legislation authorizing United States Commissioners, in prohibition and misdemeanor cases in which the defendant failed to file a written demand for jury trial, to receive guilty pleas, hear evidence on not guilty pleas, and file reports in court accompanied by recommended judgments. Several members of the Conference doubted its constitutionality. The matter was finally tabled after the chairman of the Conference committee charged with drafting a bill on the subject indicated his plight if "its constitutionality was challenged before him."[185]

Few issues raised the "commissioner bill" dilemma. Most recommendations for legislation related to purely administrative subjects. They included mundane matters such as the Post Office weight limits for court records[186] and places of holding court.[187] Others urged uniform district court rules[188] and enlargement of the rule-making power of the Supreme Court.[189] And still others sought to effect changes

---

[182] "Report of the Third Conference," p. 3.
[183] *Ibid.*
[184] *Judicial Conference Report, 1933,* p. 5.
[185] "Report of the Third Conference," p. 24.
[186] *Judicial Conference Report, 1928,* p. 5.
[187] *Ibid., 1937,* p. 14.   [188] *Ibid., 1939,* p. 7.
[189] *Ibid., 1932,* p. 12.

in procedural aspects of bankruptcy,[190] criminal,[191] and probation laws.[192]

By and large, the Hughes Conferences "rather closely held to the view that they would make no suggestions to Congress except in matters that need judicial help and matters of procedure that seemed to justify such a step."[193] Endorsement of legislation for a public defender system by the 1937 Conference, however,[194] constituted a major departure from existing policy,[195] and foreshadowed vast expansion of the Conference's jurisdiction following creation of the Administrative Office of the United States Courts in 1939.

Conference endorsements of legislative proposals were differently perceived by different congressmen. One school contended that they were simply gratuitous pronouncements, "only advisory"[196] and "not necessarily binding."[197] In justification of this position, Congressman George Graham, Chairman of the House Judiciary Committee, rejected the view "that it is necessary to get the imprimatur of that board," because, he argued, "we did not surrender our legislative function when we created this board."[198]

At the opposite pole were those who asserted that Congress "can not give too much weight to the recommendation of . . . the judicial conference."[199] Congressman Francis Walter of the House Judiciary Committee once went so far

[190] Ibid., 1924, facing p. iii. [191] Ibid., 1929, p. 7.
[192] Ibid., 1931, p. 11.
[193] Kimbrough Stone, "Transcript of the Judicial Conference of the United States Courts of the Eighth Circuit," January 4-6, 1940, p. 84, Kimbrough Stone Papers, Box 26 (cited hereafter as Stone, "Transcript").
[194] Judicial Conference Report, 1937, p. 17.
[195] Stone, "Transcript," p. 84.
[196] Emanuel Celler, House, Subcommittee No. 1 and 3 of the Committee on the Judiciary, Hearings, Additional United States Judges, part 1, 1938, p. 65.
[197] Ibid., p. 4.
[198] Congressional Record, 70th Cong., 2d Sess., 1929, vol. 70, part 2, 1743.
[199] Robert L. Bacon, ibid., 1745.

as to question whether his committee should inquire into "the reasons that impel the council to make the recommendation. I cannot," he said, "imagine a body of that sort making a recommendation that would not be proper and fitting and necessary."[200] To ignore the Conference's recommendations "unless the case is most urgent and most unusual" or unless "we find that the facts do not warrant the conclusions that the Conference makes," would be, thought Walter, detrimental to "the dignity and position of our courts."[201]

The recommendations of that institution should be accepted by Congress because it was competent in a way that Congress could never be. "If . . . we were not able to accept the report of the conference of senior circuit judges with reference to the needs within the respective circuits, one would wonder upon whose word and whose report we could rely," commented a Connecticut senator in 1939.[202]

That Congress did accord deference to Conference resolutions became evident during the Taft era when advocates of legislation affecting the judiciary, particularly additional judgeships, cited the support of the Conference for their proposals.[203] One Maryland congressman, seeking a judgeship for Baltimore, which had won the senior circuit judges' endorsement in 1924, reminded the Judiciary Committee chairman that "you told me that if they did this you thought you could get me a favorable report on my bill for this purpose."[204] Once out of committee, Conference recommendations constituted "one of the yardsticks used by the House

---

[200] House Subcommittee No. 1 and 3 of the Committee on the Judiciary, *Hearings, Additional United States Judges*, part 1, 1938, p. 24.

[201] *Ibid.*

[202] John A. Danaher, *Congressional Record*, 76th Cong., 1st Sess., 1939, vol. 84, part 9, 9815.

[203] "Resolution of the Maryland Bar Association," in U.S., Congress, House, Committee on the Judiciary, *Hearings, on H.R. 10821, Additional Judges*, 69th Cong., 1st Sess., 1926, p. 7.

[204] John P. Hill to George S. Graham, November 28, 1924, Legislative Files on H.R. 5083, 68th Cong.

Rules Committee to clear bills for action on the floor of that chamber."[205]

Between Supreme Court and Trial Benches

From the outset, the clearance function of the Judicial Conference extended beyond the confines of Congress to encompass the Supreme Court and the federal district courts. Conferences under Taft and Hughes promoted an ever-increasing exchange of information with these tribunals and rendered advice on rules, housekeeping matters, and court administration.

The members of the Supreme Court were not participants in the Judicial Conference; the Chief Justice, however, acted as their spokesman.[206] When it was suggested that one district judge disposed of his cases most expeditiously because "he never wrote an opinion,"[207] Taft objected. The Supreme Court, he observed, "relied very strongly on the opinions of the courts below."[208] Trial court efficiency should not be purchased at the High Court's expense.

Supreme Court efficiency was not the Chief Justice's only concern. The Conference provided an apt vehicle for pronouncements on issues of law which had not yet reached the highest court for adjudication. Aided and abetted by the Chief, the Conference could, as the Supreme Court could not, issue advisory opinions. In 1925 the senior circuit judges condemned use by federal prosecutors "of conspiracy indictments for converting a joint misdemeanor into a felony."[209] Because the conspiracy charge rendered "the

[205] Bernard H. Snell, *Congressional Record*, 70th Cong., 2d Sess., 1929, vol. 70, part 2, 1743.

[206] "Report on the Third Conference," p. 38. Chief Justice Taft informed the Conference of Justice Brandeis' opposition to the appointment of receivers by arrangement in a bill by a creditor who was not a judgment creditor in the federal courts.

[207] *Ibid.*, p. 14.   [208] *Ibid.*

[209] *Judicial Conference Report, 1925,* p. 5.

71

aborted plan a greater offense than the completed crime,"[210] the Conference employed due process language in voicing its belief "that this method of prosecution [was] used arbitrarily and harshly."[211]

The Conference's position on the issue was very much the handiwork of Chief Justice Taft. He told the assembled judges that "there will probably be an expression from the Supreme Court . . . if a proper case permits it. Some of our members are just bursting for expression on it."[212] But a "proper case" could prove quite elusive. The judges of his Court, Taft explained, had "got themselves tied up with so many decisions that they can not reverse."[213] A Conference resolution offered a way out of this Blackstonian dilemma. It provided, in addition, a means by which Taft could meet demands made on him by his Court constituency, several members of which, he related, would "read this [resolution] with the utmost satisfaction."[214]

In the realm of rule-making over which the Supreme Court exercised formal and virtually conclusive power, the Conference played a consultant's role. Recognizing the usefulness of such a role, the 1922 Conference established committees on bankruptcy and equity rules to assist the Court in exercising its power to promulgate these rules.[215] Not only did Chief Justice Hughes continue the practice, begun in the Taft period, of clearing proposed changes in equity and bankruptcy,[216] but the Conference under his leadership expanded this function as additional rule-making powers devolved on the Supreme Court.[217] Thus Conferences in the mid-1930s devoted major portions of their sessions to the mechanics of implementing the Court's newly granted

[210] *Ibid.*   [211] *Ibid.*, p. 6.
[212] "Report of the Fourth Conference," p. 141.
[213] *Ibid.*, p. 142.
[214] *Ibid.*, Resolution approved 9 to 1, Buffington voting nay.
[215] "The Federal Judicial Council," p. 459.
[216] *Judicial Conference Report, 1931*, p. 11.
[217] *Ibid.*, *1933*, pp. 5-6.

power to draft and promulgate uniform rules of civil procedure.[218] After their drafting by the Supreme Court's Advisory Committee, the 1936 and 1937 Conferences then studied and commented on various drafts of the rules.[219]

The power of the Conference of senior appellate judges to make "recommendations to the District Judges," said Chief Justice Taft, "gives a unity to the Federal judicial force that I think is valuable."[220] To this end the first Conference established a Committee on Recommendations to District Judges of Changes in Local Procedure to Expedite Disposition of Pending Cases and to Rid Dockets of Dead Litigation.[221] Conferences in subsequent years recommended that dockets be called annually, thereby dismissing unprosecuted cases a year after docketing; that continuances be granted only for "good cause"; and that motion and settlement of issues be heard at "fixed times at frequent intervals."[222] Implicit in these formal recommendations was the policy that the flow of judicial business should be under the courts' rather than the litigants' control and that there was a "best way" of realizing this control.[223] Thereafter successive Conferences unloosed a barrage of recommendations to once wholly autonomous district and even appellate judges.[224] What cases should receive preference on the docket,[225] whether to use masters,[226] and how to devise simple and uniform rules of court[227] were among the suggestions received in the districts.

[218] Act of June 19, 1934, 48 *Stat.* 1064. *Judicial Conference Report, 1934,* p. 6. See also Chandler, "Some Major Advances," pp. 485-87.

[219] *Judicial Conference Report, 1936,* p. 7; *ibid., 1937,* p. 19. See Chandler, p. 498, n. 86.

[220] William Howard Taft to Felix Frankfurter, February 23, 1926, Taft Papers.

[221] "The Federal Judicial Council," p. 459.

[222] *Ibid.;* see also *Judicial Conference Report, 1926,* p. 7; *ibid., 1927,* p. 4.

[223] See Chandler, p. 346.

[224] *Judicial Conference Report, 1927,* p. 6.

[225] *Ibid.*   [226] *Ibid., 1935,* p. 6.

[227] *Ibid., 1938,* pp. 22-23.

The Conference also clarified the state of the law for uncertain trial judges. An 1895 Supreme Court decision had been interpreted by at least one appellate court as making bail after a conviction a constitutional right.[228] Not so, declared the 1925 Conference. A constitutional right to bail existed only before conviction.[229] Chief Justice Taft contended that judges had no constitutional obligation to grant bail after conviction. "They must," he said, "exercise a discretion and [they] have a right to."[230] But how trial judges were to exercise their discretion was specifically stated by the Conference,[231] and further elaborated by Circuit Justice

[228] "Report of the Fourth Conference," p. 135. Senior Circuit Judge Henry Wade Rogers cited *Parker v. Hall* as the case in point. No case involving parties so named has ever been decided by the Supreme Court of the United States. He was apparently referring to *Hudson v. Parker*, 156 *U.S.* 277 (1895) in which the Court considered for the first time the issue of bail pending appeal after conviction. It granted a writ of mandamus compelling a district court to grant bail pending appeal to a defendant convicted of a felony. The Sixth Circuit Court of Appeals subsequently construed *Hudson* as holding that there existed a constitutional right to bail pending appeal in all except capital cases. *Knight v. United States*, 113 Fed. 451 (C.C.A. 6th, 1902). Other courts of appeals held to the contrary. *Garvey v. United States*, 292 Fed. 591 (C.C.A. 2nd, 1923); *United States v. St. John*, 254 Fed. 794 (C.C.A. 7th, 1918).

[229] Adopted 8 to 2, Sanborn and Waddill voting nay. Both believed bail was a constitutional right until judgment became final.

[230] "Report of the Fourth Conference," p. 102.

[231] *Judicial Conference Report, 1925*, p. 6. "B. . . . the right to bail after conviction . . . is not a matter of constitutional right. The acts of Congress make provision for allowance of bail after conviction by court and judges to release the convicted defendant upon the exercise of their judicial discretion, having in mind the purpose of the Federal statutes not to subject to punishment anyone until he has been finally adjudged guilty in the court of last resort. But the judicial discretion of the Federal courts and judges in granting or withholding bail after conviction should be exercised to discourage review sought, not with hope of new trial, but on frivolous grounds merely for delay." Chief Justice Taft perceived discretionary access to bail as a means of preventing affluent criminal defendants, particularly "bootleggers," from delaying the administration of justice. It would also equalize conditions for rich and poor defendants alike by incarcerating all

74

Pierce Butler eight months later in a decision of the Seventh Circuit Court of Appeals.[232] Ethical problems arising from the activities of lower court judges likewise came before the early conferences. Taft informed the 1924 session of an inquiry from the Assistant Attorney General inquiring "whether Judge [William H.] Atwell of the Northern District of Texas might properly accept the position of . . . Chief Exalted Elk, and [spend] . . . a year . . . visiting all parts of the country on his duties."[233] The Chief's negative reply to the Justice Department then received the senior circuit judges' warm endorsement.[234] No formal public resolution was issued in this instance nor in any similar instances arising during the conferences under Taft and Hughes. Instead, the senior circuit judges privately sanctioned action proposed or already taken by the Chief Justice in the sensitive realm of judicial ethics.

The Attorney General and Congress

Policies established by the Judicial Conference were obviously not self-executing. Resolutions calling for legislation

defendants after conviction and pending appeal. Such incarceration, Taft believed, would promote judicial efficiency because a jailed defendant would "get a quick trial, because his counsel will ask for it. . . . If he does not stay in jail, he does not want a trial." "Report of the Fourth Conference," p. 101.

[232] *United States v. Motlow*, 10 Fed. 2d 657 (C.C.A. 7th, 1926). Of the resolution of the 1925 Conference, Mr. Justice Butler said: "That statement will be taken as a guide in this case. . . . It reflects the purpose of the federal statutes and the rules of court . . . and it adopts the substance of the rule laid down by the Supreme Court in *Hudson v. Parker* . . ." (*ibid.*, p. 662). After reviewing the merits of the defendant's case, Butler paraphrased the resolution's language in holding that "it does not appear that these applicants seek review, not with the hope of a new trial, but on frivolous grounds merely for delay" (*ibid.*, p. 663).

[233] "Report of the Third Conference," p. 39. Judge Atwell served as "Grand Exalted Ruler of the Elks" from 1925 to 1926.

[234] *Ibid.*

usually passed through the hands of the Attorney General, who acted as the Conference's liaison with Congress. To strengthen the value of this intermediary, Chief Justice Taft not only developed extraordinary rapport with several attorneys general, but sought to influence their appointment in the first place.[235] No sooner had he become Chief Justice than he cultivated Harding's Attorney General, Harry M. Daugherty, with whom he shortly "established a very pleasant relation."[236] Daugherty, reported Taft, was "only too willing to follow suggestions from me. In other words, I think he wants to do right, and he wants to be told what is right."[237]

After Daugherty's inglorious departure, the Chief immediately forged lines of communication to Attorney General Harlan Fiske Stone.[238] Stone's tenure proved short and John G. Sargent, who followed him, fell far short of Taft's ideal incumbent for the office. A Vermonter like President Coolidge, Sargent reportedly regarded it as "his business to carry out the law that Congress makes, and not to say what Congress shall do. . . ."[239] Unsympathetic with this timid attitude, Taft never developed a satisfactory association with Sargent, whom he considered "stupid and slow."[240] Improvement came when President Hoover appointed William D. Mitchell whom Taft promptly hailed as "a first class Attorney General."[241]

A typical example of the relationship between the Chief

[235] Murphy, *Elements of Judicial Strategy*, pp. 152-54.
[236] William Howard Taft to Clarence H. Kelsey, July 21, 1921, Taft Papers.
[237] Taft to Charles P. Taft, January 2, 1923, *ibid.*
[238] Taft to Helen H. Taft, April 10, 1924, *ibid.*
[239] John M. Robinson, U.S., Congress, House, Subcommittee of the Committee on the Judiciary, *Hearings, on H.R. 11088, H.R. 16471, and S. 4162, Southern Judicial District of Kentucky*, 69th Cong., 2d Sess., 1927, p. 73.
[240] Taft to Charles P. Taft, February 14, 1926, Taft Papers.
[241] Taft to Charles P. Taft, April 20, 1929, *ibid.*

Justice as chairman of the Conference and the Attorney General occurred late in 1923 when Congressman Leonidas C. Dyer of Missouri requested justification for an additional judgeship in the Eighth Circuit. Assistant Attorney General Rush Holland promptly conferred with Chief Justice Taft, who informed him that the subject had arisen at "the most recent session of the Judicial Council . . . and that the Judicial Council was unanimously of the opinion that the Eighth Circuit should have six judges, which would require legislation for two. . . ."[242] Attorney General Daugherty then told the congressman that "it would be a good thing if you would introduce a bill providing for two additional judges, get the bill in early, and this Department will prepare data in support of it."[243]

Daugherty's successors continued this transmission function with varying degrees of skill.[244] Some legislation required a high degree of coordination on the part of the Attorney General and the Chief Justice. Appropriations requests were preceded by conferences between Taft and members of the Justice Department's budget section, joined by the director of the Bureau of the Budget.[245] On other issues, Taft and the Attorney General worked hand in hand as indicated by an entry in the Chief's "Daily Calendar" reminding him to "Call up Attorney General and arrange for

[242] Memorandum for the Attorney General from Rush L. Holland, November 23, 1923, Administrative Office Correspondence, 52-A-18, Box 148.

[243] Harry M. Daugherty to L. C. Dyer, November 23, 1923, *ibid.*

[244] See John G. Sargent to C. W. Ramseyer, November 30, 1926, Legislative Files, H.R. 10821, 69th Cong.; William D. Mitchell to George S. Graham, November 19, 1930, Department of Justice Central Files, OX11, Sec. 1; John G. Sargent to Arthur C. Denison, November 30, 1927, *ibid.*; Homer S. Cummings to Chairman of Senate Judiciary Committee, May 2, 1933, *Congressional Record,* 73d Cong., 1st Sess., 1933, vol. 77, part 6, 6159.

[245] "Statement of Honorable William Howard Taft, Chief Justice," February 16, 1923, Speeches and Articles, Taft Papers.

a talk with him about the bill for increase of Judges and arrangement with New York Democrats."[246]

The Attorney General could also be used to "front" for the Chief Justice with congressional committees. "Chief Justice Taft . . . would be very helpful to your Committee," wrote Daugherty to the chairman of the Senate Judiciary Committee. "Of course he is reluctant to suggest this, but if you could ask him to attend the meeting I will appreciate it and am sure he would be delighted to sit in."[247]

Just as Chief Justice Taft made extensive use of the Attorney General in carrying on liaison with Congress, so too did his successor; but Charles Evans Hughes operated in a different manner. The informal telephone calls and consultations so common under Taft vanished and were replaced by a much more formal relationship. Conference policies once directed to Congress were more often formally directed to the Attorney General for submission to Congress.[248]

When no Conference position existed on a pending legislative measure relating to the judiciary, Attorney General Cummings would write Hughes, suggesting that "it may be that you would feel justified in making a favorable recommendation to the President, so that he, in turn, could submit the matter to the appropriate Committee of the Congress."[249] The Chief Justice then dispatched the requested letter, carefully noting that he had been informed by the Attorney General that "you would like to have my views as to the necessity of the appointment of additional Judges."[250]

[246] Taft, Daily Calendar, December 18, 1926, Speeches and Articles, ibid.

[247] Harry M. Daugherty to Knute Nelson, September 30, 1921, Department of Justice Files, Record Group 60, No. 144446, Sec. 2.

[248] Judicial Conference Report, 1931, pp. 11-12; ibid., 1937, pp. 17-18.

[249] Homer S. Cummings to Charles Evans Hughes, February 20, 1935, Charles Evans Hughes Papers, Box 51 (Library of Congress, Washington, D.C.; cited hereafter as Hughes Papers).

[250] Charles Evans Hughes to Franklin Delano Roosevelt, May 30,

Thereafter, word of the Chief's position reached Congress through the Attorney General,[251] who, in one instance, sent Hatton Sumners, chairman of the House Judiciary Committee "a letter which I have received from the Chief Justice recommending the enactment of the pending bill."[252] This cooperative, but discreet, relationship between Hughes and the Attorney General was to prove short-lived. In the wake of the Supreme Court-packing crisis of 1937, it disappeared altogether.[253]

The Chief Justice and Congress

Personally intervening in the congressional process was a role both important and congenial to Chief Justice Taft. No question of propriety gnawed at Taft's conscience, for he considered it part of his "duty, as head of the Federal Judicial system, to suggest needed reforms, and to become rather active in pressing them before the Judiciary Committees."[254] This task included much lobbying facilitated by an effective information network. Thomas Shelton, Washington lobbyist for the American Bar Association and chairman of that group's Committee on Uniform Judicial Procedure, supplied Taft with a continuous flow of news concerning the status of various bills and alignments of congressional forces.[255] So, too, did Associate Justice Willis Van Devanter, who apparently had independent sources of information.[256]

1934, Department of Justice Files, OX11, Sec. 1; Hughes to Roosevelt, February 22, 1935, Hughes Papers, Box 51.

[251] Homer S. Cummings to William H. King, May 9, 1935, Department of Justice Files, OX11, Sec. 2.

[252] Cummings to Hatton W. Sumners, March, 1935, Records Administration Branch, Department of Justice Files, 109X11, Sec. 2.

[253] See Chandler, "Some Major Advances," pp. 373-74.

[254] William Howard Taft to Frank H. Hiscock, April 12, 1922, Taft Papers.

[255] Taft to Thomas W. Shelton, March 23, 1924, Taft Papers; Shelton to Taft, March 25, 1924, ibid.; George W. Norris to Shelton, April 23, 1928, ibid.

[256] Taft to Henry W. Taft, April 21, 1928, ibid.

Eagerly Taft accepted invitations to testify before the Judiciary Committees "on behalf of the Conference of Senior Circuit Judges, of which I am Chairman, in behalf of this bill which the Conference recommended."[257] The Appropriations Committees were also graced with his presence. In 1923, he appealed to one of them for $300,000 "to concentrate six or seven judges from other parts of the country in that District and work on that docket."[258] Even some of his prominent colleagues on the Supreme Court were pressed into service. In one instance, Associate Justices Oliver Wendell Holmes, Jr. and Louis D. Brandeis, both from Massachusetts, appeared with the Chief Justice before an appropriations subcommittee in the hope, said Taft, that "with such big guns . . . we can impress the Committee."[259] There they appealed for funds to purchase a law library for the federal court building in Boston.[260]

Although Taft reported that "some of my enemies on the [Judiciary] Committee resent my being prominent in pressing legislation,"[261] his personal appearances had a profound effect on legislators. Perhaps it was because of their novelty; more likely it was due to the great esteem which they accorded the former President. Congressman Hatton Sumners described the experience:

. . . and there we were in the Judiciary Committee room. The way things were fixed up it looked somewhat like the Supreme Court. . . . Pretty soon the Chief Justice of the United States himself in his own proper person came be-

[257] Taft to G. S. Jameson, January 6, 1924, Legislative Files, H.R. 661, 68th Congress.
[258] "Statement of Honorable William Howard Taft, Chief Justice," February 16, 1923, Speeches and Articles, Taft Papers. See also Taft to Henry Wade Rogers, February 2, 1923, ibid.
[259] Taft to George W. Anderson, May 12, 1926, ibid.
[260] Taft to Louis D. Brandeis, May 11, 1926, ibid. See also "Deficiency Act, Second, Fiscal Year 1926," Appropriations Budget Estimates, etc., Senate Doc. No. 159, 69th Cong., 1st Sess., 1926, p. 92.
[261] Taft to Charles P. Taft, January 27, 1924, Taft Papers.

80

fore us. Well, of course, we were not robed like members of the Supreme Court. It gave us a sort of insufficiently dressed feeling sitting up there without any robes and the Chief Justice down there telling us about it. He told us we needed these judges. The Attorney General told us we needed them. I am afraid we were just a bit flabbergasted, so we accepted. . . .[262]

Taft did not confine his legislative strategies to formal appearances before committees. Informal meetings with chairmen and members of the Judiciary and Appropriations committees were not uncommon.[263] And the legislators appreciated them. Assessing the need for additional judgeships in 1928, the chairman of the Senate Judiciary Committee, George W. Norris, reported that "Chief Justice Taft met with us and took quite an interest in the matter and was of very great assistance to us. He secured his information from various Circuit Judges and I think we had a rather definite idea of the conditions over the country when we got through."[264]

Aside from face-to-face meetings with members of Congress, the Chief Justice dispatched suggestions to key members of the Judiciary committees.[265] In 1926 he sent Senator Albert Cummins, chairman of the Senate's committee, a memorandum with the thought that it would "perhaps aid you in saying what you have to say on this point."[266] Such participation in the legislative process knew no bounds as Taft engaged in various stratagems to promote legislation.

[262] *Congressional Record*, 67th Cong., 2d Sess., 1922, vol. 62, part 6, 6407.

[263] See George S. Graham, in *Congressional Record*, 69th Cong., 1st Sess., 1926, vol. 67, part 10, 10942. See also 1922 minutes of Conference, p. 18, in Chandler, "Some Major Advances," p. 361.

[264] George W. Norris to James C. Kinsler, February 10, 1928, Tray 42, Box 2, Norris Papers.

[265] George S. Graham to William Howard Taft, February 20, 1925, Taft Papers.

[266] Taft to Albert B. Cummins, May 31, 1926, *ibid.*

In one instance, he came "within an ace of getting through that additional Circuit Judgeship," after contacting a senator "who attempted to get it through" and after having made arrangements "to push it through the House."[267]

Chief Justice Hughes engaged in little of the congressional maneuvering that had been the hallmark of his predecessor's reign. By and large, he sought to influence congressional action indirectly by enhancing the prestige of the Judicial Conference[268] and by relying on the Attorney General to perform the necessary footwork on Capitol Hill. Nevertheless, on issues vitally affecting the Supreme Court, Hughes took his case directly to Congress. Together with Justices Van Devanter and Brandeis, he testified in 1935 before the Senate Judiciary Committee against Senator Hugo Black's bill providing for a direct appeal to the Supreme Court from any district court decision enjoining the enforcement of an act of Congress.[269] Two years later, he dispatched his famous letter to Senator Burton K. Wheeler which seriously undercut President Franklin Roosevelt's justification for the Court-packing plan.

Chief Justice Taft had no qualms about approaching the White House in quest of support for his legislative program, some of which was utterly unrelated to the federal courts. He urged his views on many subjects on the residents of 1600 Pennsylvania Avenue. Labor and farm policies, disarmament, bonus bills, pardons, appointments to the Cabinet and even to minor posts in the Treasury Department as well as the filling of vacancies in the judiciary were among the topics which Taft, personally or by letter, took up with Presidents Harding, Coolidge, and Hoover.[270]

Some subjects brought to the White House clearly in-

[267] Taft to Augustus N. Hand, April 21, 1927, *ibid.*

[268] *New York Times*, September 30, 1931, p. 26.

[269] U.S., Congress, Senate, Committee on the Judiciary, *Hearings, on S. 2176, Appeals from Federal Courts*, 74th Cong., 1st Sess., 1935, pp. 2-8.

[270] See Mason, *William Howard Taft*, chs. VI, VIII.

volved the lower federal courts, although not the official activities of the Judicial Conference. A bill submitted by Senator Thaddeus H. Caraway of Arkansas and aimed at barring federal judges from commenting to jurors on the credibility of witnesses appeared in several Congresses during the 1920s and 1930s. Taft took the matter up with President Coolidge, personally giving him a twelve-page memorandum attacking the Caraway bill as detrimental to law enforcement and as probably unconstitutional.[271] Two years later, when Caraway's bill[272] once again threatened, Taft came away from a conference with Coolidge certain he had "enlisted the assistance of the President in suppressing the bill."[273]

In other interviews with the President, he sought affirmative executive support for higher judicial salaries and additional judges. "The first thing [Coolidge] said to me, showing the trend of his mind," recounted Taft, "was that an increase from $7,500 to $12,500 [for District Judges] was a pretty big jump."[274] The meeting was not futile, for the President agreed to remain neutral. That same year, a Conference-endorsed bill to create much-needed judgeships became deadlocked because of partisan animosities in Congress. Acting as a legislative broker, Taft conferred with the President "to see if we cannot arrange to have some kind of an informal agreement to let the Democrats have some of the Judicial places created."[275]

The organized bar was also recruited by Taft to reinforce his own lobbying efforts. To him the American Bar Association constituted a group potentially capable of exerting "a tremendous influence through the country,"[276] and one able

[271] Memorandum, December 2, 1924, Taft Papers. See also Murphy, *Elements of Judicial Strategy*, pp. 163-65.
[272] S. 455, 69th Cong.
[273] Taft to Henry W. Taft, May 18, 1926, Taft Papers.
[274] Taft to Charles Evans Hughes, March 19, 1926, *ibid.*
[275] Taft to Learned Hand, August 1, 1926, *ibid.*
[276] Taft to Clarence Kelsey, August 17, 1923, *ibid.*

"to influence legislative bodies to real reform measures."[277] Thus Taft displayed little reticence in invoking the bar's aid in promoting legislation. Anxious to obtain three district judgeships for the hard-pressed Southern District of New York, he suggested to Charles Evans Hughes "that you and my brother Henry as the President and recent President of the Association of the Bar [of the City of New York] and a number of other influential men, should organize a movement to attack the Judiciary Committee of Congress!!"[278] Brother Henry complied. He established a Special Committee of the Bar on Congested Calendars of which he was chairman. Not surprisingly, its report, issued in May 1926, advocated more judgeships for the Southern District,[279] and a month later a bill for three new judges passed the House of Representatives.[280] The American Bar Association itself became useful to Taft when the Caraway bill appeared in the House in 1924. Wrote the Chief Justice to his wife: "I got hold of Wade Ellis today. He is on the Law Enforcement Committee of the American Bar Association, and I made him wise to the situation. He went over to see Nick Longworth [Republican floor leader] and he telephoned me he has got the thing fixed so that the bill can not come up until next session."[281]

A major legislative strategy employed by Chief Justice Taft was "grass roots" lobbying. In pursuit of an additional judgeship for the Northern District of Georgia recommended by the 1924 Conference,[282] he wrote the editor of the Atlanta *Constitution* who "got the Bar stirred up."[283] Local lawyers, judges, congressmen, and senators became

[277] Taft to Charles Evans Hughes, April 27, 1926, in *American Bar Association Journal*, 12 (May 1926), 326.

[278] Taft to Charles Evans Hughes, March 25, 1925, Taft Papers.

[279] *Congressional Record*, 69th Cong., 1st Sess., 1926, vol. 67, part 10, 10943.

[280] *Ibid.*, p. 10959.

[281] Taft to Helen H. Taft, May 11, 1924, Taft Papers.

[282] *Judicial Conference Report, 1924*, facing p. iii.

[283] "Report of the Fourth Conference," p. 52.

Taft's typical targets whenever legislation was needed for new judges.[284]

Few campaigns rivaled that which Taft launched against Senator George Norris's bill to curtail federal jurisdiction in diversity of citizenship cases.[285] To Taft, this was "the most radical bill that has been introduced in either House,"[286] for it allegedly placed out-of-state corporations at the mercy of unsympathetic state courts and impeded the work of the Supreme Court.[287] When the measure slipped out of Norris's Senate Judiciary Committee, without dismissal and without a dissent to the favorable report, the Chief Justice went into action. Desiring to spark such an outpouring of opposition that the bill's introduction in future Congresses would cause "a very profound kick,"[288] Taft wrote Casper Yost, editor of the St. Louis *Globe-Democrat*. It was a forceful letter detailing the bill's evils, explaining the theoretically helpless position of the Chief Justice, and invoking Yost's "influence in maintaining the protective power which citizens may secure from the Federal Judiciary in defense of their rights."[289] Yost cooperated; within little more than a week two editorials had appeared, both of which the grateful Chief Justice thought "very much in point" and sure to attract attention.[290] At the same time, he contacted his brother, Henry W. Taft, a leading New York lawyer. The attention of the *Times* and *Tribune* should be called to the Norris bill, the Chief Justice told him. "I think you ought to go to the *New York Times* and to the *Tribune* and explain the effect of the bill and have editorials printed on the subject."[291] Shortly thereafter two editorials appeared in the *Times*.[292]

[284] See *ibid.*, p. 42. [285] S. 3151, 70th Congress.
[286] Taft to Casper S. Yost, April 5, 1928, Taft Papers.
[287] Taft to Henry W. Taft, April 5, 1928, *ibid.*
[288] Taft to Henry W. Taft, April 7, 1928, *ibid.*
[289] Taft to Casper Yost, April 5, 1928, *ibid.*
[290] Taft to Yost, April 16, 1928, *ibid.*
[291] Taft to Henry W. Taft, April 5, 1928, *ibid.*
[292] *New York Times*, April 22, 1928, sec. III, p. 4; *ibid.*, May 10, 1928, p. 26.

The Chief Justice and the Lower Courts

The Conference faced not only toward Congress and, to some extent, toward the Attorney General but also toward the lower federal courts. The Conference was the one integrative element in a decentralized judiciary, the one element which could make district judges "feel that they are under real observation by the other judges and the country."[293] Said Chief Justice Hughes: "We are here because we are not geographical units, wholly independent . . . .[294] There is a responsibility resting upon us, in view of our investigation and examination of the different circuits."[295] From its inception, then, an important function of the Conference lay in restricting the once total autonomy of the district judges and pressing for a degree of uniformity in their non-judicial actions. But the impact of Conference actions varied.

The Act of 1922 only empowered the Conference to make "suggestions" to the trial courts.[296] Both Taft and Hughes construed that language broadly. To them it included speaking out on a broad range of shortcomings which would ordinarily never reach the appellate courts in the form of a case or controversy. And it constituted a source of some power. Consequently, Taft objected to a senior circuit judge's proposal "that the Conference merely urge the District Judges to get rid of dead stuff" on their dockets.[297] Citing the relevant language of the 1922 Act, Taft convinced members of the 1924 Judicial Conference that "a formal suggestion, and that was all a resolution of the Conference could be, was more likely to get attention."[298]

[293] Taft to Robert A. Taft, October 2, 1927, Taft Papers.
[294] 1936 Judicial Conference transcript, p. 125, in Chandler, "Some Major Advances," p. 348.
[295] 1934 Judicial Conference transcript, p. 62, in *ibid.*, p. 351.
[296] 42 *Stat.* 839.
[297] "Report of the Third Conference," p. 23.
[298] *Ibid.*; Resolution approved 9 to 1, Sanborn voting nay.

Both Taft and Hughes dealt with charges of maladministration in a similar way. When confronted by dilatory behavior on the part of a district judge, Taft told the 1928 Conference: "I think a gentle intimation from the Senior Circuit Judge, followed up by some word from here, usually helps in those cases."[299] The "word" sometimes came hard on the heels of the Conference as in 1927, when Taft learned that a district judge in Maine was holding a patent case submitted more than four years before. Wrote the irate Chief Justice:

As a fellow member of the Federal Judiciary, I urge that you drop everything else and decide this case. We none of us can afford to justify the complaints of delays in awarding just rights to litigants. Of course I write this letter with no assumption that I may exercise direct authority over you in the discharge of your duties, but as the head of the Federal Judiciary I feel that I do have the right to appeal to you, in its interest and in the interest of the public whom it is created to serve, to end this indefensible situation.[300]

The "right" decision in a case was important, contended Taft, "but there are many civil questions which arise between individuals in which it is not so important the controversy be settled one way or another as that it be settled."[301] After all, appellate courts existed to remedy "wrong" decisions.[302]

Ethical behavior and the perennial problems associated with lazy and superannuated judges moved Taft, as leader of the federal judiciary and chairman of the Judicial Conference, to act. When a district judge inquired about the propriety to assuming the presidency of a large fraternal

[299] 1928 Judicial Conference transcript, pp. 1-2, in Chandler, p. 350.
[300] Taft to John A. Peters, October 11, 1927, Taft Papers. See reply, Peters to Taft, October 24, 1927, *ibid.*
[301] Taft, "Adequate Machinery for Judicial Business," *American Bar Association Journal,* 7 (September 1921), 453.
[302] Taft to William N. Runyon, March 19, 1928, Taft Papers.

87

order in the United States, Taft replied that "by no means ought he to accept the position."[303] Likewise, District Judge George A. Carpenter's failure to clear his docket or resign provoked the Chief Justice to threaten an ultimatum to him for "his refusal to do any team work or to be interested in his work."[304]

Among trial judges, a mixed reception greeted resolutions of the newly-established Judicial Conference in Washington. One former critic of the Conference hailed that organization's work as resulting "in much public good."[305] Others objected. To them, Chief Justice Taft tactfully explained that Conference recommendations "were to be taken neither as mandatory nor as rigid. They were only intended to stimulate the District Judges to a knowledge that the whole Federal Judiciary is interested in promoting the dispatch of business."[306] Otherwise, he observed, "we are apt to fall into methods of delay just through inertia, and constant agitation of the necessity for dispatch helps."[307]

Compliance sometimes came hard. The 1927 Conference noted its recommendation for annual docket calls was being widely followed, but that "it has not been followed by all."[308] At the same time, the Conference called on those courts "which have neglected it . . . [to] see that it is enforced,"[309] and on the senior circuit judges to determine the scope and results of the practice within their respective circuits.[310] Even Taft admitted that his efforts fell short of success on the sensitive issues of ethics and retirement. "The fate of a Chief Justice in attempting to make District and

[303] 1928 Judicial Conference transcript, p. 61, in Chandler, "Some Major Advances," p. 351.
[304] Taft to Evan A. Evans, March 26, 1928, Taft Papers.
[305] Henry D. Clayton to William Howard Taft, December 3, 1924, ibid. See also Henry D. Clayton, "Popularizing Administration of Justice," American Bar Association Journal, 8 (January 1922), 45-46.
[306] Taft to J. Foster Symes, December 12, 1924, Taft Papers.
[307] Taft to Robert T. Ervin, December 4, 1924, ibid.
[308] Judicial Conference Report, 1927, p. 5.
[309] Ibid.   [310] Ibid.

88

Circuit Judges do what they are not disposed to do is a difficult one," he said.[311] His suggestions, in fact, might go utterly unheeded which, thought the Chief Justice, was "a pretty good indication that I have no function to perform in the matter of disciplining judges."[312]

Hughes, who, like Taft, perceived the Conference as "a disciplinary body," believed that "an appeal to the conscience of the individual judge is justified . . . in a case where there is an inexcusable delay."[313] The procedure was "for the Senior Circuit Judge, after he has taken such steps as he feels he is at liberty to take, to bring that matter to the attention of the Conference . . . and for the Chief Justice, as the presiding officer of the Conference, to take such measures as might be deemed wise to rectify such a situation."[314] One measure was for the Chief Justice to write "a direct letter to a judge that did not decide cases for a year or two."[315]

On more than one occasion the personal prestige of the Chief Justice was brought to bear on recalcitrant district judges—sometimes at the request of the senior circuit judge. When all the judges of one district court in the Eighth Circuit threatened to leave for summer vacations simultaneously, thereby closing the court, Senior Circuit Judge Kimbrough Stone appealed to Hughes. He suggested that "if you thought [it] proper to write me a letter . . . concerning this matter I would use it or the substance thereof as you might desire."[316] The Chief Justice promptly com-

[311] Taft to George W. Wickersham, November 23, 1929, Taft Papers.

[312] 1928 Judicial Conference transcript, p. 61, in Chandler, "Some Major Advances," p. 351.

[313] 1934 Judicial Conference transcript, pp. 56-60, in *ibid.*, p. 350.

[314] *Ibid.*, pp. 350-51. See *Judicial Conference Report, 1937*, p. 14, senior circuit judge to act if a district judge fails to hear motion.

[315] 1934 Judicial Conference transcript, pp. 56-60, in Chandler, p. 350.

[316] Kimbrough Stone to Charles Evans Hughes, May 29, 1936, Hughes Papers, Box 6.

plied,[317] and Stone reported the Chief's views to the district judges.[318]

In the relatively tractable realm of case flow, such admonitions from the Chief Justice made an impact. Related one senior circuit judge who had received a letter about a delayed case from Hughes:

> I went to see the district judge and asked him when he was going to decide, and he did not give me any very definite information. I said, "Here, here is a communication from the Chief Justice, wanting to know what you are going to do about this lawsuit. When are you going to decide it?" He said, "You may report that it will be decided by the 15th of November." That was two weeks and it was [decided].[319]

Under the vigorous leadership of Chief Justices Taft and Hughes, the Conference of the Senior Circuit Judges became, in the years after 1922, an increasingly important element in the administration of the federal courts. It brought, declared Taft, "all the district judges within a mild disciplinary circle,"[320] although, as his successor noted, Conference policies were only advisory.[321] But, stated the *American Bar Association Journal*, the policies were "not merely the expression of a pious hope, but the program of a body with reason for what it does . . . and with prestige great enough to insure that its proposals will receive careful attention."[322] Nevertheless, the Conference had no staff of its own nor could it operate as a bureaucracy. That role lay with the Department of Justice.

[317] Hughes to Kimbrough Stone, June 2, 1931, *ibid.*
[318] Kimbrough Stone to John E. Martineau, June 5, 1936, *ibid.*
[319] Xenophon Hicks, "Minutes of the Judicial Conference of the United States, 1940, Division of Procedural Studies and Statistics," p. 347, negative photographic reproduction, Administrative Office Correspondence, 60-A-328, Box 27.
[320] Taft to Robert A. Taft, October 2, 1927, Taft Papers.
[321] 1936 Judicial Conference transcript, p. 142, in Chandler, p. 348.
[322] "The Judicial Council," *American Bar Association Journal*, 11 (August 1925), 508.

CHAPTER 3

The Justice Department as Judicial Administrator: Problems, Protest, and Reform Proposals

The Administrative System

ESTABLISHMENT of the Judicial Conference in 1922 built into the federal judiciary a new administrative dimension. Yet its addition affected only in a small way the extensive role played by the Department of Justice in the administration of the United States courts, a role it would continue to play until 1939. The Attorney General, as head of that department, stood at the center of a far-flung administrative network. As chief law officer for the United States government, he was responsible for the prosecution of all government cases and supervised the work of his agents—the United States attorneys.[1]

In a similar relationship to the Attorney General were the United States marshals. Assigned to each district court as were the attorneys, they, like the attorneys, were appointed by the President with the advice and consent of the Senate for four year terms. Essentially, the marshals and their deputies were administrative officers for the courts even though under the Attorney General's control. They executed processes and judgments, provided courtrooms, found chambers for the judges, secured utilities and supplies, and disbursed the funds allocated to the courts.[2]

The clerks of the federal courts, on the other hand, bore a relationship to the Attorney General and to the courts different from that of the attorneys and marshals. The clerks

[1] Albert Langeluttig, *The Department of Justice of the United States* (Baltimore, 1927), pp. 75-81.
[2] *Ibid.*, pp. 82-89.

were officers of the court, appointed and removable by the judges alone. Their functions, essentially of a housekeeping character, included the maintenance of court records, issuance of process, entry of judgments and orders, the counseling of lawyers on the intricacies of administrative procedures, and the performance of a myriad of other tasks.[3] Although considered officers of the courts, bailiffs were appointed by the marshals with the approval of the judges. They served under the marshals in preserving order in the courts and performing other duties assigned by the marshals or the judges. Also appointed by the courts and considered officers of the courts were the criers. These officers performed various ceremonial functions such as announcing the opening of court, its adjournment, and other public proclamations ordered by the judges.[4] Messengers, however, were employees of the judges and rendered personal services for them.

Probation officers and bankruptcy referees were included among the officers of the courts. Though under the general supervision of the superintendent of prisons in the Department of Justice, probation officers were appointed by the courts, investigated cases for the courts, and supervised probationers at the discretion of the courts.[5] So, too, bankruptcy referees who administered the assets of bankrupt estates, were appointed by the district judges for two-year terms; hence, they too were officers of the courts rather than agents of the Attorney General. These referees were even more autonomous than other personnel. They supplied their own quarters and equipment, hired their own staffs, and received compensation and expenses from fees, indemnity funds, and charges against the assets of estates under rules set by the district courts.[6]

As the Washington-based administrator for the federal

[3] *Ibid.*, pp. 90-96.   [4] 36 *Stat.* 1088.   [5] 43 *Stat.* 1259-60.

[6] See Henry P. Chandler, "Some Major Advances in the Federal Judicial System: 1922-1947," *Federal Rules Decisions*, 31 (1963), 455.

judiciary, the Attorney General and the Department of Justice had contact with, if not direct responsibility for, these officials of the courts. From the department's Division of Supplies came files, furniture, sheet forms, dockets, and calendars not only for the marshals and attorneys but also for the judges and clerks.[7] The Division of Accounts in the Office of the General Agent audited claims, accounts, and vouchers of all court personnel from the judges to the messengers. It prepared and reviewed authorizations for expenditures from funds allocated to the Attorney General. Preparation of the budget estimates fell to this division as did the compilation of statistical data on the volume of judicial business and the expenditure of the appropriations by the Department of Justice and the courts.[8]

The Division of Examiners, also a part of the general agent's office, was staffed by field auditors. Appointed by the Attorney General, they visited the judicial districts and spent months scrutinizing the books, records, and accounts as well as the conduct of personnel attached to the courts. But they performed a communication function as well as an investigative one; they were, in essence, "the connecting links between the Department and the courts."[9] Thus with their experience and knowledge of practices in other courts, the examiners suggested "to the court rules and orders for the conduct of the business,"[10] a practice which fostered some uniformity in the organization and procedures of the court officers.[11]

The quality of their work, however, was a topic of unremitting controversy. Examinations had been of a rather perfunctory nature in the early years when appointments were

[7] Langeluttig, p. 28.   [8] Ibid., p. 30.
[9] John W. Gardner, U.S., Congress, House, Subcommittee of the House Committee on Appropriations, Hearings, on Department of Justice Appropriation Bill for 1935, 73d Cong., 2d Sess., 1934, p. 97.
[10] J. D. Harris, U.S., Congress, House, Subcommittee of the House Committee on Appropriations, Hearings, on Appropriations, Department of Justice, for 1925, 68th Cong., 1st Sess., 1924, p. 113.
[11] Langeluttig, pp. 30-33.

on a patronage basis, supervision was nominal and service desultory.[12] Yet in 1915 a spokesman for the department told the House Appropriations Committee that "the examinations made now are very real indeed, and during the last four or five years there has been almost a revolution in the way the clerks of the courts . . . have been required to handle trust moneys in their hands."[13] This description reflected reforms instituted during the Taft administration, when Attorney General George W. Wickersham formally established the "Bureau of Investigation." Replacing a miscellaneous group of operatives drawn from various government agencies,[14] the bureau began systematic investigations of the courts, which by the end of 1911, had uncovered criminal practices in clerks' offices across the land.[15]

In spite of their successes, these investigations manifested inherent weaknesses. The examiner force was small, rarely more than two dozen men,[16] its examinations sporadic, and the quality of its work suspect. At the root of the problem lay the examiner himself who was described as "a little second-rate employee that nobody pays much attention to," and whom "the Referee knows . . . does not know much bankruptcy."[17]

[12] See Homer Cummings and Carl McFarland, *Federal Justice: Chapters in the History of Justice and the Federal Executive* (New York, 1937), p. 375.

[13] A. Bruce Bielaski, U.S., Congress, House, Subcommittee of the Committee on Appropriations, *Hearings, on the Legislative, Executive, and Judicial Appropriation Bill for 1915*, 63d Cong., 2d Sess., 1914, pp. 539-40.

[14] See Cummings and McFarland, p. 380.

[15] U.S., *Annual Report of the Attorney General of the United States for 1911* (Washington, 1911), p. 22. (Cited hereafter as *Attorney General's Report.*)

[16] J. D. Harris, U.S., Congress, House, Subcommittee of the Committee on Appropriations, *Hearings, on Appropriations, Department of Justice, for 1927*, 69th Cong., 1st Sess., 1926, p. 113.

[17] "Annual Conference of the United States District Judges of the Eighth Circuit," January 4-5, 1932, stenographic transcript, p. 42,

Growth of Administrative Control

However efficient or defective the administrative system maintained by the Department of Justice, stresses developed. Given the tenuous relations between the Attorney General and various officers of the courts, not to mention the judges themselves, conflicts were all but inevitable.

Springing from the fertile soil provided by a highly decentralized court system staffed with lifetime judges and their appointees, conflicts between the Attorney General and the far-flung courts had been a feature of judicial administration ever since the founding of the Department of Justice in 1870.[18] The new agency inherited at that time the task of preventing indifferent record keeping, waste of funds, and embezzlement of moneys deposited with court officials.[19] These proved no simple duties for clerks, who, with the support or, at least, connivance of their judges, resisted demands from Washington for compliance with statutory obligations to report financial transactions.[20] Complained Attorney General William H. Moody in 1905: "The inability of the Department to require clerks of court to keep proper records or make an accounting . . . together with the serious defects, incompleteness, and great variety of existing records, are conditions not only rendering it exceedingly difficult to detect and punish, those misappropriating the funds in question, but affording such extensive opportunities for wrongdoing that they demand immediate and radical improvement."[21] Shortly thereafter the Attorney General was permitted, by statute, to prescribe rules and

Kimbrough Stone Papers, Box 26. Cited hereafter as "Annual Conference," Kimbrough Stone Papers.

[18] 16 *Stat.* 162.

[19] Cummings and McFarland, pp. 148-49, 534-35.

[20] See Langeluttig, p. 22.

[21] "Letter from the Attorney General," in U.S., Congress, House, *Fees of United States Court Clerks*, House Doc. 97, 59th Cong., 1st Sess., 1905, p. 2.

regulations for the accounting of all funds, disbursements, collections, and trusts.[22]

Following World War I, the Department of Justice launched a concerted drive to establish a degree of central agency control over remote and relatively autonomous court personnel. Abolition of the fee system, creation of salary classifications, and the setting of objective appointment standards were seen as a prerequisite for uniform administration of the courts and for professionalization of court personnel.

Enlargement of executive department power over these aspects of judicial administration naturally evoked anguished cries of protest from congressmen and judges opposed to infringing upon the judge's absolute appointment power, "which power, from almost time immemorial, the judge has had."[23] Such a change, warned the eminent judges of the United States Court of Appeals in the Second Circuit conflicted with "the uniform policy of the Government from the organization of the Federal Courts by placing it within the power of the Attorney General to force out of office an efficient and trustworthy Clerk by fixing his salary below what should be paid and thus forcing him to resign his office."[24]

Whether the issue of administrative control involved court reporters, clerks, or bankruptcy referees,[25] it seemed to judges "very much like the Attorney General was taking the matter over."[26] Administrative power once lodged in the

[22] 34 Stat. 754.

[23] Royal H. Weller, Congressional Record, 70th Cong., 1st Sess., 1928, vol. 69, part 2, 1693.

[24] Judges Charles M. Hough, Martin T. Manton, Julius M. Mayer, Henry Wade Rogers to Harry M. Daugherty, April 15, 1922, Administrative Office Correspondence, 52-A-116, Box 3. Daugherty's response was negative: Daugherty to Warren Harding, April 24, 1922, Administrative Office Correspondence, 52-A-18, Box 3.

[25] George C. Scott, "Annual Conference," p. 66, Kimbrough Stone Papers, Box 26.

[26] Ibid., p. 69.

individual courts was centered elsewhere with the result that there appeared a "growing tendency," exclaimed Senator Thomas Walsh, "to reduce the officers charged with the administration of justice locally to the position of mere clerks, to act in accordance with directions which emanate from the city of Washington."[27]

In spite of opposition and amid charges that centralized administration fostered department interference in the appointment of court officers,[28] reflected on the integrity of federal judges,[29] and actually prevented the employment of personnel "acceptable to the court,"[30] central agency control increased. The salaries of district court clerks and deputies were placed under the Attorney General's supervision in 1919,[31] and three years later he gained control over the compensation received by clerks in the courts of appeals, instituting a salary system.[32] Then, in 1925, Congress created a professional probation service with lines of authority running both to the courts and to the Department of Justice.[33] With most court personnel becoming subject to its administrative control, the department, in the 1930s, pressed hard for drastic reforms in the administration of the bankruptcy system which would enable it to supervise the appointment and work of the referees.[34]

[27] Congressional Record, 67th Cong., 2d Sess., 1922, vol. 62, part 6, 5720.

[28] Joseph Hutcheson, Jr., in Henry P. Chandler, "Report of the Conference of the Fifth Circuit," May 23-24, 1941, pp. 22-23, Administrative Office Correspondence, 57-A-122, Box 1.

[29] Milton W. Shreve, Congressional Record, 70th Cong., 1st Sess., 1928, vol. 69, part 2, 1262-63.

[30] William H. Stafford, ibid., 71st Cong., 2d Sess., 1930, vol. 72, part 2, 2165.

[31] 40 Stat. 1182.

[32] 42 Stat. 616.

[33] 43 Stat. 1259.

[34] See U.S., Congress, Senate, Strengthening of Procedure in the Judicial System, 72d Cong., 1st Sess., 1932, Senate Doc. 65, pp. 104-07.

The trend was unmistakable even if fully satisfactory results eluded the administrators. Effective administration, whether involving salaries, personnel classifications, or appointment standards required a "central authority that [would] bring together all the threads and weave them."[35] Said a department spokesman, "Somebody has to be the spider,"[36] and that somebody necessarily became the Department of Justice.[37]

Administrative Power and Realities

Statutory authority to administer the courts, however, marked for the department only a beginning, not an end. Exercise of its administrative functions proved no easy task for the department in spite of the impression given by a departmental memorandum circulated during Harry Daugherty's administration which noted that the federal courts are "for administrative purposes . . . subject, in a degree at least, to regulating rules by the Department of Justice."[38]

But the department's ambiguous position in administering the court system became obvious in a multitude of delicate situations unrelated to those acts constituting grounds for impeachment or to judicial views on substantive legal issues vitally important to the government's side. The Attorney General might discipline his own attorneys. Judges and court employees, however, fell into a different category. Even the failure of a judge to honor his private financial obligations[39] stirred little activity in the Justice Depart-

[35] Luther C. White, House Subcommittee of the Committee on Appropriations, *Hearings, Appropriations, Department of Justice, 1927,* 1926, p. 331.

[36] *Ibid.*

[37] Andrew Volstead, *Congressional Record,* 67th Cong., 4th Sess., 1923, vol. 64, part 6, 5497.

[38] "Memorandum for Colonel Goff, Re: Plan for Reducing Federal Court Dockets to Normal," April 8, 1922, Department of Justice Files, No. 144446, Sec. 3.

[39] Lloyd Thurston to John G. Sargent, February 6, 1928, Department of Justice Central Files, Judicial Districts Administration Files,

ment of the 1920s. Then, an assistant attorney general disclaimed any "administrative control over United States Circuit or District Judges."[40] The Attorney General's reluctance to approach federal magistrates sprang, in part, from a fear of damaging relations between judge and prosecutor,[41] from recognition of a dispute's triviality, or from a sense of sheer futility, often accompanied by a feeling of impropriety in recommending courses of action to judges. Thus when Chief Justice Taft suggested that the senior circuit judge of the Ninth Circuit was contemplating retirement from the bench, Attorney General William D. Mitchell excused himself from making an investigation because "I would seem to be anticipating Judge [William B.] Gilbert's retirement, and some of these judges are very sensitive about having other people handing in their resignations for them."[42] The efficiency of a judge in disposing of cases on his docket likewise proved a refractory problem for the Attorney General. "What would he think," said Homer Cummings in 1938, "if I wrote him a letter saying 'Why don't you speed up?' He will think I am impertinent and will probably tell me so."[43]

And rebuff the Attorney General was what judges did, regardless of their formal subjection to the department's "regulating rules." They ignored qualification standards set by the Attorney General in their appointment of probation officers.[44] And they resisted the department's fiscal policies.

1912-1938, 6-W-2, Record Group 60 (National Archives, Washington, D.C.; cited hereafter as Department of Justice Central Files).

[40] John Marshall to Lloyd Thurston, February 9, 1928, *ibid.*

[41] E. S. Wertz to Harry M. Daugherty, November 9, 1922, Department of Justice Central Files, 36-N-20.

[42] William D. Mitchell to William Howard Taft, November 5, 1929, Administrative Office Correspondence, 52-A-18, Box 149.

[43] U.S., Congress, Senate, Committee on the Judiciary, *Hearings, on S. 3212, Administrative Office of the United States Courts,* 75th Cong., 3d Sess., 1938, p. 13.

[44] Sanford Bates, "The Establishment and Early Years of the Federal Probation System," *Federal Probation,* 14 (June 1950), 20.

When, in the midst of the Depression, an official of the department urged a district judge to withhold mileage allowances from jurors who traveled only short distances, the magistrate coolly replied: "The practice prevailing in my district is more exposed to the criticism that it is too generous to the government in view of the present meager compensation for both jurors and witnesses."[45]

With judicial finances, the department could ill afford to remain neutral. Yet at the same time, its leverage was rather limited by the very nature of the court system. Unlike the budgetary requirements of executive agencies, those of the federal courts were unpredictable; they depended on the volume of judicial business and on the use of witnesses, jurors, and other court personnel which varied directly with the number of cases processed,[46] all of which lay beyond the department's control.[47] Although the Attorney General, as one district court clerk so aptly put it,

has responsibility as fiscal agent of the Courts, and would not be warranted in approving any item of expenditure by the Courts that was not in complete accordance with the laws and regulations governing such expenditures, the Attorney General's responsibility ceases when the appropriate officer of the Courts certifies as to payrolls and other expenditures of the Courts. It is my view that the Attorney General must assume that all laws and regulations affecting such expenditures have been complied with, and if there be errors of omission or commission,

[45] J. Stanley Webster to Charles E. Stewart, July 19, 1933, Department of Justice Central Files, OX 313. See also Stewart to Webster, July 12, 1933, ibid.

[46] Walter W. Warwick, U.S., Congress, House, Subcommittee of the Committee on Appropriations, Hearings, Appropriations, Department of Justice, 1924, Part 2, 67th Cong., 4th Sess., 1922, p. 153.

[47] See E. M. Kennard, "Statement," U.S., Congress, House, Subcommittee of the Committee on Appropriations, Hearings, Appropriations, Department of Justice, 1926, 68th Cong., 2d Sess., 1925, p. 152.

the responsibility then rests upon the Courts, and not upon the Court's fiscal agent.[48]

Once Congress had appropriated the funds, the sole function of the Attorney General was to dispense them. Each judge, not the central administrator, was, in this view, responsible for the moneys. Thus, when the department ordered a court clerk to establish reserves in his 1938 appropriations pursuant to a Presidential Order directing the creation of such reserves in all executive agencies, the irritated clerk promptly invoked the separation of powers doctrine. The Order, he observed, "is addressed to the heads of the executive departments." Thus, it could not "be the intention of the Executive branch . . . to fix any sum whatever that must be saved in the strictly court appropriations or to seek in any manner to curtail the activities of the Judicial Service by withholding funds appropriated by Congress."[49]

Except for its power to cut the judiciary's budget requests, the department had little room in which to maneuver. On one side Congress demanded responsibility in the allocation of appropriated funds; on the other, virtually autonomous judges resisted, contending that executive officials were "obsessed by a delusion that federal courts are little more than appendages of . . . the executive office."[50]

At the root of many executive-judiciary stresses was the relatively insignificant place of the courts in the department's total administrative realm, and the nature of the court system's problems. These often hampered the department's exercise of authority and engendered misgivings and antagonisms among the magistrates. Officials in the Justice

[48] Charles E. Stewart to T. D. Quinn, January 20, 1938, Harold M. Stephens Papers, Box 37 (Library of Congress, Washington, D.C.; cited hereafter as Stephens Papers).

[49] Charles E. Stewart, "Memorandum to Mr. S. A. Andretta, Acting Administrative Assistant to the Attorney General," July 2, 1937, *ibid.*

[50] *In re: Conciliation Commissioner,* 5 *Fed. Supp.* 131 (1933). Cited in Cummings and McFarland, *Federal Justice,* p. 539.

Department found certain aspects of judicial administration unique and episodic, hence difficult to meet effectively. Facilitating the intercircuit assignment of judges was typical. "No one," said a member of the department in 1926, "is charged with the responsibility of studying docket conditions and requesting assignment of judges where the docket is light to districts where it is heavy. . . . What is everybody's business becomes nobody's."[51]

Such treatment led judges to regard the Justice Department as an indifferent bureaucracy, a view articulated at the 1926 Judicial Conference. There, one senior circuit judge decried "the difficulties that the district judge has in a formal communication to the attorney general where they so frequently get inadequate attention."[52]

Exacerbating this feeling of alienation was a failure or inability on the part of the Attorney General to engage in timely consultation with the judges. Hence, legislation affecting the federal courts might be proposed and pressed upon Congress by the department without the endorsement or even the knowledge of the judges.[53] In fact, the Attorney General might even refuse to support and to submit to Congress recommendations of the Conference of Senior Circuit Judges.[54]

Important too as a source of conflict between the department and the federal judges were real and imagined threats to the integrity of the judiciary's substantive work. As the prosecutor for the government, the Justice Department's fundamental interests did not invariably coincide with

[51] Unsigned Memorandum to Walton R. Moore, April 22, 1926, Administrative Office Correspondence, 52-A-18, Box 3.

[52] 1926 Judicial Conference transcript, pp. 62-63. In Chandler, "Some Major Advances," p. 365.

[53] See "Annual Conference," pp. 2, 30, 61-62, Kimbrough Stone Papers.

[54] *Ibid.*, p. 85. See also Testimony of Kimbrough Stone, U.S., Congress, Senate, Subcommittee of the Committee on the Judiciary, *Hearings, on S. 188, Administration of United States Courts*, 76th Cong., 1st Sess., 1939, p. 21.

those of the courts and any coincidence might not be purely fortuitous. "In different ways and by different methods other than by the usual practice judges are given to understand the views of the Government as to what the law is and what the decision should be," suggested Senator William E. Borah of Idaho.[55]

Within the department's power lay various means of influencing the impartial administration of justice. Selection and promotion of judges constituted a potent weapon in the hands of the Attorney General.[56] Investigations were another. Whatever their intrinsic value, investigations afforded or were perceived as affording the prosecuting department immense leverage in its relations with the judges. Aware of their potential, especially during Prohibition, one legislator thought they "should not be ordered by the executive department because the theory of our Government is that those departments are separate."[57] Another wondered how a federal judge "under constant scrutiny of the Department of Justice . . . can make a fair and upright and honest judge."[58]

Attorney General James C. McReynolds stoutly defended his department's scrutiny of judicial conduct. Citing the department's responsibility for providing the House of Representatives with facts preliminary to impeachment pro-

[55] *Congressional Record*, 63d Cong., 1st Sess., 1913, vol. 50, part 4, 3166-67.

[56] See James E. Babb to William E. Borah, February 19, 1914, William E. Borah Papers (Library of Congress, Washington, D.C.), Box 163.

[57] George H. Tinkham, U.S., Congress, House, Subcommittee of the House Committee on Appropriations, *Hearings, Appropriations, Department of Justice, 1923*, part 2, 67th Cong., 2d Sess., 1922, pp. 158-59.

[58] Kenneth McKellar, *Congressional Record*, 71st Cong., 2d Sess., 1930, vol. 72, part 10, 10883. See correspondence between Senator McKellar and Attorney General William Mitchell respecting a Justice Department investigation of District Judge Harry B. Anderson, *ibid.*, pp. 10881-83.

103

ceedings,[59] he protested that "the suggestion that the Department of Justice is maintaining a system of espionage of the courts and judges of the country is entirely without foundation."[60] A few years later, the department discharged an employee who had taken it upon himself to investigate a United States judge.[61] These congressional reactions revealed the dichotomic nature of such investigations. On the one hand, the surveys promoted improved administration of justice; on the other, they could pose real dangers to judicial integrity.

The assignment of judges was of reciprocal advantage to judge and prosecutor alike. Both were anxious to dispose of congested dockets. Yet the department's attitude was not necessarily neutral. "When certain departments . . . are interested in a question they have a system by which they get for a particular cause a judge off the bench that they want off and another on that they want on," charged one senator whose own impartiality on questions of law lay open to doubt.[62]

Nevertheless, when the Act of 1922[63] enlarged the assignment power of the Chief Justice, Taft was wary of the role played by the Department of Justice in the transfer of judges—and with good reason. No sooner had the law become effective than he felt constrained to complain vigorously to Attorney General Daugherty after an official of the department had transferred, on his own initiative, a district judge to try a criminal case in another circuit.[64]

[59] "James C. McReynolds to President of Senate, August 6, 1913," U.S., Congress, Senate, *Report on Courts and Judges: Letter from the Attorney General*, 63d Cong., 1st Sess., 1913, Senate Doc. 156, p. 2.

[60] *Ibid.*, p. 3.

[61] Rush L. Holland, House Subcommittee of the Committee on Appropriations, *Hearings, Appropriations, Department of Justice, 1923*, part 2, p. 163.

[62] William E. Borah, *Congressional Record*, 62d Cong., 1st Sess., 1911, vol. 47, part 4, 3686.

[63] 42 *Stat.* 839, sec. 3.

[64] William Howard Taft to Harry M. Daugherty, November 28, 1923, Taft Papers.

Depression Economies

In this environment of headquarters-field conflicts over routine administrative matters and of executive intervention in the essence of the judicial process itself, a devastating crisis engulfed the courts. The Great Depression, reducing government revenues and necessitating far-reaching economies in all branches of government, affected the judiciary as well as its fiscal agent, the Department of Justice.

The department had never enjoyed any largess from Congress. Long before, during Grover Cleveland's administration, Attorney General Richard Olney had complained that "the treatment received by the Department is . . . of the most niggardly character."[65] Retrenchment characterized the department's budgetary policy during the Harding and Coolidge administrations when Attorney General Daugherty informed all court personnel that "It is not our desire, nor the intention of Congress, to increase appropriations, notwithstanding ever increasing business. The President of the United States and the Attorney General are opposed to requests for more funds for present needs."[66]

Nevertheless, expansion of federal jurisdiction continued unabated, and, with its growth, the department's budget increased. From $11.7 million in 1920, the estimates for 1933 rose to $53.9 million, an increase of over 400 percent. But with the onset of the Depression the gulf between the estimates prepared by the department and the amount actually appropriated by Congress widened. The 1933 estimate had been based upon the $51.6 million appropriated for the previous fiscal year. It was, however, cut to $44 million, to $31.6 million for the 1934 fiscal year, and then increased slightly to $34.9 million for the 1935 fiscal year.[67]

[65] Richard Olney to George F. Hoar, October 23, 1894, Letter Book, Richard Olney Papers (Library of Congress, Washington, D.C.).

[66] Harry M. Daugherty to All United States Attorneys, United States Marshals, and Clerks of Court, Circular No. 1484, January 15, 1924, Department of Justice Files, 58-A-839, Box 93.

[67] Homer C. Cummings, U.S., Congress, House, Subcommittee of

THE JUSTICE DEPARTMENT AS ADMINISTRATOR

The budgetary deflation of these years capped economy efforts which had begun at the end of the 1929 fiscal year. Rising deficits that year had caused President Hoover to notify his able Attorney General, William D. Mitchell, in July 1930 that "It is of the utmost importance in this time of national depression that we should reduce outlays in every possible direction as a contribution from the Government to the national situation, and thus [bring about] the avoidance of increased taxation."[68] Acting Attorney General Thatcher replied that the judiciary's appropriations were virtually uncontrollable, and that "it would be difficult and inexpedient to halt even temporarily judicial activities, or to delay expenditures in appropriations contributing thereto."[69]

Deepening economic chaos led to a revision in departmental thinking. Terms of district courts in isolated locations had been canceled in the past for lack of travel funds.[70] Now, with a deficiency threatening before the end of the fiscal year, an official of the department, in March 1932, urged one district judge to "avoid the summoning of jurors, except in an emergency, during the last two weeks of June, and that . . . all court officials remain at headquarters, as much as possible, in order to incur a minimum amount of travelling expenses."[71] Judges made little objection to these moves, because the consequences involved nothing more than an enforced vacation.[72]

---

the Committee on Appropriations, *Hearings, on Department of Justice Appropriation Bill for 1937*, 74th Cong., 2d Sess., 1936, p. 2.

[68] Herbert Hoover to William D. Mitchell, July 29, 1930, Department of Justice Files, 58-A-839, Box 93.

[69] Thomas D. Thatcher to Herbert Hoover, August 12, 1930, *ibid.*

[70] 1927 Judicial Conference transcript, pp. 44-46, in Chandler, "Some Major Advances," p. 363.

[71] Charles P. Sisson to William H. Barrett, March 30, 1932, Department of Justice Files, 58-A-839, Box 93.

[72] Luther B. Way to William D. Mitchell, May 9, 1932, *ibid.*; C. F. Amidon to William D. Mitchell, October 1, 1932, *ibid.*

Other steps to curtail judicial expenses, no less drastic, proved quite unpalatable. Judges expressed annoyance with the Budget Bureau's rejection of requests for additional judges on grounds that creation of such new positions would impair the President's conservative financial program.[73] Assaults on their exposed financial flanks by the comptroller general further roused the ire of judges. They regarded his application of the Economy Act of 1932[74] to the *per diem* allowances fixed by the Judicial Code as no less obnoxious because he was an agent of Congress rather than of the President as was the Bureau of the Budget. From the $10-a-day rate of reimbursement permitted under the earlier Code, federal judges were reduced to the $5-a-day allowance provided by the Economy Act for all government officials. A heated response from leading judges greeted this interpretation, and in 1935 a committee of the Judicial Conference presented a report disapproving the opinion of the comptroller general and recommending that the provision of the Judicial Code be re-enacted or litigated. However, apprehension over the potential criticism from opponents of recent federal judicial decisions led them to table the proposal.[75]

Likewise, elimination by Attorney General Mitchell of bailiffs, criers, and messengers came as a bitter blow to many judges. The loss of these often aged messengers was especially hard, and the Attorney General's explanation for his action provided no balm. "Messengers," he said, "are a great convenience and aid to the judges, but many of them perform more or less personal services for the judges which are very desirable and comfortable but not absolute-

[73] Lewis W. Douglas to Homer Cummings, February 7, 1934, Department of Justice Central Files, OX 11.

[74] Act of June 30, 1932. 47 *Stat.* 405, sec. 207. See Act of March 4, 1911. 36 *Stat.* 1161, sec. 259; *Decisions of the Comptroller General of the United States*, 12 (1933), 190-92.

[75] See 1935 Judicial Conference transcript, pp. 241-56, in Chandler, p. 365.

ly essential."[76] Although he noted that the "desperate slashes" of Congress had produced hardships throughout the government,[77] judges bombarded him with protests over their messenger's "sudden dismissal under orders from Washington."[78] Discontent with these policies spanned the nation. "Federal Judges from New York to Fargo," declaimed one judge, "are all distressed over the results of the economy campaign. They feel that the courts have been reduced in dignity and efficiency and that the Judges have been seriously embarrassed in the performance of their duty."[79]

With inception of the New Deal came further indignities. President Roosevelt's Attorney General ordered a 25 percent reduction in expenditures for the 1934 fiscal year from those of the previous year.[80] Salaries of secretaries to retired judges were halved with the explanation that such judges would only render occasional service. That the work of those sitting full time would suffer was dismissed as another Depression casualty.[81] Then the Independent Offices Appropriation Act of 1933 administered the *coup de grâce* to the pride of retired United States judges.[82] That measure, reducing their salaries 15 percent, evoked from the judges protests and threats "to enforce payment of all sums held

[76] William D. Mitchell to C. F. Amidon, October 7, 1932, Department of Justice Files, 58-A-839, Box 93.

[77] *Ibid.*

[78] Curtis D. Wilbur to Charles E. Stewart, November 16, 1933, Administrative Office Correspondence, 52-A-18, Box 150.

[79] C. F. Amidon to William D. Mitchell, October 1, 1932, Department of Justice Files, 58-A-839, Box 93.

[80] "Memorandum in Connection with Statement Showing Appropriations or Actual Expenditures for the Department of Justice for the Fiscal Years 1920, 1933, 1935, and the Estimates for 1936," U.S., Congress, House, Subcommittee of the House Committee on Appropriations, *Hearings, on Department of Justice Appropriation Bill for 1936,* 74th Cong., 1st Sess., 1935, p. 19.

[81] Charles E. Stewart to Robert W. Walker, January 3, 1934, Administrative Office Correspondence, 52-A-18, Box 145.

[82] 48 *Stat.* 307, sec. 13.

back."[83] The wait was brief, for the Supreme Court soon declared the provision unconstitutional.[84]

Reform Proposals

The crisis of the Great Depression only emphasized the administrative position of the federal courts which had prevailed for many years. During that time judges had sought to meet challenges to their budgets and administrative prerogatives by proposing various adaptations in the judiciary's administrative institution. As early as 1926 Senior Circuit Judge Arthur C. Denison had called for a separate appropriation for each circuit court of appeals, explaining that the necessity for Justice Department authorization of administrative expenses had become "a most aggravating thing."[85] Three years later, the Judicial Conference recommended that complete control of the clerks' offices in the appellate courts, including power over salaries and disbursements, be lodged in the senior circuit judges.[86]

Emphasis upon the upper courts rather than on the entire judicial institution reflected a peculiar perception of the changing relationships between the Supreme Court, the inferior federal courts, and the Department of Justice. The Act of February 13, 1925[87] had made the courts of appeals tribunals of final review for many matters previously part of the Supreme Court's appellate jurisdiction. This substantial increase in judicial responsibility enlarged the role and prestige of these intermediate courts. Yet, almost simultaneously, their administrative independence had suffered inglorious erosion with extension of the Attorney General's

[83] John E. Sater to Homer Cummings, January 4, 1934, Administrative Office Correspondence, 52-A-18, Box 3. See also Charles E. Stewart to John E. Sater, January 8, 1934, *ibid.*

[84] *Booth v. United States, Amidon v. United States*, 291 U.S. 339 (1933).

[85] 1926 Judicial Conference transcript, p. 158, in Chandler, p. 367.

[86] *Judicial Conference Report, 1929*, p. 6.

[87] 43 *Stat.* 936.

109

power over the salaries of court clerks. This development left the circuit courts administratively on a plane with the inferior trial courts; a wide gulf separated them from the kind of administrative independence and status enjoyed by the Supreme Court.[88]

That tribunal alone among the federal courts continued to regulate its personnel independently of other branches of government. The number and salaries of its clerks, marshals, and reporters remained within the discretion of the Chief Justice or the court if not fixed by law.[89] Chief Justice Taft had further strengthened this autonomy by making approval of the marshal's accounts by the Chief Justice, rather than by the comptroller general, conclusive on the General Accounting Office.[90] In the minds of some appellate judges, the nation's highest court had effectively preserved its institutional integrity because of its budgetary independence. For the appellate courts, inferior, but not much inferior, to the Supreme Court, a similar course seemed desirable.

Separation of the appellate court budgets from the Department of Justice's appropriation became a more prominent issue in the mid-thirties. Then, a committee of the Judicial Conference composed of Martin T. Manton of the Second Circuit, and his counterpart from the Fifth Circuit, Nathan P. Bryan, pressed the proposal upon the Attorney General who looked askance at its fragmenting influence on judicial administration.[91] Even so enthusiastic an advocate of severing administrative relations between the courts and

---

[88] Memorandum of Martin T. Manton, "Regulation of Personnel of United States Courts; Purpose: To Determine How Far Control of Personnel, at First Almost Wholly in the Courts, Has Been Shifted to the Executive Branch of Government," Department of Justice Files, No. 236508, Sec. 1.

[89] 36 *Stat.* 1152-3.

[90] See E. M. Kennard, House Subcommittee of the Committee on Appropriations, *Hearings, Appropriations, Department of Justice, 1927*, p. 221.

[91] Memorandum, Alexander Holtzoff to Charles E. Stewart, January 29, 1934, Department of Justice Files, No. 236508, Sec. 1.

the executive branch as Judge Bryan entertained doubts, fearing "that there would be great disparity as between the courts in the compensation allowed for the same work."[92] A bill drafted by the Attorney General's office which provided for the optional participation of the Judicial Conference partially met his objections.[93] As for the district courts, their administration remained unattractive, especially to Hughes,[94] and Judge Manton had no great interest in their inclusion.[95] Neither did Attorney General Cummings, who felt that an independent circuit appropriation was "probably as far as we should care to go for the present at least."[96]

No approval of this proposal came from the Conference in either 1934 or 1935. Inaction persisted despite the Justice Department's presentation of a draft bill, described by one of its spokesmen as "a plan of allotment of funds which will . . . materially solve the problems which have been in the past most annoying."[97] A majority of the Conference found neither the plan advanced nor its justification persuasive for they believed that the Department of Justice was better situated to secure appropriations from Congress than were the courts acting on their own.[98]

While proposals for changes in the administrative structure of the federal judiciary were going into limbo, the long paralyzed procedural reform campaign displayed new strength. Culmination of that campaign in the 1930s

[92] Nathan P. Bryan to Martin T. Manton, January 5, 1934, *ibid.*
[93] 1934 Judicial Conference transcript, p. 97, in Chandler, p. 369.
[94] 1930 Judicial Conference transcript, pp. 336-37, *ibid.*, p. 368.
[95] 1933 Judicial Conference transcript, p. 273, *ibid.*, p. 369.
[96] Homer C. Cummings to William Stanley, October 10, 1933, Department of Justice Files, No. 236508, Sec. 1.
[97] William Stanley to Martin T. Manton, March 6, 1934, *ibid.*
[98] Memorandum, Alexander Holtzoff to Homer Cummings, November 12, 1937, *ibid.*, Section 2. Their preferences reportedly coincided with partisan loyalties, with the five Democratic members voting in favor of the Manton recommendation and the five Republicans against. See William Denman to Stanley Reed, September 5, 1936, *ibid.*

111

brought to a virtual end one of the two major responses to attacks from without and to discontent from within the court system. Thereafter, bench and bar were compelled to deal with the other reform thrust, namely, further development of the judiciary's administrative institution. Hitherto stalled because of conflicting opinions among the senior circuit judges, in 1937 administrative reform suddenly took on a new and vigorous life. Then the dramatic events occurring early in President Franklin Roosevelt's second term shattered the deadlock on the Judicial Conference which had doomed earlier proposals.

Crisis and the Court Plan

The fate of the New Deal at the hands of the Supreme Court generated a major political crisis involving the entire federal court system. Neither the 1935 nor the 1936 terms of the Court had been happy ones for Roosevelt's legislative program. One after another, its components had been struck down as unconstitutional by the Hughes Court, a development which caused the President to castigate one decision as a return to the "horse-and-buggy" age.[99]

Early in 1937, the President unveiled his plan for mitigating the Court's obstruction of his congressional program. In what Secretary Harold Ickes described as a "sensational document,"[100] he proposed the appointment of an additional Supreme Court justice for each justice who had served ten years and had not resigned or retired within six months after reaching the age of seventy.

Although clearly aimed at the Supreme Court,[101] the

[99] See *A.L.A. Schechter Corporation v. United States*, 295 U.S. 495 (1935); Samuel F. Rosenman, ed., *The Public Papers and Addresses of Franklin D. Roosevelt*, vol. 4, *1935* (New York, 1938), p. 209. (Cited hereafter as *Public Papers of FDR*.)

[100] Harold L. Ickes, *The Secret Diary of Harold Ickes: The Inside Struggle, 1936-39* (New York, 1954), II, 65.

[101] See *ibid.*, II, 66.

President's "Court-packing" bill made a broad appeal to all who were disenchanted with any or all levels of the federal judicial hierarchy. These critics were legion. Slightly less than a year before the bill's introduction, Circuit Judge William Denman of the Ninth Circuit had charged that "the administrative side of the Federal courts is as sluggish and inefficient and its tendency as likely to destroy public confidence, as that of England in the time when Dickens' poignant novels stimulated the procedural reform movement there."[102] Inertia on the part of court personnel, overworked judges indifferent to administration, and dispersion of administrative responsibility and authority between the courts and the Attorney General, in his opinion, contributed significantly to this condition.[103]

Lawyers, too, had little enthusiasm for the manner in which the lower federal courts functioned. After the Court fight, the President of the American Bar Association, Arthur T. Vanderbilt, would admit "that while lawyers generally had the highest respect for the Supreme Court . . . there was a feeling that the district courts were not keeping abreast of their work, and there was a much greater tendency to criticize the district courts."[104] It was not merely the fact that the courts were slow which irritated lawyers, but that many trial judges seemed "as a class, arrogant, domineering and tyrannical . . . a group of public dictators and tyrants and without responsibility to anyone."[105]

[102] William Denman, "The Denial of Civil Justice in the Federal Courts and a Suggested Remedy; Submitted March 9, 1936, to the Administration, the Attorney General, and the Chairmen of the Judiciary Committees of the Senate and House," p. 6, private print, Stephens Papers, Box 12. (Cited hereafter as Denman, "The Denial of Civil Justice.")

[103] Ibid., pp. 6-10.

[104] U.S., Congress, House, Subcommittee of the Committee on the Judiciary, Hearings, on the General Subject of the Administration of the Federal Courts, stenographic transcript, 75th Cong., 3d Sess., 1938, p. 44. In Legislative Files, H.R. 2973, 76th Cong.

[105] Stephen M. Young, Congressional Record, 74th Cong., 1st Sess., 1935, vol. 79, part 7, 7536.

113

The public behavior of some judges during the Depression did nothing to improve the congressional mood. Congressmen resented the exemption of the judicial salaries from the operation of the Economy Acts. A plea for voluntary contributions up to 15 percent of their salaries went virtually unheeded by the judges, a seemingly unpatriotic response to a crisis analogized to war.[106] The prestige of the judiciary fell further when Depression-generated scandals in bankruptcy administration twice compelled the Senate to hold full-dress impeachment trials,[107] and when Thomas E. Dewey's investigation of Martin Manton, senior circuit judge of the esteemed Second Circuit Court of Appeals, revealed case after case of justice sold to the highest bidder.[108]

Thus, the legislative environment was one conducive to judicial reform, even drastic reform. As never before, congressmen seemed receptive to demands for "a vigorous, exhaustive and complete administration of the Federal Judiciary and an executive control of its acts, while preserving, at the same time, the freedom of its judicial decision."[109]

Taking cognizance of widespread discontent with the administration of justice in the lower federal courts, the President advanced his Court plan not merely as an attack on the Supreme Court, but as a constructive step toward reform. "A growing body of our citizens," he said, as had unnumbered judicial reformers before him, "complain of the complexities, the delays, and the expenses of litigation in United States Courts. . . . Only by speeding up the processes

[106] See John W. Gardner, House Subcommittee of the Committee on Appropriations, *Hearings, Department of Justice Appropriation Bill for 1935*, pp. 180-81.

[107] See Acquittal of District Judge Harold Louderback, *Congressional Record*, 73d Cong., 1st Sess., 1933, vol. 77, part 4, 4088; Conviction of District Judge Halstead L. Ritter, *ibid.*, 74th Cong., 2d Sess., 1936, vol. 80, part 5, 5606-07.

[108] See Borkin, *The Corrupt Judge*, ch. II.

[109] Harry A. Toulmin, Jr. to Hatton Sumners, June 9, 1937, Legislative Files, H.R. 2271, 75th Cong.

of the law and thereby reducing their cost, can we eradicate the growing impression that the courts are chiefly a haven for the well-to-do."[110] Efficiency and economy in the administration of justice required, Roosevelt asserted, "the same kind of reorganization of the Judiciary as has been recommended . . . for the Executive Branch of the Government."[111] Thus he publicly equated his Court plan with that for reorganization of the executive branch submitted by his Committee on Administrative Management less than a month before presentation of the Court proposal.[112] This distinguished committee, headed by Louis Brownlow, had been created in March 1936 to analyze government administration in the light of needs generated by the Depression, the nation's growth, the rising totalitarian menace abroad, and by "the vexing social problems of our times."[113] After intensive study it concluded that the canons of efficiency required "the establishment of a responsible and effective chief executive as the center of energy, direction, and administrative management, the systematic organization of all activities in the hands of a qualified personnel under the direction of the chief executive; and to aid him in this, the establishment of appropriate managerial and staff agencies."[114]

The thrust of this managerial reform movement, then prominent in official thinking, was reflected in the Judicial Reorganization Bill. Key members of the Roosevelt administration had been impressed with "the failure of some judges whose time was not fully occupied in their own districts to relieve temporary congestion in others."[115] Thus President

[110] *Public Papers of FDR*, vi, 52.
[111] *Ibid.*, p. 35.
[112] See *The President's Committee on Administrative Management: Report of the Committee with Studies of Administrative Management in the Federal Government* (Washington, 1937; cited hereafter as *Report of the President's Committee*).
[113] *Ibid.*, p. 2.   [114] *Ibid.*, p. 3.
[115] Unsigned Memorandum, "Judicial Reform," p. 3, Department of Justice Files, No. 235773, Sec. 5.

Roosevelt had declared that any new "system should be flexible and should permit the temporary assignment of judges to points where they appear to be most needed."[116] To this end the bill revived the hoary idea of judges-at-large and enhancement of the Chief Justice's discretionary power. Section 2 provided for the assignment by the Chief Justice of any circuit or district judge, thereafter appointed, to any circuit. Only an objection from the senior circuit judge of the assigned judge's home circuit could bar the Chief Justice's action. However, such an objection could not bind the Chief, who might use his own judgment in determining the sufficiency of the senior circuit judge's argument.[117]

Strengthening the Chief Justice's administrative power was not enough; he, like the President, needed help.[118] Years of experience had revealed inherent deficiencies in the much-vaunted intercircuit transfer of judges and the proposed appointment of judges-at-large offered no great advance in efficiency unless accompanied by other administrative reforms.[119] Just as the Brownlow committee recommended adequate staff assistance for the President,[120] so Roosevelt urged creation of a judicial administrator "known as Proctor . . . to be appointed by the Supreme Court and to act under its direction."[121]

Although unveiled in a climate of unprecedented administrative reorganization, the idea of a judicial administrator broke no new ground. For nearly three decades, leading members of the legal community had been advancing such a proposal. As early as 1909 the American Bar Association had recommended that a mobile judiciary be created "un-

[116] Public Papers of FDR, vi, 38.   [117] Ibid., vi, 64.
[118] Report of the President's Committee, p. 5.
[119] See Unsigned Memorandum, "The New Court Bill," p. 8, Department of Justice Files, No. 235773, Sec. 5.
[120] Report of the President's Committee, p. 5.
[121] Public Papers of FDR, vi, 38.

der the direction of someone whose duty it is to see that the work of the court is provided for and disposed of." This, it thought, "would make a real judicial department."[122] Two decades later, a scholar advanced a similar suggestion, in recommending establishment of "an administrative bureau . . . with a competent administrative officer at its head who, under the general supervision of the Supreme Court or the Chief Justice, would conduct the administrative affairs of the entire judicial branch of the federal government."[123]

Then, in 1931, the Judicial Conference considered a proposal for "the formal organization of the Judicial Branch of the Government, to be presided over by a 'Chancellor of the United States,' to be appointed by the Supreme Court."[124] One of the duties of this officer would be to determine "the needs . . . of the various circuits and districts [and] where they may have special need [giving] them special attention."[125]

Four years later, Judge Denman unveiled a similar proposal, reputed to be the immediate ancestor of the President's "Proctor" provision.[126] In March 1936 he presented it to ranking Administration officials and to the chairmen of the Judiciary Committees of Congress. But, first, Denman discussed his plan with Felix Frankfurter, then professor of law at Harvard.[127] Subsequently he spoke "with two of

[122] "Report of the Special Committee to Suggest Remedies and Formulate Proposed Laws to Prevent Delay and Unnecessary Cost in Litigation," *Report of the 32nd Annual Meeting of the American Bar Association*, 34 (1909), 593.

[123] Langeluttig, *The Department of Justice*, p. 179.

[124] Louis Fitz Henry to Samuel Alschuler, September 2, 1931, 1931 Judicial Conference transcript, pp. 378-79, in Chandler, "Some Major Advances," p. 368.

[125] 1932 Judicial Conference transcript, pp. 255-56, in *ibid.*, p. 369.

[126] Joseph Alsop and Turner Catledge, *The 168 Days* (Garden City, 1938), p. 35.

[127] William J. Denman to John J. Parker, February 20, 1940, Parker Papers, Box 54.

the so-called liberal Justices of the Supreme Court,"[128] reportedly Stone and Brandeis.[129] Both gave the proposal their blessing.[130] Denman's plan reflected the influence on judicial reformers of the Act of February 13, 1925, which permitted the Supreme Court to control the volume of its business. That act demonstrated "that under a centralized administrative control over an adequate number of judges, similar effectiveness is possible in our trial courts."[131] Denman then suggested the creation of a powerful central administrator who "should rank any Judge under the Supreme Court . . . [and] who should be able to undertake far-reaching investigations of courts, to press delinquent judges in clearing their dockets, and to supply judges-at-large to congested courts."[132]

So, too, Section 3 of Roosevelt's bill empowered a Proctor to secure from the courts and publish, with the highest Court's consent, information on the business of the district and circuit courts, to "investigate the need of assigning district and circuit judges to other courts and to make recommendations thereon to the Chief Justice; (3) to recommend, with the approval of the Chief Justice, to any court of the United States, methods for expediting cases pending on its dockets; and (4) to perform such other duties consistent with his office as the Court shall direct."[133] Later,

---

[128] William R. Wallace, "Judge Denman's Contribution to the Reorganization of the Lower Federal Courts and Its Relation to the Court Enlargement Bill of 1937," reprinted from *The Record* (San Francisco), April 7, 1939, Stephens Papers, Box 12.

[129] Denman to Parker, February 20, 1940, Parker Papers, Box 54.

[130] *Ibid.*

[131] Denman, "The Denial of Civil Justice," pp. 11-12.

[132] William Denman, U.S., Congress, Senate, Committee on the Judiciary, *Hearings, on S. 1392, Reorganization of the Federal Judiciary*, Part 2, 75th Cong., 1st Sess., 1937, p. 483; William Denman to Stanley Reed, September 5, 1936, Department of Justice Files, No. 236508, Sec. 2.

[133] *Public Papers of FDR*, vi, 65.

during hearings on the measure, it became apparent that a staff as well as a Proctor was contemplated to examine caseloads in eighty-five districts,[134] and to expose if not to the general public, then to their peers, "laggard judges . . . and those who lack the capacity to organize the business of their individual courts."[135]

Counterattack and Reappraisal

Ultimately, the administration's court bill suffered mortal blows, some of them emanating from the Supreme Court itself,[136] as well as from the September 1937 Judicial Conference.[137]

Section 2 of the court bill likewise came under attack from the Chief Justice. He adamantly opposed the creation of judges-at-large because such an innovation would necessarily require an enlargement of his own assignment power. Such power, he feared, would compel him to "practically determine who should try cases for the Government in the circuits or districts of the country."[138]

The Proctor proposal evoked sharper and more widespread criticism. Judges saw it as a threat to an independent and decentralized judiciary. One of the more influential among them contended that "the effort to reconstitute the Supreme Court was only part of a general effort to appoint what was called a 'Court Proctor' to supervise the work of the district judges and generally exercise power in relation to their duties and functions which, in the opinion of most

[134] Denman, Senate Committee on the Judiciary, *Hearings on S. 1392*, 1937, p. 482.

[135] *Ibid.*, p. 484.

[136] U.S., Congress, Senate, Committee on the Judiciary, *Reorganization of the Federal Judiciary*, Report to Accompany S. 1392, S. Rept. 711, 75th Cong., 1st Sess., 1937, pp. 38-40.

[137] *New York Times*, September 29, 1937, p. 17.

[138] 1937 Judicial Conference transcript, p. 220, in Chandler, pp. 343-44.

people, would have totally destroyed the independence of the courts."[139]

Following defeat of the President's bill, prominent federal judges reappraised the judiciary's adequacy as an administrative institution. Publicly, they acknowledged the validity of arguments founded on the existence of congestion and delay in the courts.[140] But in private they admitted the creditability of broader criticisms. At the 1938 Conference, Chief Justice Hughes noted the geographical isolation of federal judges, an environment which "in some instances, tends to the creation of a disposition to exercise an individual will which some critics have characterized as 'czar-like and arbitrary.' "[141]

Institutional means for meeting such administrative and ethical problems seemed desirable, if not vital. "Once given authority as well as the responsibility," Circuit Judge Harold M. Stephens believed that the judges "would be much more effective in their duties than they have been in the past because they would feel the responsibility and having also authority to express it and to make the responsibility effective, they would be quickened to do it."[142] But the existing absence of a staff equipped to perform essential bureaucratic functions rendered it simply impossible for "any body of men, highly specialized in contemplative work, whose whole energy is completely absorbed in a struggle to keep pace with their calendars, to manage in a week's session in Washington, the huge business of an annual filing of

[139] D. Lawrence Groner to Orie L. Phillips, July 17, 1944, Groner Papers, Box 4.

[140] D. Lawrence Groner, U.S., Congress, Senate, Committee on the Judiciary, *Hearings on S. 188*, 1939, p. 11.

[141] " 'Administration in the Federal Courts—Administrative Office Bill,' Extract from the Proceedings of the Judicial Conference: September 30, 1938, pp. 174-92," mimeograph (Washington, n.d.), p. 10. (Cited hereafter as "Extract, Administration in the Federal Courts.")

[142] Senate Subcommittee of the Committee on the Judiciary, *Hearings on S. 188*, 1939, p. 33.

78,000 cases in courts scattered through 48 states."[143] Reorganization would strengthen the Conference by providing it with a permanent secretariat, a reform innovation which found favor with the Chief Justice.[144] Hughes saw in such an administrative agency a means for improving the judiciary's far-flung communications system established in 1922. Primarily, he regarded it as affording an instrument for securing the specialized information on judicial business so vital to rational administration, and especially for improving the quality of judicial statistics.

To other judges a separate administrative agency seemed an ideal instrument for improving liaison with Congress.[145] It could counter, said Judge Denman, "the feeling that it is *infra dig* for the Federal judiciary, constitutionally equal with Congress, to make a direct approach to their coordinate brethren in the legislature in matters regarding the discharge of their constitutional functions."[146]

With effective liaison, judges anticipated tangible results. More money appropriated by a Congress whose heart would melt at the sight of the judiciary's minuscule requests was forecast by the California jurist.[147] Moreover, an administrator responsible only for the courts would, thought some judges, insure a more equitable allocation of funds finally appropriated.[148]

Undoubtedly, these positive advantages associated with

[143] William Denman to Henry F. Ashurst, January 31, 1938, Senate Committee on the Judiciary, *Hearings on S. 3212*, 1938, p. 69.

[144] "Extract, Administration in the Federal Courts," pp. 19-20.

[145] Harold M. Stephens, Senate Subcommittee of the Committee on the Judiciary, *Hearings on S. 188*, 1939, p. 33.

[146] William J. Denman, "Proposals for Part of the Agenda for the Conference of Federal Circuit and District Judges, Ninth Circuit Conference," undated, Department of Justice Files, No. 236508, Sec. 2.

[147] William J. Denman to Martin T. Manton, September 26, 1936, Groner Papers, Box 8.

[148] D. Lawrence Groner to Wiley Rutledge, April 17, 1939, *ibid.*, Box 22.

a separate administrative institution motivated leading members of the courts, especially Chief Justice Hughes. Its appeal, however, was a narrow one. Programs for building into the judiciary an efficient administrative agency and enhancing accountability held limited attraction for many members of the courts.

On the other hand, the Roosevelt onslaught elicited powerful negative responses founded essentially on ideological grounds. And in the crisis of 1937, the significance of the doctrine of separation of governmental powers came to the fore.

Although the Department of Justice had been involved in judicial administration since 1870, feelings ran so high in the wake of the Court fight that one leading spokesman for the legal community protested that "any influence over judicial administration by the department for prosecution is an odious usurpation."[149] Suddenly there was something insidious in the Justice Department's control of judicial finances. Warned one judge:

> The fact . . . is that if an Attorney General or a Budget Director or Secretary of the Treasury were hostile to the courts and their independence, he could cripple their independence seriously by refusing to include necessary items for their support and equipment. By a process of attrition upon the estimates of the courts he could ultimately cripple their powers seriously.[150]

Favoring the separation of judicial administration from the Justice Department, Attorney General Cummings took the same approach.[151]

This administrative tyranny argument contained some

149 Herbert Harley, "Forced Retirement of Federal Trial Judges," *Journal of the American Judicature Society*, 21 (October 1937), 89.

150 Harold M. Stephens to William H. King, March 14, 1938, Stephens Papers, Box 208.

151 See Senate, Committee on the Judiciary, *Hearings on S. 3212*, 1938, p. 14.

truth. The Bureau of the Budget had, in fact, revised and reduced the estimates for the courts.[152] The Department of Justice had, perhaps, treated the courts indifferently. "The requirements of the courts for more judges, with properly salaried law clerks . . . and for their libraries and their chambers are," charged Judge Denman, lost in the unit consideration . . . with the executive need for assistant attorneys general, lawyers, and clerical force all for the United States as litigant."[153] Seemingly inequitable allocation of funds between courts as well as between branches of the government had occurred and was similarly protested by another eminent judge.[154]

Finally, normal administrative authorization of supplies and travel expenses had irritated many judges. But Learned Hand thought this issue "theoretical talk, pure and simple." He had been on the bench for nearly three decades and had "come to be suspicious of executive pressure . . . but it has never come in the form of shutting off my stationery. This . . . is to me the veriest claptrap."[155] Chief Justice Hughes substantially agreed with Hand's view.[156]

Myth and reality merged imperceptibly. Nevertheless, to a large number of judges one thing was clear: their prestige had fallen. Whatever the fundamental cause, whether the Depression, administrative disorganization and indifference, or an outright executive conspiracy against the courts of which the Court bill was but one manifestation, many judges felt a loss of self-esteem and status. They wanted "a

[152] Harold M. Stephens to Charles E. Stewart, December 23, 1937, Stephens Papers, Box 208.

[153] William Denman, "Critical Study of United States Trial Courts: What the Legislature Owes the Judiciary," *Journal of the American Judicature Society*, 21 (December 1937), 122-23.

[154] D. Lawrence Groner, U.S., Congress, House, Committee on the Judiciary, *Hearings, on H.R. 2973, H.R. 5999, Administration of United States Courts*, 76th Cong., 1st Sess., 1939, p. 7.

[155] Learned Hand to D. Lawrence Groner, December 26, 1938, Groner Papers, Box 4.

[156] "Extract, Administration in the Federal Court," p. 8.

restoration of the authority, jurisdiction, privileges and prestige of the district judges to what they were no longer than ten years ago."[157]

Federal judges, in short, felt threatened. At home, they confronted a "movement for centralization or control."[158] Around the world the strident sounds of totalitarian political systems echoed. "We are living in a time when all legal processes, all processes of reason, here and abroad throughout the world, are more or less subject to attack," Chief Justice Hughes asserted. "We are living at a time when the disposition to exercise authority, to control by executive force, makes a strong appeal to a multitude of people."[159] The need for adaptations in the judicial institution had become self-evident and the time for meeting it perhaps short.

To meet the challenge to a government of laws resting upon an independent judiciary and to maintain the people's confidence in their courts, the judges moved "to clean their own house, rather than be subject to the embarrassment and destruction of our theory of government by having it done by someone else."[160] They sought to build "up ourselves, among ourselves, our own controlling organization as far as might be necessary."[161] To this end, the Administrative Office Act of 1939 would be the judiciary's substitute for the Court bill introduced by President Roosevelt in 1937.

[157] Merrill Otis, "Conference of the United States Circuit and District Judges of the Eighth Circuit," 1939, stenographic transcript, p. 343, Kimbrough Stone Papers, Box 26.

[158] *Ibid.*, p. 319.

[159] "Extract, Administration in the Federal Court," p. 12.

[160] D. Lawrence Groner, Senate Subcommittee of the Committee on the Judiciary, *Hearings on S. 188*, 1939, p. 9.

[161] D. Lawrence Groner to Orie L. Phillips, July 17, 1944, Groner Papers, Box 4.

CHAPTER 4

The Administrative Office Act of 1939

New Plans and New Proponents

THE aspirations and apprehensions which stirred federal judges during the court fight of 1937 induced some of their number to sponsor a reform program of their own. With the endorsement of the American Bar Association,[1] and the active support of its president, Arthur T. Vanderbilt,[2] a bill drafted in the spring of 1936 by Judge Martin T. Manton and Charles E. Stewart of the Department of Justice was revived.[3]

Unlike the administration's proctor proposal, this measure was the successor to earlier Conference proposals for the separation of appellate court administration from the Department of Justice. Transferring the department's administrative functions to the judiciary, it provided for the establishment of an Administrative Office of the United States Courts with a director appointed by the Chief Justice. As administrative officer of the federal judiciary, the director was charged with the performance of duties prescribed by the Judicial Conference and supervised by the Chief Justice and a committee selected by him. These duties included control of all fiscal and business services then under the Department of Justice as well as "the preparation

[1] William L. Ransom, "Members and Non-Members of the American Bar Association Take Same Stand on Court Issues," *American Bar Association Journal*, 23 (May 1937), 384-85.

[2] See Henry P. Chandler, "Some Major Advances in the Federal Judicial System: 1922-1947," *Federal Rules Decisions*, 31 (1963), 373-74.

[3] Martin T. Manton to Kimbrough Stone, May 22, 1936. Quoted in Kimbrough Stone to Elmore Whitehurst, November 20, 1953, Kimbrough Stone Papers, Box 11.

of statistical data and reports of the business transactions of the courts."[4]

This plan had been presented to the Judicial Conference in the fall of 1936 where it was discussed at length by the senior circuit judges.[5] But they took no formal action at that time,[6] perhaps because of protests emanating from the trial benches. At least one district judge feared that the bill's language would permit transfer of supervisory power over subordinate court personnel from the courts to "an executive officer in Washington whose lack of knowledge in the situation or political bias might cause him to go counter to the wishes of the courts."[7]

If the Manton plan threatened judicial autonomy, it appeared minimal when contrasted with President Roosevelt's court reorganization proposal. Following defeat of that measure, Judge Manton, in November 1937, forwarded the Conference's 1936 draft to President Roosevelt and to officials in the Justice Department.[8] They received it favorably. The plan, observed one high-ranking member of the Attorney General's staff, would not only transfer administrative duties to the judiciary, but "would confer on the Director all of the duties which were contemplated for the Proctor by the court bill."[9]

The now chastened Attorney General was reluctant to press another court reform plan. Not only had his own proposal suffered crushing defeat, but it had ignited the wrath of bench and bar.[10] Bridging this wide gulf was Arthur T.

[4] Bill in File of Judicial Conference, 1936, in Chandler, "Some Major Advances," p. 370.

[5] 1936 Judicial Conference transcript, p. 292; Chandler, p. 371.

[6] Ibid., p. 155; Chandler, p. 371.

[7] Henry H. Watkins to John J. Parker, July 21, 1936, Parker Papers, Box 53.

[8] Alexander Holtzoff, "Memorandum for the Attorney General," November 12, 1937, Department of Justice Files, No. 236508, Sec. 2.

[9] Ibid.

[10] See Annual Report of the American Bar Association, 62 (1937), 415-28, 904-11.

Vanderbilt, then president of the American Bar Association. He successfully took the case for judicial reform to Chief Justice Hughes, who agreed to withhold objections to further reform efforts.[11]

The path now cleared, Attorney General Cummings pressed for reform of the judiciary's administrative system. In his *Annual Report*, issued on January 3, 1938, he urged that "serious thought . . . be given to increasing . . . flexibility by appropriate measures that will involve a greater coordination of the judicial machinery, a better method of assembling data and continuous oversight by the judiciary itself of its functions and efficiency."[12]

Little more than a week later, Senator Henry F. Ashurst of Arizona, chairman of the Senate Committee on the Judiciary, introduced a bill conforming to the recommendations of the Attorney General.[13] The major features of the Ashurst Bill resembled those of the 1936 Conference draft, but the Supreme Court was included within the scope of the proposed reform. That Court, rather than the Chief Justice, would appoint the director, whose duties included recommending to the Chief Justice assignment of judges as well as examining dockets and preparing statistical data.

Ultimate responsibility for the functioning of the director would rest with the Chief Justice and the Judicial Conference.[14] To this suggestion, Hughes reported that "there was a very preponderant sentiment vigorously expressed in the conference of the members of the Supreme Court in opposition to the adoption of the measure."[15] The Chief Justice, too, had misgivings about the role of the Court in supervis-

[11] Interview of Arthur T. Vanderbilt by Henry P. Chandler, February 6, 1957, Newark, New Jersey, in Chandler, "Some Major Advances," p. 374.

[12] U.S., *Annual Report of the Attorney General of the United States for 1938* (Washington: Government Printing Office, 1937), p. 5.

[13] *Congressional Record*, 75th Cong., 3d Sess., 1938, vol. 83, part 1, 304.

[14] S. 3212, 75th Congress.

[15] "Extract, Administration in the Federal Courts," p. 4.

ing judicial administration in general or the director in particular.[16]

Another measure, this one sponsored by the Judicial Conference and introduced in the Seventy-sixth Congress, conformed with the Chief's views. It provided for a formally decentralized administrative institution and removed the Supreme Court and even the Chief Justice from direct responsibility for the administration of the inferior federal courts.[17] Yet its provision for the appointment of the director by the Supreme Court and the continued participation of the Chief Justice in the Judicial Conference led Justice Brandeis to oppose even the modified bill on grounds "that it was the duty of the Court to adjudicate, not to administer."[18] Lacking unanimity, the members of the Supreme Court withheld their official support,[19] but a congressional spokesman for the bill would state that they generally favored it.[20]

In the end, all the senior circuit judges with the exception of Martin Manton, then preoccupied with Thomas Dewey's investigation of his judicial conduct, supported the measure and signified a willingness to testify on its behalf.[21] However, Manton's successor, Learned Hand, extended his approval only reluctantly; at least he promised to remain neutral.[22] Thus on the eve of a major adaptation in the judi-

[16] *Ibid.*, p. 5.

[17] S. 188, H.R. 2973, H.R. 5999, 76th Cong.; Act of August 7, 1939, 53 *Stat.* 1223.

[18] Charles E. Clark to Lester B. Orfield, November 25, 1942, Charles E. Clark Papers (in possession of Elias Clark, Yale University, New Haven, Connecticut; cited hereafter as Clark Papers).

[19] *Ibid.*

[20] Henry F. Ashurst, *Congressional Record*, 76th Cong., 1st Sess., 1939, vol. 84, part 9, 9807.

[21] D. Lawrence Groner to Alexander Holtzoff, January 6, 1939, Groner Papers, Box 4. See also Xenophon Hicks to D. Lawrence Groner, January 7, 1939, *ibid.*; D. Lawrence Groner to Hatton Sumners, February 15, 1939, Legislative Files, H.R. 2973, 76th Cong.

[22] Learned Hand to D. Lawrence Groner, December 26, 1938, Groner Papers, Box 4.

ciary's administrative institution not only the Attorney General but the Conference as well stood almost unanimously behind it. This consensus apparently prevailed only among the higher levels of the judicial hierarchy for Chief Justice Hughes reported that many trial judges looked askance at the proposal.[23]

The Conference as a whole did not act on this bill until its meeting in the fall of 1938. Then, a special committee of its members was created to secure reform of the federal court system acceptable to the judges and to legislators who had balked at the administration's far-reaching proposals. Chief Justice Hughes selected as chairman a conservative Virginia Republican, D. Lawrence Groner, then chief justice of the Court of Appeals for the District of Columbia Circuit.[24] He would be strongly influenced by a non-

[23] "Minutes of the Judicial Conference of the United States, 1940, Division of Procedural Studies and Statistics," p. 331, negative photographic reproduction, Administrative Office Correspondence, 60-A-328, Box 27 (cited hereafter as "Minutes of the Judicial Conference, 1940"). The Chief Justice's information was probably based, in part, on intuition as well as empirical data. He may have inferred opposition to the Administrative Office bill in its final form, S. 188, H.R. 2973, H.R. 5999, 76th Cong., from objections to the earlier Manton bill. See Henry H. Watkins to John J. Parker, July 21, 1936, Parker Papers, Box 53.

[24] The presiding judge of the United States Court of Appeals for the District of Columbia Circuit was designated "chief justice" by the Act of February 9, 1893, 27 Stat. 434. By Sec. 2 of the Act of June 25, 1948, 62 Stat. 985 as amended by Sec. 51 of the Act of September 3, 1954, 68 Stat. 1245, his designation became "chief judge," as did that of all "senior" circuit and district judges. The 1948 revision of the Judicial Code designated the members of the United States Court of Appeals for the District of Columbia as " 'judges' rather than as 'justices,' thus harmonizing [section 44] with the provisions of section 41 [of Title 28] . . . , which specifically designates the District of Columbia as a judicial circuit of the United States. In doing so it consolidates sections 11-201, 11-202 of the District of Columbia Code, 1940 ed., which provided for one 'chief justice' and five associate 'justices.' " U.S., Congress, House, Committee on the Judiciary, Revision of Title 28, United States Code, H. Rept. 308 to accompany H.R. 3214, 80th Cong., 1st Sess., 1947, p. A5.

129

member of the Conference, Judge Harold M. Stephens. Groner's colleague on the District of Columbia bench, Stephens had formerly held the post of Assistant Attorney General under Homer Cummings. Other members of the committee included the senior circuit judge of the Eighth Circuit, Kimbrough Stone, and Judge John J. Parker of the Fourth Circuit, both of whom would be influential in shaping the reform legislation. Evan A. Evans and Martin T. Manton, senior circuit judges of the Seventh and Second Circuits, respectively, would exercise less influence, the latter resigning his judicial commission four months after the committee's establishment. These judges of the Conference coordinated their efforts with a committee of lawyers headed by Arthur T. Vanderbilt which represented the Attorney General.[25]

The Separation

In the wake of the dramatic clash between the executive and judicial branches, all parties agreed on the desirability of separating judicial administration from the Justice Department. In the eyes of the judges who had experienced the department's Depression-inspired economies, a primary objective of both the 1936 Conference draft and the later Ashurst Bill was "to relieve the courts of Executive control over its finances."[26] This objective was of paramount importance to Judge Stephens who had been strongly impressed by the power of the Bureau of the Budget to slash the financial estimates of the courts.[27] Encouraged by his colleague, Groner told key members of the House Judiciary Commit-

[25] The members were Arthur T. Vanderbilt, chairman; George M. Morris, chairman of the House of Delegates, American Bar Association; Herschel W. Arant, dean of law, Ohio State University; Assistant Attorneys General Alexander Holtzoff and Gordon Dean.

[26] Charles E. Stewart, Memorandum, May 21, 1939, p. 2, Legislative Files, S. 188, 76th Cong.

[27] Harold M. Stephens to William H. King, March 14, 1938, Stephens Papers, Box 208.

tee that "It is the purpose of the administrative office bill to make the inferior Federal courts responsible for their own fiscal and administrative efficiency, and they should therefore have the power to present to the Congress without interference or elimination of items by the Executive Branch the estimates which they regard as necessary to their fiscal and administrative efficiency."[28] His plea was successful. The Act of 1939 would prohibit the Budget Bureau from revising the judiciary's estimates although it permitted that agency to make negative recommendations.[29]

Not all ties to the executive branch were severed, however. The employees of the Administrative Office, like those of the Department of Justice, remained under the jurisdiction of the Civil Service Commission. Although this provision of the bill[30] generated little controversy, at least one member of Groner's committee thought it "fundamentally wrong for an executive commission to have anything to do with the personnel or employees in the judicial department. Beyond the requirements in the Constitution," Senior Circuit Judge Kimbrough Stone believed, "the three departments should be carefully kept apart." Stone argued that "the moving force in the creation of the Administrative Office was to take from the Department of Justice its former limited control over inferior personnel and supplies of the judiciary."[31]

No great controversy arose over the transfer to the Administrative Office of various "housekeeping" duties long performed by the department and of administrative re-

[28] D. Lawrence Groner to House Conferees on S. 188 (Emanuel Celler, Walter Chandler, Samuel Hobbes, Earl C. Michener, John W. Gwynne), July 22, 1939, Groner Papers, Box 4.

[29] 53 *Stat.* 1224, sec. 305.   [30] 53 *Stat.* 1223, sec. 303.

[31] Kimbrough Stone to Chief Justice and Members of the Judicial Conference, "Minority Report, Report of the Judicial Conference Committee to Consider the Desirability of Extending the Merit System to Cover Personnel of the Clerks Offices," 1942, mimeographed (Administrative Office of the United States Courts, Washington, D.C.), pp. 9-10.

131

sponsibility for most court employees. However, a proposed change in control of the probation service stirred a storm of protest. Although appointed by the judges, the probation officers had not been included in earlier versions of the Administrative Office Bill; their inclusion in the final stages of the legislative process was almost fortuitous. It came about as a result of a combination of peculiar circumstances. Transfer of the service had been considered by the Interdepartmental Committee to Coordinate Health and Welfare Activities, a group whose genesis lay with the New Deal's administrative reorganization campaign. The report of that committee's Technical Committee on Probation, Parole, and Crime Prevention noted that

> the close relationship of the functions of such a Bureau of Prisons, Probation, and Parole to the courts and to the detecting, apprehending and prosecuting agencies is favorable to the retention of its services in the Department of Justice. On the other hand, the close relationship of the methods and treatment resources used in probation, parole and institutional supervision to other social-work functions argues for its placement in a Department of Welfare.[32]

Meanwhile, the Department of Justice, pressed by Congress,[33] sought to enhance the caliber of probation officers appointed by the courts. This effort required some administrative centralization and in January 1938, the Attorney General issued a memorandum entitled "Minimum Standards for the United States Probation Service." It supplemented and reiterated the language of the 1938 appropriations act which had stipulated that no portion of its funds "shall be used to defray the salary or expenses of any probation officer whose work fails to comply with the standards

[32] "Report of the Technical Committee," 1938, p. 8, Department of Justice File, No. 220602, Sec. 5.

[33] "Conference Report [on S. 188]," *Congressional Record*, 76th Cong., 1st Sess., 1939, vol. 84, part 10, 10387.

promulgated by the Attorney General, and no part may be used for the payment of compensation of new probation officers, who in the judgment of the Attorney General, do not have proper qualifications as prescribed by him."[34]

The standards so prescribed were at least suspect, if not rejected outright, by the judges. And so, to clothe them with some legitimacy, James V. Bennett, director of the Bureau of Prisons, encouraged the chairman of the Senate Judiciary Committee to grant either the Supreme Court or the Judicial Conference power to establish standards of appointment. These, he said, would guide both the courts and the Department of Justice in the selection and compensation of officers.[35] But, in the House, Congressman Sam Hobbes of Alabama adamantly opposed the power of the Attorney General to influence the appointment of probation officers. In the Judiciary Committee he "moved that the committee offer on the floor, as committee amendments, amendments to clarify the relation of probation officers to the district judges and to repeal the provision in the recently enacted Department of Justice appropriation bill, which in effect gave the Department of Justice a veto power over the appointment of probation officers."[36] The motion carried[37] and the Administrative Office Bill subsequently passed the House with the committee amendments.[38] These deleted the language in Section 304 (1) in all the previous bills[39] which had saved to the Attorney General authority over "United States marshals and their deputies, United States attorneys

[34] *Federal Probation*, 3 (February 1939), 14.

[35] James V. Bennett to Henry F. Ashurst, June 12, 1939, Legislative Files, S. 188, 76th Cong.

[36] Extract from Minutes of House Judiciary Committee Hearing on H.R. 5999, June 30, 1939, in Memorandum by Mr. Shupienis, "Supervision of Probation Officers," p. 6, in Groner Papers, Box 11.

[37] *Ibid.*

[38] H.R. 5999 (S. 188 as amended), in *Congressional Record*, 76th Cong., 1st Sess., 1939, vol. 84, part 9, 9310.

[39] S. 3212, 75th Cong.; S. 188 (as originally introduced), H.R. 2973, 76th Cong.

and their assistants and probation officers." A new section was inserted which "repealed a small portion of an appropriations bill which contained straight legislation covering probation officers."[40] This "small portion" was, of course, the provision barring payment to any probation officer whose work failed to conform with orders and regulations issued by the Attorney General and whose qualifications when appointed by the district judge did not conform with those prescribed by the Attorney General.[41]

Thus probation officers, long excluded by Section 304, were included by implication in the category of "other employees of the courts" and transferred to the control of the Administrative Office by Section 6. With this development, the Justice Department expressed deep disappointment. "Nevertheless," reported Harold M. Stephens, "the Department regards this as incidental as compared with the primary objectives of the bill and will in consequence interpose no objection [to the President]."[42]

Administrator and Supreme Court

More obscure than the intended relationship between the judiciary and the Department of Justice was that between the Administrative Office and the judges. In framing this relationship, legislative drafters in the judiciary considered the historic character of the federal judiciary, the attitude of its judges toward control of the administration of their

[40] Emanuel Celler, *Congressional Record*, 76th Cong., 1st Sess., 1939, vol. 84, part 9, 9696.

[41] H.R. 5999, Sec. 304 (2).

[42] Harold M. Stephens to Walter Chandler, August 3, 1939, Stephens Papers, Box 208. See also D. Lawrence Groner to Charles Evans Hughes, August 19, 1939, Groner Papers, Box 4. For a detailed study of separation of probation from the Justice Department, see Peter G. Fish, "The Politics of Judicial Administration: Transfer of the Federal Probation System," *The Western Political Quarterly*, 23 (December 1970), 769-84.

134

courts, and their reaction to the economic crisis of the early 1930s and to the political hurricane of 1937.

Even before introduction of the Court Bill in 1937, the Judicial Conference had been concerned with the problem of ultimate administrative responsibility. Its members wanted an administrator "on tap" but not "on top." To insure preservation of the traditional autonomy of individual courts, judges, not administrators, were to reign over the judiciary's administrative institution.

The administrator's initial selection by an organ of the judiciary thus appeared of critical importance. That judges would choose him was never in question. The 1936 Conference draft had provided for his appointment by the Chief Justice[43] while the Supreme Court was to select the proctor stipulated in President Roosevelt's court plan.[44] Later versions alternated between these two appointing authorities.[45]

Chief Justice Hughes favored vesting the appointment power in himself and in his successors.[46] But there were constitutional objections to placing it in the hands of a single judge rather than in a court.[47] After consulting Associate Justice George Sutherland of the Supreme Court,[48] Judge Groner reported to the clerk of the House Judiciary Committee the lack of any authoritative precedents on the subject. He predicted, however, that "if the question should ever be raised, it would be held by the court that the vest-

[43] Bill in File of the Judicial Conference, 1936, in Chandler, "Some Major Advances," p. 370.

[44] S. 1392, sec. 3(a), 75th Cong.

[45] S. 3212, 75th Cong. (Supreme Court); S. 188, 76th Cong. (Chief Justice).

[46] D. Lawrence Groner to John J. Parker, November 30, 1938, Groner Papers, Box 21.

[47] See U.S., Constitution, Art. II, sec. 2, c. 2: ". . . the Congress may by law vest the appointment of such inferior officers, as they may think proper, . . . in the courts of law, or in the heads of departments."

[48] D. Lawrence Groner to George Sutherland, March 23, 1939, Groner Papers, Box 4.

THE ACT OF 1939

ing of the appointment in the Chief Justice is a sufficient compliance with the provision authorizing the vesting in the courts of law."[49] The senior circuit judge also suggested that the words "Heads of Departments" might be construed to include the Chief Justice as head of the judicial department and, hence, empowered to appoint subordinate officers.[50] In spite of Groner's advisory opinion, the House Judiciary Committee preferred to follow a cautious path,[51] and the bill in final form fixed the power in the Supreme Court[52] rather than in the Chief Justice.[53]

Much more significant than the appointment power was the power of the judges to exercise control over the acts of the administrator. Originally, the Supreme Court and the Chief Justice were regarded as the natural locus for ulti-mate responsibility in judicial administration. The Ashurst Bill of 1938 had provided for a sharing of this responsibility between the Chief Justice and the Judicial Conference.[54] At the Senate hearings on that measure, Arthur Vanderbilt as-sailed this bifurcation of responsibility with its unfavorable implications for effective administration. He urged that the bill be "recast in such a way that the supervision of the Chief Justice is understood to be continuous . . . . so that the Chief Justice has the sole responsibility."[55]

Hughes, however, objected to this plan. Not only was his tribunal divided on the subject but also he sought to segre-gate administrative responsibility for the lower courts from the lofty heights of the Supreme Court. In the wake of Pres-

[49] D. Lawrence Groner to Elmore Whitehurst, April 8, 1939, *ibid.*
[50] *Ibid.*
[51] U.S., Congress, House, Committee on the Judiciary, *Hearings, on H.R. 2973, H.R. 5999, Administration of United States Courts,* 76th Cong., 1st Sess., 1939, pp. 49-52.
[52] See: 53 *Stat.* 1223, sec. 302.
[53] S. 188, sec. 302, 76th Cong.
[54] S. 3212, sec. 304, 75th Cong.
[55] U.S., Congress, Senate, Committee on the Judiciary, *Hearings, on S. 3212, Administrative Office of the United States Courts,* 75th Cong., 3d Sess., 1938, p. 52.

ident Roosevelt's assault on the Supreme Court, thinly veiled by more valid criticisms of inadequacies in the lower federals courts,[56] the Chief Justice bent every effort to avoid tying the Supreme Court into an integrated system of judicial administration. Above all, he wanted to insulate himself and his Court from any future politically-inspired campaigns against the judiciary.

As he told the 1938 Conference, the Chief Justice, as a responsible administrator, would be required to receive endless complaints and settle innumerable disputes which lay beyond the director's competence.[57] Scandals in budgetary matters or problems in far-away courts would reflect upon the Chief Justice "as the responsible officer who apparently had been neglectful in a matter which did not seem important perhaps at the time, but later developed importance because of some irregularity that was disclosed."[58] He reported that "the members of the Court strongly opposed the imposition of that burden, . . . possibly making the Chief Justice and the Court itself a center of attack."[59]

His desire to segregate the Supreme Court from the lower courts was advanced by Groner's committee. A provision permitting either the Chief Justice or the Conference to assign duties to the director raised doubts in the mind of Judge Kimbrough Stone. He thought the provision injected the Chief Justice "as a separate entity into the control of the Director in a way which might be objectionable to him or to members of the Supreme Court."[60] A later version substituted the Supreme Court for the Chief Justice, an ac-

[56] *Public Papers of FDR,* VI, 52.
[57] "Extract, Administration in the Federal Courts," p. 5. See also D. Lawrence Groner to John J. Parker, November 30, 1938, Groner Papers, Box 21; Groner to Evan A. Evans, December 1, 1938, *ibid.,* Box 4.
[58] "Extract, Administration in the Federal Courts," pp. 5-6.
[59] *Ibid.,* p. 6.
[60] Kimbrough Stone to D. Lawrence Groner, December 9, 1938, Groner Papers, Box 4.

tion which induced another Circuit Judge to note that the language would permit the Supreme Court "to give orders to the Director in conflict with the orders of the Conference of Senior Circuit Judges."[61] By changing the alternative construction to a complementary one, this problem was obviated. As finally enacted, the provision charged the director with performing such duties as were assigned to him, not by the Supreme Court alone, but by the Court and the Conference acting together.[62] These modifications, some pressed by the Chief Justice and others by the senior circuit judges, effectively eliminated the Supreme Court as a vital force in judicial administration.

Administrator and the Judicial Conference

Attention now turned to the Judicial Conference as an instrument of ultimate administrative responsibility. In the past, its peculiar nature had always seemed to place its real or potential role in doubt. During discussion of the Manton proposals for separating the appellate court budgets from the Department of Justice and of the 1936 Conference bill, the Conference as a locus of authority had come under consideration.

In 1933 Senior Circuit Judge Manton had remarked to Attorney General Cummings that the Conference's "existence and successful operation suggest that there might be built around it a central coordinated judicial means of administration of the federal courts."[63] Again, prior to the 1936 Conference an official of the Justice Department had recommended that the Conference play a part because, as

[61] Memorandum, Harold M. Stephens to D. Lawrence Groner, May 4, 1939, pp. 4-5, Legislative Files, S. 188, 76th Cong.

[62] 53 *Stat.* 1224, sec. 304 (7); see also: *ibid.*, 1223, sec. 304, lines 1-3.

[63] Martin T. Manton to Homer Cummings, October 5, 1933, Department of Justice Files, No. 236508, Sec. 1.

he explained, "the Senior Circuit Judges representing both the Circuit and District Courts perhaps should have some voice in administering the affairs of the courts."[64]

This conception of authority founded on representation encountered skepticism based not on the Conference's composition, but on its potential for action of any kind. "I am inclined to the notion," the chairman of the House Judiciary Committee told President Roosevelt, "that while these senior circuit judges may constitute a very helpful advisory council, it does not seem to me that they fit into the administration picture."[65]

Arthur Vanderbilt took a more emphatic position. An untiring advocate of centralized administration, he thought participation by an eleven-member Conference singularly inappropriate. It convened but once a year, and "with its members spread all over the country, [it] cannot function either legally or effectively by correspondence."[66] Moreover, he continued, "inasmuch as this director would have to supervise circuit courts of appeals as well as district courts, he ought not to be placed in any respect under their jurisdiction, but should respond solely to the Supreme Court, particularly to the Chief Justice."[67]

In the end, the views of Chief Justice Hughes prevailed. He told Vanderbilt and the Attorney General's committee "that if he were ever called upon to administer this bill as an act, he would route the work through the senior circuit

[64] Charles E. Stewart to Martin T. Manton, June 8, 1936, *ibid.*

[65] Hatton Sumners to Franklin D. Roosevelt, January 27, 1938, *ibid.*, Sec. 2.

[66] Arthur T. Vanderbilt, "Our Main Order of Business: The Administration of Justice," *American Bar Association Journal*, 24 (March 1938), 189.

[67] Arthur T. Vanderbilt, U.S., Congress, House, Subcommittee of the Committee on the Judiciary, *Hearings, on the General Subject of the Administration of the Federal Courts*, stenographic transcript, 75th Cong., 3d Sess., 1938, following p. 47, p. 9, in Legislative Files, House, H.R. 2973, 76th Cong.

court judges, because they were the logical men to attend to it."[68] Such a procedure might appear to eliminate the Chief Justice as an influential actor in the administrative process. This was a fallacious assumption, contended Hughes. "A capable Chief Justice," he informed a doubting Vanderbilt, "could always be assured of the support of a very strong majority of the Conference of senior circuit judges, and . . . he would always find it to his great advantage to work through them."[69]

The attitude of the Chief Justice compelled the senior circuit judges to seek an alternative agency of ultimate responsibility. Convinced that real "control should remain unimpaired in the judiciary," the Conference, noted one such judge, "is the only existing central body representing the entire country."[70] It alone offered a bulwark "against development of a bureaucratic spirit in the [administrative] organization,"[71] and had the capacity, as Groner later put it, "to keep a rein on the 'Office' and maintain the theory on which the bill creating the Office passed, viz., to make it an agency, and not a master of the courts."[72]

The clearly articulated intent of key framers of the Administrative Office Bill[73] determined the eventual relationship between the director of the Administrative Office of the United States Courts and the Judicial Conference. No opportunities for enhancing the Conference's checking capacities were ignored as judges strove to build into the judiciary's administrative institution the concept of a government of limited powers.

Before Chief Justice Hughes had removed himself from

[68] Ibid.   [69] Ibid.

[70] "Suggestions of Judge [Kimbrough] Stone," October 14, 1938, p. 2, Groner Papers, Box 4.

[71] Ibid.

[72] D. Lawrence Groner to Harlan Fiske Stone, September 8, 1941, ibid., Box 12.

[73] See D. Lawrence Groner, House Committee on the Judiciary, Hearings on H.R. 2973, 1939, pp. 56-57.

140

a position of administrative responsibility, Assistant Attorney General Charles E. Stewart questioned the necessity for language in the Ashurst Bill placing the director "under the supervision of the Chief Justice."[74] Presuming that the proposed administrator merely replaced the Attorney General as administrator of the federal courts, he suggested that the director be "under the Chief Justice of the United States and Conference of Senior Circuit Judges, instead of under the supervision of the same."[75] In this way the director's position would be analogous to that of the Attorney General who performed his duties "under the President of the United States."[76] Such was decidedly not the view of the judges. They had not defended their independence against the proposed court proctor only to succumb to the self-inflicted consequences of an unrestrained director.

Thus, even a later draft which actually placed the director under the Conference's supervision evoked protests from Judge Groner. He assailed its failure to include language enabling the Conference to direct as well as to supervise the administrator.[77] This omission, observed his colleague on the Circuit Court, Harold M. Stephens, constituted an important limitation on the power of the Conference over the new agency. Supervision was defined as overseeing or inspection; but he noted that the word "direct" meant "to give direction; to point out a course; to act as a guide or director."[78]

His presiding judge easily grasped the significance of this omission. Two months later he wrote several key congressmen then completing their consideration of the legislation:

[74] S. 3212, sec. 304, 75th Cong.
[75] Charles E. Stewart to Martin T. Manton, June 29, 1938, Department of Justice Files, No. 236508, Sec. 2.
[76] Charles E. Stewart to Harold M. Stephens, July 1, 1938, Stephens Papers, Box 208.
[77] See H.R. 5999, sec. 304, 76th Cong. Compare H.R. 2973, sec. 304, 76th Cong.
[78] Memorandum, Harold M. Stephens to D. Lawrence Groner, May 4, 1939, pp. 2-3, Legislative Files, S. 188, 76th Cong.

141

"The whole scheme of the bill places the Director under the supervision of the Conference of Senior Circuit Judges and it would be unfortunate if, after his appointment, he were to assume that he would be entirely independent of the slightest control, for that would strike at the very heart of the purpose of the bill."[79] Although made in the last stages of the legislative process, this appeal proved successful. The opening lines of Section 304, Act of August 7, 1939, would read: "The Director shall be the administrative officer of the United States Courts . . . under the supervision and direction of the Conference of Senior Circuit Judges."[80]

The Administrator's Powers

Establishment of a superior-subordinate relationship between the Judicial Conference and the Administrative Office was strengthened still more by a careful delineation of the administrator's formal powers. In the hands of Judge Groner's committee, powers once contemplated for the court proctor and even for the director described in the 1936 Conference draft and its successor, the Ashurst Bill, underwent drastic revision, if not emasculation. So extensive was the change that Judge Stephens could assure a vacillating senator who had fought the President's Court plan that "the bill has no connection whatever, either in source or in content, with the so-called court packing bill. The Director to be established under the bill has no such powers as were thought to exist in the Proctor."[81]

The language of the 1939 bill in final form specifically prohibited the director from controlling the appointment

[79] D. Lawrence Groner to House Conferees on S. 188, July 22, 1939, Groner Papers, Box 4.

[80] 53 *Stat.* 1223.

[81] Harold M. Stephens to William H. King, March 14, 1938, Stephens Papers, Box 208.

[82] See 53 *Stat.* 1223, sec. 304 (1).

or removal of subordinate personnel in the various courts.[82] This provision had been inserted after Judge Manton, who favored a highly centralized administrative system, intimated that such functions might lie within the scope of the director's power.[83] Nor did the measure sponsored by the Judicial Conference mention any role for the director in the assignment and designation of judges. A feature of the Ashurst Bill, its existence had led Judge Manton to argue that the director could act "without embarrassment . . . as assignment commissioner."[84] But his colleagues on the Conference regarded this interpretation as "exceedingly dangerous."[85] In the face of their opposition, a legislative draftsman in the Department of Justice deleted the power of the director to "recommend" the transfer of judges even before introduction of the 1939 bill in Congress.[86]

Naturally, the capacity of the director to coerce individual judges came under sharp scrutiny. Statements made at the hearings on the Ashurst Bill aroused their apprehensions over such power lodged in an aggressive administrator. Then, Attorney General Cummings had told the assembled senators that "if you want continuous administrative pressure brought to bear to bring the business of the judiciary up to date, you have got to have a continuous administrative officer, clothed with authority and so completely independent from the Department of Justice, so completely a part of the judiciary itself that his suggestions and recom-

[83] Martin T. Manton, Senate Committee on the Judiciary, *Hearings on S. 3212*, 1938, p. 38; see also D. Lawrence Groner to Manton, December 27, 1937, Groner Papers, Box 21.

[84] Manton, Senate Committee on the Judiciary, *Hearings on S. 3212*, 1938, p. 37.

[85] Kimbrough Stone, U.S., Congress, Senate, Committee on the Judiciary, *Hearings, on S. 188, Administration of United States Courts*, 76th Cong., 1st Sess., 1939, p. 23.

[86] Charles E. Stewart to Harold M. Stephens, July 1, 1938, Stephens Papers, Box 208.

143

mendations . . . will be regarded as amounting to directions."[87] At the same time the Attorney General mentioned the possibility of a director writing letters to judges on the sad condition of their dockets,[88] roving around the country and recommending changes in a court's administration,[89] and spreading the derelictions of inferior federal judges on records submitted to the Supreme Court.[90]

Strategically placed judges sought an effective and innocuous administrator; they wanted someone who confined his orders to his own staff and interfered not at all with the work of independent judges.[91] Least of all did they want him to encourage coercion by external agencies such as the bar, labor, and civic organizations. To this end Chief Justice Groner successfully secured removal from a draft of the House Judiciary Committee's report of language which appeared to permit this kind of pressure on the judges, pressure which could emanate from outside the legal community.[92]

The Administrative Office was "not an executive establishment."[93] The director, an official of the new Administrative Office would say, possessed "no authority to tell any judge what he should or should not do, nor will he have any authority to recommend to the Chief Justice of the Supreme Court in regard to the assignment or designation of judges to serve temporarily in circuits or districts other than those for which they were appointed."[94]

---

[87] Homer S. Cummings, Senate Committee on the Judiciary, *Hearings on S. 3212*, 1938, p. 13.

[88] *Ibid.*, pp. 16-17.   [89] *Ibid.*, p. 19.   [90] *Ibid.*

[91] Curtis D. Wilbur, quoted in *San Francisco Examiner*, July 6, 1940, p. 12, in Stephen S. Chandler, "The Role of the Trial Judge in the Anglo-American Legal System," *American Bar Association Journal*, 50 (February 1964), 130.

[92] D. Lawrence Groner to Walter Chandler, May 27, 1939, Groner Papers, Box 4.

[93] "Address of the Honorable Charles Evans Hughes," *American Law Institute, Proceedings*, 17 (1940), 29.

[94] Will Shafroth, "New Machinery for Effective Administration of

THE ACT OF 1939

As the framers conceived it, the Administrative Office was a medium for improved intra-judiciary communications rather than a source of real administrative power. Its director would, in the opinion of a member of the Attorney General's committee, "simply be a compiler and adjuster, a person who acts as a go-between or intermediary."[95] It was the information he conveyed and the "good offices" he provided which would promote more effective administration—by the judges themselves.

The Circuit Judicial Conferences

"As stated by the Chief Justice," related Judge Kimbrough Stone, "one of the purposes of the Administrative Office Act was to decentralize control of the Judiciary," and to Stone that purpose was "of cardinal importance."[96] He, like Hughes, had regarded as examples of "undue centralization" the power of the director and the great responsibility placed on the Chief Justice as provided in the Ashurst Bill.[97]

In proposing creation of a decentralized administrative system, the Chief Justice was motivated by a desire to distribute responsibility to the circuits as a defense against political forays centered on the establishment in Washington. Perhaps, too, the philosophy and practice of federalism held a powerful attraction for him. "My thought," declared the former New York governor, "is that . . . there should be a greater attention to local authority and local responsibility. It seems to me that, as we have the States as *foci* of administration with regard to local problems pertaining to the

Federal Courts," *American Bar Association Journal*, 25 (September 1939), 738.

[95] George M. Morris, House Subcommittee of the Committee on the Judiciary, *Hearings on the General Subject*, 1938, p. 2, following p. 47.

[96] Kimbrough Stone to John Biggs, Jr., November 14, 1940, Groner Papers, Box 16.

[97] "Extract, Administration in the Federal Courts," p. 14.

States, we have in the various Circuits of the country *foci* of federal action from the judicial standpoint."[98]

To this end, annual conferences in each circuit, composed of circuit and district judges and of members of the bar invited by the judges, were formalized.[99] Such conferences had been recommended by Attorney General Daugherty during the hearings on the Act of September 14, 1922.[100] There he predicted "that a meeting every two years of the district judges of the United States would be most beneficial to the Government and most profitable."[101]

A conference of federal trial judges in the Sixth Circuit met in 1924 to consider procedures for expediting litigation.[102] Then, with the newly-created Judicial Conference in Washington as a model, Senior Circuit Judge Arthur C. Denison convened, the following year, a conference of both the circuit and district judges of that circuit.[103] Later, at the October 1929 meeting of the senior circuit judges, the presiding judge of the Eighth Circuit, Kimbrough Stone, consulted with Judge Denison on the advisability of holding a similar meeting in his region.[104] In January 1930, that circuit held a conference which its senior circuit judge would later claim as the first of its kind anywhere in the country.[105] Convinced of the value of these circuit gatherings, the

[98] *Ibid.*   [99] 53 *Stat.* 1224, sec. 307.   [100] 42 *Stat.* 838.

[101] Harry Daugherty, U.S., Congress, House, Committee on the Judiciary, *Hearings, on H.R. 8875, Additional Judges, United States District Courts*, 67th Cong., 1st Sess., 1921, p. 6.

[102] Arthur C. Denison, "Report on the Third Conference of Senior Circuit Judges Called by the Chief Justice Pursuant to the Act of September 14, 1922," October 1924, p. 40, Parker Papers, Box 53.

[103] Arthur C. Denison to Lewis W. Morse, January 27, 1942, cited in Lewis W. Morse, "Federal Judicial Conferences and Councils: Their Creation and Reports," *Cornell Law Quarterly*, 27 (April 1942), 360.

[104] Kimbrough Stone, "History of Federal Judicial Administration," draft of address to Missouri Bar Association, undated, p. 8, Kimbrough Stone Papers, Box 31.

[105] Kimbrough Stone to Glenn A. McCleary, November 5, 1941, *ibid.*, Box 16.

Washington Conference gave its warm endorsement to them in 1930 and again in 1931 and in 1932,[106] but the Depression deterred their development.

In addition to providing a forum for relaxation and entertainment, such meetings facilitated the integration of judicial administration. They offered an instrument for meeting criticism of unnecessary diversity in "sentences, customs, rules, and regulations in the district courts."[107] Forward-looking judges, said John J. Parker, had "devised improvements in administration and procedure and put them into effect within their districts, but because of lack of contact with other judges the effect . . . rarely extended beyond their districts."[108] Now, as Denison observed, the "weak sisters" among the judges had an opportunity to learn "what the others were doing."[109]

Thus, the circuit judicial conferences served to enhance intra-circuit communications. This was particularly valuable in geographically large circuits such as the Fourth, Sixth, and Eighth. At the annual forum, judges, lawyers, and United States attorneys exchanged ideas and criticisms. Occasionally, graced with the presence of the circuit justice from the Supreme Court, these conferences impressed upon the then isolated district judge a realization that he was "engaged in a Nation-wide undertaking, and not just a little potentate off by himself."[110] "They brought," Parker said, "the Judges of the Circuit into closer contact and [tended]

[106] *Judicial Conference Report, 1930,* p. 7; *ibid., 1931,* p. 11; *ibid., 1932,* p. 12.

[107] Harry Daugherty, House Committee on the Judiciary, *Hearings on H.R. 8875,* 1921, p. 6.

[108] "Report of the Judicial Circuit Conference of the United States Court of Appeals and the United States District Court [for the District of Columbia Circuit]," May 24-25, 1940, unnumbered page of stenographic transcript, Groner Papers, Box 8 (cited hereafter as "Report of the D. C. Judicial Conference," 1940).

[109] Arthur C. Denison, "Report on the Third Conference," p. 40.

[110] John J. Parker, House Committee on the Judiciary, *Hearings on H.R. 2973,* 1939, p. 24.

to prevent the jealousies and misunderstandings which sometimes occur."[111]

Some circuit conferences conducted what Judge Parker termed a "school of jurisprudence."[112] Such sessions discussed general problems arising from the development of jurisprudence. "In other words," Parker explained, "the conference has become not only an instrumentality for expediting the work in the circuit, but has become a means by which we inform ourselves of worth-while movements in the field of law."[113]

At the same time, the conferences provided a convenient forum for presentation of legal briefs by interested parties. Then Special Assistant to the Attorney General Alexander Holtzoff came to the 1939 Conference in the Fourth Circuit and sought to assure the assembled judges of the constitutionality of the 1938 Federal Juvenile Delinquency Act.[114] Answering the charge that the measure's provision for prosecution by information violated the Fifth Amendment, Holtzoff reviewed federal case law on the issue. He contended that "logic inescapably leads to the conclusion that the right not to be prosecuted except by indictment is a right that may be waived. . . . Consequently the possible objections . . . to the validity of the Act can be completely met, and hence the Federal Juvenile Delinquency Act must be regarded as constitutional."[115]

[111] "Annual Report of Senior Circuit Judges for the Fourth Judicial Circuit Submitted to the Judicial Conference of Senior Circuit Judges, September 27th to September 29th, 1934," p. 4, Parker Papers, Box 53.

[112] John J. Parker, House Committee on the Judiciary, *Hearings on H.R. 2973*, 1939, p. 24.

[113] "Minutes of the Ninth Annual Meeting of the Federal Judicial Conference of the Fourth Circuit Held at Asheville, North Carolina, June 8, 9, 10, 1939," p. 3, Parker Papers, Box 53 (cited hereafter as "Minutes of the Ninth Annual Meeting").

[114] *Ibid.*, pp. 247ff. Holtzoff referred to the Act of June 16, 1938, 52 *Stat.* 764.

[115] *Ibid.*, p. 262.

148

The early conferences centered much of their attention on the disparate and sometimes conflicting and redundant local rules of court.[116] Sentencing,[117] administration of the probation system,[118] and shortening of appellate records[119] constituted other subjects considered at these meetings. By the mid-thirties, however, consideration of the proposed rules of civil procedure began to dominate them as did the criminal rules later in the decade.[120] To the conferences in these years came leading experts on rule-making such as Homer Cummings and William Mitchell. In the ensuing exchanges of views, constituency desires were revealed to the Supreme Court and to its Advisory Committee on the Rules and their proposals sanctioned.[121]

The significance of this function had been perceived by the Washington Conference even before the rule-making debates brought the circuit meetings into prominence. With the senior circuit judge as chairman, these conferences were a natural source of information for transmission via the presiding circuit judge to the Conference of Senior Circuit Judges in Washington and from the national conference to the local judges.[122] The efficacy of such a procedure was evident to the judges who met with the Chief Justice in October 1931. At that Conference, the solicitor general unveiled some reforms in bankruptcy administration which the Justice Department had incorporated in a proposed

[116] John B. Sanborn, "Conference of Circuit and District Judges of the Eighth Circuit," 1939, p. 275, stenographic transcript, Kimbrough Stone Papers, Box 26.
[117] John J. Parker, House Committee on the Judiciary, *Hearings on H.R. 2973*, 1939, p. 23.
[118] Memorandum, "The Conference of the Fourth Circuit," November 1, 1938, Groner Papers, Box 21.
[119] "Minutes of the Fifth Annual Meeting of the Federal Judicial Conference of the Fourth Circuit," June 6-8, 1935, p. 167, stenographic transcript (Law Library, University of Virginia).
[120] See Chandler, "Some Major Advances," p. 498; D. Lawrence Groner to Alfred A. Wheat, June 19, 1938, Groner Papers, Box 8.
[121] See Chandler, pp. 491-93.
[122] "Minutes of the Ninth Annual Meeting," p. 246.

149

bill.[123] "Members of the conference," recounted Senior Circuit Judge Kimbrough Stone, "of course, had no opportunity because of time, if nothing else even to read the report."[124] Stone, however, "thought that the judgment and advice of the District Judges would be much more valuable to those who might be framing such legislation than the suggestions of the Conference."[125]

And so, at the Judicial Conference of the Eighth Circuit held in January 1932, an official of the Department of Justice appeared and presented the bill, explained its purpose, and received suggestions from "the Judges who handle hundreds and hundreds of these bankruptcy proceedings every year."[126] The value of such a function was not lost on the Judicial Conference in Washington. In the fall of 1932, it endorsed such procedures, stating that "from the several districts . . . well-considered proposals may be brought to circuit conferences and thence to this conference of senior circuit judges. The advantage to this conference of having before it proposals which have been carefully matured in this way is manifest."[127]

As administrative agency for the courts, the Department of Justice received criticism in the circuit conferences, often by irate district judges. After a trial judge had called on his brethren to flood the Attorney General with letters demanding retention of court messengers,[128] the 1932 session of the Fourth Circuit Conference resolved: "That in the judgment of the Judges of this Circuit, it would naturally inconvenience the District Judges in the performance of their duties and would delay and impair their efficiency in the prompt

[123] Kimbrough Stone, "Annual Conference of the United States District Judges of the Eighth Circuit," January 4-5, 1932, p. 64, stenographic transcript, Kimbrough Stone Papers, Box 26.

[124] Ibid.   [125] Ibid.   [126] Ibid., p. 65.

[127] Judicial Conference Report, 1932, p. 12.

[128] "Minutes of the Second Annual Meeting of the Federal Judicial Conference of the Fourth Circuit Held at Asheville, North Carolina, June 9, 10, 11, 1932," p. 16, Parker Papers, Box 53.

dispatch of judicial business, if the position of messenger to the District Judges is abolished."[129]

By 1939 the utility of these circuit conferences as vehicles for socializing district judges and for facilitating communications within the circuits and between the circuits and both the Judicial Conference and Attorney General in Washington was recognized. Chief Justice Hughes, who had presided over several meetings in the Fourth Circuit, and Senior Circuit Judge John J. Parker enthusiastically advocated their establishment in all circuits.[130] However, some judges contended that in the absence of congressional authorization the conferences were unlawful.[131] To meet this objection, the Act of 1939 formally authorized these pre-existing organizations. In statutory language almost identical to that suggested by Parker to Judge Groner,[132] the conferences were created "for considering the state of the business of the courts and advising ways and means of improving the administration of justice within the circuit."[133] It granted them no additional authority other than that which had already accrued by custom. Such authority as existed took the form of persuasion by fellow judges and prominent members of the bar, publicity of different judicial techniques and performances, as well as self-recognition by individual judges of the compelling nature of this criticism.

Although integrative agencies of administration, the circuit conferences were hardly authoritative. Like the Admin-

[129] *Ibid.*, p. 18. See *ibid.*, p. 19, for resolution re: salaried probation officer and clerical assistance for probation officer.

[130] See Charles Evans Hughes, "Report of the D. C. Judicial Conference," 1940; see also: John J. Parker, "Schools of Jurisprudence in the Federal System," *Journal of the American Judicature Society*, 23 (June 1939), 6; John J. Parker to D. Lawrence Groner, October 25, 1938, Parker Papers, Box 27.

[131] John J. Parker, House Committee on the Judiciary, *Hearings on H.R. 2973*, 1939, p. 23.

[132] John J. Parker to D. Lawrence Groner, October 25, 1938, Parker Papers, Box 27.

[133] 53 *Stat.* 1225, sec. 307.

151

istrative Office, they were never so intended. "Not even the Judicial Conference itself," remarked Senior Circuit Judge Kimbrough Stone, "can do more than make recommendations and suggestions which may or may not be followed, as the judges affected may elect."[134]

The Circuit Councils

"The Act creates," declared Stone, "one and only one agency with any disciplinary powers, that is, the Circuit Council."[135] Composed of the judges of the courts of appeals in each circuit, the councils were the handiwork of Chief Justice Charles Evans Hughes, and their design reflected his conception of the ideal administrative model. The councils constituted, he told the 1938 Conference, "a mechanism through which there could be a concentration of responsibility in the various Circuits—immediate responsibility for the work of the courts in the Circuits, with power and authority to make the supervision all that is necessary to insure competence in the work of all of the judges of the various districts within the Circuit."[136]

More than six years before, he had indicated a strong preference for such an administrative organization. "We are apt to look too far away for the accomplishment of reforms," he told an early judicial conference in the Fourth Circuit.[137] "Improvement," he said, "is generally a personal and local matter."[138] Later, the former Republican presidential candidate would explain to his own Judicial Con-

[134] Kimbrough Stone to John Biggs, Jr., November 14, 1940, Groner Papers, Box 16.

[135] *Ibid.*

[136] "Extract, Administration in the Federal Courts," pp. 14-15.

[137] "Chief Justice Hughes Addresses Judicial Conference of the Fourth Circuit," *American Bar Association Journal*, 18 (July 1932), 447.

[138] *Ibid.*

ference the benefit inherent in local responses to complaints and to instances of inept or corrupt administration.[139]

Fundamentally, it lay with the circuit judges' knowledge of their domain. "When you come to the supervision of the work of the judges," he asserted, "there you have the great advantage of the supervision of that work by the men who know. The Circuit judges know the work of the district judges by their records that they are constantly examining. . . . And the Circuit judges know the judges personally in their districts; they know their capacities. And if complaints are made, they have immediate resort to the means of ascertaining their validity."[140] Such direct and on-the-spot supervision could, he believed, "be made very effective . . . far more so than the more remote supervision, entailing a great deal of labor and circumlocution, imposed upon the Chief Justice."[141]

This plan, presented to the 1938 Conference, represented a minimal adaptation in the existing institution, and manifested the influence of contemporary practices and proposals. In their appellate capacity, judges of the circuit courts of appeals had always exercised their power of reviewing the substantive judicial decisions of the district judges. They had also reviewed their behavior as administrators and as individuals;[142] as one senior circuit judge recalled, his court had once "had to issue a mandamus to compel the judge to decide a case he had under submission for about two years. Of course, we do not issue the mandamus. We just write the opinion, indicating he ought to decide."[143]

Legislative feeling as well as judicial experience may also have influenced the establishment of circuit councils as instruments of administrative responsibility and authority.

[139] "Extract, Administration in the Federal Courts," p. 18.
[140] *Ibid.*, pp. 17-18.   [141] *Ibid.*, p. 18.
[142] John J. Parker, House Committee on the Judiciary, *Hearings on H.R. 2973*, 1939, p. 22.
[143] Rufus E. Foster, "Minutes of the Judicial Conference, 1940," Administrative Office Correspondence, 60-A-328, Box 27.

Following the drawn-out impeachment trial of District Judge Halstead Ritter, which had left the 1936 congressional schedule in shambles, these proceedings came under attack from scholars and congressmen alike.

Members of Congress cast about for alternatives, and in the midst of the Court-packing crisis, a committee of the House Judiciary Committee held hearings on a bill entitled "Trial of Good Behavior for United States District Judges."[144] This measure, introduced by the committee chairman, Hatton Sumners, permitted the removal of judges for lesser offenses than high crimes and misdemeanors. Article III of the Constitution allowed judges to hold office only during "good behavior." Hence, they might be removed, but not impeached, for conduct defined as other than "good behavior."[145] Judges, not congressmen, would perform the delicate task of removing derelict judges.

This procedure had been advocated by Professor Burke Shartel of the University of Michigan Law School[146] who, in 1937, urged Sumners "to invest the circuit courts with a definite duty to supervise the conduct of district judges. If such supervision were exercised as it should be," he added, "I believe that most of the complaints against the federal judges would soon be eliminated."[147]

To Shartel's proposal the chairman replied that he had "some notion of that sort in my own mind."[148] The bill which he introduced provided for a court composed of three circuit judges convened at the call of the Chief Justice. Before it, district judges accused by the House of Representatives of misbehavior would be prosecuted by the At-

[144] H.R. 2271, 75th Cong.

[145] See William McAdoo, *Congressional Record*, 74th Cong., 2d Sess., 1936, vol. 80, part 6, 5934.

[146] Burke Shartel, "Retirement and Removal of Judges," *Journal of the American Judicature Society*, 20 (December 1936), 134.

[147] Burke Shartel to Hatton Sumners, February 18, 1937, Legislative Files, H.R. 2271, 75th Cong.

[148] Hatton Sumners to Burke Shartel, March 10, 1937, *ibid.*

torney General.[149] Undoubtedly, Chief Justice Hughes was aware of this bill, and, said Shartel, "appreciates the need for . . . supervision and . . . would gladly see such supervision extended in the Federal system."[150]

A third source of the circuit council idea proposed by Chief Justice Hughes was a legacy of Martin Manton's campaign for separate administration of the courts of appeals. The influence of this factor became apparent in the support initially given by Hughes to extreme decentralization of budgetary and statistical administration. Each circuit council, he suggested to the 1938 Conference, should have "direct control" of its budget.[151] He argued that "the questions relating to all the different needs of the district judges could be directly worked out, threshed out by the judicial council composed of men who have an immediate understanding of those needs."[152] As it later turned out, the original Hughes plan also envisioned an administrative officer attached to each circuit council. It would be the duty of this officer "to keep abreast of the dockets and like matters" and to report that information to a council.[153]

Powerful opposition greeted this plan. Influential judges at the 1938 Judicial Conference protested its diffusion of administrative authority, and Judge Parker emphatically told Chief Justice Groner that "the preparation of the budget and the gathering of statistics should certainly be conducted from a central agency."[154] The council's role should be advisory, not executory. The key administrative entities

[149] H.R. 2271, sec. 1 and 2, 75th Cong.

[150] Burke Shartel to Hatton Sumners, March 24, 1937, reprinted in U.S., Congress, House, Committee on the Judiciary, *Hearings, on H.R. 2271, Trial of Good Behavior of United States District Judges*, part II, 75th Cong., 1st Sess., 1937, p. 42.

[151] "Extract, Administration in the Federal Courts," p. 16.

[152] *Ibid.*, p. 17.

[153] D. Lawrence Groner to John J. Parker, November 30, 1938, Groner Papers, Box 21.

[154] John J. Parker to D. Lawrence Groner, December 1, 1938, Groner Papers, Box 4.

would be the Conference and the senior circuit judges.[155]

Such objections were partially effective. The plan advanced by Hughes underwent revision before its introduction in the Seventy-sixth Congress.[156] The bills then submitted omitted mention of council staffs. However, Chief Justice Groner, in testimony before the House Committee, raised the possibility of staffing the councils with an administrator responsible to the Administrative Office in Washington.[157]

Powers of the Councils

Although Learned Hand was never "much in love with the general supervision given to [the circuit courts] over the district judges,"[158] the councils became repositories of vast responsibilities in accordance with the view of Chief Justice Hughes. Section 306 of the Act of August 7, 1939 vested the councils of circuit judges with responsibility for insuring the effective and expeditious transaction of district court business, and required "the district judges promptly to carry out the direction of the council as to the administration of the business of their respective courts."[159]

The statutory language indicated a broad grant of power, and, at the hearings, judges acknowledged this intent. "Do you put any restraint on the council at all?" inquired Congressman Emanuel Celler. Replied Judge Parker: "I do not think this bill does."[160] Like the senior circuit judge, Chief Justice Hughes considered the councils as vested with

[155] John J. Parker to D. Lawrence Groner, October 25, 1938, Parker Papers, Box 27.

[156] See S. 188 and H.R. 2973, 76th Cong.

[157] D. Lawrence Groner, House Committee on the Judiciary, *Hearings on H.R. 2973*, 1939, p. 46.

[158] Learned Hand to D. Lawrence Groner, April 27, 1939, Groner Papers, Box 4.

[159] 53 *Stat.* 1224.

[160] House Committee on the Judiciary, *Hearings on H.R. 2973*, 1939, p. 22.

156

sweeping power to "see that any necessary steps are taken to correct procedural defects and to expedite the work of the courts."[161] Within the scope of its intended competence lay a multitude of administrative functions: assigning judges to congested districts,[162] and to particular types of cases,[163] directing them to assist infirm judges,[164] ordering them to decide cases long held under advisement,[165] requiring a judge to forego his summer vacation in order to clear his congested docket,[166] compelling multi-judge courts to arrange staggered vacations,[167] and setting standards of judicial ethics.[168] The only limitation on the sweeping powers of the councils which was cited at the hearings was an obvious one, namely, that they possessed no competence to issue irrational or unreasonable directives to district judges.[169]

Although wide agreement existed on the scope of the councils' powers, differences arose over their manner of exercising this power and over the degree of coercion permissible. Opposing conceptions of the councils' actual authority as distinguished from their legal powers involved contrasting ideas on the composition of these circuit organs.

[161] "Address of the Honorable Charles Evans Hughes," *American Law Institute, Proceedings*, 17 (1940), 31.

[162] John J. Parker, House Committee on the Judiciary, *Hearings on H.R. 2973*, 1939, p. 21; Arthur T. Vanderbilt, Senate Committee on the Judiciary, *Hearings on S. 188*, 1939, p. 18.

[163] Insertion by Judge Groner, "Senior Judges Plan to Integrate Federal System," *Journal of the American Judicature Society*, 22 (December 1938), 161, in Senate Committee on the Judiciary, *Hearings on S. 188*, 1939, p. 48.

[164] D. Lawrence Groner, House Committee on the Judiciary, *Hearings on H.R. 2973*, 1939, p. 11; Arthur T. Vanderbilt, Senate Committee on the Judiciary, *Hearings on S. 188*, 1939, p. 18.

[165] Groner, House Committee on the Judiciary, *Hearings on H.R. 2973*, 1939, p. 13.

[166] *Ibid.*, pp. 14, 18.

[167] Kimbrough Stone, Senate Committee on the Judiciary, *Hearings on S. 188*, 1939, p. 26.

[168] Groner, House Committee on the Judiciary, *Hearings on H.R. 2973*, 1939, pp. 18, 53-54.

[169] John J. Parker, *ibid.*, p. 22.

On one side were the activists favoring single-member councils. On the other stood the passivists supporting councils with broad-based memberships. Learned Hand objected to both alternatives.

To activists, the statutory language was clear and the only remaining problem was to centralize responsibility and authority in a single judge, thereby guaranteeing maximum effectiveness. Among the centralizers was Martin T. Manton, who assailed the apparent attempt to destroy or, at least, dilute the power of the presiding circuit judge to assign district judges, or, in his own case, himself, to the district courts.[170] Shortly after the 1938 Conference, he requested committee chairman Groner to vest in the senior circuit judge alone "the obligation of directing the business of the circuit in the various district courts to the end that the work of such courts be effectively and expeditiously transacted. Provision should be made for obedience by all judges of the district courts to any assignment made by the senior circuit judge as well as to carry out his directions as to the conduct of business of their respective courts."[171]

This position elicited support from Parker. To him a multi-judge administrative council with or without an administrator constituted "a mere 'fifth wheel to the coach' which would breed confusion without corresponding benefit."[172] Senior Circuit Judge Evan A. Evans of the Seventh Circuit took a similar view because "this is an efficiency measure, and efficiency is most always promoted where responsibility

[170] See 1938 Judicial Conference transcript, p. 193, in Chandler, "Some Major Advances," p. 380. See also Martin T. Manton to D. Lawrence Groner, December 13, 1938, Groner Papers, Box 4.

[171] Martin T. Manton to D. Lawrence Groner, October 24, 1938, ibid.

[172] John J. Parker to D. Lawrence Groner, December 1, 1938, ibid. Parker favored a purely advisory role for a council composed of the senior circuit judge "and the two circuit judges next in order of seniority." John J. Parker to D. Lawrence Groner, October 25, 1938, Parker Papers, Box 27.

is located squarely on the shoulders of one person."[173] The centralizers clearly regarded a concentration of responsibility and authority in the senior circuit judge as preferable to a diffusion of it throughout the court of appeals. Such a dispersion would invariably be aggravated by the difficulty of communications common in the larger circuits and the time-consuming nature of group decison-making.[174]

In lonely opposition was Circuit Judge Learned Hand. For him, only the *status quo* was acceptable. As his predecessor, Martin Manton, slipped into an ignominious darkness, the distinguished jurist asserted: "I am very strong for the autonomy of each court; at least I don't want the District Judges under the authority of a Senior Circuit Judge, or for that matter, of a whole bunch of Circuit Judges. If we are to have it, at least let's keep the hands of Senior Circuit Judges or any other God damn Circuit Judges off their fellows."[175]

However, the influence of Chief Justice Charles Evans Hughes proved decisive. His initiation of a campaign for multi-judge circuit councils placed proponents of a single locus of administrative responsibility and authority, as well as Learned Hand, in an untenable position. At the 1938 Conference, he made plain his feelings on the subject.[176] Several months later, Judge Groner informed all his colleagues on the Conference that "the Chief Justice thought it would be very unwise to impose upon the Senior Circuit Judge all of the corrective power over District Judges."[177]

He and his supporters offered several compelling explanations for multi-member administrative agencies in the

[173] Evan A. Evans to D. Lawrence Groner, November 17, 1938, *ibid.*
[174] "Suggestions of Judge [Kimbrough] Stone," October 14, 1938, *ibid.*
[175] Learned Hand to D. Lawrence Groner, December 26, 1938, *ibid.*
[176] "Extract, Administration in the Federal Courts," pp. 15-16, 18.
[177] D. Lawrence Groner to Senior Circuit Judges, December 21, 1938, Groner Papers, Box 4.

circuits. Such an organization alleviated the serious problems associated with one-man control, namely physical or mental incapacity, indifference, or dictatorial attitudes.[178] At the Senate hearings in 1939, Judge Kimbrough Stone recalled the administrative breakdowns which had flowed from such failings.[179] Provision for a council of judges guaranteed continuity "in case of emergencies which arise in the course of human events."[180]

Of greater importance was the Chief Justice's singular perception of the kind of authority available to the councils as well as the sort of administrative techniques they might exercise. Under administration by the several circuit judges, Hughes believed "that the district judges would not feel that they were dependent upon a single individual, a particular circuit judge, and they would feel their requests had consideration of the organization in the circuit."[181] Similarly, he told Judge Groner that in meeting administrative problems "there would be greater confidence on the part of the bar and public if the matter was handled by two or three rather than one judge."[182] In short, the authority of the councils was perceived as more legitimate than that of a single senior circuit judge.

Utilization of the plural circuit courts instead of the presiding judge alone clothed administrative directions with that body's status achieved from its role as an appellate court of review. To enhance its prestige, both Chief Justice Hughes and Judge Groner considered the value of incorporating peer-group representation into the councils. Variously, they studied and then rejected the idea of bar partici-

[178] "Suggestions of Judge [Kimbrough] Stone," October 14, 1938, p. 4, *ibid.*

[179] Kimbrough Stone, Senate Committee on the Judiciary, *Hearings on S. 188*, 1939, p. 26.

[180] *Ibid.*, pp. 26-27.

[181] 1938 Judicial Conference transcript, p. 203, in Chandler, "Some Major Advances," p. 380.

[182] D. Lawrence Groner to John J. Parker, November 30, 1938, Groner Papers, Box 21.

pation,[183] attendance of the circuit justice,[184] and inclusion of district judges possibly selected on the principle of seniority.[185]

This emphasis upon the composition of the responsible administrative agency acknowledged the nature of authority in the judiciary. As members of a professional guild, with its own process of socialization and with its own recognized standards of conduct and ways of doing things, judges accepted as legitimate those actions resting on acceptable premises. After all, said one senior circuit judge, "we are not dealing with plumbers or ditch diggers when we are dealing with Federal judges."[186] With such individuals, unabashed exercises of administrative power were not only unacceptably, but, hopefully, unnecessary.

Confidence in voluntary compliance was widely expressed at the time of the council's establishment. Judge Groner found it hard to conceive of a district judge's refusal to follow the admonitions of the circuit judges.[187] "You don't have to threaten judges to get them to carry out the directions of the councils," asserted his colleague Judge Parker, "they carry them out because the judges are good men, they want to do what is right."[188]

In any case, the councils were not expected to make impossible demands on the trial judges. "Except in mere routine," stated Groner, "the authority will be utilized very

183 "Extract, Administration in the Federal Courts," p. 16.

184 D. Lawrence Groner to John J. Parker, November 30, 1938, Groner Papers, Box 21.

185 *Ibid.*; see also 1939 Judicial Conference transcript, p. 183, in Chandler, p. 385.

186 Evan A. Evans to D. Lawrence Groner, November 17, 1938, Groner Papers, Box 4.

187 D. Lawrence Groner, House Committee on the Judiciary, *Hearings on H.R. 2973*, 1939, p. 14.

188 U.S., Congress, House, Special Subcommittee on Bankruptcy and Reorganization of the Committee on the Judiciary, *Hearings, on H.R. 4394, Administration of the Bankruptcy Act: Referees in Bankruptcy*, 77th Cong., 1st Sess., 1941, p. 91.

161

infrequently."[189] It was not its use, but its mere existence which, Parker thought, would foster improved administration in the federal court system.[190]

Whenever the councils did invoke their compulsory power, the framers of the Act of 1939 had a definite conception of the means at their disposal. Coercion, Judge Groner had told the House Committee on the Judiciary, unquestionably constituted the object of the Administrative Office Bill.[191] He offered a short list of coercive instruments. Consultation, reasoned arguments and persuasion, and publicity, but not penal sanctions, loomed large in his mind. More could be accomplished, observed his counterpart from the Seventh Circuit, Evan A. Evans, "by a diplomatic handling of a bad situation where cooperation of the district judges is necessary than by coercion under authority of law."[192]

Publicity within the legal guild offered another acceptable technique. "Just turning the light of day on the judges probably in most instances would be all that is required."[193] Peer-group ostracism would do the rest. So thought Arthur Vanderbilt, who told the Senate Judiciary Committee that "no judge likes to have the fact that he is not abreast of his work held up to public notice."[194]

Sanctions more dramatic than these were never intended

[189] D. Lawrence Groner to Senior Circuit Judges, December 21, 1938, Groner Papers, Box 4; Arthur Vanderbilt, Senate Committee on the Judiciary, *Hearings on S. 188*, 1939, p. 19.

[190] House, Special Subcommittee on Bankruptcy and Reorganization of the Committee on the Judiciary, *Hearings on H.R. 4394*, 1941, pp. 91-92.

[191] House Committee on the Judiciary, *Hearings on H.R. 2973*, 1939, p. 15.

[192] Evan A. Evans to D. Lawrence Groner, November 17, 1938, Groner Papers, Box 4.

[193] 1938 Judicial Conference transcript, p. 227, in Chandler, "Some Major Advances," p. 382.

[194] Arthur Vanderbilt, Senate Committee on the Judiciary, *Hearings on S. 188*, 1939, p. 18.

by the judges,[195] although one congressman regarded their absence as a "grave defect."[196] Articulating the view of the judges, Senior Circuit Judge Orie Phillips admitted that "there may be instances you cannot cure at all, but I don't believe you can do it by force."[197] If, said Vanderbilt, "after all the admonition that may come from the circuit judges, a district judge still persists in neglecting his work, still holds up cases from decision when they should be decided, then everything has been accomplished by mild measures that could be accomplished."[198] Meaningful sanctions were for Congress to apply, but no augmentation of congressional power accompanied the reform of 1939. As it had since 1789, Congress continued to possess only the power of impeachment for "high crimes and misdemeanors."[199]

An alternative source of administrative authority received little consideration. During discussion of the Ashurst Bill in early 1938, many members of the legal community assumed that the problem of dealing with obdurate and misbehaving judges would not fall to the circuit judges alone. In spite of the status of the intermediate appellate tribunals, some reformers recognized their limits as instruments of final administrative responsibility. They saw the need for authority exercised not by a local organ like the councils, but a prestigious national forum.

Until Chief Justice Hughes eliminated the Supreme Court from any significant role in federal judicial adminis-

[195] John J. Parker, House Committee on the Judiciary, *Hearings on H.R. 2973*, 1939, p. 22.
[196] Vanderbilt, Senate Committee on the Judiciary, *Hearings on S. 188*, 1939, p. 18.
[197] 1938 Judicial Conference transcript, p. 227, in Chandler, p. 382.
[198] Vanderbilt, Senate Committee on the Judiciary, *Hearings on S. 188*, 1939, p. 18.
[199] D. Lawrence Groner, House Committee on the Judiciary, *Hearings on H.R. 2973*, 1939, p. 14; John J. Parker, *ibid.*, p. 22; Arthur Vanderbilt, Senate Committee on the Judiciary, *Hearings on S. 188*, 1939, p. 18.

tration, it was naturally thought that this organ or its presiding officer would act in the "hard cases." Hence, the senior circuit judges and their colleagues on the courts of appeals would constitute something less than a repository of final administrative responsibility; they would be instead "a combination buffer and strainer."[200] In operation, one member of the Attorney General's Committee on the Administrative Office Bill explained how the system would meet a real problem in administration. He stated: "In the first instance, the judges in the circuit court would handle it, the senior circuit judge being the principal administrative officer, and not until he was unable to handle the situation successfully, cooperating with the director, would there be any trouble and grief upon the bench or before the Supreme Court or its Chief Justice."[201] Clearly, an appellate system of judicial administration analogous to that prevailing in matters of law was reflected in this conception.

Removal of the Supreme Court as a factor in administration necessarily destroyed any such possibility. Substitution of the Judicial Conference commanded virtually no attention. However, at the critical 1938 Conference, Chief Justice Hughes may have dimly perceived its role in meeting the problem of non-conforming judges. There he suggested that "as to all questions which would require uniformity of action, or where there would be differences between the various organizations of the Circuits, or where there would be any need for the intervention of a central body, we have here a Judicial Conference ready to give the supervision and to make the requirements that are needed."[202] In short, the Judicial Conference in Washington afforded in matters of judicial administration what the Supreme Court did in the sphere of substantive law, a locus of effective authority. However, other than as a check on the Administrative Of-

[200] George Morris, House Subcommittee of the Committee on the Judiciary, *Hearings on the General Subject*, 1938, p. 46.
[201] *Ibid.*, following p. 47, p. 2.
[202] "Extract, Administration in the Federal Courts," p. 19.

fice, the Conference as a coercive force in administration was all but ignored during the formative years.

As conceived by Chief Justice Hughes and by leading members of the Judicial Conference, the circuit councils, established by the Act of 1939, were the cornerstone of the federal judiciary's administrative institution. The Act endowed appellate judges with responsibility and statutory power to promote adequate standards of administrative behavior in the trial courts of the several circuits. If any agency within the court system could act upon traditionally autonomous judges to rectify their conduct as individuals or as administrators, it was the councils. Although limited in their real competence, the mere existence of these formal organs was an important innovation. Attesting to this fact, Senior Circuit Judge John J. Parker told a congressional committee:

What you have done is to make a fundamental change in the judicial system of the country. Heretofore the judicial system rested upon the district judge alone. He was responsible for administration in his district. But you have placed in the council of the circuit responsibility for supervision of the administration.[203]

[203] U.S., Congress, Senate, Subcommittee of the Committee on the Judiciary, *Hearings, on S. 1051, S. 1052, S. 1053, S. 1054, H.R. 138, Administration of United States Courts*, 77th Cong., 1st Sess., 1941, p. 27.

CHAPTER 5

The Administrative Office
of the United States Courts, Part I

Appointment of the Director

ALTHOUGH judges and legislators alike regarded the circuit councils as the real locus of administrative power, the immediate effect of the Act of 1939 was the organizing of the judiciary's housekeeping agency—the Administrative Office of the United States Courts. To this end, selection of a director and assistant director constituted the first order of business. Under the Act, they were to "be appointed by the Supreme Court of the United States and hold office at the pleasure of and be subject to removal by the aforesaid court."[1] Once the Court had chosen them, it became "functus officio,"[2] for thereafter, the Conference, not the Court, "supervised and directed the Office."[3]

The statute made clear the role of the Court in the appointment process, but that of the Judicial Conference remained vague. Notwithstanding the Act's lack of ambiguity on the subject, many senior circuit judges assumed that because of the Conference's responsibility "for the administration of the Act, the appointees would be persons known to and agreeable to the members of the Conference."[4] They fully expected to have a voice, perhaps a decisive voice, in the appointments.[5] At the very least, they expected, in the words of one congressman, that "before making an appointment, the members of the Supreme Court would undoubt-

[1] 53 *Stat.* 1223, sec. 302.
[2] Harold M. Stephens to Thomas L. Marshall, December 9, 1939, Stephens Papers, Box 28.
[3] *Ibid.*   [4] *Ibid.*
[5] Stephens to Charles E. Stewart, December 21, 1939, *ibid.*, Box 37.

edly confer with the members of the judicial conference."[6]

Confident that the views of the federal judges, and especially of the senior circuit judges, would count heavily, candidates for the directorship lobbied the judges for support, and by October 1939 more than fifty names had been advanced.[7] The most active among them was Charles E. Stewart, then clerk of the United States District Court for the District of Columbia Circuit. A relatively old but vigorous man, he had long held the post of administrative assistant to the Attorney General and in that capacity had aided courts in securing appropriations, personnel, and supplies. Tapping a large reservoir of good will,[8] he generated endorsements from district and circuit courts across the country and by September 1939 could claim support from nine of the eleven senior circuit judges and from sixty senior district judges.[9] Stewart was the overwhelming choice of the federal judges for director.[10] For the position of assistant director, Sal Andretta, Stewart's successor in the Department of Justice, commanded widespread grass-roots support.[11]

In spite of this groundswell, key senior circuit judges

[6] Edward R. Burke, U.S., Congress, Senate, Committee on the Judiciary, *Hearings, on S. 3212, Administrative Office of the United States Courts,* 75th Cong., 3d Sess., 1938, p. 37.

[7] D. Lawrence Groner to William P. Boehmer, October 6, 1939, Groner Papers, Box 4.

[8] Interview with Henry Hull, December 17, 1964, Washington, D.C.

[9] Charles E. Stewart to Harold M. Stephens, September 28, 1939, Stephens Papers, Box 37. See also (all in Groner Papers, Box 4) John J. Parker to D. Lawrence Groner, March 1, 1938, May 20, 1939, and May 23, 1939; Curtis D. Wilbur to D. Lawrence Groner, May 12, 1938; Orie L. Phillips to D. Lawrence Groner, March 3, 1938; Learned Hand to D. Lawrence Groner, March 10, 1939; William P. James to D. Lawrence Groner, August 26, 1939; Robert C. Baltzell to D. Lawrence Groner, September 6, 1939.

[10] Charles E. Stewart to Rufus E. Foster, September 17, 1939, Stephens Papers, Box 37.

[11] Charles E. Stewart to Harold M. Stephens, September 18, 1939, *ibid.*

questioned "the propriety of the Conference or anybody else making recommendations to the Supreme Court as to whom it shall appoint."[12] Even Chief Justice Groner of the Court of Appeals in the District of Columbia made no move to press any candidate on Hughes or the Supreme Court,[13] confident that whomever the Court appointed would prove satisfactory because that body would surely delegate to the Chief Justice "the task of finding the right man."[14] But rumors reached him during the summer of 1939 that the Chief's grip on the appointment process might be weaker than expected and that the director's selection had become a political football.[15] Under these circumstances, an uncertain Groner presented to Hughes the names of Stewart and Andretta.[16]

Premonitions of political maneuvering on the high court were at least partly justified. "Every member of the Court was expected to suggest any person whom he thought suitable" for the directorship, recalled Associate Justice Stanley Reed.[17] While McReynolds apparently solicited the views of some Conference participants,[18] Reed organized a cabal among the four New Deal justices. This group then proposed the candidacies of several lawyers associated with the executive branch, one of whom the ubiquitous fixer, Thomas "The Cork" Corcoran, was assiduously promoting.[19]

[12] Kimbrough Stone to Andrew Miller, September 6, 1939, Kimbrough Stone Papers, Box 10.

[13] Stewart to Foster, September 17, 1939, Stephens Papers, Box 37.

[14] D. Lawrence Groner to Charles Evans Hughes, July 19, 1939, Groner Papers, Box 4.

[15] Ibid.

[16] Charles E. Stewart to Harold M. Stephens, September 19, 1939, Stephens Papers, Box 37; see also Stephens to Stewart, September 21, 1939, ibid.

[17] Stanley Reed to Peter G. Fish, January 8, 1965, in possession of author.

[18] Interview with John Biggs, Jr., February 28, 1965, Wilmington, Delaware.

[19] Merlo Pusey, Charles Evans Hughes (New York, 1951), II, 687.

Hughes, however, had his own ideas. He told the 1939 Conference that the director "ought to be one who, while not known at the time of his appointment, will be well-recommended. . . . He ought to have the caliber of a judge. . . . He ought to be a man who is not essentially a bureaucrat in the making. He has got to be a real executive, with a knowledge of legal affairs, and a man who will be regarded favorably by the judges with whom he comes in contact."[20]

After a delay, the Chief Justice offered the directorship to several prominent lawyers, who declined.[21] Then from different sources came recommendations for the selection of Henry P. Chandler, a lawyer and civic reformer in Chicago and a former president of the Chicago Bar Association and Union League Club. He made a favorable impression on the Chief Justice, proved acceptable to the other members of the Court, and received the appointment.[22]

For assistant director, the Court chose Elmore Whitehurst, not Andretta. Whitehurst had been secretary to the chairman of the House Judiciary Committee, Hatton Sumners, and later clerk of that committee. His appointment to the office enabled Chief Justice Hughes to reward, in this limited manner, the powerful Texas congressman who had vigorously and decisively opposed the Court-packing bill.[23]

These appointments, especially that of the director, came as a profound shock to some of the ranking federal judges. Informed of Chandler's selection, a bewildered Judge Groner told Hughes that he hoped "it's a case of . . . all's well that ends well, but I confess the experience has shaken some of my fixed convictions."[24] His colleague on the appel-

[20] 1939 Judicial Conference transcript, pp. 225-26, in Chandler, "Some Major Advances," pp. 393-94.

[21] Grenville Clark to Peter G. Fish, August 16, 1965, in possession of the author.

[22] Pusey, *Hughes*, II, 687-88.

[23] Interview with Henry P. Chandler, August 1, 1963, Chevy Chase, Maryland.

[24] D. Lawrence Groner to Charles Evans Hughes, November 24, 1939, Groner Papers, Box 4.

late court bench, was even more emphatic in venting his displeasure. "The fact is," complained Judge Stephens, "that we suddenly find that we have a Director in the person of Mr. Chandler whom most of the judges of the country and most of the members of the Conference do not know and in respect of whose appointment the Conference had no voice. To put it bluntly, the views of the judges of the country as expressed through the Conference were in effect ignored in this appointment so that the Conference is in the position of having to carry out its duties to administer the Act through a man whom it had no voice in selecting."[25]

The appointment of the first director clearly demonstrated the reality of the Supreme Court's prerogative. Moreover it established a precedent to be followed two decades later in the selection of the successor to Director Chandler. Then, though Chief Justice Earl Warren consulted with members of the Conference,[26] the candidate preferred by the rank and file judges failed to receive the crown. Their choice was the former assistant director and then acting director of the office, Elmore Whitehurst. He received the endorsement of the circuit council in several circuits including that in the Second, which "expressed [the] belief and hope that Mr. Whitehurst should succeed Mr. Chandler."[27] Moreover it directed Chief Judge Charles E. Clark to "express our views to our Circuit Justice, Justice [John M.] Harlan, together with the suggestion that we should be glad to have him transmit our views to his colleagues [on the Supreme Court]."[28] Whatever Harlan may have transmitted to the Chief Justice, it had little effect, for Warren Olney III, not Whitehurst, received the appointment early in 1958.

[25] Harold M. Stephens to Thomas L. Marshall, December 19, 1939, Stephens Papers, Box 28.

[26] Interview with John Biggs, Jr., August 12, 1965, Washington, D.C.

[27] "Minutes of the Judicial Council of the Second Circuit," November 15, 1956, p. 6, Clark Papers.

[28] Ibid.

Olney was very much the personal choice of Chief Justice Warren. The son of one of the Chief's closest friends and a loyal protégé of the former California governor, he had been chief counsel of Warren's Special Crime Study Commission and in 1953 had joined the Eisenhower administration as assistant attorney general in charge of the Criminal Division of the Justice Department. In this capacity, he had come to the assistance of his former superior when old California adversaries attacked Warren during the congressional hearings on his confirmation as Chief Justice.[29]

The Director and the Chief Justice

Once the director's and assistant director's posts had been filled, the active role of the Supreme Court virtually disappeared. However, that of the Chief Justice remained paramount despite an early prediction that "rarely, if ever, will he be needed for considering interim policies or any details."[30] Acting on this assumption, the 1939 Conference established an Advisory Committee of four of its most influential members "to advise and assist the Director in the exercise of his duties."[31]

Director Chandler, however, depended less on this committee than on the Chief Justice. As Judge Groner warned then newly-appointed Chief Justice Harlan Fiske Stone, "The principal burden on you will be the constant appeals to you by the Director for advice. We have in the present set-up an Advisory Committee . . . but Chandler prefers to take his problems to the Chief Justice, and Chief Justice Hughes was always available to him."[32] Moreover, Hughes maintained an "open-door" policy and actively encouraged

[29] New York Times, February 21, 1954, p. 18.

[30] "Senior Judges Plan to Integrate Federal System," Journal of the American Judicature Society, 22 (December 1938), 161.

[31] "Report of the Judicial Conference," Judicial Conference Report, 1939, p. 18.

[32] D. Lawrence Groner to Harlan Fiske Stone, September 8, 1941, Groner Papers, Box 12.

171

the director "to bring to him any matters . . . of importance."[33] By memoranda and conferences, Chandler carried his questions to the Chief Justice for a "judgment."[34] Hughes' successors, too, found that they were expected to be available and to pass on a steady stream of detailed suggestions and inquiries.[35]

With Warren Olney, however, this relationship between the director and the Chief Justice underwent a distinct change. Instead of passing judgment on specific problems submitted to him by the director as had Chief Justices since Hughes, Warren gave the office a relatively free rein. But, not surprisingly, the director usually consulted with the Chief in shaping broad policies relating to the office and the work of the Judicial Conference.[36]

Early Organization and Functions

The initial organization of the Administrative Office reflected the major functions conferred on the new agency by the Act of 1939. They were twofold, as Chief Justice Hughes explained to Henry P. Chandler shortly before his appointment. First were the administrative duties then being performed by the Department of Justice for the courts, and second were the collection and reporting of judicial statistics.[37] In consultation with representatives of the Brookings Institution, a budget expert from the Agriculture Department, and a member of the Civil Service Commission, the director and his assistant, Elmore Whitehurst, hammered

[33] Chandler, p. 412.

[34] Henry P. Chandler to Harrison Tweed, October 13, 1954, Administrative Office Correspondence, 59-A-48, Box 137.

[35] Henry P. Chandler to Harlan Fiske Stone, January 13, 1946, *ibid.*, 59-A-532, Box 2; Henry P. Chandler to Fred M. Vinson, April 29, 1953, *ibid.*, 59-A-48, Box 122; Henry P. Chandler to Earl Warren, December 8, 1954, *ibid.*, 59-A-48, Box 122.

[36] Interview with Will Shafroth, February 18, 1965, Washington, D.C.

[37] Chandler, "Some Major Advances," p. 398.

172

out a suitable organization. They conceived of two divisions, one entitled the Division of Business Administration,[38] and the other designated as the Division of Procedural Studies and Statistics, a name suggested by Hughes, who perceived a broader function than mere statistical compilation.[39]

The Division of Business Administration constituted the business-managerial agency of the courts, performing a multitude of housekeeping and staff functions for the courts and for the Judicial Conference.[40] As these duties formerly lay within the domain of the Administrative Division of the Department of Justice, the new division's organization largely mirrored that of its predecessor.[41] The Budget and Accounting Section set up the books, allotted authorized funds, supervised their expenditure, and provided estimates for the judicial appropriations.[42] The accounts and vouchers of court personnel including court clerks, referees in bankruptcy, United States commissioners, and conciliation commissioners were audited by the Audit Section[43] preliminary to their submission to the General Accounting Office for review.[44] The Service Section distributed supplies ranging from typewriter ribbons to law books and negotiated with such government agencies as the General Services Administration and Public Buildings Service for court accommodations in federal buildings.[45] Shortly after the

[38] *Ibid.*, p. 400.   [39] *Ibid.*, p. 401.
[40] Fred M. Vinson, "The Business of Judicial Administration," *Journal of the American Judicature Society*, 33 (October 1949), 77.
[41] Chandler, "Some Major Advances," p. 400.
[42] Henry P. Chandler, "The Administrative Office of the United States Courts," *Journal of the National Association of Referees in Bankruptcy*, 15 (October 1940), 50-51.
[43] *Judicial Conference Report, 1940*, special session, p. 15.
[44] Melville LaMarche, "The Work of the Audit Section of the Administrative Office of the United States Courts as it is Related to Bankruptcy," *Journal of the National Association of Referees in Bankruptcy*, 19 (October 1944), 26.
[45] Henry P. Chandler, "The Administrative Office of the United States Courts," pp. 611-12.

office began operations, a personnel officer joined the division and became, in effect, the fourth section, charged with meeting personnel problems and maintenance of all judicial personnel records including those of judges and supporting personnel.[46]

The Division of Procedural Studies and Statistics assumed the task of collecting data on cases in the federal courts and, depending on their nature, reporting them to the Judicial Conference and its committees, to circuit conference committees, and as required by the Administrative Office Act, in quarterly reports to the senior circuit judge of each circuit.[47] At first, only responsibility for those statistics relating to civil and bankruptcy cases devolved upon the division.[48] Court clerks collected data for these classes of cases while the United States attorneys gathered information on criminal cases. As the Justice Department had originally designed the latter group of statistics for supervision of its attorneys, the Administrative Office soon discovered that "many of the requests for information concerning criminal statistics of the federal courts could not be accurately answered."[49] Thus the collection of all judicial statistics fell to the Administrative Office on July 1, 1941, when the court clerks were instructed to assemble material on the disposition of criminal cases in their courts.[50]

The division took over the department's statistical system which had been inaugurated in 1935 and which, in the words of Director Chandler, was "the result of careful

[46] Chandler, "Some Major Advances," p. 400.

[47] See "Report of Committee on Operation of the Jury System," Excerpt from Agenda 13, September 1953, mimeograph (Administrative Office of the United States Courts, Washington, D.C.), pp. 13-14.

[48] Will Shafroth, "Federal Judicial Statistics," *Law and Contemporary Problems*, 13 (Winter 1948), 205.

[49] Ronald H. Beattie, "Memorandum Regarding the Statistical Work of the Administrative Office," January 5, 1944, pp. 4-5, Administrative Office Correspondence, 60-A-328, Box 23.

[50] Shafroth, "Federal Judicial Statistics," p. 205.

thought and some experience."[51] Thus the division continued to provide "case flow" statistics on the relationship between the number and types of cases commenced and the number terminated, the median time intervals from filing to disposition and from joinder of issue to trial, and the length of trials.[52] An early and important statistical innovation was the compilation of cases held under advisement in each district more than thirty days.[53] These statistics, together with the "case flow" data, comprised the quarterly reports.

In addition, the division assembled statistics on pending cases held for more than sixty and ninety days and for longer than six months classified according to the reasons for their delay.[54] Information on the volume and types of probationers[55] and on various aspects of the bankruptcy system were also gathered.[56] At the request of the Conference, the division made special statistical studies of the selection and use of jurors,[57] of the methods and effect of pretrial proceedings,[58] and of the comparative times spent by representative judges in disposing of cases.[59]

Collecting, coding, correlating, tabulating, and publishing judicial statistics constituted but one function of the division. It also used them "in connection with personal inspections of each district to draw a clear picture of the

[51] Chandler, "The Administrative Office of the United States Courts," p. 615.

[52] See "Report of the Judicial Conference Committee on Statistics," September 15, 1951, mimeograph (Administrative Office of the United States Courts, Washington, D.C.), p. 6 (cited hereafter as "Report on Statistics"). *Judicial Conference Report, 1945*, p. 77.

[53] *Judicial Conference Report, 1940*, pp. 20-21.

[54] William H. Speck, "Statistics for the United States Courts: An Indispensable Tool for Judicial Management," *American Bar Association Journal*, 38 (November 1952), 936-37.

[55] *Judicial Conference Report, 1945*, pp. 115-19.

[56] *Ibid., 1948*, pp. 180-97.

[57] "Report on Statistics," p. 10.

[58] *Judicial Conference Report, 1941*, p. 29.

[59] Speck, "Statistics for the United States Courts," p. 970.

condition of judicial business in each district, the reasons for delay, if any, and suggested means of clearing up congestion."[60] Such inspections were made.[61] But the division never organized a permanent field staff, in spite of the urging, in 1939 and 1940, of Henry N. Wiseman, a personnel and management expert from the Bureau of the Budget. Such field representatives, Wiseman believed, could "make a somewhat broader study of their general procedures than the fiscal examination . . . made by examiners of the Department of Justice, recommend improvements, and then visit the offices from time to time thereafter to see that the recommendations were carried out."[62]

The idea of a central office with its own field staff to survey the offices of judge-appointed officials generated little enthusiasm among key judges.[63] Judge Groner, for instance, thought it posed a real danger "that the judges who are directly responsible for the clerks would resent it."[64] His advice "was that it would be wise to expand slowly,"[65] a suggestion which received a warm, and conclusive, reception from Chief Justice Hughes.

Of all the functions transferred from the Department of Justice, that of administrative responsibility for the probation system caused the greatest controversy.[66] Part of the

[60] Unsigned memorandum, "Re: Additional Personnel to be Included in the Requested Budget for 1941," February 19, 1941, p. 1, Administrative Office Correspondence, 57-A-122, Box 4.

[61] Ibid.

[62] Henry P. Chandler to Charles E. Hughes, November 1, 1940, ibid.

[63] See Henry P. Chandler, U.S., Congress, House, Subcommittee of Committee on Appropriations, Hearings, Judiciary Appropriations Bill for 1943, 77th Cong., 2d Sess., 1941, pp. 117-19.

[64] Chandler to Charles E. Hughes, November 1, 1940, Administrative Office Correspondence, 57-A-122, Box 4.

[65] Chandler, "Some Major Advances," pp. 400-01.

[66] For a detailed study of this issue, see Peter Graham Fish, "The Politics of Judicial Administration: Transfer of the Federal Probation System," The Western Political Quarterly, 23 (December 1970), 769-84.

difficulty lay with the language and legislative history of the Administrative Office Act and part with the nature of the probation officers' functions.[67]

Faced with the necessity of deciding whether or not the 1941 appropriations for the system should be carried in the Justice Department's budget, Director Chandler "concluded from the provisions of the [Administrative Office Act] and the history of the legislation that it vests the administration of probation in the Administrative Office."[68] As he read the Act, it granted the agency all administrative powers and duties previously conferred on the Department of Justice or the attorney general, respecting clerks of courts, other specified judicial employees, "and such other employees of the courts not excluded by Section 304 of Chapter XV." That section excluded from the scope of the office's responsibility "United States marshals and their deputies, United States attorneys and their assistants." Probation officers were not among those excepted.[69]

Furthermore, they fell within the office's administrative system because their selection and functions were judicial in character. Judges appointed them, and, noted Director Chandler, they performed tasks which were fundamentally judicial, "probation being in the nature of a suspension of sentence on condition, and probationers being within the jurisdiction of the court during the term of probation."[70]

James V. Bennett, director of the Bureau of Prisons, objected. He contended that "the determining question ought to be where probation can be most effectively administered for the good of the probationers and the public." And to him the optimum locus of control should reside in the executive rather than the judicial branch, because "probation needs central direction by an officer who can coordinate the work with other corrective methods of the Department of

[67] 43 *Stat.* 1260 and 46 *Stat.* 503.

[68] Henry P. Chandler to Charles E. Hughes, January 6, 1940, copy, Groner Papers, Box 15.

[69] *Ibid.*   [70] *Ibid.*

Justice, specifically commitment and parole."[71] As for the mode of appointment, it, said Alexander Holtzoff, special assistant to the attorney general, "is by no means determinative [as] it is entirely proper to vest in the courts the authority to appoint executive officers."[72]

Hence, the status of probation officers could not be established by the mode of their appointment, but only by the character of their functions.[73] Not surprisingly, Holtzoff found these functions wholly executive. Even the supervision of probationers was "a form of executing the judgment and order of the court,"[74] thereby placing probation officers in a position analogous to that of the marshal, an executive official, in executing a civil judgment of the courts. In conclusion, Holtzoff argued:

> It was not within the purview of the draftsmen of the Act of August 7, 1939, that the probation system should be wrenched out of its connection as an essential part of the integrated Federal penal and correctional system and transferred to the Administrative Office of the Courts. The constitutional separation of powers forbade any such intention, for the transfer of executive functions to the judicial branch of the Government would manifestly be an invalid delegation of executive power.[75]

Notwithstanding these objections, the January 1940 Special Session of the Judicial Conference agreed with Chandler's interpretation of the organic act and directed him to commence administration of the probation system "as soon as practicable."[76] On July 1, 1940, the office assumed administrative responsibility for the probation service after its director had given assurances "that the service so well devel-

---

[71] *Ibid.*, p. 2.
[72] Alexander Holtzoff, memorandum, "Re: Status of Probation Officers," January 20, 1940, p. 2, *ibid.*
[73] *Ibid.*, p. 3.   [74] *Ibid.*   [75] *Ibid.*, p. 5.
[76] *Judicial Conference Report, 1940*, special session, p. 16.

oped by the Bureau [of Prisons] will be continued without a break."[77]

Composed of a chief, an assistant chief, and two stenographers, the Probation Division acted in much the same capacity toward the probation officers as did the Business Administration Division toward such court employees as clerks, secretaries, and messengers. It met the needs of probation personnel for supplies, passed upon requests for additional personnel and increases in salaries, prescribed the form of reports, and composed and collated questionnaires on vital issues relating to the system.[78]

Together with the Justice Department, the division issued a house organ, *Federal Probation*, intended to keep probation officers informed of contemporary developments in the field of corrections and for promoting higher standards of performance on the part of individual officers.[79] In addition, the division promoted regional in-service training institutes under the auspices of leading universities, and in 1949 it organized, with the cooperation of the District Court for the Northern District of Illinois and the School of Social Service Administration of the University of Chicago, a training center for newly-appointed officers.[80]

As did the ranking members of the Division of Procedural Studies and Statistics, their counterparts in the Probation Division undertook field work. Staff supervision was given on personal visits and at small group meetings held at headquarters offices or at other points in the field. There, the Administrative Office's representatives sought to de-

[77] Henry P. Chandler, "Court Administration Agency to Supervise Federal Probation," *Federal Probation*, 4 (May 1940), 4. (Cited hereafter as "Agency to Supervise Federal Probation.")

[78] "Qualifications of Probation Officers," *Federal Probation*, 6 (January-March 1942), 7-16.

[79] Chandler, "Agency to Supervise Federal Probation," p. 4.

[80] Richard A. Chappell, "The Federal Probation System Today," *Federal Probation*, 14 (June 1950), 39-40; see also *Judicial Conference Report, 1945*, p. 41.

179

velop and improve casework techniques and administrative procedures.[81]

The same session of the Judicial Conference which directed the transfer of the probation system also construed the language of the Administrative Office Act as charging the new agency "with the responsibility of supervising the administration of the Bankruptcy Act by all officers of the bankruptcy courts, including the referees in bankruptcy."[82] The director immediately began collecting financial reports from the referees as ordered by the Conference,[83] but no separate division was created in 1940 while judges and administrators awaited the results of a Justice Department study of the bankruptcy system.

Late in 1940, the Attorney General's Committee on Bankruptcy Administration released its report. It chronicled a long list of administrative shortcomings and concluded that "the present system of supervision and coordination does not work. There are far too many illegal acts, far too much unjustified expense, . . . far too much unwarranted delay, far less confidence in bankruptcy than it should and can have."[84] The remedy lay, in part, with the establishment of a bankruptcy division in the Administrative Office. Such a division would exercise a continuing scrutiny of bankruptcy administration.[85]

Shortly after release of the report, a special session of the Judicial Conference met in January 1941 primarily to consider its recommendations. Without modification, the Conference approved the committee's proposal for a bankruptcy division in the Administrative Office.[86] Among the

[81] Louis J. Sharp, "Inservice Training in Probation and Parole," *Federal Probation*, 15 (December 1951), 29.

[82] *Judicial Conference Report, 1940*, special session, p. 16.

[83] *Ibid.*

[84] "Administration of the Bankruptcy Act," *Report of the Attorney General's Committee on Bankruptcy Administration, 1940* (Washington, 1941), p. 50.

[85] *Ibid.*, pp. 117-20.

[86] *Judicial Conference Report, 1941*, special session, p. 20.

functions of what became another three-man division was the examination and audit of bankruptcy reports and accounts, the collection of bankruptcy statistics, the investigation of rules and practices of bankruptcy administration as well as of complaints.[87] The division also maintained liaison with the Judicial Conference, its Bankruptcy Committee, as well as with the district judges and referees in each judicial district. As conceived by the senior circuit judges, the small bureau would recommend to them "changes in the Bankruptcy Act, changes in the general orders [in bankruptcy of the Supreme Court] and official forms, and changes in local bankruptcy rules, practice and procedure, and the recommending to the Circuit Council of a Circuit any changes with respect to local rules, particular practices and procedures in any court or before any referee in bankruptcy in that Circuit."[88] These responsibilities were augmented by the Referees Salary Act of 1946[89] which required the director to undertake nationwide studies of bankruptcy business, after which he would "recommend to the district judges, the councils and the Conference the number of referees to hold appointment and the territory which each shall serve."[90]

Creation of the Bankruptcy Division completed the initial, and major, stage of organization. The framework then established largely defined the nature of the office's basic functions, although others were gradually assumed during the Chandler administration. The new agency early absorbed responsibility for United States park commissioners from the Interior Department[91] and, much more significantly, it centralized the new compensation programs for

[87] Ibid.

[88] Judicial Conference Report, 1941, p. 20. See also Chandler, "The Administrative Office of the United States Courts," p. 51.

[89] 60 Stat. 323.   [90] 60 Stat. 325, sec. 4.

[91] See Harold I. Ickes to Clarence Cannon, February 9, 1943, in U.S., Congress, House, Committee on Appropriations, Hearings, on Interior Department, Appropriations Bill for 1944, part I, 78th Cong., 1st Sess., 1943, pp. 816-17.

judicial employees. Court criers, long paid on a *per diem* basis,[92] and bankruptcy referees, who had historically been compensated by fees drawn from indemnity funds created by the interested parties,[93] were both placed on salaries administered by the Administrative Office.[94] Establishment of an official court reporter system in 1944 with its salary and transcript fee plan of compensation,[95] salaried district court law clerks,[96] and reorganization of the commissioner system in 1946[97] all entailed new and additional tasks for the office.

The Unseparated Functions

Not all responsibilities for the administration of the courts were transferred to the new Administrative Office. Some remained with the Department of Justice in apparent conflict with the theory of the Act of 1939. Among the functions not separated from the department were the field audits of the accounts maintained by court personnel. They clearly lay within the jurisdiction of the office.[98] However, Chief Justice Hughes and Director Chandler encountered insuperable difficulties in separating this function from the department and placing it either in an agency independent of the executive branch or in the office itself.

To a suggestion advanced by the marshal of the Supreme Court that the General Accounting Office assume the task, a department spokesman replied that such a course was impossible "for the very sufficient reason that [the GAO] representatives would be invading a field which belongs exclusively to the Department of Justice."[99] The department, on

[92] See Chandler, "Some Major Advances," pp. 422-23.
[93] *Judicial Conference Report, 1950*, p. 46.
[94] Criers in 1944, 58 *Stat.* 796-97; referees in 1944, 58 *Stat.* 517.
[95] 58 *Stat.* 5-7.
[96] Chandler, "Some Major Advances," pp. 421-22.
[97] 60 *Stat.* 752-53.
[98] 53 *Stat.* 1224, sec. 304 (5); *Judicial Conference Report, 1940*, special session, p. 15.
[99] T. D. Quinn to Thomas E. Waggaman, September 18, 1939, Department of Justice Files, No. 236508, Sec. 2.

the other hand, would be happy to continue its examination of judicial as well as executive offices in the courts.[100] Combined with the resistance of the department, the high cost of establishing Administrative Office counterparts to the executive auditors discouraged further efforts to transfer this function.[101]

Thus, after 1939, Justice Department representatives continued to make the examinations and compose the reports which were provided to the Administrative Office for its use. That office then prepared memoranda

condensing the various reports. The original reports with copies of the memoranda are then transmitted by the Administrative Office to the Chief Judge of the district with a letter calling attention to salient points of the report. Copies of the memoranda and of the transmitted letter are also sent to the member of the Judicial Conference of the circuit in which the district is located. When the office of the clerk of a court of appeals is examined, the report is sent to the Chief Judge of the Circuit.[102]

The status of this audit power came into question during the 1950s and at one point the judiciary was compelled to fight off a congressional effort to remove its unexercised right to make such audits.[103] The tables turned completely several years later when the deputy attorney general offered to transfer the function to the office, explaining that the department's examiners devoted 67.2 percent of their

[100] Ibid.

[101] Henry P. Chandler, U.S., Congress, House, Subcommittee of the Committee on Appropriations, Hearings, Department of Justice Appropriation Bill for 1942, 77th Cong., 1st Sess., 1941, p. 637. See also Judicial Conference Report, 1944, p. 55.

[102] Memorandum, Elmore Whitehurst to Earl Warren, February 12, 1957, Administrative Office Correspondence, 60-A-328, Box 27.

[103] S. 2864, 81st Cong.; see also: memorandum, Leland Tolman to Henry P. Chandler and Elmore Whitehurst, April 21, 1950, Administrative Office Correspondence, 60-A-328, Box 5.

time to scrutiny of court records.[104] Moreover, the examiner's section was undergoing a reorganization "after which the section will not be equipped to continue making examinations for the courts."[105] Finally, the department again invoked the hoary separation of powers doctrine, this time to justify its contention that the examinations were "not a proper function of the Department of Justice."[106]

The Judicial Conference Committee on Court Administration agreed; it observed "that it was desirable for the United States Courts to have their own housekeeping done through their own agency, the Administrative Office."[107] However, no transfer ever took place largely because the powerful House Appropriations Subcommittee, in the words of its chairman, Congressman John Rooney, had "always been impressed by the fact that it is good and healthy to have one Department checking on another Department."[108] Once rebuffed, the committee and the Conference as a whole gave a cool reception to later transfer efforts.[109]

The disbursement of judicial funds constituted another function which remained with the Department of Justice even though the Act of 1939 provided that such funds might be disbursed by the judiciary "directly and through the sev-

[104] "Report of Attorney General Herbert Brownell," in *Judicial Conference Report*, 1957, p. 301.

[105] Memorandum, "Re: Letter of Deputy Attorney General William Rogers," December 6, 1956, Administrative Office Correspondence, 60-A-328, Box 27; memorandum, Elmore Whitehurst to Earl Warren, February 12, 1957, *ibid.*

[106] *Ibid.*

[107] "Report of the Committee on Court Administration," March 5, 1957, mimeograph (Administrative Office of the United States Courts, Washington, D.C.), p. 4. See also: *Judicial Conference Report, 1957*, p. 271.

[108] U.S., Congress, House, Subcommittee of Committee on Appropriations, *Hearings, Departments of State, Justice, and Commerce, the Judiciary, and Related Agencies, Appropriations for 1965, the Judiciary*, 88th Cong., 2d Sess., 1964, p. 68. See also *Judicial Conference Report, 1966*, pp. 25, 37.

[109] *Ibid., 1967*, p. 14.

184

eral United States marshals."[110] In the early 1960s, the department sought to shed its role as the judiciary's disbursing agent. The Committee on Court Administration again agreed to the idea in principle, but queried the cost of establishing a separate system.[111] The House Appropriations Committee likewise objected to the cost even though an Administrative Office study had shown the feasibility and economy of a centralized data processing system for payrolls, payments, and allowances.[112] Congressman Rooney decided "to help President Johnson,"[113] and thus the disbursement work remained in the Department of Justice.[114]

The Office and the Courts

The Act of 1939 did not create "a central-office executive agency like the F.B.I."[115] with a "program" and to which the

[110] 53 *Stat.* 1223, sec. 304 (3).

[111] *Judicial Conference Report, 1962*, pp. 6, 51; *ibid., 1963*, p. 7; *ibid., 1964*, p. 10.

[112] Warren Olney III, U.S., Congress, Senate, Committee on Appropriations, *Hearings, on H.R. 11134, Departments of State, Justice, Commerce, the Judiciary, and Related Agencies Appropriation for 1965*, part I, 88th Cong., 2d Sess., 1964, pp. 90-91; see also Olney, House Subcommittee on Appropriations, *Hearings on Appropriations for 1965*, pp. 66-67.

[113] *Ibid.*, p. 68.

[114] Controversy with the Justice Department arose during the 1950s and 1960s over the proper locus of appropriations for the compensation of and resulting administrative supervision over, masters, special masters, condemnation commissioners, and other finders of facts for the federal courts. See Memorandum from Leland Tolman, April 12, 1954, Stephens Papers, Box 229; Warren Olney, U.S., Congress, House, Subcommittee of Committee on Appropriations, *Hearings, Departments of State and Justice, the Judiciary, and Related Agencies, Appropriations for 1961*, 86th Cong., 2d Sess., 1960, pp. 68-72; *Judicial Conference Report, 1960*, pp. 419-20; *ibid., 1961*, pp. 51, 106; *ibid., 1962*, p. 30; *ibid., 1963*, p. 22.

[115] William L. Ellis to Warren Olney III, November 30, 1960, Administrative Office Correspondence, 61-A-298, Box 2.

supporting personnel in the courts were subordinate.[116] Even with the Administrative Office, there still existed in the federal judiciary "no centers of authority nor lines of authority in the usual administrative sense."[117] Such authority lay initially with the chief judges of the district and circuit courts, the Judicial Conference, and the circuit councils not with the office.[118]

That the agency enjoyed only very limited jurisdiction and power became abundantly clear in its first year of life. Then a far-reaching controversy over the administration of the bankruptcy system raised the issue of the relationship between the director and the individual courts.[119] It came on the heels of the highly critical report of the attorney general's Committee on Bankruptcy Administration,[120] which, among other recommendations, urged that the director be empowered to make recommendations for changes in the bankruptcy system directly to the district judges who appointed the referees in bankruptcy.[121]

Agreeing with one district judge that "suggestions emanating from the Administrative Office . . . may not enjoy the self-enforcing quality that would attach to suggestions emanating from the Court itself," the committee urged that the director be given limited power to request that a recommendation not accepted by a district judge be reviewed

[116] See Aubrey Gasque to Warren Olney III, December 1, 1960, ibid.

[117] "Statement of the Administrative Office, Judicial Salary Plan," in Senate, Committee on Appropriations, Hearings on Appropriations for 1965, p. 73.

[118] See Henry P. Chandler to William C. Mathes, February 13, 1953, Administrative Office Correspondence, 60-A-328, Box 32.

[119] For an extended discussion of this controversy, see Peter G. Fish, "Toward a Judicial Administrator of Limited Powers: Bankruptcy Crisis and the Administrative Office of the United States Courts," Journal of the National Conference of Referees in Bankruptcy, 44 (October 1970), 123-32.

[120] "Administration of the Bankruptcy Act," Report of the Attorney General's Committee on Bankruptcy Administration, 1940.

[121] Ibid., part III, sec. II E, pp. 130-31.

and, if accepted on review, be enforced by the appropriate Circuit Council.[122] In addition, the director, acting alone, would determine "the exact number of referees and the territory over which each shall exercise jurisdiction."[123]

Finally, the director would play an important role in the removal and appointment of referees. Removal was "to be by the district judge or judges who appointed him, upon the written recommendation of the director to the district judge or judges, or by such judge or judges."[124] Either the referee affected or the director might then appeal a district judge's action or lack thereof to the circuit council.[125] Similar recourse existed following rejection or acceptance of the director's recommendations for or against reappointment of incumbent referees.[126]

These proposals, which would have given the nascent Administrative Office a dramatic infusion of power, invoked an immediate and negative response. Judges, from the policy-makers on the Judicial Conference to the remotest district court, voiced loud objections. Groner warned against the development of "an overlordship of bankruptcy administration in the Administrative Office" which would subject historically independent district judges to "some understrapper in the Administrative Office."[127] Not only would this new administrative power, exercised by non-judges, "create a feeling of tremendous opposition to the Office itself both on the part of judges and their friends in Congress," but it could well spawn a bureaucratic monster.[128] In fact, its history might read like that of those nefarious New Deal agencies which had manifested a "tendency . . .

[122] *Ibid.*, pp. 131-32.
[123] *Ibid.*, part III, sec. III B(1), p. 139; see also p. 141.
[124] *Ibid.*, part III, sec. III D(1), pp. 162-63.   [125] *Ibid.*
[126] *Ibid.*, part III, sec. III D(2), pp. 163-64.
[127] D. Lawrence Groner to John J. Parker, November 9, 1940, Groner Papers.
[128] D. Lawrence Groner to John Biggs, Jr., November 13, 1940, *ibid.*, Box 11; see also: Groner to Kimbrough Stone, November 12, 1940, *ibid.*, Box 16.

187

to draw power to themselves, [and to] grow and grow and expand and expand and demand and demand."[129] Groner's colleague on the Conference, Kimbrough Stone, emphatically agreed. To him, the Attorney General seemed " 'hell bent' on augmenting the power of the Director and in centralizing matters in Washington [and] nothing could be more dangerous to the independence of the Judiciary than a concentration of any effective method of control in the Administrative Office or elsewhere."[130]

In the midst of these protests, a special session of the 1941 Judicial Conference went to work on the Attorney General's recommendations, largely emasculating them. The senior judges interposed the Judicial Conference and circuit councils between the director and individual judges. The Conference, not the director, would be "vested with authority to determine, in the light of recommendations from the Director as well as from the Circuit Councils, the exact number of referees to be appointed, the territory over which they shall exercise jurisdiction, the salaries they shall receive, and any changes which may be made thereafter as to their respective numbers, territories, or salaries."[131] This modification reflected Judge Stone's belief that "the Director should have no power of *determination* even though qualified,"[132] and the desire of other judges that the Conference not rely solely on his findings.[133]

At the same time, the role of the circuit councils was expanded by requiring the director to transmit his recommendations for changes in local bankruptcy rules, particular practices and procedures in any court or before any

[129] Groner to Biggs, November 13, 1940, *ibid.*; Groner to Parker, November 9, 1940, *ibid.*

[130] Kimbrough Stone to Groner, November 14, 1940, *ibid.*, Box 16.

[131] *Judicial Conference Report, 1941*, special session, p. 21; see sec. III B(1).

[132] Kimbrough Stone to Henry P. Chandler, March 13, 1941, Groner Papers, Box 16.

[133] "Statement," Henry A. Bundschu, *Journal of the National Association of Referees in Bankruptcy*, 15 (July 1941), 133.

188

referee in bankruptcy to the relevant circuit council rather than directly to the judges or referees involved.[134] Chief Justice Hughes pressed this modification, contending that "the responsibility of having the administration of justice proper and appropriate is not that of the Director in the various districts," but that of the council.[135] The director, he said, was an investigator and once he obtained the required data, "the responsibility is with the circuit council of the circuit."[136]

Finally, the Conference diluted the director's power to "recommend the removal of incumbent referees by directing him to report to the district court and to the circuit council any knowledge of incompetency, misconduct, inefficiency, or neglect of duty on the referee's part.[137] This change coincided with Chandler's "strong desire . . . that the function of the Director in reference to the removal or reappointment of a referee, would be completed when he makes his report which will go to the district court and judicial council of the circuit. He will be in no sense a prosecuting officer but rather in the nature of a special master, presenting facts as he sees them for appropriate action of the court."[138] Said the director: "I look to the court; I must look to the court . . . to take such measures as [it] may deem necessary."[139]

[134] "Administration of the Bankruptcy Act," *Report of the Attorney General's Committee on Bankruptcy Administration, 1940*, p. 20; see sec. II E.

[135] 1941 Judicial Conference transcript, special session, p. 153, in Henry P. Chandler, "The Beginning of a New Era in Bankruptcy Administration: 1939-1947," *Journal of the National Association of Referees in Bankruptcy*, 34 (January 1960), 25.

[136] *Ibid.*

[137] "Administration of the Bankruptcy Act," *Report of the Attorney General's Committee on Bankruptcy Administration, 1940*, p. 21; see sec. III D(1).

[138] Henry P. Chandler to John M. Niehaus, Jr., November 14, 1941, Administrative Office Correspondence, 59-A-532, Box 3.

[139] Henry P. Chandler, "Proceedings," *Journal of the National Association of Referees in Bankruptcy*, 17 (October 1942), 26.

The office was neither a policeman nor a prosecutor, but purely an investigator. When alleged cases of dilatory, unethical, or illegal conduct in the courts arose, the director might undertake inquiries under the supervision of the Conference, or more likely "under the supervision and very likely with the direction of the Judicial Council of the Circuit, within such limits as are practicable for the Director to observe."[140] However, information on such subjects occasionally reached the director from the Justice Department examiners[141] and even from his own quiet investigation.[142]

In the end it was the judges, not the Administrative Office, which acted or failed to act. Thus the administrators reported their findings and recommendations to the district judge involved or to the chief judge of the relevant court of appeals.[143] Whether or not a lazy judge was relieved "of all duties of any kind, including hearing of motions, until he has decided all matters now pending," or a congested court utilized pretrial procedures, as recommended by the office, rested with the judges or the circuit council.[144] If, however, the alleged conduct involved criminal as distinguished from merely unethical acts, then the director thought it "best . . . to say to the Department of Justice, without consulting the court served by the officer or employee involved, that the

[140] "Excerpt from the Proceedings of the Judicial Conference, October 3, 1940, A Method for Dealing with Complaints Against Judges Made to the Administrative Office," pp. 2-3, Groner Papers, Box 15.

[141] See Leland Tolman to Eugene Rice, February 16, 1950, Administrative Office Correspondence, 60-A-328, Box 22.

[142] Henry P. Chandler to Edwin H. Cassels, May 14, 1941, ibid., 59-A-532, Box 3.

[143] See Henry P. Chandler to Elmore Whitehurst, June 23, 1955, ibid., 59-A-48, Box 142; Henry P. Chandler to Calvert Magruder, February 12, 1954, ibid., 60-A-427, Box 100; Leland Tolman to John J. Parker, April 27, 1953, Clark Papers.

[144] "Report to the Director of the Administrative Office of the United States Courts with Reference to the United States District Court at Newark, New Jersey, by Will Shafroth," January 17-19, 1940, p. 12, Administrative Office Correspondence, 60-A-328, Box 36; see also: Judicial Conference Report, 1940, p. 24.

190

matter seems to be one wholly for the determination of the Department; that if in its opinion there is reasonable cause to believe that offenses have been committed, it should investigate and if evidence warrants, should prosecute."[145]

These early decisions on the scope and nature of the office's power proved definitive. Clearly the Administrative Office was not an independent agency subject only to subsequent supervision by the Conference, but an executive office with strictly limited power. It could not act directly upon the entire range of court personnel from the senior circuit judges to the court clerks;[146] it reached them, if they were reached at all, only through and with the authorization of judge-controlled agencies—the Judicial Conference, the councils, and the individual courts[147]—or with the voluntary consent of judges and their supporting personnel.[148]

Employees of the courts were not employees of the Administrative Office. Their appointment and removal rested not with that agency, but with the individual courts. "Unless the court concerned . . . expressly requested it, I do not propose to volunteer suggestions of persons for appointment," said Director Chandler.[149] That was a prerogative of the judges. Once appointed, an employee's performance on the job lay beyond the director's cognizance. "I really cannot come between him and the judge," asserted Chandler, for "in our judicial system we must rely upon the good

[145] Henry P. Chandler to Harlan F. Stone, October 1, 1941, Administrative Office Correspondence, 57-A-122, Box 2; Henry P. Chandler to Matthew F. McGuire, October 4, 1941, *ibid.*

[146] Henry P. Chandler, "The Administrative Office," *Journal of the National Association of Referees in Bankruptcy*, 16 (October 1941), 18.

[147] Chandler, "The Administrative Office of the United States Courts," *ibid.*, 15 (October 1940), 50.

[148] Edwin L. Covey, "Referees and Their Indemnity Funds and Accounts," *Journal of the National Association of Referees in Bankruptcy*, 17 (October 1942), 9.

[149] Henry P. Chandler, "Report of the Conference of Federal Judges in the Fifth Circuit, May 23-24, 1941," p. 22, Administrative Office Correspondence, 57-A-122, Box 1.

191

faith, the integrity of the judges, to see that proper persons are appointed in their courts."[150] In short, the Administrative Office lacked "the leverage for bringing about the adoption of more efficient procedures that . . . the Department of Justice has in relation to the United States Attorneys and United States marshals who are appointed and subject to removal by the President on the recommendation of the Attorney General."[151]

In spite of the dearth of formal powers over court personnel, the director was charged with broad but often routine administrative responsibilities involving court personnel.[152] Here the office acted in a partial fashion, for like bureaucracies, it sought to "promote uniformity and efficiency and . . . to avert the development of divergent practices."[153]

Nowhere was this administrative philosophy more apparent than in the realm of personnel management. Although the director exercised little direct influence over appointments, he did fix job classifications and authorize compensation levels.[154] This duty compelled him to establish and maintain, against pressure from the courts, fair standards of classification among and between clerks, probation officers, referees, and reporters. "Any substantial change in the grade levels of one of these groups," he warned, "will be

[150] U.S., Congress, House, Subcommittee of Committee on Appropriations, *Hearings, the Judiciary Appropriation Bill For 1948*, 80th Cong., 1st Sess., 1947, pp. 160, 189.

[151] Henry P. Chandler to Philip Young, August 2, 1956, Administrative Office Correspondence, 60-A-427, Box 105A.

[152] See "Report of the Judicial Conference Committee on Ways and Means of Economy in the Operation of the Courts," 1948, mimeograph (Administrative Office of the United States Courts, Washington, D.C.).

[153] Elmore Whitehurst to Henry P. Chandler, August 11, 1949, Administrative Office Correspondence, 60-A-328, Box 3.

[154] Henry P. Chandler, U.S., Congress, House, Subcommittee of Committee on Appropriations, *Hearings, the Judiciary Appropriation Bill for 1944*, 78th Cong., 1st Sess., 1943, p. 35.

likely to cause discontent in the others unless similar adjustments with respect to their grades are made."[155]

Although sanctioned by the Judicial Conference or by law, the office's personnel policies stirred hostility among some judges. They objected to the increasingly centralized character of the administrative system, a trend which continued throughout Chandler's tenure as the traditional part-time, patronage-oriented, and essentially amateur court staffs gave way to those with full-time, salaried professionals.[156] This centralization placed in the director's hands "a means (and a very powerful means) of controlling Circuit Judges and particularly District Judges through the granting or withholding of 'favors.'"[157] Not only that, but, contended District Judge John McDuffie of Alabama, it constituted only the first stage in "a subtle design on the part of those who believe in bureaucracy or statism, which with a deadly grasp is gradually strangling and destroying the ideals of our American form of government . . . [and] the independence, as well as the judicial functions of the District Courts, which are destined to become administrative offices."[158]

Against a background of circumscribed powers, wide responsibilities, and judicial hostility, the Administrative

[155] Elmore Whitehurst, "Memorandum for the [Judicial Conference] Committee on Supporting Personnel with Respect to the Survey of the Clerk's Office, September, 1950," p. 4, Stephens Papers, Box 216.

[156] See minority opinion in "Report of the [Judical Conference] Committee to Consider the Desirability of Extending the Merit System to Cover Personnel of the Clerk's Offices," 1942, mimeograph (Administrative Office of the United States Courts, Washington, D.C.), p. 9; Chandler, "The Beginning of a New Era in Bankruptcy Administration," pp. 3-4; Chandler, "Some Major Advances," pp. 422-23.

[157] John P. Barnes, Philip L. Sullivan, Michael L. Igoe, William J. Campbell, Walter J. LaBuy, Elwyn R. Shaw to the United States District and Circuit Judges, March 29, 1948, negative photostatic copy, Stephens Papers, Box 209.

[158] John McDuffie to Hatton Sumners, July 30, 1945, Legislative Files, H.R. 3338, 79th Cong.

Office attempted to perform its duties. Relatively few strategies were available. Unlike other central agencies, it shaped its efforts largely in terms of "guidance, not directives; of coordination, not command; of suggestions, not instructions; of assistance, not management; of counsel, not superintendence."[159] Clearly the support of judges and court personnel was essential for the office itself enjoyed no coercive powers whatsoever. As Director Chandler so aptly put it, the administrator "must speak softly and carry virtually no stick at all."[160]

To win the support of his clients, the director early established procedures intended "to promote good will."[161] These included presenting to other government agencies such as the Justice Department the needs of judges too remote from Washington to make their own case,[162] as well as prompt and individualized responses to inquiries from the courts.[163] In a similar vein, the director and other members of the office made themselves visible to the far-flung judicial establishment. They purposely visited districts in the Far West to allay the prevailing belief in those remote areas "that because of their distance from Washington they do not have our ear to the extent that nearby districts have; that the eastern districts have an inside track."[164] Visits from agency officials would, declared the assistant director, "dispel that

[159] William L. Ellis to Warren Olney III, November 30, 1960, Administrative Office Correspondence, 61-A-298, Box 2.

[160] Henry P. Chandler, "The Administration of the Federal Courts," *Law and Contemporary Problems*, 13 (Winter 1948), 195.

[161] Chandler, "Some Major Advances," p. 414.

[162] Elmore Whitehurst to Henry P. Chandler, March 12, 1942, Administrative Office Correspondence, 60-A-328, Box 36, stationing an assistant United States attorney at Bay City, Michigan. Some requests were rejected because of the impropriety of influencing the substantive policies of another governmental agency. See Henry P. Chandler to Fred Vinson, June 30, 1952, *ibid.*, 59-A-48, Box 122.

[163] Chandler, "Some Major Advances," p. 414.

[164] Elmore Whitehurst to Henry P. Chandler, undated (1940?), Administrative Office Correspondence, 60-A-328, Box 36.

feeling, would be appreciated; and would contribute materially to the cooperation of those offices with us."[165]

Attendance at, and often participation in, the judicial conferences of the circuits and gatherings of court officials, such as those of the court clerks, referees in bankruptcy, court reporters, and probation officers was also aimed at developing "between the Administrative Office and the personnel of the courts in the field from high to low, a sense of working together and of understanding and sympathy."[166]

To the same end, strategic positions in the various divisions of the Administrative Office were initially filled by appointees clearly acceptable to important blocs of court personnel. Edwin L. Covey, the president of the National Association of Referees in Bankruptcy, became chief of the Bankruptcy Division in an acknowledged bid for the referees' cooperation.[167] Appointment of the supervisor of probation in the Bureau of Prisons as head of the Probation Division was likewise designed to win the loyalty of the probation officers and to assure them of the intention of the new agency "to conserve the values that have been achieved in federal probation by the Bureau."[168]

Even if the leaders of every group affected by the office's policies did not become an integral part of that agency, they were at least co-opted on an *ad hoc* basis. Thus, from numerous meetings between the office and small groups of court clerks, submissions of drafts by their spokesmen, and ratification of the final draft by the clerks themselves, a *Clerk's Manual* emerged.[169]

[165] *Ibid.*; see also Henry P. Chandler to Elmore Whitehurst, August 9, 1952, *ibid.*, Box 35.

[166] Chandler, "Some Major Advances," pp. 419-20.

[167] Henry P. Chandler, "The Administrative Office and the Referees," *Journal of the National Association of Referees in Bankruptcy*, 19 (October 1944), 16.

[168] Henry P. Chandler, "Agency to Supervise Federal Probation," p. 4.

[169] Elmore Whitehurst to Henry P. Chandler, memorandum, August

Co-optation constituted but one strategy; persuasion was another. This strategy assumed many forms, some quite subtle. It included demonstrations of the "best techniques" or of special equipment installed in the offices of cooperative clerks and judges. The results were publicized and officials of other courts encouraged to avail themselves of the new methods and machinery.[170] In a similar vein, the clearing-house function of the office was employed to promote selected administrative practices. It "sought information with respect to improved procedures and short cuts,"[171] and then gave wide publicity to those "methods that seem to be successful in meeting particular problems and overcoming particular difficulties . . . so that the best practice of any district may become known to all."[172] As the chief of the Bankruptcy Division put it to a gathering of referees: "We . . . say to you and to the judges . . . 'we believe this way is perhaps a better way of doing it than any other way; not that your way is wrong, but on the basis of our study and investigation, and from our experience, and from our contacts with many referees and judges, these practices seem to be the better.' "[173]

The campaign of persuasion was carried into the field by examiners from the Department of Justice and personnel from the Administrative Office. The office instructed the examiners to assist the clerks by suggesting improved prac-

---

11, 1949, Administrative Office Correspondence, 60-A-328, Box 3. *Judicial Conference Report, 1949*, p. 50.

[170] Elmore Whitehurst, "Business Administration of the United States Courts," *Federal Rules Decisions*, 3 (1944), 314. Elmore Whitehurst to John A. Lowther, November 30, 1956, Administrative Office Correspondence, 60-A-594, Box 3; Lowther to Whitehurst, January 31, 1957, *ibid.*

[171] Whitehurst, "Business Administration," p. 315.

[172] Chandler, "The Administrative Office and the Referees," *Journal of the National Association of Referees in Bankruptcy*, 17 (October 1942), p. 5; Henry P. Chandler to Carroll C. Hincks, February 6, 1943, Administrative Office Correspondence, 60-A-328, Box 36.

[173] Edwin L. Covey, "Referees and Their Indemnity Funds and Accounts," p. 9.

tices and procedures,[174] a task performed with widely divergent skill by different examiners.[175] Likewise the small staff of the Administrative Office traveled about the country advising court personnel on the most efficacious methods of administration.[176]

The voice of the Administrative Office was usually one of exhortation as it struggled "to promote compliance with the standards of qualifications recommended by the Judicial Conference,"[177] and with requirements firmly set by law.[178] Its officials called on courts to experiment with new administrative procedures[179] and to adopt new rules of court such as those in bankruptcy intended to "make the court practice so plain that no referee with any intelligence could mistake it."[180]

Publicity constituted the ultimate weapon available to the office. Judges found it difficult to ignore the publication of statistics reflecting the judicial output of the courts, for such publicity exposed derelict judges to the censure of their peers.[181] Thus when an "Appendix" attached to one quarter-

[174] Leland Tolman, "Address to the Judicial Conference of the Tenth Circuit," 1951, Administrative Office Correspondence, 60-A-328, Box 1.

[175] Elmore Whitehurst to Henry P. Chandler, December 29, 1943, ibid., Box 35.

[176] Chandler, "The Beginning of a New Era in Bankruptcy Administration," pp. 46-47.

[177] "Comments in the Report of the Senate Subcommittee on Juvenile Delinquency on the Federal Probation Service," April 12, 1954, mimeograph (Administrative Office of the United States Courts, Washington, D.C.), pp. 2-3.

[178] Chandler, "The Beginning of a New Era," p. 5.

[179] Henry P. Chandler, House Subcommittee of Committee on Appropriations, Hearings, Department of Justice Appropriation Bill for 1942, p. 640.

[180] Henry P. Chandler, House Subcommittee of Committee on Appropriations, Hearings, the Judiciary Appropriation Bill for 1944, 1943, p. 65.

[181] See Henry P. Chandler, "An Administrative Office for State Courts," Journal of the American Judicature Society, 26 (June 1942),

ly report from the agency emphasized the disparities among judges in cases decided, one irate judge remarked that the report distinguished those "who made the 'dean's list' [and] the goats in the Federal Judiciary."[182] Nevertheless, the pointed publicity given judicial shortcomings in the director's reports brought results. "That the district judges are under supervision as to the volume of work they get out, how long it takes, the period of pendency, and that sort of thing has the greatest effect on the dispatch of business that I know of," declared Senior Circuit Judge William Denman of the Ninth Circuit.[183] "The very fact," he continued, "that they are conscious that it is being watched, that these reports come into us, results in the necessary pressure on a judge to catch up with his work."[184]

But persuasion, education, and publicity did not always suffice. Judges flatly refused to comply with policies of the office[185] and invoked the aid of friendly congressmen to secure their modification, sometimes successfully.[186] Under these circumstances, the centripetal impulses brought to

---

9; James W. Morris to Bolitha Laws, October 11, 1950, Stephens Papers, Box 35.

[182] Vincent L. Leibell to the Judges of the United States Court of Appeals, Second Circuit, February 26, 1951, Clark Papers.

[183] U.S., Congress, Senate, Subcommittee of Committee on Appropriations, *Hearings, Departments of State, Justice, Commerce and the Judiciary Appropriation Bill for 1952*, part I, 82d Cong., 1st Sess., 1951, p. 421.

[184] *Ibid.*

[185] Charles E. Clark to John M. Harlan, October 27, 1954, Clark Papers.

[186] See "Supplemental Memorandum in Connection with the Estimates for the Annual Appropriations for 1955, September 15, 1953," mimeograph (Administrative Office of the United States Courts, Washington, D.C.); for congressional intervention in the personnel program, see the following exchanges (all in Administrative Office Correspondence, 60-A-594, Box 3): E. L. Allen to Elmore Whitehurst, May 21, 1956; Whitehurst to Allen, May 25, 1956; Olin D. Johnston to Whitehurst, June 4, 1956; Whitehurst to Johnston, June 6, 1956; Whitehurst to Allen, June 6, 1956; Whitehurst to Johnston, June 25, 1956.

bear on the federal courts by the Administrative Office were ever confronted by an imposing array of centrifugal pressures. Nevertheless, the years of the Chandler administration witnessed a rising tide of administrative centralism, however halting and impotent it appeared.

CHAPTER 6

The Administrative Office
of the United States Courts, Part II

Staff and Liaison: The Judicial Conference

IN addition to administering an increasing number of programs for the courts, the Administrative Office performed
crucial staff and liaison functions. It became the secretariat
for the Judicial Conference and its committees and an instrument of liaison between the judicial system and Congress, individual judges, professional organizations, and
other governmental agencies. Thus the office undertook
tasks which had been either performed by the Justice Department, however inadequately, or not performed at all.
And so from its earliest years, the agency rendered a wide
variety of staff services to the Judicial Conference and the
many committees of that body. The Division of Procedural
Studies and Statistics, for instance, provided the Conference, as had attorneys general since Harry Daugherty, with
data on the volume of business in the federal courts together with analyses of congested districts.[1] Similarly, the
director gathered information on the availability of judges
for intercircuit assignments, "indicating the district judges
who are available for such assignments and the relative
needs of the districts to which assignments are to be
made."[2]

As important, if not more so, the agency acted as a reception center and clearing house for information and proposals directed to the Conference. These demands for
changes in the *status quo* emanated from a multitude of
sources. Conference committees and their chairmen, indi-

[1] "Report of the Judicial Conference," *Judicial Conference Report,*
1940, pp. 19-23.
[2] *Ibid., 1941*, p. 30.

200

vidual judges, congressmen, circuit conferences, court employees, the bar, and legal scholars and newspapermen all constituted fertile sources.[3] And this flow of suggestions, objections, and information emanated with the encouragement of the office. As Director Chandler told the 1942 meeting of the National Association of Referees in Bankruptcy: "If it should be the judgment of this association . . . if it should be the thought of the national bankruptcy conference, or if it should be the thought of any individual referee or judge that changes should be made in the bankruptcy act . . . the Administrative Office would be very glad to receive such suggestions, and if . . . deemed . . . sufficiently weighty, submit them to the Judicial Conference."[4]

During the Chandler administration, the office was more than a conduit for such information. Its director also drew up tentative agenda for Conference sessions,[5] presented them to the Chief Justice,[6] and "after he approves, with

[3] Henry P. Chandler to Members of the Judicial Conference, August 3, 1948, Stephens Papers, Box 211. John J. Parker to Henry P. Chandler, September 14, 1954, *ibid.*, Box 233; Claude McColloch to John Biggs, telegram, March 22, 1949, *ibid.*, Box 213; Will Shafroth, memorandum, undated, *ibid.*, Box 219; Memorandum on the Judicial Conference of the Sixth Circuit, January 12 and 13, [?], Administrative Office Correspondence, 59-A-532, Box 1. "Statement," Irwin Kurtz, *Journal of the National Association of Referees in Bankruptcy*, 19 (October 1944), 4; "Report of the Committee on Jurisprudence and Law Reform," *Annual Report of the American Bar Association*, 66 (1941), 143; Henry P. Chandler to Members of the Judicial Conference, September 9, 1942, Groner Papers, Box 17. Henry P. Chandler to Chief Justice and Members of the Advisory Committee of the Judicial Conference of Senior Circuit Judges, August 3, 1948, mimeograph (Administrative Office of the United States Courts, Washington, D.C.).

[4] Henry P. Chandler, "The Administrative Office and the Referees," *Journal of the National Association of Referees in Bankruptcy*, 17 (October 1942), 7.

[5] Henry P. Chandler to the Chief Justice and Members of the Advisory Committee, August 3, 1948.

[6] Henry P. Chandler to Charles E. Clark, September 13, 1951, Clark Papers.

such changes as he may wish," Chandler submitted them to the Conference Advisory Committee for approval. "When that is accomplished," related the director, "the agenda are sent to all of the circuit and district judges with an invitation to submit any comments on any of the topics or any other subjects which they think should have the attention of the Judicial Conference."[7]

In addition to organizing and circulating the Conference agenda, the office suggested discussion assignments for the several senior circuit judges,[8] as well as likely candidates for appointment to posts on the Conference committees.[9] Once constituted, the committees, usually through their chairmen, sought and received advice from the office. The agency never really staffed the committees in the sense that it could perform any and all research tasks necessary for effective committee performance.[10] But hope sprang eternal. The 1968 Conference "agreed that the staff of the Administrative Office should be augmented in order that [it] may perform fully and adequately the staff functions required by the Conference committees and subcommittees. . . ."[11] In the meantime, the Conference contented itself with a request that agency representatives "attend all committee and subcommittee meetings, record the minutes of such meetings and under the guidance of committee chairmen prepare necessary preliminary studies as well as the drafts

[7] Henry P. Chandler to Earl Warren, July 16, 1954, Administrative Office Correspondence, 59-A-48, Box 122.

[8] Henry P. Chandler, undated memorandum, "The Work of the Judicial Conference and Suggestions for its Discussion," ibid., 59-A-1536, Box 1.

[9] Henry P. Chandler to Harlan Fiske Stone, October 7, 1942, ibid., 60-A-328, Box 4.

[10] Interview with John Biggs, Jr., February 28, 1965, Wilmington, Delaware. See also Leland Tolman to Members of the Judicial Conference Committee on Pretrial Procedure in the Federal Courts, November 19, 1943, mimeograph (Administrative Office of the United States Courts, Washington, D.C.), pp. 1-8.

[11] Judicial Conference Report, 1968, p. 45.

of committee reports and any other staff functions required for the proper implementation of committee work."[12]

Even in earlier years, however, the Office had performed many services for committees; so many, in fact, that Assistant Director Whitehurst could confidently state that "the availability of the machinery and staff of the Administrative Office has . . . contributed to the effective functioning of these committees."[13] However, a major share of this "machinery and staff" was devoted to housekeeping functions, such as the duplication of questionnaires, memoranda, and committee reports, their circulation among the judges, collation of the replies,[14] and the facilitating of communications between committee chairmen and their membership[15] and between the Conference and committee chairmen.[16]

As might be expected, the Division of Procedural Studies and Statistics made its facilities available to the committees of the Conference.[17] These resources proved of particular assistance to committee chairmen in their legislative liaison role. From the division, they received data to support their arguments presented to the several committees of Congress.[18] Formal statements and letters of explanation accom-

[12] *Ibid.*, pp. 45-46.

[13] Elmore Whitehurst, "Business Administration of the United States Courts," *Federal Rules Decisions*, 3 (1944), 317.

[14] See "Memorandum Regarding the Court Reporting System," September 10, 1947, mimeograph (Administrative Office of the United States Courts, Washington, D.C.).

[15] Wilson F. Collier to Charles E. Clark, May 31, 1956, Clark Papers.

[16] Henry P. Chandler to Members of the Judicial Conference, May 5, 1954, Administrative Office Correspondence, 60-A-328, Box 27.

[17] See Harry E. Watkins to Leland Tolman, April 13, 1953, *ibid.*, Box 29, and Tolman to Watkins, April 17, 1953, *ibid.*; Will Shafroth to Harold M. Stephens, January 23, 1952, Stephens Papers, Box 179; "Report of the Committee on the Operation of the Jury System, Excerpt from Agenda 13," September, 1953, mimeograph (Administrative Office of the United States Courts, Washington, D.C.), p. 9.

[18] Will Shafroth to Harold M. Stephens, December 27, 1954, Stephens Papers, Box 118; Kimbrough Stone to Pat A. McCarran, January 8, 1946, Kimbrough Stone Papers, Box 24.

panying proposed legislation also originated in the office, even though it was the judges, not the administrators, who transmitted them to Congress.[19]

Advice on legislative strategies also originated in the Administrative Office. When Director Chandler received word of impending hearings on a bill later disapproved by the Judicial Conference,[20] he alerted Senior Circuit Judge John J. Parker. The director reported that Chief Justice Hughes believed Parker should be given an opportunity to testify. "I do not urge you to come," Chandler wrote. "Nevertheless I know that if you do you will present most strongly the undesirable consequences that would be likely to flow from the proposed measure and you will have much weight with the Committee."[21]

Instructions on other lobbying techniques also emanated from the Office. Chief of Business Administration, Leland Tolman, once urged Judge John C. Knox, then chairman of the Committee on the Operation of the Jury System, to "write to those members of the Senate and House who have shown an interest in the [jury] legislation, reminding them of it and asking them to do their best to secure its passage."[22] Then followed a list of likely candidates for the judge's pen, as well as the recommendation that he per-

[19] Elmore Whitehurst to Harold M. Stephens, March 11, 1952, Stephens Papers, Box 211; Stephens to Whitehurst, March 15, 1952, *ibid.*

[20] H.R. 138, 77th Cong., limited the conditions under which circuit judges might sit in district courts and district judges might sit in circuit courts. It also prohibited assignment of circuit judges to sit in district courts without request or consent of the relevant senior district judges. *Judicial Conference Report, 1941*, pp. 34-35.

[21] Henry P. Chandler to John J. Parker, March 27, 1941, Parker Papers, Box 54. Parker testified against H.R. 138 on April 23 and May 7, 1941. See U.S. Congress, Senate, Subcommittee of the Committee on the Judiciary, *Hearings, on S. 1050, S. 1051, S. 1052, S. 1053, S. 1054, and H.R. 138, Administration of United States Courts*, 77th Cong., 1st Sess., 1941, pp. 23-31, 44-47.

[22] Leland Tolman to John C. Knox, January 22, 1948, Administrative Office Correspondence, 60-A-328, Box 4.

sonally confer with the chairman of the House Judiciary Committee.[23]

Although some judges warned against "a director who could formulate policy,"[24] the office never confined itself to mere data-gathering. In fact, the Act of 1939 required the director to submit to the Conference a report on the activities of his office as well as his recommendations,[25] and from the beginning the new agency initiated policies later considered by the Conference and its committees. It did so with the encouragement of the judges. Ranking members of the Conference fully expected the office, in the words of Judge Albert Maris, chairman of the Committee on Revision of the Laws, "to cooperate by giving us many useful suggestions as to modifications of the present [judicial] code."[26] One "activist" judge articulated this expectation even more forcefully. The Administrative Office, he argued, should not "look to the Judicial Conference as 'a starter.' To the contrary . . . the Judicial Conference, if it is to be vital and worthwhile, must have someone to 'start them.' . . . 'The flow of ideas, suggestions, improvements, et cetera' should be *from* the Administrative Office *to* the Judicial Conference and not vice versa."[27]

In this judge's mind, the single greatest criticism of the Office under Chandler's leadership was "that it did not 'step out enough.' "[28] Not all judges sided with this view, however; and so the director followed a "middle way." It was a way which permitted him to "step out" but only within

[23] *Ibid.*; see also Henry P. Chandler to Xenophon Hicks, April 20, 1950, *ibid.*, 59-A-532, Box 1.

[24] Harold R. Medina, "The Work of the Administrative Office of the United States Courts," *Federal Rules Decisions*, 11 (1952), 357.

[25] 53 *Stat.* 1224, sec. 305.

[26] Albert Maris to Harold M. Stephens, November 29, 1944, Stephens Papers, Box 71.

[27] Charles E. Clark, quoted in Aubrey Gasque to Warren Olney III, memorandum, June 6, 1958, Administrative Office Correspondence, 59-A-48, Box 141.

[28] *Ibid.*

rather severely circumscribed limits. Usually, this meant the power of positive suggestions, suggestions of "rather definite ways in which the recommendations of the committee [on economies in the operation of the jury system] may be carried out,"[29] suggestions that the committee challenge the failure of the congested district court in the Southern District of New York to utilize a jury pool effectively,[30] and suggestions that the existing jurors' manual required revision.[31]

Liaison with Congress

Establishment of the Administrative Office also created a new medium for liaison between the Judicial Conference and Congress. The agency had initial responsibility for presenting to congressional leaders and to the committees of Congress recommendations of the Conference, especially those pertaining to additional judgeships and appropriations.[32] It also acted as a clearing house for legislation pending in Congress by reporting to the Conference on those measures relating to the federal judiciary. But the system had its faults because occasionally during the 1940s and 1950s, "legislative matters, in which the Judiciary had a very vital interest, have been acted upon by the Committees of the Congress without an opportunity having been extended to the Judiciary for the purpose of making known

[29] Henry P. Chandler to Chief Justice and Members of the Judicial Conference, September 15, 1950, mimeograph (Administrative Office of the United States Courts, Washington, D.C.), p. 3.

[30] Leland Tolman to Members of the Judicial Conference Committee on Operation of the Jury System, July 2, 1953, Administrative Office Correspondence, 60-A-328, Box 29.

[31] Leland Tolman to Harry E. Watkins, December 9, 1952, ibid.

[32] Harold M. Stephens to Chief Justice and Members of the Judicial Conference, March 21, 1955, Stephens Papers, Box 234; Henry P. Chandler to Pat McCarran, December 30, 1948, Administrative Office Correspondence, 60-A-328, Box 5.

its views concerning the proposals."[33] To obviate such over-sights, the 1952 Conference successfully urged congressional committees to "call upon the Judiciary, through the Director of the Administrative Office, for an expression of views on proposals which have been presented that may affect the Judiciary."[34] The Conference, not the office, expressed these views for the latter stood in relation to the Conference as an agent rather than as a principal. Interpreting the Act of 1939, which placed the director "under the supervision and direction of the Judicial Conference,"[35] the 1940 Conference construed "supervision" to mean ratification by the full complement of senior circuit judges of the "action of the . . . Director . . . in reference to the estimates for the appropriations."[36] This review of the 1941 appropriations, said Director Chandler, set "a firm precedent . . . for direct control by the entire body of the Judicial Conference of the estimates for the appropriations . . . and for the principles to govern all actions of the Director of consequence."[37] It soon came to mean that he exceeded his power should he advance "any opinion concerning a bill pending in Congress without prior authority from the Judicial Conference."[38]

This requirement posed difficulties when a measure appeared in Congress on which no Conference position existed but on which one was requested by Congress during the long Conference recess. Several alternatives lay

[33] *Judicial Conference Report, 1952*, p. 224.

[34] *Ibid.* This usually meant an expression of the Conference's views. However, legislation establishing new places of holding court went to the circuit councils, a procedure prescribed for the director by the Conference. See Henry P. Chandler to William Langer, May 21, 1954, Administrative Office Correspondence, 59-A-1536, Box 1.

[35] See Act of August 7, 1939, 53 *Stat.* 1223.

[36] *Judicial Conference Report, 1940*, Special Session, p. 14.

[37] Henry P. Chandler, "Some Major Advances in the Federal Judicial System: 1922-1947," *Federal Rules Decisions*, 31 (1963), 413.

[38] Henry P. Chandler to D. Lawrence Groner, June 17, 1943, Groner Papers, Box 16.

open to the director in such a circumstance. He might infer the Conference's attitude from a previous resolution relating to the subject matter of the pending bill.[39] Or, his response could be couched in neutral terms, thereby risking passage of the bill because "it might appear to the Congress that the Judicial Conference has no interest in the legislation."[40] More commonly, however, he consulted with and sought a new delegation of power from at least one member of the Conference's Advisory Committee and the Chief Justice, or from the members of the Conference by means of a poll.[41]

In its liaison role, the office performed more than routine communications functions. Its officials labored to smooth the way for Conference policies. They intervened in the politics of the American Bar Association and actively sought that organization's endorsement of Conference policies.[42] After some early stumbling, they strove to ameliorate conflicts with the Department of Justice over proposed legislation,[43] conflicts often rooted in the department's ignorance of the Conference's views.[44] They also worked closely with the Judiciary and Appro-

[39] Ibid.

[40] Harold M. Stephens to Henry P. Chandler, July 29, 1954, Stephens Papers, Box 182; Harold M. Stephens to William Langer, July 8, 1954, ibid. The bill involved was S. 3517, 83d Cong.

[41] Henry P. Chandler to Members of the Judicial Conference, "Memorandum in Reference to the Mileage Rate for the Use of Privately Owned Automobiles by Personnel of the Courts while on Official Travel, September 16, 1948," mimeograph (Administrative Office of the United States Courts, Washington, D.C.).

[42] Henry P. Chandler to Albert E. Jenner, Jr., February 10, 1956, Administrative Office Correspondence, 59-A-532, Box 3; on subject of Chandler's letter, see Judicial Conference Report, 1956, pp. 100-01.

[43] See Henry P. Chandler and Alexander Holtzoff, U.S., Congress, Senate, Subcommittee of the Committee on the Judiciary, Hearings on S. 1050, 1941, pp. 14-15.

[44] Leland Tolman to John J. Parker, February 1, 1952, Administrative Office Correspondence, 60-A-328, Box 15. See also H.R. 6157, 82d Cong.

priations Committees of Congress, providing them with a steady stream of information, chiefly statistical compilations,[45] and, in more direct fashion, lobbying congressmen. When, in 1954, the Circuit Council of the Ninth Circuit protested a measure introduced by Senate Majority Leader William Knowland of California which established a new division of court, Leland Tolman, a member of the office's staff, carried the council's case to Capitol Hill. Prior to the convening of the Senate, he "called the Ninth Circuit Council Resolution to the attention of members of the staff of the Senate Judiciary Committee and took a copy to the floor of the Senate." He then spent the remainder of the day "following the progress of the calendar call."[46] When his efforts failed in the Senate, he turned to the House. Letters were written to key California congressmen alerting them to the council's position[47] and to the chairman of the House Judiciary Committee.[48] Meanwhile, Director Chandler found the California congressman from the affected district, assured him "that the Judiciary Committee of the House would not touch the resolution, . . . read him some of the recitals of the [council] resolution, and emphasized . . . that the Judicial Council recommends that the Congress do not enact the House Resolution, [and] said that at a time when the Congress was stressing the policy of economy it would be inconsistent and extravagant to divide the quarters and the judges."[49] A majority of the Judiciary Committee agreed and pigeonholed the measure.[50]

Although the Administrative Office maintained liaison

[45] See Elbert D. Tuttle to Will Shafroth, August 16, 1949, Stephens Papers, Box 38.

[46] Leland Tolman to Louis E. Goodman, August 10, 1954, Administrative Office Correspondence, 59-A-1536, Box 1; the measure involved was S.J. Res. 158, 83d Cong.

[47] Ibid.

[48] Leland Tolman, memorandum to Henry P. Chandler, August 11, 1954, ibid.

[49] Henry P. Chandler to Louis E. Goodman, August 16, 1954, ibid.

[50] Chandler to Goodman, August 19, 1954, ibid.

with both the Judiciary and Appropriations Committees, the truly vital relationship existed with the latter committee. Administrative policies set by the Conference largely revolved about the issues of money and manpower for the courts. Both depended on the budget, and the budget, though subject to Conference review and amendment, was largely a product of the office,[51] and more particularly of its director.[52] And in the formulation and presentation to Congress of the highly complex budget, the influence of the director and his staff was decisive.

Reflecting the conservative influence of Chief Justice Hughes[53] and, in the eyes of some judges, the "overconservative" attitude of the director himself,[54] Chandler's administration invariably produced "rock bottom" budgets.[55] His policy was "to fix appropriations requested at amounts sincerely believed to be necessary, and to refuse to add something on the theory that reduction is inevitable and that if there is a margin in the amounts asked there will be a better chance that what is left will be enough."[56] According to Chandler, "Nothing was added for the contingency of adverse action in the Congress."[57]

The estimates were not merely "honest." They were conservative to begin with, because, said Chandler, this offered "the course most likely to win the respect and good will of the Congress and to promote the interests of the courts in

[51] Henry P. Chandler to Chief Judges of the United States Courts of Appeals and District Courts, March 5, 1952, mimeograph (Administrative Office of the United States Courts, Washington, D.C.).

[52] Chandler, "Some Major Advances," pp. 417-18.

[53] Evan A. Evans to Henry P. Chandler, May 17, 1947, Administrative Office Correspondence, 59-A-532, Box 2.

[54] "Address of Harold M. Stephens," *Nebraska Law Review*, 34 (January 1955), 410.

[55] Chandler, "Some Major Advances," pp. 416-18.

[56] Henry P. Chandler, "The Administration of the Federal Courts," *Law and Contemporary Problems*, 13 (Winter 1948), 193.

[57] Chandler, "Some Major Advances," p. 416.

the long run."[58] But even the "honest" and conservative Chandler budget was subject to further reduction by the Conference and its committees. These bodies pared requests to the level at which favorable congressional action might be anticipated,[59] which, lamented one judge, meant taking them "down almost to the bone."[60] Nevertheless, the paring process continued even after the estimates cleared the Conference. The Bureau of the Budget, although unable to reduce the judiciary's estimates, might well note, in its transmittal letters to the appropriations committees, discrepancies between the estimates and the requirements of the President's program and suggest specific reductions.[61]

Ultimately, this budget, comprising less than one percent of the total federal budget,[62] came before a subcommittee of the powerful House Appropriations Committee. The representatives of the courts who presented and defended the budget constituted "as a practical matter the only [contact] between the people of the United States, through their representatives in the Congress, and the judiciary so far as the needs of the courts for efficient operation are concerned."[63]

[58] Henry P. Chandler to Chief Justice and Members of the Judicial Conference, "Ways and Means of Conforming Expenditures with the Appropriations for Salaries of Supporting Personnel and Travel and Miscellaneous Expenses in 1955," September 13, 1954, mimeograph (Administrative Office of the United States Courts, Washington, D.C.), p. 15.

[59] See Bolitha Laws to John Rooney, June 19, 1952, Stephens Papers, Box 24.

[60] John Biggs, Jr., U.S., Congress, House, Subcommittee of Committee on Appropriations, Hearings, on Third Supplemental Appropriation Bill for 1952, 82d Cong., 2d Sess., 1952, p. 32.

[61] Harold M. Stephens to Judges of the Circuit Court of Appeals for the District of Columbia, memorandum, April 8, 1953, Stephens Papers, Box 89; Louis Ludlow, U.S., Congress, House, Committee on Appropriations, Hearings, on Second Deficiency Appropriation Bill for 1946, 79th Cong., 2d Sess., 1946, p. 140.

[62] See Judicial Conference Report, 1953, p. 9.

[63] Harold M. Stephens, U.S., Congress, Senate, Subcommittee of

211

There, the judiciary made its case before a committee, none of whose members sat on the Judiciary Committee which had originally authorized the programs to be funded,[64] few of whom knew anything about them,[65] and all of whom perceived every agency's budget merely as "an asking price"[66] ready for the proverbial axe.

From these legislators emanated a broadside of critical inquiries, remarks, and observations:

Are these positions really needed, or are they sinecures?[67] Jurors are called and not used, and that amounts to a great many hundreds of thousands of dollars.[68]

Here is one branch which should be able to practice some economy.[69]

These remarks, and many others like them, combined with outright insults placed on the defensive a director "not authorized to express opinions on questions of policy without consulting with the Judicial Conference."[70] Somewhat

---

Committee on the Judiciary, *Hearings, on Senate Concurrent Resolution 4-5, Invitation to the Chief Justice of the United States to Address the Congress*, 84th Cong., 1st Sess., 1955, p. 37.

[64] Richard F. Fenno, "The House Appropriations Committee as a Political System: The Problem of Integration," *American Political Science Review*, 56 (June 1962), 310-24.

[65] D. Lawrence Groner to John J. Parker, June 6, 1944, Groner Papers, Box 18.

[66] Peter Wyden, "The Man Who Frightens Bureaucrats," *Saturday Evening Post*, January 31, 1959, p. 87.

[67] Clarence Cannon, U.S., Congress, House, Subcommittee of Committee on Appropriations, *Hearings, on First Deficiency Appropriation Bill for 1946*, part I, 79th Cong., 1st Sess., 1946, p. 65.

[68] Frank T. Bow, U.S., Congress, House, Subcommittee of Committee on Appropriations, *Hearings, on the Second Supplemental Appropriation Bill for 1959*, 86th Cong., 1st Sess., 1959, p. 17.

[69] John Rooney, House Subcommittee of Committee on Appropriations, *Hearings on Third Supplemental, 1952*, p. 32.

[70] Henry P. Chandler, U.S., Congress, Senate, Subcommittee of Committee on Appropriations, *Hearings, on Legislative and Judiciary Appropriation Bill for 1944*, 77th Cong., 2d Sess., 1943, p. 23; for

verbose by nature and possessed of detailed knowledge,[71] Chandler felt "especially baffled in efforts to explain the court's needs by the short time which the subcommittee of the House Appropriations Committee can give."[72] Enjoying "no standing with Congress,"[73] the director found the endorsement of the Judicial Conference carried little weight in the Appropriations Committees,[74] while the comments of the Budget Bureau, or even the lack thereof, invariably hurt.[75] In no case did the judiciary have the kind of "clout" enjoyed by the F.B.I., nor even that which it once had as an appendage of the executive branch.[76]

In these circumstances, Director Chandler perceived himself less as an agent of the judiciary than as a neutral broker, as one "able to act as a medium of interpretation reciprocally to the courts and to Congress of the point of view of the other."[77] It was his conviction that "what Congress

director's complaints of treatment, see Henry P. Chandler to Harlan Fiske Stone, February 13, 1946, Administrative Office Correspondence, 59-A-532, Box 2; for examples of the insult strategy see Kenneth McKellar, U.S., Congress, Senate, Subcommittee of the Committee on Appropriations, *Hearings, on First Deficiency Bill for 1946*, 79th Cong., 1st Sess., 1946, p. 12, and Prince H. Preston, House Subcommittee of Committee on Appropriations, *Hearings on Third Supplemental, 1952*, p. 35.

[71] Chandler, "Some Major Advances," pp. 417-18.

[72] Henry P. Chandler, Address, "Legislation Affecting the Courts," p. 4, 1947, Administrative Office Correspondence, 60-A-328, Box 27.

[73] Harold M. Stephens to George C. Sweeney, April 30, 1945, Stephens Papers, Box 85.

[74] John Rooney, U.S., Congress, House, Subcommittee of Committee on Appropriations, *Hearings, on the Judiciary Appropriation Bill for 1953*, 82d Cong., 2d Sess., 1952, p. 73.

[75] See 63 *Stat.* 78; John Rooney, House Subcommittee of Committee on Appropriations, *Hearings on Third Supplemental, 1952*, pp. 31-32.

[76] Stephens, "Address of Harold M. Stephens," *Nebraska Law Review*, 34, 412. See also Harold M. Stephens, Senate Subcommittee of Committee on Judiciary, *Hearings on Senate Concurrent Resolution 4-5*, 1955, p. 36.

[77] Henry P. Chandler, "The Administrative Office of the United States Courts," *Federal Rules Decisions*, 2 (1943), 59.

thinks of the way the courts function will count for legislation more than any direct efforts at persuasion."[78] But the more he identified with the near-at-hand and singleminded congressional constituency, the more his displeased judicial constituency suspected that their director was not so much an advocate of their cause before the House Appropriations Committee, as an "agent for [the] committee in keeping down expenses."[79]

Change and Status Quoism

Whether they involved relations with individual courts and judges, assistance to the Judicial Conference and its committees, or liaison with Congress, new demands were placed upon the Administrative Office during the Chandler years. To them, the office typically responded in a conservative and hesitant fashion. Nevertheless, by the late 1940s, the necessity for some changes had become apparent.

A major share of the duties of the office then fell on the director and especially on his assistant, Elmore Whitehurst, who also served as chief of the Division of Business Administration. The original plan of organization had called for separate individuals to hold each position,[80] as the former involved developing general policies for the agency while the latter required close attention to highly detailed administrative problems relating to legislation and salary classification. With the growth of the office's responsibilities, the expected occurred.

More and more, Chandler found himself swamped with decisions on general policies, but deprived of the services of "Mr. Whitehurst, bound down as he is with these [de-

---

[78] Chandler, "Legislation Affecting the Courts," p. 11, Administrative Office Correspondence, 60-A-328, Box 27.

[79] Albert B. Maris, U.S., Congress, House, Subcommittee of Committee on Appropriations, *Hearings, on Legislative-Judiciary Appropriation for 1955*, 83d Cong., 2d Sess., 1954, p. 66.

[80] Chandler, "Some Major Advances," p. 400.

tailed administrative] duties."[81] The Judicial Conference, too, evinced dissatisfaction with the agency's supervision of office management by the court clerks and in 1948 urged "the appointment of an additional member to the staff of the Administrative Office to be charged with the duty of conducting a continuous study of the processes used in handling the business matters of the courts."[82] Shortly thereafter, the posts of assistant director and chief of the Business Administration Division were completely separated.[83]

Effective legislative liaison had been among the functions of the office deemed paramount by the framers of the Administrative Office Act. At least one had seen the director as "a means of direct contact with Congress, which we have never had before," and he expressed the hope that "it will be made one of his duties to keep a very careful track of any legislation introduced which might affect the courts in any way."[84]

The judge's expectations were only partially realized,[85] and the consequent unsatisfactory results induced Chief Judge Harold Stephens of the Court of Appeals in the District of Columbia to call for employment of a lawyer "charged with informing the Conference of the nature and status of pending legislation."[86] The suggestion met with a lukewarm reception from Director Chandler who was "desirous of keeping the staff . . . as moderate as possible."

[81] U.S., Congress, House, Subcommittee of the Committee on Appropriations, *Hearings, on the Judiciary Appropriation Bill for 1948,* 80th Cong., 1st Sess., 1947, p. 218.

[82] *Judicial Conference Report, 1948,* p. 37.

[83] *Ibid.,* 1949, pp. 54-55.

[84] Kimbrough Stone, Judicial Conference of the United States Courts of the Eighth Circuit, January 4 and 6, 1940, stenographic transcript, p. 282, Kimbrough Stone Papers, Box 26.

[85] Harold M. Stephens to Members of the Judicial Conference, March 21, 1955, Stephens Papers, Box 234.

[86] Harold M. Stephens to Henry P. Chandler, April 9, 1954, *ibid.,* Box 90.

215

Moreover, he expressed apprehension "that by following this suggestion we should add a person at increased cost to the government without very much advantage to the courts."[87] When the judges disagreed, Chandler changed his mind and urged the September 1954 Conference to authorize his employment of a "lawyer of substantial experience and capacity and at substantial compensation."[88] After some delay, the new position was filled in 1958.[89]

The director's reaction to Stephens' suggestion had been very much in character. Throughout his nearly two decades as head of the agency, he successfully sought to keep it small and personal. Thus during his first decade, the staff of the Administrative Office had increased from a mere 91 employees at the end of 1941 to 118, a rise of approximately 30 percent.[90] To some members of the Judicial Conference, this conservative policy, reflecting the ideological preferences of Chief Justice Hughes and Judge Groner, placed the office "on extremely short rations from the standpoint of manpower."[91] But, as Chandler's assistant director stated, "We are definitely not 'Empire Builders.' We don't want to be. We think that when you get larger something is lost."[92] Not least among the "something lost" would be the highly

[87] Memorandum, Henry P. Chandler to Elmore Whitehurst, April 16, 1954, Administrative Office Correspondence, 60-A-328, Box 27.

[88] Henry P. Chandler to Members of the Judicial Conference, memorandum, "Suggestion by Judge Stephens and Judge Biggs that a Legislative Lawyer be Added to the Staff of the Administrative Office," September 14, 1954, mimeograph (Administrative Office of the United States Courts, Washington, D.C.).

[89] Judicial Conference Report, 1958, p. 65.

[90] Ibid., 1950, p. 48.

[91] John Biggs, Jr., U.S., Congress, Senate, Subcommittee of Committee on Appropriations, Hearings, on H.R. 7343, Departments of State, Justice, the Judiciary, and Related Agencies Appropriations for 1960, 86th Cong., 1st Sess., 1959, p. 526.

[92] Elmore Whitehurst, "Address by Elmore Whitehurst," Journal of the National Association of Referees in Bankruptcy, 27 (April 1953), 66.

personal control over the office exercised by a director who "made it a point to familiarize [himself] with what all the divisions of the office were doing and to understand and take the responsibility for all actions."[93] Not only did Chandler know the functions of every member of his staff, but he "passed upon all action out of the ordinary before it was taken and thus was protected against surprise or embarrassment because of something done by someone else in the office under delegated authority." The budget, the "delicate matter of quarters and equipment for the courts," statistical reports, and "in fact . . . every phase of the work of the office" reached his desk for final approval.[94] This kind of personal control would end with Chandler's retirement in 1956, and with its termination would come an infusion of specialization and a climate more receptive to innovation.

The Olney Administration

Warren Olney's tenure as director, unlike that of his predecessor, began amid demands that the office "must expand the reach and scope of its work beyond the keeping of statistics and housekeeping."[95] The new director agreed, candidly admitting that "heretofore the service rendered by the Administrative Office to the district courts has amounted to little more than housekeeping and the maintenance of statistical records."[96] Yet even in performing these functions, the office fell short of expectations.[97]

[93] Chandler, "Some Major Advances," p. 413.
[94] Ibid., p. 414.
[95] Warren E. Burger, "Courts on Trial: A Call for Action Against Delay," Federal Rules Decisions, 22 (1958), 83.
[96] U.S., Congress, House, Subcommittee of the Committee on Appropriations, Hearings, Departments of State and Justice, the Judiciary, and Related Agencies Appropriations for 1960, The Judiciary, 86th Cong., 1st Sess., 1958, p. 58.
[97] See Warren Olney III to Charles E. Clark, May 29, 1958, Administrative Office Correspondence, 60-A-427, Box 100.

Partly responsible was the small size of the office's staff, particularly in the Division of Procedural Studies and Statistics where, said Judge Biggs, "we do not have enough force to enable us to tell where we are going and what, for example, would be the effect on the diversity jurisdiction if other provisions were inserted in the Judicial Code which might restrict that jurisdiction."[98] Much less could it "make on the spot surveys in order that basic difficulties in the courts can be pinpointed, in order that the cumbersome procedures and obsolete practices can be detected and eliminated, and in order that remedial action can be taken to achieve maximum efficiency in the operation of [the] courts."[99] Yet there existed a "crying need in nearly every one of [the] large district courts for a careful study of the court's administration."[100] Such a task appeared to lie well within the domain of the office.

Hopes for a significant enlargement of the agency and establishment of a centralized research staff were dashed during the 1950s, thereby eliminating any possibility of dramatically expanding its functions.[101] Nevertheless, the early years of Olney's administration witnessed a reorganization of the office and a slight increase in its staff and programs.[102] The duties of the new personnel included on-the-spot examinations of court dockets, surveys of individual courts including the operation of the clerks' offices and calendar control systems, field studies of the jury system, the

[98] U.S., Congress, House, Subcommittee of Committee on Appropriations, *Hearings, Departments of State, Justice, the Judiciary, and Related Agencies Appropriations for 1959*, 85th Cong., 2d Sess., 1958, p. 144.

[99] Charles E. Clark, *ibid., for 1960*, 86th Cong., 1st Sess., 1959, p. 53.

[100] *Ibid.*, p. 58.

[101] Interview with James W. Moore, November 18, 1964, New Haven, Connecticut.

[102] Warren Olney III, "New Directions in Judicial Administration," *Federal Probation*, 22 (December 1958), 3.

bankruptcy and probation system as well as study of the Federal Rules of Practice and Procedure.[103] With the additional staff and under pressure from the judges,[104] the Administrative Office accelerated its traditional studies of pretrial procedures, sentencing, use of jurors, and calendar systems,[105] and offered more advice than ever before, something Chandler had sometimes feared "would be thought officious."[106] To the judges in 1961 Olney's office "recommended the use of the best methods of judicial administration, including calendar control, insuring completion of discovery, prompt decisions of motions, careful pretrial conferences and effective judicial supervision of the proceedings at all stages of litigation."[107]

The goal was, as it had been under Chandler, an enhanced degree of centralized direction for the fragmented federal court system. Such became clear when the office issued a forty-page monograph for probation officers entitled "The Presentence Investigation Report."[108] Adherence to its principles would, commented Director Olney, result in "greater uniformity in report writing," and in "reports of higher quality." It would also aid the courts "in

[103] See Senate Subcommittee of Committee on Appropriations, *Hearings, Appropriation for 1960*, 1959, S. Rept. 424 to accompany H.R. 7343, p. 10; see also *Judicial Conference Report, 1959*, pp. 59-60.

[104] Sylvester Ryan, U.S., Congress, Senate, Subcommittee of Committee on Appropriations, *Hearings, on H.R. 11666, Departments of State, Justice, the Judiciary, and Related Agencies Appropriation for 1961*, 86th Cong., 2d Sess., 1960, p. 527.

[105] Interview with John C. Airhart, September 30, 1963, Washington, D.C.

[106] Henry P. Chandler to Elmore Whitehurst and Leland Tolman, July 20, 1953, Administrative Office Correspondence, 59-A-48, Box 142.

[107] "Court Congestion: Problems and Progress Throughout the Nation," *Journal of the American Judicature Society*, 45 (December 1961), 144.

[108] *Judicial Conference Report, 1965*, p. 136.

219

understanding the problems, needs, and concerns of the individual defendant and in arriving at an appropriate sentence."[109] Likewise, new efforts to reduce disparities in criminal sentences stimulated the office's Division of Procedural Studies and Statistics to overhaul the criminal statistics and devise measurements to determine the most effective disposition and sentence for the rehabilitation of different defendants.[110] The resulting studies, said Director Olney, "will make it possible to measure the results of probation, parole, and institutional correctional practices. They are a beginning in an effort to find out what kind of people are processed through the Federal criminal courts and what actually happens to those released on probation under varying terms, to those who are incarcerated in institutions for varying periods, and to those who are placed on parole or on conditional release."[111]

As distinguished from these traditional studies which were essentially judicial in nature, the office initiated managerial or purely administrative surveys in 1959. In cooperation with the Budget Bureau and the Air Force, it made management surveys of the court reporter system and the court clerks office. Their purpose in the latter instance was to "review and analyze methods, systems, procedures, and paper flow . . . to determine possible areas for management improvement [and to] provide a prototype against which other clerks could compare their own organization and methods."[112] This prototype, in turn, was discussed in a manual which "set forth in some detail the best ways of performing the various functions of the clerks office."[113] With it, "individual clerks could review their respective offices

[109] "Administrative Office of the United States Courts Publishes New Presentence Monograph," *Federal Probation*, 29 (June 1965), 77.
[110] See *Judicial Conference Report, 1961*, p. 140; *ibid., 1962*, p. 75; *ibid., 1964*, p. 119.
[111] *Ibid.*   [112] *Ibid., 1961*, p. 129.   [113] *Ibid., 1959*, p. 63.

and make any adjustments and modifications which to himself and to his court, seemed worthwhile."[114]

Reorganization of the judiciary's personnel system in the early 1960s further standardized administration. Prior to 1958, the application of Conference-approved personnel policies had been diffused through the several divisions of the Administrative Office with ultimate responsibility in the hands of Chandler and his assistant director.[115] Thus, even so small a matter as changing a court employee from Grade 4 to Grade 5 came before them, a practice which one observer considered "an uneconomical and unbusinesslike way of running a railroad."[116]

With Chandler and Whitehurst gone, the traditional personnel system had become completely unmanageable. "There was an obvious need for a Division of Personnel in which to centralize the responsibilities and functions relating to personnel within the judiciary," Olney told the 1958 Judicial Conference.[117] "As a consequence, a new and separate Division of Personnel was created in the Administrative Office and placed in charge of a professional personnel director."[118] It was his task "to see to the intelligent, consistent and fair classification of all supporting personnel of the courts."[119]

Consolidation of the existing diverse and somewhat inequitable classification systems was the first step. To this end, the Conference directed the office to prepare a report on "the appropriate grading and classification of personnel in the clerks' offices, the probation offices, and the referees' offices of the district courts."[120] Thereafter, the Conference

[114] Ibid. [115] Ibid., 1958, pp. 63-64.
[116] William Ellis, House Subcommittee of Committee on Appropriations, Hearings on Appropriations for 1959, 1958, p. 146.
[117] Judicial Conference Report, 1958, p. 64.
[118] Ibid.
[119] Warren Olney III, "The Administrative Office of the United States Courts," Journal of the American Judicature Society, 42 (October 1958), 82.
[120] Judicial Conference Report, 1960, p. 384.

221

adopted the judicial salary plan presented by the office.[121] It established a "general" salary level which took cognizance of "the wide variations in administrative practices found among the courts"[122] and provided education and experience requirements for all key positions, duty and responsibility statements for all positions, common classification standards, and a basis for furthering the concept of a career service for supporting personnel in the federal courts.[123] Ostensibly, the plan offered no threat to the venerable principle of judicial autonomy because, declared Olney, "the authority as heretofore for administering the plan is located in the courts themselves."[124] The director, however, enjoyed great power in allocating the grades "based upon the duties and responsibilities assigned to each individual position and the qualifications of the occupant."[125]

All aspects of legislative liaison came under sharp scrutiny early in the Olney administration. Then, the old problem of obtaining advance notice of Justice Department policies was resolved after Olney wrote Deputy Attorney General Lawrence Walsh of the Conference's need to receive copies of and supporting statements for the department's legislative proposals which related to the judiciary. This, he said, should be done "as a matter of routine"[126] and by 1962 the automatic referral of bills drafted in the department had become the usual practice.[127]

A legislative liaison officer appeared in 1958.[128] His duties included strengthening communications between the judicial and legislative branches and reducing liaison burdens on select members of the Judicial Conference. C. Aubrey Gasque, who resigned as chief counsel of the Senate Judi-

[121] *Ibid., 1961*, p. 73. [122] *Ibid.*, p. 127.
[123] *Ibid.*, pp. 126-27. [124] *Ibid.*, p. 127.
[125] *Ibid., 1965*, p. 91.

[126] Warren Olney III to Lawrence E. Walsh, March 12, 1958, Administrative Office Correspondence, 60-A-427, Box 105A.

[127] *Judicial Conference Report, 1962*, p. 2.

[128] *Ibid., 1958*, p. 65.

ciary Committee, assumed the new post. He reputedly knew ". . . the ropes and [was] personally familiar with the staff members as well as [with] most of the Congressmen and Senators."[129] However, his lobbying tactics on Capitol Hill generated antagonism toward the judiciary,[130] and his tenure was short. When he left, his duties reverted primarily to the deputy director.[131]

More enduring were the changes in liaison with the powerful House Appropriations Committee. Under Chandler, the agency had "never put in for a nickel in the way of leeway or room for growth, room for adaptation, room for change."[132] Not only did the office alter its budgetary policy after 1958 but it also played a lesser role in its presentation. It continued to perform "detail work" on the annual budgets, but the major actor in the hearing was the newly-created Budget Committee of the Judicial Conference; the director spoke on its "instructions."[133]

Even though it became "traditional that whatever is asked by the judiciary is allowed and forwarded to the Congress by the Bureau of the Budget,"[134] the now somewhat fattened judicial budget still received close scrutiny before presentation. It was, said Judge William Campbell of the Conference's Budget Committee, "carefully analyzed by our Committee . . . and gone over very carefully and cut

[129] Warren Olney III, "New Directions in Judicial Administration," p. 4.

[130] Interview with Ronald Beattie, September 30, 1963, Washington, D.C.

[131] Interview with John Biggs, Jr., August 12, 1965, Washington, D.C.

[132] William Ellis, House Subcommittee of Committee on Appropriations, Hearings, on Appropriations for 1959, 1958, p. 140.

[133] Warren Olney III, Senate Subcommittee of Committee on Appropriations, Hearings, on Appropriations for 1960, p. 463.

[134] John Rooney, U.S., Congress, House, Subcommittee of Committee on Appropriations, Hearings, on Departments of State, Justice, and Commerce, the Judiciary, and Related Agencies, Appropriations for 1965: The Judiciary, 88th Cong., 2d Sess., 1964, p. 41.

down by the Administrative Office as well as by our Committee, then presented to the Judicial Conference . . . where it received full discussion and careful consideration."[135] A new façade of legitimacy had enveloped the judiciary's budget strategy. In the process, it reduced the visibility of the unprestigious Administrative Office. At the same time it transformed the hearings from desperate salvage operations to exercises in appropriations gamesmanship.[136]

But the federal courts never received munificence from Congress. The judiciary appropriations for the 1969 fiscal year were approximately half that authorized for the Federal Bureau of Investigation.[137] Even in the relatively early stages of large-scale American intervention in the Vietnam War, the annual budget of the federal judiciary would reportedly have fallen short of underwriting one week's expenditures in that theater.[138] Piqued at the unending and unrewarding struggle for funds, the retiring Chief Justice, Earl Warren, blamed congressional penury for the rising criminal trial dockets.[139] "Other branches of government proliferate without end," he noted. "But not the courts."[140] It was "next to impossible" for them to "get something from Congress."[141] Why? Because, asserted Warren, "we can't trade anything with the Committees."[142]

[135] *Ibid.*, p. 29.   [136] See *ibid.*, p. 53.

[137] The judiciary's new obligational authority for the 1969 fiscal year was $109,945,000 while that of the Federal Bureau of Investigation for the same period was $219,591,000. U.S., *The Budget of the United States Government, Fiscal Year 1971* (Washington, 1970), pp. 212, 377.

[138] William J. Campbell, U.S., Congress, House, Subcommittee of the Committee on Appropriations, *Hearings, on Departments of State, Justice, and Commerce, the Judiciary and Related Agencies Appropriations for 1967, The Judiciary*, 89th Cong., 2d Sess., 1966, p. 48.

[139] *Washington Post*, March 16, 1969, p. A4.

[140] *Ibid.*   [141] *Ibid.*, p. A1.

[142] *Ibid.*, p. A4. Warren E. Burger, then a judge of the United States Court of Appeals for the District of Columbia Circuit, similarly charged Congress with failing to provide funds for adequate staffs to

The Olney years from 1958 to 1967 witnessed changes in the organization and functions of the Administrative Office. But these changes were incremental at best. None resulted in a transformation of the relationship between the courts and the House Appropriations Committee nor between the agency and courts. Judges might worry that the "Administrative Office may get away from us,"[143] but the office, in fact, bore no more resemblance to a central executive agency than it had under Chandler.

Not only did the office and its several divisions remain relatively small, but the agency also lacked real power to supervise court officers. It was true, conceded the director in 1963, "that the Administrative Office . . . has a Division of Probation to provide leadership, organization, and form for a more efficient probation service, [but] that Division consists of only the chief, three assistant chiefs, one editorial assistant, and three clerical personnel."[144] The Office under Olney gained no additional administrative power. It continued to lack authority to terminate unilaterally the employment of court personnel.[145] Neither did it enjoy power "to reallocate any positions between courts."[146] Declared the Assistant Director, William A. Sweeney, "We cannot take from one and give to another."[147] The judges, not the office, constituted the fundamental source of administrative power.

Nor did judges or congressmen manifest any desire to strengthen the role of the office. The Criminal Justice Act

administer the Bail Reform and Criminal Justice Acts. See *Washington Post*, November 1, 1967, p. C10.

[143] Interview with Orie L. Phillips, February 22, 1965, Washington, D.C.

[144] Warren Olney III, "The Federal Probation System in 1963: Where We Stand," *Federal Probation*, 27 (September 1963), 4.

[145] U.S., Congress, House, Subcommittee of the Committee on Appropriations, *Hearings, on Departments of State, Justice, and Commerce, the Judiciary and Related Agencies Appropriations for 1970*, part I, 91st Cong., 1st Sess., 1969, p. 124.

[146] *Ibid.*   [147] *Ibid.*

225

of 1964 provided indigent defendants with paid counsel, yet administration of the system was centered in each circuit, not in Washington. The office, asserted one judge, had responsibility neither for the Act's interpretation nor "for issuing directives for the administration of the various district and circuit plans. That . . . is the function of the court itself in each instance, subject, however, to such guidelines as the Judicial Conference . . . may see fit to recommend."[148]

The office, for its part, simply collected vouchers and dispensed payments. It received court-approved bills for services rendered by attorneys and then undertook "to check to see that there was no mistake in arithmetic, to check that the amount comes within the provisions of the act as to amounts authorized to be paid, and to guard against as many mistakes as could possibly occur."[149] The Administrative Office thus provided the courts with a centralized auditing system. Such a control was demanded by the exigencies of the appropriation process[150] and by the felt need to avoid scandals associated with the judiciary's novel duty of disbursing public funds to private parties.[151]

And so, when Warren Olney's directorship came to an end on October 31, 1967, one congressman could say of the office that it "has done an excellent job of providing the judiciary with valuable fiscal and housekeeping services, but it . . . is handicapped in its efforts to engage in continuing the in-depth research necessary to provide long-term answers to the administrative and training problems of our courts."[152] Even the agency's traditional role as the unofficial secretariat for the Judicial Conference and its commit-

[148] John S. Hastings, "Report on the Criminal Justice Act," *Federal Rules Decisions*, 39 (1966), 403.

[149] Harvey M. Johnsen, U.S., Congress, House, Subcommittee of the Committee on Appropriations, *Hearings, on Departments of State, Justice, and Commerce, the Judiciary, and Related Agencies Appropriations for 1966: The Judiciary*, 89th Cong., 1st Sess., 1965, p. 101.

[150] *Ibid.*, p. 100.   [151] *Ibid.*, p. 102.

[152] James C. Corman, *Congressional Record*, 90th Cong., 1st Sess., 1967, vol. 113, part 26, 35141.

tees came under fire from Senator Joseph D. Tydings, chairman of the Senate Subcommittee on Improvements in the Judicial Machinery. He thought the various "makeshift arrangements" which marked its role "unsatisfactory and [they] ought to be abandoned."[153]

Breaking out of the mold set under Chandler loomed as no easy task; in fact, it had proved impossible despite the efforts of Chief Justice Warren and Director Olney. A partial solution, by the late 1960s, seemed to lie not with the rigidified Administrative Office. Rather it appeared to rest with creation of a new agency which would perform a multitude of education and research functions then beyond the competence of the Administrative Office and other existing judicial institutions.

[153] *Ibid.*, part 24, 33099.

CHAPTER 7

The Judicial Conference
of the United States, 1939–1969

New and Expanded Roles

THE Administrative Office Act of 1939 made a profound impact on the quantity and quality of business considered by the Judicial Conference. In the words of Chief Justice Hughes, it "greatly enlarged the responsibilities of the . . . Conference of Senior Circuit Judges"[1] which, contended Judge D. Lawrence Groner, now included "many activities which were never thought of in the original scheme of things."[2] These new functions related to duties previously performed by the Department of Justice or, in the case of clerks' fees, by the Supreme Court. Only rarely had the old Conference given them much, if any, attention.[3] Now, their transfer to the courts fundamentally altered that body's role from one which was chiefly advisory to a vital agency of administrative integration. On issues affecting more than one judicial district or circuit, the Conference would come to act as a centralized policy-making institution. Nowhere was this role more clearly manifested than in the relationship between the Conference and the Administrative Office,

[1] "Address of the Chief Justice," *The American Law Institute, Proceedings,* 18 (1941), 27. The Conference was formally designated the Judicial Conference of the United States by Act of June 25, 1948, 62 *Stat.* 902, sec. 331.

[2] D. Lawrence Groner to Harlan Fiske Stone, September 8, 1941, Groner Papers, Box 12.

[3] "Report of the Judicial Conference," in U.S., *Annual Report of the Attorney General for 1942* (Washington, 1942), p. 30; *Report of the Judicial Conference of Senior Circuit Judges* (Washington, 1946), pp. 15-17. (Cited hereafter as *Judicial Conference Report*; for a complete title-source listing, see Appendix A.)

the jurisdiction of which extended throughout the court system.

Clothed with the power to approve the judiciary's budget, initially formulated by the Administrative Office, and to supervise and direct that office, the Conference considered and set policies on new as well as old subjects. Such became manifest in the Conference agenda, the format of which was "determined in the main by the statutory requisites for the annual appropriations and subjects of study by committees of the Conference."[4]

The Conference, through its power over the budget, authorized salary scales and promotional policies for the supporting personnel in the federal courts[5] and established qualification standards intended to guide the appointing judges in their initial classification of such employees.[6] This function was clearly evident in the setting of standards for probation officers. Spurred on by Chief Justice Hughes,[7] the 1940 Conference declared that "probation officers should be appointed solely on the basis of merit without regard to political considerations; and that training, experience, and traits of character appropriate to the specialized work of probation officers should in every instance be deemed essential qualifications."[8] This very general statement proved inadequate, and in 1942 the Conference issued explicit minimum qualifications. These included standards of character, health, and age as well as possession of a college degree and two years' experience in welfare work or professional training.[9]

---

[4] Henry P. Chandler to Chief Justice and Members of the Advisory Committee of the Judicial Conference of Senior Circuit Judges, August 3, 1948, mimeograph (Administrative Office of the United States Courts, Washington, D.C.).

[5] *Judicial Conference Report, 1940*, p. 15; *ibid., 1941*, pp. 32-33.

[6] *Ibid., 1945*, pp. 9-10.

[7] Henry P. Chandler to Peter G. Fish, July 7, 1967, letter in possession of author.

[8] *Judicial Conference Report, 1940*, p. 26.

[9] *Ibid., 1942*, pp. 26-27.

Under Conference auspices, new staff positions in the courts were created and the essential character of existing ones changed. Salaried law clerks for district judges and crier-messengers, authorized by the senior circuit judges,[10] appeared in the courts by the mid-1940s[11] as did court reporters. Until 1944 no official court reporting system existed in the federal courts and provision for reporters had varied from court to court. Most simply left it to the litigants to contract with private reporters for transcripts of their trials.[12]

To rectify the inequities arising from this system, the Conference sponsored and Congress ultimately adopted legislation for the appointment of official court reporters by each district court.[13] Its provisions required the Conference to set the number, qualifications, and general salary classifications as well as the salaries of reporters in individual districts and their transcript fees initially established by the district courts.[14]

Reorganization of bankruptcy administration in 1946 followed somewhat the same pattern as had that of the court reporter system and it, too, expanded the Conference's responsibility for judicial personnel.[15] Until that year, the administrative system in bankruptcy had been characterized by a large number of referees, many with little work, short tenure, compensation by fees, the size of which depended on their decision in each case, and loose and unsupervised means for the payment of their expenses.[16] Under pressure from creditors, judges, and even the referees themselves, then hard-pressed by a sharp war-inspired decline in bankruptcy litigation, Congress enacted the Referee's Salary Act

[10] *Ibid.*, p. 24; *ibid.*, *1943*, pp. 56-68.
[11] Henry P. Chandler, "Some Major Advances in the Federal Judicial System: 1922-1947," *Federal Rules Decisions*, 31 (1963), 421-23.
[12] *Ibid.*, p. 437.   [13] 58 *Stat.* 5-7.
[14] See *Judicial Conference Report, 1944*, pp. 55-57.
[15] 60 *Stat.* 323.
[16] Chandler, "Some Major Advances," p. 455.

of 1946.[17] It abolished the "fee and commission" system of compensation and substituted a salary system aimed at "creating and maintaining a system of full-time referees."[18] Under its provisions, the Judicial Conference determined "in the light of the recommendations of the Director [of the Administrative Office] and of the [circuit] councils, the number of referees, full-time and part-time, to be appointed, the respective territories which they shall serve, including the regular place of office and the places at which courts shall be held, their respective salaries, and schedules of graduated fees to be charged in asset, arrangement and wage-earner cases."[19]

The Acts of 1944 and 1946 largely transformed highly decentralized personnel systems, which had developed to meet the exigencies of the nineteenth century, into centralized ones under the ultimate control of the Judicial Conference. Later reorganizations of other personnel systems in the federal judiciary would be patterned after those established for the court reporters and referees in bankruptcy.[20] Thus by the final year of Chief Justice Warren's tenure the Conference had begun implementing the Federal Magistrates and Criminal Justice Acts, both of which involved setting selection standards and national job performance guidelines.[21]

Conference control over the vital salary lever had remained incomplete until the Warren era. Language carried in successive appropriation acts during the 1940s and 1950s required the director of the Administrative Office to fix the

[17] 60 *Stat.* 323.

[18] *Judicial Conference Report, 1947*, p. 224.

[19] "Memorandum on the Court Reporter System," undated, Administrative Office Correspondence, 60-A-323, Box 4.

[20] See U.S., Congress, Senate, Subcommittee on Improvements in Judicial Machinery of the Committee on the Judiciary, *Hearings, on the United States Commissioner System*, part i and ii, 89th Cong., 1st Sess., 1965; *ibid.*, part iii, 89th Cong., 2d Sess., 1966; Federal Magistrates Act, 82 *Stat.* 1107.

[21] *Judicial Conference Report, 1969*, pp. 29-34, 36-38.

compensation of individual law clerks and secretaries as "the appointing judge shall determine subject to review by the judicial council of the circuit if requested by the Director, such determination by the judge otherwise to be final."[22]

Thus the Conference was left in the anomalous position of initially establishing personnel grades and qualifications, but "helpless to police its standards."[23] Enforcement power lodged in the regional circuit councils hardly guaranteed compliance with Conference policies; in fact it threatened them.

The issue underwent a catharsis in 1956 after a western judge promoted his faithful secretary to a position requiring legal education and bar membership, neither of which she possessed. Denied reclassification by the Administrative Office, the judge appealed to his circuit council which loyally upheld his action.[24] The entire program was threatened. If one judge's unqualified secretary could be so promoted, said Circuit Judge Albert Maris, "there is probably not any reason why any judge's secretary who has been with him 10 years or so, might not be similarly reclassified."[25] To eliminate this possibility, the 1957 Conference recommended that the power of final review be lodged in it rather than the several circuit councils.[26]

The Judiciary Appropriation Act for 1958 carried the

[22] 61 *Stat.* 305; see also Clifton Matthews to Henry P. Chandler, August 15, 1945, Groner Papers, Box 15; Harold M. Stephens to Henry P. Chandler, June 8, 1945, Stephens Papers, Box 85; *Judicial Conference Report, 1948*, p. 21.

[23] Albert B. Maris, U.S., Congress, House, Subcommittee of the Committee on Appropriations, *Hearings, on Departments of State and Justice, the Judiciary, and Related Agencies, Appropriations for 1958*, 85th Cong., 1st Sess., 1957, pp. 61-62.

[24] *Judicial Conference Report, 1957*, p. 19.

[25] House Subcommittee of the Committee on Appropriations, *Hearings on Appropriations for 1958*, p. 61.

[26] *Judicial Conference Report, 1957*, p. 278.

new language.[27] Under it the director has referred personnel disputes to the Conference; it, in turn, has passed them on to its Court Administration Committee which, in a 1960 case, determined that one secretary lacked "qualifications for any grade of secretary to a federal judge" and recommended that the Conference instruct the director to remove him from the payroll.[28] Similar treatment has been authorized for derelict court reporters. A 1957 appellate court decision,[29] which interpreted a section of the Judicial Code,[30] held that court reporters must transcribe their notes and file transcripts of all proceedings on arraignment, plea, and sentence in criminal cases without additional compensation. An Administrative Office survey three years later revealed that fewer than 25 per cent of the federal district courts had complied with the law.[31] Yet, Director Olney observed that such transcripts were absolutely essential when criminal defendants challenged their convictions on newly-created collateral grounds many years after judgment.[32] Once again, the Conference resorted to the salary lever and directed the Office to "withhold the payment of salaries of court reporters" who failed to comply with the law.[33]

An important function of the Conference after 1939 lay in transfer of its prestige, or more accurately, of its "protection" to the acts of the Administrative Office.[34] Even so

[27] Ibid., p. 19.
[28] Ibid., 1960, p. 9; Warren Olney III, U.S., Congress, Senate, Subcommittee of Committee on Appropriations, Hearings, on H.R. 11666 Departments of State, Justice, the Judiciary, and Related Agencies Appropriation Bill for 1961, 86th Cong., 2d Sess., 1960, p. 508.
[29] Poole v. United States, 250 F.2d. 369 (C.C.A., D.C., 1957).
[30] 28 U.S.C. 753(b).
[31] Judicial Conference Report, 1961, p. 71.
[32] Ibid., p. 70.   [33] Ibid., 1963, p. 12.
[34] See "Transcript of the Proceedings . . . upon an Application of the Conference of United States Court Reporters on Behalf of all Federal Court Reporters before the Committee on Supporting Personnel of the Judicial Conference of the United States," August 9,

seemingly trivial a task as securing statistical data from judges and court clerks brought Will Shafroth, the office's chief of the Division of Procedural Studies and Statistics, before the Judicial Conference. There he requested a special session of the 1940 Conference to pass "a motion . . . either directing or authorizing us to [collect the data], so that when it comes to the district judge it does not come as something we are doing ourselves, but as something which the Conference of Senior Circuit Judges wants us to do."[35]

How helpful such a resolution could be became apparent when the senior circuit judge of the Ninth Circuit objected that the collection procedure undercut his prerogatives and those of his counterparts in other circuits.[36] His authority challenged, Director Chandler sought advice from Chief Justice Hughes who promptly ordered him to dispatch a copy of the Conference transcript in order that the judge might "be advised of the facts." Furthermore, declared the Chief, if any district judge should refuse "to answer upon the ground that the questionnaire was not authorized inform him that it was authorized duly by the Conference."[37]

In a similar fashion, if the office encountered resistance to one of its administrative actions, it looked to the Judicial Conference to enunciate a general policy on the issue. When some court reporters refused to report earnings derived from their private reporting business,[38] the agency,

1950, pp. 21-26, Stephens Papers, Box 216. (Cited hereafter as "Transcript, Conference of Court Reporters.")

[35] "Excerpt from the Transcript of the Proceedings of the Meeting of the Judicial Conference on January 23, 1940, pp. 356-64," p. 6, Groner Papers, Box 15; see also *Judicial Conference Report, 1940,* p. 17.

[36] Henry P. Chandler to Charles E. Hughes, telegram, July 20, 1940, Groner Papers, Box 15; Curtis D. Wilbur to Charles E. Hughes, July 25, 1940, Administrative Office Correspondence, 60-A-328, Box 27.

[37] Charles E. Hughes to Henry P. Chandler, telegram, July 22, 1940, Groner Papers, Box 15.

[38] See Elmore Whitehurst to Henry P. Chandler and Leland Tolman, February 4, 1948, Administrative Office Correspondence, 60-A-

pressed by Congress for the information, requested and promptly received Conference support.[39] Thereafter the reporters were required to list in their quarterly reports to the Administrative Office their earnings derived from private as well as public business.[40]

The director's reminders of Conference endorsement of his policies have not invariably convinced recalcitrant judges. And so he has occasionally called upon influential members of the Conference and its committees to lend their prestige to his cause. When one California judge bitterly assailed the personnel policies pursued by Director Chandler and even questioned his good faith, a Conference spokesman came to the defense, asserting that the disgruntled judge had "already pursued this matter to the point of absurdity, and beyond." Further he suggested "that you refrain from bombarding Mr. Chandler with any more letters on the subject and that you address further communications to the Judicial Conference, the members of which . . . fully approve of what Mr. Chandler has done."[41]

The Administrative Office Act augmented the role of the Judicial Conference by encouraging it to act formally on ethical problems once left to the individual judges in their separate courts. Some judges objected to this new function, contending that the power of the Conference extended no further than to the promotion of uniformity and expedition of judicial business.[42] This "strict constructionist" view persisted. In 1969 the chairman of the Judicial Conference Committee on Court Administration told a Senate subcommittee that there existed "considerable doubt that the Conference had any legal authority to regulate the conduct of

---

328, Box 8; Leland Tolman to Henry P. Chandler, August 1, 1950, *ibid.*, 59-A-48, Box 141.

[39] See "Transcript, Conference of Court Reporters."

[40] *Judicial Conference Report, 1948*, p. 27.

[41] Calvert Magruder to Clifton Matthews, April 29, 1948, Stephens Papers, Box 209; Matthews to Magruder, May 7, 1948, *ibid.*

[42] Charles E. Clark to Sam O. Clark, Jr., October 28, 1942, Clark Papers.

judges."[43] He thus urged Congress to delegate to the Conference power to "adopt standards and promulgate rules prohibiting judges from engaging in activities which are in conflict with or which may interfere with the discharge of their official duties."[44]

Lack of specific statutory authority notwithstanding, Conferences early established ethical standards for judges and their supporting personnel.[45] Under Chief Justice Stone, the senior judges acted vigorously on issues posing a conflict of interest question. They responded in 1942 to a bar association complaint that one district judge permitted his two sons and two nephews to practice before him.[46] The Conference promptly condemned his conduct and called on "the circuit councils to inquire whether such a practice exists in their respective circuits, and if so, to take appropriate action."[47] Apparently reflecting Stone's well-known attitude toward extra-judicial activities,[48] the 1942 Judicial Conference also resolved "that it would be incompatible with the obligations of the judicial office for a United States judge to accept a position as arbitrator in cases pending before the National War Labor Board."[49] The following year

[43] Robert A. Ainsworth, U.S., Congress, Senate, Subcommittee on Improvements in Judicial Machinery of the Committee on the Judiciary, *Hearings, on S. 1506, S. 1507, S. 1508, S. 1509, S. 1510, S. 1511, S. 1512, S. 1513, S. 1514, S. 1515, and S. 1516, Judicial Reform Act,* 91st Cong., 1st and 2d Sess., 1970, p. 10.

[44] *Ibid.*

[45] *Judicial Conference Report, 1940,* p. 31, prohibiting circuit and district judges from appointing relatives as law clerks or secretaries.

[46] Henry P. Chandler to Harlan F. Stone, April 27, 1942, Administrative Office Correspondence, 57-A-122, Box 15.

[47] *Judicial Conference Report, 1942,* p. 31.

[48] Alpheus T. Mason, *Harlan Fiske Stone: Pillar of the Law* (New York, 1956), ch. 42.

[49] *Judicial Conference Report, 1942,* p. 31; see "Memorandum of Charles E. Clark in Support of a Request for Reconsideration of a Resolution of the Judicial Conference, September Session, 1942, in re: 'Federal Judges as Arbitrators for the National War Labor Board,' " December 1, 1942, Clark Papers; Charles E. Clark to Henry P. Chandler, August 12, 1943, Groner Papers, Box 16.

it condemned political activities and candidacies of judicial officers and employees similar to those "forbidden to employees of the executive branch of the Government by the Hatch Act. . . ."[50] Many years later, spurred on by unfavorable newspaper publicity[51] and pending legislation,[52] the 1963 Conference reaffirmed its role in setting behavior standards for judges. It declared that "no justice or judge appointed under the authority of the United States shall serve in the capacity of an officer, director, or employee of a corporation organized for profit."[53] Then in the aftermath of Justice Abe Fortas's resignation from Warren's Court and in the midst of controversy over Justice William O. Douglas's extra-judicial activities and income,[54] a special session of the 1969 Conference sought to establish new ethical standards for federal

[50] *Judicial Conference Report, 1943*, pp. 69-70.

[51] See *The Wall Street Journal*, May 2, 1963, p. 1.

[52] H.R. 6048, 88th Cong., to amend 28 *U.S.C.* 454 by providing criminal penalties for a justice or judge of the United States who participated other than in the capacity of a stockholder in a profit-making enterprise.

[53] *Judicial Conference Report, 1963*, p. 62. No enforcement procedures were specified. The Judicial Conference has supervisory authority only over judges of the inferior federal courts. It may exercise no such authority over justices of the Supreme Court, language in the 1963 Conference resolution to the contrary notwithstanding. The language of that resolution appears to control the conduct of justices of the Supreme Court of the United States, thereby implying an intention to extend substantially the Judicial Conference's jurisdiction. No such intention existed. Inclusion of the word "justice" was inadvertent as the Committee on Court Administration and the Conference as a whole simply adopted the language of H.R. 6048, 88th Congress. Thus, failure to excise "justice" was purely a drafting error and no implications may flow from it. See Senate Subcommittee on Improvements in Judicial Machinery, *Hearings, Judicial Reform Act*, 1970, pp. 135-39.

[54] On the Fortas-Douglas controversy and related issues, see U.S., Congress, Senate, Subcommittee on Separation of Powers of the Committee on the Judiciary, *Hearings, on S. 1097, S. 2109, Nonjudicial Activities of Supreme Court Justices and Other Federal Judges*, 91st Cong., 1st Sess., 1969.

judges. It sharply restricted compensation received for extra-judicial services, and required that each judge file an annual report with the Conference of his income, investments, and assets.[55]

Many policies set by the Judicial Conference have related to the expeditious dispatch of judicial business, a venerable goal of federal judicial administrators since the time of William Howard Taft. Specifically, the Conference has called on circuit councils to investigate delayed cases and to increase the use of intra-circuit assignments to achieve that end.[56] Even more specific was the request of the 1961 Conference that each council develop a plan which included "mustering the available judges of the circuit to pretry, try," and dispose of those cases pending on the federal docket for more than three years.[57] But judicial efficiency may be impeded by the behavior of judges. Six sun-drenched months spent in the West Indies by a Third Circuit judge proved no boon to the work of his court and led to congressional criticism as well.[58] The Conference under Warren reacted by directing "that in those circuits or districts in which the disposition of judicial business is not upon a current basis, judge's vacations should not exceed one month per annum." It further requested "the Judicial Councils of the respective circuits to inquire into the matter of vacations, and if any be excessive, to take appropriate action in respect thereto."[59]

In theory "the conception is pretty well established that the Judicial Conference deals with questions of general policy." On the other hand, remarked Director Chandler, "a

[55] *Judicial Conference Report, 1969*, pp. 42-43; *ibid.*, p. 51, suspending the resolution of June 10, 1969.

[56] *Ibid., 1954*, p. 29.

[57] *Ibid., 1961*, p. 63. See also "Court Congestion: Problems and Progress throughout the Nation," *Journal of the American Judicature Society*, 45 (December 1961), 144.

[58] Charles E. Clark to Irving R. Kaufman, September 17, 1956, Clark Papers.

[59] *Judicial Conference Report, 1956*, p. 12.

238

question concerning the application of the general policy in a particular case involving the interpretation and enforcement of the policy locally . . . would seem to be clearly a matter for the court concerned and the judicial council of the circuit."[60] But in reality the Judicial Conference together with its committees began, in the post-1939 period, to act as an administrative tribunal for the final adjudication of those controversies which had defied settlement at the lower levels. When a bailiff in the Third Circuit, wrongly appointed as an appraiser in bankruptcy, threatened the judiciary with a scandal, the council considered the issue, but refused to criticize the district court appointment.[61] On appeal by the director of the Administrative Office, the Conference, acting on the recommendation of its Committee on Bankruptcy Administration, "disapproved the practice as improper and detrimental to the proper administration of justice in bankruptcy cases."[62]

Most, but not all, of the great expansion of the Conference's business after 1939 can be laid at the doorstep of the Administrative Office Act of that year. However, the transfer of the rule-making power, long exercised by the Supreme Court Advisory Committee on the Rules of Civil Procedure and Practice, was largely unrelated to the Act as was Conference consideration of subjects only tangentially related to the administration of the federal courts.

The changed locus of the rule-making power occurred after years of agitation over the Supreme Court's role, agitation initiated by Justice Louis Brandeis[63] and continued by Justices Frankfurter and Black. For his part, Frankfurter objected to the Court's duty to examine and place its imprimatur on a stream of amendments to the rules because

---

[60] Henry P. Chandler to John Biggs, Jr., September 29, 1949, Administrative Office Correspondence, 60-A-328, Box 8.

[61] Interview with John Biggs, Jr., February 28, 1965, Wilmington, Delaware.

[62] *Judicial Conference Report, 1961*, p. 42.

[63] See *Orders re Rules of Procedure*, 302 U.S. 783 (1937).

"he was unwilling to be a 'dummy director,' and . . . that was what the Court really became, since it did not have, or at least take, time to become itself master of proposed rules."[64] Thus both he and Black "refused to sit on the rules in any form."[65]

Soon after his arrival on the bench, Chief Justice Earl Warren cast his crucial support to the Black-Frankfurter faction which favored termination of the Advisory Committee's life.[66] Influencing his decision were not only the objections posed by his two brethren but also growing and widespread dissatisfaction with the work of the old committee and the rising volume of Judicial Conference business relating to the rules.[67]

"The Conference," said Warren, "is the best functionary which could be utilized by the Court to process proposals for changes in the rules."[68] Echoing Frankfurter, he argued that "the existing personnel and facilities of the Supreme Court are in no sense adequate to the great responsibility for rule-making in the fields of civil and criminal procedure, admiralty, bankruptcy, and tax appeals. With the ever increasing length of our calendars it becomes more difficult for any of the members of the Court to give continuous attention to the spadework essential to the formulation of new rules and amendments to existing rules."[69] The Judicial Conference, on the contrary, "would be in a position to know whether there was need for change."[70] The Chief's

[64] Charles E. Clark to Lester B. Orfield, November 25, 1942, Clark Papers.
[65] Charles E. Clark to Leland L. Tolman, September 27, 1954, *ibid.*; see also dissent of Black, J., *Amendments to the Federal Rules of Civil Procedure*, April 17, 1961, 368 U.S. 1012-1014 (1961); dissent of Black, J., *Amendment of the Copyright Rules*, June 5, 1939, 307 U.S. 652 (1939).
[66] Charles E. Clark to John J. Parker, October 1, 1954, Clark Papers.
[67] See "Statement of the Chief Justice," *Federal Rules Decisions*, 21 (1958), 118; "Observations of Chief Judge Biggs," *ibid.*, p. 123; "Address of James W. Moore," *ibid.*, p. 130.
[68] *Ibid.*, p. 118.   [69] *Ibid.*   [70] *Ibid.*

1. Members of the Second Conference of Senior Judges of the United States Courts of Appeals calling on President Calvin Coolidge at the White House, September 23, 1923. *Left to right*: Richard W. Walker, with face hidden (C.C.A. 5th); Henry Wade Rogers (2nd); George H. Bingham (1st); William B. Gilbert (9th); Harry M. Daugherty, Attorney General; William Howard Taft, Chief Justice; Joseph Buffington (3rd); Walter H. Sanborn (8th); Loyal E. Knappen (6th); Francis E. Baker (7th); Charles A. Woods (4th).

2. Chief Justice Charles Evans Hughes and members of the Conference of Senior Circuit Judges following a meeting with President Franklin D. Roosevelt at the White House, September 27, 1934. *Left to right*: Kimbrough Stone (C.C.A. 8th), Curtis D. Wilbur (9th), Nathan P. Bryan (5th), John J. Parker (4th), George H. Bingham (1st), Martin T. Manton (2nd), Chief Justice Hughes, Charles H. Moorman (6th), Joseph Buffington (3rd), Evan A. Evans, substituting for Samuel Alschuler (7th), Robert E. Lewis (10th).

3. Judges lobbying Congress. Chief Justice Hughes, flanked by Associate Justices Willis Van Devanter and Louis D. Brandeis, testifying before the Senate Judiciary Committee, March 26, 1935. They opposed Senator Hugo Black's bill enlarging the Supreme Court's appellate jurisdiction in certain injunction cases. *Left to right*: Senators Warren Austin, George W. Norris, William E. Borah, Chairman, Henry E. Ashurst, Pat McCarran, Justices Van Devanter, Hughes, Brandeis.

4. President Franklin Roosevelt signing into law the bill establishing an Administrative Office of the United States Courts and the circuit judicial councils, August 7, 1939. *Left to right*: former Attorney General Homer S. Cummings, the President, Attorney General Frank Murphy.

5. Interchange among judges of the appellate courts at the Judicial Conference of the Third Circuit, 1945. *Left to right*: Chief Judge John Biggs, Jr. (C.C.A. 3rd), former Circuit Justice Owen J. Roberts, and his successor, Circuit Justice Harold H. Burton.

6. Unveiling of the dedicatory plaque in the courtyard of the Federal Judicial Center, November 1, 1968. *Left to right*: Lawson B. Knotts, Jr., Administrator of the General Services Administration; Justice Tom Clark, first Director of the Center; Chief Justice Earl Warren.

7. A session of the Judicial Council of the District of Columbia Circuit in the 1960s. *Left to right (as seated at table)*: Charles Fahy, Warren E. Burger, Spottswood W. Robinson, III, Chief Judge David L. Bazelon, J. Skelly Wright, Harold Leventhal, Carl McGowan, John A. Danaher, Edward A. Tamm.

8. The Judicial Conference Committee on Court Administration meeting on June 8, 1969, in the Federal Building in San Francisco to consider extra-judicial services performed by federal judges. *Left to right*: William E. Foley, Deputy Director of the Administrative Office; James R. Browning (C.C.A. 9th); Bernard M. Decker (N. Dist. Ill.); Ernest Friesen, Director of the Administrative Office; Edward T. Gignoux (Dist. Me.); Senior Judge and former Chairman John Biggs, Jr. (C.C.A. 3rd); Robert A. Ainsworth, Jr., Chairman (C.C.A. 5th); J. Skelly Wright (C.C.A. D.C.); A. Sherman Christensen (Dist. Utah); Chief Judge Bailey Brown (W. Dist. Tenn.); Chief Judge J. Edward Lumbard (C.C.A. 2nd); Chief Judge Edwin M. Stanley (M. Dist. N.C.); Elmo B. Hunter (W. Dist. Mo.).

**"Why Ain't You Keeping Up With
All Those Criminals?"**

9a, b. Causes and conse-
quences of docket congestion
and delays in administering
justice, two views: (a, *top*)
by Herblock in *The Washington Post*, March 19, 1969;
(b, *bottom*) by LePelley in
*The Christian Science Moni-
tor*, March 13, 1971.

There's such a thing as being too blindfolded

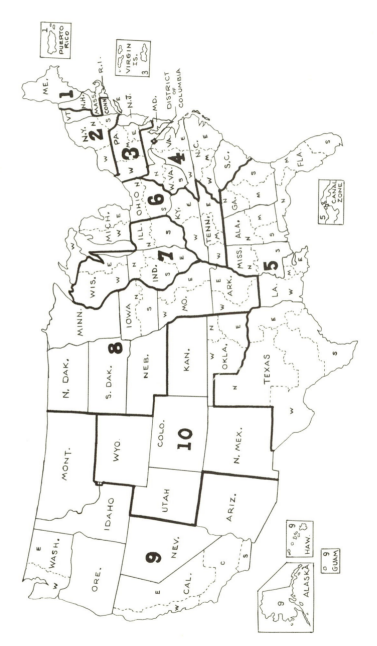

10. The United States Courts of Appeals and the United States District Courts. Large numerals indicate Courts of Appeals, and heavy lines represent each circuit's jurisdictional boundaries. Broken lines denote boundaries of District Courts in states with two or more districts. Districts are designated geographically: North, East, South, West, Middle, and Central. Portions of Yellowstone National Park within Montana and Idaho are in the District of Wyoming. (Map by John W. Winkle, III, based on *The United States Courts: Their Jurisdiction and Work*, G.P.O., 1967.)

hopes became reality in mid-1958 when Congress formally empowered the Conference to make continuing studies of the operation and effects of the general rules of practice and procedure and to recommend to the Supreme Court proposed changes in them.[71]

But in the absence of a case or controversy the high court's word on procedural rules was not necessarily the last one. On at least one occasion, the Judicial Conference overruled the Supreme Court. The latter had rejected a proposal of its Advisory Committee on the Rules of Criminal Procedure that submission of detailed government briefs to trial judges, but not to defense counsel, be eliminated.[72] The justices believed that the recommended rule "was an affront to the dignity of the trial judges(!)."[73] The senior circuit judges and Chief Justice Fred Vinson felt quite differently; they called for "the immediate discontinuance of such practice."[74]

[71] 72 *Stat.* 356. Justices Black and Douglas remained dissatisfied. They contended: "The present rules produced under 28 U.S.C. § 2072 are not prepared by us but by the Committees of the Judicial Conference designated by the Chief Justice, and before coming to us they are approved by the Judicial Conference pursuant to 28 U.S.C. § 331. The Committees and the Conference are composed of able and distinguished members and they render a high public service. It is they, however, who do the work, not we, and the rules have only our imprimatur. The only contribution that we actually make is an occasional exercise of a veto power. If the rule-making for Federal District Courts is to continue under the present plan, we believe that the Supreme Court should not have any part in the task; rather, the statute should be amended to substitute the Judicial Conference. . . . Transfer of the functions to the Judicial Conference would relieve us of the embarrassment of having to sit in judgment on the constitutionality of rules which we have approved and which as applied in given situations might have to be declared invalid." *Amendments to Rules of Civil Procedure for the United States District Courts*, 374 U.S. 861, 870 (1962).

[72] Arthur T. Vanderbilt, *The Challenge of Law Reform* (Princeton, 1955), p. 68.

[73] *Ibid.*

[74] *Judicial Conference Report, 1946*, p. 21.

The relationship was a reciprocal one, for the binding decisions of the Supreme Court also had an impact on the Judicial Conference. That Court's 1966 decision in *Sheppard v. Maxwell*[75] brought the fair trial-free press issue to the fore. It held that a defendant may be denied due process of law by prejudicial trial publicity even in the absence of proof that the jury was in fact prejudiced by the publicity. Thereafter, the Conference, through its Committee on the Operation of the Jury System, took the lead in urging trial judges to "enact rules relating to the free press-fair trial problem in accordance with a report made to the September 1968 meeting. . . ."[76] Other controversial Supreme Court decisions generated congressional legislation and corresponding responses by the Conference. The judiciary's administrative policy-makers came to the defense of the "Mallory rule" excluding all evidence obtained from defendants who, after arrest, had not been brought before a magistrate without unnecessary delay.[77]

Even more far-reaching was the Conference's endorsement of crime control legislation. At the September 1967 session the judges threw their support behind one of six pending Senate and House bills permitting court-supervised electronic surveillance.[78] And a year later, they noted recent Supreme Court rulings on the subject, and stated "that there are areas of law enforcement in which the use of wiretapping and eavesdropping devices should be permitted provided that any legislation therefor meets the Constitutional standards of *Berger v. New York*, 388 U.S. 41 (1967) and *Katz v. United States* 389 U.S. 347 (1967)."[79]

[75] 384 U.S. 333 (1966).

[76] *Judicial Conference Report, 1969*, p. 15; see also *ibid., 1968*, pp. 16-17, 66-67.

[77] *Mallory v. United States*, 354 U.S. 449 (1957); the 1963 Conference condemned S. 1012, 88th Congress which sought to abrogate *Mallory*. See *Judicial Conference Report, 1963*, p. 80.

[78] *Ibid., 1967*, p. 80; see also *ibid., 1965*, p. 72.

[79] *Ibid., 1968*, p. 28.

Conference action on this "bugging" legislation as well as on bills to overturn Supreme Court criminal law rulings and "war on crime" bills for federal aid to law enforcement agencies[80] immediately prompted queries as to "the proper role of the Conference, the administrative arm of the federal judiciary, when Congress is considering controversial legislation that touches on the duties of judges."[81] The 1968 Conference took cognizance of this criticism but voted to adhere to the existing practice of gratuitously presenting to Congress "its views on pending legislation which affects or is of interest to the judiciary."[82] Qualitative expansion of Conference business had thus brought the judiciary to a politically sensitive penumbra area. Judges in their administrative capacity were speaking authoritatively on subjects which might later come before them in their judicial capacity. Although it is the judicial decision which is final, the latter may in fact, determine the former, whether the subject matter relates to rules of procedure or substantial constitutional questions. The Judicial Conference operates in the misty realm where "lawmaking" shades into that which is wholly judicial at one pole and that which is wholly legislative at the other. It ever stands, then, at the very brink of the "political thicket."

Conference Composition

Proliferation of Conference responsibilities after 1939 dramatically altered the structure and composition of that institution. For the first time since its establishment in 1922, so-called special sessions were held by the senior circuit judges in January 1940 and 1941. Subsequently, such sessions were called in March or April and became annual affairs after 1948 even though they retained their "special

[80] *Ibid.*, approved policy statement contained in Sec. 2 of S. 917, 90th Congress ("Safe-Streets" Bill).
[81] *Washington Post*, October 15, 1967, p. F1.
[82] *Judicial Conference Report, 1968*, p. 33.

session" designation until 1961. Typically, these special sessions lasted for two days although some met for only one,[83] while from 1940 to 1946 the regular September session lasted four days. Thereafter its duration declined to three days during the 1950s and to two in the following decade, as changes in the organization of the Conference improved the efficiency of that institution.

Similarly, changes in the substance of court and conference business brought to the sessions new participants as well as presiding judges of the courts of appeals with new titles, for the 1948 revision of the Judicial Code renamed the senior circuit judge. Henceforth, he would be chief judge of the circuit "in recognition of the great increase in administrative duties of such judge."[84]

At every meeting, beginning with that held in January 1940, the director of the Administrative Office and members of his staff attended. As their presence indicated the new supervisory functions granted the Conference by the Act of 1939, so, too, the appearance of the chairmen and members of the House and Senate Judiciary Committees reflected the Conference's enlarged legislative clearance role. Their attendance had been specifically authorized by the 1941 Conference[85] on the initiative of Senior Circuit Judge John J. Parker. The presence of ranking members of the Judiciary Committees would prove most beneficial because, as Judge Parker told Chief Justice Stone, "with a better understanding on the part of the Congress of the problems of administration in the federal courts, and with a better understanding by the members of the Conference of the complaints that come to Congress, there would be less dan-

[83] See *ibid., 1949; ibid., 1950.*

[84] U.S., Congress, House, Committee on the Judiciary, *Revision of Title 28, United States Code,* H. Rept. 308 to accompany H.R. 3214, 80th Cong., 1st Sess., 1947, p. A6 revising Section 45(a).

[85] *Judicial Conference Report, 1941,* pp. 28-29. No member of the critical House Appropriations Committee attended a Conference until 1951; see *ibid., 1951,* p. 1.

244

ger of the passage of legislation out of harmony with the great purposes of the Administrative Office Act, and there would be less need for legislation to remedy defects and delays in administration."[86]

Consideration of the Conference's legislative and administrative programs encouraged attendance of representatives from assorted interest groups within and without the judiciary. Referees in bankruptcy and the chairman of the American Bar Association's Committee on Bankruptcy and Liquidation appeared at the 1944 Conference, then considering fundamental changes in bankruptcy administration.[87] At the Conference the following year, the president of the National Shorthand Reporters Association and ten court reporters from across the country lobbied the assembled judges for salary and transcript rate increases.[88] With further evolution of the Conference's committee system, these interest group representatives attended less often during the Vinson era.[89] However, spokesmen for such governmental agencies as the Securities and Exchange Commission and the Public Buildings Service appeared before the Warren Conference.[90]

The presence of visiting district and circuit judges did

[86] John J. Parker to Harlan F. Stone, September 3, 1941, Parker Papers, Box 54. See Harlan F. Stone to John J. Parker, September 7, 1941, in *ibid.* Parker's proposal came in the wake of congressional-judicial conflict over H.R. 138, introduced in the 77th Congress by Representative Hatton Sumners, Chairman of the House Judiciary Committee. The bill restricted the ability of judges of the United States Courts of Appeals to sit in trial courts. Both Senior Circuit Judge Martin Manton and Joseph Buffington had abused this power, according to Congressman Francis E. Walter of Pennsylvania, thereby stripping the district courts of their independence. See Henry P. Chandler to John J. Parker, August 5, 1941, in *ibid.*; U.S., Congress, Senate, Subcommittee of the Committee on the Judiciary, *Hearings, on H.R. 138, Administration of United States Courts*, part 2, 77th Cong., 1st Sess., 1941.
[87] *Judicial Conference Report, 1944*, p. 47; see also *ibid.*, *1945*, p. 2.
[88] *Ibid.*, pp. 2, 7-9.   [89] *Ibid.*, *1952*, p. 2.
[90] *Ibid.*, *1954*, pp. 2, 230-31.

245

not decline. Under every Chief Justice from Stone, with whom the tradition began in 1942,[91] to Warren their numbers steadily increased. From 4.6 per Conference during Stone's chairmanship, the visitors' ranks rose to 7 under Vinson and to 10.8 in each of the first twelve years of Chief Justice Warren's fourteen-year reign as head of the Conference.[92] The appearance of these judicial visitors reflected not only a growth in the Conference's jurisdiction but also the development of its internal organization.

Those who came to the Stone and Vinson Conferences generally fell into two categories. One class was composed of emissaries from individual circuits who, ordinarily in the name of their circuit's conference, advocated changes in Conference policies or in laws or in both.[93] Members of the various Conference committees comprised another, and larger, segment of the visitors. Their appearance evidenced, first of all, the growth of the committee system which occurred under Chief Justice Stone and, secondly, the expansion of committee membership to include judges other than those on the Conference itself.

Because of the visitor's role, as an emissary or as a member of what was most likely an *ad hoc* committee, high turnover marked the roster of visitors during the Stone period. The number of these one-Conference transients declined sharply under Vinson and stabilized in his successor's chairmanship as standing committees with relatively static composition, including many retired or senior judges in active service, emerged. (See Table 1.)

[91] *Ibid., 1942*, p. 21.

[92] The data includes judges of the United States district courts, circuit courts of appeals, Court of Claims, Customs Court, Court of Customs and Patent Appeals. For the Stone Conference, 1941-1945 inclusive, N = 23; for Vinson, 1946-1953 inclusive, N = 56; for Warren, 1954-1966 inclusive, N = 130.

[93] *Judicial Conference Report, 1942*, p. 21. See Carl Baar, "When Judges Lobby: Congress and Court Administration" (unpub. Ph.D. dissertation, Department of Political Science, University of Chicago, 1969), p. 210.

Table 1.
Index of Judicial Conference Visitor Turnover, 1941-1966 inclusive.*

	District Judges	Circuit Judges	Retired or Senior Judges
Stone Conference	88.9%	66.7%	—
Vinson Conference	56.6%	34.8%	—
Warren Conference	41.5%	38.2%	22.2%

* Turnover (%) = $\dfrac{\text{Number of different visiting judges}}{\text{Total number of visiting judges exclusive of judges of special courts}}$

As for the official delegates and their substitutes, they became increasingly more Democratic and more advanced in years than had ever been true in the Taft and Hughes Conferences. The overwhelming Democratic tide, which had overtaken the nation in the 1930s, made its influence felt in the Conferences under Chief Justice Stone. Then the former Republican majorities vanished and were replaced first by a 50-50 parity and then a 3-2 Democratic majority under Vinson. This increased to 2-1 in the Warren period. (See Table 2.)

Table 2.
Political Party Affiliations of the Official Delegates and Substitutes to the Judicial Conference of the United States, 1941-1966 inclusive.

	Democrats	Republicans	Unidentified
Stone Conference	50%(7)	50%(7)	—
Vinson Conference	56%(14)	44%(11)	—
Warren Conference	64.1%(59)	28.3%(26)	7.6%(7)

At the same time, progressive aging characterized the membership of the Conference. Under Stone, the median age rose steadily from 67 in 1941 to 72 in 1945 and the average median age reached 69, while during his successor's eight years the judges' median age ranged from 64 to 74. More indicative of the Conference's composition, however, was the average median age; it increased slightly to 69.5. Dramatic reversal of this trend would await the appointment of Chief Justice Earl Warren.

District Judge Representation

As chairman of the Judicial Conference, the former California governor sponsored a major reorganization of that institution which doubled the number of official delegates by the addition of district court representatives. Trial court representation had been a goal of some articulate judges since District Judge Merrill E. Otis told the Circuit Conference of the Eighth Circuit in 1939 that he and his colleagues needed

> a voice, a spokesman, an organization to represent them. The Chief Justice speaks for the Supreme Court, in *tones of thunder.* The Conference of Senior Circuit Judges speaks for the circuit courts of appeals. *And when it speaks it is heard.* The Chief Justice and the Conference do what they can for the district courts . . . But their interest in the district courts necessarily is secondary. Their information concerning them is often hearsay and hazy. The result is, district judges have as much influence in the councils of the nation as have the Hottentots of South Africa in the Government of the British Empire.[94]

As he saw it, the solution lay in establishing an organization of district judges in each circuit which would then dis-

[94] "Conference of the United States Circuit and District Judges of the Eighth Circuit, 1939," stenographic transcript, p. 348, Kimbrough Stone Papers, Box 26.

patch representatives to "a national council of judges meeting annually in Washington with the Chief Justice and the Senior Circuit Judges."[95]

District judge demands for more effective access to the Conference grew louder during the early 1940s in the wake of highly controversial policies adopted by the last Conferences under Chief Justice Charles Evans Hughes. These included the setting of standards for the appointment of probation officers,[96] endorsement of the Attorney General's proposal that the circuit councils play a prominent role in the removal and reappointment of referees in bankruptcy,[97] and, as the *coup de grâce*, the extending of its support to a proposed federal indeterminate sentence law which would have curtailed the historic discretion enjoyed by trial judges in fixing sentences.[98]

These apparent efforts to erode in the name of more effective justice historic prerogatives enjoyed by the district judges evoked a storm of protest at the "grass roots."[99] Even a modified indeterminate sentence law was greeted by the Circuit Conference of the Seventh Circuit with "vigorous discussion [and] . . . a full and frank (though not always friendly) criticism of the proposed change."[100] Members of the national Conference echoed this criticism, admitting, in the words of one senior circuit judge, that they had "gone pretty far in recommending to Congress radical changes in the law itself."[101]

The Conference initially sought to meet the challenge by improving its communication system.[102] But the basic issue

[95] *Ibid.*
[96] *Judicial Conference Report, 1940*, pp. 26-27.
[97] *Ibid., 1941*, pp. 21-22; see particularly proposed sections III D1 and III D2.
[98] *Ibid., 1940*, pp. 27-28.   [99] *Ibid., 1941*, pp. 36-37.
[100] Evan A. Evans, "Judicial Conference of the Seventh Circuit," *American Bar Association Journal*, 29 (February 1943), 81.
[101] Xenophon Hicks to D. Lawrence Groner, April 11, 1944, Groner Papers, Box 11.
[102] *Judicial Conference Report, 1941*, p. 31.

was not one of agenda circulation and transmission of lower court views to the Conference. It was one involving the very structure of that body. As then composed, the Conference, observed one judge, was "more representative of what might be termed the administrative function of the judges than . . . of other . . . rapidly developing functions."[103] With expansion of the Conference's business, he thought "a conference composed only of those judges who are oldest in point of service and most removed from the activities of practice, of public life and social policy, and, indeed, from district court activity, must give a one-sided representation of many points of view."[104]

To the district judges, then, the solution lay in their actual participation. They, together with one circuit conference after another echoed this demand during the early 1940s, and transmitted it to the Judicial Conference, and even to influential members of Congress.[105] One of the recipients was Hatton Sumners,[106] chairman of the House Judiciary Committee, who called on the senior circuit judges to "work out some plan to satisfy the demands of the District Judges to proper representation."[107]

Under pressure from all sides, important members of the Conference told their colleagues that they had "about reached the conclusion that something affirmative must be

[103] Charles E. Clark to Learned Hand, October 17, 1944, Clark Papers.

[104] Ibid.

[105] Judicial Conference Report, 1943, p. 71; "Portion of the Transcript of Proceedings of the Judicial Conference of the Ninth Circuit, Recommendations to the Judicial Conference of Senior Circuit Judges, September 9-11, 1943," Administrative Office Correspondence, 59-A-532, Box 2 (cited hereafter as "Judicial Conference of the Ninth Circuit, Recommendations," 1943); D. Lawrence Groner to Members of the Judicial Conference, April 4, 1944, Groner Papers, Box 11.

[106] Allen Cox to Hatton D. Sumners, May 15, 1944, Legislative Files, House, H.R. 2140, 78th Cong.

[107] D. Lawrence Groner to Members of the District Court for the District of Columbia Circuit, April 4, 1944, Groner Papers, Box 11.

done to keep peace in the judicial family"[108] and to over-come "the hard sleddings that our recommendations are having in the Congress."[109] Thus the 1943 Conference estab-lished a three-judge Committee on the Representation of District Judges, chaired by Senior Circuit Judge Orie L. Phillips.[110] Although Phillips favored direct representation of the trial judges, his two colleagues objected,[111] and, as a result, the committee successfully presented a compromise proposal to the Judicial Conference.[112] Known as the "Phil-lips Plan," the measure made no fundamental change in the Conference structure. Instead, it simply created a well-de-fined communications system intended to guarantee consul-tation by the senior circuit judges with the district judges on issues of interest to the latter.[113] The media were the cir-cuit conferences, specially created circuit legislative com-mittees, and committees of the Judicial Conference com-posed equally of district and circuit judges.[114]

Refusal of the senior circuit judges to do more than mere-ly tinker with the Conference procedures reflected a nat-ural desire to retain power as well as their belief in the fundamental adequacy of the existing system of representa-tion,[115] in the real inability of the Conference to threaten the independence of district judges through punitive sanc-tions,[116] and in the absolute necessity of having a "compact

[108] Ibid.

[109] Xenophon Hicks to Groner, April 11, 1944, Groner Papers, Box 11.

[110] Judicial Conference Report, 1943, p. 71. Other members: D. Lawrence Groner and John J. Parker.

[111] Orie L. Phillips to Peter G. Fish, August 12, 1965, in possession of the author.

[112] Ibid.

[113] Judicial Conference Report, 1944, p. 59.

[114] Ibid., 1945, pp. 6-7.

[115] D. Lawrence Groner to Members of the District Court for the District of Columbia Circuit, October 18, 1944, Groner Papers, Box 11.

[116] "Report to the Judicial Conference of the Committee to Con-sider the Representation of District Judges in the Judicial Confer-

and mobile rather than large and cumbersome" Conference.[117] Moreover, democratization of that institution would only establish "a form of political organization within the judiciary which is not based on a definite line of division of thought."[118] If the differences between trial and appellate judges were few and far between, then any formalized distinctions founded on them rested, in fact, upon "a false dichotomy."[119] If, on the other hand, there did exist such differences, then the very presence of trial judges posed the danger that the district and circuit judges might "square off at the other ... without getting anywhere."[120]

The advantages inherent in the *status quo* seemed overwhelming when weighed against the uncertain benefits of change. And so ranking judges in the Conference were confident that minor modifications in the system would prove satisfactory and with them "the District judges, with one or two exceptions, will be entirely content."[121] But the district judges never became "entirely content" nor, in their eyes, did the "Phillips Plan" further enhance the legitimacy of Conference policies. Six years after inauguration of the plan, the assistant director of the Administrative Office reported that "under the present system the district judge is given an opportunity to express his views, but if the final action is adverse to what he thinks it ought to have been, it is sometimes difficult to persuade him that consideration of his views is an adequate substitute for a vote by himself or

---

ence," 1944, mimeograph (Administrative Office of the United States Courts, Washington, D.C.), p. 5.

[117] D. Lawrence Groner to Orie L. Phillips, July 17, 1944, Groner Papers, Box 4.

[118] Charles E. Clark to Learned Hand, October 17, 1944, Clark Papers.

[119] *Ibid.*

[120] *Ibid.*

[121] D. Lawrence Groner to Orie L. Phillips, July 17, 1944, Groner Papers, Box 4.

by someone whom he has selected to vote for him."[122] For their part, district judges opposed further grants of power to the circuit councils or the national Conference "until such time as District Judges have representation—and adequate representation—on the Judicial Council and on the Judicial Conference."[123] Serious agitation erupted in the Ninth Circuit, where in the early 1950s that circuit's Judicial Conference adopted a resolution favoring direct district judge representation.[124] Although the Vinson Conference turned a deaf ear to the proposal, the judges of the Ninth Circuit continued their efforts with undiminished enthusiasm.

Then in March 1955 the chairman of a Ninth Circuit Conference Committee created to implement that circuit's endorsement of district judge representation on the Judicial Conference of the United States circulated a statement of grievances among all federal judges. Reiterating the hoary demand for an enlarged Conference, it pointedly noted that never had "any Committee of the Judicial Conference, upon which *District Judges* were represented, investigated or reported upon the question of representation of the District Judges on the Conference."[125] This proposal now found a strong supporter in Chief Justice Earl Warren. The addition of district judges and concomitant expansion of the size

[122] Elmore Whitehurst to Joseph C. Hutcheson, Jr., October 12, 1951, Administrative Office Correspondence, 60-A-328, Box 27.

[123] John P. Barnes to All Circuit and District Judges of the Seventh Circuit, June 9, 1948, p. 2, copy, Administrative Office Correspondence, 60-A-328, Box 7.

[124] See "Statement of United States District Judge Louis E. Goodman, Chairman of a Committee Appointed by the Judicial Conference of the Ninth Circuit at its July 1954 Session, to Implement its Resolution for Representation of United States District Judges on the Judicial Conference of the United States, March 1955," Stephens Papers, Box 235 (cited hereafter as "Statement of Judge Louis E. Goodman"). See also *Judicial Conference Report, 1951*, p. 33.

[125] "Statement of Judge Louis E. Goodman."

253

of the Conference appealed to him as a means of diluting the strength of vested interests often represented by aged magistrates.[126] And so the March 1955 Conference referred the Ninth Circuit's resolution to the Committee on Court Administration for action.[127]

Presenting the report of that committee to the March 1956 session, the chairman, Chief Judge John Biggs, Jr., noted the widespread support among the judges for trial judge representation and reported unanimous committee endorsement of their participation in the Conference.[128] To this end, he proposed enactment by Congress of legislation providing "for membership on the Judicial Conference of the United States of one district judge from each of the eleven circuits to be elected for a term of three years by the circuit and district judges at the annual circuit conference."[129] The following year, Congress made the recommendation law with the Act of August 28, 1957, and brought to an end the long and sometimes bitter campaign of the district judges for representation on the federal judiciary's highest administrative policy-making institution.[130]

Special Court Representation

Although the addition of trial judges constituted by far the most significant change in the organization of the Judicial Conference since its founding in 1922, there were other additions albeit of far less importance. These new members came from the special courts and, like the district judges, they appeared during the Warren era. By then, both the Court of Claims and the Court of Customs and Patent Appeals had become constitutional rather than legislative

[126] Telephone interview with John C. Airhart, February 5, 1965, Washington, D.C.
[127] *Judicial Conference Report, 1955*, pp. 255-56, 259.
[128] *Ibid., 1956*, p. 313.   [129] *Ibid.*
[130] 71 *Stat.* 476.

254

courts;[131] as such they were Article III tribunals and eligible for Conference membership.[132]

Like the campaign for district judge representation, that for the representation of the special courts sprang from the expanded administrative responsibilities of the Judicial Conference and the work of the Administrative Office. "At one time or another," Director Henry P. Chandler told the then newly-appointed Chief Justice, Earl Warren, "the special courts . . . have raised a question whether the power vested in the Director . . . to regulate the compensation and official expenses of supporting personnel of the United States Courts . . . applies to the special courts or whether the special courts have in reference to their personnel the ultimate control of these matters."[133] The ability of these courts to fix their own subsistence rates for their personnel nullified the congressional demand for "central control of the travel expenses within each department," and meant that "anything like a uniform administration of the travel appropriations . . . as well as effective control of the rates of expenditure would become impossible."[134] The Judicial Conference sided with Chandler and formally supported

[131] See Act of July 8, 1953, 67 *Stat.* 226 (Claims); Act of July 28, 1958, 72 *Stat.* 848 (Customs and Patent Appeals). Upheld by Supreme Court in *Glidden Co. v. Zdanok,* 370 U.S. 530 (1962).

[132] See U.S., Congress, Senate, Committee on the Judiciary, *Amending Title 28, United States Code, With Respect to the Duties of the Judges of the United States Court of Claims,* 84th Cong., 2d Sess., 1956, S. Rept. 1817 to accompany S. 977, p. 2. See also U.S., Congress, Senate, Committee on the Judiciary, *Providing Representation for the Court of Customs and Patent Appeals on the Judicial Conference of the United States,* 87th Cong., 1st Sess., 1961, S. Rept. 887 to accompany H.R. 176, p. 2.

[133] Henry P. Chandler to Earl Warren, February 2, 1954, Stephens Papers, Box 229.

[134] Henry P. Chandler, "Memorandum Concerning Action Taken by the Administrative Office under the Travel Expense Act of 1949, September 9, 1949," mimeograph (Administrative Office of the United States Courts, Washington, D.C.), pp. 3-4.

him against the challenge leveled by the special courts, specifically by the Court of Claims.[135]

The reaction of that court was as emphatic as it was predictable. Chief Judge Marvin Jones complained to a ranking member of the Senate Judiciary Committee that "the Director . . . is given wide administrative authority over the business of all courts, including the Court of Claims; yet our court is not represented on the Conference. . . . This is unjust," he cried, evoking the Spirit of '76. "It is similar in principle to taxation without representation."[136]

Thereupon, judges of the Court of Claims lobbied the Judicial Conference for a place on it. Their "personal presence in the [Conference] room, . . . apparently firm convictions, plus the distinguished support of one of [the Conference's] best members" won over that body.[137] With the Conference's endorsement, Congress acted, and the chief judge of the Court of Claims became an official delegate to the Judicial Conference beginning in 1956. But the Conference exacted a price. It required a waiver by that court of its power to present its own appropriation estimates to Congress without prior Conference approval.[138] Thereafter, its budget estimates were submitted to that body as were those of other Article III courts.

Although the judges of the Court of Customs and Patent Appeals had rejected admission to the Conference with the Court of Claims,[139] they changed their minds six years later. Unanimously favoring representation,[140] they won a place

---

[135] *Judicial Conference Report, 1949*, p. 9.

[136] Marvin Jones to Harley M. Kilgore, undated, in Senate Committee on the Judiciary, *Amending Title 28*, S. Rept. 1817, 1956, p. 3.

[137] Charles E. Clark to Henry P. Chandler, September 14, 1955, Clark Papers; see also *Judicial Conference Report, 1955*, p. 259.

[138] 70 *Stat.* 497.

[139] Henry P. Chandler to Harley M. Kilgore, May 5, 1955, in Senate Committee on the Judiciary, *Amending Title 28*, S. Rept. 1817, 1956, p. 4.

[140] See Senate Committee on the Judiciary, *Providing Representation*, S. Rept. 887, 1961, p. 2.

on the Conference in 1961 under the same conditions as the Court of Claims.[141]

A Changed Appearance

The addition of district judge representatives and judges from the special courts swelled the Judicial Conference from a gathering of twelve official delegates in 1954 to one of twenty-five members in 1966.[142] This transformation, however, proved more profound than a mere change in membership size, for the impact of trial court representation on the Conference had been augmented by the Act of August 6, 1958. This measure required the presiding judges of the circuit and district courts to relinquish that post at age 70.[143] Although this law left the district court representatives to the Conference unaffected as their delegate status was not achieved through seniority, it did ensure that the age of the circuit representatives, who automatically acted as presiding judges of their respective courts of appeals, would fall beneath the 70-year limit.

The effect of this statutory requirement immediately altered the composition of the Warren Conference. What had once been an "assembly of ancients," with a member such as 92-year-old Chief Judge Archibald K. Gardner of the Eighth Circuit, absorbed an infusion of youth. Whereas in the first five years of Warren's chairmanship, the average median age of the chief circuit judges had surpassed that of the Vinson Conference, rising to 69.8 years, it declined dramatically after 1958. That year the median age of the delegates fell below 65 for the first time in nearly a decade, while the average median age during the seven years 1959 through 1966 reached 63.4 years.[144]

[141] 75 Stat. 521.
[142] See Judicial Conference Report, 1966, p. 29.
[143] 72 Stat. 497.
[144] See John R. Schmidhauser, "Age and Judicial Behavior: American Higher Appellate Judges," in Wilma Donahue and Clark Tibbitts, eds., Politics of Age (Ann Arbor, 1961), pp. 108-13.

If the Warren Conference lost its aged members, it also experienced a greatly increased turnover in its official delegates and their substitutes. From 1922 through 1956 the median Conference tenure of individual judges had been 8.0 years and the mean 8.8,[145] while in the decade 1957 through 1966, median tenure declined to 3.0 years and the mean to 3.4.[146] In the same manner the proportion of judges who had sat on the Conference for ten or more years fell from 39.2 percent in the period 1922 through 1956 to practically zero in the years 1957 through 1966.[147] In fact, during that decade only 24.6 percent of the sixty-five judges on the Conference remained for five years or longer.[148]

Reduction of the average age of Conference members, the increased number of participants, and their turnover largely destroyed the system of seniority which had prevailed since the days of William Howard Taft. Gone were the venerable judges with influence achieved through long years of service on the Conference. Gone, too, was the kind of judicial "power elite" which had emerged so clearly in the Vinson era when judges like John Biggs, Jr., Orie L. Phillips, and John J. Parker dominated the Conference. In its stead appeared a mature institution organized around a system of committees.

Inside the Conference

Leadership of the post-1939 Judicial Conferences rested with three very different Chief Justices: Harlan Fiske

[145] N = 51. Data includes: the Chief Justice, excluding Senior Associate Justice Hugo Black, Acting Chief Justice and chairman of the Judicial Conference, September session, 1953, presiding judges of the United States courts of appeals, Circuits One through Nine from 1922, Circuit Ten from 1928, the District of Columbia Circuit from 1937, and the Court of Claims from 1956.

[146] N = 65. Data includes members of courts listed in n. 145 and the Court of Customs and Patent Appeals from 1961.

[147] Seventeen official delegates, N = 51.

[148] Sixteen official delegates, N = 65.

Stone, Fred M. Vinson, and Earl Warren. Although circumstances beyond their control often influenced the business and organization of their Conferences, these prestigious chairmen largely set the tone of the meetings and exercised the decisive power.

That their leadership styles differed became evident in the transition from Charles Evans Hughes to Chief Justice Stone. This changeover in Conference chairmen was as sharp for the Judicial Conference as it was for the Supreme Court.[149] "There is quite a contrast between him and Chief Justice Hughes," wrote Senior Circuit Judge Orie L. Phillips, who found the new chairman not only able but "human" as well.[150] Stone's conception of his role as chairman emphasized this contrast. To him, his primary task was simply "to focus discussion and [to dispatch] the business of the Conference without being too much of a Czar."[151]

This conception of the chairman's duties combined with the great expansion of Conference responsibilities in the wake of the Administrative Office Act turned the sessions into veritable "town meetings" in which "debate went on and on."[152] Even though the judges eventually took decisive action, much to the surprise of one visitor to the 1943 Conference,[153] the proceedings were enervating for the participants. They complained of the large volume of relatively trivial subjects considered. One judge reported especially widespread criticism of the half-day which the 1942 Conference devoted to the problem of a park commissioner whom the director of the Administrative Office had "met

[149] Mason, *Harlan Fiske Stone*, ch. 47.

[150] Orie L. Phillips to Henry M. Bates in Henry M. Bates to Harlan Fiske Stone, December 17, 1945, Harlan Fiske Stone Papers, Box 3 (Library of Congress, Washington, D.C.; cited hereafter as H. F. Stone Papers).

[151] Harlan F. Stone to D. Lawrence Groner, August 17, 1941, Groner Papers, Box 12.

[152] Interview with John Biggs, Jr.

[153] Statement of Paul J. McCormick, "Judicial Conference of the Ninth Circuit, Recommendations," 1943, p. 5.

out in one of the national parks and who wanted some relief whereby the Park Commissioners could work nearly full time."[154]

Despite the wandering nature of Conference discussions under Stone, the Chief Justice exercised his prerogatives as chairman, even if in a far less autocratic and authoritarian fashion than had his predecessor. He took the initiative in Conference policies relating to judicial ethics and Supreme Court jurisdiction,[155] and successfully labored for their endorsement by the senior circuit judges.[156] Temperamentally unable to dictate to these judges, the Chief utilized a different strategy: he appealed to reason. In the words of one Conference member, Stone "just persuaded and persuaded until he got his way."[157] Even on issues which stirred great heat among federal judges, such as extra-judicial duties performed by sitting judges, his deep convictions on the subject and his persistence won over reluctant Conference members.[158]

Chief Justice Vinson brought to the Conference an intimate acquaintance with the legislative process as well as an abiding interest in and detailed knowledge of judicial administration.[159] Even so, the Conference continued to be

[154] Evan A. Evans to Henry P. Chandler, November 17, 1942, Administrative Office Correspondence, 59-A-532, Box 2.

[155] Harlan F. Stone to John J. Parker, August 22, 1943, copy, Kimbrough Stone Papers, Box 23.

[156] Kimbrough Stone, memorandum, "Habeas Corpus Bill, June 1946," ibid., Box 24.

[157] Interview with Orie L. Phillips, February 22, 1965, Washington, D.C. See Henry P. Chandler to John F. Finerty, November 25, 1944, Administrative Office Correspondence, 57-A-122, Box 15; Judicial Conference Report, 1945, p. 12, on subject of Chandler's letter.

[158] See Sam O. Clark to Charles E. Clark, October 24, 1942, Clark Papers; Learned Hand to Charles E. Clark, October 24, 1942, ibid.; Judicial Conference Report, 1942, p. 31, on subject of Clark's correspondence.

[159] Interview with Orie L. Phillips; interview with Will Shafroth, February 18, 1965, Washington, D.C.

marked by the "town meeting" atmosphere which had been so characteristic of the Stone period. Agenda grew, debate rambled, and voluble senior circuit judges filibustered at the meetings.[160] Aggravating, if not causing, this condition was the increasing sensitivity of the Vinson as well as of the Stone Conferences to the demands of the district judges. These were the years of the "Phillips Plan" and endless polling of the trial judges.[161] If referenda proved inadequate,[162] the doors of the Conference were flung open to itinerant judicial and non-judicial petitioners.

Thus, the Conference became a kind of appellate tribunal for those individuals and interests who suffered defeat in the committees of the Conference.[163] When one chief district judge, seeking increased salaries for his staff, met rebuff from the Committee on Supporting Personnel, his counterpart on the circuit court advised him "to take an appeal, so to speak, to the Judicial Conference from the ruling of the Personnel Committee against your proposed reclassification of present personnel."[164] He did, appearing at the 1954 Conference "prepared to carry the ball" for his court.[165]

Further contributing to the "town meeting" atmosphere

[160] Interview with John Biggs, Jr.

[161] Irving Kaufman, "Appellate Review of Sentences: A Symposium at the Judicial Conference of the United States Court of Appeals for the Second Circuit," *Federal Rules Decisions*, 32 (1963), 261-63.

[162] See "Report of the Committee on Procedure in Antitrust and Other Protracted Cases, September 22, 1954," mimeograph (Administrative Office of the United States Courts, Washington, D.C.), pp. 1-2; *Judicial Conference Report, 1954*, p. 24; *ibid., 1955*, pp. 26-71.

[163] See Peter B. Olney to Harlan F. Stone, September 27, 1943, H. F. Stone Papers, Box 16; Stone to Olney, November 3, 1943, *ibid.*; Kimbrough Stone to E. Marvin Underwood, June 1, 1943, Kimbrough Stone Papers, Box 23.

[164] Harold M. Stephens to Bolitha Laws, March 31, 1954, Stephens Papers, Box 228.

[165] Joseph Paull to John Biggs, Jr., April 8, 1954, *ibid.*; *Judicial Conference Report, 1954*, p. 237.

of the Vinson Conferences were sharply divergent views of the role of the institution in making recommendations to Congress for money and manpower. On one side stood those like Chief Judge Harold M. Stephens of the District of Columbia, who held the conviction "that we must have a vast expansion in the Federal Judiciary if we are going to do our work in a manner which will not only dispose of the cases carefully, but promptly."[166] At the other pole were the advocates of administrative self-restraint, led by Chief Judge Joseph C. Hutcheson, Jr., of the Fifth Circuit, who "consistently opposed requested increases of judicial personnel . . . when I thought them unsupported by a reasonable view of available statistics."[167]

The presence of such articulate adversaries was tempered by the existence of a triumvirate of judges which had emerged in Chief Justice Stone's time and rose to dominance in the Vinson and early Warren Conferences. Consisting of John J. Parker of the Fourth Circuit, John Biggs, Jr. of the Third, and Orie L. Phillips of the Tenth Circuit, it exercised vast influence by virtue of its members' expertise, committee chairmanships, seniority, and strong personalities.[168]

In fact, the work of the Conference largely revolved about the Parker-Biggs-Phillips axis if for no other reason than that these judges were recognized as leaders to whose judgment others on the Conference deferred. They deferred because of expertise and knowledge, and because,

[166] "Address of Harold M. Stephens," *Nebraska Law Review*, 34 (January 1955), 411; see also Harold M. Stephens to Fred M. Vinson, January 6, 1949, Stephens Papers, Box 211.

[167] In Henry P. Chandler to Members of the Judicial Conference, June 8, 1951, mimeograph (Administrative Office of the United States Courts, Washington, D.C.), p. 2.

[168] Interview with Ronald C. Beattie, January 19, 1965, Washington, D.C. See also Henry P. Chandler, undated memorandum, "The Work of the Judicial Conference and Suggestions for its Discussion," Administrative Office Correspondence, 59-A-1536, Box 1.

in one instance, they were "impressed by the insistence of Judge Biggs . . . as to the attitude of Congress."[169]

But, as might be expected, members of the triumvirate sometimes carried the day in Conference only after modifying their own views. Thus Parker, as a committee chairman, changed his position during the course of one Conference in order to "present a united [committee] recommendation, which will stand a much better chance of approval [by Congress] than a proposal as to which there is a division of [committee] opinion."[170]

Nevertheless, some issues lay beyond compromise even by members of the triumvirate and here conflict among the Conference titans raged, especially if the Chief Justice remained neutral. One such issue involved a proposed restriction of federal habeas corpus jurisdiction designed to favor the jurisdictional integrity of state court systems. Parker led the restriction campaign and, as described by Chief Judge Charles E. Clark, the struggle was a furious one. With final success in sight, "Judge [William] Denman defected, and the verbal battles between him and Judge Parker . . . with . . . Judge Hutcheson taking over for Judge Parker after Denman had worn Parker out . . . were fearful and wonderful."[171]

Despite the clear dominance of the Parker-Biggs-Phillips bloc, Chief Justice Vinson played a vital and sometimes aggressive role as chairman of the Conference. At strategic moments he would decisively, if not always tactfully, intervene in the proceedings to advocate or even to impose his own views.[172] Suggestions of other participants were "rejected out of hand,"[173] and when one Conference committee

[169] Charles E. Clark to Irving R. Kaufman, September 21, 1956, Clark Papers.

[170] John J. Parker to Kimbrough Stone, April 28, 1947, Kimbrough Stone Papers, Box 24.

[171] Charles E. Clark to Walter L. Pope, July 24, 1962, Clark Papers.

[172] Interview with John Biggs, Jr.

[173] Harold M. Stephens to Louis Goodman, September 8, 1951, Stephens Papers, Box 82.

favored submission of confidential trial briefs to the judges but not to the opposing attorney, the Chief Justice reportedly "expressed horror at the practice and an administrative order was made prohibiting confidential briefs."[174]

Vinson's tendency to take forthright positions on some issues did not guarantee success, for he was one of the few chairmen to suffer an outright defeat at the hands of his Conference.[175] But more often than not it resulted in victory and when it did there existed little recourse for the losers. Criticized for the policy adopted by the Conference on confidential briefs, Vinson simply dismissed the complaint, stating that he did "not care to enter into a discussion of the action. . . . In my view the language is clear."[176]

Largely responsible for his success among the assemblage of presiding circuit judges was the Chief's prestige derived from his previous career as a politician. This status gave him a strong hand in the formulation of Conference legislative policies[177] for he commanded great deference from members of the Conference, as witnessed by Chief Judge Calvert Magruder's lecture to a trial judge embittered by the Conference's congressional tactics. "Chief Justice Vinson strongly urged us out of his long Congressional experience," declaimed Magruder, "that we could not ignore the rebuke contained in the report of the House Committee on Appropriations and again submit a budget calling for appropriations in excess of the salaries for law clerks authorized by law." Pragmatism rather than idealism had paid rich dividends, for, observed the ranking judge, "The result has amply demonstrated the wisdom of the Judicial Con-

[174] Arthur T. Vanderbilt to Leland L. Tolman, August 27, 1954, Administrative Office Correspondence, 60-A-328, Box 2; see also *Judicial Conference Report, 1946*, p. 21.

[175] Interview with John Biggs, Jr.

[176] Fred M. Vinson to Charles E. Clark, December 3, 1946, Clark Papers.

[177] See Fred M. Vinson to Xenophon Hicks, December 30, 1948, Stephens Papers, Box 211.

264

ference in following the advice of Chief Justice Vinson in this matter."[178]

After 1958, the Conference under Chief Justice Earl Warren bore only a faint resemblance to that under his predecessor. The now younger and much enlarged policy-making body, despite predictions to the contrary, manifested little tendency to postpone decisions and even less willingness to tolerate filibusters which had bedeviled earlier Conferences.[179] Instead, it became what one judge termed a "receptacle for Committee reports,"[180] most of which won Conference endorsement without amendments.[181] The enhanced efficiency founded on youth, numbers, and a revitalized committee system was purchased at a price, namely the price of careful Conference review of committee recommendations.[182] In short, the Conference after 1958 became far more of a "rubber stamp" than had ever been true during its preceding thirty-five years of existence.[183]

Over this transformed Judicial Conference presided Chief Justice Earl Warren, a former political leader and

[178] Calvert Magruder to Clifton Matthews, June 4, 1948, Stephens Papers, Box 211.

[179] Telephone interview with John C. Airhart, February 5, 1965; interview with Matthew McGuire, January 6, 1965, Washington, D.C.

[180] Charles E. Clark to J. Edward Lumbard, November 6, 1959, Clark Papers.

[181] Interview with Matthew McGuire. Exceptions involve fundamental changes in the structure or jurisdiction of the federal courts. See *Judicial Conference Report, 1956*, p. 11; *ibid., 1958*, pp. 34-35; *ibid., 1961*, pp. 67-68; *ibid., 1962*, pp. 5-6, 50-51; *ibid., 1963*, pp. 7, 63; *ibid., 1964*, p. 7.

[182] *Washington Post*, October 15, 1967, p. F1, F4.

[183] An exception occurred at the first Conference chaired by Chief Justice Warren E. Burger when the judges acted on a controversial issue which had bypassed regular committee channels. See *Judicial Conference Report, 1969*, p. 85; U.S., Congress, Senate, Subcommittee on Separation of Powers of the Committee on the Judiciary, *Hearings, on the Independence of Federal Judges*, 91st Cong., 2d Sess., 1970, pp. 57, 316.

THE JUDICIAL CONFERENCE, 1939-1969

chief executive of California. At his first Conference in the spring of 1954, the new chairman made a favorable impression on the assembled judges, one of whom remarked on his "executive ability" and described his conduct of the meeting as "very businesslike, very pleasant."[184] Although not regarded as an especially voluble chairman nor as an active initiator of discussion,[185] the Chief was, according to Judge Harold Stephens, "a good listener and . . . decisive."[186] As described by one student of the Conference, Warren's administrative style was to "lend encouragement to those with new ideas, give private support, but withhold public commitment until a new scheme had won broader acceptance."[187]

Once support had developed and been manifested in a Conference Committee recommendation, the Chief's position could be decisive. Before the 1965 Conference began discussion of the controversial division of California's judicial districts, Warren said, "Let me tell you about California." He then explained the nature and growth of the state's economy and population "since I was Governor." Commented one judge: "The old boy said it was necessary." In this manner the Chief settled the question to his satisfaction in spite of the objections of some Conference members to district division.[188]

On other issues Warren routed all opposition including that based upon committee recommendations.[189] For instance, late in 1955 controversy erupted in Congress over the University of Chicago's Jury Project which involved the

184 Harold M. Stephens to Frank S. Richards, May 25, 1954, Stephens Papers, Box 83.
185 Interview with John C. Airhart, December 22, 1964.
186 Harold M. Stephens to Frank S. Richards, May 25, 1954, Stephens Papers, Box 83.
187 Baar, "When Judges Lobby," p. 417.
188 Ibid., p. 435.
189 Interview with J. Edward Lumbard, December 30, 1964, New York, New York.

266

"bugging" of jury rooms in federal courthouses.[190] At the March 1956 meeting of the Judicial Conference, the Chief Justice, in the words of one participant, "showed himself as emotional as any senator about the observation of juries and really took away any chance of real discussion."[191] The thoroughly chastened Conference then "went out of its way to take prompt action," endorsing a pending bill intended to curb such "bugging."[192]

A similar steamroller strategy emerged at the last Conference chaired by Chief Justice Warren. Stung by the Fortas debacle[193] and threatened with unwanted congressional legislation,[194] he hurriedly convened a Special Session of the Judicial Conference in June 1969. It adopted guidelines proposed by the Court Administration Committee,[195] but not without "spirited debate" and sharp dissension.[196] Some members favored delay and further study pending the appearance of Warren E. Burger as chairman.[197] They resented the haste with which the Chief had "rammed through" the proposal "without adequate notice. . . ."[198] Others felt that judges of the inferior federal courts were being made scapegoats for off-the-bench activities of Supreme Court justices. Yet the Conference had no jurisdiction over the High Court magistrates.[199] Nevertheless, Warren mustered decisive two-to-one support among Conference members by dropping strong hints that the Supreme Court justices would adopt similar guidelines.[200] At least a

---

[190] New York Times, October 12, 1955, p. 1.
[191] Charles E. Clark to Edward H. Levi, March 15, 1956, Clark Papers.
[192] Ibid.; Judicial Conference Report, 1956, p. 319; see H.R. 8328, 84th Cong.
[193] See above, n. 54.   [194] New York Times, June 11, 1969, p. 1.
[195] See above, n. 53.   [196] New York Times, July 3, 1969, p. 15.
[197] Ibid., June 13, 1969, p. 16.
[198] Ibid., p. 1.   [199] Ibid., p. 16.
[200] Washington Evening Star, June 13, 1969, in Congressional Record, vol. 115, part 12, 91st Cong., 1st Sess., 16043.

Conference resolution would give him "clout" in pressing his independent-minded colleagues on the Court to curb their own non-judicial activities.[201]

Warren's capacity to influence the members of the Judicial Conference was no less, and was perhaps more, than that of his predecessors. He had, declared one judge, "but to state his position,"[202] and he could expect to win the support of his Conference "999 times out of 1000."[203] But he could often achieve his ends in a less overt manner than could previous chairmen. Through his hand-picked director of the Administrative Office, the Chief could communicate his views to the Judicial Conference and its committees. Director Olney, in turn, then worked to "grease the tracks" for these views long before discussion in the Conference ever began.[204] Even more significant as a lever of power has been the committee system which, under Warren, served to reduce his visibility as a policy-maker without endangering his ultimate control of the policy-making process.

[201] *Ibid.* The Supreme Court substantially rebuffed Warren. See *New York Times*, June 18, 1969, pp. 1, 54; *Washington Post*, June 24, 1969, p. A13. Ultimately, opposition among judges of the inferior courts would compel the Conference under Chief Justice Warren Burger to modify, if not emasculate, the guidelines established at the June 10, 1969 Special Session. See *Judicial Conference Report, 1969*, pp. 50-52.

[202] Interview with Richard H. Chambers, January 26, 1965, Washington, D.C.

[203] Interview with John C. Airhart, December 22, 1964.

[204] *Ibid.*

CHAPTER 8

The Committee System
of the Judicial Conference

Organization

POST-1939 changes in the Judicial Conference as a whole were accompanied by equally significant modifications in that institution's committee system. Committees had existed since 1922, but those established under Taft and Hughes were relatively few in number and typically select rather than standing committees. Once the work of the Conference expanded in the wake of the Administrative Office Act, this system became inadequate.

Thus a proliferation of committees marked the work of the early Conferences presided over by Chief Justice Stone. At the first held under his chairmanship, seven committees were created as contrasted to the three authorized by the final two Hughes Conferences.[1] The September 1942 meeting established another twelve, and that held in 1943 set up seven more.[2]

However, the significance of these committees was not confined to their quantity. Many were qualitatively different from those common to the Taft and Hughes Conferences, because an increasing proportion had the status of standing committees intended to deal with permanent subjects such as personnel policies for judicial employees and administration of the bankruptcy system.[3] Ad hoc or select committees continued to exist, but the trend toward permanent committees to consider ongoing issues had become unmistakable.

[1] "Report of the Judicial Conference," in *Judicial Conference Report, 1941,* pp. 36-41.
[2] *Ibid., 1942,* pp. 24-35; *ibid., 1943,* p. 71.
[3] *Ibid., 1942,* p. 24.

In addition, all the committees during Stone's tenure began to utilize revamped procedures. Their reports, the initial presentations of which were once orally rendered to the Conference by committee chairmen, now appeared in mimeograph form. Moreover, by a rule adopted at the 1944 Conference, they were "submitted at least thirty days in advance of the September Session of the Judicial Conference."[4] This procedure bore rich fruits; in fact, Stone wrote Charles A. Beard, it "is giving results far beyond my expectations."[5]

Under Chief Justice Fred Vinson, the general character of the committee structure remained unchanged, although his formal power to shape it was strengthened when the 1948 Conference authorized him "to take whatever action he deemed desirable with respect to . . . the appointing of new committees."[6] Not until the chairmanship of his successor, Earl Warren, however, did the committee system undergo a major reorganization. In Warren's second year as chairman, the 1955 Judicial Conference discharged every existing committee and replaced them with ten new committees, eight of which were permanent.[7] Later, these specialized committees, endowed with broad subject-matter jurisdiction, would be joined by the standing Committee on Rules of Practice and Procedure. Including Advisory Committees on Civil Procedure, Admiralty, Bankruptcy, Appellate Rules, Evidence, and Criminal Rules, this committee assumed the rule-making functions of the now defunct Advisory Committee to the Supreme Court.[8]

Early in his tenure, Warren reshaped the committee system into one composed of a relatively small number of

[4] Ibid., 1944, p. 65.
[5] Harlan Fiske Stone to Charles A. Beard, November 12, 1943, H. F. Stone Papers, Box 3.
[6] Judicial Conference Report, 1948, p. 43.
[7] Ibid., 1955, pp. 30-32.
[8] See ibid., 1961, pp. 21-31; ibid., 1963, pp. 19-21.

standing committees.[9] Over time, however, even this system grew ragged as the natural process of committee genesis increased the number of such bodies to "some fifteen or sixteen" by 1967.[10] That year, the Conference took the novel step of creating a Committee on Committees to make "a complete survey of its committee structure as to status, number and functions."[11]

The propensity toward committee proliferation demonstrates the vital role played by these bodies. As important links in the administrative chain, they exercise an often decisive influence over the policy-making process.[12] Thus committee genesis reflects new and changing demands made on the federal judiciary. It has been related to the exigencies of the congressional process[13] as well as to demands for change emanating from the "grass roots," from circuit conferences and councils, and individual state and federal judges.[14]

Committee genesis constitutes, in short, a vital means of access to the Judicial Conference. This has been especially true for those to whom other channels are closed. When Judge Jerome Frank of the Second Circuit Court of Appeals sought enlarged grounds for appeal of interlocutory orders to the courts of appeals, he was rebuffed by the old Supreme Court Advisory Committee on the Rules.[15] "This

[9] See "Agenda for the Judicial Conference of the United States, Special Session Beginning March 18, 1965," mimeograph (Administrative Office of the United States Courts, Washington, D.C.).

[10] *Judicial Conference Report, 1967*, p. 66.

[11] *Ibid.*

[12] See *ibid., 1962*, p. 46; *ibid., 1957*, p. 293.

[13] Re: Maintenance Expenses of Judges. See Walt Horan, U.S., Congress, House, Subcommittee of the Committee on Appropriations, *Hearings, Second Supplemental Appropriation Bill, 1953*, 83d Cong., 1st Sess., 1953, p. 427; *Judicial Conference Report, 1953*, pp. 230-31.

[14] *Ibid., 1950*, p. 18; see also John J. Parker to Kimbrough Stone, December 2, 1942, Kimbrough Stone Papers, Box 23.

[15] See Henry P. Chandler, "Memorandum on the Proposal to Enlarge the Provision of the Present Statute for Appeals from Interlocu-

sort of upper-court policing of trial court activity is not a sound appellate function," declared that committee's reporter, Judge Charles E. Clark, "and, in view of its haphazard and freezing characteristics, can only be detrimental to effective court administration."[16] To Frank's request for establishment of a new committee of the Conference to study the issue, Clark retorted: "The Advisory Committee [of the Supreme Court] by virtue of its study, experience, and past activities is the proper body to consider proposals of this general nature, and should not be ousted or subjected to conflicts of jurisdiction by the appointment of a new committee."[17] But ousted it was, for Judge Frank successfully persisted in his quest for a new committee.[18]

By the end of Chief Justice Warren's chairmanship, however, reorganization and consolidation of the committee system restricted much *ad hoc* committee genesis and longevity. The September 1968 Conference abolished a number of vintage committees.[19] It established in their place committees of three types. Foremost were *general committees* with subcommittee networks. With membership broadly based, their primary function lay in serving the "overall requirements of the Conference."[20] *Standing committees*

---

tory Decisions," 1951, mimeograph (Administrative Office of the United States Courts, Washington, D.C.), p. 1.

[16] *Ibid.*, p. 11.

[17] *Ibid.*; see also Charles E. Clark to Henry P. Chandler, September 14, 1951, Clark Papers.

[18] See *Judicial Conference Report, 1951*, p. 32; *ibid.*, *1952*, p. 203; *ibid.*, *1953*, p. 27.

[19] Abolished were: the Advisory Committee; the Habeas Corpus Committee; the Special Committee on the Geographical Organization of the Courts; the Committees on Judicial Statistics, Supporting Personnel, and the Revision of the Laws; and the Subcommittee on Discovery and Multiple Litigation of the Committee on Trial Practice and Technique, *ibid.*, *1968*, p. 44.

[20] *Ibid.* The general committees were: "a) A Committee on Court Administration, with subcommittees on statistics, on judicial salaries, annuities, and tenure; on supporting personnel of the courts and on federal jurisdiction, as well as such other subcommittees as it may

ranked next in the new hierarchy. They had a somewhat smaller and not necessarily representative membership. Such groups were to serve specific Conference needs.[21] Finally, the Conference could create *special committees* "for a specific limited purpose . . . ," with a normal life expectancy of two years or less.[22]

Composition

Positions on committees of the Judicial Conference are coveted by federal judges. In spite of the often arduous and unpaid labor involved, judges seek them because a committee appointment constitutes one of the few means of status differentiation available within the judicial system.[23] Through membership on committees, judges gain esteem in the eyes of their peers, a condition materially advanced when tangible benefits flow from committee activities to the courts of their fellow judges.[24] Moreover, committee participation enhances self-esteem. "One of the pleasantest and most rewarding tasks to which I was assigned," related a judge from New York, "resulted from my appointment by the late Chief Justice Harlan Fiske Stone as a member of the Judicial Conference Committee . . . to assist the Con-

---

determine; b) A Committee on the Administration of the Criminal Law with subcommittees as it may determine; c) A Committee on the Operation of the Jury System with such subcommittees as it may determine."

[21] *Ibid.* The standing committees were: "a) A Committee on the Budget; b) A Committee on the Administration of the Bankruptcy System; c) A Committee on the Administration of the Probation System; d) A Committee on Intercircuit Assignments; e) A Committee on Trial Practice and Techniques."

[22] *Ibid.* The special committee was: "A Special Committee on the Implementation of the Criminal Justice Act of 1964."

[23] Telephone interview with John C. Airhart, February 5, 1965, Washington, D.C.

[24] *Ibid.*; Archibald K. Gardner to Harold M. Stephens and John Biggs, Jr., June 11, 1954, Stephens Papers, Box 228.

gressional Committee on the Revision of the Federal Judicial Code."[25]

Such appointments are very much the prerogative of the Chief Justice, a prerogative which was formalized in 1948 when the Judicial Conference authorized Chief Justice Vinson to "take whatever action he deemed desirable with respect to increasing the membership of existing committees, . . . the filling of any existing committee vacancies . . . and the designation of membership."[26] This power was absolute as Chief Judge Charles E. Clark discovered late in 1959. Then, after fifteen years as chairman of the Statistics Committee, he learned that his committee had been reconstituted by Chief Justice Warren. Nowhere on the list of members was Clark's name. "I guess there isn't much question that the Chief did not like my point of view on statistics and was rather happy to eradicate it," commented the chagrined and committeeless judge.[27]

In utilizing their appointment prerogative, Chief Justices have usually followed certain criteria. Long before district judges acquired official delegate status on the Conference, Charles Evans Hughes "had the idea . . . that the committees should contain judges [from] outside of the Judicial Conference as well as those [from] within it, and that in all matters affecting the district courts there should be a liberal representation of district judges."[28] Inclusion of non-members of the Conference, which became a fixed practice under Stone,[29] had "the double advantage that the Judicial Conference receives the benefit of the opinions of judges throughout the country, and the judges who serve on the committees gain a perspective of the Federal judicial ad-

[25] Clarence G. Galston, *Behind the Judicial Curtain* (Chicago, 1959), p. 129.

[26] *Judicial Conference Report, 1948*, p. 43.

[27] Charles E. Clark to Will Shafroth, December 18, 1959, Clark Papers; see also Clark to Earl Warren, September 18, 1959, *ibid.*

[28] *Judicial Conference Report, 1950*, p. 65.

[29] *Ibid., 1942*, pp. 34-35.

ministration as a whole."[30] And, it might be added, their participation would have a legitimizing effect on the policies ultimately adopted by the senior circuit judges.

However, as Henry P. Chandler, director of the Administrative Office, told Chief Justice Stone, the presence on each committee of at least one member of the Judicial Conference was advisable because it permitted "the district judges to know what the general attitude of the Conference is likely to be."[31] Further, it guaranteed "that when the committee report comes before the Judicial Conference there will be at least one member of the Conference who is thoroughly familiar with the recommendations and who can see that they are adequately supported in any discussions before the Conference."[32]

Representation of particular geographical regions or particular courts has sometimes been a determining factor in committee selections. For committees considering such subjects as public defender systems or budgetary proposals, Chief Justices sought out judges from metropolitan areas where indigent defendants were many and budgets large.[33] Thus reorganization of the Budget Committee in 1960 reflected Warren's conviction that its majority "should probably be district judges and particularly judges of the larger metropolitan districts which have the greatest budgetary problems."[34]

Important, too, as a criterion for appointment has been the candidate's interest. "In view of your interest in the matter [of sentencing]," Chief Justice Warren wrote one judge, "and at the suggestion of our mutual friend, John Parker,

[30] *Ibid.*, p. 65.
[31] Henry P. Chandler to Harlan Fiske Stone, October 7, 1942, Administrative Office Correspondence, 60-A-328, Box 4.
[32] *Ibid.*
[33] Henry P. Chandler to Harrison Tweed, December 30, 1954, *ibid.*, 59-A-18, Box 137; Chandler to Elmore Whitehurst and Leland Tolman, October 28, 1947, *ibid.*, 60-A-328, Box 27.
[34] Earl Warren to Charles E. Clark, November 30, 1959, Clark Papers.

who is already aware of your interest, I would like to appoint you a member of the Committee on the Administration of the Criminal Law."[35]

Interest alone is insufficient; it must be known to the Chief Justice. Through good words from committee chairmen like Parker,[36] the Advisory Committee of the Judicial Conference,[37] members of the Conference,[38] the Administrative Office,[39] and through judicial opinions reaching the Supreme Court on appeal[40] as well as through his personal acquaintance with the judges, the Chief Justice gains a knowledge of likely appointees.

But the actual appointment may be based on other qualities: seniority on the Conference,[41] personal loyalty to the Chief,[42] and coincidence of views with those of the Chief Justice on particular issues.[43] On the other hand, some judges have received committee posts for the specific purpose of integrating them into the national administrative system, thereby reducing internal resistance to Conference policies.[44]

[35] Earl Warren to Carl A. Hatch, January 15, 1957, Administrative Office Correspondence, 60-A-328, Box 25.

[36] See Leland Tolman to Charles E. Clark, October 25, 1951, *ibid.*, Box 4.

[37] *Judicial Conference Report, 1955*, p. 30.

[38] D. Lawrence Groner to Harlan F. Stone, October 6, 1945, Groner Papers, Box 6.

[39] Henry P. Chandler to Harlan Fiske Stone, October 7, 1942, Administrative Office Correspondence, 60-A-328, Box 4; Henry P. Chandler to Elmore Whitehurst and Leland Tolman, October 28, 1947, *ibid.*, Box 27.

[40] Interview with Albert B. Maris, December 29, 1964, Philadelphia, Pennsylvania.

[41] Telephone interview with John C. Airhart.

[42] Interview with Richard H. Chambers, January 26, 1965, Washington, D.C.

[43] Earl Warren to Carl A. Hatch, January 15, 1957, Administrative Office Correspondence, 60-A-328, Box 25. See Baar, "When Judges Lobby."

[44] William C. Mathes to Arthur F. Lederle, January 15, 1953, Stephens Papers, Box 225.

More typically, however, the Chief Justice recruits committee members because of their demonstrated expertise and experience. Thus a judge, widely recognized for his competence in legislative drafting, found himself on the committee to revise the Judicial Code;[45] another with long experience in judicial statistics, first with the Wickersham Commission and later with the American Law Institute, was appointed to the Statistics Committee, later becoming its chairman.[46] Likewise, judges with prior experience in the Department of Justice[47] and those wise in the ways of congressional politics[48] have been apt candidates for committee slots.

Finally, personal qualities loom large in the appointments, particularly for committee chairmanships. Effectiveness in small group situations and in interpersonal relations was considered so essential by Director Chandler that he urged on Chief Justice Stone "the desirability of securing strong men who . . . can be relied upon to bring out good reports from their committees."[49] Senior Circuit Judge Orie L. Phillips met this qualification. Chandler described him as having "admirable judgment in council, [and as one who] usually takes a median position between extremes, which . . . is desirable in a chairman who is trying to accomplish something; he has a faculty for bringing people

[45] Interview with John Biggs, Jr., August 12, 1965, Washington, D.C.

[46] Charles E. Clark to D. Lawrence Groner, March 16, 1940, Groner Papers, Box 21; *Judicial Conference Report, 1943*, p. 71; *ibid., 1944*, p. 64.

[47] Henry P. Chandler to Elmore Whitehurst and Leland Tolman, October 28, 1947, Administrative Office Correspondence, 60-A-328, Box 27; also interview with Matthew McGuire, January 6, 1965, Washington, D.C.

[48] Interview with Albert B. Maris, December 29, 1964, Philadelphia, Pennsylvania; Charles E. Clark to Earl Warren, September 18, 1959, Clark Papers.

[49] Henry P. Chandler to Harlan F. Stone, October 7, 1942, Administrative Office Correspondence, 60-A-328, Box 4.

together and he showed by his work on the committee on punishment for crime that he is ready to devote a very large amount of time and energy to promoting the efficiency of the federal judicial system."[50]

Chief Justices from Stone to Warren staffed their Conference committees with interested, skilled, and personally effective members, who, with some exceptions, were ideologically in what one judge termed as "the middle of the road."[51] Avoided have been those judges regarded as "chronic dissenters and odd balls."[52]

The selection criteria themselves were wholly unpublicized and non-specific until 1968. That year the Conference established for the first time formal selection criteria. It ordered that the reorganized "general committees normally have a member from each circuit and that standing committees and special committees should have seven members, at least four of whom should be district court judges." The committees themselves became exclusive. With exceptions made by the Chief Justice, each appointee could serve on no more than one committee at the same time nor could non-members of the committee serve on subcommittees. Finally, terms of office were set at six years and were non-renewable "except as the Chief Justice may otherwise determine for special reasons."[53] Thus, by the end of the Warren era, the committee system had become a thoroughly institutionalized part of federal judicial administration.

Committee Functions

As key elements in the policy-making process of the Judicial Conference, committees consider, in the first instance,

[50] *Ibid.*
[51] Interview with Roszel C. Thomsen, January 11, 1965, Baltimore, Maryland.
[52] *Ibid.*; also interview with Ronald C. Beattie, January 19, 1965, Washington, D.C.
[53] *Judicial Conference Report, 1968*, p. 45.

those items of business which ultimately come before the Conference itself.[54] When the work of the latter expands, that of the committees follows a similar course. Thus the Act of 1939 affected the committees as it affected the Conference; it substantially increased their business.

That year, the Conference established the Advisory Committee to act as an official "watchdog" over the new Administrative Office;[55] others were intended primarily as research and information sources for the agency as well as instruments for reviewing the work of its various divisions. The Statistics Committee emerged following an expressed desire on the part of the chief of the Division of Procedural Studies and Statistics to "be benefitted by occasional consultation with and advice from a committee on statistics composed of a small group of individuals who have had some experience in judicial statistics and whose counsel as to particular policies would be valuable."[56]

This research role would gain increasing importance during the Warren era, and would encompass much more than mere consultation and advice with the Administrative Office. Then it came to include promotion of and participation in scientific policy studies undertaken by public and private research agencies. For example, in cooperation with the National Institute of Mental Health and the School of Criminology of the University of California, the Conference's

[54] Jurisdiction of Judicial Conference committees has never been clearly defined. To resolve questions of committee jurisdiction, Chief Justice Warren E. Burger appointed an Executive Committee in 1970. See "Report of Special Committee Regarding Jurisdiction of Committees and Procedures," reprinted in U.S., Congress, Senate, Subcommittee on Separation of Powers of the Committee on the Judiciary, *Hearings, on the Independence of Federal Judges*, 91st Cong., 2d Sess., 1970, pp. 60-61. J. Edward Lumbard, *ibid.*, p. 57.

[55] *Judicial Conference Report, 1939*, p. 18.

[56] Will Shafroth, "Memorandum to Henry P. Chandler," September 18, 1940, Administrative Office Correspondence, 60-A-328, Box 7; see also Charles E. Clark to Henry P. Chandler, August 12, 1943, Groner Papers, Box 16; *Judicial Conference Report, 1943*, p. 71.

Committee on the Administration of the Probation System, reported another committee of the Conference in 1967, "has been concerned with evaluating the effectiveness of the federal probation and parole system in supervising persons in the community."[57]

Other committees sought similar studies. They urged "a systems analysis of court processes in the light of modern methods of data recordation and retrieval," a study of "the use of computers in the jury system, both to obtain a random selection of jurors and to avoid wasteful calling of jurors," and a project "to identify and manage the civil litigation on the court dockets which can be disposed of without trial and with a minimum of judicial effort."[58] But without resources other than their own efforts and those of their secretaries and law clerks together with the very limited assistance available from the small staff in the Administrative Office, judges on the committees labored under real handicaps.

Such handicaps had been unknown and inconsequential in the years immediately after 1939 when committees had centered their attention on the Administrative Office, on the performance of its several divisions, on expanding that agency's jurisdiction over court personnel, and on legitimizing and sanctioning the office's efforts to execute administrative policies authorized by the Conference. When these policies embodying uniform national standards evoked re-

---

[57] "Report of the Special [Judicial Conference] Committee on Continuing Education, Research, Training and Administration to the Chief Justice of the United States, Chairman, and the Members of the Judicial Conference of the United States," in U.S., Congress, Senate, Subcommittee on Improvements in Judicial Machinery of the Committee on the Judiciary, *Hearings, on S. 915 and H.R. 6111, Crisis in the Federal Courts*, 90th Cong., 1st Sess., 1967, p. 35. See also *Judicial Conference Report, 1967*, p. 38.

[58] Senate Subcommittee on Improvements in Judicial Machinery, *Hearings on S. 915*, 1967, pp. 35-36.

sistance at the lower levels of the judiciary, the office looked to the committees and their members to "front" for it.[59] An exchange between District Judge John McDuffie of the Southern District of Alabama and Judge John Knox, chairman of the Committee on Selection of Jurors in the Federal Courts, illustrated this committee role. To Mc-Duffie, the committee's *Handbook for Petit Jurors*, distributed by the Administrative Office, "was written, in part at least, by one who has limited experience with courts and juries."[60] Moreover, it constituted but one more example "of a tendency toward too much reformation, standardization, and . . . centralization of control over duties and functions which are and should be solely the responsibility of the judges of the District Courts."[61] To these charges, Knox replied that his committee had invited suggestions from all the district judges, but that "you failed to express yourself as you have now done."[62] If we had known, needled the chairman, "that a man as experienced as yourself was convinced of the worthlessness of this subject matter, your views . . . would have had the serious consideration of the Committeemen, each of whom is a judge of long and wide experience."[63] McDuffie, now thoroughly chastened, confessed that "my experience on the Bench is so limited compared with yours and the learned Judges of your Committee, I do not seek now an argument with you about the *Handbook*."[64]

[59] Harry E. Watkins to Stephen W. Brennan, April 21, 1953, Administrative Office Correspondence, 60-A-328, Box 29.

[60] John McDuffie to Henry P. Chandler, December 3, 1943, Groner Papers, Box 15.

[61] John McDuffie to United States Judges, January 6, 1944, *ibid.*, Box 15.

[62] John C. Knox to John McDuffie, December 18, 1943, Groner Papers, Box 15.

[63] *Ibid.*

[64] John McDuffie to John C. Knox, December 29, 1944, *ibid.*, Box 15.

In addition to such "fronting" functions as the Knox Committee performed and the more traditional policy-making and coordinating tasks, promotional-educational efforts became a feature of committee work after 1939. The Committee on Pretrial Procedure, established in 1943,[65] undertook major promotional campaigns to encourage district judges to use pretrial, particularly in protracted cases. From numerous local and regional forums, members of the committee sponsored live demonstrations of the recommended techniques.[66] Ultimately, these techniques were compiled in a handbook and given wide circulation among the federal judges.[67]

The same committee carved out a new function in 1959 when it organized the "Brooklyn Experiment" in the congested Eastern District of New York. Here, to test its methods of pretrial and calendar control, it enlisted teams of visiting judges under the direction of a single administrative judge. The director of the Administrative Office could say for the first time, "Federal judges . . . organized and conducted an actual experiment in judicial administration under controlled conditions and according to scientific principles."[68]

A somewhat analogous, though more sophisticated, role was played by a subcommittee of the Pretrial Committee. Known as the Co-ordinating Committee for Multiple Litigation, this nine-judge panel sought to meet on a national scale the flood of antitrust cases which appeared after the government's successful prosecution of the electrical equipment manufacturers in 1960.[69] It coordinated and consoli-

[65] *Judicial Conference Report, 1943,* p. 71.

[66] Henry P. Chandler, "Some Major Advances in the Federal Judicial System, 1922-1947," *Federal Rules Decisions,* 31 (1963), 451.

[67] Warren Olney III, U.S., Congress, House, Subcommittee of Committee on Appropriations, *Hearings, Departments of State and Justice, the Judiciary, and Related Agencies, Appropriations for 1960,* 86th Cong., 1st Sess., 1959, p. 64.

[68] *Judicial Conference Report, 1959,* p. 66; *ibid., 1961,* pp. 136-39.

[69] *United States v. Westinghouse Elec. Corp.,* Criminal No. 20399

dated pretrial discovery proceedings by issuing uniform pretrial orders for the nearly 1800 cases filed in more than thirty judicial districts, establishing a central depository for the one million or more documents involved, and, most significantly, by communicating to all parties information on its activities as well as those of the several trial courts involved in this litigation.[70]

As operating agencies, the Conference committees suffer from a pervasive absence of power. They can sponsor demonstration projects and "crash programs" staffed by judge-volunteers to relieve court congestion. The Intercircuit Assignments Committee, however, has never realized its potential for routinely meeting congestion because not all federal judges adhere to "the concept of the national Federal judicial system."[71] The few committee successes have involved discouraging unnecessary and frivolous assignments.[72] Rarely has it assumed the initiative in securing manpower for busy metropolitan courts.[73] "When it comes to . . . getting judges to serve in cases of need," Chairman Jean S. Breitenstein told a Senate committee, "I am frank

---

(E. D. Pa. 1960), cited in Myron W. Watkins, "Electrical Equipment Antitrust Cases—Their Implications for Government and for Business," *The University of Chicago Law Review*, 29 (Autumn 1961), 98.

[70] See Phil C. Neal, Perry Goldberg, "The Electrical Equipment Antitrust Cases: Novel Judicial Administration," *American Bar Association Journal*, 50 (July 1964), 621-28. The Committee in 1968 organized an eleven-judge task force to relieve congested civil jury dockets in the Southern District of New York. See *New York Times*, March 12, 1968, pp. 1, 34.

[71] U.S., Congress, Senate, Subcommittee on Improvements in Judicial Machinery of the Committee on the Judiciary, *Hearings, on Temporary Judicial Assignments*, 90th Cong., 2d Sess., 1968, p. 40.

[72] *Judicial Conference Report, 1969*, p. 28. See also Senate Subcommittee on Improvements in Judicial Machinery, *Hearings on Temporary Judicial Assignments*, 1968, p. 40.

[73] Joseph Tydings, Jr., *Congressional Record*, 90th Cong., 2d Sess., vol. 114, part 23, 30019. But see: *Judicial Conference Report, 1968*, pp. 63-66.

to say that it has been up to the chief judge."[74] Neither the committee nor the Conference enjoyed the wherewithal other than persuasion to transfer judges when challenged by candidates for assignment or by their chief judges.[75] Congress had authorized the assignment system. But, "all I can say," Breitenstein confessed, "is that . . . it is kind of hard to make it work."[76]

Legislative drafting and liaison gained new importance after 1939. Formulating policies for presentation first to the Judicial Conference and then, with its approval, to the committees of Congress became the major function of such Conference committees as those on Court Reporters, Supporting Personnel and Court Administration, Bankruptcy Administration, and Punishment for Crime. After intensively studying and drafting legislation providing for an indeterminate sentencing system, Senior Circuit Judge John J. Parker's Punishment for Crime Committee followed a set procedure: It secured approval of the Director of the Bureau of Prisons and the Attorney General, recirculated the draft to all Committee members, submitted the proposal to the district judges, discussed introduction of the bill with the Chairman of the House Judiciary Committee, and then obtained the bill's introduction in both houses of Congress.[77] Thereafter, the committees and, most prominently their chairmen, would engage in a variety of lobbying tactics designed to promote passage of their program.[78]

In hammering out legislative proposals, however, some committees shared jurisdictions, thereby strengthening intra-Conference "checks and balances." The Statistics and

[74] Senate Subcommittee on Improvements in Judicial Machinery, *Hearings on Temporary Judicial Assignments*, 1968, p. 40.

[75] 28 *U.S.C.* 292(c)(d), 295.

[76] Senate Subcommittee on Improvements in Judicial Machinery, *Hearings on Temporary Judicial Assignments*, 1968, p. 43.

[77] Bolitha J. Laws to Orie L. Phillips, December 11, 1944, Parker Papers, Box 62.

[78] See generally: Chapter 9, "The Judicial Conference and Congress."

Court Administration Committees considered questions of additional judgeships, but each applied different criteria in developing its recommendations. The former traditionally perceived its role as that of promoting objectivity. Its function, said long-time Chairman Charles E. Clark, lay not in "making *recommendations* for judges in individual cases, but rather . . . [in] presenting *facts* based on docket conditions in various federal courts together with estimates of additional manpower."[79] These estimates, in turn, were based on "a simple standard of definite need."[80]

In contrast to the cold objectivity of the Statistics Committee, the recommendations of the Court Administration Committee were infused with subjective considerations. That Committee applied "the human equation to statistics."[81] Its members scrutinized such data as personal problems afflicting individual judges in various courts, the number of places of court and the distances traveled, the health and ages of judges, population trends, the character of local economies,[82] and the political expediency of creating "pork barrel" judgeships.[83] Thus the Court Administration Committee not only reviewed the suggestions advanced by the Statistics Committee but, complained Clark, would "very likely . . . tear them to pieces."[84] By late in the Warren period, however, this particular inter-committee conflict had

---

[79] Charles E. Clark to Members of the Committee on Court Administration, October 31, 1955, p. 15, Administrative Office Correspondence, 60-A-328, Box 31.

[80] Charles E. Clark to Alfred P. Murrah, September 27, 1955, Clark Papers.

[81] Warren Olney III, "Procedures Used by the Judicial Conference to Arrive at Recommendations for Additional Judgeships," in U.S., Congress, House, Subcommittee No. 5 of the Committee on the Judiciary, *Hearings, on Federal Courts and Judges,* 87th Cong., 1st Sess., 1961, p. 436.

[82] *Ibid.*

[83] John Biggs, Jr., to Willis W. Ritter, May 29, 1953, Stephens Papers, Box 184.

[84] Charles E. Clark to J. Edward Lumbard, August 3, 1959, Clark Papers.

285

largely disappeared. Now, the Conference presented a judgeship package to Congress every four years,[85] and even the Statistics Committee was constrained to view the manpower requirements of the federal courts prospectively.[86]

Creation of the Budget Committee,[87] allegedly on the recommendation of Congressman John Rooney of the House Appropriations Committee,[88] added a formal intermediate level of review to the judiciary's policy-making system. Unlike the Court Administration Committee, which shared jurisdiction with that on Statistics, the Budget Committee acts as the Budget Bureau of the federal courts. It receives estimates from every other committee of the Judicial Conference, considers them against the total budgetary requirements of the judiciary,[89] and finally tailors the budget, subsequently presented to the Conference for its approval, to fit the perspectives of the House Appropriations Committee. Such tailoring may well entail rejecting the budget recommendations of other committees of the Judicial Conference.[90]

Distinguished from most functions performed by committees are those of an executive-adjudicatory nature. From time to time the Conference has been called upon to settle issues of judicial behavior. Under intense congressional

[85] Harvey M. Johnsen, U.S., Congress, Senate, Subcommittee on Improvements in Judicial Machinery of the Committee on the Judiciary, *Hearings, on S. 952, S. 567, S. 474, S. 585, S. 852, S. 898, S. 1036, S. 1216, S. 1509, S. 1646, S. 1712, S. 2040, Federal Judges and Courts*, 91st Cong., 1st Sess., 1969, pp. 55-56.

[86] *Ibid.*, p. 59.

[87] *Judicial Conference Report, 1957*, p. 26.

[88] William J. Campbell, U.S., Congress, House, Subcommittee of the Committee on Appropriations, *Hearings, on Departments of State, Justice, and Commerce, the Judiciary, and Related Agencies Appropriations for 1969*, part I, 90th Cong., 2d Sess., 1968, pp. 70-71.

[89] William J. Campbell, U.S., Congress, House, Subcommittee of the Committee on Appropriations, *Hearings, on Departments of State, Justice and Commerce, the Judiciary, and Related Agencies, Appropriations for 1965*, part I, 88th Cong., 2d Sess., 1964, p. 74.

[90] *Ibid.*

pressure,[91] its 1953 session established an *ad hoc* Committee on the Maintenance Expenses of Judges, and charged it with investigating allegations that four federal district judges had unlawfully received *per diem* subsistence payments.[92] The committee was directed to "hold hearings and afford an opportunity to be heard to such judges as may desire to appear." If the payments were in order, then the committee and the Conference "should defend the judges who are presently under attack." On the other hand, if the judges concluded that the compensation had been "mistakenly made, then acknowledgement of that should be made and steps be taken through Mr. Chandler to have the money repaid."[93]

Following an "exhaustive study," the committee made its report, which, reflecting internal compromises,[94] "concluded that, with few exceptions, charges made for maintenance by the judges have been clearly within both the letter and spirit of [Title 28, *United States Code*] section 456."[95] Nevertheless, the committee passed judgment on the propriety of the judges' past conduct. Three were fully exonerated, while the fourth was placed in the shadows with the committee merely implying unlawful activity on his part. This indecisive judgment irritated at least one administrative "activist" who urged a broader prosecutor-adjudicator function for the committee. It should, he contended, "direct the Administrative Office to request Judge Healy to repay the illegally charged moneys, and if he does

[91] John Biggs, Jr. to Fred M. Vinson, February 5, 1953, Stephens Papers, Box 195.

[92] "Report of the Committee on Maintenance Expenses of Judges," April 30, 1953, mimeograph (Administrative Office of the United States Courts, Washington, D.C.; cited hereafter as "Report of the Committee on Maintenance Expenses of Judges").

[93] Harold M. Stephens, "Draft of Motion to the Judicial Conference," undated, Stephens Papers, Box 224.

[94] William Denman to Orie L. Phillips, May 6, 1953, *ibid.*, Box 226.

[95] "Report of the Committee on Maintenance Expenses of Judges," p. 11.

not respond affirmatively, [it] should refer the matter to the appropriate authorities, presumably the Comptroller General and the Department of Justice."[96]

More decisive have been those judgments of committees against court employees as distinguished from judges. Here committees have recommended sanctions with greater alacrity than in cases involving magistrates themselves. Thus in 1960 the Committee on Supporting Personnel found that a judge's secretary lacked "the qualifications for any grade of secretary to a federal judge" and advised the Conference to instruct the director of the Administrative Office to remove his name from the payroll.[97]

Behind Committee Doors

Conference committees provide forums for the airing of divergent points of view and, ultimately, for the formulating of policy proposals considered by the Conference as a whole. They constitute, in short, vital institutionalized means of access to the Conference. And so, to their doors come not only the issues, trivial and major, but also advocates ranging from the Chief Justice of the United States to the lowliest court employee. However, access is not the same for all interested parties. "Your committee has been reluctant . . . to take reporters and reporters' organizations into their confidence," complained one court reporter to John J. Parker, then chairman of the Court Reporters Committee, and, he continued, "it should be apparent that those who may gain or suffer from wise or unwise provisions, and whose economic interests are deeply involved, should have been afforded the opportunity of voicing their views."[98]

[96] Harold M. Stephens, memorandum, May 26, 1953, Stephens Papers, Box 89.

[97] *Judicial Conference Report, 1960*, p. 9.

[98] Joseph Van Gelder to John J. Parker, May 20, 1942, Groner Papers, Box 12.

In general, committee practice and indeed that of the Conference run counter to that followed by Parker. Few restraints have been placed on efforts to influence committee policies. Interested groups have used the mass media,[99] scholarly journals,[100] and members of Congress[101] to impress committeemen and Conference members with the validity of their views. Court employees have circularized their fellows in courts throughout the land and urged them to press their judges to support particular programs then pending before committees.[102]

And judges have followed the same strategy, lobbying their colleagues on the Conference and its committees.[103] When the propriety of this conduct arose in the Vinson era, the politically astute Chief "immediately assured" the inquiring judge "that he had never heard it suggested that all the district judges should not join in an effort for a . . . change, and that it was proper for a group of district judges to seek the support of others."[104]

As a matter of course, Conference committees seek out the views of those affected by proposed legislative or ad-

[99] Bolitha Laws to Harold M. Stephens, January 17, 1953, mimeograph copy, p. 6, Stephens Papers, Box 225.

[100] O. L. McCaskill to Pierson Hall, July 8, 1951, Stephens Papers, Box 17; see also O. L. McCaskill "The Modern Philosophy of Pleading: A Dialogue Outside the Shades," American Bar Association Journal, 38 (February 1952), 123-26, 174-75.

[101] See Baar, "When Judges Lobby," p. 419.

[102] Committee of Secretaries to United States Circuit Judges [of the Ninth Circuit] to All Secretaries, July 19, 1954, Stephens Papers, Box 232.

[103] See Henry P. Chandler to Charles E. Clark, November 18, 1942, Clark Papers; Harold M. Stephens to Circuit Court of Appeals Judges, March 21, 1949, Stephens Papers, Box 87.

[104] "Memorandum by Chief Judge [William] Denman to the Judges and Members of the Judicial Conference and the Members of the Judicial Conference of the Ninth Circuit Re: The action of the Judicial Conference of the United States on matters affecting the Ninth Circuit," October 10, 1951, Samuel Driver Papers (University of Oregon, Eugene, Oregon), pp. 5-6.

ministrative changes. They poll judges,[105] and, more typically, entertain petitions from individual judges,[106] circuit conferences and councils,[107] and from court employees.[108]

In other instances, committees have held formal hearings resembling those of congressional committees, hearings which have occasionally lasted for several days.[109] Testifying before them have been judges, court employees, spokesmen for executive agencies, primarily the Justice Department, and even laymen who, in one case, supported a district judge's campaign for additional personnel in his court.[110]

Finally, co-optation of certain interests has facilitated their access to the committees. By means of committee-created advisory groups, members of the Conference committees have availed themselves of information and expertise commanded by the ultimate consumers of Conference policies while enabling these same consumers to exert maximum influence on the very substance of the policies.[111]

[105] John Biggs, Jr., to All District and Circuit Judges, August 10, 1955, mimeograph (Administrative Office of the United States Courts, Washington, D.C.).

[106] Judicial Conference Report, 1958, p. 241.

[107] See Henry P. Chandler to Members of the Judicial Conference of Senior Circuit Judges, February 11, 1942, mimeograph (Administrative Office of the United States Courts, Washington, D.C.).

[108] See "Petition to the Judicial Conference Signed by the Chairman of the Committee on Legislation and Regulations of the Conference of United States Court Reporters," in memorandum of Leland L. Tolman, "Supplementary Material on the Court Reporting System," September, 1949, p. 1, Stephens Papers, Box 214. See also Judicial Conference Report, 1956, p. 80.

[109] Bolitha Laws, "Adequate Personnel for the Courts," The Journal of the Bar Association of the District of Columbia, 20 (April 1953), 187.

[110] See Judicial Conference Report, 1958, p. 241; "Report of the Committee on Protracted Cases," April 21, 1951, mimeograph copy (Administrative Office of the United States Courts, Washington, D.C.), p. 1; Bolitha Laws to Harold M. Stephens, January 17, 1953, Stephens Papers, Box 225.

[111] Galston, Behind the Judicial Curtain, p. 130.

When the Bankruptcy Committee decided "that the views of the Referees in Bankruptcy on a number of the matters coming before [it] would be extremely helpful," the judges called for the appointment of an advisory committee of three referees "to which may be referred such questions as the committee may deem appropriate for study and report."[112]

As could be expected, the degrees of influence exercised by different actors over the committee policy-making process varies markedly. That of the associate justices of the Supreme Court has been limited,[113] as indicated by Justice Felix Frankfurter's disengagement from one controversy for fear of "entering into what may or may not be a public fight."[114] That of Chief Justices from Stone to Warren, on the contrary, has sometimes been forceful and decisive. They have manifested little hesitation in pressing their views upon committee members.

Even so restrained a Conference chairman as Chief Justice Stone invoked the power of his position to alter the substance of committee recommendations. During the spring and summer of 1943, a committee led by Judge John J. Parker hammered out proposed changes in habeas corpus procedures.[115] Intended to restrict federal jurisdiction, thereby allowing wide scope to that of the state courts,[116]

[112] "Report of the Committee on Bankruptcy Administration," August 27, 1948, mimeograph copy (Administrative Office of the United States Courts, Washington, D.C.), p. 12.

[113] See "Report of the Judicial Conference Committee on Court Administration," March 5, 1957, p. 10, mimeograph (Administrative Office of the United States Courts, Washington, D.C.; cited hereafter as "Report of the Committee on Court Administration"). See also Judicial Conference Report, 1957, p. 273; Thomas W. Swan to Charles E. Clark, September 3, 1951, Clark Papers.

[114] Felix Frankfurter to Charles E. Clark, September 28, 1951, Clark Papers.

[115] Judicial Conference Report, 1942, p. 35.

[116] John J. Parker, "Memorandum," undated, Kimbrough Stone Papers, Box 23; see also U.S., Congress, House, Subcommittee No. 3

the committee's proposals evoked a sharp reaction from Stone, who charged that "there are state courts in which an impartial trial of issues of fact in certain classes of habeas corpus cases cannot be had." He had sometimes reluctantly affirmed a questionable judgment of the state courts when it reached the Supreme Court, but he did so "with the conviction that if the case had been tried by a federal judge with the care and skill which we have a right to expect of federal judges the result would have been different and that we would have sustained it." As for the committee report, he specifically objected to its final sentence which would mean "that men will be sent to their deaths because they are denied an impartial tribunal to try issues of fact when the evidence is notoriously conflicting, evasive and perjured."[117]

Parker and the Chief Justice continued their exchanges as the committee chairman strove to meet Stone's objections. The Chief Justice, for his part, tactfully expressed the hope that Parker would "not accept any of my suggestions merely because I have made them," but only that he accord them "serious consideration on their merits."[118] Whether because of the substance of Stone's arguments or because of the shadow cast by his official position or both, Parker told his committeemen that "all of the suggestions of the Chief Justice with one possible exception . . . should be adopted."[119]

Chief Justice Fred Vinson, like his predecessor, intervened in the work of Conference committees. Like Stone, he too was caught up in the habeas corpus dispute. A proposed bill fixing federal court jurisdiction had been drafted after protracted negotiations between the Habeas Corpus

of the Committee on the Judiciary, *Hearings, on H.R. 5649, Habeas Corpus*, 84th Cong., 1st Sess., 1955, p. 7.

[117] Harlan F. Stone to John J. Parker, August 22, 1943, Kimbrough Stone Papers, Box 23.

[118] Harlan F. Stone to John J. Parker, September 6, 1943, *ibid.*

[119] John J. Parker to Kimbrough Stone and Orie L. Phillips, December 9, 1943, *ibid.*, Box 24.

Committee and the Department of Justice. When it was finally presented to him for his comments, Vinson promptly announced that he did not "favor the provision requiring three-judge federal courts to hear such cases" because he believed "that the tendency should be rather to reduce or eliminate the device of three-judge district courts rather than to extend it."[120] Thereupon, the committee secured the department's consent to remove the objectionable provision.[121]

Although Chief Justice Earl Warren preferred to influence committee action through his appointment prerogative and through an intermediary such as his director of the Administrative Office,[122] he resorted to more direct communication in at least one instance. Again the issue involved habeas corpus; the committee had urged legislation which would have encouraged a flood of habeas corpus litigation in the Supreme Court in the absence of review by any lower federal tribunals.[123] To prevent this possibility, Warren charged the Committee on Habeas Corpus with bringing out a report endorsing his position, namely that district courts hear habeas corpus cases in the first instance.[124]

Although the views of rank and file judges are considered, they are not necessarily decisive especially if they conflict with a standing Conference policy. A bill creating a new middle district of Louisiana enjoyed the support of both the past and present chief judge of the Fifth Circuit as well as that of the judicial council. Nevertheless, the Judicial Conference followed the negative recommendation of the Court Administration Committee, whose Chairman deemed the proposal "really . . . unjustifiable."[125]

[120] Henry P. Chandler to Kimbrough Stone, March 28, 1946, *ibid.*
[121] Kimbrough Stone to Members of the Judicial Conference, April 15, 1946, *ibid.*
[122] Interview with Orie L. Phillips, February 22, 1965, Washington, D.C.
[123] *New York Times*, May 9, 1959, p. 19.
[124] Interview with Orie L. Phillips.
[125] John Biggs, Jr., Senate Subcommittee on Improvements in Judi-

The committee chairman, who bears a major share of his committee's workload, enjoys extensive and sometimes absolute power over the policies ultimately adopted by it. Judge Parker, for instance, reportedly almost "always carried his committees."[126] His counterpart from the Third Circuit, Judge John Biggs, Jr., also proved a vigorous chairman. "Vested with the right of casting a vote to break a tie," related one committee member, "John, with his characteristic humility and modesty, not only breaks the ties, but frequently casts the vote for the entire Committee."[127] Other chairmen dominated their committees to a lesser extent, a fact reflected in non-unanimous reports.[128]

But chairmen are responsive and the reports of their committees are products of extensive bargaining and a multitude of compromises. Even so dominant a chairman as Judge John J. Parker tried to draw the report of his Committee on Habeas Corpus "in such a way as to do justice to the views of those who are not in agreement with me; and . . . to accomplish this result by omitting all argument as to which we are not in agreement." Throughout the report, in fact, he had endeavored "to avoid argument, even as to matters that we are agreed on, and to state merely the present state of the practice and the purpose of the amendments proposed."[129]

Such committee compromises are often testimony not only to the persuasive power and prestige of the chairman but also to the strength of forces external to the judiciary, not the least of which is Congress. "While the various mem-

---

cial Machinery, *Hearings, Federal Judges and Courts*, 1969, p. 69; see also p. 75.

[126] Interview with Orie L. Phillips.

[127] John S. Hastings, "Report on the Criminal Justice Act," in "Proceedings of the Twenty-Eighth Annual Judicial Conference: Third Judicial Circuit of the United States," *Federal Rules Decisions*, 39 (1965), 400.

[128] Interview with Orie L. Phillips.

[129] John J. Parker to Kimbrough Stone, May 23, 1943, Kimbrough Stone Papers, Box 23.

bers of your Committee have held somewhat different views on some minor features of the proposed legislation," reported a committee to the Conference, "it has seemed . . . so important to secure the passage of the legislation . . . that they have thought it wise to abandon further consideration of the statutes heretofore under consideration and join in recommending the adoption of the provisions of the Judicial Code."[130]

The ever-present threat of congressional inaction or negative action and the need for building and maintaining an alliance composed of several groups may require more than subordination of individual judges' preferences. It may demand that a majority of committee members acquiesce to the position held by an important element of the alliance, often the Department of Justice. A wide range of legislative issues affect both the Department and the judiciary. Some primarily concern the courts or are "politically sensitive," in which case the Attorney General may defer to the Judicial Conference.[131] But others are deemed vital to the Department's programs. "I cannot agree to a change in the language I had suggested," wrote Attorney General Francis Biddle to Judge Parker, Chairman of the Committee on Punishment for Crime.[132] Although Committee members had levelled policy and even constitutional objections at the amendments which Biddle offered to a then pending bill,[133] the Attorney General protested that any retraction on his part would permit interference "with the powers of the Attorney General vested in the Director [of the Bureau of

[130] "Report of the Habeas Corpus Committee," September 20, 1947, mimeograph (Administrative Office of the United States Courts, Washington, D.C.), p. 1.

[131] See Baar, "When Judges Lobby," p. 250.

[132] Francis Biddle to John J. Parker, June 2, 1943, Parker Papers, Box 62.

[133] H.R. 2140, 78th Cong., 1st Sess., "A Bill to Provide a Correctional System for Adult and Youth Offenders convicted in Courts of the United States" (Federal Corrections Act).

Prisons] in administering the prisons."[134] Parker, faced with an unyielding Justice Department position, called upon objectors on his committee to accept the amendments. It was, he told Judge Orie L. Phillips, "a matter of prime importance . . . [to] present a united front in advocacy of the bill. . . ."[135] It would thus "be unwise to jeopardize the bill by allowing a controversy with the Attorney General to develop."[136]

Decisive, too, has been the influence of advocates of highly technical and specialized interests. Committees have sometimes virtually co-opted these groups, as did the Committee to Consider Amendments of the Admiralty Rules Proposed by the Maritime Law Association of the United States. Its 1947 report to the Judicial Conference noted that "the changes which the Committee has adopted are mainly for clarification and in substance follow the proposals of the Maritime Law Association of the United States."[137] Likewise the patent bar exercised a veto power over proposals before the Court Administration Committee to establish a new court for patent appeals.[138]

At the heart of much conflict within the Judicial Conference lie issues relating to court personnel; such conflict emerges initially at the committee level where differences are resolved, often after highly tendentious adversary proceedings. Typically in dispute are proposals developed by the Administrative Office and supported by its studies or those of cooperating agencies such as the Civil Service Commission and the Justice Department. Once presented, these proposals, stressing enhanced administrative uniformity applied nationwide, become a target for dissatisfied

[134] Francis Biddle to John J. Parker, June 2, 1943.
[135] John J. Parker to Francis Biddle, June 3, 1943, Parker Papers.
[136] John J. Parker to C. C. Hincks, June 8, 1943, in *ibid.*
[137] "Report of the Committee to Consider Amendments of the Admiralty Rules Proposed by the Maritime Law Association of the United States," September, 1947, mimeograph (Administrative Office of the United States Courts, Washington, D.C.), p. 2.
[138] "Report of the Committee on Court Administration," p. 9.

local and regional groups of clerks, secretaries, court reporters, referees in bankruptcy, and their allies among the judges.

The recommendations of the office, argue these dissidents, "cannot be statistically justified or supported,"[139] were all but "plucked . . . out of the air,"[140] and were "written with the purpose of discrediting the court as a whole."[141] They query whether it is "the function of the Administrative Office to administer a policy, [or] to establish a policy."[142] The answer is self-evident; the agency's report merely furnishes "a factual basis upon which the Committee and the Judicial Conference must proceed . . . to make an independent examination and appraisal of the facts submitted by the Administrative Office, in order to arrive at their own conclusions."[143] But the data supplied can reflect the fact that congressional liaison is a reciprocal relationship. Interested members of Congress and judges may intercede with the Administrative Office to describe the needs of courts in their constituencies with suitable adjectives.[144]

With no staffs of their own, key committees have taken their cues largely from the Administrative Office rather than from petitioning judges and court personnel. "I can not lose sight of the fact," commented one committeeman, "that what [the judge] is urging upon us necessarily is not his personal survey but the recommendations made to him by his agency heads."[145] Thus the recommendations of Confer-

---

[139] "Memorandum in Behalf of the Official Court Reporters in the United States District Courts Concerning the Report Dated July 14, 1951, from the Administrative Office of the United States Courts to Members of the Judicial Conference Committee on the Court Reporting System," August 17, 1951, p. 1, Stephens Papers, Box 219. (Cited hereafter as "Memorandum in Behalf of the Official Court Reporters.")

[140] *Ibid.*, p. 2.

[141] Harold M. Stephens to E. Barrett Prettyman, September 18, 1953, Stephens Papers, Box 89.

[142] "Memorandum in Behalf of the Official Court Reporters," p. 3.

[143] *Ibid.*, pp. 3-4.   [144] Baar, "When Judges Lobby," p. 168.

[145] "Statement of Harvey M. Johnsen as to Chief Judge [Bolitha]

ence committees are attuned to the views of administrators in the office, and they often deviate little from those urged by the agency.[146]

Laws' Request for Additional Personnel," April 5, 1954, p. 1, Stephens Papers, Box 228.

[146] See "Report of the Judicial Conference Committee on the Court Reporting System," 1951, p. 2, mimeograph (Administrative Office of the United States Courts, Washington, D.C.; cited hereafter as "Report of the Committee on the Court Reporting System"). See also *Judicial Conference Report, 1959*, p. 16.

For comparison of the efficacy of recommendations for additional personnel for the District Court for the District of Columbia Circuit by (1) Chief Judge Bolitha Laws, (2) a Layman's Committee organized by the district court, (3) the Administrative Division of the Department of Justice whose recommendations were endorsed by the Administrative Office, and (4) the Judicial Conference Committee on Supporting Personnel, see tables below. (Extracted from "Report of the Committee on Supporting Personnel of the United States Courts," February 27, 1952, mimeograph [Administrative Office of the United States Courts, Washington, D.C.], pp. 11-29.)

Clerk's Office
Number recommended by:
1) Chief Judge	14
2) Layman's Committee	11
3) Justice Department	5
4) S. Personnel Comm.	7

Register of Wills and Clerk of the Probate Court
Number recommended by:
1) Chief Judge	8
2) Layman's Committee	6
3) Justice Department	6
4) S. Personnel Comm.	6

Domestic Relations Commissioner
Number recommended by:
1) Chief Judge	5
2) Justice Department	2
3) S. Personnel Comm.	2

Office of Assignment Commissioner
Number recommended by:
1) Chief Judge	2
2) Layman's Committee	1
3) Justice Department	1
4) S. Personnel Comm.	1

Committee support of Administrative Office proposals as against those of other interested parties reflect a perception of judicial administration as a whole, and a recognition of the need "to preserve a proper relationship between the compensation of the reporters and other highly essential and skilled supporting personnel of the courts."[147]

That recommendations of the Administrative Office command great respect from the committees hardly means that they control in every case. Sheer lobbying by aggressive and persistent judges may win over their colleagues on committees and turn the tide against the administrators. From 1951 to 1953, the Committee on Supporting Personnel resisted attempts by Chief Judge Bolitha Laws of the federal trial court in the District of Columbia to secure increases in his court's staff.[148] His vehement attacks on the office's recommendations, his persistence, and his "passionate sincerity" in pressing his case combined with aid and comfort rendered by Harold M. Stephens, chief judge of the Court of Appeals for the District of Columbia Circuit, ultimately won over a majority of the committee.[149]

During Warren's chairmanship, the adversary character of many committee proceedings was complemented by a growing investigation and research orientation. In the absence of staff support from the Administrative Office and of federal funds, committees enlisted support from public and private agencies. Thus a major function of committee members, and especially of the chairman, lay in formulating project proposals and securing sponsors. As the chairman of the Committee to Implement the Criminal Justice Act told a congressional committee, it was his task to obtain from the legal defender program "some money, so that we

---

[147] "Report of the Committee on the Court Reporting System," p. 6.

[148] "Separate Statement of Ben C. Connally," in "Report of the Committee on Supporting Personnel of the United States Courts," April 5, 1954, mimeograph (Administrative Office of the United States Courts, Washington, D.C.), p. 3.

[149] Ibid., p. 21. See also "Separate Statement of Harvey M. Johnsen," in ibid., pp. 1-3.

may contract with their money, with a nationally recognized law school, to make this survey and study" on the feasibility of a public defender system.[150]

This mendicant role seemed most unsatisfactory to him. "We should not have to go around . . . with our hat in hand," he argued, "begging foundations and other projects that have money to spend for worthwhile purposes, to underwrite the business of the Judicial Conference."[151] A partial solution lay in establishment of a Federal Judicial Center which "will furnish a staff organization that we can go to, and . . . can contract with such agencies as it determines is advisable . . . if there aren't [sufficient] appropriated funds."[152]

[150] John S. Hastings, Senate Committee on Improvements in Judicial Machinery, *Hearings on S. 915*, 1967, p. 17.
[151] *Ibid.*, p. 17. [152] *Ibid.*

CHAPTER 9

The Judicial Conference and Congress

The Conference Role

"SINCE the establishment of the Administrative Office, Congress has more and more come to rely upon the Judicial Conference for recommendations in relation to the general subject of administration of justice in the Federal Courts," observed Judge D. Lawrence Groner in 1944.[1] The Judicial Conference, now enjoying the expertise of the Administrative Office and an expanded committee system, packaged and presented to the committees of Congress more legislative proposals than ever before. Reflecting this enlarged liaison role, the Conference received formal authorization for what had heretofore been mere custom. The 1948 revision of the Judicial Code required that the Chief Justice "submit to Congress an annual report of the proceedings of the Judicial Conference and its recommendations for legislation."[2]

Increasingly congressional committee chairmen looked to the Conference for cues, for authoritative pronouncements of the judiciary's legislative program. When such was unavailable, they took the initiative and called on the Chief Justice to "request the Judicial Conference of the United States to express its current wishes on the legislation, especially in view of the varied views which have been ex-

[1] D. Lawrence Groner to Orie L. Phillips, July 17, 1944, Groner Papers, Box 4.
[2] U.S., Congress, House, Committee on the Judiciary, *Revisions of Title 28, United States Code*, H. Rept. 308 to accompany H.R. 3214, 80th Cong., 1st Sess., 1947, p. A45. The new paragraph of sec. 331 was inserted, according to the official explanation, "to authorize the communication to Congress of information which now reaches that body only because it is incorporated in the annual report of the Attorney General."

pressed by individual judges."[3] Even if Congress did not ask them, the Conference felt empowered to offer gratuitous suggestions. When this practice came under attack late in the Warren period, the courts' administrative policymakers publicly took the position "that it is appropriate for the Conference to study legislation affecting the judiciary and that the views of the Conference should be given in advance of consideration on such legislation even though its views have not specifically been sought."[4]

So accepted was the cooperative relationship between courts and Congress, that when the Johnson administration pressed for passage of its 1966 civil rights bill, including a portion reforming the federal jury selection system, without first clearing it with the Judicial Conference, a torrent of complaints emanated from key legislators, the Chief Justice, and the rank and file judges.[5] "I am under the impression from many years' service on the Senate Judiciary Committee," declared a surprised Senator Sam Ervin, "that virtually all proposed legislation which the Committee considers, which has to do with matters of court procedure and the like, are considered by the Judicial Conference before we are requested to act upon it."[6]

[3] Olin D. Johnston to Earl Warren, March 8, 1962, and Earl Warren to Olin D. Johnston, March 8, 1962, U.S., Congress, Senate, Subcommittee on Improvements in Judicial Machinery of the Committee on the Judiciary, File on H.R. 6690, 87th Cong. (cited hereafter as Senate Subcommittee File on H.R. 6690).

[4] *Report of the Proceedings of the Judicial Conference of the United States, Annual Report of the Director of the Administrative Office of the United States Courts, 1968* (Washington, 1969), p. 33. Cited hereafter as *Judicial Conference Report*. For a complete title-source listing, see Appendix A.

[5] See Title I, S. 3296, H.R. 14765, 89th Cong., in U.S., Congress, Senate, Subcommittee on Constitutional Rights of the Committee on the Judiciary, *Hearings, on S. 3296, Amendment 561 to S. 3296, S. 1497, S. 1654, S. 2845, S. 8846, S. 2923, and S. 3176, Civil Rights*, part I, 89th Cong., 2d Sess., 1966, pp. 19-23, 46-48.

[6] *Ibid.*, p. 198; Attorney General Nicholas Katzenbach held a dif-

302

With institutionalization of the Conference's legislative role, there emerged "a disposition on the part of Congress to accept the Conference reports,"[7] although it sometimes took "action wherein not all of a Judicial Conference report is approved and embodied in legislation."[8] And congressional sponsors of bills were quick to avail themselves of Conference endorsements. Pressing for House approval of the Federal Magistrates Bill,[9] Judiciary Committee Chairman Emanuel Celler emphatically stated the significance of Conference action. "It means," he asserted, "that the imprimatur of approval has been placed on this bill by the Chief Justice of the United States, by 10 chief judges of the courts of appeals of the 10 circuits."[10] Then, warming to his subject, he challenged "any Member on the other side of the aisle to pit his knowledge of this bill, much less his wisdom . . . , against that huge array of judicial talent."[11]

If Congress deferred to the judges' reputed expertise, members of the Conference have bowed to political realities in formulating their legislative program. When a California congressman obtained in writing the support of 35 of his state's 38 members of Congress for creation of new judicial districts, the Conference saw the proverbial handwriting on the wall; it reversed its historic opposition to additional districts.[12]

---

ferent view—that "not all legislation that affects the administration of justice is put to the Judicial Conference." *Ibid.*

[7] D. Lawrence Groner to Orie L. Phillips, July 17, 1944, Groner Papers.

[8] Roman L. Hruska, *Congressional Record*, 87th Cong., 1st Sess., 1961, vol. 107, part 3, 3163.

[9] S. 945, 90th Congress.

[10] *Congressional Record*, 90th Cong., 2d Sess., 1968, vol. 114, part 21, 27328. Celler neglected to include as members of the Judicial Conference district court representatives and judges of the special courts.

[11] *Ibid.*

[12] Baar, "When Judges Lobby," pp. 359-60. See also *Judicial Conference Report, 1964*, p. 8.

On issues of less intensity and duration than district divisions, judges feel that "we can get nothing—practically—out of the Congress without the recommendation of the Conference."[13] Without it, the very effectiveness of the judiciary's legislative liaison officers suffered. "In the absence of an endorsement by the Conference," confessed Chief Circuit Judge Harold M. Stephens, neither judges nor administrators could "in making representations to the Leaders and Committees in the Senate and House speak with any authority." Rather, they could "speak only with such weight as the Leaders and Committee Members are willing to recognize because of past acquaintance with our efforts in behalf of legislation benefitting the Judiciary."[14] Moreover, lack of official status raised questions about the "possibility of embarrassment under the Lobbying Act" which required "some official warrant" for the time spent and expenses incurred by the judges.[15]

Court personnel made the same discovery as the judges. "It became apparent, and strikingly demonstrated," la-

[13] William Denman, "Excerpt from Proceedings of the Conference of Judges and Lawyer-Delegates of the Ninth Judicial Circuit, July, 1954," p. 66, Stephens Papers, Box 233.

[14] Harold M. Stephens to the Chief Justice and Judicial Conference Members, March 2, 1955, p. 2, ibid., Box 234.

[15] "Outline of Remarks by Harold M. Stephens Before the Judicial Conference of the United States," April 15, 1954, ibid., Box 229. See also Harold M. Stephens, "Agenda, Conference with Chief Justice," March 12, 1954, ibid., Box 90. The relevant law is 18 U.S.C. 1913: "No part of the money appropriated by any enactment of Congress shall . . . be used directly or indirectly to pay for any personal service, advertisement, telegram, telephone, letter, printed or written matter, or other device, intended or designed to influence in any manner a Member of Congress to favor or oppose, by vote or otherwise, any legislation or appropriation by Congress, whether before or after the introduction of bill or resolution proposing such legislation. . . ." There are several exceptions. A public official may communicate with a Member of Congress on the request of any such member, and may communicate "to Congress, through the proper official channels, requests for legislation or appropriations which they deem necessary for the efficient conduct of the public business."

mented representatives of the National Association of Referees in Bankruptcy after a futile appeal to one congressional committee, "that recommendations of the Judicial Conference are very persuasive with Congress."[16] Without these recommendations, the bankruptcy referees met rebuff at the hands of Congress, as did the court reporters, who, in turn, took their case to a Conference committee where their spokesmen expressed certainty "from what has been said to us before the Congressional Committees that they defer to your judgment." If the judges thought "that we should be taken care of just as everyone else is, Congress will agree with you."[17]

As could be expected, Chief Justices, as Conference chairmen, value this legislative clearance role. In the first place, the Conference's endorsement usually ensures that a proposal has been acted upon "very considerately and consistently."[18] Moreover, it gives the Chief Justice a major control over the contents of the legislative program, a point not overlooked by Chief Justice Warren who was reportedly "quite meticulous in working for Judicial Conference support in ordinary course."[19]

Circumventing the Conference

Despite the best efforts of Chief Justices and the fact that legislative liaison has become highly centralized in the Ju-

[16] "Report of Special Committee on Salaries," *Journal of the National Association of Referees in Bankruptcy,* 30 (January 1956), 34.

[17] "Transcript of Proceedings at Washington, D.C., on July 26, 1951, upon an application of the Conference of United States Court Reporters on behalf of the official court reporters in the United States District Courts, Before the Committee on the Court Reporting System of the Judicial Conference of the United States," p. 35, Stephens Papers, Box 219.

[18] Harold M. Stephens to Fred M. Vinson, January 6, 1949 [not sent], *ibid.,* Box 211.

[19] Charles E. Clark to J. Joseph Smith, March 12, 1955, Clark Papers.

dicial Conference and its committees, the system remains eminently porous. Judges and judicial employees who have lost or fear the loss of their cause in the Conference arena continue to carry their case to Congress without Conference authorization. Federal district judges occupy a strategic political position. The selection process, the proximity of their offices in federal buildings to those of congressmen, the likelihood of their acquaintance with local representatives in Washington, and their ties with county and state bar associations which in turn provide links with the decentralized American political system—all contribute to the trial judges' access to and influence on Congress.[20]

Their lobbying strategies have been multifarious. Congress may initiate them by polling those judges affected by pending legislation.[21] Or judges may take the initiative and solicit Congress. They have secured the introduction of favorable bills, either through direct contact with Congress[22] or through friendly intermediaries such as the Attorney General.[23] They have provided legislators with information rebutting that transmitted by the Administrative Office and Judicial Conference.[24] They have appeared before sympathetic congressional committees "to put before you both what our plight is and what we are trying to do about it."[25]

[20] See Baar, "When Judges Lobby," pp. 565-67, 583.

[21] See Henry P. Chandler to John J. Parker, April 25, 1945, Parker Papers, Box 62.

[22] See Henry P. Chandler to United States District and Circuit Court Judges, "Memorandum Concerning the Proposal to Give to Secretaries and Law Clerks of Judges Involuntarily Separated from Their Employment under Specified Conditions a Civil Service Status," September 20, 1948, mimeograph (Administrative Office of the United States Courts, Washington, D.C.).

[23] Bolitha Laws to Harold M. Stephens, March 23, 1949, Stephens Papers, Box 213.

[24] Baar, "When Judges Lobby," p. 217.

[25] John Brown, U.S., Congress, Senate, Subcommittee on Improvements in Judicial Machinery of the Committee on the Judiciary, *Hearings, on S. 952, S. 567, S. 474, S. 585, S. 852, S. 898, S. 1036, S. 1216,*

Such hearings afforded petitioners "a good forum."[26] As one judge confessed: "I do better here . . . than I do among judges."[27]

Often done to force the hand of the Conference,[28] even by Conference committee chairmen anxious to apply pressure on the Conference,[29] self-directed lobbying may threaten Conference policies with defeat. Such a result loomed when the first revision of the Judicial Code in nearly forty years neared enactment in 1948. Then some district judges enlisted an Oregon senator to prevent its passage "unless those in charge of H.R. 3214 will consent to an amendment to the Code enlarging the Conference to include the eleven Senior District Judges." Forewarned of the senator's intention to "do all within his power . . . to defeat the Code as a whole," one judge observed that "at this eleventh hour in the session, unless the Code can get through on a consent basis, it is quite unlikely that it can be passed."[30]

Consequently, political leverage exercised by federal judges at the local level may require compromises and "trade-offs" by the national Judicial Conference and its committees. Emergence of omnibus judgeship bills has tended to centralize judicial manpower decisions in the specialist committees of the national Judicial Conference thereby diluting the effect of local demands for additional judgeships. Yet because such bills can be threatened by judges operating on a local (district) and regional (circuit) basis with members of Congress, the cost of success has been de-

S. 1509, S. 1646, S. 1712, S. 2040, Federal Judges and Courts, 91st Cong., 1st Sess., 1969, p. 315.

[26] Ibid.   [27] Ibid.

[28] Richard J. Martin to the Chief Justice, the Members of the Judicial Conference, and the Director of the Administrative Office, March 15, 1952, ibid., Box 222.

[29] Interview with Hubert H. Finzel, January 13, 1965, Washington, D.C.

[30] Harold M. Stephens to Frank E. Tyler, May 31, 1948, Stephens Papers, Box 86.

centralization of Conference control over various issues of court organization such as places of holding court and consolidation or division of districts.[31]

On some issues, however, neither "trade-offs" nor compromises are feasible. Here district judge opposition can be decisive. They struck with devastating effect when threatened with enactment in the 78th Congress[32] of an indeterminate sentence bill, a bill which had been endorsed by the Judicial Conference.[33] Many trial judges perceived the measure as a vehicle for replacing elements of localism, diversity, and judicial prerogatives with those of nationalism, uniformity, and executive control in the sentencing process.[34] Among those actively antagonistic to the corrections bill were the three judges of the Northern District of Texas.[35] This district happened to include House Judiciary Chairman Hatton Sumner's Fifth Congressional District (Dallas County). In a vitriolic letter to the President of the Dallas Bar Association[36] and through their participation in that organization's proceedings, these judges mobilized the local bar.[37] Its condemnation of the measure received front page coverage in the *Dallas Morning News* which editorialized that the sentencing bill was only "further evidence of the Washington itch to bring everything in all three

[31] See Carl Baar's excellent case study of this subject: "When Judges Lobby," pp. 577-79, 582-85.

[32] H.R. 2140.

[33] *Judicial Conference Report, 1944*, p. 57.

[34] See Wayne L. Wilson, "The Federal Corrections Act: A Case Study of Judicial Lobbying" (unpub. thesis, Department of Political Science, Duke University, 1971), pp. 29-30, 88-101. (Cited hereafter as Wilson, "The Federal Corrections Act.")

[35] The three judges were William H. Atwell, James C. Wilson, and T. Whitfield Davidson.

[36] *Dallas Morning News*, February 27, 1944, sec. II, p. 1. Cited in Wilson, "The Federal Corrections Act," p. 98.

[37] *Ibid.*

branches of the Federal Government under its immediate control."[38]

The impact of the anti-sentencing bill movement on Sumners was telling indeed. He reportedly appeared "to have been quite upset by the criticism of him in his own bailiwick in an election year, the more so as he is instinctivly not sympathetic to the philosophy of [the] bill." As for its legislative fate, "the incident . . . practically killed any chance that . . . Sumners [would] let the bill be reported out."[39] Ultimately district judge opposition, of which the Dallas bar incident proved a critical manifestation, and the bleak prospects of success led the Conference to drop its campaign even though "individual members of the Judicial Conference still favored the bill. . . ."[40]

Anti-Conference judicial lobbying is differently perceived by different judges. To those occupying the policy-making heights, "bypassing the usual channels for a sharp surprise attack 'betrays a lamentable lack of confidence in the intellectual and deliberative processes which should distinguish our profession."[41] But to those on the outside of the policy-making process, the strategy is seen as quite legitimate, in spite of the "feeling in some quarters that District Judges are in 'lèse-majesté' when they write directly to Senators and Congressmen."[42] To these judges, it is emphatically his responsibility "if any legislation is pending which I think will affect or concern the administration of justice in the District Courts, to make my views known not only to the

[38] *Dallas Morning News*, March 1, 1944, sec. II, p. 2. Quoted in Wilson, "The Federal Corrections Act," p. 38.
[39] John R. Ellingston to Orie L. Phillips, March 25, 1944, Parker Papers, Box 62.
[40] Elmore Whitehurst to John J. Parker, January 8, 1947, *ibid.* See generally, Wilson, "The Federal Corrections Act," pp. 41-45.
[41] Charles E. Clark to Stevens Fargo, June 12, 1952, Stephens Papers, Box 17.
[42] Pierson Hall to Olin D. Johnston, February 5, 1962, Senate Subcommittee File on H.R. 6690.

309

Judicial Conference, but to the Congressmen and Senators as well."[43]

In practice, if not in theory, this strategy has been sanctioned by members of the Judicial Conference itself. Loyal to their courts and localities, rather than to the evanescent Conference, they have carried their cause directly to Congress after suffering defeat at the hands of their colleagues.[44]

Sabotage of a Conference policy by discontented members of that body became a *cause célèbre* during the life of the 87th Congress. A bill providing for district judge representation on the circuit councils was introduced.[45] Endorsed by the attorney general and the Department of Justice,

> it was overwhelmingly approved by the Judicial Conference of the United States at its September 1961 session, upon the recommendation of two separate committees of the Conference, the committee on court administration composed of both appellate and trial judges, and the committee on multiple judge courts composed of the chief judges of the district courts having five or more judges. Moreover, in addition to unanimous approval by the Committee on the Judiciary of the House of Representatives, the bill was approved by the House of Representatives without a single dissenting vote. . . .
>
> Thereafter, in the Senate, it was approved by the Subcommittee on Improvements in Judicial Machinery, and

[43] *Ibid.*

[44] J. Edward Lumbard to Kenneth Keating, September 22, 1961, *ibid.*; Richard H. Chambers to Hubert H. Finzel, December 19, 1961, *ibid.*; John J. Parker, U.S., Congress, Senate, Subcommittee of the Committee on the Judiciary, *Hearings, on S. 1050, 1051, 1052, 1053, 1054, H.R. 138, Administration of United States Courts*, 77th Cong., 1st Sess., 1941, p. 26.

[45] H.R. 6690, 87th Cong.

unanimously reported by the Full Committee on the Judiciary.[46]

Nevertheless, reported Senator Olin D. Johnston, then chairman of the subcommittee, "when H.R. 6690 was reached on the calendar, there was an objection, and the bill was passed over. It now appears that the objection was made to accommodate Judge J. Edward Lumbard of the Court of Appeals for the Second Circuit, and Judge Richard H. Chambers of the Court of Appeals for the Ninth Circuit."[47] These judges had waged "an active campaign at random among the Members of the Congress, including an organized effort of letters and telephone calls from other judges."[48] In addition Chambers had contacted Senator Carl Hayden of Arizona, president pro tempore of the Senate, while Lumbard had gone over the head of Senator Johnston and won the support of Senator Sam Ervin, a ranking member of the Judiciary Committee.[49]

The Lumbard-Chambers strategy led Johnston to condemn those who, "the moment the Conference adjourned . . . rush over to Congress to undermine and undercut the Conference action."[50] Such strategy affected his prestige as a congressional leader and weakened "the long and completely harmonious relationship which has existed between the Congress and the Judicial Conference of the United States."[51] It made absolutely clear, however, the utility of judicial lobbying.

[46] Olin D. Johnston, *Congressional Record*, 87th Cong., 2d Sess., 1962, vol. 108, part 3, 3615-16.

[47] *Ibid.*

[48] *Ibid.*, p. 3616. See also Richard H. Chambers to Hubert H. Finzel, December 19, 1961, Senate Subcommittee File on H.R. 6690; J. Edward Lumbard to Olin D. Johnston, January 29, 1962, *ibid.*

[49] Pierson Hall to Olin D. Johnston, March 16, 1962, *ibid.*; see complaint of Olin D. Johnston, *Congressional Record*, 88th Cong., 1st Sess., 1963, vol. 109, part 15, 19735-36.

[50] *Congressional Record*, 87th Cong., 2d Sess., 1962, vol. 108, part 3, 3616.

[51] *Ibid.*

311

Liaison: The Chief Justice

"If the recommendations of the Judicial Conference for legislation are not to be fruitless," observed an official of the Administrative Office in 1942, the exigencies of the congressional process required that "they be followed up by representations before the appropriate . . . committees."[52] Such representation has typically fallen to Conference committee chairmen or to "the accessible members of the Advisory Committee of the Judicial Conference,"[53] which in the Vinson and Warren eras included Chief Judge Harold M. Stephens of the District of Columbia Court of Appeals and John Biggs, Jr. of the Third Circuit.

Neither the Administrative Office nor the Chief Justice assumed as prominent a liaison role as that played by leading members of the lower courts. It was true, said Judge Stephens, that the prestigeless office maintained routine contact with Congress, but "we are obliged to give a good deal of time ourselves to the questions . . . which arise."[54]

The Chief Justice, on the contrary, commanded great prestige, but development of the Administrative Office and the Conference committee system permitted him to remain aloof from the legislative labyrinth and to leave the intricacies of legislative maneuvering to the director and Conference committee members.[55] Even so, Chief Justices have never completely isolated themselves from the legislative process. They submit to Congress the Conference's legisla-

[52] Elmore Whitehurst to Henry P. Chandler, December 14, 1942, Administrative Office Correspondence, 60-A-328, Box 36.

[53] Harold M. Stephens to Xenophon Hicks, April 11, 1950, Stephens Papers, Box 56.

[54] Harold M. Stephens to Dan B. Shields, January 24, 1951, *ibid.*, Box 81.

[55] See D. Lawrence Groner to John Biggs, Jr., John J. Parker, and Kimbrough Stone, June 18, 1943, Groner Papers, Box 11; Kimbrough Stone to Harlan Fiske Stone, February 16, 1946, Kimbrough Stone Papers, Box 24.

tive program,[56] and as chairman of that Conference, their views on pending legislation are solicited by congressional leaders.[57] In fact, every Chief Justice from Stone to Warren has personally intervened in the legislative process. Stone, for instance, followed this course in order to prevent the House Committee on Revision of the Laws from inserting in the Judicial Code a habeas corpus provision, which, he thought, was "not an adequate way of dealing with the matter."[58]

Vinson was even closer to the congressional scene than his predecessor had ever been and, to some degree, revived the legislative role once played by Chief Justice Taft. Like Taft, "his knowledge of the legislative branch and his personal acquaintance with the leaders of that branch enabled him to develop between [the] Conference and the Congress a relationship which . . . resulted in a better understanding of problems affecting the judiciary and the passage of legislation which has done much to improve the courts and the administration of justice therein."[59] Regarding him as a fountain of knowledge on the congressional process, judges looked to Vinson for advice on the likely responses of congressmen to various types of legislation[60] as well as on the nature and timing of legislative maneuvers.[61] He was, in effect, the judiciary's chief legislative strategist.

[56] 62 *Stat.* 902.

[57] Earl Warren to Olin D. Johnston, May 26, 1964, in U.S., Congress, Senate, Committee on Post Office and Civil Service, *Hearings, on H.R. 11049, Federal Pay Legislation*, 88th Cong., 1st and 2d Sess., 1963-64, p. 292; Earl Warren to Tom Murray, October 11, 1963, *ibid.*, pp. 293-94.

[58] Henry P. Chandler to Kimbrough Stone, March 28, 1946, Kimbrough Stone Papers, Box 24; Harlan Fiske Stone to Eugene J. Keogh, March 25, 1946, in Kimbrough Stone, "Habeas Corpus Bills," June 1946, p. 4, *ibid.*

[59] *Judicial Conference Report, 1953*, pp. 1-2.

[60] Henry P. Chandler to Fred M. Vinson, February 11, 1948, Administrative Office Correspondence, 60-A-328, Box 5.

[61] Harold M. Stephens, "Memorandum for Conference with Chief Justice Vinson," May 24, 1949, Stephens Papers, Box 40.

Should all judges buttonhole their senators to support a pending bill? "It was the Chief Justice's judgment that it is not desirable at the present time for members of the judiciary to get in touch with their respective senators."[62] Should serious attempts be made to win over an influential senator hostile to a bill favored by the judges? Again, "The Chief Justice is of the view that we should take no steps at all in respect of obtaining the Senator's support. He thinks it unlikely that the Senator will give the bill his support, and that if we attempt to secure his support he will probably again attack the Judiciary on the floor of the Senate."[63] Was a statement in support of a pending bill prepared by the chairman of the Senate Judiciary Committee adequate? "Fred thought we should have a more workmanlike and persuasive presentation."[64]

Not only did Vinson advise, but he also acted. His lobbying activities were multifarious and took him to executive as well as legislative doorsteps. He conferred with the director of the Budget Bureau when that agency's negative comments on the judiciary's budget threatened to stimulate an unfavorable congressional response,[65] pleaded with Judiciary Committee chairmen to restore on the floor of Congress budget cuts made by the Appropriations Committees,[66] and personally intervened with congressional leaders like Senate Majority Leader Scott Lucas, House Majority

[62] Harold M. Stephens to Kimbrough Stone, September 8, 1951, *ibid.*, Box 38.

[63] Harold M. Stephens to John J. Parker, April 9, 1952, *ibid.*, Box 89.

[64] Harold M. Stephens to John Biggs, Jr., October 15, 1951, *ibid.*, Box 88.

[65] Interview with Henry P. Chandler, August 1, 1963, Chevy Chase, Maryland.

[66] Henry P. Chandler, "Address of the Honorable Henry P. Chandler," in *Journal of the National Association of Referees in Bankruptcy*, 25 (January 1951), 22.

314

Leader John McCormack, and Speaker Sam Rayburn to promote enactment of Conference-sponsored bills.[67]

Even so reserved a Chief Justice as Earl Warren[68] occasionally lobbied individual congressmen for their support of a Conference-endorsed bill. Shortly after taking office, some ranking judges pressed him to contact the Senate Republican leader, William Knowland of California, and encourage that senator to throw his weight behind a then stalled judicial salary bill. That the Chief did, in fact, communicate with Knowland seemed certain to one Conference member, who expressed "no doubt . . . that he really did speak to Knowland." In the Conference "Warren said that he had 'spoken to such persons as he could properly speak to on the subject,' or words to that effect."[69]

At the end of Vinson's chairmanship and during the first years of Warren's, leading members of the Judicial Conference made a major attempt to elevate the visibility of the Chief Justice and to give his relationship with Congress a formal status. Such an official liaison role would remedy the existing lack of "a spokesman whose voice not only is heard but penetrates," asserted Judge John Biggs, Jr., "and who will be listened to far more than anything that Judge Stephens and I can say, or that Mr. Chandler . . . can say." What the judiciary needed, he argued, was "someone at the head of this coordinate branch of the Government to speak for that branch."[70] That someone was necessarily the Chief

[67] "Memorandum for Discussion with the Chief Justice," Harold M. Stephens, November 22, 1950, Stephens Papers, Box 81. See also Stephens to Bennett Champ Clark, August 21, 1950, ibid.

[68] Although seemingly in favor of creation of a new federal judicial district in California, Chief Justice Warren refused the request of a lawyer-lobbyist to intervene in the struggle. See Baar, "When Judges Lobby," p. 96.

[69] Harold M. Stephens to William M. Byrne, May 12, 1954, ibid., Box 198.

[70] U.S., Congress, Senate, Subcommittee of the Committee on the Judiciary, Hearings, on Senate Concurrent Resolution 4-5, Invitation

Justice, who could carry the Conference's program beyond the House and Senate subcommittees to the full Congress and to "the people themselves."[71]

Although the proposed "State of the Judiciary" speech commanded wide support, including that of Chief Justice Warren,[72] it encountered a cool reception in Congress. There, critics attacked it as "a political plot to get Chief Justice Warren an opportunity to advertise himself for the 1956 Presidential nomination if President Eisenhower should not run,"[73] and as smacking "of . . . the aping of British custom by our American Government."[74] When the suggestion failed to win the approval of Emanuel Celler, chairman of the House Judiciary Committee,[75] it became moribund.

However, the voice of the Chief Justice was hardly silenced. Denied an official forum, Warren availed himself of those provided by circuit conferences, cornerstone-laying ceremonies, and meetings of the American Bar Association.[76] Use of the latter declined, however, during the 1950s

---

to the Chief Justice of the United States to Address the Congress, 84th Cong., 1st Sess., 1955, p. 53.

[71] Harold M. Stephens to J. Earl Major, July 31, 1954, Stephens Papers, Box 90; Stephens to the Chief Justice and Members of the Judicial Conference, March 21, 1955, ibid., Box 233.

[72] See S. Con. Res. 4 and 5, 84th Cong.; H. Res. 60 and 69, 84th Cong.; H. J. Res. 46, 85th Cong.; S. J. Res. 80, 86th Cong.; S. J. Res. 43, 87th Cong. Chief Justice Vinson rejected the proposal; Harold M. Stephens to Kimbrough Stone, December 3, 1954, Stephens Papers, Box 90; Earl Warren to Estes Kefauver, February 4, 1955, in Senate Subcommittee of Committee on the Judiciary, Hearings on S. Con. Res. 4-5, 1955, pp. 60-61. Endorsements: ibid., p. 66; Journal of the American Judicature Society, 40 (October-December 1956), 68.

[73] Harold M. Stephens to James F. Byrnes, January 26, 1955, Stephens Papers, Box 90.

[74] William Langer, Senate Subcommittee of the Committee on the Judiciary, Hearings on S. Con. Res. 4-5, 1955, p. 2

[75] Ibid., p. 58.

[76] New York Times, November 1, 1958, p. 8.

in the wake of scathing attacks by the association's leaders on the series of controversial decisions handed down by the High Court.[77]

Foremost among Warren's platforms was that provided by the American Law Institute. It had fallen into disuse during the Stone period, but was reoccupied by Warren. In his annual address to that organization, he discussed not only the condition of the federal court system, but also presented the Judicial Conference's program, including its legislative proposals.[78] In addition, this forum provided an apt means of alerting the bench and its present and potential allies in and out of Congress of pending legislation which the Chief deemed inimicable to the judiciary's interests.[79] The ALI address, with its attendant publicity, thus afforded the Chief Justice a nonpartisan vehicle for articulating the needs and plans of the federal judiciary.

Liaison: Inferior Court Judges

With the Chief Justice largely removed from the legislative tumult, and the Administrative Office confined to routine functions, judges of the inferior courts have forged the vital links between the Conference and Congress. Typically responsibility for congressional liaison devolved upon the chairman and perhaps selected members of Judicial Conference committees. Often enjoying long tenure as commit-

[77] *Ibid.*, July 7, 1956, p. 11; *ibid.*, August 26, 1958, p. 15; *ibid.*, January 6, 1959, p. 23, on his resignation from the ABA.
[78] *Ibid.*, May 21, 1959, p. 20.
[79] Chief Justice Earl Warren, in his 1966 ALI address, assailed as "ill-advised" the then pending Administration-endorsed Title I of the Civil Rights Act of 1966 (S. 3296, H.R. 14765, 89th Cong., 2d Sess.) relating to jury selection. See *New York Times*, May 19, 1966, p. 1. His statement brought forth charges that he was prejudicing a case that might be brought to his Court for statutory and/or constitutional interpretation. See summary of issue from *Washington Post*, May 22, 1966, excerpt quoted in, Senate Subcommittee on Constitutional Rights, *Hearings, Civil Rights*, part i, pp. 47-48.

317

tee members and as chairmen, these judges develop a clientele relationship with the Appropriations and Judiciary Committees as well as with their several chairmen, subcommittee chairmen, and members of their staffs.[80] Thus Judicial Conference committee chairmen have played a role analogous to that played by heads of executive departments and agencies. They organize and coordinate lobbying campaigns[81] and act as the judiciary's spokesmen on Capitol Hill.

Their staff work includes preparing memoranda in support of bills proposed by the Conference, in itself no small task. "We put in one eighteen-hour stretch," related Judge Stephens, "myself, Biggs, three secretaries, and a law clerk, from 9:30 in the morning until 12:30 at night, to get the statutes and memorandum drafted in time for a deadline for their presentation to Senator McCarran [chairman of the Senate Judiciary Committee] and Congressman Celler [chairman of the House Judiciary Committee]."[82]

Some memoranda were exhaustively detailed. One to accompany a judicial salary bill considered "the nature and importance of the work of the Federal bench, the history of Federal judicial salaries, a comparison of such salaries with those of other court systems, including the English, . . . the relation of the cost of living to salaries and of taxation on a reduction of salaries."[83] Another assailed the constitutionality and wisdom of a Senate-passed bill requiring the chief judge of the Court of Appeals for the District of Columbia Circuit to appoint three district judges to arbitrate a dispute between the Willmore Engineering Company and the United States Maritime Commission.[84] These scholarly

[80] See Baar, "When Judges Lobby," p. 563.

[81] See Wilson, "The Federal Corrections Act," p. 55.

[82] Harold M. Stephens to Henry W. Edgerton, January 17, 1949, Stephens Papers, Box 13.

[83] Harold M. Stephens to Willis Smith, December 3, 1945, ibid., Box 85.

[84] Harold M. Stephens to the Chief Justice and Members of the Judicial Conference, March 21, 1955, ibid., Box 234.

memoranda occasionally constituted the basis for congressional committee reports[85] and even served as the report
itself.[86]

Collaboration, even intimacy, has characterized relations
between Conference and congressional committees. Conference committees like that on Codification and Revision of
the Laws were created primarily to act as an expert advisory staff to a congressional committee and its staff, in this
instance the House Committee on Revision of the Laws.[87]
Other judges on other Conference committees have collaborated with congressional committees, rewriting the latter's
reports[88] and even preparing their title pages and specific
committee recommendations.[89]

More commonly, however, the relationship is one simply
of access to congressional committees and legislative leaders. Judges of conference committees, like their counterparts in the executive branch, testify before the committees
of Congress, and organize the appearance of their supporters who, on important measures, may reach parade
lengths.[90] As described by one participant, the Administrative Office would inform him that the committees of Congress "want to get your views on this [legislation] as Chairman of the Committee on Court Administration and the

[85] D. Lawrence Groner to John C. Knox, February 10, 1945, Groner
Papers, Box 9.

[86] Harold M. Stephens to D. Lawrence Groner, August 2, 1945,
Stephens Papers, Box 125.

[87] "Report of the Committee on Codification and Revision of the
Judicial Code," 1947, mimeograph (Administrative Office of the
United States Courts, Washington, D.C.), pp. 1-2.

[88] Harold M. Stephens to Henry W. Edgerton, November 1, 1950,
Stephens Papers, Box 13.

[89] Harold M. Stephens to D. Lawrence Groner, August 2, 1945,
ibid., Box 125.

[90] Harold M. Stephens to the Circuit Court of Appeals of the District of Columbia, August 17, 1949, ibid., Box 87; Harold M. Stephens
to D. Lawrence Groner, August 29, 1949, ibid.

Committee on Supporting Personnel. Can you come down?"[91]

But judges like Biggs and Stephens hardly needed to await a committee call; they engineered invitations[92] by virtue of their personal acquaintance with committee chairmen.[93] Or they invited themselves. "I would greatly appreciate the opportunity," Biggs wrote one committee chairman, "of appearing before your Committee at such time as might be convenient, if you would be so good as to afford me a hearing."[94] Once in the congressional committee hearing room, such judges command great respect from the assembled legislators by virtue of their previous political experience and present status both as federal magistrates and as ranking members or chairmen of a specialized Judicial Conference Committee.[95] The judge as witness was thus a "big gun" because of what he symbolized and because of his abilities as an advocate which had possibly led the Chief Justice to extend a committee appointment to him in the first place. Not surprisingly, he could seemingly make "a deep impression on the [congressional] committee . . ."[96] and the hearings themselves could be described as "most imposing and quite impressive."[97]

Intervention in the legislative process has not always ended with testimony before the substantive committees. Unfavorable measures may slip out of the busy Judiciary

[91] John Biggs, Jr., U.S., Congress, House, Subcommittee of the Committee on Appropriations, Hearings, on Departments of State and Justice, the Judiciary, and Related Agencies, Appropriation Bill for 1960, 1959, 86th Cong., 1st Sess., p. 140.

[92] Harold M. Stephens to William H. Timbers, May 5, 1953, Stephens Papers, Box 195.

[93] Harold M. Stephens, "Memorandum for Discussion with Judge Biggs and the Chief Justice," June 9, 1949, p. 3, ibid., Box 40.

[94] John Biggs, Jr., to Matthew M. Neely, March 2, 1952, ibid., Box 221.

[95] See Wilson, "The Federal Corrections Act," pp. 58-59.

[96] John J. Parker to Orie L. Phillips, May 21, 1943, Parker Papers, Box 62.

[97] James V. Bennett to John J. Parker, June 14, 1943, in ibid.

committees without warning, thus requiring dexterous footwork on the part of judges. When a bill[98] disapproved by the Judicial Conference[99] silently emerged from the House Judiciary Committee during the Eighty-second Congress, the chairman of the Conference Committee on the Operation of the Jury System "communicated to the House Committee on Rules, where the favorable report of the Judiciary Committee was under consideration, . . . and requested that no rule for House debate . . . be granted until the Judiciary could be heard."[100]

Judges have buttonholed legislators and even prepared floor speeches for delivery by friendly congressmen[101] in order to smooth the path for Conference-endorsed bills. To quell fierce Republican opposition to an Omnibus Judgeship Bill stalled in the last months of the Truman administration, Biggs and Stephens called on House Republican leaders, Joseph Martin and Charles Halleck. "We presented the compliments of the Chief and the Judicial Conference," related Judge Stephens, "and expressed the hope that they would aid in getting the bill through."[102] They lobbied the Democratic leadership as well, and worked "actively . . . with members of the Democratic Policy Committee of the Senate in the hope of getting a place on the floor for a vote on the Widows Pension Bill."[103]

[98] H.R. 287, 82d Congress.
[99] *Judicial Conference Report, 1952*, pp. 209-11.
[100] "Report of the Committee on the Operation of the Jury System," September 11, 1952 (Administrative Office of the United States Courts, Washington, D.C.), p. 13.
[101] Harold M. Stephens to Charles Halleck, May 21, 1946, Stephens Papers, Box 190; see speech of Charles Halleck, *Congressional Record*, 79th Cong., 2d Sess., 1946, vol. 92, part 8, 9570.
[102] Harold M. Stephens to Emanuel Celler, April 14, 1952, Stephens Papers, Box 179. See Wilson, "The Federal Corrections Act," p. 79, where he notes another instance in which judicial lobbyists contacted congressmen who were either neutral or opposed to a Conference-sponsored bill.
[103] Harold M. Stephens to John C. Knox, May 16, 1952, *ibid.*, Box 89. On the Policy Committee, behind which façade Floor Leader Lyn-

No stone was left unturned. As one major Conference bill on the consent calendar neared a Senate vote, Biggs, Stephens, and the Chief Justice made "every possible effort personally and through friends to secure the general support of the Senate, and to avoid objection." And this strategy included getting "the two Republican official objectors to agree not to object."[104]

Rank and File Support

Although only a handful of judges shape and execute the judiciary's strategy within the halls of Congress, rank and file judges may also play a role. Primarily, it has been that of a supporting cast for the Conference and its operatives on Capitol Hill. Such support may constitute little more than neutrality on the part of dissident judges who threaten Conference programs with letters to Congress or through resolutions of their circuit conferences.[105] Thus in the midst of legislative crises, judges of the Conference assiduously court their acquiescence to a form of "democratic centralism."[106]

A united front may prove unobtainable, but campaigns for it have produced some conversions. Seeking broad-based support for a judicial salary bill, Judge Stephens reported to Biggs receipt of a letter from "one of the Texas judges that cussed you and me out when we wrote them."[107] The judge had always thought that "if a man did not like

---

don Johnson operated, see Hugh A. Bone, *Party Committees and National Politics* (Seattle, 1958), pp. 170ff.

[104] Harold M. Stephens to Bennett Champ Clark, August 21, 1950, Stephens Papers, Box 81.

[105] Harold M. Stephens to Joseph C. Hutcheson, Jr., July 19, 1949, *ibid.*, Box 87; Albert Maris to Fred M. Vinson, April 9, 1948, *ibid.*, Box 209.

[106] Albert Maris to Homer T. Bone, February 3, 1948, *ibid.*, Box 175.

[107] Harold M. Stephens to John Biggs, Jr., April 30, 1953, *ibid.*, Box 89.

the salary he was getting, it was his privilege to quit."[108] Now he had to confess that the arguments advanced in behalf of the bill were "unanswerable." Federal income taxes continued to rise and thereby reduce judicial incomes. This, he declared, was a condition "not only quite burdensome, but unfair in the light of fundamental constitutional provisions."[109]

Rank and file judges provide positive support for Conference policies, by bringing influence to bear on key legislators. During one campaign to raise judicial salaries, Judge Stephens maintained a detailed record of the position of individual representatives and senators, whether "for, against, or uncommitted," together with a listing of those judges with whom they were acquainted.[110] These judges, in turn, afforded useful channels of communication with legislators but superficially known to the judiciary's Washington spokesmen.[111] And so when Senator James Eastland of the Judiciary Committee opposed a Conference-endorsed bill, Stephens contacted the chief judge of the Fifth Circuit, who "was able to get some of the judges in Mississippi to intervene with Eastland, and as a result he did support the bill in the Subcommittee and in the full Committee when it was voted out."[112] Similarly, when a member of the Rules Committee took a position unfavorable to the Conference's program, a remote district judge was urged "to get his Congressman, who used to be his referee in bankruptcy, to see Congressman [Leo E.] Allen of the Rules Committee."[113]

[108] William H. Atwell to Harold M. Stephens, John Biggs, Jr., and Henry P. Chandler, April 18, 1953, ibid., Box 195.

[109] Ibid.

[110] See File on H.R. 2181, July 15, 1946, ibid., Box 188.

[111] Albert Maris to Harold M. Stephens, April 26, 1944, ibid., Box 27.

[112] Harold M. Stephens to Bennett Champ Clark, August 21, 1950, ibid., Box 81. See also Wilson F. Collier to Charles E. Clark, May 31, 1956, Clark Papers.

[113] Harold M. Stephens to D. Lawrence Groner, March 26, 1946, Stephens Papers, Box 185; Shackelford Miller, Jr., to Harold M. Stephens, April 30, 1946, ibid., Box 190.

Washington-based judges may buttonhole individual legislators and blanket Congress with form letters urging support for a particular bill.[114] However, only resolutions of circuit conferences and waves of letters and telephone calls from the dispersed judicial membership can demonstrate the scope and intensity of the measure's constituency.[115] Mass lobbying efforts have been rare, if for no other reason than because of the degree of organization and coordination required. Nevertheless, in some instances, the judiciary has launched nationwide lobbying efforts. Then judges of each circuit court of appeals[116] and legislative committees of the circuit conferences[117] have assumed directing roles. But ultimate responsibility rested with Stephens and Biggs in Washington. They "armed their judges with material . . . with which to bombard their Congressmen and Senators."[118]

Signals on specific "grass roots" strategies also emanated from the same source. With the vote on a critical bill close at hand, Stephens issued the final order to all federal judges:

1) If you have not heretofore talked with your Congressman about the bill, do so now and request that he support it *by voice* and *by vote.*

2) If you have heretofore talked with your Congressman, *do so again,* reiterate your interest, and request that he support the bill *by voice* and *by vote.*

[114] See Harold M. Stephens to Leonard W. Hall, July 15, 1946, *ibid.*, Box 85.

[115] See D. Lawrence Groner to Kimbrough Stone, October 18, 1941, Groner Papers, Box 16; D. Lawrence Groner and Kimbrough Stone to Senior Circuit Judges, March 28, 1946, *ibid.*, Box 9.

[116] Kimbrough Stone and J. C. Collet to George H. Moore, February 4, 1954, Stephens Papers, Box 197.

[117] John E. Miller to Circuit and District Judges of the Eighth Circuit, May 4, 1953, *ibid.*, Box 195.

[118] Memorandum of Harold M. Stephens' Secretary to Harold M. Stephens, August 22, 1949, *ibid.*, Box 189.

324

3) If your Congressman does not return home for recess, *telephone him.*

In conclusion, he predicted that "If you will act as suggested, I believe the bill will pass."[119]

Executive Branch Aid

Support of the executive branch, especially the Attorney General, for Conference programs has been an important goal for the judges. Usually this support is won at the Judicial Conference committee stage where legislative proposals have been tailored to coincide with the views of the Department of Justice.[120] In addition, judges have availed themselves of the Attorney General's good offices to promote publicly their programs[121] and even to act as an intermediary between the Conference and the President. "The bill is now at the White House for the President's attention," wrote Stephens to Truman's Attorney General, James P. McGranery, suggesting that the judges would be grateful "if you will speak to the President favorably on the subject of this bill."[122]

Positive Presidential assistance to the Conference has been limited in the modern period. However, judges have made infrequent efforts to secure public endorsements from the Chief Executive. During the Truman administration, they considered the possibility of evoking a favorable Presidential statement on higher judicial salaries at one of his press conferences.[123] Shortly after Eisenhower's election in 1952, a concerted attempt was made to secure his public

[119] Harold M. Stephens to All Judges, April 19, 1946, *ibid.*

[120] Interview with Albert B. Maris, December 29, 1964, Philadelphia, Pennsylvania.

[121] See *New York Times,* January 28, 1956, p. 1.

[122] Harold M. Stephens to James P. McGranery, June 24, 1952, Stephens Papers, Box 180.

[123] Harold M. Stephens to D. Lawrence Groner, June 13, 1945, Groner Papers, Box 9.

support for the still live salary issue. Then, a federal judge in New York approached Governor Thomas Dewey, an early and enthusiastic Eisenhower backer, and successfully urged him to broach the subject to the President-elect.[124]

When Congress failed to act on the measure, the judges launched a campaign to include a reference to the subject in the President's State of the Union Address. Although only President Coolidge had ever mentioned a Judicial Conference recommendation in this address,[125] the judges through the Attorney General and leading members of the American Bar Association, met with success.[126] The intermediaries took their case to Bernard Shanley, Eisenhower's speechwriter,[127] who included an endorsement of increased congressional and judicial salaries in the 1955 address.[128] Thereafter President Eisenhower used his annual budget message to impress upon successive Democratic-controlled Congresses the urgency of Judicial Conference recommendations especially those urging creation of additional judgeships.[129] Similarly, President John Kennedy included such recommendations among his various communications to Congress.[130]

[124] Harold M. Stephens, memorandum re: Telephone Call to Judge Irving Kaufman, November 20, 1952, Stephens Papers, Box 194.

[125] *Congressional Record*, 68th Cong., 1st Sess., 1923, vol. 65, part 1, 98. See William H. Taft to Robert A. Taft, December 2, 1923, Taft Papers.

[126] "Memorandum of Conference in Judge Stephens' Chambers," November 4, 1954, Stephens Papers, Box 198.

[127] Harold M. Stephens to Eugene D. Bennett, January 5, 1955, *ibid.*

[128] Morris Mitchell to Harold M. Stephens, January 3, 1955, *ibid.*; State of the Union Address, 1955, *Public Papers of the Presidents: Dwight D. Eisenhower* (Washington, 1956), p. 27.

[129] See Annual Budget Message to Congress for Fiscal Year 1958, *ibid.*, 1957, pp. 56-57; for Fiscal Year 1960, *ibid.*, 1959, p. 111; for Fiscal Year 1961, *ibid.*, 1960, p. 105; for Fiscal Year 1962, *ibid.*, 1961, p. 1023.

[130] President Kennedy included similar subject matter in letters to the President of the Senate and to the Speaker of the House. See *Pub-*

Invoking the Mass Media

If judges sought to publicize their case through the President, they also took it directly to the mass media. In print and over the air, they rebutted unfavorable publicity and promoted their own programs. The ultimate target, as always, remained Congress. Only the strategy changed.

Sensitive to press criticism which "might react very unfavorably in getting our bill . . . through the House of Representatives,"[131] judges worked to counter it. An editorial in the *Saturday Evening Post* attacking an increase in federal judgeships on the grounds that the existing intercircuit assignment power offered adequate relief led Biggs to protest to the editor.[132] Mincing no words, he told him that the magazine's proposed remedy was *"putting the matter bluntly . . . a medicine which has long been tried and has effected no cure. . . .* The subject should be re-examined, and another editorial of a different tenor published."[133]

Later Biggs, in company with a prominent federal judge from Philadelphia, home office of the *Post*, "called on . . . the head of the editorial department of the Saturday Evening Post . . . and talked with him for about an hour and a half."[134] They came away, he reported to the Chief Justice, with "the impression that we have won him over to

---

lic Papers of the Presidents: John F. Kennedy, Letter of February 10, 1961, pp. 83-84; *ibid.*, Letter of March 8, 1963, p. 244.

[131] John Biggs, Jr., to Harold M. Stephens, November 8, 1951, Stephens Papers, Box 179. See also Harold M. Stephens to Philip L. Graham, July 26, 1949, *ibid.*, Box 87.

[132] "Federal Courts Could Use Improvement in Routine," *Saturday Evening Post*, November 10, 1951, pp. 10-12.

[133] John Biggs, Jr., to Ben Hibbs, November 2, 1952, Stephens Papers, Box 179, italics in original. See also John Biggs, Jr., to Ben Hibbs, December, 1951, Administrative Office Correspondence, 60-A-328, Box 5.

[134] John Biggs, Jr., to Fred M. Vinson, January 2, 1952, Stephens Papers, Box 179.

our view and we hope that there may be a countervailing editorial."[135] A month later, one appeared.[136]

Key judges have also initiated favorable editorials. This strategy was used to promote a major item of legislation, after the then Senate majority leader, Lyndon B. Johnson, expressed "some disappointment" to Judges Biggs and Stephens over "the lack of newspaper support for the proposed salary increase legislation . . . and . . . suggested that it would be well to try to secure the support of the *New York Times* and of the Scripps-Howard papers, also to obtain more editorial support throughout the country."[137] With such encouragement, veritable bundles of propaganda were dispatched to editors. These included copies of statements made by favorable witnesses before congressional committees, copies of letters from prominent judges attesting to the need for the particular bill, and memoranda explaining its merits.[138] In a previous effort of this sort, judges "planted" editorials in leading publications, as did Judge Stephens in the *Washington Post* under Merlo Pusey's name.[139]

Publicity efforts assumed gigantic proportions in 1953 and 1954 when ranking judges joined with the American Bar Association to bombard newspaper editors across the country in quest of favorable editorials. At that time five

[135] *Ibid.*
[136] See Editorial: "Fair Deal Laws Create Need for More Judges," *Saturday Evening Post*, February 2, 1952, pp. 10 and 12. For other efforts to create a favorable press, see: Harold M. Stephens to Philip Graham, Benjamin McKelway, Frank C. Waldrop, Arthur Krock, George B. Packer, Whitelaw Reid, August 9, 1949, Stephens Papers, Box 87; Harold M. Stephens to John F. Fitzpatrick, June 9, 1953, *ibid.*, Box 89; Harold M. Stephens to Fred M. Vinson, September 2, 1949, *ibid.*, Box 192.
[137] Harold M. Stephens to Lyndon B. Johnson, January 18, 1955, *ibid.*, Box 198.
[138] Harold M. Stephens to Philip L. Graham, June 6, 1951, *ibid.*, Box 73.
[139] Harold M. Stephens to Sam Hobbes, May 24, 1945, *ibid.*, Box 85.

thousand editors of rural newspapers, always eager for filler material, received a packet of information including a "canned" editorial on the case for increased salaries, while the editors of five hundred daily newspapers received all but the editorial.[140] At the same time, key judges utilized radio and television. Stephens, for instance, arranged for a radio broadcast by Walter Winchell, in which the renowned commentator urged his listeners to write their congressmen and senators and request passage of a judicial salary bill.[141] Meanwhile, Bernard Segal of the American Bar Association, closely cooperating with the judges, reported he had "had personal conversations with officials of NBC and CBS." In addition, he held "a long meeting with Ed Murrow, who is going to put on a one-half hour television program on his national CBS hook-up on the subject, and . . . talked with Ted Granick, who is planning to devote one whole program on the Forum of the Air to Congressional and Judicial salaries."[142]

Co-opting the ALI and the ABA

Judges have elicited support for the Conference's legislative policies from a broad spectrum of labor, business, and fraternal interest groups.[143] But organizations representing the national interests of the legal profession have been their most consistent and effective allies. Both the

[140] Harold M. Stephens to John C. Collet, June 19, 1953, *ibid.*, Box 89.
[141] Harold M. Stephens to Bernard Segal (telegram), February 2, 1954, *ibid.*, Box 197.
[142] Bernard Segal to Don Hyndman, February 3, 1954, *ibid.*
[143] See Harold M. Stephens to Sam Hobbes, May 19, 1945, *ibid.*, Box 85; Harold M. Stephens to Judges of United States Courts of Appeals, District Courts, Court of Customs and Patent Appeals, Court of Claims, and Customs Court, July 31, 1945, *ibid.*, Box 189; D. Lawrence Groner to John C. Knox, November 9, 1944, Groner Papers, Box 9.

American Law Institute and the American Bar Association have been useful in alliances seeking congressional enactment of Conference-sponsored bills.

The American Law Institute has provided the Conference with services commonly associated with private interest groups rather than with public agencies, namely those of a full-time paid "Washington lobbyist." Faced with legislative roadblocks impeding passage of a federal corrections bill,[144] a member of John J. Parker's Conference Committee on Punishment for Crime reported that William Draper Lewis, Director of the Institute, "had received information which caused him to doubt that the Corrections Act would pass at this session of the Congress, unless someone was delegated to go to Washington and press for its passage."[145] That "someone" was John R. Ellingston, the organization's Special Advisor on youth offenders.[146] Funded by the ALI, his credentials were established by Parker who spoke with Congressman Francis Walter of the House Judiciary Committee.[147] Thus the senior circuit judges' good offices, developed through a continuing relationship with Walter's committee, enabled Ellingston "to get on with work in support of the Federal Corrections Act, with the approval of key people."[148] And work he did, performing a wide variety of liaison duties as well as direct and indirect lobbying. He monitored legislative developments, kept open lines of communication with Parker's committee, the House Judiciary Committee, the Chief Justice, and the Department of Justice, drafted, in consultation with Parker, reports on the pending bill for the House committee's use, arranged meetings between Parker and members of Congress, and sug-

[144] H.R. 2140, 78th Cong.
[145] Orie L. Phillips to John J. Parker, June 27, 1943, Parker Papers, Box 62.
[146] *Ibid.*
[147] John J. Parker to Orie L. Phillips, June 29, 1943 in *ibid.*
[148] John R. Ellingston to John J. Parker, July 24, 1943, in *ibid.*

gested timely lobbying strategies to Parker and his commit-tee.[149] Many of these strategies were similar to those performed by the judges themselves, when the judiciary's legislative demands failed to overlap those of a well-organized interest group such as the ALI. Thus Ellingston urged that judges write their congressmen,[150] sought the support of United States attorneys,[151] and ghost-wrote a magazine article to be published under Representative Walter's name,[152] as well as drafts of letters to be sent, over a judge's signature, to a newspaper editor, a county bar president, and the chairman of the House Judiciary Committee.[153] As did the judges, he worked for favorable media publicity, and an editorial in the *Saturday Evening Post* bore testimony to his efforts.[154]

Like the American Law Institute, the American Bar Association has collaborated with the Judicial Conference in quest of congressional enactment of measures important to the federal courts. Unlike the ALI, the ABA purports to be a representative organization with a capacity for action in local and national political arenas. The association, in the words of its leaders, is "the congress of the American bar with representation from all parts of the Nation,"[155] "so that [it] can speak with authority for the lawyers of America."[156] State and local bar associations may be requested to sup-

[149] See Wilson, "The Federal Corrections Act," pp. 73-80.

[150] John R. Ellingston to John J. Parker, July 24, 1943, Parker Papers, Box 62.

[151] *Ibid.*   [152] *Ibid.*

[153] John R. Ellingston to Orie L. Phillips, March 25, 1944, in *ibid.*

[154] John R. Ellingston to John J. Parker, October 28, 1943, in *ibid.* See "For a Better Deal in Criminal Justice," *Saturday Evening Post,* December 11, 1943, p. 116.

[155] Bernard Segal, U.S., Congress, Senate, Commission on Judicial and Congressional Salaries, *Hearings, before the Commission on Judicial and Congressional Salaries,* 83d Cong., 2d Sess., 1954, Senate Doc. 104, p. 19.

[156] Morris Mitchell, *ibid.*

port judicial policies,[157] especially additional judgeships,[158] but it is the prestigious American Bar Association which has commanded close attention.

The association has been so important that leading members of the Judicial Conference have worked for the election of those candidates for its presidency who would turn "the strength of the Association to aiding the Federal Judiciary in improving the administration of justice."[159] They have, similarly, sought to influence the composition of ABA committees,[160] as have officials of the Administrative Office, some of whom have been members of them.[161]

On a wide variety of issues, judges seek to enlist the active support of the bar association.[162] Launching a major campaign for the association's endorsement of the judge's widows pension plans during the Vinson era,[163] Judges Biggs and Stephens personally appealed to 30 lawyers in

[157] Pierson M. Hall to James C. Sheppard, May 4, 1961, Clark Papers.
[158] Harold M. Stephens to Archibald K. Gardner, June 7, 1949, Stephens Papers, Box 211.
[159] Harold M. Stephens to Franklin Ritter, February 24, 1954, ibid., Box 83.
[160] Harold M. Stephens to John G. Buchanan, December 3, 1952, ibid., Box 89; D. Lawrence Groner to Thomas B. Gay, December 7, 1945, ibid., Box 191.
[161] See Director's Membership, American Bar Association Reports, 66 (1941), 492; Articles Editor, ibid., p. 458; Secretary of the Section on Judicial Administration, ibid., 73 (1948), 55; ibid., 75 (1950), 57; ibid., 76 (1951), 61; Member of the Section Council, ibid., 73 (1948), 55; ibid., 75 (1950), 59; ibid., 76 (1951), 61; ibid., 77 (1952), 61; ibid., 79 (1954), 60.
[162] Ibid., 72 (1947), 192-93; "Report of the [Judicial Conference] Committee on Rule 71A(h) of Rules of Civil Procedure and Pending Bill S. 1958," January 16, 1952, mimeograph (Administrative Office of the United States Courts, Washington, D.C.); Henry P. Chandler to Albert E. Jenner, Jr., February 10, 1956, Administrative Office Correspondence, 59-A-532, Box 3; New York Times, August 10, 1966, p. 28. See also American Bar Association Reports, 82 (1957), 438, 393; ibid., 88 (1963), 637-38; Baar, "When Judges Lobby," p. 566.
[163] American Bar Association Reports, 77 (1952), 501-06.

the House of Delegates. The delegates from the District of Columbia were buttonholed by district and circuit judges from the District's federal court. Then by telephone calls, correspondence, and personal conferences, key members of the association were enlisted, as were all former American Bar Association presidents still living, and the officers of the Section on Judicial Administration.[164] Lists of state delegates were dispatched to other federal judges with the suggestion that they contact them.[165] Meanwhile Judges Biggs and Stephens arranged for introduction of a favorable resolution through the association's Committee on Selection, Tenure, and Compensation and contacted a strategically placed ABA officer on the efficacious use of parliamentary procedure.[166]

Bar committees and prominent members of the association may act as intermediaries between the Conference and Congress.[167] With the creation of additional judgeships blocked by the Republican Eightieth Congress, an official of the Administrative Office informed a leading association figure that "the preliminary job is to convince Senator [Irving M.] Ives and Congressman [Frederic R.] Coudert that new judgeships are needed and should be promptly provided for. I think that your committee and others of the

[164] Harold M. Stephens to Chief Justice [Fred M. Vinson], February 15, 1952, Stephens Papers, Box 89.

[165] Harold M. Stephens to Judge Clark, February 13, 1952, ibid., Box 89.

[166] Harold M. Stephens to Chief Justice [Fred M. Vinson], February 15, 1952, ibid.; Harold M. Stephens to Cody Fowler, December 14, 1951, ibid., Box 88. Much the same strategy has been followed in defeating association actions. See Harold M. Stephens to Fred M. Vinson, August 4, 1953, ibid., Box 229; Harold M. Stephens to Frank E. Holman, December 4, 1951, ibid., Box 88; Harold M. Stephens to John J. Parker, December 4, 1951, ibid.; Harold M. Stephens to Fred M. Vinson, December 21, 1951, ibid.

[167] Harold M. Stephens to Morris Mitchell, memorandum re: telephone call, May 11, 1953, ibid., Box 195; Harold M. Stephens to Joseph J. Daniels, May 22, 1946, ibid., Box 190.

333

Association will be far more influential in this respect than we can ever hope to be."[168]

On a politically sensitive issue like increased judicial salaries, which is invariably tied to those of the legislators, congressional leaders have called upon the judges for "some sort of campaign in the field which will impress upon the members of Congress that there really is wide support for the increase proposal."[169] For such a "grass roots" effort, the judges were singularly ill-equipped and looked to the bar for assistance. Late in 1952, Morris Mitchell, chairman of the ABA's Standing Committee on Judicial Selection, Tenure, and Compensation, together with Judge Stephens, mapped out a nationwide salary campaign unique in the annals of congressional liaison. They virtually co-opted the ABA in creating two organizations: one in Washington composed of prominent local lawyers and Judge Stephens, and a "grass roots" network composed of the 48 associate and advisory committee members (one from each state) of the ABA's Committee on Judicial Selection, Tenure and Compensation, the ten Federal Judicial Circuit Committees, and the Committee on Federal Judicial Salaries of the Conference of Bar Association Presidents.[170]

The latter group headed by Bernard Segal, was organized on a federal pattern, with the country divided into areas. "Each area chairman was made responsible for appointing a chairman of each of the circuits in his area," and as Segal described it, "either himself or through them appointing a Chairman for each State comprising the Circuit." The state chairman, in turn, would be "expected to appoint

[168] Leland Tolman to Samuel M. Lane, December 23, 1947, Administrative Office Correspondence, 60-A-328, Box 6.

[169] Morris Mitchell, "Memo re Suggested Program for Bar Support of S. 1663, re: April 22, 1953, Session of the Senate Judiciary Committee," Stephens Papers, Box 195.

[170] Morris Mitchell to Harold M. Stephens, December 4, 1952, *ibid.*, Box 194.

a state-wide committee."[171] Finally, the Committee on Judicial Selection, Tenure, and Compensation would act as the "clearing house" for the grass roots committees and would coordinate their work and provide liaison with the Washington committee.[172]

Although the lawyers in the Washington organization imparted great prestige to it, Judges Biggs and Stephens dominated the scene.[173] "One of the primary purposes of the organized Bar in stepping into the picture was to relieve the Judges of the burdens and embarrassment of carrying the ball"; yet, admitted lawyer Segal, these two judges "had so much experience in their field and by virtue of their activity for the Federal Judicial Conference are continually working with the respective Judiciary Committees of the Senate and of the House, [that] they have been active participants . . . [and] Judge Stephens has also been serving as the Washington clearing house for all of us."[174]

At the grass roots level, however, it was the bar groups which stood out. Their job, declared Morris Mitchell, was to "really get letters, resolutions, etc. pouring into Congress in large volume,"[175] and particularly to the congressmen

[171] Bernard Segal to the Members of the Committee on Federal Judicial Salaries of the National Conference of Bar Association Presidents, August 18, 1953, ibid., Box 196.

[172] Morris Mitchell to Harold M. Stephens, December 4, 1952, ibid., Box 194. See "Report of the Standing Committee on Judicial Selection, Tenure and Compensation," American Bar Association Reports, 79 (1954), 233-34, containing a description of ABA activities re: judicial and congressional salaries, and "Appendix I: Judicial-Congressional Salary Program Organization," pp. 237-39.

[173] Harold M. Stephens to Webster J. Oliver, March 12, 1953, Stephens Papers, Box 89; Harold M. Stephens to Carl A. Hatch, May 25, 1953, ibid., Box 195.

[174] Bernard Segal to the Members of the Committee on Federal Judicial Salaries of the National Conference of Bar Association Presidents, August 18, 1953, ibid., Box 196.

[175] Morris Mitchell to James D. Fellers, July 17, 1953, ibid., Box 196.

who were indifferent to the proposal.[176] Thus when Democratic floor leader Lyndon B. Johnson was reported as taking a lukewarm attitude, Mitchell promptly telephoned the chairman of the Texas committee who had "a good committee of 22 lawyers located throughout Texas." The state chairman agreed with alacrity "to . . . get each of them to try to get favorable editorials in their local papers, of which they will send copies to Senator Johnson."[177]

Meanwhile, salary propaganda flooded the country.[178] Under the auspices of the ABA, a fifty-page portfolio of editorial reprints was assembled and distributed to congressmen. With them went Mitchell's assurance "that public opinion throughout America favors these salary increases."[179] But Robert A. Taft, then Senate Republican leader, was unconvinced and "indicated a definite desire that Congress be fortified with the opinion of an independent commission concerning the propriety of the increase in salaries for members of Congress."[180] And so a Salary Commission emerged. As finally established, it contained eighteen members, six appointed by the President (including the chairman), six by the Chief Justice, three by the speaker of the House, and three by the Vice President with a nine-member advisory staff on which the commission would be wholly dependent.[181] In its composition and operation, the ABA again played a vital part. "We must," wrote Bernard

[176] Harold M. Stephens to Kurt Panzer, July 24, 1953, *ibid.*, Box 89.
[177] Morris Mitchell to Harold M. Stephens, January 18, 1955, *ibid.*, Box 198.
[178] These are reproduced in the Senate Commission on Judicial and Congressional Salaries, *Hearings*, 1954, "Appendix I: Editorials and Articles," pp. 463-540; "Appendix II: Resolutions," pp. 541-90; "Appendix III: Letters and Statements," pp. 591-668.
[179] Morris Mitchell to all members of Congress, January 15, 1954, Stephens Papers, Box 197.
[180] John Caskie Collet to Harold M. Stephens, June 5, 1953, *ibid.*, Box 195.
[181] 67 *Stat.* 485. See Draft of Minutes of Organizational Meeting of the Commission on Judicial and Congressional Salaries, November 30, 1953, Stephens Papers, Box 196.

336

Segal to Morris Mitchell, "do everything in our power to assure the appointment of a strong Commission, which will have wide public acceptance, and will not include any mavericks . . . [for] it would be regrettable if there were to be dissents to the report by people who start with strong prejudices."[182] Thus leading ABA members became immediately involved in the selection process.[183] However, Chief Justice Warren, at the urging of Mitchell and Stephens, took the lead in constituting the full commission,[184] and undoubtedly influenced the President's appointees as well as his own.[185]

With clockwork precision, the commission went about legitimizing the salary increase. Behind the scene, the ABA's "Hearing Team" assembled witnesses and, during three days of testimony, paraded 63 witnesses, 60 of whom were favorable, before the commission.[186] A month later, the commission issued its final report,[187] terminating what Chairman Segal termed "a monumental job."[188]

[182] Bernard Segal to Morris Mitchell, August 5, 1953, *ibid.*

[183] Morris Mitchell to Herbert Brownell, September 2, 1953, *ibid.*; Morris Mitchell to William J. Tyson, September 2, 1953, *ibid.*; Harold M. Stephens to William C. Mathes, October 28, 1953, *ibid.*, Box 89.

[184] Harold M. Stephens to Morris Mitchell, September 3, 1953, *ibid.*

[185] See "Minutes of Organization Meeting of the Commission on Judicial and Congressional Salaries," November 30, 1953, in Senate Commission on Judicial and Congressional Salaries, *Hearings*, 1954, pp. 6-8.

[186] Morris Mitchell to Preston C. King, Jr., December 23, 1953, Stephens Papers, Box 197. The three who gave adverse testimony were Rep. William A. Dawson (Utah), Senate Commission on Judicial and Congressional Salaries, *Hearings*, 1954, pp. 101-27; Rep. Usher L. Burdick (North Dakota), *ibid.*, pp. 271-84; and Rep. Clare E. Hoffman (Michigan), *ibid.*, pp. 329-37.

[187] See U.S., Congress, Senate, Commission on Judicial and Congressional Salaries, *Reports of the Task Forces of the Commission on Judicial and Congressional Salaries*, Senate Doc. 97, 83d Cong., 2d Sess., 1954.

[188] Bernard Segal to Hugo Black, January 16, 1954, Stephens Papers, Box 197. See: P. L. 9, March 2, 1955, 84th Cong.

View from the Hill

"The courts have no lobby," contended Chief Judge Harold M. Stephens. "They cannot exert pressure on the Congress."[189] In spite of his disclaimer, judges, acting in the name of the Judicial Conference or through assorted interest groups, have done just that. They have played the role of "Washington lobbyist" because the decentralized organization of the federal judiciary required some centralization of legislative liaison. "We are so far away from the seat of government," wrote one West Coast judge, "that we have little knowledge of what the undercurrents are or what is really going on."[190] They have lobbied Congress because the realities of the congressional process demanded it. Commented Judge Stephens, why any congressman "should expect the bill to pass if the judges are not interested in it, I do not know."[191]

Legislative criticism and the ever-present danger of becoming entangled "in the politics between the two parties in the Congress"[192] has not deterred them.[193] Nor have judges been discouraged by the cost of lobbying, costs in out-of-pocket expenses[194] and in time, which, remarked Stephens, if otherwise available, "would have made it possible for us to write many more opinions for our courts."[195]

[189] Harold M. Stephens, Senate Subcommittee of the Committee on the Judiciary, *Hearings on S. Con. Res. 4-5*, 1955, p. 39.

[190] William Healy to Harold M. Stephens, April 24, 1950, Stephens Papers, Box 56.

[191] Harold M. Stephens to Bennett Champ Clark, August 21, 1950, *ibid.*, Box 81; Harold M. Stephens to William C. Coleman, May 1, 1946, *ibid.*, Box 85.

[192] Olin D. Johnston, *Congressional Record*, 87th Cong., 2d Sess., 1962, vol. 108, part 3, 3616; see also: Paul Douglas, *ibid.*, 82d Cong., 2d Sess., 1953, vol. 98, part 1, 478.

[193] Harold M. Stephens to John E. Miller, memorandum, May, 1953, Stephens Papers, Box 195.

[194] Harold M. Stephens to Albert B. Maris, November 5, 1946, *ibid.*, Box 27.

[195] Harold M. Stephens to Chief Justice Earl Warren and the Mem-

Finally, they have labored on Capitol Hill even though beset by doubts that "perhaps if I had let things ride . . . [they] might have gotten through anyway. But," said Stephens, "in foresight one can never take this position because it is just the constant nudging of this Congressman and that Senator and the appearances before Committees and the letters one writes which may cumulatively result in success."[196]

And such has been the outcome of innumerable legislative efforts. "Generally speaking," stated an official of the Administrative Office, "Judicial Conference recommendations, both in regard to judgeship positions and other matters, have had considerable standing, and have received favorable consideration in the Congress."[197]

---

bers of the Judicial Conference, March 21, 1955, pp. 3-4, *ibid.*, Box 234.

[196] Harold M. Stephens to Wilbur K. Miller, August 18, 1947, *ibid.*, Box 85.

[197] Joseph F. Spaniol, Jr. to Peter G. Fish, September 16, 1966 (letter in possession of the author).

CHAPTER 10

Administrative Regionalism and Centralism: From Circuit Conferences to the Federal Judicial Center

INNOVATION at the center of the judiciary's administrative network predictably influenced the development of those on the periphery. Thus emergence of the Administrative Office of the United States Courts and far-reaching changes in the structure and work of the Judicial Conference and its committees vitally affected the nature and functions of the circuit conferences, stimulated the growth of additional forums of education and communication, and ultimately spurred establishment of a new central agency for research and development in judicial administration as well as for education. Some of these agencies, particularly those on a circuit level, strengthened the voice of parochial interests; others acted as vehicles of administrative integration. These latter agencies, developed during the nearly three decades after 1939, were incremental and highly pragmatic responses to the apparent needs of an ever busier judicial system. Foremost among them were the circuit conferences, sanctioned by the Administrative Office Act, and utilized, modified, and, in some instances, supplemented by new administrative institutions.

Circuit Conferences: Organization

Wide variations characterize the organization and functions of different circuit conferences, although by statute all consider "the business of the courts and . . . means of im-

340

proving the administration of justice within [the] circuit."[1] These conferences are supposed to meet annually at the call of the chief judge of each circuit. The clear and mandatory language of the statute notwithstanding, some chief judges have cancelled them,[2] while others have labored through what they regarded as "tedious" gatherings at which "everything under the sun" was discussed.[3]

Success depended on the chief judge. If he had, as some did, an "ever-lasting enthusiasm" for the conferences,[4] they came off well. If not, they proved less than satisfactory. The latter condition tended to prevail as noted by one prominent federal judge in 1958, who found that only a minority of circuits "have consistently held meaningful conferences and in some places the conferences which are held fall far short of what Congress intended."[5]

District and circuit judges are required by law to attend their respective conferences unless excused by the chief judge.[6] Again, this is a rule which has been honored in the breach. So few judges appeared at the 1944 District of Columbia conference that the secretary reported: "When most of the voting [on the new Federal Rules of Criminal Procedure] took place the number of judges from both [circuit and district] courts ranged between 3 and 6 [making] it . . . difficult to say that the action was that of the Conference."[7]

[1] 28 U.S.C. 333.
[2] Cancelled in the First, Second, and Eighth Circuits in 1953; see Thomas W. Swan to Circuit and District Judges of the Second Circuit, May 25, 1953, Clark Papers.
[3] Evan A. Evans to Henry P. Chandler, November 17, 1942, Administrative Office Correspondence, 59-A-532, Box 2.
[4] Ibid.
[5] Warren E. Burger, "Courts on Trial: A Call for Action Against Delay," Federal Rules Decisions, 22 (1958), 79.
[6] Ibid., pp. 74-75.
[7] Justin Miller to D. Lawrence Groner, Harold M. Stephens, Henry W. Edgerton, Thurman Arnold, September 25, 1944, Groner Papers, Box 13.

Attendance of the Attorney General, United States attorneys, representatives or deans of law schools within the circuit, chief justices of the state Supreme Courts, and referees in bankruptcy has been permitted by formal rule in many circuits.[8] Members of Congress as well as circuit justices from the Supreme Court may also attend.[9] Bar participation has been mandatory since 1948, when an act of Congress directed the courts of appeals in each circuit to "provide by its rules for representation and active participation . . . by members of the bar of such circuit."[10] Yet as late as 1961 two of the eleven circuits had failed to promulgate the rule, although one maintained an informal "open door" policy for anyone wishing an invitation. The other had "never had any rules providing 'for representation and active participation at such Conferences by members of the Bar of such circuit' as required by 28 U.S.C. 333."[11]

Selection of lawyer delegates in the overwhelming majority of circuits conforming with the law differs. Some provide by formal rule for representation by members of the principal bar association within the circuit. These members have variously been the bar presidents, delegates selected by the association, their presidents, or representatives selected by joint committees of lawyers and judges.[12] The bulk of bar representatives, however, are chosen by the judges themselves. In some circuits both the trial and appellate judges invite equal numbers of lawyers. In others each of the less numerous appellate judges select twice as many delegates as each district judge, or the trial and appellate judges invite equal numbers, but the court of appeals as a

[8] Robert W. Graham to the Chief Judges of the Circuits, July 10, 1961, mimeograph, Clark Papers.

[9] Carl Baar, "When Judges Lobby: Congress and Court Administration" (unpub. Ph.D. dissertation, Department of Political Science, University of Chicago, 1969), pp. 293-94.

[10] 62 *Stat.* 903.

[11] Robert W. Graham to the Chief Judges, July 10, 1961, p. 11, Clark Papers.

[12] *Ibid.*

whole is empowered to choose a designated number as well. Further weighting the selection process in favor of the appellate courts has been the power of the chief judge to issue an unlimited quantity of invitations and reject candidates nominated by the judges.[13]

Little uniformity characterizes the size of the non-judicial contingent, even within the circuits, much less among them. For instance, the Second Circuit adopted a flexible membership rule permitting its conference to meet special circumstances and to conform with the capacities of hotels in different cities.[14] In the Third Circuit, however, faithful attendance has been rewarded by permanent membership, a custom tending to expand the size of that conference.[15]

Although some circuits follow a policy of rotating lawyer-delegate participation among different bars within the circuit,[16] lawyer-delegate membership has often become static. Even in the Second Circuit, where rotation was encouraged, the chief judge reported in 1961 that "a study of the Conference attendance records indicates that many members of the bar are attending the Conference year after year." Regarding this practice as undesirable, he called on the judges "to see that invitations are extended to as many members of the bar as possible."[17]

Although chief judges, particularly in the pre-Warren era, often organized the program of their conferences,[18] this responsibility was usually delegated to judges or lawyers,

[13] *Ibid.* See also *Judicial Conference Report, 1949*, p. 52.

[14] Charles E. Clark to J. Edward Lumbard, November 25, 1959, Clark Papers.

[15] *Ibid.*

[16] Samuel M. Driver to S. J. Olson, March 25, 1950, Samuel M. Driver Papers (University of Oregon, Eugene, Oregon; cited hereafter as Driver Papers).

[17] J. Edward Lumbard to All Circuit and District Judges of the Second Circuit, December, 1961, p. 2, Clark Papers.

[18] Kimbrough Stone, Conference of United States Circuit and District Judges of the Eighth Circuit, January 5 and 6, 1939, stenographic transcript, Kimbrough Stone Papers, Box 26.

or some combination of the two. Named by Chief Judge Groner as secretary of the 1944 District of Columbia conference, Judge Justin Miller formulated the program and submitted it to Groner with the request that he communicate the discussion assignments to each judge, accepting no excuse "short of ill health."[19]

During the Warren era, efforts were made to enlarge bar participation in order to transform the circuit conferences into "a meaningful and dynamic medium of communication between the Bench and Bar."[20] To realize this goal, the Seventh and Ninth Circuits simply allot a portion of the Conference sessions to the lawyer-delegates who then assume full responsibility for the program.[21] The program of the Third Circuit's conference "has been arranged by one of the judges of the Circuit who has called upon the lawyer-delegates for advice and assistance."[22] Other circuits, including the Second, Fifth, and Ninth, have admitted members of the bar to the program or arrangements committees once composed solely of judges.

Inclusion of the elements of the bar as an integral part of the conference organization has typically accompanied attempts to reform these institutions. When Charles E. Clark became chief judge of the Second Circuit Court of Appeals, he found a moribund and widely criticized conference in his circuit. Leading members of the bar, judges, and even Supreme Court Justice Robert H. Jackson assailed its "barren nature" and its "noncompliance with the statutory requirements."[23] Under Clark's leadership, the Second Circuit council established a lawyer-dominated Planning and Program Committee charged with formulating "plans for a re-

[19] Justin Miller, Memorandum to D. Lawrence Groner, April 8, 1944, Groner Papers, Box 13.
[20] Burger, "Courts on Trial," p. 83.
[21] Robert W. Graham to the Chief Judges, July 10, 1961, Clark Papers.
[22] *Ibid.*
[23] "Minutes of the Council of the Second Circuit," October 7, 1954, p. 1, Clark Papers.

invigorated Conference."[24] Judges not lawyers, however, continued to exercise veto power over conference agendas. Such became apparent when several members of the council of the Second Circuit "expressed disapproval of the subject of jury trials for panel discussion at the Conference," thereby effectively killing the proposal.[25]

On the other hand, the availability of lawyers has provided personnel for circuit conference committees. Several such committees established by the District of Columbia conference have been research-oriented. Staffed largely by lawyers and legal scholars, and funded, they have engaged in rather long term conference-sponsored projects.[26]

The role of the Administrative Office in the program planning has never been extensive. Under Director Chandler, it was the agency's policy not to "make up programs of the conferences and . . . not even [to] make suggestions with reference to them unless requested to do so."[27] When invited, the office provided limited staff services, chiefly statistical data,[28] suggested likely discussion topics as well as possible speakers,[29] and even educated at least one conference secretary on the general nature of his record-keeping duties.[30]

[24] *Ibid.*

[25] "Minutes of the Council of the Second Circuit," November 20, 1963, p. 4, Clark Papers.

[26] See David L. Bazelon, U.S., Congress, Senate, Subcommittee on Separation of Powers of the Committee on the Judiciary, *Hearings, on the Independence of Federal Judges*, 91st Cong., 2d Sess., 1970, pp. 326-27.

[27] Elmore Whitehurst to John McDuffie, November 21, 1946, Administrative Office Correspondence, 60-A-328, Box 25.

[28] Sumter D. Marks, Jr. to Henry P. Chandler, May 19, 1950, and Henry P. Chandler to Sumter D. Marks, Jr., May 10, 1950, *ibid.*, 59-A-532, Box 1.

[29] See Henry P. Chandler, Memorandum for Leland Tolman, January 13, 1955, *ibid.*, 60-A-328, Box 1; Henry P. Chandler to Frederick V. Follmer, January 12, 1955, *ibid.*, 60-A-328, Box 1.

[30] Henry P. Chandler to Elwyn R. Shaw, November 30, 1944, *ibid.*, 59-A-532, Box 2. See also Henry P. Chandler, "Memorandum in Refer-

Circuit Conferences: Programs

The programs of the conferences held in each of the eleven circuits are a potpourri of activities, most of them intended to enhance the administration of justice within the respective circuits. Some, however, have been essentially social,[31] "designed primarily for interest and entertainment rather than for direct application to the work of the courts."[32] Thus, conferences in the Ninth Circuit featured addresses on the laudatory topic "In Praise of Judges,"[33] and in 1947, a more jingoistic one entitled "China Confronts Western Civilization."[34] The Third Circuit once staged a debate between William Crosskey and H. M. Hart on "The Constitutional and Intended Role of the National Courts."[35]

The programs of the executive sessions, restricted to the judges, have emphasized the work of the courts within the circuits, and particularly the work of the federal trial courts. "The District Judges have, outside of the Conference, no opportunity for . . . discussion," observed one senior circuit judge in 1940. Hence the agenda items at his circuit's conferences were "nearly always such as particularly concern the trial courts."[36]

---

ence to the Deposit of Copies of Minutes of the Judicial Conferences of the Circuits in the Administrative Office, Part I," September 9, 1949, Stephens Papers, Box 315.

[31] See Charles E. Clark to J. Edward Lumbard, December 26, 1962, Clark Papers.

[32] Henry P. Chandler to Frederick V. Follmer, January 12, 1955, Administrative Office Correspondence, 60-A-328, Box 1.

[33] "Minutes of the Judicial Conference of the United States Circuit and District Judges of the Ninth Circuit," August 31-September 1, 1948, p. 3, Driver Papers (cited hereafter as "Minutes of the Judicial Conference of the Ninth Circuit," 1948).

[34] "Judicial Conferences, Sixth, Ninth, and D.C.," *American Bar Association Journal*, 33 (October 1947), 980.

[35] Memorandum, "Judicial Conference," undated, Administrative Office Correspondence, 60-A-328, Box 1.

[36] Kimbrough Stone to Robert G. Simmons, January 12, 1940, Kimbrough Stone Papers, Box 10.

Reports by the chief judges of the district courts traditionally constitute an early order of business.[37] Thereafter the district judges in the Second Circuit, together with the appellate judges, have considered problems of court congestion, use of pretrial procedures and electronic recording equipment in lieu of reporters, summer sittings, bail bonds, and defense of indigent defendants,[38] while at one District of Columbia conference, they discussed such parochial subjects as court housing and libraries, as well as means of improving the judiciary's public image.[39]

Consideration of case law has apparently been relatively limited, although participants sometimes discussed "trends in judicial decisions," which, said Henry P. Chandler, "doubtless conduce toward uniform attitudes of the judges toward similar problems in cases coming before them."[40] However, he quickly added that no precedent existed "in the federal system for conferences of judges of different circuits for the direct purpose of considering how they shall decide similar questions of law in specific cases pending before them and I can conceive that there would be objection to such a practice."[41]

Thus the major subjects considered by the judges in their executive sessions emphasize administrative and procedural problems rather than substantive judicial issues. But the consideration given the former typically extends little beyond the discussion and resolution stage, because any rem-

[37] See "Fourteenth Annual Judicial Conference of the Third Judicial Circuit of the United States," July 17-18, 1951, Agenda, mimeograph, Clark Papers; "Meeting of the United States Judges of the Second Circuit," June 25, 1964, Agenda, mimeograph, in possession of of the author.

[38] "Annual Judicial Conference of the Second Judicial Circuit of the United States, 1955-63 Executive Session," Clark Papers.

[39] "Proceedings of the Judicial Circuit Conference of the United States Court of Appeals and the District Court of the United States for the District of Columbia," 1941, Groner Papers, Box 13.

[40] Henry P. Chandler to John H. Yauch, Jr., May 12, 1944, Administrative Office Correspondence, 59-A-328, Box 4.

[41] *Ibid.*

edies ultimately chosen to meet difficulties in administration or procedure will be chosen by the individual courts
or circuit councils, or possibly recommended by the Judicial
Conference of the United States. They will not be settled
by an evanescent assemblage of judges from every district
in the circuit.[42] Even so, debate among the judges may be
heated and the impact of far-reaching significance.[43]

As indicated, the conferences are instruments of education and persuasion to the end of achieving greater administrative integration on the circuit level, a fact recognized
by Administrative Office Director Chandler when he declared that "one of the great things about these Judicial
Conferences is their opportunity for exchange of experiences between judges."[44]

That such exchanges were perceived as a means of overcoming excessive parochialism in the federal trial courts
was evident in a statement by Senior Circuit Judge Kimbrough Stone to the 1940 conference of the Eighth Circuit.
During a discussion of the local rules of court required by
the then recently promulgated Federal Rules of Civil Procedure, he admitted that the power to adopt them rested
with each court. However, he suggested that "a discussion
of the rules while the Judges are together here might prove
enlightening and also it might be found that a certain degree of uniformity could be reached."[45]

Similarly, the conference forum is employed to promote

[42] Interview with J. Edward Lumbard, December 30, 1964, New
York, New York.

[43] See Frank L. Kloeb to James C. Wilson, May 12, 1944, House
Legislative Files, on H.R. 2140 to accompany papers H.R. 78A-D17,
78th Cong. (National Archives, Washington, D.C.; cited hereafter as
House Files on H.R. 2140).

[44] Henry P. Chandler to the District of Columbia Circuit Conference, 1944, p. 10, Administrative Office Correspondence, 60-A-328,
Box 36.

[45] "Judicial Conference of the United States Court of the Eighth
Circuit," January 4-6, 1940, p. 10, stenographic transcript, Kimbrough
Stone Papers, Box 26.

within the circuit the "better interpretation" of the rules of procedure[46] and the "better method" of court administration. The technique has been one of persuasion through education, a strategy for which the conferences are admirably suited. At several of them held during the 1940s, Director Chandler reported that "three extremely able and efficient judges have spoken on the methods which they have employed to keep their dockets current."[47]

In many respects the subjects discussed at the general sessions of the conferences with the lawyer-delegates in attendance resemble those considered in the executive session from which non-judges are usually excluded.[48] But with lawyers outnumbering judges three to one in the Ninth Circuit conference, leaders of that conference have tried to avoid issues salient to only a segment of that large and diverse circuit.[49] Avoided, too, if possible, are fights among bench and bar factions. The circuit councils, not the conference, possess administrative power. Consequently long and acrimonious debate in open sessions can be expected to yield little fruit.[50]

Court congestion and the utilization of various procedures to alleviate it often dominate the general sessions.[51] As Chief Justice Earl Warren put it, the conferences pro-

[46] "Judicial Conference for the Fifth Circuit: Report of Interesting Discussions and Actions," *American Bar Association Journal*, 34 (August 1948), 673.

[47] Henry P. Chandler, "Address to the District of Columbia Circuit Conference," 1944, p. 10, Administrative Office Correspondence, 60-A-328, Box 36.

[48] Practices differ: no closed sessions in the Ninth Circuit. Interview with Richard H. Chambers, January 26, 1965, Washington, D.C. None also in the Second Circuit until attendance of lawyer members of the Conference's Program and Planning Committee was discouraged by the Circuit Council in 1960. "Minutes of the Second Circuit Council," June 15, 1960, Clark Papers.

[49] Baar, "When Judges Lobby," p. 486.

[50] *Ibid.*, p. 485.

[51] See Henry P. Chandler to Frederick V. Follmer, January 12, 1955, Administrative Office Correspondence, 60-A-328, Box 1.

349

vided arenas in which "lawyers and judges sitting down together [could] do something toward ending congestion on court calendars in most of our metropolitan centers."[52] Thus summer court terms, use of arbitration, central calendar systems, and pretrial procedures have been perennial topics of discussion at the conferences.[53] At the 1951 conference in the Third Circuit, a committee of lawyers reported on the use of interrogatories, discovery procedures, depositions, subpoenas and special verdicts as well as the merits of changes in venue requirements, the jurisdictional amount and diversity jurisdiction.[54]

Other topics considered at the general sessions of the conferences reflect the special interests of the bar. They have included the rules for admission to the federal bar,[55] limitations on contingent fees,[56] compensation for counsel appointed to represent indigent litigants,[57] allocation of trial costs,[58] and abridgement of the record on appeal.[59]

As might be expected, landmark judicial decisions which vitally affect the work of judges and lawyers have been vig-

[52] Speech to the Second Circuit Conference, reported in the *New York Times*, September 10, 1955, p. 11.

[53] See "Agenda, Annual Judicial Conference of the Second Circuit of the United States," 1951, 1955, Clark Papers. See also "Memorandum for Chief Justice Groner from Justice Miller," Arrangement Committee's Recommendation for the 1944 Circuit Conference of the District of Columbia, March 3, 1944, Groner Papers, Box 13.

[54] "Fourteenth Annual Judicial Conference of the Third Judicial Circuit of the United States," Agenda, July 17-18, 1951, mimeograph, Clark Papers.

[55] "Judicial Conferences," *American Bar Association Journal*, 33 (1947), 980.

[56] Agenda, "Annual Conference of the Second Judicial Circuit," 1957, Clark Papers.

[57] Henry P. Chandler to Frederick V. Follmer, January 12, 1955, Administrative Office Correspondence, 60-A-328, Box 1.

[58] Agenda, "Annual Conference of the Second Judicial Circuit," 1962, Clark Papers.

[59] Memorandum, "Annual Conference of the Third Judicial Circuit," n.d., Administrative Office Correspondence, 60-A-328, Box 1.

350

orously debated. In the wake of *Durham v. United States*,[60] the use of insanity as a defense occupied the attention of one circuit conference,[61] while in the 1960s, conferences turned their attention to the issue of criminal justice. Thus the 1966 conference in the Third Circuit heard several law school professors discuss the meaning of *Miranda v. Arizona*,[62] the problems it posed for law enforcement, and the kind of judicial issues likely to arise from it.[63]

The conferences, as a medium of communication and education for the bar as well as for the judges, also play the role of complaint bureaus. For instance, lawyers have been requested "to present uninhibited suggestions for the improvement in the administration of the work of the courts within the circuit." This complaint function, which Judge Biggs termed "by far the most useful contribution lawyer-delegates can make,"[64] has found a place in the typical conference agenda. The 1963 agenda of the conference of the Second Circuit, for instance, included a panel entitled

Open Season on Bench and Bar. A frank and open discussion of questions and critical suggestions that members of the Bench and Bar may have for each other; mutual spirited interrogation of the Bar by the Bench and *vice-versa* on areas of possible improvement of the practices of judges and lawyers in the administration of justice in the Second Circuit. While questions may be civil or criminal, they need not be courtly.[65]

[60] 214 F. 2d 862 (D.C. Circuit, 1954).

[61] Henry P. Chandler to Frederick V. Follmer, January 12, 1955, Administrative Office Correspondence, 60-A-328, Box 1.

[62] 384 U.S. 436 (1966).

[63] Louis B. Schwartz and Paul M. Bator, "Criminal Justice in the Mid-Sixties: Escobedo Revisited," *Federal Rules Decisions*, 42 (1967), 463-78.

[64] Robert W. Graham to the Chief Judges of the Circuits, July 10, 1961, mimeograph, Clark Papers.

[65] "Agenda, Panel Discussion, Annual Judicial Conference of the Second Judicial Circuit of the United States," 1963, mimeograph, Clark Papers.

Although much of the business of the circuit conferences relates to the problems experienced by bench and bar within that circuit, the conferences also constitute an integral segment of the national judiciary's administrative system. In this respect, they provide platforms for spokesmen of national stature. To them have come Chief Justices of the United States as well as circuit justices. The presence of these judicial luminaries, though customary in some circuits,[66] is hardly automatic. "I have written a letter to Justice [Frank] Murphy asking him to come and attend the meeting," related the presiding judge of the Seventh Circuit late in 1944, but "once before when [Felix] Frankfurter was assigned to this circuit, I asked him to attend our conference, and he never answered my letter."[67]

For the members of the Supreme Court who have attended, the circuit conferences afforded an opportunity to publicize the administrative problems confronting the federal courts and to decry the judiciary's inability "to get Congress to appreciate the problems."[68] Likewise, the Chief Justice and his associates use the conference forum to press reforms on the lower federal judges and to threaten as did Chief Justice Warren that "if the judiciary does not become forward-looking and willing to accept new methods, they will be forced on them by the Congress."[69]

Also presenting a national viewpoint are the representatives from the Administrative Office. Their presence has become institutionalized although Director Chandler initially worked to avoid obtruding "our presence" at the circuit

[66] "Meeting of the United States Judges of the Second Circuit," June 25, 1964, Agenda, mimeograph, Clark Papers; "Proceedings of the Twenty-Ninth Annual Judicial Conference, Third Judicial Circuit of the United States, 1966," Federal Rules Decisions, 42 (1967), 440.

[67] Evan A. Evans to D. Lawrence Groner, November 21, 1944, Groner Papers, Box 11.

[68] Chief Justice Warren, New York Times, September 30, 1957, p. 17.

[69] New York Times, September 26, 1959, p. 10.

conferences unless "it is really desired that we do so."[70] Nor did he wish to flood the meetings with Administrative Office personnel.[71] However, few circuit conferences have been held in the Vinson-Warren era without the attendance of the director or one or more of his subordinates. They have discussed the state of the federal judiciary, the use of judicial statistics, economical use of jurors,[72] and more efficient administrative methods, invariably citing the successful use of various practices in other jurisdictions.[73] They have enumerated the problems faced by the judiciary's legislative program and called on conference leaders to inform their judges of congressional criticism of judicial behavior and to stimulate a sentiment "that would lessen the grounds for these criticisms."[74] To the same end, Director Chandler once commended to the judges assembled in their conferences "more general and definite plans to make the members of the Congress in your different areas acquainted with your work and problems."[75]

Such spokesmen, whether from the Administrative Office or the Department of Justice, were hardly neutral. When invited to address a circuit conference during the indeterminate sentence controversy of the early 1940s, Attorney General Robert H. Jackson asked Director Chandler for a likely speech topic. Unhesitatingly, Chandler replied that Jackson "could do a good deal to promote a correct understanding of the subject and to strengthen the sentiment for it among federal judges of that circuit by attending and

[70] Henry P. Chandler to Louis W. Strum, March 1, 1944, Administrative Office Correspondence, 59-A-532, Box 1.

[71] Henry P. Chandler to Joseph C. Hutcheson, Jr., April 5, 1948, *ibid.*

[72] "Memorandum Re: Judicial Conferences," undated, *ibid.*, 60-A-328, Box 1.

[73] "Tentative Program of the Judicial Conference of the Second Circuit," September 8-9, 1955, Clark Papers.

[74] Henry P. Chandler to Kimbrough Stone, February 8, 1946, Administrative Office Correspondence, 59-A-532, Box 2.

[75] Henry P. Chandler, "Legislation Affecting the Courts," 1947, p. 10, *ibid.*, 60-A-328, Box 27.

presenting the difficulties with the present system of fixed sentences in federal courts and gains to be expected from an indeterminate sentence law along the lines that you suggested at . . . the Judicial Conference of the Senior Circuit Judges."[76]

Circuit Conferences: Liaison Mechanism

Not only are the conferences in the circuits sounding boards for proponents of Judicial Conference policies, but they are also an integral part of that Conference's policy-making process. This development began in earnest in the 1940s when the national committees began to establish links with counterpart committees in the circuits. Thus, the Judicial Conference Committee on Ways and Means of Economy in the Operation of the Federal Courts urged "that the chief judges of each circuit appoint a committee to investigate the use of jurors in the various district courts in the circuit and make recommendations to increase the efficiency of that use."[77]

The Conference Committee on Pre-Trial Procedure followed the same strategy. Circuit committees were established because the national committee believed that "localized work may be most efficiently performed by active pretrial committees erected and functioning within each of the several Judicial Circuits of the United States, aided occasionally and discreetly by this committee or one or more of its members."[78] The task of the Judicial Conference com-

[76] Henry P. Chandler to Robert H. Jackson, November 18, 1940, *ibid.*, 59-A-532, Box 2.

[77] "Report of the Committee on Ways and Means of Economy in the Operation of the Federal Courts as Amended by the Judicial Conference of the United States," September 1, 1948, p. 7, mimeograph (Administrative Office of the United States Courts, Washington, D.C.). See also "Report of the Committee on the Operation of the Jury System, Excerpt from Agenda No. 13," September 1953, p. 15, mimeograph, *ibid.*; *Judicial Conference Report, 1953*, p. 19.

[78] "Report of the Committee on Pre-Trial Procedure," September 15, 1952, mimeograph (Administrative Office of the United States Courts, Washington, D.C.), p. 2.

354

mittee, in addition to developing models of pretrial procedures for recommendations to judges, was "to do everything possible to stimulate activity on the part of circuit committees," and to educate judges in its use by giving live demonstrations of pretrial proceedings at the circuit conferences.[79]

However, the circuit pretrial committees were not mere agents of the national committee; they acted quite autonomously. The Conference committee, declared the Pre-Trial Subcommittee of the Ninth Circuit, should not "presume that it has any authority, either supervisory or advisory over any circuit committee." Although the objectives of the two committees might coincide, the national committee should be "prudently helpful," and should avoid attempting "to control or direct that work, or save by discreet suggestions, to influence it."[80]

Nor have the circuit conferences been relegated to the status of repositories for policies adopted by the Judicial Conference and advocated by its spokesmen. They and their committees have long been conduits for "grass roots" sentiment, acting as "clearing houses" for policy proposals submitted to the Judicial Conference of the United States. As early as 1942, the new director of the Administrative Office, Henry P. Chandler, began to encourage the conferences to discuss subjects pending before the Judicial Conference and its committees,[81] an obvious response to lower

[79] "Minutes of the Meeting of the Pretrial Committee of the Judicial Conference of the United States," February 24, 1951, Administrative Office Correspondence, 60-A-328, Box 26. See also "Report of the Meeting of the Committee on Pre-Trial Procedure of the Judicial Conference of the United States," February 20, 1953, Administrative Office Correspondence, 60-A-328, Box 16, p. 4; *Judicial Conference Report, 1955*, p. 26.

[80] "Report of the Pre-Trial Subcommittee [of the Ninth Circuit Conference] to the Chairman and other members of the Pretrial Committee under authority of the Judicial Conference of the United States," February 1956, p. 4, Driver Papers.

[81] See Henry P. Chandler to Curtis D. Wilbur, March 6, 1942, Administrative Office Correspondence, 59-A-532, Box 2.

court criticisms of the unrepresentative and arbitrary nature of the judiciary's policy-making system. Two years later, he informed a presiding circuit judge that "the Chief Justice would very much like to see the matters which are referred by the Judicial Conference of the Senior Circuit Judges to committees of the Conference for study and recommendations discussed at the judicial conferences in the circuits. The reflection of the views of the judges on the various questions would be helpful to the committees and would make for conclusions in accordance with the consensus of judgment."[82]

Inauguration of the "Phillips Plan" in 1945 made circuit conference participation mandatory, and generated a proliferation of committees concerned with national administrative policies. Under it, each circuit conference appointed a legislative committee with which Judicial Conference committees were required to consult. These circuit legislative committees were, in turn, charged with receiving reports of Judicial Conference committees and copies of proposed bills at least 120 days before the Washington conference met. District and circuit judges would also receive this information. Then, the circuit legislative committees or individual judges on their own initiative transmitted to the relevant Judicial Conference committee their "views, suggestions, and criticisms of the Judicial Conference committee report and draft of bills." These expressions ultimately accompanied the report of the national Conference committee to the Judicial Conference and were included in any Conference recommendations to Congress.[83]

Endorsement by the broad-based circuit conferences of programs sponsored by the national Conference or by its committees serves to legitimize those programs, both in the eyes of the Judicial Conference and, more importantly, of

[82] Henry P. Chandler to Joseph C. Hutcheson, February 12, 1944, *ibid.*, Box 1.
[83] *Judicial Conference Report, 1945*, p. 7.

Congress.[84] At the same time, it works to render the conferences hotbeds of "judicial politics," as representatives of the national Conference's committees lobby for endorsement of their programs. Thus when the Judicial Conference Committee on Supporting Personnel proposed a salary increase for the United States commissioners in Alaska, aptly described as the "'poobahs' of the judiciary system," its chairman went before the circuit conference of the Ninth Circuit,[85] and urged adoption of a resolution supporting his committee's proposal.[86] His appearance could as well have constituted an effort to quell "grass roots" resistance to his committee's proposals.[87] Or he might have acted by proxy as did Senior Circuit Judge John J. Parker when the district judges in the First Circuit presented their conference with a resolution opposing the "Phillips Plan." Parker, a member of the committee which had drafted the plan, urged his counterpart in that circuit to pigeonhole the resolution, thereby delaying action until the plan became effective.[88]

For those seeking to change existing policies, the circuit conferences have provided an institutionalized means of gaining access to the Judicial Conference of the United States and its committees, and of reaching the ears of sympathetic congressmen. Individual judges seeking to take their case directly to the national conference have usually found "that the national Judicial Conference is likely to give

[84] See Bernard G. Segal, U.S., Congress, House, Committee on Post Office and Civil Service, *Hearings, on H.R. 7552, H.R. 7814, and Similar Bills, Federal Employees Salary Act of 1963*, part I, 88th Cong., 1st Sess., 1963, p. 261.

[85] See John Biggs, Jr., to Members of the Committee on Judicial Personnel, December 18, 1950, Stephens Papers, Box 217.

[86] "Minutes of the Circuit Conference of the Ninth Judicial Circuit," June, 1950, p. 3, Driver Papers.

[87] See Speech of John Biggs, Jr., on Salaries of Secretaries and Law Clerks in "Minutes of the Judicial Conference of the Ninth Circuit," 1948, p. 3.

[88] John J. Parker to Calvert Magruder, November 17, 1944, Groner Papers, Box 11.

more thorough consideration to suggestions . . . if they orig-
inate in a circuit conference than if they are brought to
their attention simply on the suggestion of one judge."[89] In
this manner, "the merits of the idea would be fully explored
and the [Judicial] Conference would be in a position to recommend legislation if that is necessary."[90]

This procedure assumed the cooperation of each circuit's
representative to the Judicial Conference. To assure such
cooperation one conference "instructed the Senior Circuit
Judge to convey its disapproval [of a pending bill] to the
next succeeding Judicial Conference in Washington."[91] Similarly, the 1950 District of Columbia meeting, formally expressed "its views to Judge [Harold M.] Stephens that he
should vote at the Judicial Conference . . . to direct Mr.
Chandler not to make deductions from judicial salaries for
the proposed Civil Service retirement benefits."[92] But some
representatives proved recalcitrant and when one flatly refused to present a resolution of his circuit conference to the
Judicial Conference, the former conference promptly
elected another judge to present its case.[93]

As a general purpose "grass roots" organization, the circuit conference affords a propitious arena for those elements discontented with existing or proposed administra-

[89] Leland Tolman to Theodore Levin, February 6, 1950, Administrative Office Correspondence, 60-A-328, Box 2.
[90] Leland Tolman to Lawrence E. Walsh, March 29, 1955, ibid.
[91] Frank L. Kloeb to James C. Wilson, May 12, 1944, House Files
on H.R. 2140.
[92] "Memorandum Concerning the Action of the Circuit Conference
[of the District of Columbia]," February 9, 1950, Stephens Papers,
Box 88. See also "Minutes of the Judicial Conference of the Ninth
Circuit," 1948, p. 4.
[93] "Memorandum by Chief Judge [William] Denman to the Judges
and Members of the Judicial Conference and Members of the Judicial
Conference of the Ninth Circuit Re: The action of the Judicial Conference of the United States on matters affecting the Ninth Circuit,
October 10, 1951," ibid. (Cited hereafter as "Memorandum by Chief
Judge Denman.")

358

tive policies or rules of procedure.[94] Here those injured by administrative centralization have found a platform from which to lob attacks against the Administrative Office and to protest its policies as "the pernicious results of the 'Manton Bill.' "[95]

Here, too, district judges, faced with loss of their prerogatives in sentencing, protested and eventually beat down a Conference-endorsed indeterminate sentence proposal.[96] Senior Circuit Judge John J. Parker described consideration of that measure in the executive session of the Fourth Circuit Judicial Conference: "All of the Judges in attendance, with the exception of myself, expressed themselves as opposed to the indeterminate sentence law and adopted a resolution to the effect that the passage of such a law would not be in the public interest. I expressed as best I could the views entertained by [the Judicial Conference of the United States], but the judges were not impressed by them."[97] Subsequently, Parker urged the national conference to reconsider its position,[98] because he thought the "reasoned opin-

[94] "Discussion Concerning Report of the Committee on Rule 8 of the Federal Rules of Civil Procedure," Circuit Conference of the Ninth Circuit, June 26-29, 1951, Stephens Papers, Box 17 (cited hereafter as "Discussion on Rule 8").

[95] Will Shafroth, "Memorandum Re: Seventh Circuit Conference, June 16, 1949," Administrative Office Correspondence, 59-A-532, Box 2.

[96] *Judicial Conference Report, 1940*, pp. 27-28; *ibid., 1941*, pp. 36-37; *ibid., 1942*, pp. 25-26; John J. Parker, "The Integration of the Federal Judiciary," *Harvard Law Review*, 56 (January 1942), 570. A detailed analysis of the ill-fated legislation, H.R. 4581, 77th Cong., and its successor, H.R. 2140, 78th Cong., is provided in Wayne L. Wilson, "The Federal Corrections Act: A Case Study of Judicial Lobbying" (unpub. thesis, Department of Political Science, Duke University, 1971).

[97] John J. Parker to Chief Justice of the United States and the Judges in attendance at the 1941 Session of the Conference of Senior Circuit Judges, Washington, D.C., September 23, 1941, p. 3. Parker Papers, Box 54.

[98] *Ibid.*

ion of so many experienced judges is entitled to great weight. . . ."[99]

The 1969 Judicial Conference of the Second Circuit followed the pattern set nearly three decades before in the Fourth Circuit. Forty-three district and nine circuit judges condemned the June 10, 1969 resolution of the Judicial Conference of the United States, which had set forth certain ethical standards for inferior federal court judges and established procedures for clearing extra-judicial activities and reporting financial assets.[100] Hastily passed in the wake of the Abe Fortas affair[101] and in the last days of Chief Justice Warren's chairmanship of the Conference, the resolution excited opposition among federal judges, who resented its application to them but not to Supreme Court justices.[102] They demanded suspension of the resolution.[103] And they obtained results, for the September Conference, chaired by the new Chief Justice, Warren E. Burger, at least partially met their demands.[104]

Responding to pressure from judges and/or assorted court employees, such as clerks, reporters, and bankruptcy referees, circuit conferences have adopted resolutions favorable to these groups. One resolved "that there has been progressive administrative encroachment upon the functions of the federal courts to the detriment of the proper and efficient functioning thereof, particularly in relation to the appointment, classification, and salaries of the personnel of the courts." Its remedy? Nothing less than complete decentralization of the personnel system, empowering each district court to determine the salary and classification of its personnel.[105]

[99] *Ibid.*
[100] *Judicial Conference Report, 1969,* pp. 42-43.
[101] *New York Times,* May 24, 1969, pp. 1, 34.
[102] *Ibid.,* July 3, 1969, pp. 1, 15.
[103] *Ibid.*
[104] *Judicial Conference Report, 1969,* p. 51.
[105] "Minutes of the Circuit Conference of the Ninth Judicial Circuit, June 1950," p. 12, Driver Papers.

Less radical, but nevertheless threatening to uniform and centralized personnel policies, have been those resolutions seeking advantages, usually financial, for special categories of judicial personnel. For instance, reporters and referees have often succeeded in winning conference endorsements of their proposals for higher salaries and travel expenses.[106] The centrifugal tendencies of such resolutions have laid them open to the charge of one chief circuit judge that they were "absurdly conceived" and had as much chance of securing ultimate congressional approval as "the continuance ... of a snowball in Hades."[107]

During the Warren period, circuit conference resolutions as significant elements in the policy-making process waned in importance. In part this reflected the termination of the "Phillips Plan"[108] coincident with direct district judge representation on the Judicial Conference of the United States. Partly, too, it reflected the strengthening of that Conference's committee system as well as objection to the whole organization of the circuit conference; their accessibility to parochial interest groups, their lack of staff with its attendant inadequate preparation of proposals, hasty floor action, and their narrow perspectives which mirror the views of specific professional, local, and regional constituencies.[109]

[106] "Petition of the Official Court Reporters of the Southern District of California for an increase in salary and Excerpt of Transcript of the Proceedings in relation thereto at the Conference of Judges for the Ninth Circuit at San Francisco, California," June 27-30, 1950, pp. 10-19, Stephens Papers, Box 216; "Minutes of the Circuit Conference of the Ninth Judicial Circuit," June 1950, p. 8, Driver Papers; "Report of the Referees' Committee to the 1952 Circuit Conference of the Ninth Judicial Circuit," May 1952, p. 1, ibid.
[107] "Memorandum by Chief Judge Denman," pp. 6, 11.
[108] Judicial Conference Report, 1958, p. 275.
[109] Interview with John Biggs, Jr., August 12, 1965, Washington, D.C.; "Report of the Second Circuit Committee on Ways and Means of Economy in the Federal Courts," 1948, draft copy, Administrative Office Correspondence, 60-A-328, Box 7; "Discussion on Rule 8," p. 9.

Circuit Conferences: Judicial Elections

At the same time the significance of the circuit conferences in the policy-making process was declining, a new function emerged. After 1957, the district and circuit judges elected at the conferences their trial court representatives to the Judicial Conference. As might be expected, selection procedures differ markedly. Some are essentially noncompetitive, while others have involved hotly contested campaigns and close elections. Several circuits have rotated the post among district judges. This may be done at random[110] or among those judges senior in length of commission or age[111] as a sort of reward for a magistrate in the twilight of a long judicial career. Non-competitive, too, has been the selection procedure followed by the Second Circuit. There, an absolute majority of that circuit's trial judges sit in the Southern District of New York, and this large bloc has permitted the judges of the Southern District to dominate the election.[112] Almost invariably, the representative chosen has been the chief judge of that court—the so-called "mother court" of the federal trial system.

The selection process in other circuits has been characterized by competitive elections, issue-oriented platforms, and varying degrees of strategic planning and campaigning on the part of candidates. The circuit conference of the Third Circuit has elected its representative by a secret vote on a list of nominees, after which a run-off election has been taken on the two or three leading candidates.[113] Although some pre-election campaigning has occurred, such activity has not been promoted by that circuit's ranking judges.

[110] Interview with Matthew McGuire, January 6, 1965, Washington, D.C.
[111] Interview with John C. Airhart, December 22, 1964, Arlington, Virginia.
[112] Interview with J. Edward Lumbard.
[113] Interview with John Biggs, Jr., February 28, 1965, Wilmington, Delaware.

362

Elections in the Fourth Circuit, however, have assumed a distinct issue aspect. After casting his hat into the ring with the time-honored statement that he "would be honored to serve if the majority of you would so decree," Judge Oren R. Lewis of the Eastern District of Virginia then set forth his "judicial platform." In it, Lewis boldly announced that he "most probably would be characterized as a strict constructionist" who favored "maintaining the independence of the federal judiciary."[114] More specifically he called for "a major overhaul" of both the probation and prison systems and declared that a judge's "fitness to hold office should not be open to question on the informal complaint of every Tom, Dick, and Harry, as proposed by Section 378 of the Tydings bill, S. 1506, now pending in the Senate Judiciary Committee. Further, a federal judge should not be required to report his and his wife's and [minor] children's income and liabilities in the manner and form as provided for in the said Tydings bill."[115]

In some circuits elections have entailed extensive pre-election maneuvering, if not campaigning. In the Ninth Circuit, for instance, selection of the district judge representative has reportedly resembled a full-scale political campaign with candidates, assisted by campaign managers, vigorously seeking votes and building alliances with other districts in that sprawling circuit.[116] The political convention atmosphere apparently underwent some attrition by 1966 when a caucus of district judges, held prior to the opening of the Conference, developed. Its purpose, declared Judge Pierson M. Hall, included settling "among

[114] Oren R. Lewis to All Judges of the Fourth Circuit Judicial Conference, June 19, 1970, reprinted in Senate Subcommittee on Separation of Powers, *Hearings, on the Independence of the Federal Judges,* 1970, p. 981.

[115] *Ibid.*

[116] Interview with John C. Airhart. Interview with Ronald C. Beattie, January 19, 1965, Washington, D.C.

ourselves . . . without going onto the floor of the Conference, the matter of whom the District Judges desire for the District Judge Representative on the Judicial Conference."[117]

The circuit conferences, organized long before the establishment of the Administrative Office, had, by the 1960s, assumed some new functions and amplified others. Nevertheless, the traditional social, educational, and liaison activities continued to dominate the programs, and to the same end—namely that of a federal judicial system enjoying a degree of administrative cohesion albeit through highly informal means. In their methods and ends, the disparate circuit conferences are not alone.

Conventions, Seminars, and Institutes

The formal administrative system established by the Act of 1939 is surrounded and acted upon by a coterie of voluntary and statutory organizations such as the Federal Court Clerks Association, the Conference of United States Court Reporters, the Federal Probation Officers Association, and the National Conference of Referees in Bankruptcy. Lacking official status, these groups, composed of assorted court personnel, are distinguished by their scant financial resources and relatively low attendance at meetings and related activities.[118]

Nevertheless they perform several functions complementing that of the formal administrative structure. The purpose of the National Conference of Referees in Bankruptcy is "to promote better acquaintance and co-operation among the referees in bankruptcy of the United States Courts, to se-

[117] Pierson M. Hall to District Judges of the Ninth Circuit, June 7, 1966, reprinted in Senate Subcommittee on Separation of Powers, *Hearings, on the Independence of the Federal Judges*, 1970, p. 972.

[118] See *Journal of the National Conference of Referees in Bankruptcy*, 40 (October 1966), 99-100. See also Harold M. Stephens to E. M. Garrett, January 30, 1945, Stephens Papers, Box 85.

cure a greater degree of uniformity in the administration of estates in bankruptcy, to encourage expedition in the liquidation of estates and economy in the administration thereof."[119] In addition they act as pressure groups for their constituents by taking positions on legislation affecting their offices and communicating their views to the Administrative Office, the Judicial Conference, and its related committees.[120]

Finally, they, like the circuit conferences, afford spokesmen for the national organizations a platform from which to explain their policies[121] and to persuade officials in the field to adopt them.[122] Calling on the bankruptcy referees for "more innovation, more experimentation . . . to meet the demands made upon us by modern conditions," Chief Justice Warren urged them to "adapt to bankruptcy as far as practical, the techniques of pretrial and judicial control of the proceedings as they are being tried out, and proven in the district courts."[123] More general was Director Chandler's exhortation "not to grow weary in well-doing; . . . to make the bankruptcy procedure an efficient means for minimizing the loss incident to business misfortune, and

[119] *Journal of the National Association of Referees in Bankruptcy,* 40 (January 1966), 3. See also 1965 Constitution, Article II, which altered the organization's title from the National Association of Referees in Bankruptcy to the National Conference of Referees in Bankruptcy.

[120] See *Journal of the National Association of Referees in Bankruptcy,* 19 (October 1944), 15; *ibid.,* 40 (April 1966), 34.

[121] Edwin L. Covey, "A Day with the Administrative Office," *ibid.,* 23 (January 1949), 51-54; Elmore Whitehurst, "The Referees and the Civil Service Retirement Law," *ibid.,* pp. 54-55.

[122] See Henry P. Chandler, "Comments on the Report of the Senate Subcommittee on Juvenile Delinquency on the Federal Probation Service," April 12, 1954, mimeograph (Administrative Office of the United States Courts, Washington, D.C.), pp. 2-3.

[123] "Address Delivered by the Honorable Earl Warren, Chief Justice of the United States," *Journal of the National Association of Referees in Bankruptcy,* 37 (January 1963), 4-5.

strengthening among the people affection for their government as their protector."[124]

Although speeches, panel discussions, seminars, and demonstrations at the circuit conferences and conventions of court personnel had an integrative effect, the emphasis was typically on persuasion and adoption of the "better way." Training and education in specific techniques lay generally outside the scope of these gatherings. Only the probation officers enjoyed a system of continuing education. Sponsored by the Administrative Office and the Department of Justice and conducted in cooperation with leading universities, five regional four-day in-service training institutes were held at two or three year intervals. These stressed casework skills as well as methods.[125] In 1950, a national training program was established. Since then, the Federal Probation Center in Chicago has offered orientation courses to newly appointed probation officers and refresher courses to veteran officers. The five-day program includes lectures on the organization and operation of the probation system, and on psychological and social work as well as workshops on specific functions of probation officers.[126]

Establishment of the in-service training institutes and the Probation Center marked a sharp break with historical practices. Traditionally, court personnel and, for that matter, judges had been trained on the job. "What they learn is simply what is being done in the office at that time," observed Administrative Office Director Warren Olney.[127]

[124] "Henry P. Chandler to the Fifteenth Annual Conference of the National Association of Referees in Bankruptcy," ibid., 15 (October 1940), 52.

[125] Louis J. Sharp, "Inservice Training in Probation and Parole," Federal Probation, 15 (December 1951), 28. See also Richard A. Chappell, "The Federal Probation System Today," Federal Probation, 14 (June 1950), 39.

[126] See A. Kenneth Pye, George W. Shadoan, Joseph M. Siree, A Preliminary Survey of the Federal Probation System (Washington, 1963), p. 14.

[127] Warren Olney III, U.S., Congress, House, Subcommittee of the

Regional and national programs, on the other hand, offered a means of infusing the federal judiciary with national standards of administration. And in the absence of uniform qualifications for appointment, a large field staff attached to the Administrative Office, or a reorganization of the judiciary's entire administrative system, it offered virtually the only means.

Then in 1959 the Bankruptcy Committee of the Judicial Conference, noting the inadequacy of the Administrative Office's supervision of procedures used by the referees in bankruptcy, urged a four-day administrative and procedural training course for newly-appointed referees.[128] With characteristic speed, a seminar system for the referees was established five years later[129] "to standardize . . . practices and procedures wherever practical with due regard for variations necessitated by local conditions."[130]

At government expense, referees now attend an annual seminar in Washington and thereafter two-day refresher seminars held on a regional basis.[131] In papers and at roundtable discussions, referees have considered such topics as the appointment and work of trustees in bankruptcy, fees and allowances, organization of their offices, and the impact of the Uniform Commercial Code on bankruptcy law.[132]

Meanwhile a seminar system for judges has been established. Authorized by the March 1960 Judicial Confer-

Committee on Appropriations, *Hearings, on the Departments of State and Justice, the Judiciary and Related Agencies. Appropriation for 1960*, 86th Cong., 1st Sess., 1959, p. 146.

[128] *Judicial Conference Report, 1959*, p. 311.

[129] *Ibid., 1964*, p. 194.

[130] "The Referees' Seminar," *Journal of the National Association of Referees in Bankruptcy*, 38 (April 1964), 34.

[131] Royal E. Jackson, "Trends and Developments in Bankruptcy Administration," *ibid.*, 40 (January 1966), 10.

[132] "The Second Seminar for Referees," *Journal of the National Association of Referees in Bankruptcy*, 39 (July 1965), 66; proceedings published by Clark Boardman Co., Ltd., New York.

ence,[133] the initial seminar for newly-appointed judges was included in the program of the circuit conference in the Tenth Circuit. To it came twenty-two district judges from across the country. Once there, they "received a comprehensive orientation in the most up-to-date techniques of judicial administration,"[134] with the emphasis on close judicial supervision of litigation.[135] In lectures and roundtable discussions, the neophyte judges learned the intricacies of discovery procedures, motions, pretrial conferences, charges to juries, post-conviction problems, bankruptcy administration, and judicial ethics.[136]

A series of seminars was also inaugurated for veteran judges and trial lawyers. Held at the Southwestern Legal Center at Southern Methodist University starting in 1961, these seminars were intended to explore "the most effective techniques for the utilization of pretrial and trial procedures contemplated by the Federal Rules of Civil Procedure."[137]

A major innovation was the program of institutes and joint councils on sentencing. Authorized by Congress in 1958,[138] they have been held on both a circuit and regional basis, sometimes in conjunction with circuit conferences for the purpose of "studying, discussing, and formulating the objectives, policies, standards and criteria for sentencing those convicted of crimes and offenses in the courts of the United States."[139] Participating judges have analyzed sample cases,[140] learned from physicians and psychologists of institutional resources available for committed defendants,[141] and toured a federal correctional institution where

[133] *Judicial Conference Report, 1960,* p. 385.
[134] *Ibid., 1961,* p. 132.   [135] *Ibid., 1962,* pp. 93-94.
[136] See "Seminar Held for Newly Appointed Federal Judges," *Federal Probation,* 26 (March 1962), 75.
[137] *Judicial Conference Report, 1961,* p. 132.
[138] 72 *Stat.* 845.   [139] 28 *U.S.C.* 334(a).
[140] *Judicial Conference Report, 1961,* p. 131.
[141] Frank J. Remington, "The Highland Park Institute on Sentence Disparity," *Federal Probation,* 26 (March 1962), 8.

the Parole Board gave a demonstration of its preliminary hearing and the Bureau of Prisons demonstrated the methods used in formulating recommendations for those cases referred to it by the courts for observation and study.[142] Out of these sessions has come not only a plethora of publicity,[143] but also more permanent contributions such as the "Desk Book for Sentencing." Prepared by the Administrative Office and the Bureau of Prisons, it includes a compilation of current sentencing statutes as well as information intended to assist the judges in achieving greater uniformity in their sentences.[144]

These seminars and institutes were obvious "halfway measures," designed to meet the judiciary's pressing educational demands and thus avoid any far-reaching alteration in its administrative system. As such, they enjoyed a degree of popularity among their participants and achieved some success. Perhaps even more significant than their immediate results was the impetus given to further tinkering with the existing administrative apparatus.

The Federal Judicial Center

The trend toward uniformity in judicial administration received an important advance in 1967 with establishment of a Federal Judicial Center[145] initially headed by retired Supreme Court Justice Tom C. Clark.[146] Long advocated by Chief Justice Warren[147] and urged on Congress by Pres-

---

[142] *Judicial Conference Report, 1964,* pp. 34-35.

[143] See "Pilot Institute on Sentencing, Proceedings," *Federal Rules Decisions,* 26 (1961), 379-81; "Seminar and Institute on Disparity of Sentences for the Sixth, Seventh, and Eighth Judicial Circuits," *Federal Rules Decisions,* 30 (1962), 458-60; "Papers Delivered at the Institute on Sentencing for United States District Judges," *ibid.,* 35 (1964), 381-409.

[144] See *Judicial Conference Report, 1961,* pp. 131-32.

[145] 81 *Stat.* 664.

[146] *New York Times,* March 5, 1968, p. 25.

[147] *Ibid.,* December 7, 1967, p. 42.

ident Lyndon Johnson in his 1967 "Message on Crime in America," the Center, said the President, would "enable the courts to begin the kind of self-analysis, research and planning necessary for a more effective judicial system."[148] The proposal found favor with the judges, especially those at the appellate level. They confronted a torrent of criminal appeals which, stimulated by a battery of far-reaching Supreme Court decisions, had doubled in the six years between 1960 and 1966.[149] Similarly marked was the increase of cases under the "federal question" jurisdiction and judicial review of administrative agency decisions. This growth, in turn, was related to "an increasing federalism in our Government, an increasing population, an increasing number of district judges."[150]

When additional judges and a perceptible rise in cases terminated by each judge proved of little avail in reducing case backlogs, influential members of the Judicial Conference sought some "means, in concepts, machinery, and unified practices, that can alleviate our present statistical spectre or at least bring within some control the threat of future overwhelmingness."[151] The Federal Judicial Center became a step toward meeting the challenge of "congestion and delay, untrained supporting personnel, inadequate facilities, uneven distribution of caseloads, and the general absence of administrative expertise."[152]

[148] *Congressional Record*, 90th Cong., 1st Sess., 1967, vol. 113, part 2, 2566.

[149] "Survey of the United States Courts of Appeals," Report by Will Shafroth, Consultant, Administrative Office of the United States Courts, part I, in U.S., Congress, Senate, Subcommittee on Improvements in Judicial Machinery of the Committee on the Judiciary, *Hearings, on S. 915 and H.R. 6111, Bills to Establish a Federal Judicial Center*, 90th Cong., 1st Sess., 1967, p. 75.

[150] *Ibid.*

[151] Statement of Honorable Harvey M. Johnsen, *ibid.*, p. 28.

[152] U.S., Congress, Senate, Committee on the Judiciary, *Federal Judicial Center*, Senate Report 781 to accompany H.R. 6111, 90th Cong., 1st Sess., 1967, p. 9.

370

One major function of the Center lay in doing better the work of the network of regional and national conferences, institutes, and seminars which had been established by the Judicial Conference or by statute. These entities notwithstanding, Senator Joseph Tydings could argue with great force in 1967 that "generally, continuing education for members of the judiciary and supporting personnel is still in its incipiency."[153]

In typical fashion, the new agency was virtually autonomous, its activities supervised by a specially constituted board, rather than by the Judicial Conference or by the Administrative Office director, an important, and happy, consideration from the judges' point of view. The board, in turn, would formulate the Center's policies and priorities and select an administrator to serve at its pleasure.[154] On the board sit the Chief Justice and director of the Administrative Office, as well as two federal appellate court and three trial court judges elected for staggered terms by the Judicial Conference. Senior or retired judges were barred because the framers "felt that active judges would likely be more familiar with the problems that currently face the judiciary, and . . . more ready to authorize research in innovative procedures and techniques."[155] Members of the Judicial Conference were also excluded to "avoid interlocking relationships between the Conference and the Board."[156] Such a relationship could impair the Center's objectivity as the

[153] *Congressional Record*, 90th Cong., 1st Sess., 1967, vol. 113, part 24, 33099.

[154] 81 *Stat.* 666, Sec. 624(a). As with the appointment of the Director of the Administrative Office of the United States Courts, so with that of the Director of the Federal Judicial Center, the role of the Chief Justice of the United States is important and may be decisive. On the informal role of Chief Justice Warren Burger in the appointment of Alfred Murrah as Center Director, see *Hearings on the Independence of Federal Judges*, 1970, pp. 1197-99.

[155] Emanuel Celler, *Congressional Record*, 90th Cong., 1st Sess., 1967, vol. 113, part 26, 35138.

[156] *Ibid.*

agency "may be called upon to evaluate the work of the Judicial Conference or its committees."[157]

Similar considerations induced Congress to establish the Center "within the judicial branch of the Government," rather than "in the Administrative Office of the United States Courts," as had been recommended by the Judicial Conference and carried in the House version.[158] The House conferees, however, accepted the former or Senate version which emphasized "that the Federal Judicial Center was not to be a subordinate or a constituent part of the Administrative Office."[159]

In this way, Congress sought, perhaps because of their awareness of the office's past and present failings, "to make sure that the resources including personnel that are supposed to go into research and into training programs are not absorbed into the regular administrative tasks of the Administrative Office."[160] So, too, Congress sought to avoid the "chilling effects" of the office's "many and personal relationships with almost every judge in the Federal Judiciary."[161]

The Administrative Office, declared a Senate Judiciary Committee counsel, "must always operate with the confidence of the judges that it serves, and . . . it cannot hope in some circumstances to give a thoroughly objective appraisal of what needs to be done, because such an objective analysis may meet with considerable criticism from members of the judiciary. . . . Therefore, to get the objectivity that is needed, you really have to insulate the people doing the in-depth research into problems of judicial administration from those performing the housekeeping function of the

---

[157] *Ibid.*

[158] Sec. 620, H.R. 6111, 90th Cong.

[159] Celler, *Congressional Record*, 90th Cong., 1st Sess., 1967, vol. 113, part 26, 35137-38.

[160] Warren Olney III, *Hearings on S. 915 and H.R. 6111*, 1967, p. 364.

[161] John S. Hastings, *ibid.*, p. 20.

Administrative Office."[162] To this end, the Federal Judicial Center Act of 1967 formally separated the Administrative Office or "operation arm" of the judicial branch from the "research and development arm."[163] The result was two distinct institutions, equal in status, but with different functions.

The new agency would "stimulate, develop, and conduct programs of continuing education and training for personnel in the judicial branch of Government, including but not limited to, judges, referees, court clerks, probation officers, and United States commissioners."[164] The content of these programs presumably would resemble that of existing ones although House Judiciary Committee chairman Emanuel Celler stated that the continuing education for judges meant primarily keeping "judicial personnel updated on current cases."[165] Queried whether such programs included "philosophical or political nourishment,"[166] Celler noted the difficulty of separating "that which is judicial from that which is philosophical."[167]

Congressman James C. Corman, however, articulated the clear intent of the provision, arguing "that the type of education about which we are talking here goes more to [administrative] procedure than it does to philosophy."[168] In short, one function of the Center lay simply in institutionalizing, under specific congressional authorization and with permanent staff and funds, existing and future in-service programs.

In addition to its education role, the new Center was to act, in the words of Senator Tydings, as the "'research and

[162] William T. Finley, Jr., *ibid.*, p. 20.
[163] Celler, *Congressional Record*, 90th Cong., 1st Sess., 1967, vol. 113, part 26, 35138.
[164] S. 915, Sec. 620(2), 90th Cong.
[165] Celler, *Congressional Record*, 90th Cong., 1st Sess., 1967, vol. 113, part 26, 35141.
[166] William M. Colmer, *ibid.*   [167] *Ibid.*
[168] *Ibid.*, 35142.

development' arm of the judiciary, responsible for furthering the level of improved techniques of administration in
the courts of the United States."[169]

The task of the Center, in the language of the Act, was "to
stimulate, coordinate, and conduct research and tests in all
aspects of Federal judicial administration,"[170] and to "provide staff, research and planning assistance to the Judicial
Conference of the United States and its committees."[171]

As Senator Tydings, leading sponsor of the measure, put
it:

> Research into the administrative problems of the Federal
> courts and development of recommended solutions are
> the primary functions of the Center. . . . It will collect
> data, conduct research, depict the contours of each prob-
> lem. Practitioners of the arts and services of administra-
> tion will then formulate recommendations for solution to
> the problems. Management experts, systems analysts,
> data interpreters, personnel experts, as well as judges,
> academicians, and practicing attorneys, will bring the
> skill and experience of their disciplines to the Cen-
> ter. . . .[172]

The Center would provide the Judicial Conference with
the kind of staff support which many judges had once
thought the Administrative Office would render. In words
which had a familiar ring, Tydings warned against any
"equivocation of the congressional intent in H.R. 6111 as
amended." In that measure, he stressed that "Congress is
demanding that the Center bring . . . court administration
up to date [by] providing the medium, the funds, and the
moral support for the judiciary to do a topflight job." With
such resources at the judiciary's disposal, Congress, said
Tydings, would "settle for nothing less."[173]

[169] *Ibid.*, part 24, 33098.   [170] Sec. 620(1).   [171] Sec. 620(3).
[172] *Congressional Record*, 90th Cong., 1st Sess., 1967, vol. 113, part
24, 33098.
[173] *Ibid.*, 33099.

In the first years of its existence, the Center, operating with limited funds,[174] sought to execute the legislative mandate. Its goal, declared Director Clark, was "to get a uniform judicial system as far as practicable."[175] The means lay in "research, testing, and things of that kind."[176] If the new agency seemed to be encroaching on the Administrative Office's old domain, Clark replied that their roles differed. The Office constituted a mere "housekeeper";[177] it kept the statistics.[178] In fact, the older agency lost some of its functions.

Judges seminars, which had been sponsored by the Administrative Office during the 1960s, became a Center function. "What we do," said former Justice Clark, "is [to] bring in the more experienced judges, who are specially skilled in a particular area and ask them to lead discussions. . . ."[179] In three seminars for newly-appointed judges, held in the Center's first full year of operation, the judges considered a wide assortment of topics including jurisdictional problems, trial practice, discovery and pretrial settlements, jury selection and instruction, and aspects of criminal litigation.[180] As had the Administrative Office, the Center also

[174] See *Judicial Conference Report, 1969*, p. 3. The appropriations for Fiscal Year 1968 totaled $40,000 and for Fiscal Year 1969, $300,000.
[175] U.S., Congress, House, Committee on Appropriations, *Hearings, on Departments of State, Justice, and Commerce, the Judiciary, and Related Agencies Appropriations for 1970*, 91st Cong., 1st Sess., 1969, p. 201.
[176] *Ibid.*, p. 205.
[177] U.S., Congress, Senate, Committee on Appropriations, *Hearings, on H.R. 12964, Departments of State, Justice, and Commerce, the Judiciary, and Related Agencies Appropriations for Fiscal Year 1970*, 91st Cong., 1st Sess., 1969, p. 28.
[178] House Committee on Appropriations, *Hearings on Appropriations for 1970*, 1969, p. 205.
[179] *Ibid.*, p. 201.
[180] U.S., Congress, Senate, Subcommittee on Improvements in Judicial Machinery of the Committee on the Judiciary, *Hearings, on S. 952, S. 567, S. 474, S. 585, S. 852, S. 898, S. 1036, S. 1216, S. 1509,*

sponsored training sessions for court officers and supporting personnel. It arranged an educational program for new
United States Magistrates at circuit judicial conferences,
and it promoted somewhat similar experiences for district
court clerks.[181]

The Center assumed responsibility for research and development programs. It let contracts to private firms, law
schools, and other governmental agencies for "a study of the
management, docketing, case flow and causes of congestion,
obstruction, bottlenecks, etc. in the United States Courts,"[182]
for computerization of a district court's business,[183] and for
studies of bail,[184] post-conviction remedies,[185] probation,[186]
and the impact of automobile accident litigation on the federal courts.[187]

With its various training and research programs, the
Center expected to realize long-term results. Broad impact
was to be achieved by the publication of manuals for clerks,
magistrates, and judges. The *Judge's Bench Book*, for instance, provided standardized forms for the trial of criminal cases and criteria for granting habeas corpus petitions.[188] More generally, the Center moved to improve the
judiciary's communications system with inauguration of a
newsletter. Entitled *The Third Branch: A Bulletin of the
Federal Courts*, it reports on local, regional, and national

S. 1646, S. 1712, S. 2040, *Federal Judges and Courts*, 91st Cong.,
1st Sess., 1969, p. 39.

[181] House Committee on Appropriations, *Hearings on Appropriations for 1970*, 1969, p. 200.

[182] Senate Committee on Appropriations, *Hearings on Appropriations for 1970*, 1969, pp. 22-23.

[183] *Ibid.*   [184] *Ibid.*   [185] *Ibid.*
[186] *Ibid.*   [187] *Ibid.*

[188] U.S., Congress, Senate, Committee on Appropriations, *Hearings,
on H.R. 17522, Departments of State, Justice, and Commerce, the
Judiciary, and Related Agencies Appropriations for Fiscal Year 1969*,
90th Cong., 2d Sess., 1968, p. 178. A roster of 45 "Research Projects
for the Federal Judicial Center" is presented on pp. 181-82.

affairs of interest to judges, court officers, and supporting personnel.

Proselytizing constituted another vital function of the Center. Sounding much like Henry P. Chandler in the early days of the Administrative Office, former Justice Clark stated that "one of the most important phases of the Center is going out among the judges and hearing their problems and talking with them."[189] Ideas, demonstration projects, suggestions, and persuasion—these were the Center's stock in trade. Armed with them, Clark believed that the new agency had a role to play in dealing with the black sheep of the federal bench. The Center's director, informed of a dilatory judge, might write him a letter. Declared Clark:

> When in town I might say: "Well, the bar association invited me to speak here and I plan to make a little speech on the docket." That needles him.
>
> We develop new techniques he can use. Sometimes we may put on a project that involves him and other judges of greater skill; so he might adapt their techniques for use to his own abilities.[190]

Finally, the Center's first director believed that change within the judiciary might be brought about not only through demonstration, persuasion, and imitation, but also by legislation. Research would necessarily result in proposals to Congress, some of them undoubtedly affecting the substance of the law itself. Clark indicated as much when he decried the inability of federal judges "to sentence habitual offenders to longer sentences than now provided for the specific offense with which they are charged." This situation, he lamented, turned such persons "loose on the pub-

[189] House Committee on Appropriations, *Hearings on Appropriations for 1970*, 1969, p. 207.
[190] Senate Committee on Appropriations, *Hearings on Appropriations for 1970*, 1969, p. 15.

lic after service of a short sentence, even though it be the maximum." The director asserted that the Center could "be of material assistance in ferreting out such loopholes in effective administration and reporting them to the appropriate committees of Congress. This," he added, "would also be of material help in the fight against crime."[191] With establishment of the Federal Judicial Center, Congress sought to infuse the judiciary's highly decentralized administrative apparatus with a healthy dose of centralized direction—this time in the realm of research and education. But significantly neither judges nor legislators contemplated any fundamental changes in that apparatus. The Judicial Center would merely enable existing regional and national instruments of judicial administration to function in a more efficacious manner.

[191] Senate Committee on Appropriations, *Hearings on Appropriations for 1969*, 1968, p. 178.

CHAPTER 11

The Circuit Councils:
Linchpins of Administration

Council Organization and Procedures

IN the years since enactment of the Administrative Office Bill of 1939, circuit council organization has changed little from that envisioned and secured by the Act's judicial framers.[1] Committees of the several councils have, however, emerged with the increase in appellate judgeships and the need for greater specialization.[2] "Whenever a problem comes up at one of the . . . meetings of our Judicial Council in which inquiry must be made," Judge Carl McGowan of the Court of Appeals for the District of Columbia Circuit stated, "our only resource, and our invariable practice, is to appoint an *ad hoc* committee of two or three judges to look into the matter and make recommendations to the

---

[1] Its title did change. Section 306 of the Administrative Office Act, 53 *Stat.* 1224, referred to a "council." Judge Albert B. Maris of the Third Circuit, a participant in drafting the 1948 revision of the Judicial Code, stated in 1941: "We have adopted for our council the name 'Judicial Council of the Third Circuit' and we understand that a number of the other circuits are using the same name. The council is composed solely of the circuit judges and is, therefore, in the literal sense a judicial council. Furthermore, its functions are those which in many states are entrusted to bodies which are quite generally known as judicial councils; consequently, the name is one which is calculated to indicate to those interested the functions of the council. On the other hand, the term 'circuit council' is hardly descriptive. . . ." Albert W. Maris to Hatton W. Sumners, June 6, 1941, photostat copy, Parker Papers, Box 54. See 62 *Stat.* 902, 28 *U.S.C.* 332(b).

[2] "Minutes of the Council of the Second Circuit," October 17, 1957, p. 1, Clark Papers; see also J. Edward Lumbard to Robert P. Anderson, November 20, 1961, *ibid.*; "Minutes of the Meeting of the Second Circuit Council," November 4, 1961, p. 7, *ibid.*

Council for action."[3] Such committees, like the council itself, lacked any staffs until the post-Warren era.[4] Thus the judges themselves dealt with a variety of issues, many of which "are not purely judicial in nature," but which "require leg work and time-consuming conferences with persons outside the judicial circle."[5]

The static quality of the council's organization has not gone unchallenged; from diverse quarters it has been subjected to sharp criticism and reform campaigns.[6] With all the earmarks of earlier attacks on the composition of the Judicial Conference, district judges have agitated for representation on the councils,[7] a possibility clearly foreseen, and provided for, by the framers of the Administrative Office Act.[8]

Appellate judges have predictably responded by offering access rather than representation. They have polled trial judges[9] and invited them to attend council sessions devoted

[3] U.S., Congress, Senate, Subcommittee on Improvements in Judicial Machinery of the Committee on the Judiciary, Hearings, on S. 3055, S. 3060, S. 3061, S. 3062, The Judicial Reform Act, 90th Cong., 2d Sess., 1968, p. 275.

[4] The Act of January 5, 1971, 84 Stat. 1907, permitted each circuit to appoint a circuit executive to "exercise such administrative powers and perform such duties as may be delegated to him by the circuit council." Prominent among such duties were assorted staff services for the council. See U.S., Congress, House, Subcommittee No. 5 of the Committee on the Judiciary, Hearings, on H.R. 17901 and H.R. 17906, Circuit Court Executives, 91st Cong., 2d Sess., 1970.

[5] Senate Subcommittee on Improvements in Judicial Machinery, Hearings, Judicial Reform Act, 1968, p. 275.

[6] See Pierson Hall to Warren Olney III, February 21, 1962, in U.S., Congress, Senate, Subcommittee on Improvements in Judicial Machinery of the Committee on the Judiciary, File on H.R. 6690, 87th Cong.

[7] Warren Olney III to Olin D. Johnston, February 5, 1962, Clark Papers.

[8] Charles E. Hughes to D. Lawrence Groner, December 30, 1938, in U.S., Congress, Senate, Committee on the Judiciary, Hearings, on S. 188, Administration of United States Courts, 76th Cong., 1st Sess., 1939, p. 13.

[9] See Baar, "When Judges Lobby," pp. 335-36.

to legislation affecting the district courts[10] and to "the use of pre-trial practice and the holding of terms of court in such a way as to shorten the time between filing of cases and their disposition."[11] They have also requested that district judges appear and discuss specific administrative problems troubling them.[12] "Regularly," reported Sylvester Ryan, chief judge of the Southern District of New York, "I and the other Chief Judges of the circuit have attended council meetings at Chief [Circuit] Judge [J. Edward] Lumbard's invitation and have given detailed reports of the activities of our district."[13] When their participation was no longer required, they withdrew.[14]

Advocates of district judge representation regarded the presence of lower court judges on the councils as a means of improving communications between the council and district judges sitting in as many as sixteen districts within the circuit.[15] More significantly, they perceived such representation as enhancing the authority of the councils and perhaps strengthening their propensity for administrative action.[16] In the eyes of reformers, "one of the reasons why the Judicial Councils of the Circuits [have] not functioned

[10] Memorandum, "Meeting of the Judicial Council [of the District of Columbia], on Friday, April 14, 1952," Stephens Papers.

[11] John J. Parker to the Chief Justice of the United States and the Judges in attendance at the 1941 Session of the Conference of Senior Circuit Judges, Washington, D.C., September 23, 1941, p. 2, Parker Papers, Box 54.

[12] "Minutes of the Meeting of the Second Circuit Council," October 17, 1957, p. 4, Clark Papers; ibid., November 11, 1959.

[13] Sylvester J. Ryan to Pierson M. Hall, January 4, 1962, Senate Subcommittee File on H.R. 6690.

[14] "Meeting of Judicial Council [of the District of Columbia], March 14, 1952," Stephens Papers, Box 221.

[15] Olin D. Johnston, Congressional Record, 88th Cong., 1st Sess., 1963, vol. 109, part 15, 19736.

[16] See Maynard E. Pirsig, "A Survey of Judicial Councils, Judicial Conferences and Administrative Directors," The Brief, 47 (Spring 1952), 195.

more adequately in the past"[17] can be traced directly to the absence of permanent spokesmen for the interests of the district courts.

On the other hand, it has been precisely the fear that the addition of district judges was "intended to be a forerunner of pressures to increase the activity of such councils"[18] that evoked opposition. At least one chief district judge did not "take kindly to the idea of having a Judge of another district court taking part in the supervision of our administrative action."[19] Orders and directives to the trial courts, said Judge Sylvester Ryan, "should be made only by circuit Judges and . . . District Judges of coordinate jurisdictions should not as a routine procedure take part in the consideration of such matters."[20]

Circuit judges, too, had misgivings. They objected to district judges sitting "in judgment on circuit judges,"[21] and contended that district judges on the councils would only "add further paralyzing forces."[22] Furthermore, they argued that the "information gap" was illusory. Not only did council members have telephones close at hand, but many had themselves been trial judges and were well versed in the administrative problems afflicting the lower courts.[23] If they lacked such knowledge, they might easily remedy

[17] John Biggs, Jr., "Some Observations on Judicial Administration," *Federal Rules Decisions,* 29 (1962), 469.

[18] "Resolution of the Judicial Council of the Ninth Circuit: Proposed Amendment of Section 332, Title 28, U.S.C., Relating to Judicial Councils," November 13, 1959, Clark Papers (cited hereafter as "Resolution of the Judicial Council of the Ninth Circuit").

[19] Sylvester J. Ryan to Pierson M. Hall, January 4, 1962, Senate Subcommittee File on H.R. 6690.

[20] *Ibid.*

[21] Richard H. Chambers to Olin D. Johnston, December 21, 1961, *ibid.*

[22] Charles E. Clark to J. Edward Lumbard, January 5, 1961, Clark Papers.

[23] Henry P. Chandler to Harold M. Medina, January 18, 1952, Administrative Office Correspondence, 60-A-328, Box 4.

the deficiency by sitting on some of the congested district court benches in their circuit.[24]

In spite of the sharp division among judges over the inclusion of trial judges on the councils, a committee of the Judicial Conference proposed to the September 1960 Judicial Conference that two or three district judge representatives join the councils, that these councils meet quarterly, and that their supervisory powers be enlarged.[25] This recommendation drew, as might have been expected, "a lukewarm reception" from the Conference.[26]

Nevertheless, the following year witnessed increased pressure for an overhaul of the councils, this time from Congress.[27] The September 1961 Conference reacted by discussing the issue "at length" and approving then pending legislation which incorporated major features of the original Conference committee proposal.[28] The following March, it reaffirmed this recommendation[29] in the face of rising opposition within the judiciary,[30] opposition which proved decisive when the March 1963 Conference reversed its previous position and took a firm stand against formal district judge participation on the councils.[31]

In the meantime, a Special Committee of the Judicial Conference on the Responsibilities and Powers of the Judicial Councils had advanced a middle ground position

[24] *Ibid.*
[25] Biggs, "Some Observations on Judicial Administration," p. 469.
[26] *Ibid.*
[27] See Warren Olney III to Olin D. Johnston, February 5, 1962, Clark Papers.
[28] *Ibid.* See also *Judicial Conference Report, 1961*, p. 67. The vote was 17 to 5.
[29] *Ibid., 1962*, p. 3.
[30] See J. Edward Lumbard to Kenneth Keating, September 22, 1961, Clark Papers; Richard H. Chambers to Olin D. Johnston, January 31, 1962, Senate Subcommittee File on H.R. 6690; Stephen S. Chandler, "The Role of the Trial Judge in the Anglo-American Legal System," *American Bar Association Journal*, 50 (February 1964), 129-30.
[31] *Judicial Conference Report, 1963*, p. 9.

between the *status quo* and a formal statutory provision for district judge representatives. Its report, presented in March 1961, concluded that the "present statute[32] is adequate," but urged the appellate judges to invite "the district judge, who is the representative on the Judicial Conference of the United States, to attend a council meeting."[33] Although the March 1961 Conference overlooked this particular recommendation in summarizing the recommendations of the report, it did approve the report as a whole.[34] By this strategy, congressional criticism was muted, the organization of the councils remained unchanged, and the judiciary was spared the vagaries of reform. It was spared, too, the pangs of effective administrative power.

Council Procedures

More varied than their organization have been the procedures followed by different councils. They are required by law to meet twice a year at the call of the chief judge of court of appeals.[35] Some meet monthly,[36] while that in the Ninth Circuit has met an average of eight times a year since

[32] 28 *U.S.C.* 332.

[33] U.S., Congress, House, Committee on the Judiciary, *Report on the Responsibilities and Powers of the Judicial Councils*, 87th Cong., 1st Sess., 1961, H. Doc. 201, p. 10. The *Report* urged chief judges of the courts of appeals to invite "the district judge, who is the representative on the Judicial Conference of the United States, to attend a council meeting."

[34] *Judicial Conference Report, 1961*, pp. 51-53.

[35] 28 *U.S.C.* 332. Although the judicial council and the court of appeals *en banc* are similarly constituted, the latter may be convened only by a majority of the circuit judges in regular active service. 28 *U.S.C.* 46(c).

[36] Third Circuit: interview with Albert B. Maris, December 29, 1964, Philadelphia, Pennsylvania; Fourth Circuit: Clement Haynsworth, U.S., Congress, Senate, Subcommittee on Improvements in Judicial Machinery of the Committee on the Judiciary, *Hearings, on S. 952, S. 567, S. 474, S. 585, S. 852, S. 898, S. 1036, S. 1216, S. 1509, S. 1646, S. 1712, S. 2040, Federal Judges and Courts*, 91st Cong., 1st Sess., 1969, pp. 410-11.

1955.[37] At its first meeting under the Administrative Office Act, the Fourth Circuit council resolved that it would "meet on the first days of each regular term of the Circuit Court of Appeals in January, April, June, and October and November of each year and at such other times as the Senior Circuit Judge may designate."[38] In the District of Columbia Circuit, however, no council had ever been formally convened nearly five years after enactment of the statute.[39] Chief Justice D. Lawrence Groner simply "considered that the Council of this Circuit was in perpetual session and that any matter affecting the work of the Judges of the District Court known to any member of the Council would be brought to the attention of the other members."[40] His successors, however, held monthly meetings.[41] In circuits less compact than the District of Columbia, the geographical dispersion of judges and the infrequency of en banc proceedings have militated against formal council sessions.[42] Here telephone communications have largely filled the void.[43]

Councils differ, too, in their use of agendas and maintenance of records. Some circulate an agenda in advance of

[37] Richard H. Chambers to Olin D. Johnston, June 20, 1961, Senate Subcommittee File on H.R. 6690.

[38] "Minutes of the Meeting of Judicial Council of the Fourth Circuit held at Charlotte, N.C., Monday, January 8th, 1940," p. 1, Parker Papers, Box 54 (cited hereafter as "Fourth Circuit Council Minutes," 1940).

[39] Justin Miller to D. Lawrence Groner, January 27, 1944, Stephens Papers, Box 28.

[40] D. Lawrence Groner to Justin Miller, January 28, 1944, Groner Papers, Box 13.

[41] E. Barrett Prettyman, "The Duties of a Circuit Chief Judge," *American Bar Association Journal*, 46 (June 1960), 634. See also "Statement of Carl McGowan," Senate Subcommittee on Improvement of Judicial Machinery, *Hearings, Judicial Reform Act*, 1968, p. 275.

[42] Olin D. Johnston to Richard H. Chambers, undated, Senate Subcommittee File on H.R. 6690.

[43] Interview with Simon E. Sobeloff, January 18, 1965, Baltimore, Maryland.

their sessions. In the Fifth Circuit, it has contained forty or more items[44] and, stated the chief judge, "is so formal that I have reduced it to a Dewey-decimal system so we can refer to it intelligently."[45] That circuit's council also distributes copies of its minutes to all members.[46] The Third Circuit has long maintained detailed minutes of its sessions, copies of which are filed with the Administrative Office.[47] The Second's records are little more than amplified agendas.[48] But such skeletal minutes have advantages. As one chief judge noted: "Some of our most effective action in our council has been taken without being recorded in the minutes."[49]

As with records, so with the entire decision-making process. In some circuits the process is highly formal, and in others, quite the contrary. By law, circuit council approval is required for routine changes in the numbers, territories and salaries of bankruptcy referees.[50] In the Third Circuit, the council formally polls all its members,[51] while that in the Second has operated much more informally.[52] "I assume each member of our Judicial Council is in agreement with the recommendation of the Administrative Office," wrote acting Chief Judge Sterry Waterman to his colleagues, "and, though there is some doubt as to the effect of a vote

[44] John R. Brown to Peter G. Fish, June 5, 1970 (letter in possession of the author).

[45] John R. Brown, Senate Subcommittee on Improvements in Judicial Machinery, *Hearings, Federal Judges and Courts*, 1969, p. 323.

[46] *Ibid.*

[47] U.S., Congress, Senate, Committee on Appropriations, *Field Study of the Operations of United States Courts*, 86th Cong., 2d Sess., 1959, Committee Print, p. 57.

[48] See "Minutes of the Meeting of the Circuit Council," November 15, 1951, Clark Papers.

[49] Richard H. Chambers to Olin D. Johnston, June 20, 1961, Senate Subcommittee File on H.R. 6690.

[50] 11 *U.S.C.*, secs. 65, 68, 71.

[51] Interview with Albert B. Maris.

[52] Sterry R. Waterman to Warren Olney III, February 17, 1960, Clark Papers.

of only three of us in a court of six (!!), I will take your vote as sufficient authority to support the recommendations."[53]

Clearing-House Function

As already noted, the framers of the 1939 Act intended the councils as the administrative linchpin of the federal judiciary. As such, their functions approximate those of most administrative agencies, and are at once quasi-legislative, quasi-executive, and quasi-judicial. Like the circuit conferences, the councils form a link in the judiciary's policy-making system. To them report the circuit chief judges on the action of preceding Judicial Conferences and the relevance of those actions for the circuit.[54] But the councils are not mere receptacles of Conference policies; they also influence their very substance.

This advisory function is hardly novel. It became commonplace after Congress authorized the Supreme Court to draft new rules of criminal procedure.[55] Shortly thereafter, Chief Justice Hughes called on the councils to appoint committees; these, in turn, would provide the Court's Advisory Committee on the Criminal Rules with suggestions.[56] Rarely, however, have the councils dealt with the Supreme Court as distinguished from the Judicial Conference.

Their primary role since 1940 has been that of a clearing-house for Conference action on administrative and legislative policies, particularly those relating to the district courts within their circuits.[57] Proposals from these courts are

[53] Sterry R. Waterman to Charles E. Clark and Judges of the United States Court of Appeals for the Second Circuit, June 29, 1961, Clark Papers.
[54] "Minutes of the Second Circuit Council," October 17, 1957, Clark Papers.
[55] 54 *Stat.* 688.
[56] Charles E. Clark to D. Lawrence Groner, February 18, 1941, Groner Papers, Box 3; D. Lawrence Groner to Charles E. Hughes, March 17, 1941, *ibid.*
[57] *Judicial Conference Report, 1940*, p. 33.

screened by the councils, and if approved, are submitted to Congress, or more likely, to the Judicial Conference or its committees.[58] Negative use of this power is not unknown, and in the Ninth Circuit under Chief Judge William Denman, council vetoes of district judges and circuit conference recommendations were a thing to be reckoned with.[59]

The bulk of this clearing-house business involved lower court requests for more money and manpower.[60] However, since the early 1950s, requests for additional judgeships have traveled the council route on their way to the Judicial Conference,[61] as has pending legislation affecting intra-circuit judicial administration. The ability of the councils to act promptly and the wholly circuit-related nature of some legislation encouraged the 1961 Judicial Conference to direct "that any bill to create a new judicial district, . . . to authorize a new place for holding federal court, or to waive the provisions of 28 U.S.C. 142 respecting the furnishing of accommodations at places of holding court be submitted . . . first to the Judicial Council of the Circuit involved for its consideration and recommendation which shall then be transmitted by the Director to the Committee on Court Administration for its consideration and report to the Judicial Conference."[62]

Issues of greater complexity and of national rather than regional importance also pass through the councils and may in fact arise there. Making its way in the late 1950s from the Third Circuit's council was a question of the power of re-

[58] Ibid., 1962, p. 48.
[59] See Excerpt from "Proceedings of the Conference of Judges and Lawyer Delegates of the Ninth Judicial Circuit," July 1954, pp. 73-74, 254, Stephens Papers, Box 233; William Denman to Warren Magnuson, April 15, 1954, Congressional Record, 83d Cong., 2d Sess., 1954, vol. 100, part 4, 5220.
[60] "Agenda, Second Circuit Council," May 19, 1962, Clark Papers.
[61] Henry P. Chandler, "Standards for Creation of New District Judgeships, Sixth Circuit Judicial Council," April 17, 1953, Administrative Office Correspondence, 59-A-532, Box 1.
[62] Judicial Conference Report, 1961, p. 66.

tired judges on assignment to participate in the adoption of rules of court, the appointment of officers and similar functions of the court sitting *en banc*. This issue "had been raised in other circuits," the chief judge of one district court in the circuit informed his council, "and . . . the views of the Judicial Conference of the United States upon the subject would be most helpful." The council agreed, and authorized Chief Judge Biggs "to suggest to the Committees on Court Administration and Revision of the Laws of the Judicial Conference of the United States that they study the problem and, if they think it appropriate, to report upon it to the next session of the Judicial Conference."[63]

Scope of Intra-circuit Functions

Although the councils are clearly a cog in the larger policy-making process, their importance stems less from this role than from their jurisdiction over "administration of the business of the courts within the circuit."[64] This language, inserted during the 1948 revision of the Judicial Code, modified that contained in the Administrative Office Act.[65] Framers of the Act had clearly contemplated council supervision of district court administration, but had left vague its role in administering the court of appeals. Theoretically, the 1948 revision resolved the uncertainty, at least by implication.[66] Nevertheless, one senior circuit judge contended that "on its face [the law] does not apply to circuit judges";[67] when the council acts on appellate judges, it acts as a court, not as a council.

[63] "Minutes of 119th Meeting of the Judicial Council of the Third Circuit," June 11, 1958, Administrative Office Correspondence, 60-A-427, Box 101.

[64] 28 *U.S.C.* 332.   [65] See *ibid.*

[66] House Committee on the Judiciary, *Report on the Responsibilities*, 1961, p. 2.

[67] John Biggs, Jr., U.S., Congress, Senate, Subcommittee on Improvements in Judicial Machinery of the Committee on the Judiciary, *Hearings, on Judicial Fitness*, part I, 89th Cong., 2d Sess., 1966, p. 12.

However the statutory language may be construed, councils have often used their sessions to discuss and settle judicial and administrative problems peculiar to the appellate court. In fact, Chief Judge Clement Haynsworth of the Fourth Circuit reported that "[t]he regular meetings of the Council find us devoting a major part of our time to problems of the Court of Appeals. . . ."[68] Thus appellate judges meeting as a council have considered cases,[69] drafted *per curiam* opinions,[70] set summer schedules,[71] considered circuit court housing and personnel as well as proposed changes in rules of court,[72] and designated the purposes for which the fees collected from attorneys admitted to the appellate court bar may be used.[73]

The annual circuit judicial conferences claim the atten-

[68] Senate Subcommittee on Improvements in Judicial Machinery, *Hearings, Federal Judges and Courts*, 1969, p. 411.

[69] "Minutes of the Meeting of the Second Circuit Council," November 11, 1959, Clark Papers.

[70] *Ibid.*

[71] "Memorandum Concerning Summer Schedules," June 27, 1951, Stephens Papers, Box 88.

[72] "Agenda of the Circuit Council of the Second Circuit," May 9, 1962, Clark Papers; "Minutes of the Circuit Council of the Second Circuit," November 4, 1961, p. 8, *ibid.* The Fifth Circuit Judicial Council gained wide publicity for its "Summary Calendar" procedure "ordained" by the council and promulgated by the Court of Appeals as Rules 17-20 of the Fifth Circuit Rules. The procedure requires a judicial screening of every case docketed to determine whether it is frivolous and "subject to dismissal or affirmance without more," whether it may receive "disposition on briefs and record without oral argument," or whether it merits an oral argument. *Murphy v. Houma Well Service*, 409 F.2d 804, 805-808 (C.C.A. 5th, 1969). See also John R. Brown, Senate Subcommittee on Improvements in Judicial Machinery, *Hearings, Federal Judges and Courts*, 1969, pp. 254, 326-27.

[73] 28 *U.S.C., United States Courts of Appeals Rules*: Rule 6, C.C.A. (Fourth Circuit); Rule 6, C.C.A. (Sixth Circuit); Rule 6, C.C.A. (Eighth Circuit); Rule 11, C.C.A. (Ninth Circuit). This last rule requires the court clerk to disburse revenue from fees on order of the Chief Judge "pursuant to resolutions of the court prescribing the purposes for which such funds may be disbursed."

tion of councils which have come to serve as the organizing agency for the meetings. This role was especially pronounced in the Second Circuit when Chief Judge Charles E. Clark sought to overhaul that circuit's conference.[74] In some circuits, the council's role has been formalized in a rule of court. Rule 20(a) of the Court of Appeals for the District of Columbia Circuit requires that the full council approve the lawyer members named to the Committee on Conference Arrangements as well as "the proposed agenda of the public session of the Conference."[75] Rules of court in the Second and Third Circuits likewise provide for council participation in the selection of either the members of the Planning and Program Committee of the Judicial Conference in the former circuit[76] or the lawyer-delegates to be designated "life members of the conference" in the Third.[77] Unlike other circuit councils, that in the District of Columbia enjoys formal authority to take the initiative in appointing committees to report to the judicial conference "on matters pertaining to the improvement of the administration of justice within the circuit."[78]

But as perceived by the framers of the Administrative Office Act, the critical work of the councils was their responsibility for effective and expeditious administration of judicial business.[79] And in this realm, their mandate was sweeping. It meant "not merely . . . dealing with the question of the handling and dispatching of a trial court's business in its technical sense, but also . . . dealing with the

[74] See "Minutes of Meeting of the Circuit Council," November 15, 1961, Clark Papers; Harold M. Stephens to Joseph Stewart, October 18, 1951, Stephens Papers, Box 88; "Minutes of the Meeting of the Second Circuit Council," October 15, 1959, Clark Papers.
[75] 28 U.S.C., United States Court of Appeals Rules.
[76] Ibid., Section O. 22(4), C.C.A. (Second Circuit).
[77] Ibid., Rule 15(3)(g), C.C.A. (Third Circuit). Rule 15(4) permits the council to fix the registration fee for all members attending sessions of the Judicial Conference.
[78] Ibid., Rule 20(d), C.C.A. (District of Columbia Circuit).
[79] 28 U.S.C. 332.

business of the judiciary in its broader or institutional sense, such as . . . preventing . . . any stigma, disrepute, or other element of loss of public confidence occurring as to the Federal Courts or to the administration of justice by them, from any nature of action by an individual judge or a person attached to the courts."[80]

Council jurisdiction is broad, but it does not extend to the legality of judicial conduct[81] nor does it encompass "the legal correctness of the work of the respective district courts."[82] But it may, in fact, include a rather strong judicial as opposed to administrative component. Whether exercising jurisdiction of a judicial or administrative nature, the scope of council power is extensive; it contributes to that institution's potentially significant integrative role within the diffused federal judiciary.

Statutory Functions

The integrative role of the councils assumes importance in the light of the twentieth-century proclivity of Congress to delegate to the judiciary those powers once regarded as wholly within the legislative prerogative. The powers so delegated typically require that the councils either review

[80] House Committee on the Judiciary, *Report on the Responsibilities*, 1961, p. 7.

[81] When a council uncovers illegal conduct, it may, by resolution, call on the Department of Justice for an investigation and notify the House and Senate Judiciary Committees of the existence of grounds for impeachment. See John Biggs, Jr., Senate Subcommittee on Improvements in Judicial Machinery, *Hearings, on Judicial Fitness*, part I, 1966, p. 19; Henry P. Chandler to Senior Circuit Judges, September 3, 1942, mimeograph (Administrative Office of the United States Courts, Washington, D.C.).

[82] "The Judicial Council of the Third Circuit: In the Matter of the Examination by the Administrative Office of the United States Courts of the Records of Everett G. Rodebaugh, one of the Court Reporters of the United States District Court for the Eastern District of Pennsylvania," *Federal Rules Decisions*, 10 (1951), 215.

decisions made in the first instance by district judges or resolve disagreements among trial judges.

The councils' utility as instruments of integration became apparent when district judges sought general legislation enabling them to fix the time and place of holding court and to abolish places of court by a simple rule of the district court. This change would clearly have placed a major area of administration in the "uncontrolled discretion of the district judges."[83] To a committee of the Judicial Conference, the councils "should logically have a voice in the matter."[84] Alterations made by rule of court should pass muster with the relevant council thereby insuring that "proposed changes be given consideration from a wider point of view."[85]

Congressional grants of specific powers to the councils reflect this desire to render the district judges responsible to a less parochial authority. Councils must consent to pretermission by the district courts of any terms of court,[86] and under the Bankruptcy Act, the councils as well as the district judges must pass on recommendations of the Director of the Administrative Office for changes in the number, territories, and salaries of referees; these are then submitted to the Judicial Conference for final determination.[87]

[83] "Report of the Committee on Ways and Means of Economy in the Operation of the Federal Courts as Amended by the Judicial Conference of the United States," September 1, 1948, mimeograph (Administrative Office of the United States Courts, Washington, D.C.).

[84] *Ibid.*

[85] *Ibid.*, p. 3. See *Judicial Conference Report, 1948*, p. 34. See also 28 *U.S.C.* 142.

[86] 28 *U.S.C.* 140(a).

[87] 11 *U.S.C.* 65(b), (1), 68(a), (b), 71(b), (c). However, a vacancy in the office of referee may be filled, if no changes are made in salary or other arrangements, when recommended by the Director, the district judge or judges, and the circuit council without a recommendation to the Judicial Conference or its approval. 11 *U.S.C.* 71(b).

The Federal Magistrates Act of 1968,[88] which abolished the historic commissioner system characterized by many non-lawyer officeholders and a fee system,[89] largely followed the pattern established by the Bankruptcy Act. Under its terms, the director, the district courts and the circuit councils all make recommendations to the Judicial Conference on the number and salaries of full-time and part-time magistrates, the Conference then acting in the light of these recommendations.[90]

Both the Criminal Justice Act of 1964[91] and the Jury Selection and Service Act of 1968[92] provide for the traditional council review function. Councils must pass on and approve, under the Criminal Justice Act, district court plans "for furnishing representation for defendants charged with felonies or misdemeanors . . . who are financially unable to obtain an adequate defense,"[93] while under the Jury Selection Act they must similarly act on trial court plans "for random selection of grand and petit jurors."[94] Present and participating with the council is "either the chief judge of the district court whose plan is being reviewed or such other active district judge of that district as the chief judge may designate."[95] His presence is intended "to insure that any special considerations underlying particular features of the district court's plan will be given adequate weight by the reviewing panel."[96]

[88] 82 *Stat.* 1107; for a brief legislative history of the Act, see Joseph Tydings, Jr., *Congressional Record*, 90th Cong., 2d Sess., 1968, vol. 114, part 22, 29406-07.

[89] See U.S., Congress, House, Committee on the Judiciary, *The Federal Magistrates Act*, H. Rept. 1629, to accompany S. 945, 90th Cong., 2d Sess., 1968, pp. 13-14.

[90] 28 *U.S.C.* 633(b).

[91] 78 *Stat.* 552-54.   [92] 82 *Stat.* 54.   [93] 18 *U.S.C.* 3006A(a).

[94] 28 *U.S.C.* 1863(a).   [95] *Ibid.*

[96] *Congressional Record*, 90th Cong., 1st Sess., 1967, vol. 113, part 26, 35633. It should be noted that the Jury Act limits review to the issue of the district court plan's compliance with the provisions of the statute 28 *U.S.C.* 1863(a). "It is not intended," the House Judiciary Committee declared, "that the [reviewing] panel should be able to

Circuit councils have been formally designated as arbiters of disagreements over administrative policies in the lower courts. If the trial judges "are unable to agree upon the adoption of rules or orders for [dividing the district's business among themselves] the judicial council of the circuit shall make the necessary orders."[97] Provisions of the Bankruptcy Act likewise provide for council intervention whenever the judges of a district court fail to achieve a meeting of the minds. Such a failure in designating a referee to fill a vacancy in another referee's office may lead to council action[98] as would an inability on the part of the trial judges to agree on the removal of a referee for cause.[99] Similarly, the Federal Magistrates Act of 1968 permits a majority of all judges on the circuit council to remove a magistrate whenever there exists a tie vote among the district judges on the question of removing or retaining that officer.[100]

As collegial bodies in which responsibility for any given decision is diffused among as many as fifteen judges, the councils offer a ready vehicle for dealing with such sensitive issues as judicial assignments and work capacity. Judges and congressmen have recognized this function by carving out a role for the councils in the assignment of judges, a realm largely subject to the prerogatives of the chief circuit judge.[101] "The chief judge or judicial council . . . ," states the law, may designate "any retired circuit or district judge . . . to perform such judicial duties within the circuit as he is willing and able to undertake."[102] One or the other must also consent to the designation and assignment of an active

---

substitute its own plan for the district court's if the district court's plan complies with the statute." See U.S., Congress, House, Committee on the Judiciary, *Federal Jury Selection Act*, H. Rept. 1076 to accompany S. 989, 90th Cong., 2d Sess., 1968, p. 9.

[97] 28 *U.S.C.* 137. [98] 11 *U.S.C.* 71(c).

[99] 11 *U.S.C.* 62(b). [100] 28 *U.S.C.* 631(h).

[101] 28 *U.S.C.* 291(a), (b), (c); 292(a), (b), (c), 295. See J. Edward Lumbard, Senate Subcommittee on Improvements in Judicial Machinery, *Hearings, Judicial Reform Act*, 1968, p. 266.

[102] 28 *U.S.C.* 294(c).

judge from one circuit to another.[103] This ratification role has been extended to include the intercircuit transfer of other court officials such as referees in bankruptcy.[104]

Whenever special circumstances arise, chief judges tend to invoke the prestige of the councils rather than act on their own. "These designations," declared Senior Circuit Judge John J. Parker, "in . . . unusual cases are usually made at the suggestion of the council." Rarely would he "make a designation, except a routine designation, unless the council approved or authorized it."[105] Consequently when Parker's council "found that in one District disposition of cases was being delayed because of the disqualification of the judge, . . . [it] arranged for other judges to dispose of these cases."[106]

In the same category lies the cancellation of a proud and sensitive, but perhaps physically and/or mentally enfeebled, retired judge's assignment.[107] So, too, refusal of a request for intercircuit assignments of active trial judges would likely find a chief judge seeking his council's endorsement. "Naturally reluctant to decline to approve the proposed transfer," Chief Judge Harold Stephens of the Dis-

[103] 28 *U.S.C.* 295.

[104] The Bankruptcy Act as amended by the Act of September 19, 1950, 64 *Stat.* 866, requires that the chief judge or the circuit council of the circuit from which a referee in bankruptcy is designated and assigned consent to his designation and assignment to another circuit. 11 *U.S.C.* 71(c).

[105] U.S., Congress, Senate, Committee on the Judiciary, *Hearings, on S. 1050, S. 1051, S. 1052, S. 1053, S. 1054, H.R. 138, Administration of United States Courts,* 77th Cong., 1st Sess., 1941, p. 45. The practice of council assignment as distinguished from that of the chief circuit judge varies. See Richard H. Chambers to Olin D. Johnston, June 20, 1961, Senate File on H.R. 6690.

[106] John J. Parker to the Chief Justice of the United States and the Judges in attendance at the 1940 Session of the Conference of Senior Circuit Judges, Washington, D.C., October 1, 1940, p. 2, Parker Papers, Box 54.

[107] Richard H. Chambers to Olin D. Johnston, December 21, 1961, Senate File on H.R. 6690. See also 28 *U.S.C.* 294(e).

trict of Columbia Circuit wrote his counterpart in the Ninth Circuit, "I not only gave the request consideration myself, but also, . . . to make sure that my own attitude was not erroneous, placed the matter . . . before the Council."[108]

Since the Vinson era, various statutes have empowered the councils to take positive action without awaiting initial action by or disagreement among the trial judges or a waiver of his prerogatives by the chief circuit judge. For instance, in the wake of a controversy over maintenance expenses in the early 1950s,[109] Congress empowered the councils to direct a judge to maintain his abode at or near a particular place of holding court within his district.[110]

Several years later, it further strengthened the councils' hands in the realm of judicial behavior by authorizing a majority of their members to certify the permanent mental or physical disability of district and circuit judges who, though eligible to retire, refuse to step down. Thereafter, the President may appoint an additional judge in the usual fashion if he agrees with the council's findings and determines that an additional judge is "necessary for the efficient dispatch of business." The "disabled Judge," should he remain on the bench, then becomes "junior in commission" and hence less capable of impeding or disrupting this court's administrative and judicial work.[111]

Legislative and Executive Functions

The specific statutory powers given the councils describe only a part, and a minute part at that, of the actual scope of the councils' work. Section 332 of the Judicial Code constitutes a full reservoir of council powers. It provides that "each judicial council shall make all necessary orders for the effective and expeditious administration of the business

[108] Harold M. Stephens to William Denman, May 21, 1954, Stephens Papers, Box 90.
[109] See *Judicial Conference Report, 1953*, pp. 239-340.
[110] 68 *Stat.* 12; see 28 *U.S.C.* 134(c).
[111] 28 *U.S.C.* 372(b).

397

of the courts within its circuit. The district judges shall promptly carry into effect all orders of the judicial council."[112] Under this Section, councils consider a broad range of subjects which may not involve application of explicit grants found elsewhere in the Judicial Code.

The specific grants of power provided the councils by the Bankruptcy, Magistrates, Criminal Justice, and Jury Selection Acts may well be redundant. As the House Committee Report on the Jury Act observed, the "approval provision in the proposed statute . . . only make[s] crystal clear the scope of the power that the judicial councils pursuant to section 332 already have to modify or approve local plans. . . . Presumably, this authority embraces jury selection procedures as well as other matters of judicial administration."[113] Utilizing Section 332 powers, councils may pass on issues running the gamut from decisions on the most mundane housekeeping details to critical cases of judicial misbehavior on which the judiciary's reputation hangs.

The councils can become veritable receptacles for trivial issues chiefly of a housekeeping nature. One meeting in the Second Circuit found Chief Circuit Judge Charles E. Clark reporting on a proposal to grace the barren walls of the old federal courthouse in Foley Square with portraits of former luminaries of the bench and bar. The portrait hanging, however, generated surprising opposition among the district judges, perhaps because the suggestion had originated with several circuit judges. "No action was taken, as the lack of enthusiasm seemed somewhat contagious."[114]

A major function of the circuit councils lies in their supervision of the flow of judicial business in the trial courts. Prodded by the Judicial Conference for action on backlogs

[112] 28 *U.S.C.* 332.
[113] House Committee on the Judiciary, *Federal Jury Selection Act*, 1968, H. Rept. 1076, p. 9.
[114] "Minutes of the Judicial Council, Second Circuit," October 15, 1958, Clark Papers.

398

of cases,[115] and by the data contained in quarterly reports from the Administrative Office,[116] they are expected to respond to any problems so revealed. In the wake of one such report, a session of the Second Circuit's Council discussed at length "the continuing chaotic congestion in the Eastern District of New York and the lack of calendar control or administrative direction there existing, resulting in its being the district of worst delay in the country according to the report of the Administrative Director."[117]

The councils, as Chief Justice Earl Warren stated in his 1968 address to the American Law Institute, "have had their responsibilities substantially increased with actual managerial responsibilities."[118] Both the Criminal Justice Act and the Jury Selection Act impose on the councils continuing supervisory functions which cannot be avoided. Not only must they initially review district court plans and modifications thereof,[119] but also council scrutiny of the manner in whch the plans are executed is required. The Criminal Justice Act of 1964 provides that each district court and circuit council "shall submit a report on the appointment of counsel within its jurisdiction to the Administrative Office of the United States Courts."[120] Similarly, the Jury Act requires that the councils receive the names of all persons excluded from jury service "together with detailed explanations for the exclusions."[121] It is then empowered "to make any appropriate order, prospective or retroactive, to redress any misapplication" of the statutory classifications.[122]

[115] *Judicial Conference Report, 1961*, p. 63.

[116] 28 *U.S.C.* 332. See also "Minutes of the 119th Meeting," June 11, 1958, Administrative Office Correspondence, 60-A-427, Box 101.

[117] "Minutes of the Meeting of the Second Circuit Council," November 15, 1956, p. 4, Clark Papers.

[118] Reprinted in Senate Subcommittee on Improvements in Judicial Machinery, *Hearings, Judicial Reform Act*, 1968, p. 297.

[119] 18 *U.S.C.* 3006A(a); 28 *U.S.C.* 1866(a).

[120] 18 *U.S.C.* 3006A(g).   [121] 28 *U.S.C.* 1866(c).

[122] *Ibid.*

Judicial and Executive Functions

The broad powers enjoyed by the councils over "the business of the courts" has sometimes blurred the distinction between administrative and purely judicial functions. Thus councils have considered the exclusion of an interested party from a trial and a lawyer's right to appear in a case.[123] In a more narrow sense, councils have acted in a quasi-judicial capacity in matters which are more clearly administrative. "The council is the administrative agency empowered by Congress to investigate and determine the facts and fashion the appropriate remedy," stated the Third Circuit Council in a leading case.[124] This had been a role promoted by Chief Justice Hughes and one which, in the words of the first Director of the Administrative Office, Henry P. Chandler, "could put to rest many complaints that, if there is no way of dealing with them within the judicial system, are likely to be handled in a way which is much less considerate of the courts."[125]

Early constructions of council power to entertain, much less act on, such complaints were restrictive. The council of the Eighth Circuit concluded in late 1940 "that no such power is given under the section of the Administrative [Office] Act which creates and defines the duties and powers of the Council";[126] but this interpretation was gradually eroded. By the 1950s council jurisdiction over alleged untoward conduct had won wide acceptance.[127]

[123] "Appendix A, Business of the Judicial Council of the Third Circuit," in William H. Speck, "Memorandum on the Powers of the Judicial Councils," July 13, 1949, mimeograph (Administrative Office of the United States Courts, Washington, D.C.).

[124] "The Judicial Council of the Third Circuit," *Federal Rules Decisions*, 10 (1951), 216.

[125] Henry P. Chandler to Kimbrough Stone, January 3, 1941, Administrative Office Correspondence, 57-A-122, Box 2.

[126] Kimbrough Stone to Henry P. Chandler, December 18, 1940, Administrative Office Correspondence, 57-A-122, Box 2.

[127] See *Judicial Conference Report, 1956*, p. 31.

Although only occasionally called upon to review "cases of malfeasance of a judge who is able and willing but refuses to do the things that he should do,"[128] councils have often found themselves confronted with the more common problems of "advancing age, with its accompanying advance in senility, lack of mental powers, and alcoholism."[129] They have also been faced with failure of district judges to appear at conferences for newly appointed judges,[130] habitual failure on their part to submit to the Administrative Office reports on pending cases,[131] their misclassification of court personnel,[132] and, from the beginning, delays. The Fourth Circuit Council, at its first session in January 1940, resolved: "Complaint having been made through the Director of the Administrative Office of the United States Courts of delay in the decision of cases 3698 and 3699 pending in the Western District of Virginia, it is decided to request Judge [John] Paul to advise the Council forthwith as to the status of these cases, the reason for delay in decision and as to when decision may be expected."[133]

Serious charges of unethical and criminal conduct have come before the councils. Thus they have considered a judge's appointment of relatives as court officers,[134] their practice before him,[135] as well as cases of outright judicial

---

[128] Albert B. Maris, Senate Subcommittee on Improvements in Judicial Machinery, *Hearings, Judicial Reform Act, 1968*, p. 55.

[129] *Ibid.*

[130] "Minutes of the Meeting of the Second Circuit Council," June 5, 1963, p. 4, Clark Papers.

[131] "Minutes of the Meeting of the Committee on Judicial Statistics," March 29, 1946, Administrative Office Correspondence, 60-A-328, Box 4.

[132] *Judicial Conference Report, 1960*, p. 9.

[133] "Fourth Circuit Council Minutes," p. 2, Parker Papers, Box 54.

[134] See Henry P. Chandler to Elmore Whitehurst, December 2, 1940, p. 3, Administrative Office Correspondence, 60-A-328, Box 35.

[135] Harvey M. Johnsen to J. Edward Lumbard, December 14, 1960, Clark Papers.

401

corruption.[136] By resolution of the Special Session of the 1969 Judicial Conference, the councils were specifically authorized to review extra-judicial activities of the judges for which remuneration is received. When such duties were deemed "in the public interest or are justifiable by exceptional circumstances," councils could permit them; otherwise they were prohibited.[137]

Almost as sensitive for the councils are allegations of improper practices on the part of supporting personnel in the courts.[138] The refusal of a court reporter to disclose his earnings from a private reporting business for fear it would result in reducing his government compensation and establish a precedent unfavorable to the reporters became a *cause célèbre* in the Third Circuit before being settled by that circuit's council.[139] And in the Fourth Circuit the council considered allegations that the clerk of the District Court for the Southern District of West Virginia had campaigned for the nomination of a senatorial candidate in the 1946 Democratic Primary.[140]

Within their wide range of disciplinary jurisdiction, the councils act in the capacity of a *conseil d'état*. They do not ordinarily set the standard of conduct which is one of custom, Judicial Conference resolution, or statutory law, but they do bring the charges, sit in judgment on the case, de-

[136] John Biggs, Jr., Senate Subcommittee on Improvements in Judicial Machinery, *Hearings on Judicial Fitness*, part I, 1966, pp. 18-19.

[137] *Judicial Conference Report, 1969*, p. 42; but see the action of November session substantially modifying the June resolution, *ibid.*, pp. 50-52.

[138] Interview with Orie L. Phillips, February 22, 1965, Washington, D.C. See *Judicial Conference Report, 1956*, p. 31.

[139] See Henry P. Chandler to William B. Kirkpatrick, April 5, 1949, Administrative Office Correspondence, 60-A-328, Box 8; "The Judicial Council of the Third Circuit," *Federal Rules Decisions*, 10 (1951), 207-24.

[140] See Morris A. Soper, "Report to the Judicial Conference of Senior Circuit Judges of the state of business in the Fourth Judicial Circuit during the past year," October 1, 1946, Parker Papers, Box 55.

cide it, and set the penalty. "The usual process," as described by Judge Biggs, "has been to issue something in the nature of a rule to show cause or a notice to the individual judge who is involved, requesting him or asking him to appear before . . . the judicial council with attorneys of his own choosing, so that the matter can be explained and so he could be heard.[141] If other parties such as the Administrative Office or court reporters are affected, they too are notified and may be represented at the hearing.[142]

As in any proceeding of this nature, the councils may receive testimony and statements presented by the parties.[143] They lack the power of subpoena, however, a failing which one judge thought caused "difficulty in some instances in getting information which ordinarily is not available."[144] But the absence of this power has more subtle consequences, for without it councils find it difficult to discipline judges whose relations with litigants and members of the bar are of questionable propriety. "I am sure you appreciate," Chief Judge J. Edward Lumbard told a congressional committee, "the difficulty of getting members of the bar to make a formal complaint or even to communicate to a judicial council what they might know unless there is the power to compel them to give this information."[145]

Councils may adhere to customary standards of due process but they are under no obligation to do so unless the proceedings involve federal magistrates or referees in bankruptcy.[146] Thus council proceedings are sometimes *ex parte.*

[141] John Biggs, Jr., Senate Subcommittee on Improvements in Judicial Machinery, *Hearings on Judicial Fitness,* part I, 1966, p. 17. See "The Judicial Council of the Third Circuit," p. 218.

[142] *Ibid.*   [143] *Ibid.*

[144] John Biggs, Jr., Senate Subcommittee on Improvements in Judicial Machinery, *Hearings on Judicial Fitness,* part I, 1966, p. 11.

[145] Senate Subcommittee on Improvements in Judicial Machinery, *Hearings, Judicial Reform Act,* 1968, p. 265.

[146] 28 *U.S.C.* 631(h), which closely adheres to the language of 11 *U.S.C.* 62(b), respecting referees in bankruptcy reads: "Before any order or removal shall be entered, a full specification of the

A Special Session of the Tenth Circuit's Council, meeting in December 1965, felt no such obligation in disciplining Chief Judge Stephen Chandler of the Western District of Oklahoma. It gave him: "no notice of the calling of the Special Session or of its purpose, . . . no opportunity to be present during the deliberations of the Special Session, no opportunity to hear the nature of any complaint about him, no opportunity to rebut complaints, cross-examine accusers, or present explanations or evidence in his own behalf, and no opportunity to be represented at the Special Session by counsel."[147] In the words of his attorneys, "he was deprived of liberty and property by secret and summary procedures so shocking that they recall those of the British Star Chamber."[148] Ultimately, the council reversed itself and afforded Judge Chandler an opportunity to appear before it with his attorneys.[149]

Pillars of Passivity

Given their broad responsibilities, the councils would seem to constitute veritable "lightning rods" for meeting malfunctions in the federal court system. Their actual performance, however, suggests a contrary view. At a discussion on judicial administration held in 1956, Chief Judge Charles E. Clark of the Second Circuit Court of Appeals asked: "How should the circuit council try to push, to stim-

---

charges shall be furnished to the magistrate, and he shall be accorded by the judge or judges of the removing court, courts, council, or councils an opportunity to be heard on the charges." See also *Dubnoff v. Goldstein*, 385 F.2d 717, 723 (C.C.A. 2d 1967).

[147] Brief, Supreme Court of the United States, October Term, 1965, No. 1111, Miscellaneous, *Stephen S. Chandler v. Judicial Council of the Tenth Circuit of the United States*, p. 10.

[148] *Ibid.*, p. 17.

[149] See *Chandler v. Judicial Council*, 382 U.S. 1003 (1966); Judge Chandler, however, refused to appear and the hearing was cancelled. See *Chandler v. Judicial Council*, 398 U.S. 74, 80 (1969).

ulate, and to lead the various district courts?"[150] From many councils comes the reply: "not very hard." Passivity, not activity, has typically characterized the work of circuit councils.[151] There exist several reasons for this inert condition.

Much depends on the chief judge of the circuit. Without his leadership, council effectiveness wanes,[152] and his outright disinterest assures impotence. Such was the situation in the Second Circuit under Senior Circuit Judge Learned Hand. Administrative work, he once said, "I utterly loathe . . . and thoroughly despise, as 'work for the learned pig,' as John Grey used to say of conveyancing."[153] Not every chief judge takes Hand's position, but even so discretion may prove the better part of valor in supervising the work of fellow judges. The chief judges' burdens are weighty indeed. As described by Judge Clark, the presiding judge of the appellate court "must keep his own court running with full judicial personnel, appropriate calendars, reasonably prompt decisions, and smooth operation. . . . Second is his ceremonial duties, organizing and running the annual Circuit Conference, memorial and other ceremonies together with patiently listening to all sorts of complaints and suggestions from District Attorneys, court reporters, attorneys, bar associations, court librarians, court clerks and assistants, and so on."[154] His work on the Judicial Conference and its committees further consumes his time and energies as do his duties as putative administrator of the district courts

[150] Charles E. Clark, "The Role of the United States Court of Appeals in Law Administration," *Conference on Judicial Administration*, Series No. 16 (Chicago, 1956), p. 96.

[151] See Warren E. Burger, "Courts on Trial: A Call for Action Against Delay," *Federal Rules Decisions*, 22 (1958), 77.

[152] Interview with J. Edward Lumbard, December 30, 1964, New York, New York.

[153] Learned Hand to D. Lawrence Groner, April 5, 1944, Groner Papers, Box 11.

[154] Charles E. Clark to J. Edward Lumbard, January 5, 1961, Clark Papers.

405

within his circuit. In the latter role, chief judges struggle to meet complaints from the Judicial Conference as well as from litigants, prosecutors, and bar groups, all of which lack any legal recourse short of petitioning for impeachment.[155]

Conceived as grass-roots centers of administrative power, the councils operate in close proximity to the trial courts. The same judges who sit on the councils in an administrative capacity sit on the courts of appeal in a judicial capacity. They are then called upon to review the acts of judges whose courts generate much of the appellate tribunals' judicial business. They are required, in short, to consider the behavior of judges with whom they interact on a judicial and sometimes even personal basis. To avoid unnecessary friction and to maintain the institutional prestige of the courts, appellate judges adopt "a certain judicial etiquette in our dealing with judges lower in the federal system, whose acts we are called on to review on appeal. . . ."[156]

This "etiquette" is perhaps even more pronounced in administrative relations. Councils tend to practice a policy of diplomatic accommodation with the trial judges. It is a policy of formal deference in some instances. The judges of the Ninth Circuit's council have resolved, for example, not "to take any action which might be construed by the district

---

[155] Justice Stephen J. Field declared in *Bradley v. Fisher*, 80 U.S. 335, 350 (1871): "In this country the judges of the superior courts of record are only responsible to the people, or the authorities constituted by the people, from whom they receive their commissions, for the manner in which they discharge the great trusts of their office. . . . [They] . . . are not liable to civil actions for their judicial acts, even when such acts are in excess of their jurisdiction, and are alleged to have been done maliciously or corruptly." See *Pierson v. Ray*, 386 U.S. 554-55 (1966) which adheres to the *Bradley* rule.

[156] Calvert Magruder, "The Trials and Tribulations of an Intermediate Appellate Court," *Cornell Law Quarterly*, 44 (Fall 1958), 3. For an extended and excellent discussion of district court-court of appeals relations in the Second Circuit, see Marvin Schick, *Learned Hand's Court* (Baltimore, 1970), pp. 133-41.

judges as an effort to crack the whip over them."[157] As they put it, "school-masterish supervision" would entail the loss of "inestimable benefits of a judicial system handled by trial judges who are answerable to no man, and under no control other than that of their own consciences."[158] It would foster a "feeling on the part of the judge that he was just another employee taking orders from a judicial council acting as a quasi board of directors."[159]

This philosophy has been less clearly articulated in other circuits, but nevertheless operative.[160] It provides the background against which councils have failed to act, especially on problems involving judicial behavior. In this sensitive area, the council in the Ninth Circuit refused to act against judges who charged the government for maintenance expenditures of dubious validity,[161] while that in the Third Circuit defeated outright a proposal to override a district judge's appointment of bailiffs as appraisers in bankruptcy.[162] Even in so routine a matter as personnel qualifications, councils have refused to infringe upon the district judge's prerogatives in selecting trial court officers. This "hands off" attitude was summed up by one former Circuit Chief Judge who asked, "What do the circuit judges know of the man to be appointed?"[163]

Such deference to trial judges may relate to the council's remoteness from the lower courts rather than to their proximity. Although situated at the "grass roots" level, councils "are too far removed for the daily and constant supervision needed."[164] They find it difficult, in the absence of staffs, to

[157] "Resolution of the Judicial Council of the Ninth Circuit," November 13, 1959, Clark Papers.

[158] *Ibid.*   [159] *Ibid.*

[160] See Senate Committee on Appropriations, *Field Study,* 1959.

[161] Interview with Orie L. Phillips.

[162] Interview with J. Edward Lumbard.

[163] Interview with Simon Sobeloff.

[164] Charles E. Clark to John Biggs, Jr., August 22, 1955, Administrative Office Correspondence, 60-A-328, Box 15.

obtain information on conditions in the district courts, much less to exercise continuous oversight.[165] Even if adequate staff facilities existed, at least one chief judge doubted "whether we should vest in a staff officer, however competent he may be, . . . extensive supervision and authority over the daily operations of the district courts."[166]

Council inactivity is also rooted in a pervasive attachment to the ideal of local self-government and an independent judiciary, independent of the councils as well as of the more remote Judicial Conference, Administrative Office, and Congress. Responsibility for district court administration rests fundamentally, and perhaps finally, with the district judges, not with the appellate judges. "[A]bsentee management," Chief Judge William Hastie of the Third Circuit told a Senate subcommittee, "does not work well. I don't care what power you give on paper. . . . [The] council sitting at the seat of the court of appeals . . . cannot efficiently exercise management control over a large number of courts scattered in various places."[167]

And of course some chief judges and their councils did not even try. No other chief judge defended his colleagues from outside interference more assiduously than did Joseph C. Hutcheson, Jr. of the Fifth Circuit. When the Administrative Office transmitted a petitioner's complaint of delay in one of the districts of his circuit, Hutcheson "objected strenuously" and demanded that it not "follow such a course in reference to his circuit in the future."[168] Thereafter, the Office strove mightily to avoid pressing this judge who, in any case, was "inclined to support his judges."[169]

[165] "Statement of John R. Brown," Senate Subcommittee on Improvements in Judicial Machinery, *Hearings, Federal Judges and Courts*, 1969, pp. 260, 323-24.
[166] William H. Hastie, *ibid.*, p. 373.
[167] *Ibid.*
[168] Leland L. Tolman to Monte M. Lemann, November 3, 1950, Administrative Office Correspondence, 60-A-328, Box 4.
[169] Memorandum, Henry P. Chandler to Elmore Whitehurst, June 23, 1955, 59-A-48, Box 142.

So, too, the councils provide a formidable defense against congressional demands for reform or economy.[170] Their role as "insulators" became evident when word that a district judge in New York City had taken a three-month world tour induced the Senate Appropriations Committee to demand an explanation.[171] "I should think," the former chief judge of the circuit declared, "that this is not an occasion to express public criticism of the judges." In fact, he continued, "we should probably defend a judge's right to a reasonable amount of vacation as against implications of the Senate inquiry."[172] A month later, the judge involved was exonerated.[173]

For whatever reasons, councils or their chief judge remain passive in the face of administrative shortcomings. Inaction has a cumulative effect on the authority of the councils as viable institutions. "Their many failures to act," one critic contends, "have themselves contributed to a feeling on the part of many judges that Section 332 gave the councils no real power; and some judges have thereby been encouraged to defy the councils."[174]

Intervention by Higher Authority

Into the breach thus created has stepped the agency of the more inclusive community, namely the Judicial Conference and its committees. They assume an appellate role when, as Chief Justice Charles Evans Hughes perceived,

[170] See "Minutes of the Judicial Council of the Second Circuit," June 4, 1959, Clark Papers.

[171] See Warren Olney III to J. Edward Lumbard, November 14, 1960, Clark Papers.

[172] Charles E. Clark to J. Edward Lumbard, November 16, 1960, ibid.

[173] J. Edward Lumbard to Warren Olney III, December 20, 1960, ibid.

[174] J. Edward Lumbard, "The Place of the Federal Judicial Councils in the Administration of the Courts," American Bar Association Journal, 47 (February 1961), 170.

there exists "any need for the intervention of a central body."[175] That "need" arises in its starkest form whenever councils wholly fail to act or fail to act uniformly on problems well within their jurisdiction.[176]

Highly sensitive issues involving personnel management may paralyze the appellate judges. A district court which wrongly appointed its bailiff as an appraiser in bankruptcy received no rebuke from the council.[177] The Administrative Office director, charged with administering the bankruptcy system, protested to the Judicial Conference. Acting on the recommendation of its Committee on Bankruptcy Administration, that body "disapproved the practice as improper and detrimental to the proper administration of justice in bankruptcy cases."[178] Similarly, with the council remaining passive, a trial judge appointed as his secretary a man lacking the requisite qualifications for the position.[179] A committee of the Judicial Conference so found, and successfully urged that the full Conference instruct the director of the Administrative Office to "remove him from the payroll forthwith."[180]

And so as Chief Justice Earl Warren observed in a different context, an instrumentality of national administration "tends to involve itself in many things which should be pri-

[175] "Administration in the Federal Courts—Administrative Office Bill—Extract from the proceedings of the Judicial Conference: September 30, 1938, pp. 179-94," mimeograph (Washington, D.C.: United States Supreme Court, n.d.), p. 19.

[176] The June 10, 1969 Judicial Conference acted on judicial ethics, but provided no guidelines or standards for the circuit councils. Several councils subsequently rendered conflicting interpretations of "appropriate non-judicial services." Thereafter the November 1969 session of the Conference transferred somewhat narrower supervision to itself. See *Judicial Conference Report, 1969*, p. 51.

[177] Interview with John Biggs, Jr., February 28, 1965, Wilmington, Delaware.

[178] *Judicial Conference Report, 1961*, p. 42.

[179] *Ibid., 1960*, p. 9.   [180] *Ibid.*

marily of local concern."[181] But it intervenes "because the power given to local agencies to remedy admittedly bad situations is not exercised."[182] It acts too because it represents a national constituency rather than a local or regional one, and because it possesses prestige and access to sanctions unavailable to the councils.

Neither the Conference nor the Administrative Office, however, are central offices for the management of the courts. They enjoy no power to discipline misbehaving judges. On more than one occasion the Conference has felt constrained to resort to exhortation, calling on judges to use "the councils to promote efficiency . . . and to execute the administrative policies laid down by law and by the Judicial Conference."[183] But it can utilize no legal sanctions, because the Conference has never been deemed a court.[184]

Some councils have acted, but not many and not often. When they have responded positively to administrative problems in their circuits, it was because their members believed that they were duty bound "to take the initiative . . . in preventing nonfeasances and misfeasances, in anticipating difficult situations, and in taking steps to prevent difficulties which might otherwise arise."[185] But this was easier

[181] "Address of the Honorable Earl Warren," *Federal Rules Decisions*, 35 (1964), 185.

[182] *Ibid.*

[183] *Judicial Conference Report, 1960*, p. 16.

[184] That the Conference was not a court became a salient issue in 1943. At that time, Senior Circuit Judges Orie L. Phillips and John J. Parker and Chief Justice Harlan F. Stone gave serious consideration to vesting the appointment of certain "inferior" officers in a legislatively created Court of Judicial Administration of the United States. It would be composed of all members of the Judicial Conference except the Chief Justice and would exercise as much jurisdiction as Congress chose to grant it. See Wayne L. Wilson, "The Federal Corrections Act: A Case Study of Judicial Lobbying" (unpublished thesis, Department of Political Science, Duke University, 1971), pp. 75-76.

[185] Justin Miller to D. Lawrence Groner, January 29, 1944, Stephens Papers, Box 28.

said than done. As Chief Judge Charles E. Clark once observed, the councils' powers might be sweeping in principle, but in reality they were "so broad and general as to seem finally vague."[186]

Nowhere did reality depart so sharply from the ideal than when councils sought to placate demands made on them by Congress, the Judicial Conference, or local bars and thereby collided with strong-willed judges. Confronted with resistance from such trial judges, councils have been thoroughly defeated in efforts to "set up at least some summer schedules"[187] in the district courts,[188] to remove a district judge's secretary,[189] and to secure the retirement of the colorful District Judge for the Southern District of Ohio, Mell G. Underwood. He "just was not doing much work," and the chief circuit judge reported, "a number of mandamus cases were filed against him in our court."[190] When presented with the unanimous council resolution urging him to retire from the bench, Underwood allegedly retorted that "they have no authority to remove me, and they've found that out. I told them to go to hell."[191]

Strategies of Compliance

Persuasion affords councils their initial and often sole strategy in implementing administrative policies. After all district judges hold important trump cards. If they "have

[186] Charles E. Clark to J. Edward Lumbard, February 26, 1958, Clark Papers.

[187] Charles E. Clark to John W. Clancy, May 29, 1956, ibid.

[188] See John W. Clancy to Charles E. Clark, May 28, 1956, ibid.

[189] Warren Olney III, U.S., Congress, Senate Committee on Appropriations, Hearings, on H.R. 11666, Departments of State, Justice, the Judiciary, and Related Agencies Appropriation for 1961, 86th Cong., 2d Sess., 1960, p. 508.

[190] Paul C. Weick, Senate Subcommittee on Improvements in Judicial Machinery, Hearings, Federal Judges and Courts, 1969, p. 381.

[191] Quoted in Jack E. Frankel, "Case for Judicial Disciplinary Measures," Journal of the American Judicature Society, 49 (April 1966), 223.

not been sold on" a council policy, ". . . if they don't believe in it, if they are not trying to make it work . . . ," then, asserted Chief Judge Hastie, ". . . it is not going to work well."[192]

As another practitioner of the art put it, lifetime judges cannot "be bossed around—they respond to more delicate handling."[193] And more often than not this "delicate handling" must come from the busy presiding judge of the court of appeals rather than from the collegial council which he heads. That body is ill-designed to "take the initiative, but can at most give the Chief Judge a little moral support."[194] The chief judge, however, enjoys no special prerogatives as Judge Charles E. Clark, former Dean of the Yale Law School, discovered. He thought himself "in a worse business than when [he] was dean" for he now possessed "no semblance of power whatsoever."[195]

Thus chief judges must seek to execute their council's policies by "wheedling,"[196] a strategy which may bring results,[197] but which may also prove futile.[198] They appeal to flattery and to institutional loyalty in the face of congressional and judicial criticism and of threats, real and imaginary, of remedial legislation or budgetary retaliation.[199] And to bolster their case, chief judges may note the deep concern of that august body expressed at its most recent

[192] Senate Subcommittee on Improvements in Judicial Machinery, *Hearings, Federal Judges and Courts*, 1969, p. 375.
[193] Charles E. Clark to Richard A. Merrill, April 5, 1963, Clark Papers.
[194] Charles E. Clark to J. Edward Lumbard, January 5, 1961, *ibid.*
[195] Charles E. Clark to William Clark, May 31, 1956, *ibid.*
[196] Interview with Richard H. Chambers, January 26, 1965, Washington, D.C.
[197] "Minutes of the Judicial Council of the Second Circuit," June 14, 1955, Clark Papers; see also Justin Miller to D. Lawrence Groner, January 29, 1944, Stephens Papers, Box 28.
[198] Learned Hand to Frank Cooper, January 17, 1941, Administrative Office Correspondence, 60-A-328, Box 1; Cooper to Hand, January 22, 1941, *ibid.*
[199] Interview with J. Edward Lumbard.

session,[200] or urge, as did Senior Circuit Judge Learned Hand, that a district judge behind in his work "act on this case, because when I go to Washington on the conference, this very matter will be mentioned, and they will say, 'What happened here?' "[201] Hand might have added, as did his counterpart in the Fourth Circuit, that his suggestion was "not intended as in any sense a criticism of your administration of your District."[202] Parker merely wished "to show our work up to the Conference in its true light and not permit unfavorable inferences to be drawn as to what we are doing in our Circuit."[203]

A hard-pressed chief judge may even seek a Judicial Conference resolution on a particular issue in order to strengthen his hand in dealing with a recalcitrant judge.[204] Conference words and attitudes may be readily invoked, but no chief judge can normally expect the Chief Justice nor individual members of the Judicial Conference to fight his wars for him. Chief Justice Earl Warren reportedly never assisted a hard-pressed chief judge,[205] a fact which Chief Judge Clark knew when he poured out the troubles he was then encountering with an uncooperative district judge.[206] He sent the letter, Clark wrote Warren, "more that you be at all times fully informed than as a request for any action

[200] Charles E. Clark to Clarence G. Galston, March 15, 1956, Clark Papers.

[201] U.S., Congress, House, Special Subcommittee on Bankruptcy and Reorganization of Committee on the Judiciary, *Hearings, on H.R. 4394, Administration of the Bankruptcy Act: Referees in Bankruptcy,* 77th Cong., 1st Sess., 1941, pp. 244-45.

[202] John J. Parker to Frank K. Myers, September 13, 1938, Parker Papers, Box 54.

[203] *Ibid.*

[204] Telephone interview with John Airhart, February 5, 1965, Washington, D.C.; interview with J. Edward Lumbard.

[205] Telephone interview with John Airhart; interview with J. Edward Lumbard.

[206] Charles E. Clark to Earl Warren, May 15, 1956, Clark Papers.

414

on your part."[207] Warren, in reply, expressed his sympathy for Clark's difficulties and applauded his efforts, but suggested "that you have done about all you can reasonably do at the moment."[208] No gratuitous offers of aid, such as might have come from Taft or even Vinson, accompanied the Chief Justice's letter.

In the same manner that resolutions of the Judicial Conference may enhance the persuasive capacities of councils and their chief judges, so too imperative legislative language may assist them. Both the 1964 Criminal Justice Act and the Jury Selection Act of 1968 contain identical phrases stipulating that a district court "shall modify" its assigned counsel or jury selection plan when so directed by the judicial council of the circuit under the former act[209] and by "the reviewing panel" under the latter.[210]

Studies by the Administrative Office can perform a function analogous to that of Conference resolutions or statutes. Seeking to alleviate the dockets in the Eastern District of New York, seriously clogged in the mid-1950's, Chief Judge Clark called on the agency's resources after the 85-year-old court clerk allied with his chief judge blocked plans to establish a jury pool operated by an experienced calendar commissioner.[211] An Administrative Office study, thought Clark, was "one way of building a fire under the aged gentleman."[212] And when completed, the agency's recommendations were employed by him to move the clerk to action.[213] This strategy proved highly successful, for the clerk,

[207] *Ibid.*
[208] Earl Warren to Charles E. Clark, May 21, 1956, *ibid.*
[209] 18 *U.S.C.* 3006A(a).   [210] 28 *U.S.C.* 1863(a).
[211] Charles E. Clark to Will Shafroth, December 17, 1955, Clark Papers; see also Percy B. Gilkes to Elmore Whitehurst, October 7, 1955, Administrative Office Correspondence, 60-A-594, Box 3.
[212] Charles E. Clark to Will Shafroth, December 17, 1955, Clark Papers.
[213] Charles E. Clark to Elmore Whitehurst, April 12, 1957, Administrative Office Correspondence, 60-A-594, Box 3.

appointed during the presidency of Benjamin Harrison, not merely moved, but retired after 65 years of service in the Eastern District.[214]

Some difficult administrative problems necessitate more novel strategies. Persuading incompetent and senile judges to retire from active service as presiding officers of district courts ranked as the greatest challenge faced by a chief circuit judge prior to 1958 when Congress fixed a maximum age of 70 years for such officers.[215] Chief Judge Charles Clark used an assortment of techniques to induce three chief district judges then in their mid-80s to step down from their administrative posts. He applied pressure on one judge's secretary,[216] while in another case, he made "use of a sort of high-grade blackmail,"[217] by threatening "that the Bar Association was going to take the matter to the newspapers."[218] The entire proceeding is tortuous. One chief judge recalled it as being "rather unpleasant, both for the person who goes to see the aged judge and . . . for the aged judge himself."[219] So the Sixth Circuit Council had discovered in the Underwood affair. But, the chief judge declared: "We kept after him, and the largest newspaper in Ohio with statewide circulation published some accounts concerning the way he was handling his work, and he finally called me up and said his name had been 'dragged down in the mud far enough,' and that he would retire, and he did retire."[220] But one chief judge has stated his circuit council's disinclination "to handle very sensitive matters in

[214] *New York Times*, November 1, 1957, p. 18.
[215] 72 *Stat.* 497.
[216] Charles E. Clark to Samuel C. Coleman, October 18, 1954, Clark Papers.
[217] Clark, in *Conference on Judicial Administration*, series no. 16, p. 96.
[218] *Ibid.*
[219] John Biggs, Jr., Senate Subcommittee on Improvements in Judicial Machinery, *Hearings on Judicial Fitness*, part i, 1966, p. 15.
[220] Paul C. Weick, Senate Subcommittee on Improvements in Judicial Machinery, *Hearings, Federal Judges and Courts*, 1969, p. 381.

a district court by the promulgation of formal orders issuing as lofty commands from Olympus."[221] Other judges would likely agree with his belief that the chief judge alone could act more tactfully and effectively than a collegial institution.[222]

Formal Council Sanctions

Not all council policies are executed informally or by the chief circuit judge acting alone. Formal council orders may be issued and implemented. Ever since 1948, when Congress revised the Judicial Code, the circuit judicial councils have been empowered to "make all necessary orders."[223] And, stated the council of the Third Circuit, "having thus acted, its orders have the force of law."[224] Doubt has been

[221] Clement Haynsworth, *ibid.*, p. 411; see J. Edward Lumbard, U.S., Congress, Senate Subcommittee on Separation of Powers of the Committee of the Judiciary, *Hearings, on the Independence of Federal Judges*, 91st Cong., 1st Sess., 1970, p. 70.

[222] *Ibid.*

[223] 28 *U.S.C.* 332. This power was not explicit in Section 306 of the Administrative Office Act, 53 *Stat.* 1224, which provided that "It shall be the duty of the district judges promptly to carry out the *directions* of the council as to the administration of the business of their respective courts." The 1948 revision of the Judicial Code simplified the language and consolidated the delegation of power in a two sentence final paragraph: "Each judicial council shall make all necessary *orders* for the effective and expeditious administration of the business of the courts within the circuit. The district judges shall promptly carry into effect all orders of the judicial council." [Italics added.] The word "orders" was thus substituted for "directions." The only explanation offered by the House Judiciary Committee for this alteration was that "changes in phraseology were made." See U.S., Congress, House Committee on the Judiciary, *Revision of Title 28, United States Code*, H. Rept. 308 to accompany H.R. 3214, 80th Cong., 1st Sess., 1947, p. A46. And in 1961, a committee of the Judicial Conference minimized the importance of the language change. The Committee stated that it "would seem to have been one of form and emphasis rather than of substance." House Committee on the Judiciary, *Report on the Responsibilities*, 1961, p. 2.

[224] "The Judicial Council of the Third Circuit," pp. 214-16, citing

417

cast on this position by the Supreme Court's 1970 decision in *Chandler v. Judicial Council*. There, the Court found "nothing in the legislative history to suggest that the Judicial Council was intended to be anything other than an administrative body functioning in a very limited area in a narrow sense as a 'board of directors' for the circuit. . . . We find no indication that Congress intended to or did vest traditional judicial powers in the Councils."[225] Justice John M. Harlan, concurring, reached the opposite conclusion. He interpreted the legislative history to mean "that, at least in the issuance of orders to district judges to regulate the exercise of their official duties, the Judicial Council acts as a judicial tribunal. . . ."[226]

Formal orders from the council to a district court or judge are, however, very much the exception. The council in the District of Columbia "has reportedly never found it necessary or advisable to enter a formal order,"[227] while that in the Eighth Circuit has similarly relied on informal methods.[228]

When such formal orders are issued, they often relate to the more mundane aspects of administration. Freezing a district judge's regular docket assignments until he has de-

---

Yakus v. United States, 321 U.S. 414, 425 (1944). As they are not self-executing, council orders must be addressed to a judge or other officer of the court, *ibid.*

[225] 398 U.S. 74, 86 n. 7 (1969).

[226] *Ibid.*, p. 102. In fact, as Justice Harlan noted and as respondent conceded, ". . . at least one of [the Council's] enumerated powers— the power to remove referees for cause—'can properly be regarded as judicial,' and it is not at all clear that any of them is beyond the range of the permissible activities of an Article III court." *Ibid.*, p. 110. See also "Statement of Carl L. Shipley," Senate Subcommittee on Separation of Powers, *Hearings on the Independence*, 1970, p. 98.

[227] Prettyman, "The Duties of a Circuit Chief Judge," *American Bar Association Journal*, 46 (1960), 634-35.

[228] Harvey M. Johnsen to J. Edward Lumbard, December 14, 1960, Clark Papers.

cided cases already under advisement is not uncommon,[229] however unpopular it may be with trial judges.[230] More dramatic is the course of action proposed by Chief Judge Richard H. Chambers of the Ninth Circuit. He suggested to a Senate subcommittee that a problem judge should be punished by temporarily assigning him to "a nonexistent place" where court was never held or to a place of court where little judicial business was generated.[231] Utilized far less than the assignment power has been the council's power to certify a judge as physically or mentally disabled, thereby reducing him to junior status on the court and creating a vacant judgeship to be filled by the President.[232] A seemingly potent formal power, its use has sometimes involved a strong element of consent, if not on the judge's part, then on that of his wife and children.[233]

Even if a council never actually employed its formal powers, the mere threat to cancel a judicial assignment or to certify disability "has resulted in definite consequences in the form of action by the intended subjects of the orders."[234] Either order, if issued, would have reflected on the incumbent judge's physical and/or mental capacity. It constitutes a public vote of no confidence in him, and is aimed directly at his pride and vanity. A veteran magistrate, anxious to re-

[229] See Henry P. Chandler to Harold R. Medina, January 8, 1952, Administrative Office Correspondence, 60-A-328, Box 4; J. Edward Lumbard to Sylvester J. Ryan, November 29, 1960, Clark Papers.

[230] Sylvester J. Ryan to J. Edward Lumbard, December 7, 1960, *ibid.*

[231] Senate, Subcommittee on Improvements in Judicial Machinery, *Hearings, Judicial Reform Act, 1968,* pp. 249-52.

[232] 28 *U.S.C.* 372(b); Joseph Tydings, Senate Subcommittee on Improvements in Judicial Machinery, *Hearings, Judicial Reform Act, 1968,* p. 254.

[233] Clement Haynsworth, Senate Subcommittee on Improvements in Judicial Machinery, *Hearings, Federal Judges and Courts,* 1969, pp. 411-12.

[234] Richard H. Chambers to Olin D. Johnston, June 20, 1961, Senate Subcommittee File on H.R. 6690.

419

tain his hard-won reputation, can ill afford to ignore it, though some do.[235]

But the problem, which "has baffled the members of the judiciary," persists.[236] "What happens," queried Judge John Biggs, "if a Council makes a decision and an order and directs a district judge to carry out . . . that order and the judge refuses to do it?"[237]

No difficulty arises if a non-tenured officer of the court is the object of an order.[238] A council may direct that the district court remove him from office for refusal to obey the order.[239] Removal or other disciplinary steps by the trial court may be ordered notwithstanding the statutory language of Section 332, which directs compliance with council orders by the district judges rather than by the court. The Judicial Council of the Third Circuit declared this distinction merely technical because "the courts and the judges who dictate and direct its action are one."[240]

A recalcitrant court employee such as court reporter could also be disciplined by a proceeding in the district court brought "in the name of the judicial council to secure an order in the nature of a writ of mandamus to be directed to the reporter." The order so secured "would be a 'necessary' and 'appropriate' aid to the jurisdiction of the district

[235] Interview with John Biggs, Jr.

[236] John Biggs, Jr., Senate Subcommittee on Improvements in Judicial Machinery, *Hearings on Judicial Fitness*, part I, 1966, p. 11.

[237] *Ibid.*

[238] The Supreme Court of the United States has declared: "All offices, the tenure of which is not fixed by the Constitution or limited by law, must be held either during good behavior, or . . . must be held at the will and discretion of some department of the government, and subject to removal at pleasure. . . . And if removable at pleasure, . . . it would seem to be a sound and necessary rule, to consider the power of removal as incident to the power of appointment." *Ex parte Hennen*, 38 U.S. 230, 258-59 (1839).

[239] "The Judicial Council of the Third Circuit," p. 217.

[240] *Ibid.*

court for the court could not properly exercise its jurisdiction without the proper functioning of its reporter."[241]

However, deprivation of a judge's judicial power poses a truly serious issue in that it may infringe upon his judicial discretion and constitutional rights. At least one district judge has been removed from a case in which the court of appeals twice reversed him,[242] while the Third Circuit removed all criminal cases from a judge suspected of corrupt practices.[243] But such actions have often been those of the court of appeals rather than of the circuit judicial council. Expanded appellate court use of extraordinary writs to control the actions of trial judges was sanctioned by the Supreme Court in *LaBuy v. Howes Leather Co.*[244] Justice Clark for the Court minced no words about the thrust of the decision. "We believe," he concluded, "that supervisory control of the District Courts by the Courts of Appeals is necessary to proper judicial administration in the federal system. The All Writs Act confers on the Courts of Appeals the discretionary power to issue writs of mandamus in . . . exceptional circumstances. . . ."[245] Shortly thereafter the *LaBuy* case provided the legal bedrock in the running battle between the Tenth Circuit Court of Appeals and District Judge Willis W. Ritter of Utah. Contending that he could not conduct the trial of a particular case in a calm and im-

[241] *Ibid.*, p. 217; see also 28 *U.S.C.* 1651(a), the "All Writs" provision, which reads: "The Supreme Court and all courts established by Act of Congress may issue all writs necessary or appropriate in aid of their respective jurisdiction and agreeable to the usages and principles of law."

[242] "Notes, Judicial Personnel in the Fifth Circuit," *Yale Law Journal*, 73 (November 1963), 120.

[243] John Biggs, Jr., Senate Subcommittee on Improvements in Judicial Machinery, *Hearings on Judicial Fitness*, part I, 1966, p. 19.

[244] 325 U.S. 249 (1956). For an analysis of the *LaBuy* case and its implications, see Charles Allan Wright, "The Doubtful Omniscience of Appellate Courts," *Minnesota Law Review*, 41 (May 1957), 771-78.

[245] *LaBuy v. Howes Leather Co.*, 325 U.S. 249, 259-60 (1956).

partial fashion, the Court first requested that further proceedings in the lower court take place before a judge other than Ritter.[246] The Utah judge refused to comply, whereupon, the Court "ordered that further proceedings . . . be heard before a judge to be designated by the Chief Judge of this Circuit, pursuant to Section 292(b), Title 28 U.S.C. . . ."[247] The appellate judges cited *LaBuy*, but indicated that their order rested either on statutory or natural law foundations. As they put it, the exercise of appellate supervisory control was, in this instance, "found in the all-writ statute[248] or in the exercise of the inherent powers of appellate jurisdiction to effectuate what seems to us to be the manifest ends of justice."[249]

Later, the judges of the same court sought to exercise their supervisory powers as a council instead of as a court. Judge Stephen Chandler of the Western District of Oklahoma became the subject of a major test of the scope of council powers, for in his case the Judicial Council of the Tenth Circuit went even further than had the appellate court in the Ritter case.[250] It ordered that Chandler "take no action whatsoever in any case or proceeding now or hereafter pending in the United States District Court for the Western District of Oklahoma; that all cases and proceedings now assigned to or pending before him . . . be reassigned to and among the other judges of said court; that until the further order of the Judicial Council no cases or proceedings filed or instituted in the United States District Court for the Western District of Oklahoma shall be as-

[246] *United States v. Hatahley*, 257 F.2d 920, 926 (C.C.A. 10th, 1959).

[247] *United States v. Ritter*, 273 F.2d 30, 32 (C.C.A. 10th, 1959).

[248] 28 *U.S.C.* 1651.

[249] *United States v. Ritter*, above, n. 247.

[250] See Brief of Petitioner, "Motion for Leave to File Reply Brief and Reply Brief," in *Chandler v. Judicial Council*, No. 2, Misc. (1969) reprinted in Senate Subcommittee on Separation of Powers, *Hearings on the Independence*, 1970, pp. 794-824.

signed to him for any action whatsoever."[251] In short, the council had "stripped Judge Chandler of his judicial authority and powers and left him only the shell of his Office . . . his office space, his desk, his robe hanging in a closet."[252] Chandler's attorneys argued that his office had been effectively removed from him, thereby depriving him of his constitutional rights under Article III, Section 1 and infringing upon the impeachment powers of Congress.[253] An appeal to the Supreme Court in 1966 for a stay of the order brought no relief. Wary of interjecting itself into the dispute, the Court, by a 7-to-2 vote, held the issue unripe because the order was "entirely interlocutory in character pending further prompt proceedings."[254] However, both Justices Black and Douglas sharply dissented, contending that enforcement of the order would mean "that Judge Chandler is completely barred from performing any of his official duties and in effect is removed or ousted from office pending further orders of the Council."[255] The council, said the dissenters, "is completely without legal authority to issue any such order . . . that no statute purports to authorize it, and that the Constitution forbids it."[256]

Although the Supreme Court failed to hand down a definitive pronouncement on the outer limits of the council's powers under Section 332 in 1966, it heard further arguments on the still live case in 1969.[257] And on June 1, 1970 the Court again denied Judge Chandler relief on his petition for "an order under the All Writs Act [28 U.S.C. 1651, 62 Stat. 944, as amended, 63 Stat. 102] telling the Council

[251] Notarized copy of original Order of the Judicial Council of the Tenth Circuit, *In the Matter of the Honorable Stephen S. Chandler, United States District Judge for the Western District of Oklahoma* (Special Session, December 1965), pp. 3-4.
[252] Brief for Stephen S. Chandler, p. 17.
[253] *Ibid.*
[254] *Chandler v. Judicial Council*, 382 U.S. 1003 (1966).
[255] *Ibid.*, 1004; see *Booth v. United States*, 291 U.S. 339 (1934).
[256] 382 U.S. 1004.
[257] *Chandler v. Judicial Council*, 395 U.S. 956 (1969).

to 'cease acting [in] violation of its powers and in violation of [his] rights as a federal judge and an American citizen.' "[258] Chief Justice Warren Burger, speaking for the Court, emphasized a lack of jurisdiction over the case as grounds for denial.[259] But he concluded by stating that whether or not the court had jurisdiction, "plainly petitioner has not made a case for the extraordinary relief of mandamus or prohibition."[260] The substantive issue of council enforcement powers was never reached by the Court. Instead Burger called for further congressional clarification of these powers because "standing alone, §332 is not a model of clarity in terms of the scope of the judicial council's powers or the procedures to give effect to the final sentence of §332."[261] Nevertheless, in the light of Section 332's legislative history, it is manifestly clear that the framers of the Administrative Office never intended to vest in the councils any power to deprive a judge of his office. Furthermore, both before and after passage of the Administrative

[258] *Chandler v. Judicial Council*, 398 U.S. 74, 76-77 (1969); petition for rehearing denied, 399 U.S. 937 (1969).

[259] Implying that the actions of the Council were "administrative" rather than "judicial" and citing *Marbury v. Madison*, 1 Cranch 137, 173-180 (1803), Burger argued that to find "that we do have appellate jurisdiction in this case would be no mean feat," *Chandler v. Judicial Council*, 398 U.S. 74, 86 (1969). But the Court had no need to achieve such a "feat" because Chandler had failed to exhaust all possible remedies, *ibid.*, pp. 86-89.

[260] *Ibid.*, p. 89. Mr. Justice Harlan assailed this reasoning in his concurring opinion. See *ibid.*, pp. 89-94. He concluded that the Court had jurisdiction because the councils exercised "judicial power," *ibid.*, p. 102. But, argued Harlan, the council's order in this case constituted neither "a 'removal' of Judge Chandler from judicial office [nor] . . . anything other than an effort to move along judicial traffic in the District Court." *Ibid.*, p. 119. Justices Black and Douglas, dissenting, agreed with Harlan that councils exercised judicial power and thus the Supreme Court had jurisdiction. *Ibid.*, pp. 133-35. They found unconstitutional, however, the council's exercise of power which in effect removed a judge from office by means other than impeachment. *Ibid.*, pp. 136-41.

[261] *Ibid.*, p. 85, n. 6.

Office Act, Congress considered separately and in depth this very issue of judicial removal by means other than impeachment.[262] But at the time, constitutional arguments against such removal power prevailed, although scholars and judges as well as legislators have been divided on the issue.[263]

In the absence of the ultimate sanction of removal, a council defied by a district judge might invoke the "All Writs" section of the Judicial Code[264] and entertain a petition for a writ of mandamus or prohibition.[265] A trial judge's violation of the terms of such a writ presumably could be enforced by a contempt citation directed against him.[266] Yet the efficacy of this procedure remains uncertain because until the Chandler case no judge had ever disobeyed one of the rare council orders,[267] much less a writ of mandamus or

[262] See U.S., Congress, House, Committee on the Judiciary, *Hearings, on H.R. 2271, Trial of Good Behavior of United States District Judges*, 75th Cong., 1st Sess., 1937; U.S., Congress, Senate, Subcommittee of the Committee on the Judiciary, *Hearings, on H.R. 146, Trial of Good Behavior of Certain Federal Judges*, 77th Cong., 1st Sess., 1941.

[263] The definitive study of judicial removal by statute remains that of Burke Shartel, "Federal Judges—Appointment, Supervision, and Removal—Some Possibilities Under the Constitution," *Michigan Law Review*, 28 (May 1930), 870-909. Later articles have reiterated his arguments: Jon J. Gallo, "Removal of Federal Judges—New Alternatives to an Old Problem: *Chandler v. Judicial Council of the Tenth Circuit*," *University of California at Los Angeles Law Review*, 13 (1966), 1385-1407; "Case Comments: Courts—Judicial Responsibility—Statutory and Constitutional Problems Relating to Methods for Removal or Discipline of Judges," *Rutgers Law Review*, 21 (Fall 1966), 153-78.

[264] 28 *U.S.C.* 1651.

[265] See "Statement of John Biggs, Jr.," Senate Subcommittee on Improvements in Judicial Machinery, *Hearings on Judicial Fitness*, part I, p. 13.

[266] See "Notes: Judicial Performance in the Fifth Circuit," *Yale Law Journal*, 73 (1963), 122.

[267] See Lumbard, "The Place of the Federal Judicial Councils in the Administration of the Courts," *American Bar Association Journal*, 47 (1961), 169-72.

prohibition. Should a judge challenge the legality of a council order or the issuance of an extraordinary writ, it seems uncertain whether his case may be reviewed in a court of law. Congress has remained silent on judicial review of council orders. And if councils are non-judicial bodies exercising purely administrative rather than judicial power, then appellate courts, including the Supreme Court lack jurisdiction to entertain such disputes.[268] As the Supreme Court never reached the substantive issues in the Chandler case, obscurity continues to veil both the enforcement and review of council sanctions.

The formal powers and, in many instances, even council precedents are at variance with the actual practice of most councils. Informality, negotiations, bargaining, and compromise are the hallmarks of council strategy. Formal orders are the exception, reflecting a belief among judges that "the councils should act by order only when necessary,"[269] and that "cooperation . . . and . . . not purported policeman-ship"[270] is the path to effective judicial administration.

[268] See *Chandler v. Judicial Council*, 398 U.S. 74, 86 (1969).

[269] Lumbard, "The Place of the Federal Judicial Councils," p. 172.

[270] House Committee on the Judiciary, *Report on the Responsibilities*, 1961, p. 9.

426

CHAPTER 12

Politics and Administration: A Dilemma

JUDICIAL administration has long enjoyed the status of a "timely topic." Courts and judges never seem to be performing quite as well as their critics, sometimes legions of critics, think they should. Catastrophe and collapse of an independent judiciary is prophesied. And the inventory of reasons for the approaching Armageddon is long indeed: burgeoning caseloads, complex litigation, procrastinating lawyers and judges, anachronistic court structures and procedures, and the encroachment of "politics," to name a few. The traditional solution proposed is constructed around the goal of efficiency in processing judicial business. Politics is perceived as playing little or no part in setting or realizing this goal. All that courts require is an infusion of management techniques and a purge of political encumbrances. Once this condition is achieved, an independent judiciary will be in a position to dispense justice in a prompt and efficient manner.

Federal judicial administration encompasses, however, much more than the time-worn topics of delay and congestion, efficiency and economy. To be sure, homage is invariably paid to these rhetorical monuments, and many instances warrant it. Yet the politics associated with judicial administration indicate that goals other than administrative efficiency are often at stake.

Commentators have noted the great durability of the United States courts, a durability which has persisted in spite of the "undemocratic" nature of the Third Branch. Instead of abiding by the notion of electoral responsibility, federal judges cling to that of judicial independence. No one described the lodestar of judicial independence in more uncompromising terms than did Chief Justice John Marshall. "The Judicial Department," he declared, "comes home in its effects to every man's fireside; it passes on his property, his reputation, his life, his all. Is it not, to the last degree important, that [the judge] should be rendered perfectly and completely independent, with nothing to influence or control him but God and his conscience? . . . I have always thought . . . that the greatest scourge an angry Heaven ever inflicted upon an ungrateful and a sinning people, was an ignorant, a corrupt, or a dependent Judiciary."[1]

The courts, however, do not exist in isolation. They are integral parts of the political system, and in some measure they must be responsive to demands emanating from that system.[2] Judicial selection, the litigation process, and the Article III power of Congress all bear overtones of the larger political world.[3] So, too, issues of administration and procedure have borne a close relationship to the emergence of political exigencies. The Administrative Office Act of 1939 clearly constituted the judges' response to broad-based political attacks on the courts.[4] The same may well be said of the Judicial Conference's establishment in 1922 and of Chief Justice Taft's efforts to reform the rules of procedure. By such responses federal judges sought to regain an equilibrium apparently lost or threatened by executive or congressional attacks on the courts. Reform of administrative structures afforded a safe course. It gave visible evidence of the court's recognition of popular opinion. At the same time, such reform would leave intact and untouched the

[1] Quoted in *O'Donoghue v. United States*, 289 U.S. 516, 532 (1932).

[2] Robert A. Dahl, *Pluralist Democracy in the United States: Conflict and Consent* (Chicago, 1967), pp. 155-64.

[3] See generally, Richard J. Richardson and Kenneth N. Vines, *The Politics of Federal Courts* (Boston, 1970); Sheldon Goldman and Thomas P. Jahnige, *The Federal Courts as a Political System* (New York, 1971).

[4] See Peter Graham Fish, "Crises, Politics, and Federal Judicial Reform: The Administrative Office Act of 1939," *The Journal of Politics*, 32 (August 1970), 596-627.

substantive heart of the judicial decision-making process. As Leonard White observed: "Crisis puts institutions to hard tests. The crust of custom breaks and old institutions either adapt themselves to new demands or are discarded."[5] Federal judges have adapted. They have created new and adjusted existing national and regional administrative structures. They even made adjustments in the substance of the law in the acute crisis of the 1930s. Both types of changes account in some measure for the extraordinary durability of the American federal judiciary.

Other factors account for this institutional resilience, not the least of which are the linkages between federal judges and the local political system. Recent studies have indicated the close ties between local politics and judicial selection and decison-making.[6] In the realm of administration, the influence of localism is pronounced. Chapter 1 noted the diffuse character of national judicial power and the federal courts' relationship to state boundaries and politics. Subsequent chapters delineated the numerous types of center-periphery conflicts arising in part from the structure of the judiciary's administrative system. Judges tend to be individualists. Their legal training and practice emphasize legal rather than administrative skills and individual effort rather than teamwork. "As judges," a former Administrative Office Director observed, "they value their independence, recognize its importance to impartiality in decision-making, but have no awareness of their duty to the judicial organization."[7] Lower court judges thus may identify generally with the system of which they are a part. Specifically, they relate to their own courts, not to more remote national and region-

[5] Leonard White, ed., *Civil Service in Wartime* (Chicago, 1945), p. 1.

[6] See Kenneth M. Dolbeare, "The Federal District Courts and Urban Public Policy: An Exploratory Study (1960-1967)" in Joel B. Grossman and Joseph Tanenhaus, eds., *Frontiers of Judicial Research* (New York, 1969), pp. 373-404.

[7] Ernest C. Friesen, "Constraints and Conflicts in Court Administration," *Public Administration Review*, 31 (March/April 1971), 121-22.

429

al agencies such as the Judicial Conference, its committees, the Administrative Office, or the circuit judicial councils. District and even circuit judges are, quite simply, "the most important national officials who are systematically localized in the performance of their functions."[8]

Yet the institutions of federal judicial administration tend to be responsive to their clientele in Washington as well as to their dispersed judge constituency. They pay heed to demands articulated by Congress, the Executive departments, and by the Supreme Court.[9] Thereafter judges, especially district judges, may be called upon to change their ways and to conform with national administrative policies set by the Judicial Conference of the United States. Since 1922, individual trial and appellate judges have occupied, in effect, a position vis-à-vis the Judicial Conference that during the Warren years was analogous to that held by the states vis-à-vis the Supreme Court. To use the language of Judge John Minor Wisdom of the Fifth Circuit Court of Appeals, a function of the national administrative system has often been a "frictionmaking exacerbating political" one. Its "destined role" is that "of bringing local policy in line with national policy."[10]

District judge reaction to national policies varies, but it can be bitter indeed. "For a considerable number of years," lamented several dissident trial judges in 1947, "the tendency in the United States has been toward a controlled fed-

[8] Richardson and Vines, *Politics of Federal Courts*, p. 173.

[9] See Matthew G. McGuire, U.S., Congress, House, Subcommittee of the Committee on Appropriations, *Hearings, on Departments of State, Justice, and Commerce, the Judiciary, and Related Agencies for 1969*, 90th Cong., 2d Sess., 1968, p. 47; "Statement of William Campbell," U.S., Congress, Senate, *Hearings, on H.R. 12964, Departments of State, Justice, and Commerce, the Judiciary, and Related Agencies Appropriations for Fiscal Year 1970*, 91st Cong., 1st Sess., 1969, pp. 48-52.

[10] John Minor Wisdom, "The Frictionmaking Exacerbating Political Role of Federal Courts," *Southwestern Law Journal*, 21 (Summer 1967), 411.

eral judiciary."[11] Admittedly, "some central control of administrative matters [was] helpful and desirable,"[12] but the actions of the Judicial Conference, established a quarter of a century before, had far exceeded anyone's expectations. With its supervisory powers, that body now appeared to constitute "a vast step . . . toward a controlled judiciary."[13]

Given the omnipresent centrifugal impulses flowing from the grass roots, prospects of a "controlled judiciary" appear remote in spite of the development of a network of administrative institutions wholly absent when William Howard Taft became Chief Justice in 1921. Since then Congress has authorized creation of a national policy-making organ, the Judicial Conference of the United States; a bureaucracy, the Administrative Office of the United States Courts; a research and development arm, the Federal Judicial Center; "grass-roots" institutions of education, entertainment, and information, the circuit judicial conferences; and, finally, executive agencies, the circuit councils. Emergence of these institutions occurred simultaneously with the growth of professionalism among court officers and supporting personnel. Over a period of time and in response to felt needs, these developments have imposed a degree of administrative integration on the federal courts. In the same vein, the rules of civil and criminal procedure have produced nationalizing tendencies in lieu of former federal attachment to state procedures. Yet, as already noted, changes wrought have been changes in degree rather than kind. As former Senator Joseph D. Tydings, Jr. observed: "Our courts are administered today in essentially the same way that they were two centuries ago."[14]

[11] John P. Barnes, Philip L. Sullivan, Michael L. Igoe, William J. Campbell, Walter J. LaBuy, Elwyn R. Shaw to United States District and Circuit Judges, December 10, 1947, mimeograph copy, p. 6, Stephens Papers, Box 211.

[12] *Ibid.* [13] *Ibid.*

[14] *Congressional Record*, 91st Cong., 1st Sess., 1969, vol. 115, part 20, 27493.

The record of the past half century does not in fact bode well for major reforms of the federal judiciary. Such changes, whether in administrative structures and powers, procedure, or court organization and jurisdiction tend to have a centralizing effect. Among reforms proposed are: powerful chief appellate judges elected by the court or appointed by the President or Chief Justice because of their administrative expertise and activism;[15] mobile judges or a new mobile national court of appeals superior to the present courts of appeals;[16] abolition of district and circuit lines, or redrawing them such that they cut across state boundaries;[17] and establishment of a commission or court with power to pass on judicial behavior and to remove misbehaving judges outside the impeachment powers.[18] Each of these measures would exert decided centripetal impulses through the federal court system. Each would threaten or appear to threaten the hallowed ground of judicial independence. More realistically every one would be seen as subverting existing status relationships by changing the internal distribution of power within the judicial system.

Thus reform prospects are dim, given the low visibility of courts and court reform legislation in the American scheme of government. The political clout enjoyed by local magistrates standing securely on their geographical bases renders the prospects even darker.[19] Consequently, reforms

[15] John Biggs, Jr., Transcript of "Conference in re: 'Manner of the Selection of Chief Judges,' Ninth Circuit, December 20, 1955," p. 10, Administrative Office Correspondence, 60-A-328, Box 31; S. 3055, Title V, sec. 501(a) (1), 90th Cong.; *ibid.*, sec. 502(a) (1).

[16] Paul D. Carrington, "Crowded Dockets and the Courts of Appeals: The Threat to the Function of Review and the National Law," *Harvard Law Review*, 82 (January 1969), 542-617; ————, "Accommodating the Workload of the United States Courts of Appeals" (Chicago, 1968).

[17] *Ibid.*   [18] See S. 1506, Title I, 91st Cong.

[19] See Fish, "Crises, Politics, and Federal Judicial Reform"; Baar, "When Judges Lobby," pp. 645-48.

in court and administrative organization have been and will likely continue to be in the realm of "minor adaptations rather than basic changes."[20] The extent of actual changes and the feasibility of further reforms in administrative behavior and structure is, of course, always debatable. Less uncertain have been other consequences of a formal administrative system. Judges have, of necessity, become politicians operating both inside and outside that system. Much has been written about the role of interest groups in the litigation process.[21] Less has been said about judges as interest groups. This study makes clear that judges seek a favorable degree of freedom for nonconformity as against pressure for uniform national standards of behavior, qualifications of supporting personnel, pretrial proceedings, and so on. In this context, judges lobby judges with bar organization and congressional committees as interested parties. Courts need and judges want money, manpower, and assorted statutory changes in jurisdiction and court organization.

The rhetoric of judicial independence founded on the separation of powers doctrine notwithstanding, judges must look to Congress to satisfy such requirements. In administration as distinguished from judicial decision-making, the Third Branch is dependent on Congress and to a lesser extent on the executive. And Congress operates on the assumptions of pressure group theory. To obtain favorable legislative action or, conversely, to prevent unfavorable action, judges, behaving like interest groups, generally must take the initiative. In this manner selected judges associated with the judiciary's administrative system and allied groups have become deeply and continuously involved in legislative politics.

[20] Herbert Jacob, *Justice in America: Courts, Lawyers, and the Judicial Process* (Boston, 1965), p. 145.

[21] For a discussion of the literature, see C. Herman Pritchett, "The Development of Judicial Research," in Grossman and Tanenhaus, eds., *Frontiers of Judicial Research*, pp. 33-34.

Institutions of federal judicial administration thus face in two directions: toward the separate courts and toward Congress. Not surprisingly, administrative policies directed toward both forums have generated controversy founded on local-national, individuality-conformity lines. Administrative "activists" such as Associate Justice William J. Brennan, Jr. complain about the opposition of those whose thinking is "clouded by the bugaboo that centralized administration poses [a] threat to the independence of decision, which is the absolute essential of the judicial function."[22] The assumption that "to be free and independent in judicial determinations, each judge and each court must also be completely independent in matters of administration as well" is a wholly invalid one, said Brennan.[23] In fact, quite the contrary is true, for, he observed, "experience with centralized administration . . . taught us that . . . such administration often enhances the judge's independence to do right and justice in every case."[24]

On the other hand, centralization of administrative power raises important questions as to its location, accessibility, and scope. Such power initially flowed from trial courts to appellate courts in accordance with hierarchical theory. When conflicts and breakdowns were resolved in an unsatisfactory manner or left totally unresolved at the lower levels, recourse was had to the more inclusive political community. The net result of this practice tended toward centralized policy-making and control, largely in the hands of appellate judges. But such judges, dominating the circuit judicial councils, have proved unprepared to meet instances of irregular judicial conduct and nonconforming administrative practices in the trial courts. Thus many problems wend their way up to the Judicial Conference and its committees for definitive settlement. Yet even the national Con-

---

[22] William J. Brennan, Jr., Address, "The Continuing Education of the Judiciary in Improved Procedures," Tenth Circuit Judicial Conference, July 5, 1960, multilithed copy, p. 8.
[23] *Ibid.*　　　　　　　　　　　[24] *Ibid.*

ference lacks the ultimate sanctions which generally render effective the appellate use of authority.[25] It enjoys no power over the appointment, discipline, or dismissal of errant judges whose acts of malfeasance or nonfeasance may fall short of constituting "high crimes and misdemeanors" warranting impeachment. The conference lacks, therefore, any formal power to remove federal judges holding office during "good behavior." Nor do the circuit councils enjoy this power, notwithstanding any inferences which may be drawn from the action of the council of the Tenth Circuit in the Stephen Chandler case considered in Chapter 11.

Whether councils or other judge-controlled institutions should enjoy sanctions including removing judges from office by means other than impeachment is a question with far-reaching implications. Foremost among them is the possibility of using such methods to penalize judges for the substance of their judicial decisions. Mr. Justice William O. Douglas spelled out this danger in his *Chandler* dissent. The nonconformist, he asserted, would suffer "greatly at the hands of his fellow judges."[26] He argued:

The problem is not resolved by saying that only judicial administrative matters are involved. The power to keep a particular judge from sitting on a racial case, a church-and-state case, a free-press case, a search-and-seizure case, a railroad case, an antitrust case, or a union case may have profound consequences. Judges are not fungible; they cover the constitutional spectrum; and a particular judge's emphasis may make a world of difference when it comes to rulings on evidence, the temper of the courtroom, the tolerance for a preferred defense, and the like. Lawyers recognize this when they talk about "shopping" for a judge; Senators recognize this when they

[25] See Herbert Simon, *Administrative Behavior: A Study of Decision-Making Processes in Administrative Organization* (New York, 1957), p. 12.

[26] Douglas, J., dissenting in *Chandler v. Judicial Council*, 398 U.S. 74, 137 (1969).

435

are asked to give their "advice and consent" to judicial appointments; laymen recognize this when they appraise the quality and image of the judiciary in their own community.

These are subtle, imponderable factors which other judges should not be allowed to manipulate to further their own concept of the public good. That is the crucial issue at the heart of the present controversy.[27]

Douglas made a valid point; judges are clearly not above efforts to use administrative institutions to influence judicial decision-making. Chapter 2 indicated that considerations other than mere efficiency have occasionally entered into intercircuit assignments. Nor have federal judges shied away from using their administrative system to speak out on issues which may reach them at some later time in the form of a "case or controversy." Federal courts allegedly refrain from giving advisory opinions. But Judicial Conference policies, noted in Chapters 2 and 7, may, in effect, constitute such opinions. They may be intended for Congress or for judges who subsequently receive a relevant case. In any event, an agency of the federal judiciary has already spoken with authority if not with finality on the subject. The substance of the law may be determined through administrative rather than adversary processes.

Centralized judicial administration surely poses dangers, but it raises a dilemma as well. Without at least some degree of central control and clearance, the viability of the judiciary as an independent branch may be threatened by local and individual customs and behavior. That any centripetal force emerged in the first place owes much to the quantity and complexity of judicial work generated by a populous and modern industrial society with a national economy. In addition the proliferation of federal laws demanded by the development of that economy and the expansion of constitutional rights and liberties in the 1950s

[27] *Ibid.*

436

and 1960s contributes in no small part to the need to maximize administrative performance. Centralization owes much also to court personnel seeking professional status and hence uniform appointment and salary standards, to an Administrative Office pressing to rationalize bureaucratic processes, to Congress responding to constituent complaints about courts and judges and demanding responsible expenditure of public funds. And finally centralization pressures emanate from the necessity of maintaining the public image of the federal courts. Positive action by a superior agency may be required when unethical, uninterested, and incompetent judges blemish that image.

For individual judges, who may have lost some of their former autonomy, the cost of a modest degree of administrative centralization may be perceived as relatively high. For the judiciary as a whole, the cost would seem quite low and the benefits correspondingly high. Administrative institutions and politics are, after all, but means to an end; they are generally not ends in themselves. They give life to the separation of powers doctrine in that the judge-developed administrative system enables courts to adjust to changes in their legal, political, and economic environment without surrendering judicial independence. Through them, courts may obtain sufficient resources to exercise final legal authority. Administrative institutions thus foster the judiciary's long run capacity to function as a coordinate part of the national political system.

Appendix A

Judicial Conference Reports

1922-23: "The Federal Judicial Council," *Texas Law Review*, Volume 2 (June, 1924), pp. 458-63.

1924: "Addenda, recommendations of Judicial Conference," in *Annual Report of the Attorney General, 1924*. Washington, D.C.: Government Printing Office, 1924.

1925: "Additional Federal Judges [and] other recommendations of Senior Circuit Judges," in *Annual Report of the Attorney General, 1925*. Washington, D.C.: Government Printing Office, 1925.

1926-29: "Recommendations of Conference of Senior Circuit Judges," in *Annual Report of the Attorney General, 1926-29*. Washington, D.C.: Government Printing Office, 1926 to 1929.

1930: "Report of the Conference of Senior Circuit Judges." *Annual Report of the Attorney General*, Washington, D.C.: Government Printing Office, 1930.

1931-44: "Report of the Judicial Conference," in *Annual Report of the Attorney General, 1931-44*. Washington, D.C.: Government Printing Office, 1931 to 1944.

1945-47: *Report of the Judicial Conference of Senior Circuit Judges*. Issued with *Annual Report of the Director of the Administrative Office of the United States Courts*. Washington, D.C.: Government Printing Office, 1946 to 1948.

1948-53: *Report of the Judicial Conference of the United States*. Issued with *Annual Report of the Director of the Administrative Office of the United States Courts*. Washington, D.C.: Government Printing Office, 1949 to 1954.

1954-60: *Annual Report of the Proceedings of the Judicial Conference of the United States.* Issued with *Annual Report of the Director of the Administrative Office of the United States Courts.* Washington, D.C.: Government Printing Office, 1955 to 1961.

1961: *Reports of the Proceedings of the Judicial Conference of the United States.* Issued with *Annual Report of the Director of the Administrative Office of the United States Courts.* Washington, D.C.: Government Printing Office, 1962.

1962: *Annual Reports of the Proceedings of the Judicial Conference of the United States.* Issued with *Annual Report of the Director of the Administrative Office of the United States Courts.* Washington, D.C.: Government Printing Office, 1963.

1963-69: *Reports of the Proceedings of the Judicial Conference of the United States.* Issued with *Annual Report of the Director of the Administrative Office of the United States Courts.* Washington, D.C.: Government Printing Office, 1964 to 1970.

Appendix B

Judicial Conference Attendance by Year[1]

Year	Chief Justice	CIRCUIT: First	Second	Third	Fourth	Fifth	Sixth
1922	Taft	Bingham	Rogers	Buffington	Woods	Walker	Knappen
1923	Taft	Bingham	Rogers	Buffington	Woods	Walker	Knappen
1924	Taft	Bingham	Rogers	(Buffington) Woolley*	Woods	Walker	Denison
1925	Taft	Bingham	Rogers	Buffington	Waddill	Walker	Denison
1926	Taft	Bingham	Hough	(Buffington) Woolley*	Waddill	Walker	Denison
1927	Taft	Bingham	Manton	(Buffington) Davis*	Waddill	Walker	Denison
1928	Taft	Bingham	Manton	(Buffington) Woolley*	Waddill	(Walker) Bryan*	Denison
1929	Taft	Bingham	Manton	(Buffington) Thomson*	Waddill	Walker	Denison
1930	Hughes	Bingham	Manton	Buffington	(Waddill) Parker*	Bryan	Denison
1931	Hughes	Bingham	Manton	Buffington	Parker	Bryan	Denison
1932	Hughes	Bingham	Manton	Buffington	Parker	Bryan	Moorman
1933	Hughes	(Bingham) Wilson*	Manton	Buffington	Parker	Bryan	Moorman
1934	Hughes	Bingham	Manton	Buffington	Parker	Bryan	Moorman
1935	Hughes	Bingham	Manton	Buffington	Parker	Foster	Moorman
1936	Hughes	Bingham	Manton	Buffington	Parker	Foster	(Moorman) Hicks*
1937	Hughes	Bingham	Manton	Buffington	Parker	Foster	Moorman
1938	Hughes	Bingham	Manton	Davis	Parker	(Foster) Sibley*	Hicks
1939	Hughes	Wilson	Hand	Biggs	Parker	Foster	Hicks

* The indicated judge attended the Conference in place of the senior judge in parentheses.

[1] Data for this table were drawn from the following: 1922-25: the *New York Times*; 1926-6? *Judicial Conference Reports* (see Appendix A).

Seventh	Eighth	Ninth	Tenth	District of Columbia	Claims	Customs
Baker	(Sanborn) Kenyon*	Gilbert				
Baker	Sanborn	Gilbert				
Alschuler	Sanborn	Gilbert				
Alschuler	Sanborn	Gilbert				
Alschuler	Sanborn	Gilbert				
Alschuler	Sanborn	Gilbert				
Alschuler	Stone	Gilbert				
Alschuler	Stone	(Gilbert) Rudkin*	Lewis			
Alschuler	Stone	(Gilbert) Rudkin*	Lewis			
Alschuler	Stone	Wilbur	Lewis			
Alschuler	Stone	Wilbur	(Lewis) Phillips*			
Alschuler	Stone	Wilbur	Lewis			
(Alschuler) Evans*	Stone	Wilbur	Lewis			
Evans	Stone	Wilbur	(Lewis) Phillips*			
Evans	Stone	Wilbur	Lewis			
Evans	Stone	Wilbur	(Lewis) Phillips*	Groner		
Evans	Stone	Wilbur	(Lewis) Phillips*	Groner		
Evans	Stone	Wilbur	(Lewis) Phillips*	Groner		

441

Year	Chief Justice	CIRCUIT: First	Second	Third	Fourth	Fifth	Sixth
1940 Jan.ss	Hughes	none	Hand	Biggs	Parker	Foster	Hicks
Oct.	Hughes	Magruder	Hand	Biggs	Parker	Foster	Hicks
1941 Jan.ss	Hughes	(Magruder) Mahoney*	Hand	Biggs	Parker	Foster	Hicks
Sept.	Stone	Magruder	Hand	Biggs	(Parker) (Soper)	Foster	Hicks
1942	Stone	Magruder	Hand	Biggs	Parker	Sibley	Hicks
1943	Stone	Magruder	Hand	Biggs	Parker	Sibley	Hicks
1944	Stone	Magruder	Hand	Biggs	Parker	Sibley	Hicks
1945	Stone	Magruder	Hand	Biggs	(Parker) Soper*	Sibley	Hicks
1946	Vinson	Magruder	Hand	Biggs	(Parker) Soper*	Sibley	Hicks
1947 Apr.ss	Vinson	Magruder	Hand	Biggs	Parker	(Sibley) Hutcheson*	Hicks
Sept.	Vinson	Magruder	Hand	Biggs	Parker	Sibley	Hicks
1948	Vinson	Magruder	Hand	Biggs	Parker	Hutcheson	Hicks
1949 Mar.ss	Vinson	Magruder	Hand	Biggs	Parker	Hutcheson	Hicks
Sept.	Vinson	Magruder	(Hand) Swan*	Biggs	Parker	Hutcheson	Hicks
Nov.ss	Vinson	Magruder	Hand	Biggs	Parker	Hutcheson	Hicks
1950 Mar.ss	Vinson	Magruder	Hand	Biggs	Parker	Hutcheson	(Hicks) Simons*
Sept.	Vinson	Magruder	Hand	Biggs	Parker	Hutcheson	Hicks
1951 Mar.ss	Vinson	Magruder	Hand	Biggs	Parker	Hutcheson	Hicks
Sept.	Vinson	Magruder	Swan	Biggs	Parker	Hutcheson	Hicks

ss Special Sessions called by the Chief Justice.
* The indicated judge attended the Conference in place of the senior judge in parentheses.

442

Seventh	Eighth	Ninth	Tenth	District of Columbia	Claims	Customs
Evans	Stone	Wilbur	(Lewis) Phillips*	Groner		
Evans	Stone	Wilbur	Phillips	Groner		
Evans	Stone	(Wilbur) Denman*	Phillips	Groner		
Evans	Stone	Wilbur	Phillips	Groner		
Evans	Stone	Wilbur	Phillips	Groner		
(Evans) Minton*	Stone	Wilbur	Phillips	Groner		
Evans	Stone	Wilbur	Phillips	Groner		
Evans	Stone	Garrecht	Phillips	Groner		
(Evans) Major*	Stone	Garrecht	Phillips	Groner		
Evans	Stone	(Garrecht) none	Phillips	Groner		
Evans	Gardner	Garrecht	Phillips	(Groner) Stephens*		
(Sparks) Kerner*	Gardner	Denman	Phillips	Stephens		
(Major) Duffy*	Gardner	Denman	Phillips	Stephens		
Major	Gardner	Denman	Phillips	(Stephens) Prettyman*		
Major	Gardner	(Denman) none	Phillips	(Stephens) Prettyman*		
Major	Gardner	(Denman) none	Phillips	Stephens		
Major	Gardner	Denman	Phillips	Stephens		
Major	Gardner	Denman	Phillips	Stephens		
Major	Gardner	Denman	Phillips	Stephens		

443

Year	Chief Justice	CIRCUIT: First	Second	Third	Fourth	Fifth	Sixth
1952							
Mar.[ss]	Vinson	Magruder	Swan	Biggs	Parker	Hutcheson	Simons
Sept.	Vinson	Magruder	Swan	Biggs	Parker	Hutcheson	Simons
1953							
Mar.[ss]	Vinson	Magruder	Swan	Biggs	Parker	Hutcheson	Simons
May[ss]	Vinson	Magruder	(Swan) Hand*	Biggs	Parker	Hutcheson	Simons
Sept.	Black[2]	Magruder	Chase	Biggs	Parker	Hutcheson	Simons
1954							
Apr.[ss]	Warren	Magruder	Chase	Biggs	Parker	Hutcheson	Simons
Sept.	Warren	Magruder	Clark	(Biggs) Maris*	Parker	Hutcheson	Simons
1955							
Mar.[ss]	Warren	Magruder	Clark	Biggs	Parker	Hutcheson	Simons
Sept.	Warren	Magruder	Clark	Biggs	Parker	Hutcheson	Simons
1956							
Mar.[ss]	Warren	Magruder	Clark	Biggs	Parker	Hutcheson	Simons
Sept.	Warren	Magruder	Clark	Biggs	Parker	Hutcheson	Simons
1957							
Mar.[ss]	Warren	Magruder	Clark	Biggs	Parker	Hutcheson	Simons
. Sept.	Warren	Magruder	Clark Smith[3]	Biggs Forman	Parker Thomsen[3]	Hutcheson	(Simons) Allen* Jones[3]
1958							
Mar.[ss]	Warren	Magruder none	Clark Dimock	Biggs Forman	Sobeloff Thomsen[3]	Hutcheson none	(Simons) Stewart* Jones[3]
Sept.	Warren	Magruder Sweeney	Clark Dimock	Biggs Forman	Sobeloff Thomsen	Hutcheson Lynne	Allen Jones
1959							
Mar.[ss]	Warren	Magruder Sweeney	Clark Dimock	Biggs Forman	Sobeloff Thomsen	Hutcheson Lynne	Martin Jones

[ss] Special Sessions called by the Chief Justice.

* The indicated judge attended the Conference in place of the senior judge in parentheses.

[2] The senior Associate Justice, Hugo L. Black, presided at the regular September session of the 1953 Judicial Conference due to the vacancy in the office of Chief Justice created by the death c Frederick M. Vinson (28 U.S.C. 3).

[3] The Act of August 28, 1957 (71 *Stat.* 476) provided for membership of one district judge from each circuit on the Judicial Conference. Although district judges had attended the Conferenc

444

Seventh	Eighth	Ninth	Tenth	District of Columbia	Claims	Customs
Major	Gardner	Denman	Phillips	Stephens		
Major	Gardner	Denman	Phillips	Stephens		
Major	Gardner	Denman	Phillips	Stephens		
Major	Gardner	(Denman) Stephens*	Phillips	Stephens		
Major	Gardner	Denman	Phillips	Stephens		
Major	Gardner	Denman	Phillips	Stephens		
Duffy	Gardner	Denman	Phillips	Stephens		
Duffy	Gardner	Denman	Phillips	(Stephens) Edgerton*		
Duffy	(Gardner) Sanborn*	Denman	Phillips	Edgerton		
Duffy	(Gardner) Sanborn*	Denman	Bratton	Edgerton		
Duffy	(Gardner) Sanborn*	Denman	Bratton	Edgerton	Jones	
Duffy	(Gardner) Whittaker*	Denman	Bratton	Edgerton	(Jones) Whittaker*	
Duffy	(Gardner) Johnsen* Nordbye[3]	Stephens Goodman[3]	Bratton	Edgerton Laws[3]	(Jones) Whittaker*	
Duffy Campbell[3]	Gardner Nordbye	Stephens Goodman[3]	Bratton Rice	Edgerton Laws	Jones	
Duffy Campbell	Gardner Nordbye	Stephens Mathes	Bratton Savage	Edgerton (Laws) McGuire*	(Jones) Whittaker*	
Duffy Campbell	Gardner Nordbye	Pope Mathes	Bratton Savage	Prettyman Pine	Jones	

previously as members of Conference committees, none had attended in the capacity of a designated representative of the district judges in the several circuits. The 1957 Conference was the first to include an official district representative, Judge Phillip Forman. Other district judges were "invited" by the Chief Justice to attend the Conference until their election by the circuit judicial councils (those footnoted). The district judge from each circuit will hereafter be indicated by italics.

445

Year	Chief Justice	CIRCUIT: First	Second	Third	Fourth	Fifth	Sixth
Sept.	Warren	Woodbury Sweeney	Clark Ryan	Biggs Ganey	Sobeloff Thomsen	Rives Connally	(McAllister) Miller* Jones
1960							
Mar.ss	Warren	Woodbury Sweeney	Lumbard Ryan	Biggs Ganey	Sobeloff Thomsen	Rives Connally	McAllister Jones
Sept.	Warren	Woodbury (Sweeney) Ford*	Lumbard Ryan	Biggs Ganey	Sobeloff Thomsen	Rives Connally	McAllister Boyd
1961							
Mar.ss	Warren	Woodbury Sweeney	Lumbard Ryan	Biggs (Ganey) Smith*	Sobeloff Thomsen	Tuttle Connally	Miller Boyd
Sept.	Warren	Woodbury Ford	Lumbard Ryan	Biggs Madden	Sobeloff Thomsen	Tuttle Connally	Miller Boyd
1962							
Mar.4	Warren	Woodbury Ford	Lumbard Ryan	Biggs Madden	Sobeloff Thomsen	Tuttle Connally	Miller Boyd
Sept.	Warren	Woodbury Ford	Lumbard Ryan	Biggs Madden	Sobeloff Thomsen	Tuttle Simpson	Cecil Boyd
1963							
Mar.	Warren	Woodbury Ford	Lumbard Ryan	Biggs Madden	Sobeloff Thomsen	Tuttle Simpson	Cecil Boyd
Sept.	Warren	Woodbury Ford	Lumbard Ryan	Biggs Madden	Sobeloff Thomsen	Tuttle Simpson	Cecil Freeman
1964							
Mar.	Warren	Woodbury Ford	Lumbard Ryan	Biggs Madden	Sobeloff Thomsen	Tuttle Simpson	Weick Freeman
Sept.	Warren	Woodbury Ford	Lumbard (Ryan) Weinfeld*	Biggs Madden	Sobeloff Hoffman	Tuttle Simpson	Weick Freeman
1965							
Mar.	Warren	Aldrich Ford	Lumbard Ryan	Biggs Madden	Haynsworth Hoffman	Tuttle Simpson	Weick Freeman

ss Special Sessions called by the Chief Justice.

* The indicated judge attended the Conference in place of the senior judge in parentheses.

4 From 1949 through 1961 the Conference held each year a Special Session in March, April, c May. Commencing in 1962 the Conference discontinued use of the term "Special Session" for wh had become its regular spring meeting.

446

Seventh	Eighth	Ninth	Tenth	District of Columbia	Claims	Customs
Hastings	Johnsen	Chambers	(Murrah)	Prettyman	Jones	
Campbell	Nordbye	Mathes	Pickett*	Pine		
			Savage			
Hastings	Johnsen	Chambers	Murrah	Prettyman	Jones	
Campbell	Nordbye	Mathes	Savage	Pine		
Hastings	Johnsen	Chambers	Murrah	Prettyman	(Jones)	
Campbell	Nordbye	Lindberg	Savage	Pine	Whittaker*	
Hastings	Johnsen	Chambers	Murrah	Miller	Jones	
Campbell	Nordbye	Lindberg	Savage	Pine		
Hastings	Johnsen	Chambers	Murrah	Miller	Jones	Worley
Swygert	Nordbye	Lindberg	Savage	McGuire		
Hastings	(Johnsen)	Chambers	Murrah	Miller	Jones	Worley
Steckler	Vogel*	Lindberg	none	(McGuire)		
	Nordbye			Pine*		
Hastings	Johnsen	Chambers	Murrah	(Miller)	Jones	Worley
Steckler	Miller	Lindberg	Kerr	Bazelon*		
				McGuire		
Hastings	Johnsen	Chambers	Murrah	Bazelon	Jones	Worley
Steckler	Miller	Lindberg	Kerr	McGuire		
Hastings	Johnsen	Chambers	Murrah	(Bazelon)	Jones	Worley
Steckler	Duncan	Solomon	Kerr	Fahy*		
				McGuire		
Hastings	Johnsen	Chambers	Murrah	(Bazelon)	Jones	Worley
Steckler	Duncan	Solomon	Kerr	Fahy*		
				McGuire		
Hastings	Johnsen	Chambers	Murrah	(Bazelon)	Cowen	(Worley)
Grubb	Duncan	Solomon	Arraj	Fahy*		Smith*
				McGuire		
Hastings	Johnsen	Chambers	Murrah	Bazelon	Cowen	Worley
(Grubb)	Duncan	Solomon	Arraj	McGuire		
Robson*						

447

Year	Chief Justice	CIRCUIT: First	Second	Third	Fourth	Fifth	Sixth
Sept.	Warren	Aldrich Ford	(Lumbard) Waterman* Ryan	Biggs Madden	Haynsworth Hoffman	Tuttle Christenberry	Weick Freeman
1966 Mar.	Warren	Aldrich Ford	Lumbard Ryan	Kalodner Madden	Haynsworth Hoffman	Tuttle Christenberry	Weick Freeman
Sept.	Warren	Aldrich Ford	Lumbard Ryan	Staley Clary	Haynsworth Hoffman	Tuttle Christenberry	Weick Swinford
1967 Mar.	Warren	Aldrich Ford	Lumbard Ryan	Staley Clary	Haynsworth Hoffman	Tuttle Christenberry	Weick Swinford
Sept.	Warren	Aldrich Gignoux	Lumbard Ryan	Staley Clary	Haynsworth Hoffman	Brown Christenberry	Weick Swinford
1968 Feb.	Warren	Aldrich Gignoux	Lumbard Ryan	Hastie Clary	Haynsworth Hoffman	Brown Christenberry	Weick Swinford
Sept.	Warren	Aldrich Gignoux	Lumbard Sugarman	Hastie Gourley	Haynsworth Hoffman	Brown Carswell	Weick Swinford
1969 Mar.	Warren	Aldrich Gignoux	Lumbard Sugarman	Hastie Gourley	Haynsworth Hoffman	Brown Carswell	Weick Swinford
June[ss]	Warren	Aldrich Gignoux	Lumbard Sugarman	Hastie Gourley	Haynsworth Hoffman	Brown Carswell	Weick Swinford
Oct.-Nov.	Burger	Aldrich Gignoux	Lumbard Sugarman	Hastie Gourley	(Haynsworth) Winter* Hoffman	Brown Estes	Phillips Weinman

[ss] Special Sessions called by the Chief Justice.
* The indicated judge attended the Conference in place of the senior judge in parentheses.

448

Seventh	Eighth	Ninth	Tenth	District of Columbia	Claims	Customs
Hastings	Vogel	Chambers	Murrah	Bazelon	Cowen	(Worley)
Grubb	Harper	Solomon	Arraj	McGuire		Smith*
Hastings	Vogel	Chambers	Murrah	Bazelon	(Cowen)	(Worley)
(Grubb)	Harper	none	Arraj	McGuire	Whittaker*	none
Robson*						
Hastings	Vogel	Chambers	Murrah	Bazelon	Cowen	(Worley)
Robson	Harper	Wollenberg	Arraj	McGuire		Smith*
Hastings	Vogel	Chambers	Murrah	Bazelon	(Cowen)	Worley
(Robson)	Harper	Wollenberg	Arraj	McGuire	Durfee*	
Campbell*						
Hastings	Vogel	Chambers	Murrah	(Bazelon)	Cowen	(Worley)
Robson	Harper	Wollenberg	Stanley	McGowan*		Rich*
				(McGuire)		
				Curran*		
Hastings	Van	Chambers	Murrah	Bazelon	Cowen	(Worley)
Robson	Oosterhout	Wollenberg	Stanley	Curran		Rich*
	Harper					
Castle	Van	Chambers	Murrah	Bazelon	Cowen	(Worley)
Robson	Oosterhout	Wollenberg	Stanley	Curran		Baldwin*
	Harper					Rich*
Castle	Van	Chambers	Murrah	Bazelon	Cowen	(Worley)
Robson	Oosterhout	Wollenberg	Stanley	Curran		Baldwin*
	Harper					
Castle	Van	Chambers	Murrah	Bazelon	Cowen	Worley
Robson	Oosterhout	Wollenberg	Stanley	(Curran)		
	Harper			Sirica*		
Castle	Van	Chambers	Murrah	Bazelon	Cowen	(Worley)
Grant	Oosterhout	Taylor	Stanley	Curran		Lane*
	Harper					

449

Appendix C

Judges in Attendance at the Judicial Conference by Circuit

Name of Judge	Date of Birth	Age at Oath	Judicial Conference Attendance Data	
			Years	Age
Chief Justices:				
Black,* Hugo L.	1886	51	1953	67
Burger, Warren E.	1907	48	1969-	62-
Hughes, Charles E.	1862	48	1930-1941	68-79
Stone, Harlan F.	1872	53	1941-1945	69-73
Taft, William H.	1857	34	1922-1929	65-72
Vinson, Frederick M.	1890	48	1946-1953	56-63
Warren, Earl	1891	62	1954-1969	63-78
First Circuit:				
Aldrich, Bailey	1907	52	1965-	58-
Bingham, George H.	1864	49	1922-1938	58-74
Ford, Francis J. W.	1882	51	1960-1967	78-85
Gignoux, Edward T.	1916	39	1967-	51-
Magruder, Calvert	1893	46	1940-1959	47-66
Mahoney, John C.	1882	58	1941	59
Sweeney, George C.	1895	40	1958-1961	63-66
Wilson, Scott	1870	59	1933, 1939	63, 69
Woodbury, Peter	1899	42	1959-1964	60-65
Second Circuit:				
Chase, Harrie B.	1889	39	1953-1954	64-65
Clark, Charles E.	1889	50	1954-1959	65-70
Dimock, Edward J.	1890	61	1958-1959	68-69
Hand, Augustus N.	1869	59	1953	84
Hand, Learned	1872	52	1939-1951	67-79
Hough, Charles M.	1858	58	1926	68
Lumbard, J. Edward	1901	53	1960-	59-
Manton, Martin T.	1880	38	1927-1938	47-58
Rogers, Henry W.	1853	60	1922-1925	69-72
Ryan, Sylvester J.	1896	51	1959-1968	63-72
Smith, J. Joseph	1904	37	1957	53

* See n.2, Appendix B.

451

Name of Judge	Date of Birth	Age at Oath	Judicial Conference Attendance Data	
			Years	Age
Second Circuit (cont.):				
Sugarman, Sidney	1904	45	1968-	64-
Swan, Thomas W.	1877	50	1949, 1951-53	72, 74-76
Waterman, Sterry R.	1901	54	1965	64
Weinfeld, Edward	1901	49	1964	63
Third Circuit:				
Biggs, John, Jr.	1895	42	1939-1965	44-70
Buffington, Joseph	1855	52	1922-1923, 1925, 1930-1937	67-68, 70, 75-82
Clary, Thomas J.	1899	50	1966-1968	67-69
Davis, J. Warren	1867	53	1927, 1938	60, 71
Forman, Phillip	1895	37	1957-1959	62-64
Ganey, J. Cullen	1899	41	1959-1961	60-62
Gourley, Wallace S.	1904	41	1968-	64
Hastie, William H.	1904	33	1968-	64
Kalodner, Henry E.	1896	50	1966	70
Madden, Thomas M.	1907	38	1961-1966	53-58
Maris, Albert B.	1893	45	1954	61
Smith, William F.	1904	37	1961	57
Staley, Austin L.	1902	48	1966-1967	64-65
Thomson, W. H. S.	1856	58	1929	73
Woolley, Victor B.	1867	47	1924, 1926, 1928	57, 59, 61
Fourth Circuit:				
Haynsworth, Clement F.	1912	45	1965-	53-
Hoffman, Walter E.	1907	47	1964-	57-
Parker, John J.	1885	40	1930-1957	45-72
Sobeloff, Simon E.	1893	63	1958-1964	65-71
Soper, Morris A.	1873	59	1941, 1945-46	68, 72-73
Thomsen, Roszel C.	1900	54	1958-1964	58-64
Waddill, Edmund T., Jr.	1855	66	1925-1930	70-75
Winter, Harrison L.	1921	45	1969	48
Woods, Charles A.	1852	61	1922-1924	70-72
Fifth Circuit:				
Brown, John R.	1909	46	1967-	58-
Bryan, Nathan P.	1872	48	1928, 1930-34	56, 58-62

Name of Judge	Date of Birth	Age at Oath	Judicial Conference Attendance Data	
			Years	Age
Fifth Circuit (cont.):				
Carswell, G. Harold	1919	39	1968-	49-
Christenberry, H. W.	1897	50	1965-1968	68-71
Connally, Ben C.	1909	40	1959-1962	50-53
Estes, Joe E.	1903	52	1969-	66
Foster, Rufus E.	1871	54	1935-1941	67-70
Hutcheson, Joseph C.	1879	52	1947-1959	68-80
Lynne, Seybourn H.	1907	39	1958-1959	51-52
Rives, Richard T.	1895	56	1959-1960	64-65
Sibley, Samuel H.	1873	58	1938, 1942-47	65, 69-74
Simpson, Bryan	1903	47	1962-1965	59-62
Tuttle, Elbert Parr	1897	57	1961-1967	64-72
Walker, Richard W.	1857	57	1922-1929	65-72
Sixth Circuit:				
Allen, Florence E.	1884	50	1958-1959	73-74
Boyd, Marion S.	1900	40	1960-1963	60-63
Cecil, Lester L.	1893	66	1962-1963	69-70
Denison, Arthur C.	1861	50	1924-1931	63-70
Freeman, Ralph M.	1902	52	1963-1966	61-64
Hicks, Xenophon	1872	56	1936, 1938-51	64, 66-79
Jones, Paul	1880	43	1958-1960	78-80
Knappen, Loyal E.	1854	56	1922-1923	68-69
Martin, John D., Sr.	1883	57	1959	76
McAllister, Thomas F.	1896	45	1959-1960	63-64
Miller, Shackelford, Jr.	1892	53	1959-1962	67-70
Moorman, Charles H.	1876	49	1932-1937	56-61
Phillips, Harry	1909	54	1969-	60
Simons, Charles	1876	56	1950, 1952-58	74, 76-82
Stewart, Potter	1915	39	1958	43
Swinford, Mac	1899	38	1965-	67-
Weick, Paul C.	1899	61	1964-	65-
Weinman, Carl A.	1903	56	1969-	66
Seventh Circuit:				
Alschuler, Samuel	1859	57	1924-1934	65-75
Baker, Francis E.	1860	42	1922-1923	62-63
Campbell, William J.	1905	33	1958-1961, 1967	53-56, 62
Castle, Latham	1900	59	1968-	68-

	Date of	Age at	Judicial Conference Attendance Data	
Name of Judge	Birth	Oath	Years	Age

Seventh Circuit (cont.):

Duffy, F. Ryan	1888	61	1949, 1954-1959	61, 66-71
Evans, Evan A.	1876	40	1934-1947	58-71
Grant, Robert A.	1905	52	1969-	64
Grubb, Kenneth P.	1895	60	1964-1965	68-70
Hastings, John S.	1898	59	1959-1968	61-70
Kerner, Otto	1884	55	1948	64
Major, J. Earl	1887	50	1946, 1949-1954	59, 62-67
Minton, Sherman	1890	49	1943	53
Robson, Edwin A.	1905	53	1965-	60-
Sparks, William E.	1872	57	1948	76
Steckler, William E.	1913	37	1962-1964	59-51
Swygert, Luther M.	1905	38	1961	56

Eighth Circuit:

Duncan, Richard M.	1889	54	1963-1965	73-75
Gardner, Archibald K.	1867	62	1947-1959	80-92
Harper, Roy W.	1905	42	1965-	60-
Johnsen, Harvey M.	1895	45	1957, 1959-65	62, 64-70
Kenyon, William S.	1869	53	1922	53
Miller, John E.	1888	53	1962-1963	74-75
Nordbye, Gunnar H.	1888	43	1958-1962	70-74
Sanborn, John B.	1883	49	1955-1956	72-73
Sanborn, Walter H.	1845	47	1922-1928	77-83
Stone, Kimbrough	1875	42	1928-1947	53-72
Van Oosterhout, Martin	1900	43	1968-	68-
Vogel, Charles J.	1898	56	1962, 1965-67	64, 67-69
Whittaker, Charles E.	1901	55	1957	56

Ninth Circuit:

Chambers, Richard H.	1906	48	1959-	53
Denman, William	1872	63	1941, 1948-57	69, 76-85
Garrecht, Francis A.	1870	63	1945-1947	75-77
Gilbert, William B.	1847	45	1922-1930	75-83
Goodman, Louis E.	1892	50	1957-1958	65-66
Lindberg, William J.	1904	46	1960-1963	55-58

Name of Judge	Date of Birth	Age at Oath	Judicial Conference Attendance Data Years	Age
Ninth Circuit (cont.):				
Mathes, William C.	1899	46	1958-1960	59-61
Pope, Walter L.	1889	60	1959	70
Rudkin, Frank H.	1864	59	1929-30	65
Solomon, Gus J.	1906	43	1963-1965	57-59
Stephens, Albert Lee	1874	63	1953, 1957-58	79, 83-84
Taylor, Fred M.	1901	53	1969-	68
Wilbur, Curtis D.	1867	62	1931-1944	64-77
Wollenberg, Albert C.	1900	58	1966-	66-
Tenth Circuit:				
Arraj, Alfred A.	1901	56	1964-1967	63-66
Bratton, Sam G.	1888	44	1956-1959	67-70
Kerr, Ewing T.	1900	55	1962-1964	62-64
Lewis, Robert E.	1857	64	1929-1940	78-83
Murrah, Alfred P.	1904	36	1959-	55-
Phillips, Orie L.	1885	44	1932, 1935, 1937-1955	47, 50, 52-70
Pickett, John C.	1896	53	1959	63
Rice, Eugene	1891	46	1958	67
Savage, Royce H.	1904	36	1958-1961	54-57
Stanley, Arthur J.	1902	48	1967-	66-
District of Columbia Circuit:				
Bazelon, David L.	1909	39	1962-	53-
Curran, Edward M.	1903	33	1967-	64-
Edgerton, Henry W.	1888	50	1955-1958	66-70
Fahy, Charles	1892	57	1963-1964	70-71
Groner, D. Lawrence	1873	64	1937-1947	64-74
Laws, Bolitha J.	1891	47	1958	67
McGowan, Carl	1911	52	1967	56
McGuire, Matthew F.	1899	42	1961-1967	62-68
Miller, Wilbur K.	1892	53	1961-1962	69-70
Pine, David A.	1891	49	1959-1962	68-72
Prettyman, E. Barrett	1891	54	1949, 1959-60	58, 68-69
Stephens, Harold M.	1886	49	1947-1955	61-69
Court of Claims:				
Cowen, Wilson	1905	34	1964-	59-
Durfee, James R.	1897	63	1967	70

APPENDIX C.

Name of Judge	Date of Birth	Age at Oath	Judicial Conference Attendance Data Years	Age
Court of Claims (cont.):				
Jones, Marvin	1886	54	1956-1964	60-68
Whittaker, Samuel E.	1886	52	1957-1958 1960, 1966	71-72, 74, 80
Court of Customs and Patent Appeals:				
Baldwin, Phillip B.	1924	44	1968-1969	44-45
Lane, Donald E.	1909	60	1969	60
Rich, Giles S.	1904	52	1967-1968	63-64
Smith, Arthur M.	1903	56	1964-1965	61-62
Worley, Eugene	1908	42	1961-	53-

Bibliography

Bibliography

Manuscript Collections

Department of Justice, Washington, D.C.
  Department of Justice Files
Federal Records Center, Alexandria, Virginia
  Correspondence of the Administrative Office of the
    United States Courts
  Department of Justice Files
Historical Society of Pennsylvania
  Salmon P. Chase Papers
Library of Congress, Washington, D. C.
  William E. Borah Papers
  Salmon P. Chase Papers
  Charles Evans Hughes Papers
  George W. Norris Papers
  Richard Olney Papers
  Harold M. Stephens Papers
  Harlan Fiske Stone Papers
  George Sutherland Papers
  William Howard Taft Papers
  John C. Underwood Papers
National Archives, Washington, D.C.
  Department of Justice Files
  Legislative Files
Private Papers of Elias Clark, Yale University, New Haven,
Connecticut
  Charles E. Clark Papers
University of Missouri, Western Historical Manuscripts
Collection, Columbia, Missouri
  Kimbrough Stone Papers

University of North Carolina, Southern Historical Manuscripts Collection, Chapel Hill, North Carolina
  John J. Parker Papers
University of Oregon, Eugene, Oregon
  Samuel M. Driver Papers
University of Virginia, Charlottesville, Virginia
  Duncan Lawrence Groner Papers

Books

Alsop, Joseph, and Catledge, Turner. *The 168 Days.* Garden City, New York: Doubleday, Doran, and Co., 1938.
American Annual Cyclopaedia, The. Volume vii. New York: D. Appleton and Co., 1872.
Barron, William W., and Holtzoff, Alexander (revised by Charles A. Wright). *Federal Practice and Procedure with Forms,* Rules Edition. Volume i. St. Paul: West Publishing Co., 1960.
Bone, Hugh. *Party Committees and National Politics.* Seattle: University of Washington Press, 1958.
Borkin, Joseph. *The Corrupt Judge: An Inquiry into Bribery and Other High Crimes and Misdemeanors in the Federal Courts.* New York: Clarkson N. Potter, Inc., 1962.
Chafee, Zechariah, Jr. *Freedom of Speech.* New York: Harcourt, Brace and Howe, 1920.
Compilation of the Messages and Papers of the Presidents, A. Volume 17: 1907-11. New York: Bureau of National Literature, Inc., 1911.
———. Volume 18: 1911-15. New York: Bureau of National Literature, Inc., 1915.
Corwin, Edward S.; Small, Norman J.; and Jayson, Lester S., eds. *The Constitution of the United States of America: Analysis and Interpretation.* Washington, D.C.: Government Printing Office, 1964.
Cummings, Homer, and McFarland, Carl. *Federal Justice:*

Chapters in the History of Justice and the Federal Executive. New York: The Macmillan Co., 1937.

Cummings, Homer. *Liberty Under Law and Administration.* New York: Charles Scribner's Sons, 1934.

Eliot, Charles W.; Storey, Moorfield; Brandeis, Louis D.; Pound, Roscoe; and Rodenbeck, Adolph J. *Preliminary Report on Efficiency in the Administration of Justice.* Boston: The National Economic League, 1914.

Fairman, Charles. *Mr. Justice Miller and the Supreme Court: 1862-1890.* Cambridge: Harvard University Press, 1939.

Frank, John P. *Justice Daniel Dissenting: A Biography of Peter V. Daniel, 1784-1860.* Cambridge: Harvard University Press, 1964.

Frankfurter, Felix, and Landis, James M. *The Business of the Supreme Court.* New York: The Macmillan Co., 1928.

Galston, Clarence G. *Behind the Judicial Curtain.* Chicago: Barrington House, 1959.

Green, Leon. *Judge and Jury.* Kansas City, Missouri: Vernon Law Books Co., 1930.

Hurst, James W. *The Growth of American Law: The Law Makers.* Boston: Little, Brown and Co., 1950.

Ickes, Harold L. *The Secret Diary of Harold L. Ickes.* Volume 2: *The Inside Struggle, 1936-1939.* New York: Simon and Schuster, 1954.

King, Willard L. *Melville Weston Fuller: Chief Justice of the United States, 1888-1910.* Chicago: The University of Chicago Press, 1967.

Langeluttig, Albert. *The Department of Justice of the United States.* Baltimore: The Johns Hopkins Press, 1927.

Mason, Alpheus T. *Harlan Fiske Stone: Pillar of the Law.* New York: Viking Press, 1956.

―――. *William Howard Taft: Chief Justice.* New York: Simon and Schuster, 1965.

Murphy, Walter F. *Congress and the Court: A Case Study in the American Political Process.* Chicago: The University of Chicago Press, 1964.

Murphy, Walter F. *Elements of Judicial Strategy*. Chicago: The University of Chicago Press, 1964.

Pusey, Merlo J. *Charles Evans Hughes*, Volume 2. New York: The Macmillan Co., 1951.

Pye, Kenneth, Shadoan, George W., Siree, Joseph M., *A Preliminary Survey of the Federal Probation System*. Washington: Georgetown University Law Center, 1963.

Reppy, Alison, ed. *David Dudley Field: Centenary Essays*. New York: New York University Law School, 1949.

Richardson, Richard J., and Vines, Kenneth N. *The Politics of Federal Courts: Lower Courts in the United States*. Boston: Little, Brown and Co., 1970.

Roe, Gilbert E. *Our Judicial Oligarchy*. New York: B. W. Huebsch Co., 1912.

Reorganization of the Federal Judiciary: Lower Federal Court Study with Respect to Congestion of Calendars and Assignments of Judges and How the Same will be Affected by the Proposed Reforms of the Federal Judiciary. Chicago: American Bar Association, 1937.

Rosenman, Samuel I., ed. *The Public Papers and Addresses of Franklin D. Roosevelt*. Volume 4: *1937*. New York: Random House, 1938.

————. Volume 6: *1939*. New York: The Macmillan Co., 1941.

Schick, Marvin. *Learned Hand's Court*. Baltimore: The Johns Hopkins Press, 1970.

Swisher, Carl B. *American Constitutional Development*. 2d ed. Cambridge: Houghton, Mifflin Co., 1954.

————, ed. *Selected Papers of Homer Cummings*. New York: Charles Scribner's Sons, 1939.

Taft, William Howard. *Present Day Problems*. New York: Dodd, Mead, and Co., 1908.

U.S. *The Budget of the United States Government, Fiscal Year 1971*. Washington, D.C.: Government Printing Office, 1970.

U.S. *United States Government Organizational Manual*:

1969-70. Washington, D.C.: Government Printing Office, 1969.

Vanderbilt, Arthur T. *The Challenge of Law Reform*. Princeton: Princeton University Press, 1955.

Van Tassel, H. G. *The Importance of Administration in the United States Courts: An Individual Businessman's View*. Washington: The Brookings Institution Public Affairs Fellowship Program, 1962.

Warren, Charles. *The Supreme Court in United States History*. 2 volumes. Boston: Little, Brown and Co., 1926.

White, Leonard, ed. *Civil Service in Wartime*. Chicago: The University of Chicago Press, 1945.

Willoughby, William F. *Principles of Judicial Administration*. Washington: The Brookings Institution, 1929.

Zeisel, Hans, Kalven, Harry J., Buchholz, Bernard. *Delay in the Court*. Boston: Little, Brown and Co., 1959.

Articles and Periodicals

"Administration Function in Federal Courts." *Journal of the American Judicature Society*, 21 (June 1937), 5-6.

"Administrative Office of the United States Courts Publishes New Presentence Monograph." *Federal Probation*, 29 (June 1965), 77.

"Administrative Plan for Federal Judiciary." *Journal of the American Judicature Society*, 21 (February 1938), 142-45.

"Appellate Review of Sentences: A Symposium at the Judicial Conference of the United States Court of Appeals for the Second Circuit." *Federal Rules Decisions*, 32 (1963), 249-321.

"Ashurst Bill Can Conserve Judicial Independence." *Journal of the American Judicature Society*, 22 (February 1939), 187.

Bates, Sanford. "The Establishment and Early Years of the Federal Probation System." *Federal Probation*, 14 (June 1950), 16-21.

Bazelon, David L. "The Future of Reform in the Administration of Criminal Justice." *Federal Rules Decisions,* 35 (1964), 99-114.

Biggs, John, Jr. "Observations of Chief Judge Biggs." *Federal Rules Decisions,* 21 (1958), 122-25.

————. "Some Observations on Judicial Administration." *Federal Rules Decisions,* 29 (1962), 464-73.

Brown, Robert C. "The Jurisdiction of the Federal Courts Based on the Diversity of Citizenship." *University of Pennsylvania Law Review,* 78 (December 1929), 179-94.

Bundschu, Henry A. "H.R. 4394: Mr. Bundschu's Comment." *Journal of the National Association of Referees in Bankruptcy,* 15 (July 1941), 133.

Burger, Warren E. "The Courts on Trial: A Call for Action Against Delay." *Federal Rules Decisions,* 22 (1958), 71-83.

Burton, Harold H. "Judging is Also Administration." *Temple Law Quarterly,* 21 (October 1947), 77-90.

"Case Comments: Courts—Judicial Responsibilities—Statutory and Constitutional Problems Relating to Methods for Removal or Discipline of Judges." *Rutgers Law Review,* 21 (Fall 1966), 153-78.

Chandler, Henry P. "Address of Honorable Henry P. Chandler." *Journal of the National Association of Referees in Bankruptcy,* 25 (January 1951), 19-23.

————. "Administering the Federal Courts." In *Strengthening Management for Democratic Government,* pp. 28-32. Chicago: American Society for Public Administration, 1958.

————. "The Administration of the Federal Courts." *Law and Contemporary Problems,* 13 (Winter 1948), 182-99.

————. "The Administrative Office." *Journal of the National Association of Referees in Bankruptcy,* 16 (October 1941), 17-18.

————. "The Administrative Office and Bankruptcy." *Journal of the National Association of Referees in Bankruptcy,* 24 (January 1950), 9-12.

————. "The Administrative Office and the Referees." *Journal of the National Association of Referees in Bankruptcy*, 17 (October 1942), 5-8.

————. "The Administrative Office and the Referees." *Journal of the National Association of Referees in Bankruptcy*, 19 (October 1944), 16-19.

————. "An Administrative Office for State Courts." *Journal of the American Judicature Society*, 26 (June 1942), 7-10.

————. "The Administrative Office of the United States Courts." *Federal Rules Decisions*, 1 (1941), 610-20.

————. "The Administrative Office of the United States Courts." *Federal Rules Decisions*, 2 (1943), 53-66.

————. "The Administrative Office of the United States Courts." *Federal Rules Decisions*, 4 (1946), 488-91.

————. "The Administrative Office of the United States Courts." *Journal of the National Association of Referees in Bankruptcy*, 15 (October 1940), 49-52.

————. "The Beginning of a New Era in Bankruptcy Administration." *Journal of the National Association of Referees in Bankruptcy*, 34 (January 1960), 3-6, 25-26.

————. "The Beginning of a New Era in Bankruptcy Administration." *Journal of the National Association of Referees in Bankruptcy*, 34 (April 1960), 44-53.

————. "The Business of the United States Courts." *Boston University Law Review*, 21 (January 1941), 3-19.

————. "Court Administration Agency to Supervise Federal Probation." *Federal Probation*, 4 (May 1940), 4-5.

————. "The Direction of Administration of Trial Courts." *Federal Rules Decisions*, 21 (1958), 65-96.

————. "Making the Judiciary Machinery Function Efficiently." *New York Law Quarterly Review*, 22 (July 1947), 445-56.

————. "The Outlook Under the New Referee Act." *Journal of the National Association of Referees in Bankruptcy*, 21 (October 1946), 9-14.

————. "The Place of the Administrative Office in the Federal Court System." *Cornell Law Quarterly*, 27 (April 1942), 364-73.

———. "Plans for the Development of Probation in the United States Courts." *Federal Probation*, 4 (November-December 1940), 4-8.

———. "Probation and Parole Officers: The Importance of Their Work." *Federal Probation*, 20 (March 1956), 9-14.

———. "The Problem of Congestion and Delay in the Federal Courts." *Annals of the American Academy of Political and Social Science*, 328 (March 1960), 144-52.

———. "Some Major Advances in the Federal Judicial System: 1922-1947." *Federal Rules Decisions*, 31 (1963), 307-517.

———. "The Winds of Change in Federal Judicial Administration." *Journal of the American Judicature Society*, 46 (April 1963), 242-49, 266.

Chandler, Stephen S. "The Role of the Trial Judge in the Anglo-American Legal System." *American Bar Association Journal*, 50 (February 1964), 125-30.

Chappell, Richard A. "The Federal Probation System Today." *Federal Probation*, 14 (June 1950), 30-40.

"Chief Judicial Superintendent, The." *Journal of the American Judicature Society*, 1 (August 1917), 19-22.

"Chief Justice Hughes Addresses Judicial Conference of the Fourth Circuit." *American Bar Association Journal*, 18 (July 1932), 445-48.

Clark, Charles E. "Code Pleading and Practice Today." In *David Dudley Field: Contemporary Essays*, edited by Alison Reppy. New York: New York University, School of Law, 1941.

———. "The Influence of Federal Procedural Reform." *Law and Contemporary Problems*, 13 (Winter 1948), 144-64.

———. "Present Status of Judicial Statistics." *Journal of the American Judicature Society*, 14 (October 1930), 84-87.

———. "The Role of the United States Court of Appeals in Law Administration." In *Conference on Judicial Admin-*

istration, series no. 16, pp. 94-98. Chicago: University of Chicago School of Law, 1956.

————. "Two Decades of the Federal Civil Rules." *Columbia Law Review,* 58 (April 1958), 435-51.

Clayton, Henry D. "Popularizing Administration of Justice." *American Bar Association Journal,* 8 (January 1922), 43-51.

"Comprehensive Programme, Our." *Journal of the American Judicature Society,* 2 (April 1919), 165-68.

"Court Congestion: Problems and Progress Throughout the Nation." *Journal of the American Judicature Society,* 45 (December 1961), 144-46.

Covey, Edwin L. "A Day with the Administrative Office." *Journal of the National Association of Referees in Bankruptcy,* 23 (January 1949), 51-54.

————. "Referees and Their Indemnity Funds and Accounts." *Journal of the National Association of Referees in Bankruptcy,* 17 (October 1942), 9-10.

Cummings, Homer. "Immediate Problems for the Bar." *American Bar Association Journal,* 20 (April 1934), 212-14.

————. "The Value of Judicial Conferences in the Federal Circuit." *American Bar Association Journal,* 24 (December 1938), 979-81.

Daugherty, Harry M. "Congested Dockets in the Federal Courts Menace to Justice." *Central Law Journal,* 95 (December 1922), 416-17.

Davis, Robert R., Jr. "The Chandler Incident and Problems of Judicial Removal." *Stanford Law Review,* 19 (January 1967), 448-67.

Dean, Claude. "Sixth Annual Judicial Conference of Fourth Circuit Devotes Entire Time to Preliminary Draft of Rules of Procedure Prepared by Advisory Committee of Supreme Court." *American Bar Association Journal,* 21 (July 1936), 444.

Denman, William J. "Administration Is Chief Need of Fed-

eral Courts." *Journal of the American Judicature Society,*
22 (August 1938), 57-61.

―――. "Critical Study of United States Trial Courts: What
the Legislature Owes the Judiciary." *Journal of the American Judicature Society,* 21 (December 1937), 115-25.

Dix, George E. "The Death of the Commerce Court: A
Study in Institutional Weakness." *The American Journal
of Legal History,* 8 (July 1964), 238-60.

"Eighth Circuit Judicial Conference Considers Rules for
Civil Practice in Federal Courts." *American Bar Association Journal,* 21 (February 1935), 69.

Evans, Evan A. "Judicial Conference of the Seventh Circuit." *American Bar Association Journal,* 29 (February
1943), 81.

"Fair Deal Laws Create Need for More Judges." Editorial,
Saturday Evening Post, February 2, 1952, pp. 10-12.

"Federal Courts Could Use Improvement in Routine," *Saturday Evening Post,* November 10, 1951, pp. 10-12.

"Federal Judicial Council, The" (Conference of Senior Circuit Judges). *Texas Law Review,* 2 (June 1924), 458-63.

"Federal Judicial System Nears End of Reform Program."
Journal of the American Judicature Society, 24 (December 1940), 106-10.

"Federal Judicial Work in Seventh Circuit." *American Bar
Association Journal,* 7 (May 1921), 244.

Fenno, Richard F., Jr. "The House Appropriations Committee as a Political System: The Problem of Integration."
American Political Science Review, 56 (June 1962),
310-24.

Fish, Peter G. "Crises, Politics, and Federal Judicial Reform: The Administrative Office Act of 1939." *The Journal of Politics,* 32 (August 1970), 596-627.

―――. "The Politics of Judicial Administration: Transfer
of the Federal Probation System." *The Western Political
Quarterly,* 23 (December 1970), 769-84.

―――. "The Status of the Federal Probation System."
Crime and Delinquency, 12 (October 1966), 365-70.

———. "Toward a Judicial Administrator of Limited Powers: Bankruptcy Crisis and the Administrative Office of the United States Courts." *Journal of the National Conference of Referees in Bankruptcy,* 44 (October 1970), 123-32.

"For a Better Deal in Criminal Justice." Editorial, *Saturday Evening Post,* December 11, 1943, p. 116.

Fowler, Chester A. "Wisconsin's Board of Circuit Judges." *Journal of the American Judicature Society,* 4 (December 1920), 101-03.

Frank, John P. "Historical Bases of the Federal Judicial System." *Law and Contemporary Problems,* 13 (Winter 1948), 3-28.

Frankel, Jack E. "The Case for Judicial Disciplinary Measures." *Journal of the American Judicature Society,* 49 (April 1966), 218-23.

Gallo, Jon J. "Removal of Federal Judges—New Alternatives to an Old Problem: Chandler v. Judicial Council of the Tenth Circuit." *University of California at Los Angeles Law Review,* 13 (August 1966), 1385-1407.

Green, Leon. "Recent Steps in Law Administration." *Journal of the American Judicature Society,* 15 (December 1930), 113-16.

Harley, Herbert. "Administering Justice in Cities." *Annals of the American Academy of Political and Social Science,* 136 (March 1928), 87-94.

———. "Forced Retirement of Federal Trial Judges." *Journal of the American Judicature Society,* 21 (October 1937), 86-89.

Hastings, John S. "Report on the Criminal Justice Act." *Federal Rules Decisions,* 39 (1965), 399-408.

Holtzoff, Alexander. "The Administration of the Federal Judiciary." *Federal Bar Association Journal,* 3 (November 1939), 373-76.

Hughes, Charles Evans. "Address of Chief Justice Hughes." *American Bar Association Journal,* 17 (June 1931), 363-65.

Hughes, Charles Evans. "Address of Chief Justice Hughes." *American Bar Association Journal*, 22 (June 1936), 374-76.

———. "Address of Charles Evans Hughes." *American Law Institute, Proceedings*, 9 (1931), 44-50.

———. "Address of the Honorable Charles Evans Hughes." *The American Law Institute, Proceedings*, 17 (1940), 27-33.

———. "Address of the Honorable Charles Evans Hughes." *The American Law Institute, Proceedings*, 18 (1941), 24-29.

———. "The Administrative Office of the United States Courts." *Massachusetts Law Quarterly*, 25 (April-June 1940), 9-11.

———. "Chief Justice Hughes Addresses Judicial Conference of Fourth Circuit." *American Bar Association Journal*, 18 (July 1932), 445-48.

Isaac, Max. "The Relief of Federal Courts and the Pay of Federal Judges." *Central Law Journal*, 93 (October 1921), 255-256.

Jackson, Robert H. "Progress in Federal Judicial Administration." *Journal of the American Judicature Society*, 23 (August 1939), 60-62.

Jackson, Royal E. "Recent Developments in Bankruptcy Administration." *Journal of the National Conference of Referees in Bankruptcy*, 41 (January 1967), 19-21.

———. "Remarks of Royal E. Jackson." *Journal of the National Association of Referees in Bankruptcy*, 38 (January 1964), 19-21.

———. "Trends and Developments in Bankruptcy Administration." *Journal of the National Conference of Referees in Bankruptcy*, 40 (January 1966), 10-12.

"Judge Merrill E. Otis Condemns Pending Bill." *Journal of the American Judicature Society*, 22 (February 1939), 191-93.

"Judicial Conference Committee Reports on the Operation of the Federal Jury System." *Journal of the American Judicature Society*, 44 (April 1961), 213-17.

"Judicial Conference for the Fifth Circuit: Report of Interesting Discussions and Actions." *American Bar Association Journal*, 34 (August 1948), 671-73, 754-55.

"Judicial Conferences: Fifth, Eighth, and Tenth Circuits." *American Bar Association Journal*, 33 (November 1947), 1111-15.

"Judicial Conferences: First, Second, Third, Fourth, and Seventh Circuits." *American Bar Association Journal*, 33 (September 1947), 873-76.

"Judicial Conferences: Sixth, Ninth, and District of Columbia." *American Bar Association Journal*, 33 (October 1947), 979-84.

"The Judicial Council." Editorial, *American Bar Association Journal*, 11 (August 1925), 508-09.

"The Judicial Council of the Third Circuit: In the Matter of the Examination by the Administrative Office of the United States Courts of the Records of Everett G. Rodebaugh, one of the Court Reporters of the United States District Court for the Eastern District of Pennsylvania." *Federal Rules Decisions*, 10 (1951), 207-24.

Kaufman, Irving. "Appellate Review of Sentences: A Symposium at the Judicial Conference of the United States Court of Appeals for the Second Circuit." *Federal Rules Decisions*, 32 (1963), 261-63.

Kurtz, Irwin. "President's Address." *Journal of the National Association of Referees in Bankruptcy*, 19 (October 1944), 7.

LaMarche, Melville. "The Work of the Audit Section of the Administrative Office of the United States Courts as it is Related to Bankruptcy." *Journal of the National Association of Referees in Bankruptcy*, 19 (October 1944), 26-28.

Laws, Bolitha J. "Adequate Personnel for the Courts." *Journal of the Bar Association of the District of Columbia*, 20 (April 1953), 182-89.

Lumbard, J. Edward. "The Place of the Federal Judicial Councils in the Administration of the Courts." *American Bar Association Journal*, 47 (February 1961), 169-72.

McCaskill, O. L. "The Modern Philosophy of Pleading: A Dialogue Outside the Shades," *American Bar Association Journal*, 38 (February 1952), 123-26, 174-75.

Magruder, Calvert. "Foreword, First Annual Conference of the First Circuit." *Boston University Law Review*, 21 (January 1941), 1-2.

————. "The Trials and Tribulations of an Intermediate Appellate Court." *Cornell Law Quarterly*, 44 (Fall 1958), 1-13.

Maris, Albert B. "Address: John Biggs, Jr., In Appreciation." *Federal Rules Decisions*, 39 (1966), 464-70.

————. "Federal Procedural Rule-Making: The Program of the Judicial Conference." *American Bar Association Journal*, 47 (August 1961), 772-77.

Medina, Harold R. "Remarks—On Retirement of Chief Judge Charles E. Clark from His Administrative Duties." *Record of the Bar Association of New York*, 15 (1960), 16-19.

————. "The Work of the Administrative Office of the United States Courts." *Federal Rules Decisions*, 11 (1952), 353-61.

Miller, Justin. "Supporting Personnel of Federal Courts." *American Bar Association Journal*, 29 (March 1943), 130-34.

Mitchell, William D. "The Federal Rules of Civil Procedure." In *David Dudley Field: Centenary Essays*, edited by Alison Reppy. New York: New York University, School of Law, 1941.

Moore, James W. "Problems of the Federal Judiciary." *Federal Rules Decisions*, 35 (1964), 305-16.

————. "Address of Professor Moore." *Federal Rules Decisions*, 21 (1958), 125-33.

Morse, Lewis W. "Federal Judicial Conferences and Councils: Their Creation and Reports." *Cornell Law Quarterly*, 27 (April 1942), 347-63.

Murphy, Walter F. "Chief Justice Taft and the Lower

Court Bureaucracy: A Study in Judicial Administration." *Journal of Politics*, 24 (August 1962), 453-76.

Neal, Phil C., and Goldberg, Perry. "The Electrical Equipment Antitrust Cases: Novel Judicial Administration." *American Bar Association Journal*, 50 (July 1964), 621-28.

"New Law Unifies Federal Judiciary." *Journal of the American Judicature Society*, 6 (October 1922), 69-72.

"News and Editorial Comment: The Second Seminar for Referees." *Journal of the National Association of Referees in Bankruptcy*, 39 (July 1965), 66-67.

"Notes: Judicial Administration in the Federal Courts." *Harvard Law Review*, 31 (May 1918), 1011-13.

"Notes: The Exclusiveness of the Impeachment Power Under the Constitution." *Harvard Law Review*, 51 (December 1937), 330-36.

"Notes: Judicial Performance in the Fifth Circuit." *Yale Law Journal*, 73 (November 1963), 90-133.

"Notes: The Second Circuit: Federal Judicial Administration in Microcosm." *Columbia Law Review*, 63 (May 1963), 874-908.

Olney, Warren, III. "Administration in the Federal System." *Journal of the American Judicature Society*, 42 (June 1958), 21-22.

—————. "The Administrative Office of the United States Courts." *Journal of the American Judicature Society*, 42 (October 1958), 78-85.

—————. "The Federal Probation System in 1963: Where We Stand." *Federal Probation*, 27 (September 1963), 3-8.

—————. "New Directions in Judicial Administration." *Federal Probation*, 22 (December 1958), 3-6.

Otis, Merrill E. "The Business of the United States District Courts." *Journal of the American Judicature Society*, 23 (December 1939), 148-52.

"Papers Delivered at the Institute on Sentencing for the United States District Judges." *Federal Rules Decisions*, 35 (1964), 381-509.

Parker, John J. "The Federal Judiciary." *Tulane Law Review*, 22 (June 1948), 569-84.

———. "The Integration of the Federal Judiciary." *Harvard Law Review*, 56 (January 1943), 563-75.

———. "Schools of Jurisprudence in the Federal System." *Journal of the American Judicature Society*, 23 (June 1939), 5-10.

Phillips, Orie L. "Better Court Administration, A Challenge to the Bench and Bar." *Journal of the American Judicature Society*, 39 (June 1955), 9-12.

"Pilot Institute on Sentencing, Proceedings." *Federal Rules Decisions*, 26 (1961), 231-383.

Pirsig, Maynard E. "A Survey of Judicial Councils, Judicial Conferences and Administrative Directors." *The Brief*, 47 (Spring 1952), 181-205.

"Plausible Idea for Ashurst Bill Advanced." *Journal of the American Judicature Society*, 22 (August 1938), 62.

Pound, Roscoe. "The Causes of Popular Dissatisfaction with the Administration of Justice." *Journal of the American Judicature Society*, 20 (February 1937), 178-87.

———. "Organization of Courts." *Journal of the American Judicature Society*, 11 (October 1927), 69-83.

Prettyman, E. Barrett. "The Duties of a Circuit Chief Judge." *American Bar Association Journal*, 46 (June 1960), 633-36.

"Proceedings of the Twenty-Eighth Annual Judicial Conference: Third Judicial Circuit of the United States." *Federal Rules Decisions*, 39 (1965), 375-580.

"Proceedings of the Twenty-Ninth Annual Judicial Conference, Third Judicial Circuit of the United States, 1966." *Federal Rules Decisions*, 42 (1967), 437-580.

"Qualifications of Probation Officers." *Federal Probation*, 6 (January-March 1942), 7-16.

Ransom, William L. "Members and Non-members of the American Bar Association Take Same Stand on Court Issues." *American Bar Association Journal*, 23 (May 1937), 338-43, 381-88.

"Referees' Seminar, The." *Journal of the National Association of Referees in Bankruptcy*, 38 (April 1964), 34.

Remington, Frank and Newman, Donald J. "The Highland Park Institute on Sentence Disparity." *Federal Probation*, 26 (March 1962), 3-9.

"Report of the Committee on Judicial Administration and Remedial Procedures." *Report of the 35th Annual Meeting of the American Bar Association*, vol. 37, pp. 434-36. Baltimore: The Lord Baltimore Press, 1912.

"Report of the Standing Committee on Jurisprudence and Law Reform." *Annual Report of the American Bar Association*, vol. 66, pp. 240-46. Baltimore: The Lord Baltimore Press, 1941.

"Report of the Committee on the Establishment of a Permanent Organization for the Improvement of the Law Proposing the Establishment of an American Law Institute." *American Law Institute, Proceedings*, 1 (1923), 1-65.

"Report of the Committee on Uniform Judicial Procedures." *Report of the 45th Annual Meeting of the American Bar Association*, vol. 47, pp. 80-82. Baltimore: The Lord Baltimore Press, 1922.

"Report of the Committee on Uniform Judicial Procedures." *Report of the 56th Annual Meeting of the American Bar Association*, vol. 58, pp. 108-10. Baltimore: The Lord Baltimore Press, 1933.

"Report of the Special Committee to Suggest Remedies and Formulate Proposed Laws to Prevent Delay and Unnecessary Cost in Litigation." *Report of the 32nd Annual Meeting of the American Bar Association*, vol. 34, pp. 578-602. Baltimore: The Lord Baltimore Press, 1909.

"Report of the Standing Committee on Jurisprudence and Law Reform." *Report of the 46th Annual Meeting of the American Bar Association*, vol. 48, pp. 325-40. Baltimore: The Lord Baltimore Press, 1923.

Roosevelt, Theodore. "Judges and Progress." *Outlook*, January 6, 1912, pp. 40-47.

"The Rule-Making Function and the Judicial Conference of the United States." *Federal Rules Decisions*, 21 (1958), 117-41.

Schmidhauser, John R. "Age and Judicial Behavior: American Higher Appellate Judges." In *Politics of Age*, edited by Wilma Donahue and Clark Tibbits. Ann Arbor: University of Michigan Press, 1962.

Schwartz, Louis B. and Bator, Paul M. "Criminal Justice in the Mid-Sixties: Escobedo Revisited." *Federal Rules Decisions*, 42 (1967), 463-78.

"Seminar and Institute on Disparity of Sentencing for the Sixth, Seventh, and Eighth Judicial Circuits." *Federal Rules Decisions*, 30 (1962), 401-505.

"Seminar Held for Newly Appointed Federal Judges." *Federal Probation*, 26 (March 1962), 75.

"Seminar on Procedures for Effective Judicial Administration, 1961, Proceedings of the." *Federal Rules Decisions*, 29 (1962), 191-473.

"Senior Judges Plan to Integrate Federal System." *Journal of the American Judicature Society*, 22 (December 1938), 160-62, 177-78.

Shafroth, Will. "Federal Judicial Statistics." *Law and Contemporary Problems*, 13 (Winter 1948), 200-15.

————. "New Machinery for Effective Administration of Federal Courts." *American Bar Association Journal*, 25 (September 1939), 738-41.

————. "Pre-Trial Techniques of Federal Judges." *Journal of the American Judicature Society*, 28 (August 1944), 39-45.

Sharp, Louis J. "Inservice Training in Probation and Parole." *Federal Probation*, 15 (December 1951), 25-30.

————. "The Pilot Institute on Sentencing." *Federal Probation*, 23 (December 1959), 9-11.

Shartel, Burke. "Federal Judges—Appointment, Supervision and Removal—Some Possibilities Under the Constitution." *Michigan Law Review*, 28 (May 1930), 870-909.

————. "Retirement and Removal of Judges." *Journal of the*

American Judicature Society, 20 (December 1936), 133-53.

Speck, William H. "Statistics for the United States Courts: An Indispensable Tool for Judicial Management." *American Bar Association Journal,* 38 (November 1952), 936-39, 970-71.

Stephens, Harold M. "Address of Harold M. Stephens." *Nebraska Law Review,* 34 (January 1955), 401-17.

————. "The Administrative Affairs of the United States Courts: A Report to the Bar." *American Bar Association Journal,* 38 (July 1952), 555-60, 621-22.

Stone, Harlan Fiske. "Functions of the Circuit Conferences." *American Bar Association Journal,* 28 (August 1942), 519-20.

Sunderland, Edson R. "Modern Procedural Services." In *David Dudley Field: Centenary Essays,* edited by Alison Reppy. New York: New York University, School of Law, 1941.

Surrency, Edwin C. "A History of Federal Courts." *Missouri Law Review,* 28 (Spring 1963), 214-44.

Swisher, Carl B. "Federal Organization of Legal Functions." *American Political Science Review,* 33 (December 1939), 973-1000.

Taft, William Howard. "Adequate Machinery for Judicial Business." *American Bar Association Journal,* 7 (September 1921), 453-54.

————. "Address." *Chicago Bar Record,* 5 (December 1921), 8-13.

————. "Address of the President." *Report of the 37th Annual Meeting of the American Bar Association,* vol. 39, pp. 359-85. Baltimore: The Lord Baltimore Press, 1914.

————. "Attacks on the Courts and Legal Procedure." *Kentucky Law Journal,* 5 (November 1916), 3-24.

————. "Delays and Defects in the Enforcement of Laws in this Country." *North American Review,* 183 (June 1908), 851-61.

Taft, William Howard. "The Delays of the Law." *Yale Law Journal*, 18 (November 1908), 28-39.

———. "Informal Address." *Report of the 44th Annual Meeting of the American Bar Association*, vol. 46, pp. 561-66. Baltimore: The Lord Baltimore Press, 1921.

———. "Possible and Needed Reforms in Administration of Justice in Federal Courts." *American Bar Association Journal*, 8 (October 1922), 601-07.

———. Remarks, "Proceedings of the Judicial Section." *Report of the 39th Annual Meeting of the American Bar Association*, vol. 41, pp. 741-44. Baltimore: The Lord Baltimore Press, 1916.

———. "Three Needed Steps of Progress." *American Bar Association Journal*, 8 (January 1922), 34-36.

Theil, Orin. "Judicial Statistics." *Annals of the American Academy of Political and Social Science*, 328 (March 1960), 94-104.

"Thirteenth Annual Judicial Conference of the District of Columbia." *The Journal of the Bar Association of the District of Columbia*, 20 (April 1953), 176-89.

Tolman, Leland L. "The Administration of the Federal Courts: A Review of Progress During 1950-51." *American Bar Association Journal*, 38 (February 1952), 127-30.

———. "The Administration of the Federal Courts: A Review of Ten Years of Progress." *American Bar Association Journal*, 37 (January 1951), 31-34, 57.

———. "Court Administration: Housekeeping for the Judiciary." *Annals of the American Academy of Political and Social Science*, 328 (March 1960), 105-15.

Tuttle, Arthur. "The Pending Referee-in-Bankruptcy Bill: Why I Oppose It." *American Bar Association Journal*, 27 (June 1941), 390-91.

Tydings, Joseph D. "The Courts and Congress." *Public Administration Review*, 31 (March/April 1971), 113-20.

Vanderbilt, Arthur T. "For Business Management of Federal Courts." *Journal of the American Judicature Society*, 21 (April 1938), 195-97.

———. "Our Main Order of Business: The Administration of Justice." *American Bar Association Journal*, 24 (March 1938), 187-90.

Vinson, Fred M. "The Business of Judicial Administration." *Journal of the American Judicature Society*, 33 (October 1949), 73-78.

Wallace, William R. "Judge Denman's Contribution to the Reorganization of the Lower Federal Courts and its Relation to the Court Enlargement Bill of 1937." Reprinted from *The Record* (San Francisco), April 7, 1939.

Walsh, Lawrence E. "The Federal Judiciary: Progress and the Road Ahead." *Journal of the American Judicature Society*, 43 (February 1960), 155-58.

Warren, Earl. "Address Delivered by the Honorable Earl Warren, Chief Justice of the United States." *Journal of the National Association of Referees in Bankruptcy*, 37 (January 1963), 3-5.

———. "Address of the Honorable Earl Warren." *Federal Rules Decisions*, 35 (1964), 181-93.

———. "Delay and Congestion in the Federal Courts." *Journal of the American Judicature Society*, 42 (June 1958), 6-12.

———. "Statement of the Chief Justice." *Federal Rules Decisions*, 21 (1958), 118-19.

Watkins, Myron W. "Electrical Equipment Anti-trust Cases —Their Implications for Government and for Business." *The University of Chicago Law Review*, 29 (Autumn 1961), 97-110.

Whitehurst, Elmore. "Address by Elmore Whitehurst." *Journal of the National Association of Referees in Bankruptcy*, 27 (April 1953), 66-67.

———. "Business Administration of the United States Courts." *Federal Rules Decisions*, 3 (1944), 312-19.

———. "The Referees and the Civil Service Retirement Law." *Journal of the National Association of Referees in Bankruptcy*, 23 (January 1949), 54-55.

Wigmore, John H. "Wanted—A Chief Judicial Superintendent." *Journal of the American Judicature Society*, 1 (June 1917), 7-9.

Winters, Glenn R. "Herbert Harley and the American Judicature Society, Part I: Background and Beginnings." *Journal of the American Judicature Society*, 30 (October 1946), 78-82.

Wright, Charles A. "The Doubtful Omniscience of Appellate Courts." *Minnesota Law Review*, 41 (May 1957), 751-82.

Wyden, Peter. "The Man Who Frightens Bureaucrats." *Saturday Evening Post*, January 31, 1959, pp. 27 ff.

Youngdahl, Luther W. "Developments of the Federal Probation System." *Federal Probation*, 28 (September 1964), 3-9.

Unpublished Material

Baar, Carl. "When Judges Lobby: Congress and Court Administration." Ph.D. dissertation, University of Chicago, 1969.

Fish, Peter G. "The Process of Federal Judicial Administration." Ph.D. dissertation, Johns Hopkins University, 1968.

————. "Salmon Portland Chase: His Concept of the Office and Powers of the Chief Justice." Senior Thesis, Princeton University, 1960.

Wilson, Wayne L. "The Federal Corrections Act: A Case Study of Judicial Lobbying." Thesis submitted for Graduation with Distinction, Duke University, 1971.

Public Documents

Executive Branch:

"Administration of the Bankruptcy Act." *Report of the Attorney General's Committee on Bankruptcy Administration, 1940*. Washington: Government Printing Office, 1941.

Annual Report of the Attorney General of the United

480

States for: *1911-41*. Washington: Government Printing Office, 1911-41.

The President's Committee on Administrative Management Report of the Committee with Studies of Administrative Management in the Federal Government. Washington: Government Printing Office, 1937.

Proceedings of the Attorney General's Conference on Congestion and Delay in Litigation. Washington: Government Printing Office, 1958.

Public Papers of the Presidents: *Dwight D. Eisenhower.* Washington: Government Printing Office, 1956.

Public Papers of the Presidents: *John F. Kennedy.* Washington: Government Printing Office, 1964.

Judicial Branch:
Report of the Judicial Conference (variously titled).
  1922-23: "The Federal Judicial Council." *Texas Law Review*, 2 (June 1924), 248-63.
  1924-44: Reports of the Judicial Conference in *Annual Report of the Attorney General*. Washington: Government Printing Office, 1924-1944 (variously titled).
  1945-47: *Report of the Judicial Conference of Senior Circuit Judges.* Issued with *Annual Report of the Director of the Administrative Office of the United States Courts.* Washington: Government Printing Office, 1946-1948.
  1948-52: *Report of the Judicial Conference of the United States.* Issued with *Annual Report of the Director of the Administrative Office of the United States Courts.* Washington: Government Printing Office, 1949-1953. By Act of June 25, 1948, 62 *Stat.* 902, sec. 331, the Conference of Senior Circuit Judges was designated "Judicial Conference of the United States."
  1953, 1957: *Report of the Proceedings of the Annual Meeting of the Judicial Conference of the United*

States. Washington: Government Printing Office, 1954, 1958.

1954-56 and 1958-60: *Annual Report of the Proceedings of the Judicial Conference of the United States.* Issued with *Annual Report of the Director of the Administrative Office of the United States Courts.* Washington: Government Printing Office, 1955-1957 and 1959-1961.

1962: *Annual Reports of the Proceedings of the Judicial Conference of the United States.* Issued with *Annual Report of the Director of the Administrative Office of the United States Courts.* Washington: Government Printing Office, 1963.

1961 and 1963-69: *Reports of the Proceedings of the Judicial Conference of the United States.* Issued with *Annual Report of the Director of the Administrative Office of the United States Courts.* Washington: Government Printing Office, 1962 and 1964-70.

Judicial Conference Proceeding. "Administration in the Federal Courts—Administrative Office Bill. Extract from the Proceedings of the Judicial Conference, September 30, 1938, pp. 174-92," mimeograph. Washington: Administrative Office of the United States Courts.

Reports of Committees of the Judicial Conference, mimeograph. Washington: Administrative Office of the United States Courts.

"Report of the Committee on Bankruptcy Administration," August 27, 1948.

"Report of the Committee on Codification and Revision of the Judicial Code," 1947.

"Report of the Committee on Court Administration," March 5, 1957.

"Report of the Committee on the Court Reporting System," 1951.

"Report of the Committee on Maintenance Expenses of Judges," April 30, 1953.

"Report of the Committee on the Operation of the Jury System," September 11, 1952.

"Report of the Committee on the Operation of the Jury System, Excerpt from Agenda 13," September, 1953.

"Report of the Committee on Pre-Trial Procedure," September 15, 1952.

"Report of the Committee on Procedure in Antitrust and Other Protracted Cases," September 22, 1954.

"Report of the Committee on Protracted Cases," April 12, 1951.

"Report of the Committee on Rule 71A(h) of Rules of Civil Procedure and Pending Bill S. 1958," January 16, 1952.

"Report of the Committee on Statistics," September 15, 1951.

"Report of the Committee on Supporting Personnel of the United States Courts," February 27, 1952.

"Report of the Committee on Supporting Personnel of the United States Courts," April 5, 1954.

"Report of the Committee on Ways and Means of Economy in the Operation of the Courts," 1948.

"Report of the Committee on Ways and Means of Economy in the Operation of the Federal Courts as amended by the Judicial Conference of the United States," September 1, 1948.

"Report of the Committee to Consider Amendments of the Admiralty Rules Proposed by the Maritime Law Association of the United States," September 1947.

"Report of the Committee to Consider the Desirability of Extending the Merit System to Cover Personnel of the Clerks Offices," 1942.

"Report of the Habeas Corpus Committee," September 20, 1947.

"Report to the Judicial Conference of the Committee to Consider the Representation of District Judges in the Judicial Conference," 1944.

Legislative Branch:

Congressional Globe.

Congressional Record.

Senate Hearings and Reports (by Congress and Session).

Committee on Appropriations. *Hearings, on H.R. 8269, Departments of State, Justice, Commerce, and Labor Appropriation Bill for 1929,* 70th Cong., 1st Sess., 1928.

————. *Hearings, on H.R. 8319, Departments of State, Commerce, and Justice Appropriation Bill, 1941,* 76th Cong., 3d Sess., 1940.

————. *Hearings, on H.R. 4276, Departments of State, Commerce and Justice and the Federal Judiciary Appropriation Bill for 1942,* 77th Cong., 1st Sess., 1941.

————. *Hearings, on H.R. 6599, Departments of State, Commerce and Justice and the Federal Judiciary Appropriation Bill for 1943,* 77th Cong., 2d Sess., 1942.

————. *Hearings, Legislative and Judiciary Appropriation Bill for 1944,* 77th Cong., 2d Sess., 1943.

————. *Hearings, on H.R. 4414, Legislative and Judiciary Appropriation Bill for 1945,* 78th Cong., 2d Sess., 1944.

————. *Hearings, on H.R. 2603, Departments of State, Justice, Commerce, the Judiciary, and the Federal Loan Agency Appropriation, 1946,* 79th Cong., 1st Sess., 1945.

————. *Hearings, on H.R. 6056, Departments of State, Justice, Commerce and the Judiciary Appropriation Bill for 1947,* 79th Cong., 2d Sess., 1946.

————. *Hearings, on H.R. 5607, Departments of State, Justice, Commerce and the Judiciary Appropriation Bill for 1949,* 80th Cong., 2d Sess., 1948.

————. *Hearings, on H.R. 4016, Departments of State,*

Justice, Commerce and the Judiciary Appropriation Bill for 1950, 81st Cong., 1st Sess., 1949.

———. *Hearings, on H.R. 7786, Departments of State, Justice, Commerce and the Judiciary Appropriation Bill for 1951*, 81st Cong., 2d Sess., 1950.

———. *Hearings, on H.R. 4740, Departments of State, Justice, Commerce and the Judiciary Appropriation Bill for 1952*, 82d Cong., 1st Sess., 1951.

———. *Hearings, on H.R. 7289, Departments of State, Justice, Commerce and the Judiciary Appropriation Bill for 1953*, 82d Cong., 2d Sess., 1952.

———. *Hearings, on H.R. 5805, Legislative-Judiciary Appropriation for 1954*, 83d Cong., 1st Sess., 1953.

———. *Hearings, on H.R. 9203, Legislative-Judiciary Appropriation for 1955*, 83d Cong., 2d Sess., 1954.

———. *Hearings, on H.R. 5502, Departments of State, Justice, the Judiciary and Related Agencies Appropriation for 1956*, 84th Cong., 1st Sess., 1955.

———. *Hearings, on H.R. 10721, Departments of State, Justice, the Judiciary and Related Agencies Appropriation for 1957*, 84th Cong., 2d Sess., 1956.

———. *Hearings, on H.R. 6871, Departments of State, Justice, the Judiciary and Related Agencies Appropriation for 1958*, 85th Cong., 1st Sess., 1957.

———. *Hearings, on H.R. 12428, Departments of State, Justice, the Judiciary and Related Agencies Appropriation for 1959*, 85th Cong., 2d Sess., 1958.

———. *Hearings, on H.R. 7343, Departments of State, Justice, the Judiciary, and Related Agencies Appropriation for 1960*, 86th Cong., 1st Sess., 1959.

———. *Hearings, on H.R. 11666, Departments of State, Justice, the Judiciary, and Related Agencies Appropriation for 1961*, 86th Cong., 2d Sess., 1960.

Committee on Appropriations. *Hearings, on H.R. 7371, Departments of State, Justice, the Judiciary, and Related Agencies Appropriation for 1962*, 87th Cong., 1st Sess., 1961.

——. *Hearings, on H.R. 12580, Departments of State, Justice, and Commerce, the Judiciary and Related Agencies Appropriation for 1963*, 87th Cong., 2d Sess., 1962.

——. *Hearings, on H.R. 7063, Departments of State, Justice, and Commerce, the Judiciary, and Related Agencies Appropriations for 1964*, part I, 88th Cong., 1st Sess., 1963.

——. *Hearings, on H.R. 11134, Departments of State, Justice, and Commerce, the Judiciary, and Related Agencies Appropriation for 1965*, 88th Cong., 2d Sess., 1964.

——. *Hearings, on H.R. 8639, Departments of State, Justice, and Commerce, the Judiciary, and Related Agencies Appropriations for 1966*, part I, 89th Cong., 1st Sess., 1965.

——. *Hearings, on H.R. 18119, Departments of State, Justice, and Commerce, the Judiciary, and Related Agencies Appropriations for Fiscal Year 1967*, 89th Cong., 2d Sess., 1966.

——. *Hearings, on H.R. 10345, Departments of State, Justice, and Commerce, the Judiciary, and Related Agencies Appropriations for Fiscal Year 1968*, 90th Cong., 1st Sess., 1967.

——. *Hearings, on H.R. 17522, Departments of State, Justice, and Commerce, the Judiciary, and Related Agencies Appropriations for Fiscal Year 1969*, 90th Cong., 2d Sess., 1968.

——. *Hearings, on H.R. 12964, Departments of State, Justice, and Commerce, the Judiciary, and Related Agencies Appropriations for Fiscal Year 1970*, 91st Cong., 1st Sess., 1969.

——. *Hearings, on H.R. 17575, Departments of State,*

Justice, and Commerce, the Judiciary, and Related Agencies Appropriations for Fiscal Year 1971, 91st Cong., 2d Sess., 1970.

————. *Hearings, on H.R. 4805, First Deficiency Appropriation Bill for 1946,* part I, 79th Cong., 1st Sess., 1945.

————. *Hearings, on H.R. 4664, Third Supplemental Appropriation Bill, 1953,* 83d Cong., 1st Sess., 1953.

————. *Hearings, on H.R. 10743, Second Supplemental Appropriation Bill for 1960,* 86th Cong., 2d Sess., 1960.

————. *Hearings, on H.R. 9169, Supplemental Appropriation Bill for 1962,* 87th Cong., 1st Sess., 1961.

————. *Hearings, on H.R. 11038, Second Supplemental Appropriation Bill for 1962,* 87th Cong., 2d Sess., 1962.

————. *Hearings, on H.R. 5517, Supplemental Appropriations for 1963,* 88th Cong., 1st Sess., 1963.

Committee on the Judiciary. *Hearings, on S. 2432, S. 2433, S. 2523, Additional Judges, United States District Courts.* 67th Cong., 1st Sess., 1921.

————. *Hearings, on S. 2176, Appeals from Federal Courts,* 74th Cong., 1st Sess., 1935.

————. *Hearings, on S. 1392, Reorganization of the Federal Judiciary,* part I and VI, 75th Cong., 1st Sess., 1937.

————. *Reorganization of the Federal Judiciary,* Report to Accompany S. 1392, Senate Rept. 711, 75th Cong., 1st Sess., 1937.

————. *Representation of the United States Court of Appeals for the District of Columbia on the Annual Conference of Senior Circuit Judges,* Report to Accompany H.R. 2703, Senate Rept. 736, 75th Cong., 1st Sess., 1937.

————. *Hearings, on S. 3233, Additional Judges for Federal Courts,* parts I and II, 75th Cong., 3d Sess., 1938.

487

Committee on the Judiciary. *Hearings, on S. 3212, Administrative Office of the United States Courts*, 75th Cong., 3d Sess., 1938.

———. *Hearings, on S. 188, Administration of United States Courts*, 76th Cong., 1st Sess., 1939.

———. *Providing for the Administration of United States Courts*, Report to Accompany S. 188, Senate Rept. 426, 76th Cong., 1st Sess., 1939.

———. *Hearings, on H.R. 146, Trial of Good Behavior of Certain Federal Judges*, 77th Cong., 1st Sess., 1941.

———. *Hearings, on S. 1050, S. 1051, S. 1052, S. 1053, S. 1054, H.R. 138, Administration of United States Courts*, 77th Cong., 1st Sess., 1941.

———. *Hearings, on S. 2655, Designation of Circuit Judges to Circuits Other Than Their Own*, 77th Cong., 2d Sess., 1942.

———. *Hearings, on S. 620, Court Reporters*, 78th Cong., 1st Sess., 1943.

———. *Hearings, on S. Con. Res. 4-5, Invitation to the Chief Justice of the United States to Address the Congress*, 84th Cong., 1st Sess., 1955.

———. *Amending Title 28, United States Code, with Respect to the Duties of the Judges of the United States Court of Claims*, Senate Rept. 1817, 84th Cong., 2d Sess., 1956.

———. *Providing Representation for the Court of Customs and Patent Appeals on the Judicial Conference of the United States*, Senate Rept. 887, 87th Cong., 1st Sess., 1961.

———. *Hearings, on S. 3296, Amendment 561 to S. 3296, S. 1497, S. 1654, S. 2845, S. 8846, S. 2923, and S. 3176, Civil Rights*, part i, 89th Cong., 2d Sess., 1966.

———. *Hearings, on Judicial Fitness*, part i, 89th Cong., 2d Sess., 1966.

————. *Hearings, on the United States Commissioner System*, part I and II, 89th Cong., 1st Sess., 1965.

————. *Hearings, on the United States Commissioner System*, part III, 89th Cong., 2d Sess., 1966.

————. *Federal Judicial Center*, Senate Rept. 781 to accompany H.R. 6111, 90th Cong., 1st Sess., 1967.

————. *Hearings, on S. 915 and H.R. 6111, Bills to Establish a Federal Judicial Center*, 90th Cong., 1st Sess., 1967.

————. *Hearings, on S. 915 and H.R. 6111, Crisis in the Federal Courts*, 90th Cong., 1st Sess., 1967.

————. *Hearings, on S. 3055, S. 3060, S. 3061, S. 3062, the Judicial Reform Act*, 90th Cong., 2d Sess., 1968.

————. *Hearings, on Temporary Judicial Assignments*, 90th Cong., 2d Sess., 1968.

————. *Hearings, on S. 952, S. 567, S. 474, S. 585, S. 852, S. 898, S. 1036, S. 1216, S. 1509, S. 1646, S. 1712, S. 2040, Federal Judges and Courts*, 91st Cong., 1st Sess., 1969.

————. *Hearings, on S. 1506, S. 1507, S. 1508, S. 1509, S. 1510, S. 1511, S. 1512, S. 1513, S. 1514, S. 1515, S. 1516, The Judicial Reform Act*, 91st Cong., 1st Sess., 1969.

————. *Hearings, on the Independence of Federal Judges*, 91st Cong., 2d Sess., 1970.

Post Office and Civil Service Committee. *Hearings, on H.R. 11049, Federal Pay Legislation*, 88th Cong., 1st and 2d Sess., 1964.

Senate Documents and Committee Prints.
"Courts of the United States" (Letter, Edward Wetmore to George F. Hoar, February 27, 1899), Senate Doc. 142, 55th Cong., 3d Sess., 1899.

Report on Courts and Judges: Letter from the Attorney General, Senate Doc. 156, 63d Cong., 1st Sess., 1913.

Winston, Robert W. *Legal Reform, Genuine and Spurious,* Senate Doc. 377, 63d Cong., 2d Sess., 1914.

Committee on the Judiciary. *Additional Judges for the Federal Courts: Report of the Committee Selected by the Attorney General to Suggest Emergency Legislation to Relieve the Federal Courts of Their Congested Condition,* Committee Print, 67th Cong., 1st Sess., 1921.

——. *Increase of Judges of United States District Courts: Letter from Hon. Arthur C. Denison, United States Circuit Judge, to Hon. Knute Nelson, Chairman of the Committee on the Judiciary, relative to H.R. 9103, together with general comments, and suggestions on said bill and an analysis and explanatory note of a proposed substitute therefor,* Committee Print, 67th Cong., 2d Sess., 1921.

Walsh, Thomas J. *Reform of Federal Procedure,* Senate Doc. 105, 69th Cong., 1st Sess., 1926.

Strengthening of Procedure in the Judicial System, Senate Doc. 65, 72d Cong., 1st Sess., 1932.

Commission on Judicial and Congressional Salaries. *Hearings before the Commission on Judicial and Congressional Salaries,* Senate Doc. 104, 83d Cong., 2d Sess., 1954.

——. *Report of the Task Forces of the Commission on Judicial and Congressional Salaries,* Senate Doc. 97, 83d Cong., 2d Sess., 1954.

Committee on the Judiciary. *Legislative History of the United States Circuit Courts of Appeals and the Judges Who Served During the Period 1801 through March, 1958,* Committee Print, 85th Cong., 2d Sess., 1958.

Committee on Appropriations. *Field Study of the Operations of United States Courts,* Committee Print, 86th Cong., 2d Sess., 1959.

House of Representatives Hearings and Reports (by Congress and Session)

Committee on Appropriations. *Hearings, The Legislative Executive, and Judicial Appropriation Bill for 1907-1922*, 59th Cong., 2d Sess.–66th Cong., 3d Sess., 1906-1920.

——. *Hearings, Appropriations, Department of Justice, 1923-1929*, 67th Cong., 2d Sess.–70th Cong., 1st Sess., 1922-1927.

——. *Hearings, Department of Justice Appropriation Bills for 1930-1942*, 70th Cong., 1st Sess.–77th Cong., 1st Sess., 1928-1941.

——. *Hearings, The Judiciary Appropriation Bill for 1943-1954*, 77th Cong., 2d Sess.–83d Cong., 1st Sess., 1941-1953.

——. *Hearings, on Interior Department, Appropriations Bill for 1944*, part I, 78th Cong., 1st Sess., 1943.

——. *Hearings, Legislative-Judiciary Appropriation for 1955*, 83d Cong., 2d Sess., 1954.

——. *Hearings, on Departments of State and Justice, the Judiciary and Related Agencies, Appropriations for /1956-1962/*, 84th Cong., 1st Sess.–87th Cong., 1st Sess., 1955-61.

——. *Hearings, on Departments of State, Justice, and Commerce, the Judiciary, and Related Agencies, Appropriations for /1963-1965/*, 87th Cong., 2d Sess.–88th Cong., 2d Sess., 1962-64.

——. *Hearings, on Departments of State, Justice, Commerce, the Judiciary, and Related Agencies, Appropriations for /1966-1967/*, 89th Cong., 1st and 2d Sess., 1965-66.

——. *Hearings, on Departments of State, Justice, and Commerce, the Judiciary, and Related Agencies, Appropriations for /1968-1971/*, part I, 90th Cong., 1st Sess.–91st Cong., 2d Sess., 1967-70.

Committee on Appropriations. *Hearings, Second Deficiency Appropriation Bill for 1938*, 75th Cong., 3d Sess., 1938.

———. *Hearings, First Deficiency Appropriation Bill for 1946*, part I, 79th Cong., 1st Sess., 1945.

———. *First Deficiency Appropriation Bill, 1946*, 79th Cong., 1st Sess., 1945, House Rept. 1288 to accompany H.R. 4805.

———. *First Deficiency Appropriation Bill, 1946*, 79th Cong., 1st Sess., 1945, House Rept. 1468 to accompany H.R. 4805.

———. *Hearings, Second Deficiency Appropriation Bill for 1946*, 79th Cong., 2d Sess., 1946.

———. *Hearings, Third Urgent Deficiency Appropriation Bill for 1946*, 79th Cong., 2d Sess., 1946.

———. *Hearings, First Deficiency Appropriation Bill for 1947*, 80th Cong., 1st Sess., 1947.

———. *Hearings, First Deficiency Appropriation Bill for 1949*, 81st Cong., 1st Sess., 1949.

———. *Hearings, The Deficiency Appropriation Bill, 1950*, 81st Cong., 2d Sess., 1950.

———. *Hearings, Second Supplemental Appropriation Bill for 1950*, 81st Cong., 1st Sess., 1949.

———. *Hearings, Third Supplemental Appropriation Bill for 1952*, 82d Cong., 2d Sess., 1952.

———. *Hearings, Second Supplemental Appropriation Bill, 1953*, 83d Cong., 1st Sess., 1953.

———. *Hearings, Third Supplemental Appropriation Bill, 1954*, 83d Cong., 2d Sess., 1954.

———. *Hearings, the Second Supplemental Appropriation Bill, 1955*, 84th Cong., 1st Sess., 1955.

———. *Hearings, Second Supplemental Appropriation Bill, 1956*, 84th Cong., 2d Sess., 1956.

———. *Hearings, the Supplemental Appropriation Bill, 1958*, 85th Cong., 1st Sess., 1957.

———. *Hearings, Second Supplemental Appropriation Bill, 1958*, 85th Cong., 2d Sess., 1958.

———. *Hearings, Second Supplemental Appropriation Bill, 1959*, 86th Cong., 1st Sess., 1959.

———. *Hearings, Third Supplemental Appropriation Bill, 1961*, 87th Cong., 1st Sess., 1961.

———. *Hearings, Supplemental Appropriation Bill, 1962*, 87th Cong., 1st Sess., 1961.

———. *Hearings, Second Supplemental Appropriation Bill, 1962*, 87th Cong., 2d Sess., 1962.

Committee on the Judiciary. *Hearings, on H.R. 8426, Salaries of Clerks of United States District Courts*, 65th Cong., 2d Sess., 1918.

———. *Hearings, on H.R. 11134, Increase Salaries and Provide for Retirement of District and Circuit Judges*, 65th Cong., 2d Sess., 1918.

———. *Hearings, on H.R. 8875, Additional Judges, United States District Courts*, 67th Cong., 1st Sess., 1921.

———. *Additional District Judges for Certain Districts, etc.* Report to Accompany H.R. 8875, H.R. 661, House Report 482, 67th Cong., 1st Sess., 1921.

———. *Additional Judges for the Eighth Circuit*, House Rept. 102, 68th Cong., 1st Sess., 1924.

———. *Hearings, on H.R. 3318, Additional Judges for the Southern District of New York*, 68th Cong., 1st Sess., 1924.

———. *Hearings, on H.R. 10821, Additional Judges*, 69th Cong., 1st Sess., 1926.

———. *Hearings, on H.R. 11088, H.R. 16471, and S. 4162, on Southern Judicial District of Kentucky*, 69th Cong., 2d Sess., 1927.

———. *Hearings, on H.R. 5690, to Change the Judicial Circuits of the United States and to Create a Tenth Judicial Circuit*, 70th Cong., 1st Sess., 1928.

———. *Hearings, on H.R. 7730, Additional Judge for the Southern District of Florida*, 70th Cong., 1st Sess., 1928.

Committee on the Judiciary. *Hearings, on H.R. 5690, 13567, 13757, to Create a Tenth Judicial Circuit,* 70th Cong., 2d Sess., 1929.

———. *Hearings, on H.R. 2271, Trial of Good Behavior of United States District Judges,* part ɪ and ɪɪ, 75th Cong., 1st Sess., 1937.

———. *United States Court of Appeals for the District of Columbia, A Member of the Judicial Conference,* Report to accompany H.R. 2703, House Rept. 163, 75th Cong., 1st Sess., 1937.

———. *Trial of Good Behavior of United States District Judges,* Report to accompany H.R. 2271, House Rept. 814, 75th Cong., 1st Sess., 1937.

———. *Hearings, Additional United States Judges,* part ɪ and ɪɪ, 75th Cong., 3d Sess., 1938.

———. *Hearings, on the General Subject of the Administration of the Federal Courts,* stenographic transcript, 75th Cong., 3d Sess., 1938, Legislative Files, National Archives, Washington, D.C.

———. *Rules of Civil Procedure for the District Courts of the United States,* House Rept. 2743, 75th Cong., 3d Sess., 1938.

———. *Hearings, on H.R. 2973, H.R. 5999, Administration of United States Courts,* 76th Cong., 1st Sess., 1939.

———. *Providing for the Administration of United States Courts,* Report to Accompany H.R. 2973, H.R. 5999, House Rept. 702, 76th Cong., 1st Sess., 1939.

———. Special Subcommittee on Bankruptcy and Reorganization, *Hearings, on H.R. 4394, Administration of the Bankruptcy Act: Referees in Bankruptcy,* 77th Cong., 1st Sess., 1941.

———. *Hearings, on H.R. 3142, Court Reporters,* 78th Cong., 1st Sess., 1943.

———. *Hearings, on H.R. 33 and H.R. 3338, Referees in Bankruptcy,* 79th Cong., 1st Sess., 1945.

———. *Revision of Title 28, United States Code,* House

Rept. 308 to accompany H.R. 3214, 80th Cong., 1st Sess., 1947.

———. *Hearings, on H.R. 5649, Habeas Corpus,* 84th Cong., 1st Sess., 1955.

———. *Appointment of an Additional Judge on the Failure of a Disabled Judge to Retire When He Is Eligible to do so,* House Rept. 170 to accompany H.R. 110, 85th Cong., 1st Sess., 1957.

———. *A Roster of Senior Judges,* House Rept. 171 to accompany H.R. 3818, 85th Cong., 1st Sess., 1957.

———. *Providing Representation of District Judges on the Judicial Conference of the United States,* House Rept. 172 to accompany H.R. 3819, 85th Cong., 1st Sess., 1957.

———. *Federal Jury Selection Act,* House Rept. 1076 to accompany S. 989, 90th Cong., 2d Sess., 1968.

———. *The Federal Magistrates Act,* House Rept. 1629 to accompany S. 945, 90th Cong., 2d Sess., 1968.

———. *Hearings, on H.R. 17901 and H.R. 17906, Circuit Court Executives,* 91st Cong., 2d Sess., 1970.

Post Office and Civil Service Committee. *Hearings, on H.R. 7552, 7814, and Similar Bills, Federal Employees Salary Act of 1963,* parts I and II, 88th Cong., 1st Sess., 1963.

House Documents and Committee Prints

Committee on the Judiciary. *Letter from the Attorney General, Fees of United States Court Clerks,* House Doc. 97, 59th Cong., 1st Sess., 1905.

———. *President's Special Message to Congress Accompanied by a Report on the Outline of the United States Government Prepared by His Committee on Economy and Efficiency,* House Exec. Doc. 458, 62d Cong., 2d Sess., 1912.

———. *National Commission on Law Observance and Enforcement of the Prohibition Laws of the United*

495

States: Message from the President of the United States, House Doc. 722, 71st Cong., 3d Sess., 1931.

———. *Report of the Commission on Judicial and Congressional Salaries, Letter from Chairman, Commission on Judicial and Congressional Salaries*, House Doc. 300, 83d Cong., 2d Sess., 1954.

———. *United States Commission on Judicial and Congressional Salaries*, House Rept. 49, 84th Cong., 1st Sess., 1955.

———. *Report on the Responsibilities and Powers of the Judicial Councils*, House Doc. 201, 87th Cong., 1st Sess., 1961.

———. *The United States Courts: Their Jurisdiction and Work*, Committee Print, 90th Cong., 1st Sess., 1967.

Personal Interviews

John C. Airhart, former Assistant Director, Administrative Office of the United States Courts, Washington, D. C., and Arlington, Virginia.

Ronald H. Beattie, former Chief, Division of Procedural Studies and Statistics, Administrative Office of the United States Courts, Washington, D. C.

John Biggs, Jr., Chief Judge, United States Court of Appeals for the Third Circuit, Wilmington, Delaware, and Washington, D. C.

Richard H. Chambers, Chief Judge, United States Court of Appeals for the Ninth Circuit, Washington, D. C.

Henry P. Chandler, former Director of the Administrative Office of the United States Courts, Chevy Chase, Maryland.

M. Albert Figinski, Chief Counsel, Subcommittee on Improvements in Judicial Machinery of the Senate Committee on the Judiciary, Washington, D. C.

Hubert H. Finzel, former Chief Counsel, Subcommittee on

Improvements in Judicial Machinery of the Senate Committee on the Judiciary, Washington, D. C.

Henry Hull, Chief Clerk, United States District Court for the District of Columbia, Washington, D. C.

J. Edward Lumbard, Chief Judge, United States Court of Appeals for the Second Circuit, New York, New York.

Matthew F. McGuire, Chief Judge, United States District Court for the District of Columbia, Washington, D. C.

Albert B. Maris, Senior Judge, United States Court of Appeals for the Third Circuit, Philadelphia, Pennsylvania.

James W. Moore, Professor of Law, Yale Law School, New Haven, Connecticut.

Orie L. Phillips, Senior Judge, United States Court of Appeals for the Tenth Circuit, Washington, D. C.

Will Shafroth, former Deputy Director and Chief, Division of Procedural Studies and Statistics, Administrative Office of the United States Courts, Washington, D. C.

Simon E. Sobeloff, Chief Judge, United States Court of Appeals for the Fourth Circuit, Baltimore, Maryland.

Joseph F. Spaniol, Jr., Chief, Division of Procedural Studies and Statistics, Administrative Office of the United States Courts, Washington, D. C.

Rozel C. Thomsen, Chief Judge, United States District Court for the District of Maryland, Baltimore, Maryland.

Index

Laws of the United States Cited in the Text

499

Index

501

Clark, Charles E. (*cont.*)
446, 451; Judicial Conference
committees, 265, 272, 274,
277, 285; leadership style
of, 405, 415-16; E. Warren,
267, 305, 414-15
Clark, Tom C., 369, 375,
377-78, 421
Clary, Thomas J., 448, 452
Clayton, Henry D., 88
Clerk's Manual, 195
clerks of courts, 8n, 91-92,
94-95, 109-10, 173-74,
176-77, 195, 215, 220-22,
373; courts of appeals, 96-97,
390n, 405, 415; district
courts, 43-44, 55-56, 376,
402
Coffeyville Daily Journal
(Ark.), 67
Coleman, William C., 55n
Collet, John C., 336
Clyne, Charles F., 26n
Colmer, William M., 373
Columbia Broadcasting
Corporation, 329
Commerce Court Act (1910),
25
Commission on Judicial and
Congressional Salaries, 336-
37
commissioners (U.S.), 54, 68,
173, 357, 373; abolished,
394; Act (1812), 8, 10; Fees
Act (1946), 182. *See also*
magistrates (U.S.)
Committee on Conference
Arrangements (District of
Columbia), 391
Committee on Federal Judicial
Salaries of the Conference of
Bar Association Presidents,
334

comptroller general, 107, 110,
288
conciliation commissioner, 173
condemnation commissioner,
185n
Conference of Senior Circuit
Judges, *see* Judicial Conference of the United States
Conference of United States
Court Reporters, 364
conflict of interest, 401-02.
See also circuit judicial councils; Judicial Conference
Conformity Act (1872), 21-22
Congress: Administrative Office, 198, 201, 204, 206-16,
222-25; American Bar
Association, 330-37; American Law Institute, 330-31;
Chief Justice, 312-17; circuit
conferences, 150, 342, 352-
53, 356-57; circuit councils,
384, 387-89, 409, 412; courts,
3, 21, 121, 266-67, 431;
delegation of powers, 22-23,
392; Department of Justice,
75-79, 102, 183, 325; federal
judges, 27-29, 35, 306-10,
322-25, 338-39, 433; Fed-
eral Judicial Center, 372,
377-78; Hughes, 62-64, 69-
70, 78, 82; injunctions against
acts of, 82; judicial behavior,
153-55, 163, 236, 238;
Judicial Conference, 36, 61-
71, 250-51, 261-62; Judicial
Conference committees, 271,
277, 283-86, 289, 294-97,
312, 317-22, 330-31; Taft,
61-62, 65-68, 70, 77-85;
Vinson, 264-65; Warren,
315-17. *See also* Judiciary
Acts (1789); Department of
Justice

Congressional liaison, *see* Congress; Judicial Conference of the United States; Judicial Conference, committees
Connally, Ben C., 299, 446, 453
Connor, Henry G., 58
consent calendar, 322
conspiracy indictment, 71-72
Constitution (U.S.), 3, 21, 135n, 148, 154, 255, 423
contempt, 425
contingent fees, 350
continuances, 47
Coolidge, Calvin, 83, 326
Coppage v. Kansas, 17
Corcoran, Thomas, 168
Corman, James C., 226, 373
Coudert, Frederic R., 333
council of judges, *see* Judicial Conference of the United States
Court of Appeals Act (1891), 5-6, 11, 13
Court of Claims Judge's Act (1956), 255-57
Court of Customs and Patent Appeals Representation Act (1961), 255-57
Court Expenses Act (1906), 95-96
Court of Judicial Administration, 411n
Court-packing plan, 79, 82, 112-24, 135-37, 142, 169
court reporters: Act (1944), 182, 230; Administrative Office, 195, 220; circuit conferences, 347, 361; circuit councils, 402-03; expenses and compensation of, 233-35, 245, 299, 361; Judicial Conference, 233, 245, 288, 296, 305; supervision, 96, 405, 420-21

Court Salaries and Expenses Act (1922), 97
courts of appeals: district courts, 271-72, 421; *en banc*, 384n, 385; establishment of, 11-12; rules of, 390; separate administration of, 109-10, 125; Supreme Court compared, 11, 109-10; CHIEF JUDGES OF: 244, 257, 318, circuit conferences, 341-43, 358, circuit councils, 384, 387, 405, court personnel, 390n, 396n, functions, 354, 395-96, 405-06, 413, Judicial Conference, 406, selection, 432; JUDGES OF: circuit councils, 152, 382-83, 389-90, district judges, 153-55, duty in district courts, 204n, 245n, expenses of, 107, Judicial Conference, 202, 246-47, lobbying, 324, roles of, 153
Covey, Edwin L., 195-96
Cowen, Wilson, 447, 449, 455
crier-messenger, 230
criers, 92, 107, 182
Criers and Bailiffs Act (1944), 182
crime control legislation, 242-43
criminal behavior, 94-95, 180, 190-91, 392n, 401-02, 421
criminal cases, 174
Criminal Division, 171
Criminal Justice Act (1964), 224n, 225-26, 231, 394, 399, 415
criminal rights, 148
criminal procedure, 69, 149, 240-41, 341, 387. *See also* electronic surveillance; Federal Rules of Criminal Procedure

509